Securities Regulation

BY NIELS B. SCHAUMANN
William Mitchell College of Law

Seventh Edition

D1476259

THOMSON

WEST

EDITORIAL OFFICES: 1 North Dearborn St., Suite 650, Chicago, IL 60602
REGIONAL OFFICES: Chicago, Dallas, Los Angeles, New York, Washington, D.C.

PROJECT EDITOR
Steven J. Levin, B.A., J.D.
Attorney At Law

SERIES EDITOR
Elizabeth L. Snyder, B.A., J.D.
Attorney At Law

QUALITY CONTROL EDITOR
Sanetta M. Hister

Summary of Contents

Text Correlation Chart

Gilbert Law Summary SECURITIES REGULATION	Coffee, Jr., Seligman, Sale *Securities Regulation, Cases and Materials* 2007 (10th ed.)	Cox, Hillman, Langevoort *Securities Regulation, Cases and Materials* 2006 (5th ed.)	Hazen *Securities Regulation, Cases and Materials* 2006 (7th ed.)	Soderquist, Gabaldon *Securities Regulation* 2006 (6th ed.)
I. INTRODUCTION TO FEDERAL SECURITIES REGULATION				
A. Why Regulate Securities?	Page 1-8	Page 1, 3-8	Page 1-5	Page 2-4
B. The Securities Industry Generally	8-88	1-3, 14-17, 245-250, 390-394	3-4	7-9, 98-99
C. The Securities and Exchange Commission	50, 55, 1227, 1376-1406	11-14	8-10	3-9
D. Securities Acts Administered by the S.E.C.—An Overview	52, 54-55, 211-213, 1256-1259	3-11	5-8	2-3, 7-10, 546, 584-588
E. Jurisdiction and Interstate Commerce			5-8, 11-13	313
F. Self-Regulatory Organizations	57-65, 576-577, 640-643	15-16, 1021-1023, 1026-1027	10-11	6-9
II. REGULATING THE ORIGINAL DISTRIBUTION OF SECURITIES—THE SECURITIES ACT OF 1933				
A. Introduction	52, 484-487	118-125, 145-148, 161, 215-222	90-137	24, 29-31, 78-79, 96-98
B. 1933 Act Section 5—Offers and Sales	90-130, 155-169, 845-931	117-221	5-6, 90-159	32-76
C. Persons Covered by the 1933 Act	67-68	21, 118, 345-366	5-6, 90-91, 108-109, 111-112	4, 32-33, 216-243
D. Property Interests Covered by the 1933 Act	254-316, 325-335, 1030-1035	19-93	5-6, 18-86	126-176
E. The Registration Statement	154-216, 241-245	145-168, 196-214	96-108, 159-162, 278-306	8, 56-57, 61-65, 69-76, 78-125, 272-276, 296-309, 610, 731-809
F. Exemptions from Registration Requirements	335-574	259-344	86-89, 434-524	8, 70-71, 177-179, 194-195, 203-215
G. Liabilities Under the 1933 Act	845-931, 1440-1441	481-544, 645-648, 746	306-388, 520-523	244-329
III. REGULATION OF SECURITIES TRADING—THE SECURITIES EXCHANGE ACT OF 1934				
A. Overview of the 1934 Act	52-53, 575-583	5-9, 544	6-7	8, 315-316, 331-338, 342-344, 389-390
B. Civil Liability Under Rule 10b-5 of the 1934 Act	932-1041	653-744, 879-919	390-394, 525-599, 636-725	414-516, 609-610
C. Tender Offers and Repurchases of Stock	713-843, 1232-1241	978-1007	773-893	373-413, 684-685
D. Regulation of Proxy Solicitations	1210-1212	936-966	166-167, 731-750	5, 9, 345-372
E. Insider Liability for Short-Swing Profits	1185-1209	919-934	600-635	521-528, 533-546
F. Prohibition Against Insider Trades During Pension Fund Blackouts		927-928	337-338, 342-350, 355-356, 395-405, 411-413	
G. Liability of Collateral Participants in Securities Transactions	53, 900-931, 1073-1095, 1348-1351	721-722, 759-781, 831-847	347-350, 393-394, 528-534, 1056-1065	250, 288-295, 309, 311, 416, 509-516, 610-616, 627-662

Gilbert Law Summary SECURITIES REGULATION	Coffee, Jr., Seligman, Sale *Securities Regulation, Cases and Materials* 2007 (10th ed.)	Cox, Hillman, Langevoort *Securities Regulation, Cases and Materials* 2006 (5th ed.)	Hazen *Securities Regulation, Cases and Materials* 2006 (7th ed.)	Soderquist, Gabaldon *Securities Regulation* 2006 (6th ed.)
H. S.E.C. Enforcement Actions	1297-1410	800-831	7, 548-554, 894-1076	4, 6-7, 11-13, 382-386, 508-509, 584-588
I. The Private Securities Litigation Reform Act of 1995	582-583, 1042-1073	747-757	388-389, 559-567	609-610
J. Criminal Enforcement and RICO	1411-1440	873-877	859-863	616-621
IV. REGULATION OF THE SECURITIES MARKETS				
A. Regulation of the National Securities Exchanges	584-712	9, 95-99, 1010-1012, 1021-1027	2, 3, 7, 10, 894-901, 1066, 1085-1096	3-4, 6, 8-9, 558-559
B. Regulation of the Over-the-Counter Market	586-603, 700-709	14-15, 96-97, 1009, 1012, 1051-1056, 1063	2-3, 894-979, 1085-1088	3, 588-560
C. Regulation of Market Manipulation and Stabilization	576, 650-672	1009-1078	171-172, 855-893	547-557
D. Regulation of Securities Analysts	106-107, 582, 625, 1021-1029	1040-1042	995-1003	563-567
E. Regulation of Broker-Dealer Trading Activities	104-106, 644-712	304-305, 1023-1078	901-979	560-580
V. APPLICATION OF FEDERAL SECURITIES LAWS TO MULTINATIONAL TRANSACTIONS				
A. Registration Under the 1933 Act	1441-1462	224-238, 1131-1170	177-178, 587-599	698-704, 708, 710
B. Application of the 1934 Act	1441-1462	557-563, 649-650, 1131-1170	177-178, 587-599	698-701, 709-710, 722
VI. REGULATION OF SECURITIES TRANSACTIONS BY THE STATES				
A. Uniform Securities Act	1274-1278	15	4-5	664, 671-676
B. Preemption of State Securities Laws	62, 1272-1295	14-15, 247-249, 341-342	5, 183-191	664-671
C. Secondary Distribution of Securities		345-394	833-841	684-690

Capsule Summary

I. INTRODUCTION TO FEDERAL SECURITIES REGULATION

A. WHY REGULATE SECURITIES? §1

Various grounds (and criticisms) have been advanced regarding regulation of the securities markets.

1. Investor's Need for Information §2

Because the value of securities is not readily verifiable, government regulation may be the most efficient means of disclosure for investors.

2. Consumer Protection §3

Protection against fraud establishes consumer confidence and protects the health of the national economy.

3. Economic Efficiency §4

Broad disclosure rules foster accuracy with respect to prices. *Criticisms* of this ground include the argument that, because trading is speculative, extensive regulation merely adds to the cost of investing. Other critics feel that disclosure violates enterprises' interest in confidentiality, while still others endorse the idea of efficiency but consider consumer protection goals unsubstantiated.

4. Disclosure to Reduce Costs §8

Others contend that disclosure should focus on reducing agency costs, *i.e.*, shareholders should have greater control over an enterprise's managers.

5. Alternatives to Securities Markets §9

Other means of providing access to capital, *e.g.*, loans from banks, may be superior to a market-based system.

B. THE SECURITIES INDUSTRY GENERALLY

1. Private Investment and the Venture Capital Market §10

Before publicly selling its securities, a company will seek investment from private sources such as wealthy individuals, other companies interested in the start-up product (strategic investors), or investment funds (mutual funds or hedge funds).

2. Securities Markets

a. Primary markets §12

These are the facilities where the securities are *first* issued or distributed to the public.

b. Secondary markets §13

These exist for ongoing trading of securities *after* original distribution and include the following:

(1) Stock exchanges §14

These are organized facilities that have trading floors on which listed stocks are bought and sold, *e.g.*, New York Stock Exchange ("NYSE"). Stock exchanges operate as *auction markets*, in which a specialist (*i.e.*, a securities firm) determines market price based on the balance of buy and sell orders. The price goes up when there are more buy than sell orders, and vice versa.

(2) Over-the-counter trading §17

Securities not listed on an exchange are said to be traded over-the-counter (or "OTC") by broker-dealers. The National Association of Securities Dealers ("NASD") has implemented an automated quotation system ("NASDAQ") to ensure timely pricing information.

(a) OTC market is dealer market §18

Unlike stock exchange transactions—in which a specialist sets a market price in an auction—the OTC market involves a dealer acting for an investor, who seeks the lowest price for a security from dealers acting as principals for that security.

(b) "Spreads" in the dealer market §22

Several developments have occurred to prevent collusion among dealers, *i.e.*, keeping the difference between the buy (bid price) and sell (asked price) artificially high. NASD established a separate entity, NASD Regulation, Inc., to regulate spreads, while the Securities Exchange Commission ("S.E.C.") now requires that customers be allowed to place limits on buy and sell prices. Congress also contributed to narrowing spreads by requiring that securities prices be quoted in pennies (decimal pricing).

(3) Other securities markets §25

These include the "third market" wherein securities listed on national exchanges are traded over-the-counter, and the "fourth market" wherein persons owning securities trade them without the assistance of an intermediary.

3. Securities Firms—Brokers and Dealers §26

The securities laws regulate not only the securities markets but also the firms engaged in trading securities. Note the following general functional definitions.

a. "Brokers" §27

These are persons who buy and sell securities as agents for their customers on a commission basis.

b. "Dealers" §28

These persons act as principals—buying securities for their *own account* and subsequently reselling them to their customers at a marked-up price.

c. Dual functions common
The same person can be a broker in one transaction and a dealer in another transaction. Note that many firms operate both in the exchange markets (through a specialist) and in the over-the-counter market.

4. Changing Role of Banks
In 1999, the Gramm-Leach-Bliley Act effectively repealed statutes prohibiting banks from underwriting securities. Deregulation has resulted in the growth of financial holding companies, which can now legally offer many financial services, including banking, brokerage, and insurance.

5. Other Financial Markets
The U.S. securities market is increasingly affected by other financial markets, both *foreign and domestic.* The rapidly expanding domestic market includes products such as the money market, government and municipal securities markets, and derivative products markets (*e.g.*, options, futures, swaps (typically interest rates or currencies), and portfolio insurance (hedging)).

6. Levels of Regulation
Securities markets are regulated at three levels: S.E.C. regulation, self-regulatory organizations, and state blue sky regulation subject to federal preemption.

7. Regulatory Issues
The proliferation of new financial instruments has resulted in conflict between agencies as to which has jurisdiction over an instrument, *e.g.*, whether it is a security, a futures contract, or an option.

C. THE SECURITIES AND EXCHANGE COMMISSION

1. S.E.C. Functions
These include (i) adopting *substantive rules,* (ii) *interpreting* securities laws and S.E.C. rules, generally by issuing *"releases"* or giving parties *"no action" letters,* (iii) *investigating* possible violations of the laws and rules, and (iv) *initiating formal proceedings* against wrongdoers.

a. Private actions
Private plaintiffs may seek remedies when they have been injured by a violation of a securities law if the law provides for an express or implied cause of action.

2. S.E.C. Administrative Procedures
S.E.C. proceedings are conducted in accordance with the federal Administrative Procedure Act, which requires a *hearing* before an administrative law judge, followed by *review* by the full Commission on request of any party, and *appeal* to a U.S. court of appeals.

D. SECURITIES ACTS ADMINISTERED BY THE S.E.C.—AN OVERVIEW

1. Securities Act of 1933
This Act primarily regulates the *original issuance* of securities. The Act's two main purposes are to compel *full disclosure of all material facts* in public

offerings and to *prevent fraud and misrepresentation* in distributions of securities.

2. Securities Exchange Act of 1934 §64

This Act primarily governs trading of securities that are already issued.

a. Registration and reporting §65

The 1934 Act requires a company to register its securities with the S.E.C. and thereafter file periodic reports on its financial condition if the company's securities are (i) *traded on a national securities exchange* or (ii) traded over-the-counter and the company has more than *$10 million* in assets and *500 or more shareholders* of a class of equity securities; such companies are called *"reporting companies."*

b. Other functions §66

Proxy solicitation, tender offer solicitations, insider trading, and margin trading are also regulated by the S.E.C. The S.E.C. additionally conducts market surveillance of certain trading practices that are based on fraud or market manipulation.

c. Registration of securities exchanges and broker-dealers §71

National securities exchanges and broker-dealers who conduct an interstate over-the-counter securities business must register with and make periodic reports to the S.E.C.

d. Antifraud provisions §74

The 1934 Act contains a number of provisions, including rule 10b-5, that impose liability for fraud in the purchase or sale of securities.

3. Sarbanes-Oxley Act ("SOXA") §75

In response to corporate scandals, in 2002, Congress amended the 1934 Act by passing SOXA. Its objectives are to (i) *improve the reliability of issuers' disclosures*, *e.g.*, by regulation of accountants, lawyers, and securities analysts; (ii) *broaden aiding and abetting prohibitions*; and (iii) *improve the quantity and quality of enhanced corporate disclosures* (*see infra* for detailed discussion).

4. Integrated Disclosure §84

The 1933 Act and the 1934 Act originally established two distinct disclosure systems. The S.E.C. has lightened the disclosure burden by integrating the reporting requirements of the two Acts. Regulation S-K prescribes a single standard set of instructions for filing forms under the two Acts, and in some cases 1933 Act registration forms can incorporate by reference 1934 Act reports.

E. JURISDICTION AND INTERSTATE COMMERCE

1. Interstate Commerce

a. Definition under 1933 Act §86

The S.E.C. and the courts have adopted a broad interpretation of what constitutes "interstate commerce" under the 1933 Act. Any transaction involving more than one state or using any means of interstate commerce, such as *intrastate* use of the telephone or the mails, constitutes interstate commerce.

b. Definition under 1934 Act §89

Under the 1934 Act, "interstate commerce" includes trade, commerce, transportation, or communication among several states plus *intrastate* use of any facility or instrumentality of interstate commerce.

F. SELF-REGULATORY ORGANIZATIONS §91

The 1934 Act also permits self-regulatory organizations ("S.R.O.s") to regulate the securities industry in order to aid in prevention of fraud and manipulative practices. However, the S.E.C. retains power to overrule an S.R.O. if necessary, and to change an S.R.O.'s operating rules. The three most important S.R.O.s are as follows:

1. Stock Exchanges §92

The SEA requires that, upon meeting certain requirements, all national securities exchanges must be registered.

2. NASD §93

The National Association of Securities Dealers ("NASD") is the only association registered with the S.E.C. under the SEA. The SEA requires that all broker-dealers belong either to NASD or to conduct business only on a national exchange of which the broker-dealer is a *member*.

3. Public Company Accounting Oversight Board §95

All accounting firms that audit public companies must register with this board.

II. REGULATING THE ORIGINAL DISTRIBUTION OF SECURITIES—THE SECURITIES ACT OF 1933

A. INTRODUCTION

1. Distribution Process §96

Typically, the original distribution of securities involves an underwriting—*i.e.,* the passing of securities from the issuer through a syndicate of underwriters, dealers, and, ultimately, into the hands of purchasers who intend to hold the securities for investment.

a. Pattern of distribution §97

The sequence of events in a typical underwriting is as follows:

(1) The issuer *decides to issue* the securities;

(2) The issuer agrees with a securities firm to have the firm *underwrite the issue* (*i.e.*, buy the securities, arrange for a syndicate to buy them, or otherwise take responsibility for their sale);

(3) The underwriter(s) agrees with other securities firms (*i.e.*, *"dealers"*) to have them buy the securities for resale to their customers; and

(4) The dealers sell the securities to *retail customers.*

b. Initial investors §102

In a typical distribution, the initial retail investors intend to hold the securities for only a short time. The distribution continues until the securities come to rest with investors who intend to hold them for a *substantial* period of time.

c. Types of underwriting agreements

(1) "Stand-by" underwriting §104
Here, the underwriter provides advice and agrees to buy whatever the issuer cannot sell.

(2) "Firm commitment" underwriting §105
Here, the issuer sells the securities outright to the underwriter, which then resells to dealers or the public.

(3) "Best-efforts" underwriting §106
Here, the underwriter acts as a sales agent for the issuer on a commission basis.

(4) Direct offering §107
A company might not use an underwriter at all, such as when the company is either very well-established or when the company is not selling securities to the public.

2. Objectives of 1933 Act

a. Full disclosure to potential investors §108
One of the primary objectives of the 1933 Act is to provide investors with *all material investment information* relating to an original issuance of securities (*i.e.,* full disclosure). This is accomplished through the filing of a *"registration statement"* with the S.E.C. prior to an issuance of securities and distributing a *"prospectus"* (which contains the most important information in the registration statement) to investors prior to or simultaneously with delivery of the issuer's securities.

b. Prevention of fraud and misrepresentation §112
Another objective of the 1933 Act is to prevent fraud and misrepresentation. This objective is accomplished through several liability provisions affording defrauded purchasers certain advantages compared with liability at common law.

3. Scope of 1933 Act §113
The 1933 Act applies only to offers and sales in interstate commerce by issuers, underwriters, and dealers of securities. Failure to comply with the registration requirement may result in civil, and possibly criminal, liability.

B. 1933 ACT SECTION 5—OFFERS AND SALES

1. The Challenges of Section 5 §118
Recent changes to section 5 are contained in the 2005 Securities Offering Reform ("SOR") rules. While greatly reducing the regulatory burden for certain issuers, mainly those who have previously issued securities and who file regular reports with the S.E.C. as required by the 1934 Act, the SOR does so by constructing a complex set of exceptions to section 5. Because section 5

is probably the most difficult, but fundamental, provision of the 1934 Act, application of the regulations here is organized by time periods: pre-filing, waiting, and the post-effective periods.

2. Classes of Issuers §120

Some issuers will qualify for exceptions under section 5, dependent on how they are categorized.

a. Nonreporting issuers §121

Because these issuers are not required to file periodic reports under the 1933 Act, the rules are strictly applied.

b. Unseasoned issuers §122

Issuers who must file periodic reports but who are not eligible to use Form S-3 (*see below*) to register offerings are in this category.

c. Seasoned issuers §123

This category is comprised of investors who have timely filed reports for the past 12 months, have not failed to pay any dividend or required payment on preferred stock, and have not committed a material default in the current fiscal year, thus qualifying to use Form S-3.

d. WKSIs—well-known seasoned issuers §124

These issuers have met the most stringent reporting requirements and, thus, receive the largest number of exceptions from section 5 regulation.

e. Ineligible issuers §125

Issuers not eligible for the 2005 shortcuts include, *e.g.*, those who have not timely filed their 1934 Act reports, shell companies, and penny stock issuers.

3. Time Period Regulation

a. Regulation during the pre-filing period §127

Before a registration statement is filed with the S.E.C., it is unlawful for issuers, underwriters, and/or dealers *to buy, or to offer to buy, or sell, or offer to sell*, the issuer's securities by any means of interstate commerce.

(1) Exemption for agreements between issuer and underwriter §129

Negotiations and agreements between the issuer and the underwriter are exempted from the prohibition against offers and sales.

(2) Meaning of "offers" and "sales" §131

The terms "offer" and "sale" are broader under the securities laws than at common law; *e.g.*, a contract to sell is a sale under the 1933 Act. Care must be taken to avoid contract formation until the post-effective period.

(a) No conditioning of market §132

"Offer" includes the dissemination of any material that might heighten market interest in the issuer before the actual offer of securities (*e.g.*, **press releases** can be offers in violation of section 5). However, a press release in the **normal course of business** is not prohibited.

(b) **Permitted dissemination of information by issuers** §133

Communications *by issuers made more than 30 days before filing* may fall within a safe harbor if they are made by or on behalf of an issuer, they contain no reference to the securities offering, and reasonable steps are taken to prevent further dissemination during the 30 days. Exceptions also exist for some communications not qualifying under the safe harbor. Communications *by persons other than the issuer, or by the issuer and made 30 or fewer days before filing* may use a safe harbor if certain requirements are met. Even if no safe harbor exists, other provisions of the 1933 Act may permit communications by the following persons:

1) *WKSIs*. They are given the greatest latitude under the rules.

2) *Seasoned and unseasoned reporting issuers* may communicate *factual business information and forward-looking information*.

3) *Nonreporting issuers* may include regularly released *factual business information*, but *not* forward-looking information.

4) *Any issuer* has a limited opportunity to notify the public about its intention to make an offering in the future under *SA rule 135*.

(c) **Permitted dissemination of information by underwriters and dealers** §146

Underwriters and dealers generally are permitted to conduct their normal business operations, such as publishing and distributing information, recommendations, and opinions regarding an issuer's securities *if no compensation* is paid for the report. *Participating broker-dealers* are subject to certain conditions regarding a report's contents.

b. **Regulation during the waiting period** §151

After a registration statement has been filed and before the S.E.C. declares it effective, actual sales are still prohibited, but underwriters may arrange with brokers and dealers for assistance in selling to retail customers. Underwriters and dealers may also *solicit offers to purchase* using certain types of information. However, the use of any prospectus in interstate commerce is prohibited, unless it meets the requirements of SA section 10.

(1) **"Prospectus" defined** §153

A prospectus includes any *written* communication, or one communicated by radio or television, that *offers any security for sale or confirms a sale*. Note that oral offers are still permitted.

(2) Permitted offer during the waiting period §154
Oral offers and *written offers* in section 10 prospectuses are permissible. The S.E.C. has authorized the following types of prospectuses under section 10.

(a) Preliminary ("red herring") prospectus §157
This is similar to a final (section 10(a)) prospectus, but lacks some important information that is not yet available, *e.g.,* price of securities.

(b) Summary prospectus prepared by issuer §160
This prospectus has become outmoded and is seldom, if ever, used.

(c) Free writing prospectus §161
Most issuers can use this prospectus during the waiting period, and WKSIs can use one at any time. A free writing prospectus (*i.e.*, written offer) is one that is neither a preliminary section 10(b) prospectus nor a final section 10(a) prospectus, does not pertain to certain kinds of asset-backed securities, and is not exempted by the SA definition of prospectus. "Writing" includes writing, printing, and graphic (*e.g.*, radio, TV, Internet) communication. Live communications to an audience are excluded.

1) Timing of use §164
WKSIs can use a free writing prospectus *at any time* while *seasoned issuers* may use it only *after the registration statement is filed. Unseasoned and nonreporting issuers* are limited to use only *after* the registration statement is filed, and it must be accompanied by the *preliminary prospectus*.

2) Contents and filing requirements §173
The S.E.C. requires certain contents (*e.g.,* a specific legend) and allows optional information that does not conflict with information in the registration statement. A free writing prospectus *must* be filed before or on the date of its first use.

(d) Written offers that are not prospectuses §182
Written statements used after the registration statement becomes effective, if accompanied or preceded by a final prospectus and written offers that only identify the security, its price, and by whom orders will be executed are not considered prospectuses.

1) Tombstone ads §183
Tombstone ads that may also be published during the waiting period are proposed offers that must contain certain information such as the issuer's name, the kind and price of security, from whom a prospectus may be

obtained, and a statement that no offer to purchase may yet be accepted and that this is not a solicitation.

(3) Required distribution of preliminary prospectus §186
Although distribution of a preliminary prospectus is not required by the 1933 Act itself, as a practical matter the S.E.C. forces distribution of a preliminary prospectus by refusing to *accelerate* the effective date of registration statements unless a preliminary prospectus has been distributed (absent an acceleration order, the issuer must wait until the completion of a 20-day waiting period before sales can be made, and market conditions can change during this time).

c. Regulation during the post-effective period §192
Once the registration statement is declared effective by the S.E.C., sales may begin.

(1) Objective of regulation §193
The objective now is to see that all purchasers receive complete disclosure, whether by actual receipt of a written prospectus, or merely by electronic access to the prospectus.

(2) Distribution of statutory prospectus §194
After the registration statement is effective, the 1933 Act *permits* written offers in any form (free writing). However, it is important to *distinguish* a free writing prospectus from post-effective free writing. In the latter situation, if any *offering participants* want to use free writing, they will *have to ensure that the free writing is accompanied or preceded by a final prospectus*.

(a) Rule 172—access to final prospectus equivalent to delivery §203
Under 1933 Act rule 172, a confirmation of sale or a delivery of securities may be sent without being accompanied by a final prospectus, contrary to the previous rule, *if* the requirements of rule 172 are met, *e.g.*, a registration statement is in effect and a final prospectus has been filed with the S.E.C. The delivery rule has been eased since the financial world has many means to access a final prospectus (*e.g.*, S.E.C.'s web site). Note that rule 172 does *not permit post-effective free writing without delivery of a final prospectus*.

(b) Notice of registration statement §208
Even if a final prospectus is not sent with a confirmation of sale or transfer of a security, the seller must generally, within two days after the sale, provide the buyer with a final prospectus or a notice that a registration statement is in effect.

(3) Duration of post-effective regulation under section 5 §209
Section 5 continues to regulate parties to a public offering, mainly by requiring delivery of, or access to, a final prospectus. *Issuers* must comply with section 5 as long as they are offering securities to the public. *Underwriters* are subject to section 5 for as long as they continue to sell their allotted shares.

(1) Traditional *"Howey"* test   §268

The traditional test of whether a transaction constitutes an investment contract is whether the contract is a ***profit-making scheme*** whereby a person invests ***his money in a common enterprise*** and ***expects to make a profit*** solely from the ***efforts of the promoter*** or a third party who is responsible for management.

(2) Modern trend   §269

For many years cases have gone beyond *Howey* to reach situations where the investors ***participated*** to some extent in management and where the benefits received were something ***other than cash.***

(a) Factors determining "investment contract"   §270

Under the modern trend, ask:

1) Does the investor have an expectation of profit?

2) Is there a ***common enterprise*** (*i.e.*, a number of investors who stand in a similar relationship to a business in which they invest in common)?

3) Does the success of the enterprise ***depend mainly on persons other than the investors***?

4) Do the investors ***need the protection*** of the 1933 Act?

(b) Requirement of a common enterprise   §271

Under the ***"horizontal"*** test, there must be a sharing or pooling of assets by several investors and profits derived from these combined funds. All courts find the "common enterprise" requirement to be satisfied by horizontal commonality.

1) Vertical test   §272

In addition, some courts will find a common enterprise if the investment manager participates in the profits made in the account.

(c) Efforts of persons other than investors   §273

The *Howey* test requires that profits come ***"solely"*** from the efforts of others. The modern application requires only that the success of the enterprise depend ***mainly*** on the efforts of persons other than the investors. The ***timing*** of the third party's efforts may make a difference as to a court's determination.

(3) The "comparable regulation" limitation   §275

The Supreme Court has held that if a detailed scheme of federal regulation applies to a particular instrument, the 1933 Act may not apply.

c. Catchall provision   §276

The 1933 Act also covers "in general, any interest or instrument commonly known as a 'security.' "

3. Application of Definitions   §277

A property interest is a security if it is ***specifically mentioned*** in the 1933

Act, or it is an *investment contract*, or it is an interest *commonly classified as a security*.

E. THE REGISTRATION STATEMENT

as those affecting price or value of securities, risk, the issuer's status, conflicts of interest, and pending legal proceedings.

(3) "Soft" information
This covers forward-looking statements concerning matters likely to affect the value of securities. *Safe harbor provisions* exist for these disclosures. Such disclosures must be made in *good faith* and with a *reasonable basis*. Issuers have a duty to update the statements.

(a) The "bespeaks caution" doctrine
This court-developed doctrine provides that overly optimistic forward-looking statements are harmless if surrounded by cautionary statements outlining the possibilities of less favorable results. The doctrine is the basis of the 1995 safe harbor act.

(b) Two kinds of protection
Under the 1995 act, a plaintiff must prove that the forward-looking statement was made with *actual knowledge* of its falsity. A *defendant* may show *meaningful cautionary statements.*

(4) Management Discussion and Analysis ("MD&A")
Issuers *must* include an MD&A in registration statements and certain other filings. A certain amount of forward-looking disclosure is *required* to allow an investor to examine the company through the eyes of management.

3. Organization of Material
The S.E.C. closely regulates organization of the registration statement. Disclosures in the statement and prospectus must be in *"plain English,"* and the entire prospectus must be clear, concise, and understandable.

4. Liability Based on Contents
Section 11 of the 1933 Act imposes civil liability on preparers for misstatements or omissions (*see infra*).

5. Processing the Registration Statement

a. Effective date of statement
The registration statement becomes effective on the *20th* day after its filing with the S.E.C. unless it is subject to a refusal or stop order (*infra*) or becomes effective sooner under an acceleration order. (The S.E.C. will declare a registration statement effective if it is satisfied with it, even if the 20-day period has not run.) Note that if the registration statement is amended, the waiting period starts running anew.

b. Review of the registration statement
Once filed, the S.E.C. begins reviewing the registration statement to ensure that the issuer has complied with all disclosure requirements.

c. Formal proceedings by the S.E.C.

(1) Formal examination
If a serious problem is indicated by the S.E.C.'s initial review or

the issuer's responses to that review, and the issuer appears un-cooperative, a formal examination may occur with grave conse-quences—the offering is essentially returned to the pre-filing period. If completion of the examination is unreasonably delayed, a court may order the S.E.C. to either terminate the examination or issue a stop order.

(2) Refusal orders §389

If the S.E.C. finds that the issuer failed to comply with the Act's disclosure requirements, it may issue a refusal order (if the state-ment is clearly inadequate on its face) within 10 days after the statement is filed. Refusal orders are always issued **prior to** the registration statement's effective date.

(3) Stop orders §390

A stop order either delays the effective date **or** stops the selling of securities if selling has begun so that the S.E.C. can conduct an investigation.

(4) Use of acceleration power §392

As a practical matter, issuers state on the statement that it will not be effective until approved; the S.E.C. then grants accelera-tion immediately upon approval, thus bypassing formal actions.

d. Withdrawal of registration statement §393

If there are problems with the issuing company or the registration state-ment after filing, the issuer may seek to withdraw. The S.E.C. allows withdrawal if it is consistent with the public interest. A withdrawal re-quest is usually honored if filed **before** a stop order proceeding.

e. Underwriter refuses to proceed §396

If an underwriter's investigation reveals **material misstatements** by the issuer, she may refuse to proceed despite her contractual obligation.

f. Blue sky qualification §398

In some cases, issuers must be qualified under the securities law of each state in which the securities are intended to be offered, absent a state exemption.

g. NASD clearance §399

The issuer must also receive clearance from NASD that the underwrit-ing commissions being paid are "fair."

6. Post-Effective Amendments to Registration Statement

a. Errors existing at time of effectiveness §401

If the registration statement contains an error at the time it is declared effective, and the error is discovered after the effective date, the appropri-ate way to update the prospectus is to file a "post-effective" amendment with the S.E.C.

b. Errors caused by subsequent developments §402

If developments after the effective date make information in the regis-tration statement or prospectus misleading or false, a correction may be made by placing a sticker on the cover of the prospectus and supplying the correct information in the prospectus.

c. **Updating requirement** §403

The 1933 Act requires a prospectus to be updated if it is still in use nine months after its effective date, whether or not any errors are discovered.

d. **"Blank check" offerings** §404

A blank check company is defined by the 1933 Act as a development stage company issuing penny stock that either has no business plan or purpose or plans to merge with an unidentified company. To prevent misuse of the funds, the Act imposes additional requirements on such companies. The sale proceeds must be placed in *escrow* until after the issuer files a *post-effective amendment* to the registration statement, describing its acquisition of business assets, after which investors then have a right to *rescind* their purchases.

7. **Shelf Registration** §411

A shelf registration occurs when an issuer files one statement covering securities it may offer at various times in the future. Shelf registrations are generally prohibited (because of inadequate disclosure), with some exceptions, *e.g.*, *traditional shelf registrations*, some *mergers*, and *registration form S-3 companies*.

a. **Automatic shelf registration for WKSIs** §415

In addition to the traditional shelf registration exceptions, the 2005 SOR provides for automatic shelf registration for WKSIs. All shelf registrations for WKSIs are *effective immediately* upon filing and can be amended to add additional securities. Shelf registrations are *effective for three years* and a new statement may be filed, thus offering the same securities on a continuing basis.

b. **Disclosure** §420

A shelf registration issuer files a "base prospectus" as part of the registration statement. Information regarding future offerings is disseminated by distribution of the additional information or by a supplemental prospectus, or by incorporating information from 1934 Act filings, or by a post-effective amendment to the shelf registration statement.

F. **EXEMPTIONS FROM REGISTRATION REQUIREMENTS**

1. **Exempt Securities** §422

Certain types of securities are exempt from registration under section 5 of the 1933 Act, including:

a. *Bank and government* securities;

b. *Short-term notes* and other debt instruments;

c. Securities issued by *charitable organizations*;

d. Securities issued by *savings and loan institutions*;

e. Securities issued by **common carriers** to finance acquisitions of rolling stock;

f. Securities issued by **receivers or trustees in bankruptcy** with the approval of the court; and

g. **Insurance, endowment, or annuity policies** issued by companies supervised by state agencies.

2. Exempt Transactions   §430

The exempt securities above can be sold and resold without ever being subject to the section 5 registration requirements. There are also transaction exemptions that cover only one sale; resales of the same securities might be subject to registration unless the resale is also exempt. Note that an "exempt" transaction is exempt only from the registration and prospectus delivery requirements, and not from the anti-fraud provisions of the 1933 Act.

a. Integration   §431

Issuers will attempt to qualify for transaction exemptions to avoid the costs of registration. If an issuer makes several offerings fairly close together and claims that one or more are exempt, the S.E.C. might decide that the several offerings are integrated (*i.e.,* part of a single offering), which often results in a violation of section 5. There are two ways to avoid having several offerings integrated—qualify under the S.E.C.'s general five-factor test, discussed below, or qualify for the specific "safe harbor" provision applicable to the transaction exemption being used.

(1) Five-factor test   §432

The S.E.C. will consider the following in determining whether several offerings are integrated:

(a) Whether the offerings are **part of a single plan of financing;**

(b) Whether the offerings **involve issuance of the same class of security;**

(c) Whether the offerings are **made at about the same time;**

(d) Whether the **same type of consideration is to be received;** and

(e) Whether the offerings are **made for the same general purpose**.

b. Mortgage transactions   §433

Certain mortgages initiated by regulated financial institutions and participating interests in the mortgages sold to investors are exempt.

c. Transactions by particular persons

(1) Transactions by persons other than issuers, underwriters, and dealers   §434

Transactions by persons other than issuers, underwriters, and dealers are exempt. For example, sales by ordinary investors are exempt.

(2) Dealer transaction exemption—statutory delivery period   §435

Every dealer is subject to the section 5 prospectus delivery requirement during the statutory distribution period, but is exempt thereafter.

into subsequent private offering, and vice versa. However, the rule *requires* that *no securities be sold* in the public offering, and that the *offering be abandoned*.

(4)   Exemption for offerings to "accredited investors"   §477
Section 4(6) provides an exemption from registration if the offer or sale involves only *"accredited investors"* and the offering price is less than $5 million. The term "accredited investor" here is defined similarly to its definition under regulation D, *infra*.

(5)   Incentive compensation plans in nonreporting companies   §480
SA rule 701 provides an exemption to nonreporting companies that issue stock as compensation to employees but does *not* apply to issues to raise capital. There are dollar limits on the value of securities issued in any 12-month period. Such offerings are not subject to integration with other offerings.

e.   Small issue exemptions   §484
Security offerings may be exempted if protection under the 1933 Act is not required and $5 million or less in securities is involved.

(1)   Regulation D

(a)   Accredited investor   §489
Regulation D defines several key terms. An "accredited investor" includes entities such as institutional investors, corporations, and partnerships having more than $5 million in assets; natural persons with at least $1 million in net worth or $200,000 annual income, etc.

(b)   Purchasers   §490
Under regulation D, the term "purchaser" does *not* include accredited investors.

(c)   General conditions to be met

1)   Integration   §492
Regulation D provides a safe harbor for all offers and sales that take place at least six months before the start of, or six months after the termination of, the regulation D offering, as long as there are no offers and sales of securities of the same or similar class within either of these six-month periods.

2)   Information requirements   §493
Regulation D requires delivery of financial information when securities are *sold under rules 505 or 506* (*infra*) to anyone *not* an accredited investor. When securities are sold under rule 504 (*infra*) or only to accredited investors, there is no mandatory disclosure under regulation D.

3)   Manner of the offering   §499
General solicitation and *general advertising* are *prohibited* in connection with an offering under rule 505

or 506, and also in rule 504 transactions **unless** compliance with certain state law registration procedures has occurred.

4) Limitations on resale   §505
Resales of securities issued under most transaction exemptions are restricted. Issuers must exercise **reasonable care** in determining that purchasers are not underwriters.

5) Filing of notices of sales   §508
The seller must give the S.E.C. notice of the sale within 15 days after the first sale of securities under regulation D.

(d) Specific conditions of rules 504, 505, and 506

1) Rule 504   §509
Rule 504 provides an exemption for offers and sales not exceeding **$1 million** in the aggregate, over a 12-month period, for companies not registered under the 1934 Act.

2) Rule 505   §511
Rule 505 provides an exemption to any issuer that is not an investment company for offers and sales to an **unlimited number of accredited investors** and to no more than **35 nonaccredited** purchasers where the aggregate purchase price does not exceed **$5 million** during any 12-month period.

3) Rule 506   §514
Rule 506 provides an exemption for offers and sales to an **unlimited number of accredited investors** and to no more than **35 nonaccredited** investors in **any dollar amount,** but the nonaccredited investors must be **sophisticated** in financial or business matters or employ a representative who is sophisticated.

(2) Regulation A exemption   §516
Regulation A is **not a complete exemption** but instead provides a simplified form of registration. To qualify for regulation A, the issuer must (i) be a **resident of** and have its **principal place of business** in the United States or Canada, (ii) **not** be a reporting company under the 1934 Act immediately before the regulation A offering, and (iii) **not be a "blank check" company** (*i.e.*, a start-up company with no business plan). Also, **no** investment companies or issuers of oil or gas rights may use regulation A.

(a) Limitations on availability of regulation A

1) The "unworthy offering" rules   §524
Regulation A may not be used when persons involved

in the offering have engaged in (wrongful) conduct indicating that potential investors may need the protection of full registration under section 5.

2) Limitation on dollar amount of securities offered §530
The securities offered under regulation A are limited to $5 million in any 12-month period. In addition, all security holders together may not sell more than $1.5 million of securities in any 12-month period, and the securities sold by security holders are counted against the issuer's $5 million limit.

a) Limitation due to integration of issues §535
Regulation A contains a safe harbor, providing that sales made in reliance on regulation A will not be integrated with prior offers or sales of securities sold in compliance with the 1933 Act or *subsequent offers* and sales that are (i) registered under section 5, (ii) made in reliance on Securities Act ("SA") rule 701 (relating to employee benefit plans), (iii) made in reliance on regulation S (concerning unregistered offers and sales made outside the United States), or (iv) made more than six months after completion of the regulation A offering.

(b) Regulation A procedures

1) Offering statement

a) Part I §537
Part I of the offering statement under regulation A (form 1-A) is a notification which is filed with the S.E.C. and is publicly available, but is not circulated to investors.

b) Part II §538
There are three possible formats for the offering circular:

1/ *Model A* is an extensive, fill-in-the-blank form and may be used by corporations;

2/ *Model B* provides a "pool" of disclosure materials and is available for corporate and noncorporate issuers; and

3/ *Form SB-2* is available for qualified small business issuers.

c) Part III §542
Part III specifies exhibits that must be filed in a regulation A offering.

2) S.E.C. processing procedures §543
There is a 20-day waiting period before the offering statement becomes effective. The S.E.C. can review the statement and recommend changes. The S.E.C. may *accelerate* the effective date when all S.E.C. comments have been addressed.

3) Reports of sales and use of proceeds §547
An issuer under regulation A must file a report of sales and use of proceeds of the offering every six months after the offering statement is qualified and within 30 days after the offering is completed.

4) Substantial and good faith compliance §548
Failure to comply with all of the requirements of regulation A does not result in a loss of the exemption as to a sale to a particular person *if* (i) the failure did not pertain to a term *intended to protect* that particular person; (ii) the failure was *insignificant*; and (iii) there was a *good faith and reasonable attempt* to comply with all applicable regulation A requirements.

(c) Offers and sales pursuant to regulation A

1) Solicitation of interest document §549
Before committing to an offering under regulation A, an issuer may publish or deliver to prospective purchasers (and send a copy to the S.E.C.) a written document or scripted radio or television broadcast to determine whether there is any interest in a contemplated securities offer, as long as the document or script states, among other things, that no money is being solicited, that no sales will be made until delivery of an offering circular, and that an indication of interest involves no obligation or commitment by the prospective purchaser. Also, the issuer's chief executive officer must be identified and its business or products described.

2) Preliminary offering circular §553
After the offering statement is filed, but before it is qualified by the S.E.C., a solicitation of interest document may no longer be used, but the offering statement may be used in the form in which it was filed as long as it contains a legend alerting potential investors that the document has not yet been qualified under regulation A. Oral offers are also permitted, as are "tombstone" ads.

3) Final offering circular required after qualification §557
After the offering statement is qualified, written offers may be made by means of the final offering circular,

which may be accompanied or followed by other written materials. "Tombstone" ads are also permitted. Generally, a sale may not be made unless the purchaser is furnished with a copy of the offering circular.

or other remuneration for soliciting the exchange—is exempt from the registration requirements of section 5. The exemption applies to only the initial transaction; later resales must be registered or find another exemption.

(a) "Clean exchange" required　　　　　　　　　§626

Although generally, the transaction is exempt only if it involves a "clean exchange" of the old securities for the new ones, payments from security holders are allowed if necessary to ensure that all holders of a class of securities receive the same treatment. Also, the exchange may call for cash payments from the issuer.

(3) Exemption for approved reorganizations　　　§630

The 1933 Act exempts from registration approved business reorganizations in which new securities are issued in exchange for outstanding securities, claims, or property interests.

(a) Authorized agencies　　　　　　　　　　　§631

Agencies that can approve such reorganizations include the courts, an agency of the United States, and state banking or insurance commissions.

(4) Business combinations and rule 145　　　　§634

Rule 145 clarifies which transactions—such as mergers—involve offers and sales and must be registered if no exemption is available. It replaces former S.E.C. rule 133, which formalistically provided that a "sale" occurred only if there was a volitional act on the part of the seller (thus exempting many reorganizations in which a corporation, rather than its shareholders, performed this act).

(a) Transactions covered by rule 145　　　　　§640

Rule 145 provides that, unless otherwise exempt, the following involve "sales" of securities if shareholder consent is necessary to complete the transaction.

1) Any *reclassification* of securities involving the substitution or exchange of one security for another;

2) Statutory *mergers, consolidations, or similar acquisitions* of one corporation by another; and

3) Many *transfers of assets.*

(b) Proper registration under rule 145

1) Form of registration　　　　　　　　　§647

Form S-4 is used to register under rule 145. It requires details about the proposed transaction and the acquiring and acquired (or selling) company. The form also serves as a proxy statement with which the required shareholder consent can be solicited (*infra*).

2) Delivery of prospectus　　　　　　　　§649

A prospectus and proxy statement must be given to

security holders in the acquired (or selling) company who are entitled to vote on the proposed transaction.

3) Communications not subject to prospectus requirement

§650

Certain written communications made to shareholders of the selling company are **not** considered to be a prospectus (or an offer to sell). For example, acquiring companies may make an offer to sell their securities, or offer to buy the target's securities, if the written offers comply with SA requirements.

(c) "Underwriters" in rule 145 transactions

§654

Any party to a rule 145 offering other than the issuer is deemed an underwriter. "Party" includes any person whose assets or capital structure is affected by the transaction.

1) Effect on control persons of acquired company

§657

The underwriter provisions limit the subsequent transfer of securities received by control persons in a rule 145 transaction.

2) Special exemption from underwriter status

§659

Three classes of persons are not considered underwriters under rule 145: (i) a person who sells the securities in **compliance with rule 144** (*infra*); (ii) a person who has held the securities of the acquiring company for at least **one year** and who is not affiliated with the issuer, if the issuer is subject to certain periodic reporting requirements; and (iii) a person who is **not an affiliate** of the issuer and has held the securities for at least **two years**.

i. Bankruptcy exemptions

§661

Exemptions from registration can arise under chapter 11 of the Bankruptcy Code.

(1) Disclosure requirements

§663

Under Chapter 11, a debtor's debts can be restructured, usually by exchanging new debt and/or equity securities for outstanding securities. When the Bankruptcy Code applies, the issuer is exempt from state and federal securities laws. The Bankruptcy Code requires that adequate information be given to each class affected by the restructuring to enable each to make an informed judgment about the proposed exchange.

(2) Debt securities

§667

The Bankruptcy Code does not allow the sale by the debtor of equity securities to raise new capital, but debt securities may be issued.

3. Resales and "Statutory Underwriters"

§670

Because most exempt **transactions** do not involve exempt **securities**, and because nonexempt securities that were sold in an exempt transaction cannot be sold without another exemption, a resale of securities can easily violate section 5. Furthermore, under the 1933 Act, anyone who purchases from a control person and resells to the public risks becoming an underwriter, even if not in the "business" of being an underwriter *e.g.*, a broker. Such persons are called "statutory underwriters."

a. Buyer's intent important §672

Underwriter status often depends on intent. If a buyer purchases from the issuer (or a control person) intending to distribute the securities, and a distribution occurs, the buyer has become an underwriter.

(1) Traditional factors showing investment intent §673

Whether an original purchaser bought for investment or distribution is a *question of fact*. The following factors are usually considered:

(a) Whether the original purchasers gave the issuer a *letter indicating that it is buying for investment purposes* rather than resale;

(b) The *length of time* the original purchaser holds the securities; and

(c) Whether the securities certificate includes a *legend* that the certificates cannot be transferred without the issuer's permission.

(2) Proof of investment intent—rule 144 §679

Rule 144 specifies objective criteria that establish investment intent. If these factors are met, purchasers may resell "restricted securities."

(a) Scope of rule 144

1) "Restricted securities" §681

Rule 144 defines "restricted securities" to include (i) *privately offered securities* acquired from an issuer or control person; (ii) securities *issued pursuant to rules 505 or 506*, or to rule 701(c) (employee benefit plans); (iii) securities *sold under rule 144A* (*infra*); and (iv) other securities *not previously offered to the public*.

2) Sales by control persons §682

Rule 144 states when and how many securities a control person may sell without making those who purchase and resell "underwriters." The rule applies to *both restricted and nonrestricted* securities held by control persons.

(b) Requirements of rule 144 §684

The limitations of rule 144 do *not* apply to sales by persons who are *not affiliates* of the issuer and have not been so for the *last three months*, and who have *held* the securities for at least *two years*. For all other sales of restricted securities, or sales by affiliates of the issuer, the following requirements must be met:

1) **Adequate public information about the issuer** §686
   Such information must be available to the public at the time of sale.

2) **One-year holding period for restricted securities** §689
   The *restricted* securities cannot be resold until one year after they were acquired, and this period is tolled until the initial buyer has *fully paid* for the securities.

3) **Limitation on amount of securities sold** §698
   During any three-month period, the volume of restricted securities, and securities held by control persons, that can be sold may not exceed the greater of: (i) *1%* of the shares of the outstanding class, (ii) *if* the security is *traded on an exchange,* the average weekly reported volume of the security on all exchanges and/or automated securities quotations systems for the four weeks prior to the filing of a notice of sale, and (iii) *the average weekly reported volume* of trading in the securities reported through the consolidated transaction reporting system during the four weeks prior to filing the notice of sale.

4) **Limitation on manner of sale** §701
   Sales made under rule 144 must be made directly with a "market-maker" (*infra*) or in "broker's transactions." The *person selling* the securities may *not solicit orders* or pay a commission to anyone other than the broker. The *broker* may *not* do more than *execute the sale* for the customary commission or *solicit orders to buy*; she must also make a *reasonable inquiry* that the seller can sell without registration.

5) **Notice of proposed sale** §702
   Rule 144 requires that a seller who intends to sell more than 500 shares or any number of shares for more than $10,000 must file a notice of intention with the S.E.C.

6) **Nonexclusive rule** §703
   Rule 144 is *not* exclusive; sales may be made pursuant to a registration statement, another exemption, or regulation A.

(3) **Alternatives to rule 144**

(a) **Registered transactions** §705
   While this is an option, it usually is not used because of expense and the need to secure the issuer's cooperation.

(b) **Regulation A exemption** §706
   Because this is less arduous than a fully registered offering, it is sometimes used as an alternative to rule 144.

section 12(a)(1) as the result of an improper offer in the pre-filing period, failure to deliver a required prospectus in the post-effective period, or other violations of section 5.

This can arise under sections 12(a)(2) or 17.

b. Remedies for 1933 Act violations

A plaintiff entitled to damages under section 11 receives the amount lost, subject to certain limitations. Sections 12(a)(1) and (2) permit a plaintiff to rescind the sale, receiving back her purchase price.

(2) S.E.C. lawsuits

These resemble injunctions in that they direct the respondent not to violate the Act further, but a cease-and-desist order can be *issued by the S.E.C.* (an injunction must be issued by the courts), and violation of the order may result in a *civil penalty* under the Act (while violation of an injunction results in a contempt citation). Cease-and-desist orders can be temporary or permanent. In the case of a permanent order, the S.E.C. may order a respondent to furnish an accounting and to disgorge any monies received in violation of the Act.

Section 20(b) of the 1933 Act gives the S.E.C. power to seek injunctive relief (and civil fines) from the courts whenever it appears that the Act or the rules have been, or are about to be, violated.

Section 24 of the 1933 Act imposes criminal penalties for *willful violations* of any provision of the Act.

2. Express Civil Liabilities

Section 11 imposes liability on designated persons for materially false or misleading statements or omissions in an effective registration statement or prospectus. Section 11 does *not apply to a free writing prospectus* because it is not part of the registration statement.

(a) *Every person who signs the registration statement* (issuer, principal executive officers, principal financial officer, controller or principal accounting officer, and a majority of the board of directors must sign the statement);

(b) *Every director of the issuer*;

(c) **_Every person about to become a director,_** who consents to being named in the registration statement;

(d) **_Every "expert"_** who consents to being named as having prepared or certified part of the registration statement;

(e) **_Every underwriter_** involved in the distribution; and

(f) **_Control persons_** of the issuer, unless they are without knowledge of the facts on which liability is based.

(2) Elements of plaintiff's cause of action

 (a) Material misstatements or omissions   **§783**
Material facts are those to which there is a substantial likelihood that a reasonable investor would attach importance in deciding whether to purchase the security.

 (b) Limited reliance requirement   **§786**
There is **_no_** reliance requirement **_unless_** the issuer sends out an earnings statement covering the period of one year **_after_** the effective date of the registration statement (a person thereafter acquiring some of the registered securities must prove reliance on the misrepresentation or omission to recover).

 (c) Secondary market purchasers   **§788**
There is a split of authority as to whether secondary market purchasers can recover under section 11. However, most courts hold that such persons can recover if they can prove that the purchased securities were issued pursuant to the defective registration statement ("tracing"). Privity of contract is **_not_** required.

 (d) Causation and damages   **§790**
Plaintiff need **_not_** prove that the loss was caused by defendant's misrepresentation. (But **_defendant_** can prove that all or some portion of the damages is due to some cause other than the misrepresentation.)

(3) Defenses

 (a) General affirmative defenses   **§792**
Any defendant, **_including_** the issuer, may plead the following defenses.

  1) **_The alleged misstatements were true;_**

  2) The facts misstated or omitted were **_not material_**;

  3) **_Plaintiff knew_** of the misrepresentations and invested anyway; and

  4) **_The statute of limitations_** has run.

 (b) Due diligence defenses   **§793**
All defendants, **_except_** the issuer, have a due diligence defense.

1) Statements made by experts §794

Experts may avoid liability as to the portions of the registration statement they certified if they can show that they *actually believed that the statements made were true,* and that their belief was *reasonable* (*i.e.,* they made a *reasonable investigation* of the supporting facts).

2) Statements made by nonexperts §795

Nonexperts are held to the same standard as experts. A reasonable investigation for a nonexpert must be the kind of investigation that a *prudent person* in the same position, with the same responsibilities, skill, and background would have made (*e.g.,* a nonexpert director-attorney drafting part of the registration statement must conduct an independent investigation to verify the material facts stated in the registration statement).

3) Nonexperts reviewing statements by other nonexperts §801

To avoid liability under the Act for statements made in the registration statement by other nonexperts, a nonexpert not involved in the actual drafting of the registration statement (*e.g.,* an underwriter or a member of the issuer's board of directors) must show that she exercised due diligence appropriate to her position and background. The standard of diligence required is the same as for nonexperts concerning their own representations in the registration statement.

4) Nonexperts reviewing statements made by experts §806

Here the standard of care is lower. *No investigation* need normally be made by the nonexpert, because nonexperts are entitled to rely to a greater extent on the statements of experts. The reviewing nonexpert need only show that she did not believe and had no reasonable ground to believe the statements made by the expert to be false. However, an investigation is *required* if facts suggest that the registration statement contains misstatements.

(4) Measure of damages

(a) If the stock is sold prior to filing suit §811

Plaintiff may recover the difference between the price paid for the stock (but not exceeding the price at which the security was offered to the public) and the price at which it was sold prior to suit.

(b) If the stock has not been sold prior to suit §812

Plaintiff may recover *either* the *difference* between the price paid (not exceeding the offering price) and the value of the security **at the time suit is filed, or** the **price** at which the stock was sold **after suit was instituted**, but before judgment, if such damages are less than those that result from using value at the time of suit.

(c) Plaintiff not required to mitigate damages §814
The plaintiff need not sell if the market price rises.

(d) Loss causation defense §817
A defendant is not liable for damages resulting from factors other than the misstatement.

(e) Joint and several liability §818
All persons (except outside directors) who are liable under section 11 are jointly and severally liable and may recover contribution.

1) Exception §819
In actions under section 11, **outside directors** of the issuer are **jointly and severally** liable for **knowing** violations, and **proportionately liable** to their respective degrees of fault for all other violations.

b. Section 12(a)(1)—liability for offers or sales in violation of section 5 §820
Under section 12(a)(1), any person who offers or sells a security in violation of any of the provisions of section 5 of the Act is liable to the purchaser for (i) the **consideration paid** (with interest) less the amount of any income received on the securities (*i.e.*, a suit for **rescission**); or (ii) for **damages** if the purchaser no longer owns the security.

(1) Any violation of section 5 §821
Liability attaches for any violation of any provision of section 5 (*i.e.*, a sale of unregistered securities, failure to deliver the required prospectus, etc.).

(a) "Control persons" §822
Persons who control a person liable under section 12(a)(1) may be jointly and severally liable with the controlled person.

(b) Participant liability §823
"Sellers" (or offerors) liable under section 12(a)(1) include the person who **actually passes title** to the security and persons who **solicit the purchase** from the purchaser, but **not** persons whose sole motivation in acting is to benefit the buyer.

(2) Defenses to a section 12(a)(1) cause of action §827
The most common defense to a section 12(a)(1) action is that the **privity** requirement has not been met; *i.e.,* direct privity of contract between plaintiff-purchaser and the seller-defendant is necessary. **Lack of any violation** and running of the **statute of limitations** are also defenses.

(ii) obtain money or property by means of misstatements or omissions of material fact; or (iii) engage in any transaction that operates as a fraud or deceit upon the purchaser. Section 17 is generally used by the government in civil and criminal fraud cases.

III. REGULATION OF SECURITIES TRADING—THE SECURITIES EXCHANGE ACT OF 1934

A. OVERVIEW OF THE 1934 ACT
The Securities Exchange Act of 1934 ("SEA" or "1934 Act") regulates the trading of securities subsequent to their original distribution.

companies), *or* companies having assets of more than *$10 million and a class of equity security held by 500 or more persons (over-the-counter companies) must* register that class of equity securities with the S.E.C. Such companies are known as *"reporting"* companies.

when made or to disclose *misleading omissions*. Courts are divided as to whether a duty exists to update disclosures that were accurate when made but that became misleading because of subsequent events. An issuer need *not* correct misleading statements by *third parties* unless the issuer was involved.

d. Misrepresentation with respect to a material fact §959
The misrepresentation or omission must be of a material fact. Remember that forward-looking statements, *e.g.*, earnings predictions, may be protected by safe harbor provisions (*supra*). Defendants may also be liable for facts disclosed but "buried" in the text.

(1) Materiality §973
The misrepresented or undisclosed fact must be "material" to the investor's decision. Materiality exists if there is a *substantial likelihood* that a reasonable investor would consider the fact of *significance* in the investment decision.

e. "In connection with" requirement §979
Defendant's fraud must be "in connection with" the plaintiff's purchase or sale of securities. Direct involvement in the transaction is not required, but there must be a sufficiently close nexus for a court to find that defendant's fraud was "in connection with" the purchase or sale; *i.e.*, *defendant* need *not be an actual purchaser or seller*. A showing of *reliance* or *loss causation* would probably establish the "in connection with" requirement, which does *not* require *privity.*

f. Scienter §993
Plaintiff must prove that defendant had "scienter" (*intent* to deceive, defraud, or manipulate); *i.e.*, negligence is not sufficient.

(1) Reckless conduct §996
Whether reckless conduct is sufficient has not been decided by the Supreme Court, but lower courts have unanimously found it sufficient. A safe harbor provision provides that a *private plaintiff* cannot recover for a fraudulent forward-looking statement absent the defendant's *actual knowledge* of its falsity.

(2) Defense of "due diligence" §999
The lower courts have also restricted the scope of the defense of plaintiff's lack of due diligence (*i.e.*, more courts seem to require that defendant show that plaintiff's fault in relying on defendant's representations was knowing and intentional; mere *negligence* by plaintiff is *not sufficient*).

g. Standing §1005
To have standing under rule 10b-5, a *plaintiff* must be either an actual purchaser or actual seller of securities. This requirement is imposed to prevent vexatious lawsuits. Derivative suits, actions for injunctions, and forced sales are excepted from the purchase and sale requirement.

h. Reliance §1012
Reliance (sometimes called "transaction causation") requires a showing

that plaintiff **actually believed** the misrepresentation, and that it was a **substantial factor** in plaintiff's entering the transaction.

(1) Relationship to materiality §1015

It would seem that reliance would follow from a fact's materiality; however, a fact may be material but not be given any actual significance in a particular investor's decision.

(2) Face-to-face transactions §1016

In cases of **affirmative misrepresentations**, the plaintiff must show that he actually relied on the defendant's misrepresentation. In **nondisclosure cases,** reliance generally is **presumed**.

(3) Open-market transactions §1019

Courts have tended to limit the need to prove reliance where the plaintiff has no face-to-face relationship with the defendant.

(a) "Fraud on the market" doctrine §1020

Courts apply the "fraud on the market" doctrine in an attempt to address the difficulty in showing reliance in open-market (impersonal) transactions. Application of the doctrine raises a **rebuttable presumption of reliance** so that a plaintiff need only show the materiality of the misrepresentation or omission.

i. Loss causation §1026

In addition to showing that reliance on a **material** misrepresentation was a substantial factor in causing a plaintiff to enter the transaction (transaction causation), she must show that the deception also directly caused the **loss**, which was a foreseeable outcome of the deception.

(1) Nondisclosure situations §1034

In **nondisclosure cases**, courts sometimes infer loss causation upon a showing of materiality, but may not apply the presumption when it is feasible to prove actual loss causation.

j. Burden of proof §1036

In private civil damages cases, plaintiff must show the rule 10b-5 violation by a **preponderance of the evidence**.

5. Insider Trading and the Duty to Disclose §1037

Rule 10b-5 has been found to prohibit some cases of trading on the basis of "inside" information.

a. Elements of a rule 10b-5 insider trading case §1038

The elements for an insider trading case are the same as in other rule 10b-5 cases, but analysis revolves around whether the activity was fraudulent. The standard today is that a purchase or sale of a security on the basis of material nonpublic information, **in breach of a duty** owed to the issuer or shareholders, or to any person who is the source of the information, violates rule 10b-5.

(1) Insiders §1040

An insider is an officer, director, controlling shareholder, or corporate employee of an issuer. **Constructive insiders** are persons in a confidential relationship with the issuer, *e.g.*, accountants, lawyers, bankers.

    (a) Tippees §1042

        A tippee is a person who receives a tip from an insider and subsequently trades securities related to the information.

    (b) Misappropriators §1043

        Persons who misappropriate material, nonpublic information in breach of a duty to the source of the information may also be liable for insider trading.

(2) Breach of duty §1044

A defendant must have breached some **identifiable duty not to use** the information for **personal benefit**.

(3) "On the basis of" material nonpublic information §1045

The problem of whether a person violates rule 10b-5 when in possession of information without actually using it to trade was resolved by adoption of **rule 10b5-1**: A person will be deemed to have purchased or sold a security on the basis of material nonpublic information if she was **aware of it** when purchasing or selling.

    (a) Affirmative defenses §1049

        Defendant can avoid liability under rule 10b5-1 by showing that the challenged trading took place pursuant to a binding contract, trading instruction, or **plan that existed before she became aware** of the information. Nonnatural persons (*e.g.*, institutions) have an additional defense—that the person making the investment decision was not aware of the material nonpublic information and that the institution had policies in place to ensure that the person doing the trading would not violate the insider trading rules.

(4) Application

    (a) Insiders §1053

        Insiders who trade on confidential, nonpublic information are liable to the persons with whom they trade.

    (b) Issuers §1057

        An issuer may be held liable if material information is not properly disclosed to shareholders and the public before trading in the corporation's securities begins.

    (c) Tippers §1058

        Tippers can be liable even if they themselves do not trade on the inside information.

    (d) Tippees §1059

        Tippees who trade on the basis of inside information can be held liable if: (i) the **tipper breached** her fiduciary duties in giving the tip and acted from a motive of **personal benefit**; and (ii) the **tippee knows or should know** this.

(e) Misappropriators and other corporate outsiders   §1065
Typically, a corporate outsider does not owe fiduciary duties to the issuer, especially in regard to use of *"market information"* (*i.e.,* information about the likely future price of the company's stock). The S.E.C. has argued that outsiders who take information not intended for them or who misuse information lawfully in their possession breach rule 10b-5 under a *"misappropriation"* theory. The Supreme Court has endorsed the theory in a criminal case, *i.e.*, the government (but not a private plaintiff) can prosecute a person for violation of rule 10b-5 when he misappropriates confidential information for trading purposes in breach of a duty to the source of the information.

1) Rule 10b5-2—"family" misappropriation   §1075
Breach of duty by a family member occurs when the recipient agrees to keep the information in confidence, or when the source and the recipient have a practice of sharing confidences and the recipient knows that the information should remain confidential, or when the recipient obtains the information from a spouse, parent, child, or sibling, unless she can show she was unaware that the information was confidential.

2) Misappropriation not available in private actions   §1076
Although the Supreme Court has not addressed the issue, circuit courts have held that private plaintiffs cannot rely on the misappropriation theory; they must show breach of duty. The government, however, may use the theory.

b. "Selective disclosure" and regulation FD   §1077
Regulation FD ("Fair Disclosure") was promulgated to control the *selective disclosure* by insiders of material nonpublic information to securities analysts (*i.e.*, disclosure by a regulated person to a regulated person).

(1) Timing of public disclosure   §1083
In the case of an intentional regulated disclosure, there is an obligation to *simultaneously* make the information public; in the case of an *inadvertent* disclosure, the public must be *promptly* informed.

c. Specific insider trading legislation

(1) Insider Trading Sanctions Act   §1087
This Act allows the S.E.C. to seek civil penalties of up to *three times* the ill-gotten profits.

(2) Insider Trading and Securities Fraud Enforcement Act of 1988   §1088
This Act provides a cause of action for persons who sold or purchased a security in the market at the time defendant sold or

purchased a security of the same class in violation of the 1934 Act. However, damages are limited to defendant's *profit gained or loss avoided*.

6. Remedies

a. Rescission   §1091
Although most 10b-5 actions seek damages, there is some authority permitting rescission, *i.e.*, plaintiff recovers the money or securities she parted with.

b. Restitution   §1093
Most courts grant the plaintiff *damages* based on restitution (what she has lost).

(1) Defendant's profits   §1096
As an alternative measure of damages, some courts are requiring that defendant disgorge any profits made in the securities transaction that violated rule 10b-5.

(2) Benefit of the bargain   §1097
Sometimes the plaintiff may recover the benefits she expected to make in the bargain.

(3) Insider trading cases   §1098
Insider trading in an impersonal market could subject the insider to potentially huge damages that far exceed the profits realized or loss avoided (*e.g.*, class actions). Thus, courts tend to limit damages in such cases.

c. Punitive damages   §1100
Punitive damages are *not* available under rule 10b-5.

d. Liability of multiple defendants   §1101
In *private actions*, persons who knowingly commit securities fraud are jointly and severally liable; all others are liable in proportion to their respective fault. A right of *contribution* exists.

e. S.E.C. actions   §1104
When the S.E.C. brings a rule 10b-5 action, it may seek remedies different from those sought by private plaintiffs, *e.g.*, injunction, criminal penalties.

7. Defenses

a. On the merits   §1106
A defendant can assert as a defense that the elements of the cause of action have not been proved.

b. Failure to plead with particularity   §1108
Under the Private Securities Litigation Reform Act of 1995 ("PSLRA"), actions based on fraud and *filed under the 1934 Act by a private party* must meet heightened standards of specificity at the complaint stage. The plaintiff must: (i) identify each misleading statement; (ii) state the

reasons why they are misleading; (iii) specify the facts forming this belief; and (iv) specify the facts giving rise to a strong inference that the defendant acted with scienter.

Other defenses include the **statute of limitations** (two years after discovery and no more than five years after the alleged violation occurred), certain **common law defenses** (e.g., in pari delicto), and **lack of due diligence** by the plaintiff.

Sometimes both section 17(a) and rule 10b-5 may apply in an action. Although the language of the two provisions is almost identical, the scope and burdens of proof may differ.

Rule 10b-5 actions are frequently brought as class actions and are governed by the Federal Rules of Civil Procedure regarding class actions.

The Act's procedural provisions make it considerably more difficult for private plaintiffs to bring securities class actions (infra).

A "tender offer" is an offer by a person (the "bidder") to purchase the securities of a corporation (the "target"), which is made directly to the shareholders of the target.

In 1968, the Williams Act was added to the 1934 Act specifically to regulate tender offers in areas of **reporting**, **disclosure**, and **antifraud**. Although the 1934 Act does not contain **remedies** for violation of tender offer rules, courts have **implied** remedies. The most recent trend, however, is to limit implied remedies for private rights of action.

2. Preliminary Reporting Requirement—Section 13(d)

Any person (or group of persons, such as a partnership) who within 12 months acquires beneficial ownership in excess of 5% of a class of equity security registered under section 12 of the 1934 Act, must, within 10 days after the acquisition, file an information statement with the S.E.C., sending copies to the issuer of the security and to any exchanges on which the security is traded.

A group triggers the filing requirement only if it is formed for the purpose of acquiring, holding, voting, or disposing of the securities. If the disclosure requirements are circumvented by having others not subject to reporting purchase the securities (stock "parking"), the defendants are heavily penalized and profits must be disgorged.

The information statement must disclose information about the **purchasers,** the *consideration* paid, the *purpose* of the purchases, the percentage of *ownership,* and the *contracts* or other arrangements the purchaser has made regarding the issuer and its securities.

c. **Exemptions from 13(d)** §1156

(1) *Purchases made pursuant to a registered offering* under the 1933 Act;

(2) *Purchases made by the issuer of its own equity securities*; and

(3) *Acquisitions made by the exercise of state-law preemptive subscription rights* in an offering to all holders of the securities subject to the rights.

d. **Implied private rights of action** §1158
The *target* has an implied right of action against the bidder for a violation of section 13(d), and the *shareholders of the target* also have standing.

3. **Basic Tender Offer Rules—Section 14(d)** §1161
Section 14(d) contains the basic regulatory provisions concerning a tender offer.

a. **Definition of a "tender offer"** §1162
There is no explicit statutory definition of the term "tender offer," but it is generally thought to be an offer to purchase that is made "publicly" and not in normal exchange or over-the-counter market transactions. The courts look at the facts of each case and define the term broadly to effectuate the purposes of the 1934 Act.

b. **Requirements of section 14(d)** §1170
Under section 14(d) it is unlawful to use the means of interstate commerce to make a tender offer if, at consummation, the bidder will be the beneficial owner of more than 5% of the class of securities tendered, *unless* the following requirements are met:

(1) **Disclosure of information**

(a) **Schedule TO** §1172
At or before the commencement of the tender offer, the bidder must file a schedule TO, which is similar to schedule 13D, but contains additional information (*e.g.*, past contacts with the subject company, persons who will be retained or employed in connection with the offer, financial statements of the bidder (if material), etc.).

(b) **Disclosure and publication of tender offer documents** §1176
The bidder must either publish a summary of the schedule TO information in a newspaper or publish a short advertisement stating the offer's essential terms and where complete offer materials may be obtained.

(2) **Substantive requirements**

(a) **Withdrawal right** §1180
Offerees may withdraw securities they have tendered at any

time while the offer remains open. However, offer rules permit a *subsequent offering period*, extending the offer to shareholders who did not participate in the original offer, during which withdrawal rights need *not* be extended.

(b) Pro rata purchases §1182

If a greater number of shares are offered than the bidder sought to purchase, the bidder must purchase them pro rata from each person who tenders shares.

(c) Equal treatment of security holders §1183

A tender offer must be open to all holders of the securities for which the offer is made, and consideration paid to any holder must be equivalent to the highest consideration paid to any holder during the offer.

(d) Application of equal treatment rule §1184

Some courts apply the equal treatment rule *broadly* to include all contractual arrangements that depend on the tender offer's success. Other courts apply it more *narrowly*, finding that only persons selling during the tender offer period are subject to the equal treatment rule. Courts go both ways when *employment agreements* are involved in the offer.

(e) No purchases outside the offer §1187

The bidder cannot make purchases of the issuer's shares other than through the tender offer.

(f) Target company recommendations §1188

Within 10 business days after a tender offer commences, the target company must disseminate to shareholders a statement disclosing its position on the tender offer.

(g) Disclose or abstain from trading §1189

Any person who obtains information about a tender offer from the bidder or the target must disclose the information to the public *or* abstain from trading in the securities. Bidders are exempt.

(3) Registration under 1933 Act §1190

If a tender offer involves the public offer of the bidder's securities to the target's shareholders, the bidder must register the securities, absent an exemption. All other rules regarding offers of securities also apply to tender offer situations.

(4) When tender offer begins §1191

A tender offer begins at 12:01 a.m. on the date that the bidder first provides the *means to tender* to security holders. *Precommencement communications* must be filed with the S.E.C. and copies delivered to the target and any other bidder.

e. **Purchase of its own shares**   §1238

Management of the target may attempt to have the company purchase
enough of its own shares on the open market or in a self-tender to prevent
control from going to another company. When a tender offer has commenced, the target **must comply** with 1934 Act **rule 13e-1** before purchasing its own securities.

    (1) **Self-tender offers**   §1240

    If the target's program amounts to a tender offer, it must comply
    with rule 13e-4, requiring the same type of disclosure that bid-
    ders must make.

    (2) **Pre-tender offer and open-market purchases**   §1241

    If the target's open market purchases cause the price of its securi-
    ties to rise, the purchases may be deemed "manipulative" and in
    violation of the 1934 Act. The issuer can comply with rule **10b-18's
    safe harbor provisions** to avoid such treatment.

f. **"Poison pill"**   §1249

Also known as a "shareholder rights plan," this technique gives the
shareholders of a potential target the right to either purchase securities
at a low price or force a successful bidder to buy securities at a high
price.

    (1) **Proxy contests as countertactic**   §1254

    Because poison pills make it difficult or impossible to take over a
    target, it is common for bidders to negotiate with target boards to
    redeem the pill. Upon a board's refusal, the bidder may launch a
    proxy contest to replace the directors. However, the board may
    attempt to institute a pill triggered by a proxy solicitation, or a pill
    that provides it can be redeemed only by directors in office prior
    to the tender offer. Both such board actions raise possible fidu-
    ciary duty problems.

g. **"Greenmail"**   §1257

This is a payment from the target to the bidder to persuade the bidder
to abandon its takeover plans. State law generally governs the legality
of such payments, although there is a 50% nondeductible federal excise tax on profit received in a greenmail transaction.

h. **Employee stock ownership plans ("ESOPs")**   §1259

An ESOP can be structured to make it difficult for a bidder to gain control
of the target.

i. **Stock "lockups"**   §1268

An issuer may choose to issue shares to a white knight (*i.e.*, a more favorable bidder) to prevent an unfriendly takeover.

j. **"Crown jewel" lockups**   §1269

Here, the target grants an option to a white knight to purchase the target's
most valuable asset.

4. Proxy Statement Delivery Requirements §1307
Solicitation is generally **prohibited without delivery** of the proxy statement and, if directors are to be elected, an annual report.

    a. Exceptions §1311
    Delivery requirements do not apply to **public solicitations** (*e.g.*, by advertisement), if the soliciting person (other than an issuer) is **not seeking proxy authority**, or during **proxy contests** before a proxy statement is filed.

5. Proxy Statement Filing Requirements §1315
All written materials used in a solicitation must be filed with the S.E.C. Generally, both the proxy statement and the form of proxy (*i.e.*, the actual form on which shareholders grant authority to vote their shares) must be filed with the S.E.C. **at least 10 days before** definitive versions are sent to the shareholders. Preliminary copies need not be filed for meetings where only routine matters are scheduled, *e.g.*, election of directors.

6. Proxy Statement §1322
The proxy statement must include details about the solicitation and about director election, specific matters (*e.g.*, mergers), executive compensation, and some general matters (*e.g.*, significant changes in control).

7. Proxy Contests §1328
Proxy contests usually result from a fight between management and other shareholders (insurgents) for control of the company. To gain control, insurgents may solicit proxies to elect a majority of directors. To keep control, management may solicit proxies to support a merger with another company.

    a. Exception to filing requirements §1329
    Because proxy contests often require quick action, the general exception (*see supra*, §1311) is used before actually filing a proxy statement.

    b. Shareholder lists §1330
    State law normally governs the question of when a corporation must make a shareholder list available to a shareholder. The **federal** proxy rules do not require management to provide a list **except** when management is itself soliciting proxies (then it must either give the requesting shareholder complete access to the registrant's shareholder list **or** mail the shareholder's proxy solicitation material to the other shareholders).

8. Shareholder Proposals §1335
An alternative to independent proxy solicitation allows a shareholder to serve notice on management of an intention to propose action at the shareholders' meeting. In such a case, management may be compelled to include the proposal in its proxy statement.

    a. Requirements §1336
    The proponent must meet certain share ownership requirements (*e.g.*, 1% or $2,000 market value) and procedural requirements (*e.g.,* no more than 500 words).

    b. Management's omission of shareholder proposals §1350
    If management opposes the proposal and wishes to omit it from the proxy

statement, it must file the proposal and the reasons for opposing it with the S.E.C. The S.E.C. will review the proposal and state its position. Management may properly omit a shareholder proposal in the following situations:

(1) The proposal is **not a "proper subject"** for action by shareholders.

(2) The proposal is **illegal**.

(3) The proposal is **contrary to S.E.C. rules or regulations**.

(4) The proposal relates to **redress of a personal claim**.

(5) The proposal **relates to insignificant operations of the registrant** (*i.e.*, accounts for less than 5% of the registrant's total assets and net earnings and is not significant to the corporation in any other way).

(6) The proposal deals with a **matter beyond the registrant's power to effectuate**.

(7) The proposal deals with the **ordinary business operations** of the registrant and (possibly) does not involve any substantial public policy or other considerations.

(8) The proposal relates to an **election to office**.

(9) The proposal is **counter to a proposal to be submitted by the registrant** at the meeting.

(10) The proposal has been rendered **moot.**

(11) The proposal is **duplicative** of an earlier submitted proposal.

(12) The proposal or a substantially similar proposal was **rejected** within the preceding five years and received less than a specified percentage of votes.

(13) The proposal relates to **specific amounts of cash or stock dividends**.

9. **Participation of Broker-Dealers in Proxy Contests**

   a. **Stock held in "street name"** §1367
   Solicitation from banks or broker-dealers holding securities in "street name" (the name of the bank or brokerage firm rather than the beneficial owner) are governed by the national exchanges as well as the S.E.C. The S.E.C. requires proxy solicitation material to be forwarded promptly to the beneficial owners.

   b. **Solicitations by broker-dealers** §1373
   These are subject to S.E.C. rules.

10. **Exemptions from Proxy Rules** §1375
    The following are exempt from the federal proxy rules:

    a. Solicitations of 10 or fewer persons;

b. Solicitations by the beneficial owners of securities from the **registered** owners;

c. Tombstone ads;

d. Broker-dealers' impartial transmission of solicitation materials to beneficial owners;

e. Statements of intended vote, *i.e.,* written communications from a security holder stating how the holder intends to vote and the reasons therefor;

f. Solicitations by persons not seeking proxy authority; and

g. Solicitations by public broadcast, speech, advertisement, etc.

11. Enforcement Provisions §1393

There is a **private right of action** for violation of proxy rules.

a. Antifraud provisions §1395

Actions claiming a violation of the proxy rules may be brought under the antifraud provisions of the 1934 Act relating to the solicitation of proxies. [See SEA Rule 14a-9] To establish a cause of action for fraud, the following elements must be proved:

(1) Misrepresentations or omissions of fact §1396

(2) Materiality §1399

The misrepresentation or omission must be of a material fact. The **test** is whether there is a **substantial likelihood** that a reasonable shareholder would consider the fact of significance in determining how to vote.

(a) Significant information §1400

Material facts include not only information disclosed in a proxy statement, but also other information, *i.e.*, the **"total mix."** For example, **piecemeal disclosures, facts buried** in voluminous disclosure, and **conflicts of interest** may be considered significant facts.

(3) Standard of culpability §1406

Liability of a corporation and possibly its officers, directors, and employers may be based on a finding of **negligence**. **Scienter** is required for **outside accountants** in private actions.

(4) Causation §1411

Plaintiff must prove that the misrepresentation or omission of a material fact was the cause of the loss. The Supreme Court has held that the test for causation under rule 14a-9 is to be defined in terms of **materiality**.

(a) Solicitation as an "essential link" §1414

Once materiality is shown, causation is proved by showing that the proxy solicitation itself was an essential link in effecting the transaction (*i.e.*, that the votes represented by the proxies were necessary to approve the transaction).

a. **More than 10% holder** §1442

In determining whether a person is a more than 10% holder of a class of registered equity securities, all securities of the class beneficially owned by him are counted. ***For this purpose only***, beneficial ownership means having ***voting power*** over the securities.

b. **All other section 16 purposes** §1443

For all other purposes (*e.g.*, calculating profits) beneficial ownership means having a direct or indirect ***pecuniary interest in the shares***. Officers and directors are ***presumed*** to have a pecuniary interest in all securities ***owned by family members*** (*i.e.*, virtually ***all relatives who share a household*** with the insider).

5. **"Insiders" Defined**

a. **Officers and directors** §1447

Officers and directors of ***subsidiaries*** may be deemed officers of the issuer if they perform policy-making functions for the issuer. ***Timing issues*** are important in determining whether a person is an officer or director for section 16 purposes.

(1) **If the transaction takes place before a person becomes an officer or director** §1452

Section 16 does not apply.

(2) **If the transaction occurs after a person ceases to be an officer or director** §1453

Liability attaches only if it takes place within six months of a transaction that happened while the person was an officer or director.

(3) **An officer or director becomes subject to section 16** §1454

In situations where a company has no equity securities registered but then does register a class of securities and (i) the insider engaged in a second transaction after becoming subject to the reporting requirement, and (ii) the second transaction took place within six months of the first transaction, then both transactions must be reported and profits disgorged.

(4) **Deputization** §1455

Section 16 may also apply when a corporation appoints an officer or director to an inside position in a second corporation and the appointing corporation engages in a prohibited sale or purchase.

b. **More than 10% shareholder** §1458

Every person who directly or indirectly is the beneficial owner of more than 10% of any class of registered securities is subject to section 16. Remember that having or sharing the ***power to vote*** more than 10% of any class results in insider status.

(1) **Timing** §1460

A more-than-10% shareholder must be such ***both*** at the time of the purchase ***and*** at the time of the sale.

as the significant event (*i.e.*, the "purchase" or "sale") rather than the exercise of the stock option, which is considered merely a change from indirect to direct beneficial ownership.

(1) Stock appreciation rights §1496
Stock appreciation rights ("S.A.R.s") give officers a cash bonus equal to the increase in value of optional shares from the date of grant of the S.A.R. and its exercise. S.A.R.s, most employee benefit plans, and most employee compensation are usually exempt from section 16.

c. Recapitalizations §1497
Recapitalizations (*e.g.*, an exchange of a new security for an outstanding security) generally are *not* considered to involve a purchase or sale of the new stock.

d. Stock dividends and gifts §1499
When a corporation issues additional shares of common stock pro rata to its shareholders by issuing "rights" to acquire additional shares, or warrants, or the shares themselves, there is *no "purchase"* by the shareholders. However, the *exercise* of a right or warrant *is* a purchase. Similarly, a bona fide gift is *not* a purchase.

e. Reorganizations §1502
Generally, when a corporation is merged or sold in exchange for stock, there is a "sale" of the securities surrendered and a "purchase" of the securities received.

(1) Exemption for "unorthodox transactions" §1506
The Supreme Court has held that certain mergers are "unorthodox" and do *not* present the *dangers of abuse of inside information* and so are not covered by section 16.

(2) Parent-subsidiary combinations §1509
When a parent company merges with an 85% or more owned subsidiary and the shareholders of the parent receive a new security in exchange for their shares, the parent's shareholders are not treated as having made a "purchase" or "sale."

8. Within a Period of Less than Six Months §1510
Under section 16, a *fractional day counts as a full day.* Thus, the statutory period of "less than six months" begins at any time on day 1 and ends at midnight on the day that is *two days before* the date that is six months later, so that the period comprises *less* than six months. If it ended on the day before the six month anniversary, the period would be exactly six months, not "less than" six months.

9. "Profit" Under Section 16(b) §1520
The profit under section 16(b) is calculated by matching the highest and lowest prices of stock transactions of *any* purchase or sale during any six-month period. Any *loss* transactions are ignored.

a. **Matching transactions in derivative securities** §1526

The S.E.C. treats transactions in derivative securities (*e.g.*, stock options) as transactions in the underlying security.

(1) **Derivative securities with identical characteristics** §1527

If the derivatives traded have identical characteristics (*e.g.*, director trades call options several times within a six-month period), profit is determined in the normal way under section 16(b) (*i.e.*, compare the purchase and sale prices of the derivatives).

(2) **Derivative securities with different characteristics relating to the same underlying security** §1528

Here, the maximum profit recoverable is the difference in price of the *underlying security* on the relevant dates (*e.g.*, if a director purchases 10 call options, each allowing him to immediately buy 100 shares, and a few days later sells convertible debentures that may be immediately converted into 1,000 shares, the profit is based on the difference in price of the underlying stock on the days the transactions occurred).

10. Other Elements of Damages §1531

A section 16 plaintiff can recover defendant's profits. Additionally, the court has discretion to award interest on the profit made. Dividends declared on the actual shares sold while the insider held them may also be part of the profit. Attorneys' fees are usually recoverable too.

11. Strict Liability §1538

The general rule is that there are no defenses to a section 16(b) action **except** for **unorthodox transactions**.

12. Procedural Aspects of Actions Under Section 16

a. **Jurisdiction** §1540

Jurisdiction is exclusively in the federal courts.

b. **Service** §1541

Service of process is nationwide.

c. **Venue** §1542

Venue lies where any act or transaction constituting the violation occurred or where the defendant can be found or transacts business.

d. **Statute of limitations** §1543

Actions must be brought within **two years** after the profit is realized, but if the insider has not filed reports under section 16(a), the period is tolled until the profits should have been discovered.

e. **Proper plaintiff** §1545

The corporation may sue, but if it declines, **any** security holder may bring a **derivative action** on behalf of the corporation. The S.E.C. may **not** bring an action for violation of section 16(b).

13. Exemptions from Section 16(b) Liability

a. **Securities received in foreclosure on a debt previously contracted** §1552

power to bring civil actions against those who aid and abet any violators of the 1934 Act or rules thereunder.

(2) SOXA and the scandals of 2001-2002 §1573

It appears that Congress and courts are both willing to impose secondary liability. A SOXA provision directs the S.E.C. to study data from 1998 through 2001 to determine, in part, how many secondary persons (*e.g.*, accountants, lawyers, etc.) aided and abetted securities laws violations but were not sanctioned.

2. Liability of Controlling Persons §1577

Both the 1933 Act and the 1934 Act make "controlling persons" liable for the securities law violations of persons they control.

a. Liability under 1933 Act §1578

Any person who controls a person found liable under sections 11 or 12 is jointly and severally liable along with the liable party, ***unless*** the controlling person had no knowledge of, nor reasonable grounds to know of, the facts underlying the controlled person's liability. [SA §15]

b. Liability under 1934 Act §1579

Controlling persons are liable for the securities violations of persons they control, unless they acted in "good faith" and did not directly or indirectly induce the acts underlying the controlled person's liability. [SEA §20(a)]

c. "Controlling person" §1580

Whether a person is controlling depends on the degree of power and influence the person has. In general, persons have control over their ***agents***, but not necessarily over independent contractors.

d. Defenses compared §1584

Ignorance is a clear defense under section 15 of the 1933 Act, whereas section 20(a) of the 1934 Act requires a controlling person to prove that it did not induce the offense ***and*** that it acted in ***good faith***. Proving good faith might require more than proving ignorance; generally the defendant must prove that it had some reasonable procedure for supervising the primary wrongdoer.

e. Application of agency principles §1586

Central Bank (*supra*) makes it unlikely that a respondeat superior claim against an employer can be brought under federal securities laws but may possibly be brought under state law if a state law was violated.

3. Liability of "Outside" Directors

a. Under 1933 Act §1588

An outside director may be held liable under section 11 or as a controlling person under section 15.

b. Under 1934 Act

(1) Liability as an aider or abettor §1590

Outside directors might be held liable as aiders or abettors if they knowingly assist others in violations of the securities laws.

a duty to speak. The courts are split on whether the duty can arise from participation in the fraudulent scheme or whether it must be established outside the securities laws.

(3) Scope of responsibility §1637

The accountants' duty may extend to all persons they could **reasonably expect** would use the financial statements in their decisionmaking.

d. Disclosure of relationship §1642

The S.E.C. requires public accountants to disclose their **accountant-client relationship**.

6. Liability of Lawyers §1643

There are two views on the lawyer's role. Traditionally, lawyers are responsible chiefly to their clients. The S.E.C., however, maintains that lawyers owe a duty to the public and should inform the government if a client decides not to follow the lawyer's advice. However, SOXA has greatly expanded regulation of securities lawyers.

a. Liability to clients §1644

Lawyers may be held liable to their clients for intentional or negligent failure to perform properly. **Third parties** may also have a cause of action.

b. Liability as principals §1645

In addition, a lawyer may become so involved in a client's transaction that she becomes liable as a principal.

c. Liability to those affected by securities transactions §1646

Determine whether the claim results from the lawyer's involvement as a principal or as an aider and abettor.

(1) Liability as a participant §1647

If lawyers go beyond merely counseling their client (*e.g.*, where the lawyer is a **director** of the issuer, participates as an **expert**, or qualifies as a **"seller"**), liability can arise from these additional roles.

(2) Aiding and abetting liability

(a) Under 1933 Act §1652

Most of the 1933 Act's remedial provisions state specifically who may be liable and do not include aiders and/or abettors. The government, however, may claim that a lawyer aided and abetted a client's violation under section 17(a) (general fraud provision).

(b) Under 1934 Act §1653

After *Central Bank*, **private** actions are **not** permitted against an aider and abettor, although the **S.E.C. can** proceed against such persons.

d. Injunctions §1655

The S.E.C. has traditionally punished lawyers with injunctions. For rule

10b-5 actions, the S.E.C. must show that a lawyer *knowingly* violated securities laws; under many other provisions, only negligence need be shown.

e. Professional responsibility under SOXA §1657

SOXA mandates "*up-the-ladder*" reporting of a *material violation* of securities law, *breach of fiduciary duty*, or similar violations by an issuer or its agents. Thus, a lawyer is required to report violations to the issuer's chief legal officer. If that person does not *appropriately respond*, then the lawyer must report "higher up" to the audit committee or other committee. Lawyers may, in the future, be subject to a noisy withdrawal requirement. SOXA provides explicit authority for S.E.C. discipline of attorneys practicing before it.

(1) Qualified legal compliance committee ("QLCC") §1667

Most issuers will probably establish a QLCC that is responsible for legal compliance. The committee must include at least one member of the issuer's audit committee and two or more members of the board of directors who are not employed by the issuer.

(2) Sanctions for violations §1672

SOXA authorizes the S.E.C. to censure or deny a violating lawyer the privilege of practicing before it. It may additionally seek available civil penalties and remedies for violations of federal securities laws.

G. S.E.C. ENFORCEMENT ACTIONS

1. S.E.C. Investigations §1674

The 1934 Acts permits the S.E.C. to conduct investigations into possible violations. Investigations go through several stages. Once the investigation has become formal, then the S.E.C. may issue subpoenas. Witnesses have the right to be represented by counsel.

a. Section 21(a) reports §1688

This provision of the 1934 Act grants the S.E.C. discretionary power to publish information regarding probable violations of the securities laws, without any formal administrative proceedings.

2. S.E.C. Administrative Proceedings §1689

If the S.E.C. determines after investigation that an enforcement action should be commenced, it may begin an administrative proceeding in front of an administrative law judge who works for the S.E.C. In such proceedings, the S.E.C. can impose a wide variety of sanctions under the Securities Enforcement Remedies and Penny Stock Reform Act, *infra*, including civil fines, disgorgement of profits, and cease-and-desist orders.

3. S.E.C. Injunctive Actions §1695

The S.E.C. may also seek a temporary or permanent injunction in federal district court to enjoin persons who have violated or who are about to violate the securities laws. An injunction may be a severe penalty because the securities laws disqualify persons from engaging in many aspects of the securities business if the person has had an injunction entered against him. Also, as a result of an injunction, many civil actions may be filed against the defendant. Issues decided in the injunctive action cannot be relitigated in the private action for damages. Injunctions should be issued only if there is a realistic likelihood of the recurrence of future wrongdoing.

a. Ancillary relief §1708
The S.E.C. may impose other remedies for past harm and to prevent future harm, including appointment of receiver, profit disgorgement, appointment of special counsel, requiring resignation of officers and directors, appointment of independent directors, and imposition of civil fines. SOXA authorizes additional equitable relief for the benefit of investors.

4. Self-Regulatory Enforcement §1717
Self-regulatory organizations ("S.R.O.s"—such as the New York Stock Exchange and the National Association of Securities Dealers) enforce both the S.E.C.'s rules and regulations and their own rules. Disciplinary actions taken by S.R.O.s can be appealed to the S.E.C.

5. Securities Enforcement Remedies and Penny Stock Reform Act of 1990 §1721
This provision amended both the 1933 and 1934 Acts, enhancing existing remedies and providing new ones. The S.E.C. has the power to seek, in addition to disgorgement of profits, civil monetary penalties and bars against persons from serving as officers or directors of 1934 Act reporting companies. It also allows the S.E.C. to issue cease-and-desist orders, which are similar to injunctions, but unlike an injunction, can be issued without court action.

H. THE PRIVATE SECURITIES LITIGATION REFORM ACT OF 1995 §1731
In addition to its safe harbor for forward-looking statements (*supra*), the 1995 Act made several other important changes to the securities laws, mainly regarding the conduct of litigation by private parties.

1. Limitations of the 1995 Act §1732
The Act does *not apply* to actions brought by:

a. The *federal government*;

b. The *securities self-regulatory organizations*;

c. *Private plaintiffs under other federal laws* (except that private civil RICO actions based on securities law violations are limited by the Act);

d. *Private plaintiffs under state securities laws*;

e. *State securities regulators*; and

f. *Private plaintiffs under common law fraud theories*.

2. Major Provisions §1733
Provisions affecting pleadings have been discussed *supra*. However, defendants can now move for a *special verdict* on the scienter issue. Major changes in the way *class action* lawsuits are conducted were included to eliminate widespread abuses.

a. **The Securities Litigation Uniform Standards Act of 1998**   §1745
    Because of the more difficult federal requirements, the 1995 Act resulted in the movement of class actions to state courts. In response, Congress passed this 1998 Act, which preempts state law class actions that allege misrepresentation or omission of a material fact, or the use of a manipulative or deceptive device, in connection with the purchase or sale of a security. In effect, ***blue sky fraud litigation is preempted*** if it is a class action or involves consolidated actions of more than 50 plaintiffs.

b. **Discovery**

    (1) **Stay of discovery**   §1746
        A stay of discovery is entered when the defendant files a motion to dismiss, thus eliminating unnecessary costs that often forced issuers to settle. However, discovery will ***not be stayed*** when the plaintiff would suffer ***undue prejudice*** from the stay or when ***loss of evidence*** may result.

    (2) **No stay of disclosure**   §1750
        A stay of discovery is not the same as a stay of disclosure.

    (3) **"Actual knowledge"**   §1751
        Even while discovery is presumptively stayed, the court may permit discovery to show actual knowledge of falsity in a forward-looking statement that the defendant claims is exempt under the safe harbor provision.

c. **Damages capped**   §1752
    Damages in 1934 Act actions are limited to the ***difference between the price paid*** (or in a sale, the price received) and the ***average trading price*** of the security during the 90-day period beginning on the day corrective information is disseminated to the public.

d. **Contribution and proportionate liability**   §1753
    To reduce "deepest pocket" lawsuits, joint and several liability has been sharply limited:

    (1) In actions under the ***1934 Act***, joint and several liability is limited to those who ***knowingly commit*** a violation.

    (2) In ***Section 11 actions*** (***1933 Act***), joint and several liability of ***outside directors*** is limited to those who ***knowingly commit*** a violation.

    (3) In actions under ***either the 1933 or 1934 Acts***, "knowingly commit" means ***actual knowledge*** of the falsity or fraud, and defendants are provided ***express rights of contribution***.

e. **Loss causation**   §1754
    In private actions under the 1934 Act, plaintiffs must prove that the defendant caused the loss. Under section 12(a)(2) of the 1933 Act, the defendant may prove that all or part of plaintiff's loss was caused by events other than the alleged misstatement or omission.

(2) **Crimes committed "knowingly and willfully"** §1777
Knowingly and willfully failing to maintain records (for five years) and workpapers may result in a fine and imprisonment for up to 10 years. A *knowing false certification* of financial statements may result in a fine of up to $1 million and a 10-year prison term; the penalties for a *knowing and willful certification* are increased to up to a $5 million fine and a 20-year prison term.

(3) **Crimes committed corruptly** §1781
SOXA broadens the "tampering" crime to include corrupt actual or attempted alteration, destruction, or concealment of a record (or other object) to impair its availability in an official proceeding, or other actual or attempted obstruction of, or influence on, an official proceeding. A fine and up to 20 years' imprisonment may be imposed.

d. **Statute of limitations** §1782
The statute of limitations for S.E.C. actions is five years.

3. **Illegal Trading Under 1934 Act** §1783
Selling or buying securities without complying with other technical, regulatory requirements is now prosecuted, *e.g.*, *stock parking* (one person holds title to securities on behalf of another person).

4. **Mail Fraud and Wire Fraud** §1786
A criminal case for mail fraud or wire fraud requires proof of a *scheme to defraud, specific intent to defraud,* and *the mailing* of a letter or sending of a wire in furtherance of the scheme. SOXA increased prison sentences for such frauds from five years to 20 years.

5. **Racketeer-Influenced and Corrupt Organizations Act ("RICO")**

a. **Sanctions** §1795
RICO includes criminal penalties of 20-year prison terms, heavy criminal fines, forfeiture of the defendant's interest in the criminal enterprise, and a pretrial freeze on the defendant's assets.

(1) **Civil RICO** §1799
Although RICO also includes a civil cause of action for anyone injured in his business or property because of a RICO violation, civil RICO is *unavailable to private plaintiffs* for conduct actionable as fraud in the purchase or sale of securities, *unless the defendant was criminally convicted* based on the fraud.

b. **Establishing a violation** §1800
It must be proved that the defendant engaged in a pattern of racketeering activity, defined to mean *at least two acts* of racketeering activity within 10 years (excluding imprisonment time) of each other. Racketeering acts include murder, kidnapping, gambling, arson, robbery, bribery, extortion, narcotics offenses, securities fraud, and mail and wire fraud.

(1) **Relationship plus continuity** §1804
A pattern of racketeering requires proof of the *two predicate acts plus* the *relationship of the acts to one another* and that the acts

(i) **_The New York Stock Exchange_** and regional exchanges;

(ii) **_Over-the-counter markets;_** and

(iii) **_Institutional trading._**

(1) Alternative trading systems §1831

Institutional investors are allowed to trade directly with one another. Due to the rapid increase in the use of these trading systems, the S.E.C. promulgated regulation ATS, which requires a system to **_either_** register as an exchange or as a broker-dealer.

b. National market system §1833

With the development of sophisticated communications technology, a national securities market (combining all of the above markets) is now possible. Congress has directed the S.E.C. to use its authority to develop such a system.

3. Self-Regulation of Exchanges vs. S.E.C. Supervision

a. Registration with the S.E.C. §1836

Absent an exemption, a broker-dealer is prohibited from trading on an exchange not registered with the S.E.C.

b. Self-regulation with S.E.C. supervision §1837

The exchanges may adopt rules for their own regulation, but the S.E.C. has power to review such rules and to propose others. The SEA also gives the S.E.C. extensive power to impose sanctions on exchanges, their members, and associates for violations of the federal securities laws.

4. Accommodation of Exchange Rules to the Federal Antitrust Laws §1842

Traditionally, the exchanges sought to limit competition and enhance the economic position of their members.

a. Rules in restraint of competition §1843

In the past, anticompetitive practices of the exchanges have included:

(1) **_Setting fixed commission rates;_**

(2) **_Restricting membership_** on the exchange;

(3) **_Restricting the opportunity to transact business_** on the exchange exclusively to exchange members; and

(4) **_Prohibiting exchange members from executing transactions off the floor_** of the exchange.

b. Securities laws do not preempt field §1844

The Supreme Court has indicated that the securities laws should accommodate the antitrust laws. However, if there is "clear incompatibility" between the securities laws and the antitrust laws, the antitrust laws will not be enforced.

c. Fixed commission rate §1846

An S.E.C. rule now prohibits exchanges from adopting rules fixing commission rates charged by exchange members **_unless_** the rates are **_reasonable_** in relation to the services and do not impose any **unnecessary or inappropriate burden** on competition.

5. **The Specialist System**

the OTC market, and as dealers (*i.e.*, as principals owning the security and acting as either a buyer or seller in the transaction).

3. Transaction Information Systems §1898

OTC price information is disseminated by means of newspapers, the NASDAQ system, pink sheets, and the OTC Bulletin Board. The latter is operated by the NASD as an electronic interdealer quotation system. It contains quotes on stocks not available in the NASDAQ system, thus making the price information more current and accessible.

4. Regulation of Broker-Dealers §1903

The SEA requires all broker-dealers who transact a securities business in interstate commerce to register with the S.E.C. (This includes virtually all broker-dealers.) In addition, broker-dealers must be members of a national securities association which itself is registered with the S.E.C. Currently, the only registered association is the National Association of Securities Dealers ("NASD"). NASD is authorized to adopt and enforce rules for members, but the S.E.C. has authority over NASD and its members.

    a. Dealer markups §1906

    NASD regulates the profit dealers can make on transactions involving OTC securities not quoted on NASDAQ. Excessive profit subjects a dealer to NASD sanctions, S.E.C. sanctions, and private actions based on rule 10b-5.

5. Regulation of the "Penny Stock" Market §1910

The Securities Enforcement Remedies and Penny Stock Reform Act gives the S.E.C. power to regulate "penny stock" (*i.e.*, stocks worth less than $5 per share) transactions. Under the Act:

    a. Suspensions and bars §1913

    The S.E.C. may suspend or bar persons from being associated with any broker or dealer or participating in any penny stock offering if they have violated the 1933 or 1934 Act in connection with a penny stock offering.

    b. Risk disclosure document §1914

    A document setting out in detail many of the risks and dangers associated with an investment in penny stocks must be delivered to customers.

    c. Written purchase agreement §1915

    A dealer must obtain a written purchase agreement from the customer.

    d. Price information §1916

    Price information, including the wholesale bid and asked price, must be disclosed.

    e. Dealer and salesperson compensation must be disclosed §1917

    f. Account statements §1919

    These must be provided to customers monthly.

    g. Customer suitability §1920

    Dealers must learn their customer's financial situation, investment experience, and investment objectives and determine that penny stock investments are suitable for the customer.

c. **Liability provisions applicable to broker-dealers—section 15(c)** §1940

Section 15(c) of the 1934 Act is a general fraud provision, specifically applicable to transactions involving broker-dealers in the over-the-counter market.

    (1) **S.E.C. application** §1941

The S.E.C. has adopted rules pursuant to section 15(c) prohibiting certain manipulative and deceptive practices. The S.E.C. may bring disciplinary actions for violations of these rules. Note that section 15(c) contains *no* willfulness element, as does section 9.

d. **Manipulation during distribution** §1944

Regulation M forbids issuers, underwriters, participating brokers and dealers, and affiliated purchasers from purchasing or bidding for securities that are being distributed until their participation in the distribution has ended. Although several exceptions exist (*e.g.*, heavily traded securities), regulation M is *not* a safe harbor provision; *i.e.,* even compliance with regulation M may result in liability.

3. **Regulation of Market Stabilization** §1957

Market stabilization is a particular form of market manipulation.

a. **"Stabilization" defined** §1958

"Stabilization" is an attempt to set a fixed minimum price for a security in the market by purchasing all the shares that are offered at a lower price than that desired. Market stabilization usually occurs in connection with an original public distribution of shares, where the underwriters may stabilize the price until they can sell the entire securities issue.

b. **Regulation of stabilizations in public distributions** §1962

The SEA prohibits transactions aimed at pegging or stabilizing the price of a security *only* when such transactions violate rules and regulations adopted by the S.E.C. Rule 104 of regulation M is used by the S.E.C. to regulate stabilization and, unlike most of regulation M, *rule 104 is a safe harbor* provision.

    (1) **Trading generally prohibited** §1963

Stabilization violating regulation M, rule 104 is prohibited.

    (2) **Stabilization permitted to prevent price decline** §1964

Stabilization in a public distribution is permitted to prevent or retard a decline in the market price of the security being distributed.

        (a) **Stabilizing price level** §1965

Stabilization may not be commenced at a price higher than the highest independent bid price. The stabilizing bid may follow the market up and down, but cannot exceed the offering price or highest independent bid price. Offerings made "at the market" (*i.e.*, at other than a set price) may not be stabilized.

        (b) **Disclosure of stabilizing** §1966

Stabilizing of the issuer's security by the underwriters must be disclosed to a purchaser at or before the completion of the transaction (normally it is disclosed in the prospectus). Actual stabilizing transactions must also be reported to the S.E.C.

4. The "Hot Issue" Problem

a. "Hot issue" defined §1971

A "hot issue" is a security offered through a public distribution for which there is tremendous demand. There will usually be more offers to purchase than there are available shares.

b. Hot issue problems §1972

Normally, a hot issue will immediately rise to a premium price over the initial offering price, and underwriters and dealers may attempt to profit from this to the detriment of the public (*e.g.*, by holding back a portion of the initial issue to be sold later, at a higher price).

c. Violation of the securities acts §1973

Any such manipulative practices are a violation of the securities acts.

D. REGULATION OF SECURITIES ANALYSTS

1. Analysts and Regulation AC §1979

In reaction to the analyst scandal of 2001-2002 (*e.g.*, analysts were recommending securities to the public even though they privately believed the securities were not a good investment), SOXA authorizes either the S.E.C. or the S.R.O.s to adopt rules for regulating analysts and research reports. In response, the S.E.C. adopted Regulation AC ("Analyst Certification") which, among other things, requires the following.

a. *Certification of written statements that accurately reflect the analyst's personal views*;

b. *A statement attesting that the analyst's compensation is not related* to specific recommendations or views in the research report and other related disclosures; and

c. *Certifications regarding public appearances*.

2. Additional SOXA Requirements §1980

Because Regulation AC does not completely fulfill the rules for regulation required in section 501 of SOXA, more rulemaking is likely.

E. REGULATION OF BROKER-DEALER TRADING ACTIVITIES

1. Registration of Broker-Dealers with the S.E.C. §1981

Under the 1934 Act, all brokers and dealers who engage in securities transactions in interstate commerce **must register** with the S.E.C. They are regulated by both the S.E.C. or the NASD. If members of a national exchange, they are subject to the exchange's rules.

2. Regulation Under General Antifraud Provisions §1990

General antifraud provisions in the SEA and SA may be used to regulate activities of broker-dealers. [SEA Rules 10b-5, 15c1-2; SA §17(a)]

e. Agent's role; duty of execution §2028

If a broker-dealer implies that it is acting as an agent for customers, it may **not** trade as a **principal** with its customers. Broker-dealers also have a duty to exercise reasonable diligence to find the best interdealer market for a security and to buy and sell so that the resultant price to the customer is as favorable as possible (*i.e.,* best execution).

f. Prohibition against causing sales §2030

It is unlawful for a broker-dealer to cause a customer to accept a transaction not actually agreed upon.

g. Prohibition against "churning" §2032

The SEA also prohibits "churning" (*i.e.,* excessive trading by a broker-dealer in a customer's account, for the primary purpose of generating commission income).

4. Broker-Dealer's Duty to Disclose Adequate Information §2040

Broker-dealers must ascertain and disclose relevant information in making recommendations to clients.

a. "Boiler room" operations §2041

These are high pressure sales operations (*e.g.,* direct mail offers and telephone follow-up) in which the broker-dealer typically provides incomplete or false information about the security being sold.

(1) Proceeding against broker-dealer §2042

The 1934 Act authorizes the S.E.C. to proceed directly against a broker-dealer to revoke its registration for **willful** violations.

(a) Direct action against salesperson §2046

And the S.E.C. may proceed against **"any person"** (including the broker-dealer's individual salespeople) to censure or bar them from associating with **any** broker-dealer, if such person has willfully violated the securities laws.

(b) Private cause of action §2047

Customers damaged by misrepresentations or material omissions may sue for damages or rescission against the salesperson under rule 10b-5.

b. "Know thy customer" rules §2048

NASD and NYSE rules require all broker-dealers to have reasonable grounds for believing that any purchase or sale recommended to a customer is **"suitable"** to the customer.

(1) Duty applies to salespeople §2049

This rule applies to all individual salespeople employed by broker-dealers.

(2) Duty to investigate §2050

The NASD rule does not expressly require a broker to investigate the customer's financial situation. The NYSE rule requires investigation of the essential facts relative to the customer.

(3) Violations of the rules §2053

Violations include recommending a speculative security as "safe," failing to instruct sales employees of the suitability requirement, and making overly optimistic statements about a company's prospects.

(4) Violations of suitability rules §2058

Most courts do *not* allow implied causes of action, but a private plaintiff may base a *rule 10b-5 action* on misrepresentation (or omission) or on a fraud by conduct theory.

c. Duty of broker-dealers in submitting security quotations §2062

The S.E.C. has imposed a duty of care on broker-dealers in submitting quotations on over-the-counter securities to any inter-dealer quotation system or any other "publication" of such quotations. Essentially, the issuer of the security must be filing the reports required of companies registered under the 1934 Act, or the broker-dealer must obtain similar information regarding the issuer from a reliable source before making public quotations of the issuer's securities.

5. Broker-Dealer's Duty to Supervise §2064

The 1934 Act provides for the censure or, alternatively, denial, suspension, or revocation of a broker-dealer's registration for failure adequately to supervise its associates (salespeople and employees), where the result is a violation of the securities laws.

6. Margin Requirements §2068

Regulations adopted under section 7 of the 1934 Act governing the purchase of securities on credit (*i.e.*, on margin) are the province of the Federal Reserve Board, but the S.E.C. brings enforcement actions for violations by broker-dealers.

a. *Federal Reserve Board regulations* govern the various lending agencies (including broker-dealers) in loans they make to buy securities, or where securities are used as collateral.

b. *Private causes of action* are *not* provided for by section 7 or the Board regulations. Most (but not all) courts considering the issue have held that there is no implied cause of action.

7. Civil Liability for Violations of NASD, Stock Exchange, or S.E.C. Rules §2072

In the past, there were cases in which the courts implied a federal cause of action for defendant's violation of a NASD or S.E.C. rule. However, the recent trend is against implication of such causes of action.

V. APPLICATION OF THE FEDERAL SECURITIES LAWS TO MULTINATIONAL TRANSACTIONS

A. REGISTRATION UNDER THE 1933 ACT §2073

The 1933 Act applies whenever United States facilities of interstate commerce are used to effect a securities transaction, and under the 1933 Act, "interstate commerce" includes commerce between any foreign country and the United States.

U.S. interests to be protected. Most cases invoking extraterritorial application have concerned rule 10b-5.

(1) Tests used §2101

Two tests are most often used to resolve transactional jurisdiction issues. The ***substantial effects*** test bases jurisdiction on foreseeable and substantial effects within the U.S. from the transaction, regardless of where the activity occurred. The ***conduct test*** bases jurisdiction on the fact that some significant activity occurred within U.S. territorial limits. Courts have been willing to mix elements of each test in making jurisdiction determinations.

VI. REGULATION OF SECURITIES TRANSACTIONS BY THE STATES

A. UNIFORM SECURITIES ACT

1. Structure of Act §2106

The Commissioners on Uniform State Laws have adopted a Uniform Securities Act, divided into sections on (i) fraud, (ii) broker-dealer registration, (iii) registration for new securities offerings, and (iv) remedy provisions. However, (ii) and (iii) have been largely preempted by the National Securities Markets Improvement Act ("1996 Act"), and (i) has been partially preempted by the Securities Litigation Uniform Standards Act (the "1998 Act").

2. Adoption by the States §2107

In drafting their own securities laws, most states have adopted some part of the Uniform Securities Act, as well as some provisions of their own choosing and some parts of the federal acts. In cases not preempted by federal law, nearly all states regulate the original distribution of securities and the subsequent trading thereof (including the registration of broker-dealers).

B. PREEMPTION OF STATE SECURITIES LAWS

1. Introduction §2108

Section 18 of the 1933 Act effectively preempts most state securities laws (so-called blue sky laws). The 1998 Act preempts state-law securities fraud class actions.

2. Structure §2109

Section 18 covers four broad classes of securities, prohibiting states from requiring registration or qualification of any of the covered securities. States are also barred from imposing any conditions on the use of offering documents prepared by the issuer, or on disclosure documents, that must be filed with the S.E.C.

3. Four Classes of Covered Securities §2110

The four classes exempted from blue sky regulation are:

a. ***Securities of issuers registered under the Investment Company Act of 1940***;

b. ***Listed securities***;

c. ***Offers or sales to "qualified purchasers"***; and

d. ***Certain offers and sales exempt under the 1933 Act*** (*e.g.*, brokers' transactions and transactions by any person other than an issuer, underwriter, or dealer when the issuer is a 1934 Act reporting company).

4. Left to the States §2115
States still have authority to:

a. ***Regulate penny stocks***;

b. ***Regulate many small, intrastate, and other offerings*** exempt from federal regulation under the 1933 Act;

c. ***Bring actions against brokers for fraud*** and other illegal conduct; and

d. ***Require notice filings*** and payment of fees therefor.

5. State-Law Class Actions §2116
The ***1998 Act preempts*** any class action based on state law if the action alleges misrepresentation or omission of a material fact, or the use of a manipulative or deceptive device, in connection with the purchase or sale of a security, *i.e.*, state law fraud litigation is preempted if it is a class action or involves a ***consolidated action of more than 50 plaintiffs***. ***Individual lawsuits and derivative actions*** are ***not*** preempted.

a. Applies only to covered securities §2119
The 1998 Act applies only to lawsuits alleging fraud with respect to a covered security as defined in section 18 of the 1933 Act.

C. SECONDARY DISTRIBUTION OF SECURITIES §2120
Many states have statutory provisions regulating the trading of securities subsequent to their original distribution.

1. ***General fraud provisions*** have been adopted in nearly every state;

2. ***Registration of broker-dealers*** is required in many states;

3. ***Other regulatory provisions,*** such as provisions regulating ***tender offers*** made for companies domiciled within their borders, have also been adopted in many states. These tender offer rules may be held to be unconstitutional under the Commerce Clause (if they impose an ***undue burden on interstate commerce***), or if they conflict with the Supremacy Clause.

Gilbert Exam Strategies

Law school courses in Securities Regulation generally focus on two federal statutes: the Securities Act of 1933 and the Securities Exchange Act of 1934. These laws regulate: (i) the original issuance and subsequent trading of securities; (ii) the markets in which securities are traded; and (iii) the parties that do the trading.

You should use the following general approach to identify the relevant issues in exam questions. (Refer also to the Key Exam Issues at the beginning of each chapter.)

A. THE SECURITIES ACT OF 1933

1. Coverage of the Act

The 1933 Act applies to the original distribution and, in limited circumstances, the secondary distribution of securities. Thus, the first question when a fact situation involves the distribution of securities is whether there is a *"distribution of securities"* covered by the 1933 Act.

a. Original distributions

An "original distribution" is an offering by the issuer to the public of securities that have never been sold before.

b. Secondary distributions

A "secondary distribution" has two important aspects:

(1) Offering by shareholder(s)

A secondary distribution is an offering to the public of the issuer's securities, but by one or more *shareholders* of the issuer, rather than by the issuer itself.

(2) Shareholders standing in for issuer

In a secondary distribution, shareholders are standing in for the issuer; they are not merely persons who purchased the securities as a routine investment, but rather are either:

(i) "Control persons" of the issuer (*i.e.*, those who can influence the issuer); and/or

(ii) Persons who purchased the securities in a nonpublic transaction or series of transactions.

Note: A single group of selling shareholders in a secondary distribution may include persons within one or the other, or both, of the above categories.

c. Definition of "security"

The 1933 Act applies only to the distribution of securities, but the universe of possible investments is much larger. In other words, not every investment offered to the public is a security. In general, therefore, it is a good idea to verify that the exam question involves a security; if it does not, the Act does not apply.

2. Factors to Consider in Covered Distributions

If a fact situation involves an original or secondary distribution, consider the following:

a. Jurisdiction

Are the facilities or means of interstate commerce involved in the offering?

b. Exemptions from registration

If at all possible, the offeror (issuer or selling shareholder) will try to avoid by some exemption the time and expense of registering with the S.E.C.:

(1) Exemptions for original distributions

(a) Is it a "private offering"? Or, do the "small issue" exemptions apply? If so, then no registration is required.

(b) Is the offer or sale of the securities for "value"? If not, registration is not required.

(c) Is the sale pursuant to a "reorganization" or "recapitalization"? If so, there may be an exemption from registration.

(d) Is the transaction subject to approval by a court or other governmental agency? If so, there may be an exemption from registration.

(e) Is the offer or sale an "intrastate offering"? If so, the intrastate offering exemption may apply.

(f) Are brokers or dealers involved in the distribution chain? If so, an exemption from registration for these persons may be available.

(2) Exemptions for secondary distributions

(a) Is the sale a public offering? If not, the selling shareholder is exempted from the registration requirements.

(b) Is the sale exempt from registration under rule 144?

(c) Is the transaction one *not* involving an issuer, underwriter, or dealer? If so, it is exempt under 1933 Act section 4(1). *Note:* A sale by an ordinary investor of securities purchased in a routine investment transaction (and not in a private placement) is exempt because the investor can use the section 4(1) exemption, and the broker-dealer through whom the investor sells can use either the dealer's exemption in section 4(3) or the broker's exemption in section 4(4). Beware, however, of sales by persons who either are *control persons* of the issuer or who purchased the securities *in private transactions*; such sales often involve "statutory underwriters" and are therefore not exempt under section 4(1).

c. Registration

If the offering is *not* exempt, it must be registered, and the following issues may arise:

(1) Type of registration

Is the registration covered by the regulation A exemption (a shorter form for registering limited offerings), by the regular S-1 or S-3 registration (for most commercial or industrial companies), or by some other form of registration statement (*e.g.,* for "corporate act" transactions under rule 145)?

(2) Timing requirements

Have the issuer and the other parties involved in the registered offering complied with the requirements of:

(a) The pre-filing period?

(b) The waiting period?

(c) The post-effective period?

(3) Disclosure

Did the registration statement disclose all material facts concerning the issuer and its business?

(4) Processing issues

Are there issues regarding the processing of the registration statement with the S.E.C.?

(a) Has a stop order (or some other S.E.C. order) been issued?

(b) Is a post-effective amendment or a supplemental prospectus required?

d. Liability under the 1933 Act

Finally, there may be issues involving the liability provisions of the 1933

Act that apply to failure to register a nonexempt offering, and to misstatements or omissions of material facts in a covered securities offering.

B. THE SECURITIES EXCHANGE ACT OF 1934

1. Coverage of the Act

The 1934 Act generally covers the *trading of securities* in the market after the original or secondary distribution.

2. Registered Securities

The 1934 Act requires issuers to register securities meeting certain criteria.

a. Listed securities

Are the securities (equity or debt) traded on a national securities exchange? If so, they must be registered under the 1934 Act.

b. OTC securities

Does the issuer have more than $10 million in assets? If so, the issuer must register under the 1934 Act each class of equity security that is held of record by 500 or more persons.

3. Reporting Companies

All issuers with securities registered under the 1934 Act must file periodic reports with the S.E.C. Such issuers are often referred to as "reporting companies." The filed reports are public, and may be inspected and copied at the S.E.C.'s offices in Washington, D.C. These reports are of several kinds:

a. Annual reports on form 10-K (or form 10-KSB, for small business issuers);

b. Quarterly reports on form 10-Q (or form 10-QSB, for small business issuers);

c. Current reports on form 8-K (triggered by the occurrence of significant events);

d. Proxy statements (which must be sent directly to shareholders as well as filed with the S.E.C.), prior to each shareholders' meeting at which directors are to be elected; and

e. Annual reports to shareholders, which must accompany or precede each proxy statement.

4. Jurisdiction

Because most provisions of the 1934 Act apply only if *interstate commerce* is involved, has this jurisdictional requirement been met?

5. Regulation of Broker-Dealers
Does the transaction involve a broker-dealer? If so, has there been a violation of the NASD or S.E.C. rules relating to the conduct of broker-dealers?

a. Market-making
If the broker-dealer was "making a market" in the security, has she violated a duty of disclosure?

b. Margin trading
Were the securities sold on "margin" and, if so, have the rules relating to margin trading been violated?

c. "Churning"
Was there excessive trading, raising a "churning" issue?

6. Market Manipulation and Stabilization
Did any party attempt artificially to fix or determine the market price or volume of trading in a security? Or did any party unlawfully attempt to "stabilize" the market price for a security?

7. Tender Offers and Repurchases of Stock
Has there been an attempt to purchase shares of a company directly from the shareholders? If so, was this a "tender offer" subject to the 1934 Act? Were all of the rules applicable to tender offers met?

8. Short-Swing Trading
Has there been trading in an equity security by corporate "insiders" within a six-month period? If so, section 16 may apply.

9. Proxy Solicitation
Have proxies been solicited from shareholders? If so, the rules and regulations applicable to proxy solicitations may apply.

10. Rule 10b-5
In every securities transaction, consider whether rule 10b-5 is applicable. This general fraud provision is very broad and may apply whenever there is some nexus of fraud with a securities transaction.

C. LIABILITY OF "COLLATERAL PARTICIPANTS"

1. Who Is a "Collateral Participant"
Consider whether any "collateral participants" might be liable for a violation of the securities laws. "Collateral participants" are those who are involved in, but not directly responsible for, the transaction (*e.g.,* lawyers, accountants, underwriters, etc.).

2. Liability Under the 1933 Act

Although the "collateral participant" is not directly responsible for the securities transaction, has she "participated" to such a degree that she may be held liable? Could she be held liable as a "control person"?

3. Liability Under the 1934 Act

Could the person be held liable as a "control person" or co-conspirator under rule 10b-5 or under one of the other general liability provisions of the 1934 Act?

D. STATE LAW

Finally, consider whether the *statutory or common law* of one or more states might apply to regulate either an original distribution or the subsequent trading of securities.

Chapter One:
Introduction to Federal Securities Regulation

CONTENTS

Key Exam Issues

The public has a strong interest in the regulation of securities and securities markets, both because securities are an important form of private property affecting the financial well-being of a large segment of the population, and because the condition of the securities markets has a major impact on the flow of capital to industry and therefore on the economy as a whole.

This chapter provides an introduction to Securities Regulation, giving you a broad overview of the securities industry, the federal securities acts, and the Securities and Exchange Commission. Although most of the information in this chapter is important only for a general understanding of this area of law, you may find a question on your exam asking you to determine whether interstate commerce is involved and thus whether the federal securities laws apply to the particular transaction.

A. Why Regulate Securities?

1. Introduction [§1]

Although commentators are not all in agreement about why the securities markets should be regulated (or even whether they should be), a number of grounds for regulation are consistently advanced in academic writing on the subject. These are discussed below.

2. Investors' Need for Information [§2]

Unlike commodities markets, which sell products that are classified and graded for quality and marketability, the securities markets (and especially the markets for *equity* securities, *i.e.*, stocks and the like) sell intangible interests in enterprises, the important aspects of which are not subject to ready verification by the great majority of investors. Earnings, competition, fixed and contingent liabilities—all are important to the price of a security, yet the typical investor has no means by which to determine them. Without this information, presented in a somewhat standardized form to facilitate comparison among enterprises, many investors would be unwilling to risk investing. Private entities (*e.g.*, securities markets) could impose information disclosure requirements without government regulation. However, whether companies would comply is questionable, and the existence of numerous markets for securities would make consistent disclosure standards difficult to achieve. Therefore, government regulation is arguably the most efficient way to specify the format and content of disclosure for investors.

3. Consumer Protection [§3]

The public interest in an efficient, fraud-free securities marketplace includes not only an interest in protecting securities investors themselves from fraud, but also an interest in protecting the health of the national economy from the consequences of any flight from the securities markets by investors. It is no coincidence that the first federal securities regulation statutes were passed shortly after the great market crash of 1929, which not only impoverished many investors at the time, but also helped to cause the Great Depression of the 1930s. The lack of confidence in the markets prevailing in the years after 1929, in the view of many, also prolonged the Depression by making it extremely difficult for even worthy enterprises to raise capital.

4. Economic Efficiency [§4]

By ensuring broad disclosure of economically significant information about an enterprise, the securities laws foster economic efficiency in the markets. "Efficiency" in this context means, essentially, "accuracy" with respect to prices; an efficient market, in this sense, is one in which prices reflect all available information about the item traded. Not everyone agrees that current regulation results in valuable efficiency, however. Some of the more common criticisms of this basis for regulation include:

a. Trading is speculative [§5]

Some argue that much, if not most, of the trading that takes place in the securities markets is speculative; *i.e.,* driven by the belief that someone else will pay more than one has just paid for a security, simply because the price is going up, rather than because of any consideration of intrinsic value. If this view is accurate, extensive regulation would contribute little of value to the markets, but rather would represent a substantial waste of money, with the cost of regulatory compliance adding to the transaction costs borne by investors.

b. Disclosure violates enterprise's interest in confidentiality [§6]

Others, while in principle tolerating efficiency as a legitimate goal of regulation, are concerned that in many cases disclosure of the kind required by the securities laws gives competitors of the disclosing enterprise information to which they are not entitled.

c. Efficiency versus consumer protection [§7]

Finally, there are some who endorse the idea of efficiency, but resist the consumer protection goals of regulation, at least insofar as such goals result in, for example, causes of action for securities fraud. From this perspective, giving investors such potent weapons to use against enterprises invariably results in the enterprises becoming less and less willing to provide information about themselves, ultimately reducing the efficiency of the regulated market.

5. Disclosure Should Focus on Reducing Agency Costs [§8]

Still others suggest that regulation, while important, should be principally concerned with permitting the owners of the enterprise (*i.e.,* the shareholders) to gain greater control over the enterprise's managers (*i.e.,* the officers and directors). These commentators, while endorsing the idea of regulation in a broad sense, suggest that a proper focus on reducing the shareholder's cost of monitoring managers would produce a regulatory regime significantly different from that prevalent today.

6. Alternatives to Securities Markets May Be Preferable [§9]

Finally, it is at least theoretically possible that some alternative means of providing access to capital is superior to a market-based system. For example, European industry tends to rely more on banks than does American industry. However, both cultural and economic factors make it unlikely that the United States capital markets will become bank-centered any time in the near future.

B. The Securities Industry Generally

1. Private Investment and the Venture Capital Market [§10]

Before a company is ready to sell its securities to the public, it will seek investment from private sources, such as wealthy individuals ("angels"), other companies that might have an interest in the start-up company's products or services (strategic investors), or investment funds (regulated mutual funds or the largely unregulated "hedge funds") specifically set up to make such investments. The principal reason for this is that firms in their very early stages are untested and, therefore, are very difficult to value. Before selling securities to the public, more information about the company's value is usually needed. Private investors have more time to devote to assessing the value of such companies and, therefore, are in a better position to make such investments, generally with the hope that the company will become profitable and will eventually go public, with the early-stage investors cashing out and reaping a profit on their investment.

2. Securities Markets [§11]

Securities markets are the systems through which securities are bought and sold. The two basic types of securities markets are primary markets and secondary markets. Primary markets are the markets for the original distribution of securities; secondary markets are for the continuous trading of outstanding securities.

a. Primary markets [§12]

Primary markets are the facilities through which the securities are *first* issued or distributed to the public. For example, if XYZ Corp. is formed and issues some of its common stock to the public, this issuance occurs in the primary market.

b. Secondary markets [§13]

Secondary markets are markets that exist for the ongoing trading of securities *after* their original distribution. Securities already distributed may be bought and sold in one of two ways: through a stock exchange, or with the help of a securities firm in the "over-the-counter" ("OTC") market.

(1) Stock exchanges [§14]

The securities of most large corporations are traded over stock exchanges. These exchanges (the most important of which is the New York Stock Exchange—"NYSE") have physical locations with organized facilities, including trading "floors" upon which stocks are bought and sold. (Regulation of the stock exchanges is discussed *infra*, §§1816 *et seq.*)

(a) Stock exchanges are auction markets [§15]

Stock exchanges function as auction markets, in which buyers' and sellers' orders "cross"—*i.e.,* on the floor of an exchange, a securities firm called a "specialist" (*see infra,* §§1856 *et seq.*) matches orders to sell and orders to buy. The specialist determines the "market price" via the relative balance of buy and sell orders, and in this way the process resembles an auction. When there are more buy orders than sell orders, the price goes up, and vice versa. In the event there is an order to sell and no order to buy, the specialist intercedes to buy the securities, and the same is true if there is an order to buy and no order to sell (in this case, the specialist sells the security).

(b) Stock exchange "listing" [§16]

To be traded on the floor of an exchange, securities must be "listed" (*i.e.,* registered and qualified) with that exchange. (*See* further discussion *infra,* §1820.)

(2) Over-the-counter trading [§17]

Securities traded outside the stock exchanges are said to be traded "over the counter." There is no physical location or exchange facility for the over-the-counter market. Instead, securities firms in many locations are linked through various communication systems (such as computer networks) used to match buyers and sellers. (Regulation of the over-the-counter markets is discussed *infra,* §§1896 *et seq.*)

(a) OTC market is a dealer market [§18]

In stock exchange transactions, buy orders are matched with sell orders and the specialist sets a market price via auction. In the OTC market, by contrast, every transaction is with a dealer, and this market is therefore referred to as a "dealer market." That is, if an investor wants to buy a security, the investor contacts her dealer, who then seeks the lowest price from the dealers acting as principals for that security in the OTC market.

(b) NASDAQ [§19]

The National Association of Securities Dealers ("NASD") has implemented an automated quotation system—"NASDAQ"—which, by ensuring timely price information, makes the OTC market increasingly attractive to investors and issuers.

1) NASDAQ standards [§20]

Securities traded over NASDAQ must meet standards similar to (but generally less demanding than) those required of securities listed on a securities exchange.

2) NASDAQ vs. NYSE [§21]

As NASDAQ has increased in importance, it has begun to compete more directly with the NYSE. This competition does not involve sales of the same securities in each market, however. Rather, the markets compete for listings from companies that are neither very large nor very small. (The largest companies tend to list on the NYSE, with a few exceptions, while the smallest trade in the over-the-counter market.) The difference in the nature of the companies that trade on the NYSE compared with those trading in the NASDAQ system is reflected in financial data about those markets: in 1998, NASDAQ accounted for approximately 50% of all shares traded in the United States, while the NYSE accounted for about 41%. However, the NYSE accounted for roughly 51% of the total dollar volume of shares traded, while NASDAQ accounted for about 40%.

3) "Spreads" in the dealer market [§22]

One drawback of dealer markets is the possibility of collusion among dealers to keep the difference between the prices at which they buy (the "bid" price) and those at which they sell (the "asked" price) artificially high. If all dealers were to collude to maintain a bid/asked "spread" of $1 per share, for example, the cost to customers of purchasing and selling shares would be high and dealers would pocket additional profits. In the early 1990s evidence surfaced of just such collusion (although the spreads were not nearly as large as in our example). Still, the outcome was that NASD was required to establish a separate entity, NASD Regulation, Inc., to house its regulatory functions.

a) Limit orders on NASDAQ [§23]

The Securities Exchange Commission ("S.E.C.") also adopted another requirement to narrow spreads—customers must be allowed to place limit orders (*i.e.,* orders to buy or sell at a specific price) which can be between the bid and the asked price. An incoming order can then "cross" with the limit order, in effect substituting the limit order for the bid or asked price.

---

e.g. **Example:** The bid price (*i.e.,* the price a dealer will pay) for XYZ, Inc. stock is $7.80, and the asked price (*i.e.,* the price a dealer wants to get) is $8.00. This represents a spread of 20¢ per share, which is very wide. Now, suppose a customer places a limit order to sell 100 shares at $7.90. A buy order at $8.00 crosses with the sell order at $7.90, which means the effective spread for that transaction was narrowed to only 10¢ per share. Likewise, suppose a customer places a limit order to buy 100 shares at $7.90. The next sell order will cross with the buy limit order at $7.90, instead of the dealer's bid of $7.80. Again, the spread is narrowed to 10¢ per share, benefiting the customer.

---

b) **Decimal pricing [§24]**

Another major development narrowing dealer spreads was the 1998 requirement by Congress that securities prices be quoted in pennies rather than the traditional eighths of a dollar. Under the old system, the minimum spread was 1/8, or about 12-1/2¢. Now, securities prices are quoted in pennies, and the average spread on NASDAQ hovers at about 3¢.

(3) **Other securities markets [§25]**

There are also other markets for the trading of securities. One is the so-called "third market"; *i.e.,* the OTC market for securities that are also listed on a stock exchange. Another is the "fourth market"; *i.e.,* individual persons or firms owning securities trade them without the assistance of a market intermediary, such as a broker-dealer.

3. **Securities Firms—Brokers and Dealers [§26]**

Besides regulating securities markets, the federal securities laws also regulate the activities of firms engaged in trading securities. These firms function both as "brokers" and as "dealers." The definitions of "broker" and "dealer" given below are general, functional definitions. The securities acts also define the terms in several places where they are relevant to specific regulatory purposes. The definitions in the acts may or may not coincide with the general, functional definitions given here.

a. **"Brokers" [§27]**

Brokers are generally defined as agents who buy and sell securities for their customers on a commission basis. For example, assume A wishes to buy 100 shares of XYZ Corp. If B buys the shares for A at $10 per share and charges A a 5% commission, B has acted as a broker.

b. "Dealers" [§28]

Dealers, on the other hand, act as principals—buying the securities for their *own account* and subsequently reselling them to their customers at a marked-up price. Thus, in the above example, instead of charging A a 5% commission, B could have purchased the XYZ stock for $10 and resold it to A for $12 per share.

c. Dual functions common [§29]

Note that the same person or firm can be a "broker" in one transaction and a "dealer" in another transaction. Most firms in the securities business function in both capacities, and hence are referred to as "broker-dealers." Note that broker-dealers employ a variety of personnel, including salespeople, clerks, traders, and supervisory personnel.

d. Different functions on exchanges and in the over-the-counter market [§30]

When a customer executes a purchase or sale order over an exchange, the firm through which he deals acts as a broker for the customer. The broker typically executes the order through a specialist on the floor of the exchange.

(1) But note

When a customer executes a purchase or sale order in the over-the-counter market, the firm through which the customer deals may act either as a broker (buying or selling for the customer on a commission basis) or as a dealer (buying or selling for its own account and charging the customer a markup). (*See* discussion *infra*, §§1996-1997.) Note that many securities firms operate both in the exchange markets and in the over-the-counter market.

4. Changing Role of Banks [§31]

Since 1933, the Glass-Steagall Act prohibited commercial banks from underwriting corporate securities. Similarly, the Bank Holding Company Act prohibited companies that control banks from engaging in activities other than banking. However, beginning in the 1980s, federal banking regulators (including the Federal Reserve Board, the Federal Deposit Insurance Corporation and the Comptroller of the Currency) have permitted banks to engage in more and more securities-related activities. Finally, in 1999, Congress passed a financial modernization statute known as the Gramm-Leach-Bliley Act, which effectively repeals most of the Glass-Steagall Act and the Bank Holding Company Act. The result has been the growth of financial holding companies, which are legally permitted to engage in a wide variety of financial services, including banking, brokerage, and insurance.

5. Other Financial Markets [§32]

Increasingly, the operation and regulation of the United States securities markets is affected by other financial markets, both foreign and domestic.

a. Foreign markets [§33]

Growth in foreign markets, especially the so-called "Euromarket," has led the S.E.C. to seek to coordinate requirements among regulators from the United States and other countries. In particular, United States regulators are concerned that if the United States markets are seen as over-regulated, United States issuers might flee to foreign markets to raise capital, and foreign issuers might avoid the United States markets.

b. Domestic markets [§34]

There are a multitude of financial insruments trading in markets, including especially "derivative instruments," such as interest rate swaps, futures on financial indices, and options on other financial instruments. Not all of these instruments are securities. (*See* discussion of the definition of "security," *infra*, §§257-276.) But they nevertheless form an important part of the context in which the securities industry functions.

(1) The money market [§35]

The money market involves primarily "commercial paper," *i.e.*, short-term debt instruments issued by corporations.

(2) The government securities market [§36]

Government securities include direct obligations of the United States and obligations of agencies of the United States government.

(3) The municipal securities market [§37]

The market for municipal securities resembles in many respects that for government securities, except that there is a much greater risk of default by a municipality than by the United States.

(4) Derivative products market [§38]

The derivative products market includes a variety of financial products, the most important of which are discussed below.

(a) Traded options [§39]

Options are contracts giving the buyer of the option the right to buy or sell an asset at a price determined in advance. The holder of an option is *not obligated* to exercise it. Traded options are options written on standardized terms and issued by the Options Clearing Corporation, a corporation jointly owned by the exchanges on which options are traded.

(b) Futures [§40]

Futures contracts create an *obligation* to sell or to buy an asset at a future date, at a price determined in advance. Futures on stock market indices—for instance, the Standard & Poor's 500 index—give one of the parties the right to receive a sum of cash based on the price of the securities in the index. The party who gets paid depends on whether the index has risen or fallen since the parties entered into the futures contract. Futures are regulated by the Commodities Futures Trading Commission ("C.F.T.C.").

1) 1987 market crash [§41]

Most commentators attribute the October 19, 1987, stock market crash at least partly to futures trading. On that day, many investors sold stock while simultaneously purchasing index futures. The resulting flood of stock onto the market contributed to the decline of stock prices.

(c) Swaps [§42]

Swaps are agreements whereby two parties agree to make periodic payments to each other. A typical *interest rate swap* involves one side paying interest at a fixed rate, while the other side pays a floating rate (*e.g.*, the prime rate in effect on each payment date). In a typical *currency swap*, one side agrees to pay a dollar amount to the other, and the other makes its payment in a foreign currency (*e.g.*, Swiss francs). Pursuant to the Commodities Futures Modernization Act of 2000, swaps between "eligible contract participants" are essentially unregulated. This is partly because swap markets are not easily manipulated, as swaps typically involve interest rates or currencies.

(d) "Portfolio insurance" [§43]

Portfolio insurance is not really insurance at all. The term refers to a variety of complex hedging strategies, often employing one or more of the financial instruments described immediately above. The aim of these strategies is to hedge (*i.e.*, to reduce the risk of severe loss in) an investor's securities portfolio.

6. Levels of Regulation [§44]

The securities markets are regulated at three levels, each of which is discussed in this Summary:

a. The Securities and Exchange Commission [§45]

The Securities and Exchange Commission ("S.E.C.") is a federal administrative agency, and it is discussed *infra*, §§51 *et seq.*

b. Self-regulatory organizations [§46]

The regulatory aspects of self-regulatory organizations ("S.R.O.s") are discussed *infra,* §§1837 *et seq.*

c. State "blue sky" regulation and federal preemption [§47]

Every state regulates the original distribution of securities within its borders, typically by means of a requirement that distributions be registered with the state. In addition, each state offers some variety of antifraud sanction applicable to transactions in securities. However, section 18 of the 1934 Act preempts state registration with respect to securities meeting certain criteria, including securities listed on the NYSE, the American Stock Exchange ("AMEX"), the NASDAQ system, and mutual funds. (For a discussion of blue sky regulation, *see infra,* §§2106 *et seq.*)

7. Regulatory Issues [§48]

The proliferation of new financial instruments has produced conflict between the S.E.C. and the C.F.T.C., as each agency tries to assert jurisdiction over a new instrument. Which agency succeeds in a given case depends on whether the instrument in question is a security, an option on a security, or a futures contract. Many new instruments, however, fit into more than one of these categories.

a. Both a security and a futures contract [§49]

If an instrument is both a security and a futures contract, then the C.F.T.C. has sole jurisdiction. [7 U.S.C. §2a(ii); *and see* **Chicago Mercantile Exchange v. S.E.C.,** 883 F.2d 537 (7th Cir. 1989)]

b. Both an option on a security and a futures contract [§50]

If an instrument is both an option on a security and a futures contract, then the S.E.C. has sole jurisdiction. [7 U.S.C. §2a(i); *and see* **Chicago Mercantile Exchange v. S.E.C.,** *supra*]

C. The Securities and Exchange Commission

1. S.E.C. Functions [§51]

The S.E.C. is the agency responsible for administering and enforcing the federal securities laws. The basic functions of the S.E.C. are:

a. Rulemaking [§52]

The S.E.C. adopts substantive rules to implement the federal securities laws. The S.E.C. has the authority to adopt such rules pursuant to a congressional delegation of authority in the federal securities acts.

b. **Interpreting [§53]**

The S.E.C. interprets the securities laws and S.E.C. rules issued thereunder. The Commission does this in two principal ways:

(1) General policy statements [§54]

Periodically, the S.E.C. will issue "releases" to the general public which state the views of the S.E.C. on matters of current concern.

(2) No-action letters [§55]

In addition, private parties (such as lawyers for corporate clients) may inquire of the S.E.C. as to whether a specific transaction may be carried out in a specific manner without violating the securities laws. If the staff agrees that the action as described will not violate the securities laws, its response is called a "no-action" letter, since the S.E.C. staff indicates that it will not recommend enforcement action to the Commission if the transaction is carried out in the manner specified. Issues occasionally arise concerning whether no-action letters can be reviewed by a court. For example, when the S.E.C. changes a long-standing policy by means of a no-action letter, persons affected by the change may petition a court for review. The trend is to find that no-action letters are not reviewable, because they are neither rulemaking nor adjudication. [*See* **New York City Employees' Retirement System v. S.E.C.**, 45 F.3d 7 (2d Cir. 1995); **Roosevelt v. E.I. DuPont de Nemours & Co.**, 958 F.2d 416 (D.C. Cir. 1992); **Chicago Board of Trade v. S.E.C.**, 883 F.2d 525 (7th Cir. 1989)]

c. **Investigating [§56]**

The S.E.C. also investigates possible violations of the securities laws and rules.

d. **Initiating formal proceedings [§57]**

The S.E.C. initiates formal proceedings against a wrongdoer—*i.e.*, seeks statutory remedies and sanctions for violation of the securities laws. *Examples:*

(i) *Civil injunctions and civil fines* may be sought in the federal district courts;

(ii) *Criminal prosecutions* may be brought by the United States Department of Justice (generally, upon referral from the S.E.C.); and

(iii) *Administrative remedies* (*e.g.*, suspension of a securities firm from trading, or issuance of a cease and desist order) may be pursued by the S.E.C. in administrative proceedings.

Note: Private actions may be brought by private (*i.e.*, nongovernmental) plaintiffs when they have been injured by a violation of the securities laws and when the law provides for either an express or implied cause of action.

2. **S.E.C. Administrative Procedures [§58]**

All administrative proceedings brought by the S.E.C. are conducted in accordance with rules conforming to the Federal Administrative Procedure Act ("A.P.A."). These rules are designed to meet the requirements of constitutional due process—*i.e.*, proper notice, confrontation and cross-examination of witnesses, etc. (*See* Administrative Law Summary.) Briefly, the procedures are as follows:

a. **Hearing before administrative law judge [§59]**

The first step in S.E.C. proceedings is a hearing conducted by an administrative law judge appointed by the S.E.C. This judge makes the initial decision in the matter.

b. **Commission review [§60]**

Following the hearing, either or both of the parties may seek review of the administrative law judge's decision by the full Commission. Alternatively, the S.E.C. may decide to review the decision on its own motion.

c. **Appeal to the courts [§61]**

Finally, an aggrieved party may seek review of the S.E.C.'s decision by a United States Court of Appeals.

D. Securities Acts Administered by the S.E.C.—An Overview

COMPARISON OF THE 1933 AND 1934 ACTS		gilbert
	1933 ACT	**1934 ACT**
MAIN PURPOSE	To regulate the *original issuance* of securities and to *prevent fraud and misrepresentation* in interstate offerings.	To regulate the *trading* of securities that are already issued and outstanding, and to require issuers to make *ongoing disclosure* similar to that initially made under the 1933 Act.
MAIN METHOD	Compel *full disclosure* of material facts.	Require registration and regular reporting of financial information of issuers, securities exchanges, brokers, dealers, and securities associations; restrict and penalize insider trading; regulate trading of securities.

1. **Securities Act of 1933 [§62]**

   The Securities Act of 1933 ("SA" or "1933 Act"; discussed in detail, *infra*) primarily regulates the *original issuance* of securities—*e.g.,* where XYZ Corp. desires to issue 100,000 shares of its common stock to the public for $10 per share.

   a. **Purpose of the Act [§63]**

      The primary purpose of the 1933 Act is to *compel full disclosure of all material facts* in public offerings. [SA §5] A secondary purpose is *to prevent fraud and misrepresentation* in the offer or sale of securities. [SA §§11, 12(a)(2), 17]

2. **Securities Exchange Act of 1934 [§64]**

   The Securities Exchange Act of 1934 ("SEA" or "1934 Act"; also discussed at length, *infra*) governs trading in securities that are already issued and outstanding. The 1934 Act has a much broader scope than the 1933 Act, and in addition to regulating a wide variety of securities transactions, it requires ongoing disclosure by issuers. The 1934 Act regulates:

   a. **Registration and reporting [§65]**

      The 1934 Act requires a company to register its securities with the S.E.C. and thereafter to file periodic financial reports with the S.E.C. if the company's securities are (i) traded on a regulated *national securities exchange or* (ii) traded over the counter, and the company has assets of *more than $10 million and 500 or more shareholders* of a class of equity securities (such as common stock). Corporations subject to the registration and filing requirements are called "registered companies." [SEA §§12, 13; SEA Rule 12g-1]

   b. **Proxy solicitation [§66]**

      The SEA also regulates the solicitation of voting proxies from the shareholders of registered companies. [SEA §14; *and see infra*, §§1281 *et seq.*]

   c. **Tender offer solicitations [§67]**

      The 1934 Act also regulates situations in which one company seeks to acquire control of another by a direct offer to purchase stock from shareholders of the target company. [SEA §§13, 14; *and see infra*, §1127]

   d. **Insider trading [§68]**

      Provisions of the SEA restrict and penalize trading in a registered company's shares by company "insiders" (*i.e.,* company officers or directors, or owners of 10% of the outstanding shares of a registered class of equity securities). [SEA §16; *and see infra*, §§1433 *et seq.*]

   e. **Margin trading [§69]**

      The 1934 Act permits regulation by the S.E.C. of margin trading (*i.e.,* buying securities on credit). [SEA §§7, 8; *and see infra*, §1971]

f. Market surveillance [§70]

The Act likewise authorizes the S.E.C. to regulate certain securities market trading practices that are based on fraud or market manipulation. [SEA §9; *and see infra,* §§1932 *et seq.*]

g. Registration of securities exchanges, broker-dealers, and securities associations [§71]

National securities exchanges (such as the NYSE) and broker-dealers who conduct an interstate over-the-counter securities business must register with, and make periodic reports to, the S.E.C. [SEA §§6—regulation of national exchanges, 15—regulation of broker-dealers; *and see infra,* §1903]

(1) S.E.C. regulation [§72]

The 1934 Act authorizes the S.E.C. to make rules and regulations governing the activities of broker-dealers and the national exchanges. [SEA §§19(b) - (c), 15]

(2) Self-regulation [§73]

The 1934 Act also permits the exchanges to make their own self-policing rules. In addition, self-policing associations of broker-dealers may organize and register with the S.E.C. [SEA §§15, 15A, 19]

h. Antifraud provisions [§74]

The 1934 Act also contains a number of provisions that impose liability for fraud in the purchase or sale of securities—the most important of which is contained in section 10(b) and rule 10b-5 of the 1934 Act. (*See infra,* §§932 *et seq.*)

3. Sarbanes-Oxley Act ("SOXA") [§75]

In 2002, Congress reacted to a wave of corporate scandals (including those involving Enron and WorldCom) by passing a wide-ranging set of amendments to the 1934 Act, collectively called the Sarbanes-Oxley Act of 2002 ("SOXA"). SOXA had one *key objective: to improve the reliability of issuers' disclosures.* To accomplish this goal, SOXA:

a. Regulates *accountants* (*see infra,* §§1598 *et seq.*);

b. Regulates *lawyers* (*see infra,* §§1643 *et seq.*);

c. Regulates *securities analysts* (*see infra,* §§1975 *et seq.*);

d. Broadens the scope of *"aiding and abetting" prohibitions* under the securities laws (*see infra,* §§1573 *et seq.*);

e. Requires *additional and enhanced corporate disclosure* (*see infra,* §§886 *et seq.*);

f.   Reforms certain *corporate governance procedures*, notably those involving the audit committee (*see infra*, §§1616-1622); and

g.   Enhances certain *fines and penalties* for securities violations (*see infra*, §§1773 *et seq.*).

4. Other Federal Acts Administered by the S.E.C. [§76]

The S.E.C. administers certain other federal securities acts not normally covered in a law school course in Securities Regulation. Briefly, these are:

a. Public Utility Holding Company Act of 1935 [§77]

This Act is designed to prevent abuses in the financing and operation of public utility holding companies.

b. Trust Indenture Act of 1939 [§78]

This Act regulates large issues of debt securities (*i.e.*, in excess of $10 million in total value). This Act contains provisions designed to protect security holders, such as a requirement that the trust indenture covering the securities (*i.e.*, the documents stating the terms under which the securities are issued) meet certain standards insuring the independence and responsibility of the indenture trustee.

c. Investment Company Act of 1940 [§79]

This Act governs the activities of publicly owned companies that invest and trade in securities (*e.g.*, mutual funds). It regulates the composition of management, the capital structure of the company, its investment policies, etc.

d. Investment Advisers Act of 1940 [§80]

This Act provides for registration and regulation of those in the business of advising others on securities investments.

5. Other Federal Statutes [§81]

Although they are not administered by the S.E.C., the following federal statutes are also helpful to an understanding of the S.E.C.'s function and of the securities industry in general:

a. Bankruptcy Code [§82]

The Bankruptcy Code authorizes the S.E.C. to serve as an adviser to United States district courts in federal bankruptcy proceedings—involving reorganization of debtor corporations—where there is a "substantial public interest." In this capacity, the S.E.C. may be asked to advise the court on the selection of the trustee, on the appropriateness of the reorganization plans for the debtor corporation, and other related matters.

b. Securities Investor Protection Act of 1970 [§83]

This Act creates a nonprofit membership corporation to which most broker-dealers must belong. It is funded by assessments. If a securities firm fails and cannot pay its customer accounts, then (up to certain maximum amounts) this corporation makes up the difference.

6. Integrated Disclosure [§84]

As the above material makes clear, there are many disclosure requirements under the securities laws. With respect to the two main acts (Securities Act of 1933 and Securities Exchange Act of 1934), originally there were two separate and distinct disclosure systems established. This dual system spawned separate sets of registration statements, periodic reports, etc., each with its own set of instructions. Eventually, the S.E.C. lightened the burden of compliance by integrating the reporting requirements of the two Acts. Regulation S-K now prescribes a single standard set of instructions for filing forms under the two Acts, so that when the same type of information is required by the various forms under these Acts, a single set of instructions applies. Also, revisions to several rules and forms resulted in a uniform set of financial disclosure requirements for all documents required to be filed under the 1933 or 1934 Acts. Finally, the S.E.C. adopted forms for registration of offerings under the 1933 Act (*see infra*, §§310-316), which in some cases permit incorporation by reference of information in 1934 Act reports.

E. Jurisdiction and Interstate Commerce

1. In General [§85]

The provisions of the federal securities laws are based on Congress's power to regulate interstate commerce. Therefore, these acts generally apply only where the facilities or instrumentalities of interstate commerce are involved.

2. "Interstate Commerce"

a. Definition Under 1933 Act [§86]

Under the 1933 Act, "interstate commerce" is defined as "trade or commerce in securities or any transportation or communication relating thereto among the several states." [SA §2(a)(7)]

(1) Expansive interpretation [§87]

The S.E.C. and the courts have adopted a broad interpretation of what constitutes "interstate commerce."

(a) Use of means of interstate commerce [§88]

Under modern interpretations of the Act, interstate commerce is involved not only whenever a transaction touches more than one state, but also when the "means" of interstate commerce (*e.g.*, the telephone, mails, etc.) are used in any part of a securities transaction.

> **e.g.** **Example:** Thus, even *intrastate* telephone calls or mailings have been held to support federal jurisdiction under the 1933 Act, since the *means* of interstate commerce were used.

b. Definition under 1934 Act [§89]

Under the 1934 Act, the term "interstate commerce" includes trade, commerce, transportation or communication among the several states—plus *intrastate* use of any facility or instrumentality of interstate commerce, such as a national securities exchange or a telephone. [SEA §3(a)(17)]

c. Effect—nearly all transactions covered [§90]

As a result of the expansive interpretation of these definitions, very few securities transactions are exempt from the 1933 or 1934 Acts on the grounds they do not involve "interstate commerce."

F. Self-Regulatory Organizations

1. In General [§91]

Under the 1934 Act, regulation of the securities industry is accomplished not only by the government, acting through the S.E.C., but also by the industry itself, acting through self-regulatory organizations ("S.R.O.s") charged with oversight responsibility. The S.E.C., however, retains the power to overrule the S.R.O.s, if necessary, and to change the rules under which the S.R.O.s operate. [*See* SEA §19(c)] A discussion of the three most important S.R.O.s follows.

a. Stock exchanges [§92]

Stock exchanges are probably the best-known examples of S.R.O.s. Under SEA section 5, all stock exchanges must register as "national securities exchanges." And under SEA section 6, the S.E.C. cannot register a stock exchange unless certain conditions are met, including that the rules of the exchange "are designed to prevent fraudulent and manipulative acts and practices, . . . and, in general, to protect investors and the public interest." [SEA §6(b)(5); *see infra*, §§1819 *et seq.*]

b. National Association of Securities Dealers [§93]

SEA section 15A permits the S.E.C. to register "an association of brokers and dealers" as a national securities association. The National Association of Securities Dealers ("NASD") is the only such association registered under section 15A, and it is an S.R.O. much like the stock exchanges. The requirements for registration under section 15A are similar to those under section 6, discussed above, including similar requirements to protect the public and prevent fraud. [SEA §15A(b)(6); *see infra*, §§1894 *et seq.*]

(1) Broker-dealers may not conduct business unless they are NASD members [§94]

The 1934 Act requires broker-dealers to belong either to a national securities association (*see* above) or to conduct business solely on a national securities exchange of which the broker-dealer is a member. [SEA §15(b)(8)] In practice, every broker-dealer is a NASD member, because not to belong sharply limits the nature of the business in which the entity can engage.

c. Public Company Accounting Oversight Board [§95]

All accounting firms that audit public companies must register with the Public Company Accounting Oversight Board (the "PCAOB"). The PCAOB is also responsible for:

(i) *Maintaining quality control for public company audits*, including questions of ethics, independence, and other standards;

(ii) *Investigating and disciplining infractions* of its rules;

(iii) *Ensuring compliance with the securities laws and professional standards* regarding public company audits; and

(iv) *Conducting periodic inspections of the accounting firms* it registers:

    i. Annually, in the case of accounting firms that regularly audit more than 100 public companies; and

    ii. At least every three years for other accounting firms.

[SOXA §§103 - 105; *see infra,* §§1598 *et seq.*]

Chapter Two: Regulating the Original Distribution of Securities—The Securities Act of 1933

CONTENTS

Key Exam Issues

This chapter covers the Securities Act of 1933 (the "Securities Act" or "1933 Act"). A lot of material is covered here, so to help you study, the most likely topics for exam questions are discussed below.

1. **Transactions Covered by the 1933 Act**

   This part of the chapter contains very technical, detailed statutory and S.E.C. rule information. To master this material, you need to read carefully the S.E.C. rules and relevant sections of the 1933 Act. Read the rules and statute and the material in this chapter until you understand what exactly can be done to market securities that are being registered with the S.E.C. in the *pre-filing period*, the *waiting period* before the registration statement is effective, and the *post-effective period* (*i.e.*, after the registration is effective).

2. **Persons Covered by the 1933 Act**

   The registration and prospectus requirements of the 1933 Act apply to the "*issuer*," "*control person*," "*underwriter*," and "*dealer*," unless they are otherwise exempted. Be sure you understand the definition of each category. Especially remember that the person or firm *helping the issuer distribute* securities to the public may be an "underwriter" (and must comply with the registration provisions of the 1933 Act). Also, if the person selling securities to the public is *able to influence the affairs* of the company whose securities are being sold (*i.e.*, is a control person), he is treated as an issuer. Finally, be aware that people who *sell for control persons* may be underwriters.

3. **Property Interests Covered by the 1933 Act**

   Many Securities Regulation exams will have a question on whether some investment interest is a "security" and thus covered by the 1933 Act. Therefore, study this section carefully. The most likely issue would be whether an investment contract is involved. This analysis requires you to look at all of the facts of the situation and determine whether some investment interest should be treated as a security. To do this, consider four factors: (i) expectation of profit, (ii) common enterprise, (iii) risk capital test, and (iv) need for protection. (*See infra*, §270.)

   Another possible problem for an exam question would involve an investment interest that is one of the instruments *specifically named* as a security, but as to which the circumstances and economic realities of the situation make application of the 1933 Act questionable. Consider **Landreth Timber Co. v. Landreth** (*infra*, §260) (stock and the "sale of business" doctrine), **United Housing Foundation, Inc. v. Forman** (*infra*, §260) (stock in a housing cooperative), and **Reves v. Ernst & Young** (*infra*, §264) (notes).

4. **The Registration Statement**

   The main thing to note here is what type of information must be disclosed in a registration statement: financial information, information about the issuer's management, etc.

5. Exemptions from Registration Requirements

The importance of this topic cannot be overemphasized. Because registration is time-consuming and expensive, issuers generally try to avoid registering if possible. Thus, almost every exam will have at least one question asking whether one or more of the possible exemptions to registration apply to a given transaction. Some helpful hints:

a. Exempted security *transactions* are emphasized more than the exempted *securities*.

b. The *broker's exemption* is important to know because, when a security is sold outside the public offering itself, a broker is usually involved and the broker may need to appeal to this exemption.

c. The *private offering* exemption is a favorite test subject. Also likely are the *intrastate exemption* and the *Regulation D* exemptions. (Regulation A offerings or the exemptions relating to reorganizations and recapitalizations are less likely subjects, although you should study rule 145 carefully.)

d. The material on *restrictions on the resale* of securities that are first issued under a transaction exemption is very important for you to know (*e.g.*, if the issuer sells to X in a private offering, what happens if X then sells to Y?). Be sure you know the details of rule 144 (*infra*, §§679 *et seq.*).

6. Liabilities Under the Act

Be sure that you understand the various situations where the remedy provisions of the 1933 Act apply (*e.g.*, section 11 of the 1933 Act applies only to misstatements in a registration statement, while section 12(a)(2) applies more generally to securities sold by means of a fraudulent prospectus). Be sure that you understand the interrelation between the remedy provisions so that you know which might apply to a given situation and which may be preferable to sue for. Finally, integrate these remedies sections with the material on rule 10b-5 (*see infra*, §932), a general liability section.

A. Introduction

1. Distribution Process [§96]

As noted above, the Securities Act of 1933 regulates the original distribution of securities by the issuer to the general public. The distribution of securities (called an "underwriting") is a process in which securities pass from the issuer through a syndicate of underwriters, including a "managing" or "lead" underwriter, to dealers, and ultimately into the hands of those purchasers who intend to hold the securities for investment (*i.e.*, for some substantial period of time).

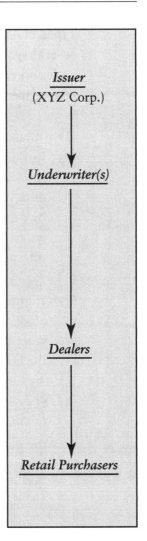

Example: XYZ Corp. contracts to have Merrill Lynch (a securities firm) underwrite 100,000 shares of its capital stock. Merrill Lynch, as the managing underwriter, may organize a group of other underwriters to help it sell the issue of XYZ securities. Merrill Lynch and the other underwriters buy the stock from XYZ at $10 per share and then arrange for other dealer firms to purchase a portion of the shares at $11 per share. The dealers then sell the securities to retail customers at $12 per share. The managing underwriter, who negotiates the deal with XYZ and assembles the underwriting group, charges each of the other underwriters in the group a commission for its services.

---

a. **Pattern of distribution [§97]**

Thus, the sequence of events in a typical underwriting is as follows:

(1) **Decision to issue [§98]**

The issuer (XYZ Corp.) decides to sell 100,000 shares of its common stock to the public in order to raise capital.

(2) **Agreement with underwriter [§99]**

XYZ goes to a securities firm (the managing, or maybe the only, underwriter) and enters into an agreement to have this firm "underwrite" the securities issue: The securities firm will either buy the securities from the issuer or take responsibility for their sale on some other basis (*see infra*, §§103-107).

(3) **Agreement with dealers [§100]**

The underwriter then enters into agreements with a number of other securities firms ("dealers") to have them buy the securities for resale to their retail customers.

(4) **Sale to retail customers [§101]**

Finally, the dealers sell the XYZ securities to their retail customers.

b. **Initial investors [§102]**

In a normal securities distribution, dealers often sell to retail customers who intend to hold for only a short time, hoping to make a quick profit by selling once the newly issued securities move up in price (which often occurs in the first hours or days of a new offering). A sale to such an investor does not mean the completion of a "distribution"; this occurs only when the securities come to rest in the hands of those investors who intend to hold them for a *substantial* period of time.

Example: XYZ Corp. issues 100,000 shares of its common stock to the public through A, an underwriter. B, a dealer who has an allotment from A to sell 10,000 shares, sells 1,000 shares to C, a retail purchaser. C holds the XYZ stock for only one day (while the price goes up) and then re-sells the stock to D, who intends to hold it for a substantial period of time. The distribution is complete only when the stock is sold to D.

---

c. Types of underwriting agreements [§103]

Several types of underwriting agreements may be used between issuers and underwriters, and the 1933 Act applies in the same manner to each of these arrangements.

(1) "Stand-by" underwriting [§104]

In this form of underwriting, the issuer itself advertises the issuance of the securities and sells directly to the public. In the event that the issuer does not sell all of its securities, the underwriter(s) agree (for a fee) to buy the unsold portion. Thus, the underwriter(s) act, in effect, as insurers of the success of the distribution. This structure is most common in offerings made only to existing shareholders of the issuer.

(2) "Firm-commitment" underwriting [§105]

Here, the issuer actually sells its securities outright to the underwriter(s), who then resell the securities to dealers and/or the general public. This is the kind of underwriting described in the examples above.

(3) "Best-efforts" underwriting [§106]

In this form of underwriting, the underwriter acts as a sales agent for the issuer on a commission basis. The underwriter agrees to use its best efforts to market the securities to the public, but makes no guarantee that the issue will be completely sold. Best-efforts underwritings usually involve only a single underwriter, which acts as the issuer's agent.

(4) Direct offering [§107]

In some situations, a company might not use an underwriter at all, even as an "insurer." Such situations generally occur when the company is well established (and does not need an underwriter) or when the company is not selling securities to the public.

TYPES OF UNDERWRITING AGREEMENTS **gilbert**

STAND-BY	The issuer advertises the issuance and sells directly to the public; the underwriter buys any unsold securities.
FIRM-COMMITMENT	The underwriter buys the securities from the issuer and then resells them to a dealer or the public.
BEST-EFFORTS	The underwriter sells the issuer's securities on a commission basis, agreeing to use its best efforts but not guaranteeing that it will sell all of the securities.

2. Objectives of 1933 Act [§108]

Congressional inquiries into the stock market crash of 1929 determined that securities were often initially distributed to investors without any disclosure of facts relevant to the buyer's investment decision, and that the remedies provided by state law for fraudulent practices in these transactions were inadequate. Enactment of the 1933 Act therefore had as its objectives: (i) *full disclosure* of all material facts in public offerings; and (ii) *prevention of fraud and misrepresentation* in the interstate offer or sale of securities.

a. Full disclosure to potential investors [§109]

The primary objective of the 1933 Act is to provide investors with all material investment information relating to the original issuance of securities.

(1) Registration statement [§110]

To accomplish this goal, the Act requires the issuer to file a "registration statement" with the S.E.C. prior to issuing its securities. This statement must disclose all material facts about the issuer and the issuer's securities. [SA §5; *see* detailed discussion *infra*, §§301-375]

(2) Prospectus [§111]

Part I of the registration statement is the "prospectus." It is the most important part of the registration statement, and it must be distributed to investors prior to (or at least simultaneously with) delivery of the issuer's securities. [SA §5(b)(2); *see infra*, §193]

b. Prevention of fraud and misrepresentation in interstate sale of securities [§112]

The second objective of the 1933 Act is to prevent fraud and misrepresentation in the interstate sale of securities. To accomplish this, the Act includes several liability provisions affording defrauded purchasers more liberal remedies than those available at common law. (*See* detailed discussion *infra*, §§747 *et seq.*)

3. Scope of the 1933 Act [§113]

The provisions of the 1933 Act apply only to certain *transactions* (offers and sales in interstate commerce) by certain *parties* (issuers, underwriters, and dealers) involving certain *property interests* (securities). The following sections of this chapter discuss the coverage of the 1933 Act in terms of these categories.

4. 1933 Act Pattern of Regulation [§114]

Under the 1933 Act, regulation is accomplished primarily by requiring disclosure by all regulated persons (primarily issuers and underwriters) to the investing public of all material information concerning the issuer and the offering.

a. Disclosure by filing a registration statement [§115]

Disclosure is accomplished by requiring the issuer to file a registration statement that registers the offering of securities. As we will see, it is usually illegal to offer or sell securities before such a registration has been filed.

b. Liability for failure to file [§116]

The 1933 Act ensures compliance by imposing civil and potentially criminal liability on those who offer or sell securities without filing a proper registration statement, as well as on those who circumvent any of the many detailed rules that specify how public offerings of securities are to be carried out.

c. Liability for fraud [§117]

The 1933 Act also seeks to eliminate (or, at least, reduce) fraud in the offering and sale of securities to the public by including a number of rather harsh provisions penalizing such fraud.

B. 1933 Act Section 5—Offers and Sales

1. The Challenges of Section 5 [§118]

Section 5 of the 1933 Act provides rules concerning the making of *offers to sell* and the actual *sale* of securities through the facilities of interstate commerce. Section 5, together with its associated rules, has never been a model of clarity. Generations of law students (and practicing lawyers, too) have struggled with its intricacies. Although the details of regulation under section 5 have changed frequently over the years, the basic concepts underlying the regulation of securities distribution have changed little. Perhaps this reflects a system that isn't broken, and thus doesn't require fixing. However, it is also true that the accretion of nuances and exceptions to the statute can make securities regulation difficult to understand for the beginner. The most recent set of changes—the 2005 Securities Offering Reform ("SOR") rules—is no exception. SOR has greatly reduced the regulatory burden for certain issuers of securities, chiefly those who have previously issued securities and who have been filing regular (and timely) reports with the S.E.C. under the Securities Exchange Act of 1934. However, SOR accomplishes this by constructing a complex set of exceptions to the prohibitions of section 5, most of which are available only to certain issuers in connection with certain kinds of transactions.

a. Organization of regulation under section 5 [§119]

Section 5 is perhaps the most difficult, and at the same time the most fundamental, section of the 1933 Act. There are many rules and exceptions, and it can sometimes be difficult to grasp the overall pattern of the statute. To try to make this material more comprehensible, we will begin by categorizing issuers into the classes in which they are regulated. The categories of issuers are subject to different rules—while the general pattern stays the same, bigger and better-known issuers tend to qualify for exceptions that are not available to smaller, less-well-known issuers. Then, we will discuss the rules that apply to the different classes of issuers. We will organize that discussion by time period: The pre-filing period; the waiting period; and the post-effective period. These time periods represent stages in a public offering, from contemplation to consummation.

2. Classes of Issuers [§120]

To understand section 5, one must understand the categories of issuers, because (as we will see below) some categories will qualify for exceptions from the general rules of section 5, which we will discuss below.

a. Nonreporting issuers [§121]

This category comprises issuers that are not required to file periodic reports under the 1934 Act. (*See infra,* §§875 *et seq.*) Because there is relatively less information available to the market concerning these issuers, they are permitted no shortcuts. The rules apply to them in the strictest manner possible.

b. Unseasoned issuers [§122]

Unseasoned issuers are issuers that are required to file periodic reports under the 1934 Act, but that do not meet the eligibility requirements for using Form S-3 to register offerings of securities (*see* below).

c. Seasoned issuers [§123]

Seasoned issuers are issuers that meet the eligibility requirements for using Form S-3. To meet these requirements, the issuer must:

(1) For the last 12 months have been reporting under the 1934 Act, and have timely filed its reports;

(2) Not have failed to pay any dividend or required payment on preferred stock; and

(3) In the current fiscal year, not have defaulted on debt or rent on a long-term lease, if the default would be material.

d. "WKSIs"—well-known seasoned issuers [§124]

Well-known seasoned issuers (or "WKSIs," pronounced "wick-sees") are issuers that meet the most stringent set of requirements—and therefore get the most leeway, and the largest number of exceptions, from regulation—under section 5. WKSIs must:

(i) Be "seasoned issuers," as described above; *and*

(ii) Have either:

    (i) A *minimum of $700 million worldwide value of common equity*, held by persons not affiliated with the issuer;

    (ii) *Issued $1 billion in nonconvertible securities* (*i.e.,* securities that cannot be converted into common stock) in the last three years, and *be issuing only nonconvertible securities (and not common stock)* in the proposed offering; *or*

    (iii) *Issued $1 billion in nonconvertible securities* in the last three years, have *a minimum of $75 million worldwide value of common equity* held by persons not affiliated with the issuer, and *be issuing common stock* in the offering.

[SA Rule 405]

e. Ineligible issuers [§125]

Finally, there are certain issuers that are not eligible for the offering shortcuts implemented in 2005, when the above categories were established. Ineligible issuers include those that:

(i) Have not timely filed their 1934 Act reports;

(ii) Were blank check companies (*i.e.,* companies with no business specifically identified);

(iii) Were shell companies (*i.e.,* companies with no or nominal operations, and either no or nominal assets, or only cash assets);

(iv) Were penny stock issuers (*i.e.,* companies with nonlisted securities that trade for less than $5/share);

(v) Have filed for bankruptcy within the preceding three years; or

(vi) Have violated the securities laws within the preceding three years.

[SA Rule 145]

3. Time Period Regulation [§126]

Section 5 does not expressly divide up the stages of a public offering, and it does not use the terms "pre-filing period," "waiting period," or "post-effective period." Nevertheless, a careful study of section 5 reveals that it divides time up into three periods (which have come to be called by these names):

(i) The *pre-filing period* is the period of time when an offering is contemplated but before a registration statement is filed with the S.E.C. The general rule at this time is "no offers, no sales." (*See infra,* §§127 *et seq.*)

(ii) The *waiting period* is the period of time that begins when the registration statement is filed and ends when the registration is declared effective by the S.E.C. (You can think of this as the period of time when one is waiting for the registration statement to become effective.) The general rule during this time is that oral—and certain written—offers may be made, but no sales may take place. (*See infra,* §§151 *et seq.*)

(iii) The *post-effective period* is the period of time that begins when the registration statement is declared effective and extends indefinitely into the future. The general rule during this period of time is that both offers and sales may be made. However, there are some specific rules that require the delivery of a package of information for some period of time after the effective date. (*See infra,* §§192 *et seq.*)

a. Regulation during the pre-filing period [§127]

During the period when an issuer is contemplating a public offering of its securities—but before a registration statement has been filed with the S.E.C. (*i.e.,* the "pre-filing" period)—it is unlawful for issuers, underwriters, and/or dealers **to buy or offer to buy** or to **sell or offer to sell** the issuer's securities (by any means of interstate commerce). [SA §5(a), (c)]

(1) Rationale—no pre-selling [§128]

Section 5 and its related rules lay out a detailed and comprehensive scheme that regulates the offering and sale of securities by the issuer to the public. Issuers cannot simply circumvent the 1933 Act's regulatory scheme by making a sales effort just before filing a registration statement, and upon filing, reverting to the statutorily permitted offering materials. If this were allowed, issuers could lure buyers to purchase securities by using materials that do not include the full information required by the 1933 Act, and then later supply a complete information package that the buyers never read. There is, of course, never any guarantee that buyers will read the complete information package. But by prohibiting offers or sales until the package is available, fewer buyers will become vulnerable to incomplete or nonexistent disclosure.

(2) Exception for agreements between issuer and underwriter [§129]

Negotiations and agreements between the issuer and an underwriter are exempted from the prohibition against offers and sales during the pre-filing period. [SA §2(a)(3)] This exception allows the issuer to make a firm contract to sell its securities to an underwriter prior to incurring the expense of preparing the registration statement.

(a) Issuers and underwriters only [§130]

Negotiations and agreements among underwriters are permitted also, but negotiations or agreements further downstream (*e.g.*, among underwriters and *dealers*) are *not* permitted during this period. [*See* SA §2(a)(3); SA Rule 141]

(3) Meaning of "offers" and "sales" [§131]

The ban against "offers or sales" in the pre-filing period encompasses more than "offers" as defined in state contract law. Because the objective is to see that all marketing activity is conducted in accordance with the 1933 Act and its rules, the terms "offer" and "sale" in section 5(a) and (c) have been given broader meaning than the contract concept of "offer," or "offer and acceptance." [SA Release No. 3844 (1957); SA §2(a)(3)]

(a) No conditioning of market [§132]

The term "offer" has been held to include the dissemination of any material that might "condition the market" prior to the actual offer of securities for public sale pursuant to a registration statement. "Conditioning the market" means whetting the public's appetite for the securities. For example, speeches by company officials, press releases, company advertising, etc., could all be "offers" in violation of section 5(c) if they had the proscribed effect.

(b) Permitted dissemination of information by issuers

1) Communications by issuers made more than 30 days before filing [§133]

Communications made more than 30 days before a registration statement is filed with the S.E.C. will not be considered "offers" and therefore will not be prohibited, if the communications:

(i) Are made *by or on behalf of the issuer* (this means that communications by other participants—*e.g.*, underwriters—are not within the safe harbor);

(ii) Do *not make any reference to the offering* of securities; and

(iii) The issuer takes *reasonable steps to prevent further distribution or publication* of the communication during the 30 days immediately before filing the registration statement.

[SA Rule 163A] Note, however, that there are a number of highly technical exceptions for certain kinds of offerings, issuers, and transactions, respectively, that are not eligible for the rule 163A safe harbor.

2) **Communications by persons other than the issuer, or by the issuer and made 30 or fewer days before filing [§134]**

Communications made by persons other than the issuer, and those made by the issuer within 30 days of filing the registration statement, are considered problematic by the S.E.C. Nevertheless, such communications may not constitute an illegal offer if certain conditions are met. In 2005, the S.E.C. adopted several "safe harbors" for these communications. In addition, there are other provisions of the 1933 Act rules that allow other kinds of communications, even if they do not qualify for the 2005 safe harbors. All of these provisions are discussed below.

a) **Communications by or on behalf of well-known seasoned issuers [§135]**

Well-known seasoned issuers are given the greatest latitude under the 1933 Act rules, and this extends to the actions they are permitted to take during the pre-filing period. SA rule 163 permits WKSIs to make unrestricted oral and written offers during the pre-filing period, nearly—but not quite—doing away with the restrictions that normally apply. For such latitude to apply:

(i) The communication must be *by or on behalf of a WKSI*;

(ii) *Written offers must be filed with the S.E.C.* if and when a registration statement is ultimately filed; and

(iii) *Written offers must contain the warning legend* specified in rule 163(b)(1) (*see infra*, §174).

Note that immaterial or unintentional failures to comply with these conditions will not cause the communication to become an illegal offer if the issuer made a good faith and reasonable effort to comply with the conditions. [SA Rules 163(b)(1)(iii), 163(b)(2)(iii)]

1/ Contrast—shelf registration [§136]

Although the S.E.C. treats WKSIs more liberally than other issuers, giving WKSIs the freedom to make oral and written offers at any time, probably an even greater benefit is given to WKSIs in the automatic shelf registration procedure, described *infra*, §§415 *et seq.*

b) Communications by seasoned and unseasoned reporting issuers [§137]

Issuers filing reports under the 1934 Act are permitted to communicate regularly released "factual business information" and "forward-looking information." [SA Rule 168] However, no communication exempt under rule 168 may contain information about the registered offering, and it may not be distributed in connection with offering activities. [SA Rule 168(c)]

1/ "Factual business information" [§138]

Factual business information includes factual information about the issuer and its business, as well as advertisements for its products or services, and dividend notices. [SA Rule 168(b)(1)]

2/ "Forward-looking information" [§139]

Forward-looking information includes the issuer's financial projections for the future, statements about the issuer's plans and future economic performance, and descriptions of the assumptions underlying such projections and plans. [SA Rule 168(b)(2)]

3/ Limited to communications by or on behalf of issuer [§140]

As with the safe harbor for WKSIs (*see* above), this safe harbor is available only for communication made by or on behalf of the issuer; communications by others, including underwriters or other participants in the offering, are not sheltered by rule 168.

c) Communications by nonreporting issuers [§141]

Even nonreporting issuers are permitted to communicate

regularly released factual business information without that becoming an illegal offer. [SA Rule 169] Although rule 169 is similar to rule 168, it is not the same: rule 169 does not permit the communication of forward-looking information, and the definition of "factual business information" is a little narrower, excluding dividend information and factual information contained in filings made with the S.E.C. (because there are no such filings in the case of a nonreporting issuer). Other factual information about the issuer is permitted, as are advertisements of its products and services. [SA Rule 169(b)] In general, the S.E.C. does not want unreasonably to interfere with an issuer conducting its business in a normal manner, and such activities are therefore permitted.

1/ Scope of rule 169

Note that SA rule 169 is technically not limited to nonreporting issuers, but is available to all issuers. However, other issuers (*i.e.*, WKSIs or reporting issuers) have broader safe harbors (rule 163 or 168, respectively) and rule 169 in practice, therefore, is a rule for nonreporting issuers.

d) Communications by any issuer under SA rule 135 [§142]

Except for WKSIs, issuers generally are not allowed to mention the proposed offering in statements intended to qualify for a safe harbor. Rule 135, however, provides a limited opportunity for issuers (even those that are not WKSIs) to notify the public about their intention to make an offering of securities in the future. [SA Rule 135] However, rule 135 is a checklist that must be followed rigorously, lest a communication become a prohibited offer.

1/ Mandatory items [§143]

Certain items *must* be mentioned in the rule 135 communication, such as the fact that the offering will be made only by means of a prospectus.

2/ Permissible items [§144]

In addition, an issuer *may* communicate certain other facts, including the title of the security, the basic terms, the time of the offering, and the name of the issuer.

3/ Prohibited items [§145]

Other facts, such as the identity of the underwriter, may *not* be mentioned in the rule 135 communication.

EXAM TIP   **gilbert**

Keep in mind that the terms *"offer"* and *"sale"* under section 5 are *broader than they are under state contract law*. Information may not be released if it would have the effect of *whetting the public's appetite* for the securities. Thus, during the pre-filing period, issuers may not publicly disclose who will be underwriting the securities or any other information designed to procure or solicit advance interest in the securities, although they may announce that they will be making an offering by means of a prospectus, and include the title of the security, its basic terms, the time of the offering, and the name of the issuer. Issuers should always check pre-filing statements against the available safe harbors.

(c) Permitted dissemination of information by underwriters and dealers [§146]

In addition to the safe harbors for issuers, the S.E.C. has established guidelines for underwriters and dealers (including those who will participate in the offering and those who will not) as to the information they may disseminate about the issuer and its securities prior to the effective date of the registration statement. In general, the S.E.C. guidelines allow underwriters and dealers to conduct their normal business operations—such as the publication of regular market reports and security analyses—as long as these do not unduly interfere with the objectives of the 1933 Act. [SA Rules 137 - 139; SA Release Nos. 5009 (1969), 5101 (1970)]

1) Broker-dealers not participating in the offering [§147]

Brokers and dealers that are not participating in the offering may, in the regular course of their business, publish and distribute information, recommendations, and opinions regarding the securities of an issuer, even during the pre-filing period. [SA Rule 137]

a) Safe harbor lost if compensation paid [§148]

If the broker-dealer receives compensation for the report, or has a special arrangement with the issuer or another participant in the distribution, the broker-dealer loses the safe harbor for ordinary-course distribution of information. [SA Rule 137(b)]

2) Participating broker-dealers

a) **Information about reporting companies and industries [§149]**

Provided the issuer is current in its required 1934 Act filings, participating broker-dealers may publish and distribute information regarding:

1/ The issuer's common stock, debt securities, or convertible preferred stock, if the offering is of only nonconvertible debt or nonconvertible, nonparticipating preferred stock. [SA Rule 138]

2/ The issuer's nonconvertible debt securities or nonconvertible, nonparticipating preferred stock, if the offering is of only common stock, debt securities, or convertible preferred stock. [SA Rule 138]

3/ The issuer's industry or sub-industry, provided the report includes similar information with respect to a substantial number of issuers in the industry or sub-industry, or contains a comprehensive list of securities recommended by the broker-dealer. [SA Rule 139(a)(2)]

b) **Information about certain seasoned issuers [§150]**

Participating broker-dealers have somewhat more freedom to disseminate information about certain seasoned issuers, subject to the conditions below. If all the requirements are met, the broker-dealer can publish and distribute information regarding *any* securities of such an issuer. The requirements are that:

1/ The issuer:

    a/ Has at least $75 million in market value of equity securities held by nonaffiliated persons; or

    b/ Is offering only investment-grade debt securities; and

2/ The broker-dealer publishes such reports in the ordinary course of its business, and the report about the issuer is not:

    a/ Its first report about the issuer; or

    b/ A re-initiation after discontinuance of its reports about the issuer.

EXCLUDED FROM DEFINITION OF "OFFER" AND "SALE"

☑ Negotiations and agreements between the issuer and one or more underwriters, or among underwriters who will be in privity of contract with the issuer

NOT CONSIDERED OFFERS

☑ Communications by or on behalf of a nonreporting issuer that: (i) are made more than 30 days before filing; (ii) contain only factual business information; or (iii) meet the requirements of the SA Rule 135 checklist

☑ Communications by or on behalf of a reporting issuer (seasoned or unseasoned) that: (i) meet the conditions for nonreporting issuers; and (ii) contain only factual business information or forward-looking information

☑ All communications made by WKSIs at any time

☑ Communications by underwriters and dealers that are: (i) not participating in the offering, when the communication is made in the ordinary course of business; or (ii) participating in the offering, if the communication is about a reporting issuer and:

(a) The issuer's common stock, debt, or convertible preferred stock, if the offering relates only to nonconvertible preferred or debt;

(b) The issuer's nonconvertible preferred or debt, if the offering relates only to common stock, convertible preferred, or debt; or

(c) The issuer's industry, if it is not the first such report (or the first in awhile), and the firm normally publishes such reports.

b. Regulation during the waiting period [§151]

Once the registration statement has been filed with the S.E.C., but before the S.E.C. declares it to be effective (so that the sale of securities pursuant to the statement may begin), the objective of regulation changes. Although actual sales of the securities are still not permitted [*see* SA §5(a)] (except between the issuer and the underwriters or among the underwriters), underwriters may now arrange with brokers and dealers for their assistance in selling the issue to retail customers. In addition, both underwriters and dealers *may solicit offers to purchase,* so that when the registration statement becomes effective, the securities may be sold very rapidly. However, only certain types of information may be used in making selling arrangements and in conducting this pre-selling. [SA Release No. 3844 (1957)]

(1) Overview of regulation during the waiting period [§152]

During the waiting period, SA section 5(c) no longer operates, because a registration statement has now been filed. SA section 5(a), prohibiting sales, remains in effect because the registration statement has not yet been declared effective. SA section 5(b) now becomes the focus. During the waiting period, SA section 5(b)(1) prohibits the use of any "prospectus" in interstate commerce, unless the prospectus meets the requirements of SA section 10. (Once a security is sold, SA section 5(b)(2) comes into play, but we will discuss that later, when we reach the post-effective period.)

(a) "Prospectus" defined [§153]

The term "prospectus" includes any communication that is *written (or communicated by radio or television)* and that *offers any security for sale or confirms the sale of any security.* [*See* SA §2(a)(10)] The breadth of this definition is no accident. Congress's intention is to regulate written or broadcast communications, while at the same time permitting oral offers to take place.

(2) Permitted offers during the waiting period [§154]

During the waiting period, SA section 5(a) prohibits sales, and section 5(b)(1) prohibits the use of any prospectus (meaning almost any kind of written offer) that *does not meet the requirements of SA section 10.* All other offers are permitted. In sum, then, the following are permitted:

(a) Oral offers [§155]

After the registration statement is filed, oral offers are allowed under SA section 5(c). SA section 5(b) does not regulate oral offers.

(b) Written offers that are section 10 prospectuses [§156]

SA section 10 authorizes two kinds of prospectuses: the section 10(a) prospectus, and the section 10(b) prospectus. The section 10(a) prospectus contains all of the information investors must receive under the 1933 Act. (Later, once the registration statement has been declared effective and sales have taken place, we will become concerned about meeting the requirements of SA section 10(a).) During the waiting period, however, participants in a public offering can deliver a less detailed section 10(b) prospectus. The S.E.C. has authorized delivery of several different kinds of prospectuses under section 10(b) during the waiting period: the preliminary, or "red herring" prospectus, the summary prospectus, and the "free writing" prospectus. Each is described below.

1) Preliminary ("red herring") prospectus [§157]

One common kind of section 10(b) prospectus is filed as part of the registration statement, and is called either a "preliminary prospectus" or a "red herring" prospectus (because the S.E.C. requires a statement to be printed in red on such prospectuses [*see* Regulation S-K Item 501(10)]). The preliminary prospectus is similar to the final, section 10(a) prospectus, but is missing some important information that is not yet available. For example, because the price of securities can change rapidly and approval of a registration statement can take a long time (*see infra,* §188), the preliminary prospectus will usually not contain the offering price or any other information that is based on the price.

a) Limited period of use [§158]

Once the registration statement becomes effective and a complete, section 10(a) prospectus is available, use of the preliminary prospectus must be discontinued. [*See* SA §§2(a)(10), 5(b)(2); SA Rule 430(a)]

b) Use when effectiveness precedes pricing [§159]

Registration statement for securities offered for cash may be *declared effective before the price of the securities is set.* Until the price is determined, the preliminary prospectus may be used for informational purposes, even after effectiveness of the registration statement. However, it may not be used to satisfy 1933 Act section 5(b)(2) (the requirement that a final prospectus be delivered with or before delivery of the securities). [SA Rule 430A(c)]

2) Summary prospectus prepared by issuer [§160]

Another kind of prospectus permitted during the waiting period is a summary prospectus. [SA §10(b); SA Rule 431] However, this variety of prospectus has become outmoded, and is seldom, if ever, used anymore.

3) Free writing prospectus [§161]

In 2005, the S.E.C. adopted rules 163, 164 and 433, which together create a new kind of section 10(b) prospectus, called a "free writing prospectus." Most issuers can use a free writing prospectus during the waiting period, and WKSIs can use one at any time, even before filing.

a) Important definitions [§162]

To help explain the new "free writing prospectus," the S.E.C. provided some important definitions:

1/ "Free writing prospectus" [§163]

A free writing prospectus is any prospectus (*i.e.,* written offer) that is neither a preliminary prospectus nor a final, section 10(a) prospectus, does not pertain to certain kinds of asset-backed securities, and is not exempted by the definition of prospectus in SA section 2(a)(10). [SA Rule 405] (As to the latter, *see infra,* §181.)

2/ "Written communication" [§164]

The term "writing" is defined in the 1933 Act itself and includes writing, printing, and any means of graphic communication. [SA §2(a)(9)] This includes "any communication that is written, printed, a radio or television broadcast, or a graphic communication." [SA Rule 405]

3/ "Graphic communication" [§165]

A "graphic communication" includes all forms of electronic media, including tape, fax, CD-ROM, email, Internet websites, and widely (rather than individually) distributed messages via telephone answering machines, computers, and the like. [SA Rule 405]

a/ Exception for live events [§166]

Graphic communications do not include communications that, at the time they are made, originate live, in real-time, to a live audience. [SA Rule 405]

---

e.g. **Example:** A live presentation by corporate officers in Miami, made to investment bankers in New York, that is transmitted via the Internet and includes both video and audio, is not a "graphic communication" under this exception. Because it is not a graphic communication, it is not written, and because it is not written, it cannot be a prospectus.

---

b/ Websites and Internet communications [§167]

Notice that emails, websites, and any other forms of non-real-time electronic communication are included in the definition of "graphic communications." Hence, any offers made through such media are regulated as "written" offers, *i.e.*, prospectuses. However, all of the possible exemptions apply, SA rules 163, 163A, 168 and 169 during the pre-filing period (*see supra*, §§127 *et seq.*), and SA rules 164 and 433 once a registration statement is filed (*see infra*, §§169 *et seq.*). Regarding the treatment of website content as a free writing prospectus, *see infra*, §§177-178.

b) Timing of use of free writing prospectus [§168]

Whether and when a free writing prospectus can be used depends on the nature of the issuer. (*See supra*, §§120-125.)

1/ WKSIs [§169]

Recall that under SA rule 163, WKSIs can make written or oral offers, *at any time, even during the pre-filing period*. [SA Rule 163; *see supra*, §135] Rules 164 and 433 give WKSIs the same freedom during the waiting period. The result is that WKSIs can freely make offers, written or oral, at any time. During the pre-filing period, such communications are excluded from the definition of "offer," even if they in fact offer securities. Once a registration statement is filed, such offers are made under SA rule 164, which defines them as section 10(b) prospectuses. Although the technique is a little different, the effect under either circumstance is that the offers do not violate section 5.

a/ Automatic shelf registration [§170]

While the ability to make oral and written offers at any time is a benefit of WKSI status, an even greater benefit might be that WKSIs qualify for the automatic shelf registration procedures, described *infra*, §§415 *et seq.*

2/ Seasoned issuers [§171]

Non-WKSI seasoned issuers may use a free writing prospectus only *after the registration statement relating to the offering is filed.*

3/ Unseasoned and nonreporting issuers [§172]

Issuers that are either unseasoned or nonreporting can use a free writing prospectus *only after the registration statement is filed,* and the free writing prospectus *must be accompanied or preceded by the preliminary prospectus* contained in that registration statement.

c) Content of free writing prospectus [§173]

The content of a free writing prospectus can be separated into two components—required and optional content. In addition, the content of a free writing prospectus relating to securities of an ineligible issuer is restricted. These rules are discussed below:

1/ Required content [§174]

The S.E.C. requires that all free writing prospectuses contain a legend referring to the fact that a registration statement has been or may be filed, and advising how the reader can obtain a copy of the preliminary prospectus (either from the S.E.C. website or from the offering participant(s)). [SA Rules 163(b)(1), 433(c)(2)] Note that for WKSIs, the content of the legend changes once a registration statement is filed and rule 163 ceases to apply. [*See* SA Rule 164]

2/ Optional content [§175]

The remaining information contained in a free writing prospectus may be different from and supplemental to the information in the registration statement, but it cannot conflict with information in the registration statement. [SA Rule 433(c)]

3/ Ineligible issuers—restricted content [§176]

Although most ineligible issuers (*see supra,* §125) are allowed to use a free writing prospectus during the waiting period, they are sharply limited in terms of the information that they may include in such a prospectus. In fact, a rule 134 tombstone advertisement (*see infra,* §183) would in almost every case accomplish the same thing as would a free writing prospectus for an ineligible issuer, so the value of free writing to such an issuer is essentially nil. [*See* SA Rule 164(e)(2)]

4/   Websites and free writing [§177]

Websites and other non-real-time Internet communications are graphic communications and as such are regulated as written materials. (*See supra,* §§165 *et seq.*) But what of materials that are not clearly offering securities, but that link to (or are linked to) materials that are offering securities? Rule 433(e) provides that an offer of securities on an issuer's website (or hyperlinked from the issuer's website) is a written offer that is subject to the filing requirements of rule 433(d) (*see infra,* §179). In other words, such a web offer is a free writing prospectus and may result in a gun-jumping violation unless the requirements of section 5 are observed. [SA Rule 433(e)(1)]

a/   Exception for historical information on issuer's website [§178]

Issuer websites often contain historical information about the issuer. Such information is *not considered a free writing prospectus* of the issuer if it:

(i)   Is identified as historical information;

(ii)   Is located in a separate section of the issuer's website;

(iii) Has not been incorporated by reference into, or otherwise included in, a prospectus of the issuer; and

(iv)   Has not otherwise been used or referred to in connection with the offering.

[SA Rule 433(e)(2)]

d)   Filing requirement [§179]

Rule 433 also requires in most cases that free writing prospectuses be filed with the S.E.C. on or before the date of first use. [SA Rule 433(d)] Compliance with the filing requirement is critical, as *failure to timely file could lead to a section 5 violation.*

e) Retention requirement [§180]

Free writing prospectuses must be retained by the person using them for three years after the initial bona fide offering of the securities. [SA Rule 433(g)]

(c) Written communications that are not "offers" [§181]

Recall that communications under SA rule 135 are by definition not "offers." (*See supra*, §§142-145.) Therefore, they also cannot be "prospectuses," and as such they can be used during the waiting period.

(d) Written offers that are not "prospectuses" [§182]

Although SA section 2(a)(10) broadly defines "prospectus" to include essentially every written offer, *it also provides two kinds of exceptions*:

(i) Written communications used after the registration statement is declared effective by the S.E.C., if accompanied or preceded by a final, section 10(a) prospectus. [SA §2(a)(10)(a)] This is a kind of "post-effective free writing" and it will be discussed in more detail in the discussion of the post-effective period, *infra*, §§194 *et seq.*;

(ii) Written communications that only identify the security, state the price, state by whom orders will be executed, and contain any other information that the S.E.C. permits by rule. [SA §2(a)(10)(b)] Pursuant to this authority, the S.E.C. has adopted rule 134, which permits so-called "tombstone" advertisements, discussed immediately below.

1) Tombstone ads [§183]

"Tombstone ads" and the slightly longer "identifying statements" are short announcements about a proposed offering of registered securities that typically appear in publications such as the *Wall Street Journal*. They, and other similar communications, may be published during the waiting period as long as they include:

(i) The *issuer's name;*

(ii) The *kind of security* that will be offered;

(iii) The *price* at which the security will be offered;

(iv) The *identity of the person who will be executing purchase orders;*

(v) The person *from whom a prospectus may be obtained;* and

(vi) A *statement that no offer to purchase can actually be accepted* during the waiting period and that the ad itself does *not constitute a solicitation* of an indication of interest from a prospective purchaser.

[*See* SA §2(a)(10)(b); SA Rule 134] The communication may also include a brief description of the issuer's business, the date on which the offering is expected to commence, and the like.

a) Sample:

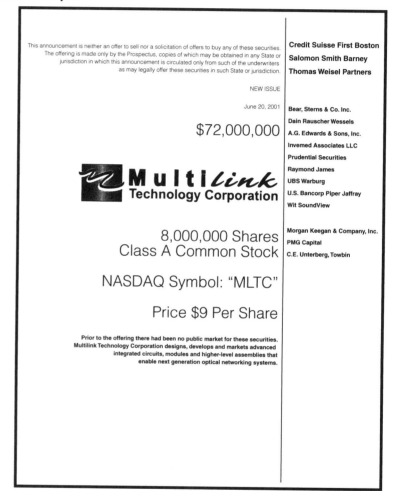

This announcement is neither an offer to sell nor a solicitation of offers to buy any of these securities. The offering is made only by the Prospectus, copies of which may be obtained in any State or jurisdiction in which this announcement is circulated only from such of the underwriters as may legally offer these securities in such State or jurisdiction.

NEW ISSUE

June 20, 2001

$72,000,000

MultiLink
Technology Corporation

8,000,000 Shares
Class A Common Stock

NASDAQ Symbol: "MLTC"

Price $9 Per Share

Prior to the offering there had been no public market for these securities. Multilink Technology Corporation designs, develops and markets advanced integrated circuits, modules and higher-level assemblies that enable next generation optical networking systems.

Credit Suisse First Boston
Salomon Smith Barney
Thomas Weisel Partners

Bear, Sterns & Co. Inc.
Dain Rauscher Wessels
A.G. Edwards & Sons, Inc.
Invemed Associates LLC
Prudential Securities
Raymond James
UBS Warburg
U.S. Bancorp Piper Jaffray
Wit SoundView

Morgan Keegan & Company, Inc.
PMG Capital
C.E. Unterberg, Towbin

Reprinted with permission of Salomon Smith Barney

b) Expanded use [§184]

Note that a rule 134 communication (including a tombstone ad) may be used to actually solicit offers if it is preceded or accompanied by a regular section 10 prospectus (other than a free writing prospectus). [SA Rule 134(d)]

(3) Impermissible communications during waiting period [§185]

As in the pre-filing period, the issuer, underwriters, and dealers must be careful not to make unlawful offers—*i.e.*, by using means or materials other than those specifically permitted above. Furthermore, no sales are permitted during the waiting period, and consequently *no offers may be accepted until the registration statement has become effective.* One technique often used to avoid inadvertently making a sale is to solicit offers to purchase (which must then be accepted by the offeror) rather than making offers to sell (which the customer might accept, creating a sale).

Example: It is an unlawful offer for the underwriter to indicate by letter to a prospective purchaser that he will sell to the purchaser "when, as, and if issued" shares in a company whose registration statement for a new offering has been filed but is not yet effective. [**Diskin v. Lomasney,** 452 F.2d 871 (2d Cir. 1971)] *Note:* The result in *Diskin* was not changed by the fact that the purchaser received and read an approved prospectus prior to actually paying for the stock after the registration statement did become effective.

Example: Where one broker-dealer agreed to sell securities of White Shield Corp. to another broker-dealer in a registered offering, and delivered a "comparison" (*i.e.,* a confirmation) of the sale to the buyer before the effective date of the registration statement, the buyer was entitled to avoid its obligation under the purchase agreement because the "comparison" constituted an illegal prospectus. [**Byrnes v. Faulkner, Dawkins & Sullivan,** 550 F.2d 1303 (2d Cir. 1977)]

---

(4) Required distribution of preliminary prospectus [§186]

Technically, the 1933 Act merely permits, and does not require, the distribution of a preliminary prospectus during the waiting period. This is because the primary aim of the statute during the waiting period is to prevent illegal offers and sales. However, most investors make their investment decisions during the waiting period, and so the S.E.C. also wants to ensure that information about the offering is distributed to all persons who should have it. To accomplish this goal, the S.E.C. uses its ability to control *acceleration* of the registration statement to influence *issuers* to cooperate in the distribution. The S.E.C. also uses its power to regulate and license brokers and dealers to obtain their cooperation in distributing the preliminary prospectus. Both of these techniques are discussed below.

(a) S.E.C. acceleration policy [§187]

As a practical matter, an issuer needs to have the effective date of its registration statement *accelerated* (*see* below). The S.E.C. will not issue an order accelerating effectiveness unless the preliminary prospectus has been distributed to certain persons.

1) Need for acceleration order [§188]

Under the 1933 Act, a registration statement becomes effective 20 days after it is filed, unless it is amended (which starts the 20-day period anew) or unless the S.E.C. declares it effective before the end of the 20-day period. [SA §8] Usually, a registration statement is amended a number of times before it is declared effective. At approximately the time the registration statement is declared effective, a price is set for the securities, based in part on prevailing market conditions. The pricing information is either included in an amendment to the registration statement, or in some cases is simply filed later with the S.E.C. Either way, once the price has been set, the underwriters will want to begin selling immediately, before market conditions change. If they have to wait 20 days until they can sell, the price will be "stale" and the registration statement will need another amendment—which of course starts the 20-day period over again. Thus, as a practical matter, acceleration of the effective date of a registration statement is a necessity.

2) Required distribution of preliminary prospectus [§189]
The S.E.C. generally will not grant acceleration unless the preliminary prospectus has been distributed to all underwriters and dealers who can reasonably be expected to participate in the distribution. [SA Rule 460; *and see* SEA Rule 15c2-8]

a) Additional distribution for new issuers [§190]
Furthermore, if the securities are being issued by a company that has never before offered its securities to the public—and hence is not a reporting company under the 1934 Act—the S.E.C. will not accelerate the offering date unless the underwriters and dealers have sent copies of the preliminary prospectus to *all persons* who are reasonably expected to become purchasers of the securities. [SA Release No. 4968 (1969)]

EXAM TIP   **gilbert**

Be sure to remember that, unless the effective date is accelerated, a registration statement is *not effective for 20 days after any amendment* is filed. The S.E.C. will not accelerate the effective date of an offering unless the issuer has distributed a preliminary prospectus to all underwriters and dealers expected to participate in the distribution and, if the issuer has never before issued securities, to all persons reasonably expected to become purchasers. Because acceleration is a practical necessity, due to market price fluctuations, the effect is that *all issuers must distribute preliminary prospectuses*.

(b) Disclosure policy of 1933 Act [§191]
Distribution of the preliminary prospectus during the waiting period is also required by the S.E.C. in some other instances:

(i) *The managing underwriter* must take reasonable steps to see that *broker-dealers* participating in the distribution receive copies of the preliminary prospectus;

(ii) *A broker-dealer* participating in the offering must take reasonable steps to see that *each salesperson* who will offer the securities gets a copy of the preliminary and final prospectus; and

(iii) *A broker-dealer* participating in the offering must take reasonable steps to see that *persons desiring a copy of* the preliminary or final prospectus get one.

[SA Release No. 5101 (1970)]

REGULATION DURING THE WAITING PERIOD — gilbert

GENERALLY, SALES ARE PROHIBITED DURING THE WAITING PERIOD, BUT *ORAL* OFFERS, AND *WRITTEN* OFFERS *THAT COMPLY WITH SECTION 10*, ARE PERMITTED:

☑ Negotiations and agreements between the issuer and one or more underwriters, or among underwriters who will be in privity of contract with the issuer, are permitted

☑ Written communications that only identify the security, state the price, state by whom orders will be executed, and contain any other information that the S.E.C. permits by rule (*e.g.*, rule 134 tombstone ads) are permitted

☑ Preliminary prospectuses under section 10(b) must be widely distributed

☑ Free writing prospectuses under SA section 10(b) and rules 164 and 433 are permitted. The rules vary depending on the kind of issuer:

(a) **Nonreporting issuer and unseasoned issuer**: Free writing prospectus *must* be accompanied or preceded by a section 10(b) preliminary prospectus

(b) **Seasoned issuer and WKSI**: Free writing prospectus need *not* be accompanied or preceded by section 10(b) preliminary prospectus

---

c. **Regulation during the post-effective period [§192]**

Once the registration statement is declared effective by the S.E.C., the "post-effective period" commences and actual sale of the registered securities may begin. Here is an overview of regulation during the post-effective period:

(i) Offers to purchase, and offers to sell, securities may now be accepted. As soon as there is an executory contract of sale, there is a "sale" under the Act [SA §2(a)(3)], but "sales" are now legal [SA §5(a)(1)].

(ii) Securities may be transported via instrumentalities of interstate commerce for the purpose of sale. [SA §5(a)(2)] A security transported in interstate commerce may be accompanied or preceded by a section 10(a) final prospectus. [SA §5(b)(2)] However, we will see that the S.E.C. has sharply limited the scope of this "requirement" and that, in many cases, "access" to a prospectus amounts to delivery of the prospectus. (*See infra*, §§193 *et seq.*)

(iii) As in the waiting period, a prospectus may be carried through the mail, as long as it meets the requirements of 1933 Act section 10. [SA §5(b)(1)] However, the section 10(b) preliminary prospectus may no longer be used. [SA Rule 430(a)—the preliminary prospectus may be used "before the effective date" of the registration statement] A free writing prospectus, on the other hand, may continue to be used. (*See infra*, §199.)

(iv) When a final prospectus must be delivered, the time during which that requirement is in effect is relatively short and varies depending on the nature of the issuer. (*See infra*, §§209-220.)

(1) Objective of regulation [§193]

The objective of the 1933 Act during the post-effective period is to see that all purchasers receive complete disclosure. For many years, disclosure was accomplished by delivering a tangible prospectus to investors, both the preliminary section 10(b) prospectus and, after effectiveness, the final, section 10(a) prospectus. Even today, the preliminary prospectus still has to be widely distributed. (*See supra*, §189.) However, today, "distribution" of the preliminary prospectus often means sending it by email or making it available on the issuer's website and providing appropriate links to it (both of which constitute "graphic communications" and, therefore, writings—*see supra*, §§165-167). As more and more information becomes available electronically, the emphasis on distribution of a tangible prospectus—including the final, section 10(a) prospectus—has waned. To be sure, issuers must still prepare and file a final prospectus. However, in many cases, access to the prospectus (*e.g.*, on the S.E.C.'s website) is equivalent to delivery of the prospectus. Once the prospectus is filed, the information rapidly penetrates the financial markets, usually making widespread delivery of a tangible final prospectus unnecessary.

(2) Distribution of statutory prospectus

(a) With written offers—"free writing" [§194]

Section 5(b)(1) of the 1933 Act prohibits the use of jurisdictional means to transport a prospectus (*i.e.*, almost any written offer) relating to a security that is the subject of a registration statement, *unless* that prospectus meets the requirements of section 10 of the Act. After the registration statement is declared effective, however, the Act *permits* written offers (*i.e.,* any kind of sales literature) in any form, as long as they are either accompanied or preceded by a copy of the final, statutory prospectus. [SA §2(a)(10)(a)] This privilege to distribute written offers that are accompanied or preceded by the final, section 10(a) prospectus is called the "free writing" privilege. This post-effective free writing privilege is different from the free writing prospectus used during the waiting period, discussed above (*see supra,* §§161-180).

1) Post-effective free writing compared with free writing prospectus [§195]

It is easy to confuse post-effective free writing with a free writing prospectus. (You have undoubtedly already noticed that sometimes the S.E.C. appears rather unconcerned with the complexity of its regulations!) There are several important differences between these two kinds of free writing:

a) Definitional differences [§196]

One important difference between the two kinds of free writing is that post-effective free writing *is excluded from the definition of prospectus* [*see* SA §2(a)(10)(a)], while free writing prospectuses are *expressly defined as prospectuses* [SA Rules 164, 433].

b) Practical differences [§197]

Besides the fact that the two kinds of free writing are defined separately, there are practical implications to the use of each kind of free writing.

1/ Post-effective free writing [§198]

The important thing to remember about post-effective free writing is that it *must be accompanied or preceded by a final section 10(a) prospectus.* If it is not, the would-be free writing itself becomes a prospectus, which does not meet the requirements of section 10 and is, therefore, illegal under section 5(b)(1).

2/ Free writing prospectus [§199]

The free writing prospectus is permitted as long as the requirements of rules 164 and 433 are met. These include the requirements that: (i) the free writing prospectus contains an appropriate legend (*see supra,* §174), and (ii) the free writing prospectus be filed with the S.E.C. (*see supra,* §179). Furthermore, nonreporting and unseasoned issuers must accompany or precede a free writing prospectus with either a section 10(b) prospectus (during the waiting period) or a section 10(a) prospectus (during the post-effective period). Thus, for these varieties of issuer, the requirements for using a free writing prospectus are very similar to those for using post-effective free writing.

2) Final prospectus needed with free writing [§200]

The upshot of the rules described above is that if any offering participants want to take advantage of the opportunity to use free writing, they will have to *ensure that the free writing is accompanied or preceded by a final prospectus* complying with SA section 10(a). Otherwise, a free writing prospectus can be used, but it will need to comply with the requirements of 1933 Act rules 164 and 433.

(b) With written confirmations [§201]

The 1933 Act defines "prospectus" as, among other things, including any written communication that confirms the sale of any security. [SA §2(a)(10)] For a long time, this meant that issuers, underwriters, and dealers had to distribute copies of the final prospectus along with confirmations of sale (which otherwise would be illegal prospectuses). Confirmations of sale are themselves mandated by the S.E.C. [*See* SEA Rule 10b-10] By delivering a final prospectus along with the confirmation, issuers, underwriters, and dealers could take advantage of the post-effective free writing privilege, which made delivery of the confirmations legal. Today, however, the requirement that a confirmation be accompanied or preceded by a final prospectus has been relaxed by 1933 Act rule 172, discussed below.

(c) With delivery of securities [§202]

As with confirmations of sale, the 1933 Act for many years required delivery of a security to be accompanied or preceded by the final prospectus. [SA §5(a)(2), (b)(2)] Today, no final prospectus need be delivered if the requirements of 1933 Act rule 172 are met.

(d) Rule 172—access to final prospectus equivalent to delivery [§203]

When a prospectus is filed with the S.E.C., its contents become widely known very quickly within the financial community, including underwriters, dealers, and investors, any of which can access the prospectus, if they wish to, by any of a large number of electronic means (not the least of which is the S.E.C.'s own website).

Rule 172 of the 1933 Act reflects this reality and treats the filing of the final prospectus with the S.E.C. as the most significant disclosure event, rather than the delivery of a final prospectus to each customer.

1) **Confirmations of sale [§204]**

   Under 1933 Act rule 172(a), a confirmation of sale (or notice of allocation of shares in an offering) may be sent without a final prospectus, as long as rule 172's requirements are met.

2) **Delivery of securities [§205]**

   Similarly, under 1933 Act rule 172(b), securities may be delivered in connection with a sale, without being accompanied or preceded by a final prospectus, if the requirements of the rule are met.

3) **Rule 172 requirements [§206]**

   In the above situations, rule 172 excuses the delivery of a final, section 10(a) prospectus if:

   (i) A *registration statement is in effect* with respect to the securities, and is *not the subject of a proceeding or examination by the S.E.C.* under the 1933 Act;

   (ii) *None of the offering participants are the subject of an S.E.C. examination* under the 1933 Act; and

   (iii) The issuer has *filed a final prospectus with the S.E.C.* and has complied or is complying with all related rules.

   [SA Rule 172(c)]

4) **Effect on free writing [§207]**

   Post-effective free writing under 1933 Act section 2(a)(10)(a), which is conditioned upon the free writing being accompanied or preceded by a final section 10(a) prospectus, is not available unless the prospectus is delivered to the recipient of the free writing. In other words, *rule 172 does not permit free writing without delivery of a final prospectus.* However, if rule 172 is used instead of delivering a final prospectus, a free writing prospectus under rules 164 and 433 can still be used.

(e) **Notice of registration statement still required [§208]**

   Although SA rule 172, discussed immediately above, generally relieves the parties to an offering of the requirement to deliver a final prospectus with a confirmation of sale or transfer of the security, under SA rule 173 the S.E.C. has retained a vestige of the former requirement by requiring that in transactions in which a prospectus would have been required, the seller must, within two days after the sale, provide the buyer with either (i) a copy of the final prospectus, or (ii) a notice "to the effect that the sale was made pursuant to a registration statement or in a transaction in which a final prospectus would have been required" but for SA rule 172. [SA Rule 173] However, if the delivery of a prospectus is excused by SA section 4(3) or rule 174 (*see infra*, §§212-220 *et seq.*), then even this notice of registration statement is not required. [SA Rule 173]

(3) Duration of post-effective regulation under section 5 [§209]

As we have seen, during the post-effective period, section 5 continues to regulate the activities of parties to a public offering of securities, chiefly by requiring delivery of (or access to) a final prospectus. How long the requirements of section 5 continue in effect depends on the party involved. Not everyone is subject to section 5. Indeed, everyone is exempt from section 5 except issuers, underwriters, and dealers. [SA Act §4(1)] How long section 5's requirements last depends in part on whether it is an issuer, underwriter, or dealer who is asking.

(a) Issuers [§210]

Issuers are subject to section 5 for as long as they are offering securities to the public. Moreover, each time an issuer offers securities to the public, it is subject to section 5. Thus, simply because an issuer has registered the sale of 5 million shares of common stock to the public, it cannot sell another 1 million shares of common stock to the public without another registration statement. [SA §5]

(b) Underwriters [§211]

Underwriters are subject to section 5 for as long as they participate in the offering, *i.e.*, for as long as they continue to sell their allotted shares. Once the allotted shares are sold, the underwriter is no longer acting as an underwriter, although it most likely will continue to buy and sell the registered securities. In that capacity, however, it is generally acting as a dealer, rather than as an underwriter (with the possible exception of underwriters engaging in price stabilization of the security by sponging up excess demand in the market—*see infra*, §§1959 *et seq.*) As a dealer, a former underwriter is subject to the dealer requirements, discussed immediately below.

(c) Dealers [§212]

Section 4(3) of the 1933 Act *exempts* from section 5 all transactions by a dealer *except* those taking place during the period of time in which the distribution is presumed to occur. Consider, for example, an offering in which many of the initial investors resell shortly after purchasing, in order to capture a quick profit. When they do so, they typically resell through securities dealers. Are such transactions part of the distribution? The fact is that such quick re-sales are indistinguishable from the sales taking place as part of the distribution, especially (but not only) when dealers that originally participated in the offering take part in the resales. For this reason, rather than attempting to trace how many retail purchasers have bought and sold a particular security, the 1933 Act simply specifies a period of time in which all dealer transactions are deemed to be part of the distribution. However, even these statutory time periods have been substantially shortened or eliminated by later S.E.C. rules. Keep in mind that these time periods specify when dealers are subject to section 5, which includes the requirement to deliver a prospectus or, when that is excused by SA rule 173, the requirement to deliver a notice of registration statement (*see supra*, §208).

1) Definition of "dealer" [§213]

A dealer in this context is a person that spends all or part of its time (directly or indirectly) as an agent, broker, or principal in the offering, buying, selling, or other trading of securities issued by another person. [SA §2(a)(12)]

a) Includes brokers [§214]

Note that for this purpose, dealers include brokers (who act as middlemen in transactions involving third-party buyers and sellers). (*See supra*, §27.)

b) Usual activity determines status [§215]

Status as a "dealer" depends on a person's usual activities and not on its role with respect to a particular transaction. In other words, a person that normally functions as a dealer could not escape regulation as a dealer by claiming that it was not acting as a dealer in the particular transaction involved.

2) Sales from unsold allotment—unlimited period [§216]

All dealers participating in the distribution are subject to section 5 (meaning that they must continue to deliver (or provide access to) a prospectus or notice of registration statement until their entire allotment is sold. [SA §4(3)(C)] There are no exceptions to this requirement, so that until a dealer's allotment is sold, section 5 will continue to apply.

3) **Initial public offerings—ninety days [§217]**

Even after a dealer has sold its allotment of securities, if the offering is an initial public offering ("IPO")—*i.e.*, the issuer has not previously sold securities to the public—then dealers continue to be subject to section 5 beginning on the effective date of the registration statement or the commencement of the public offering, whichever is later, and ending 90 days later. [SA §4(3)]

4) **Standard period—forty days [§218]**

If the offering is not an IPO, then the 90-day period is shortened to 40 days. [SA §4(3)(B)]

5) **Listed securities—twenty-five days [§219]**

If an issuer is offering securities that, as of the offering date, are listed on a securities exchange or in NASDAQ, then the period in which dealers are subject to section 5 is further shortened to 25 days. [SA Rule 174(d)] This provision would apply, for example, to IPO issuers whose securities were immediately listed.

6) **1934 Act reporting companies—zero days [§220]**

If, immediately before filing the registration statement, the issuer is a 1934 Act reporting company (*i.e.*, is an unseasoned issuer, a seasoned issuer, or a WKSI), then dealers do not have to deliver a prospectus in connection with transactions in the security.

DEALER PROSPECTUS DELIVERY REQUIREMENTS gilbert	
FACTUAL SITUATION	**REQUIREMENTS**
ISSUER IS A 1934 ACT REPORTING COMPANY	After allotment sold, no further prospectus delivery requirement
ISSUER IS NOT A 1934 ACT REPORTING COMPANY • **SECURITIES ARE "LISTED" ON OFFERING DATE**	25 days or until allotment is sold, whichever is later
• **SECURITIES ARE NOT "LISTED" ON OFFERING DATE** • **NON-IPO TRANSACTION**	40 days or until allotment is sold, whichever is later
• **IPO TRANSACTION**	90 days or until allotment is sold, whichever is later

REGULATION IN THE POST-EFFECTIVE PERIOD   **gilbert**

PERMITTED ACTIVITIES	REQUIRED ACTIVITIES
• Oral offers	• Delivery of a final prospectus
• Sales	*or*
• Communications under rule 134 (tombstone ads)	• Delivery of a rule 173 notice of registration statement
• Written offers, if they are section 10 prospectuses (but the preliminary prospectus may no longer be used). A free writing prospectus is a section 10(b) prospectus, but in the post-effective period a free writing prospectus must be accompanied or preceded by a section 10(a) final prospectus	*unless* The statutory distribution period is over or SA rule 174 (which adds the "0 days" and "25 days" provisions of the statutory distribution period) applies
• Post-effective free writing, if accompanied or preceded by the final, section 10(a) prospectus	

QUALIFICATIONS

☑ *For unseasoned issuers:* Only participants selling their allotments of securities in the offering are required to deliver a prospectus; the statutory delivery period is "0 days" but a participant selling from the original allotment always has to deliver a prospectus

☑ *For seasoned issuers:* Same rules that apply to unseasoned issuers, plus a free writing prospectus can be used without accompanying or preceding it by a section 10(a) prospectus

☑ *For WKSIs:* Same rules that apply to seasoned issuers

(4) Loophole in the 1933 Act [§221]

Note that under the above rules, sales may often be consummated in person or by telephone in the post-effective period without furnishing the buyer with a statutory prospectus in advance—as long as the preliminary prospectus is widely distributed and a final prospectus is filed. Thus, despite the objective of full disclosure, some sales of registered securities may legitimately take place even though the specific purchaser never sees a prospectus.

(5) Updating the prospectus [§222]

There are two common situations in which a prospectus must be updated—when the law requires updating and when the disclosure in the prospectus is no longer accurate.

(a) Mandatory updating [§223]

If the period of use of the statutory prospectus extends beyond nine months, the information may not be more than 16 months old. In most cases, this means that the prospectus *must* be updated. [SA §10(a)(3)]

(b) Updating to avoid liability [§224]

Furthermore, the issuer *should* update the prospectus *any time* new material facts develop, because use of a prospectus that is misleading as to a material fact can result in liability under the 1933 Act. [SA §§11, 12, 17(a)]

1) Rationale

Implicit in the statutory requirement that a prospectus contain all material information is the requirement that the information given be true and correct. According to one court, a misleading prospectus violates section 5 of the Act, and liability may result from its use. [**S.E.C. v. Manor Nursing Centers, Inc.,** 458 F.2d 1082 (2d Cir. 1972); *and see infra*, §§747 *et seq.*]

C. Persons Covered by the 1933 Act

1. In General [§225]

Although section 5 of the 1933 Act provides that a public distribution of securities by *any person* must be registered with the S.E.C., section 4(1) of the Act *exempts* from this requirement securities transactions by persons *other than* "issuers," "underwriters," or "dealers." Thus, the registration and prospectus requirements really apply only to *"issuers," "underwriters,"* and *"dealers."*

2. Issuers [§226]

The first group covered by the Act is "issuers." Section 2(a)(4) of the 1933 Act defines "issuer" as including every person who issues or proposes to issue any security. An issuer is subject to the registration requirements of the Act whenever it makes a distribution of its securities to the public. [SA §5] As we will see, persons other than the issuer may also make distributions of securities, and these people may also be regulated by SA section 5. (*See* "secondary distributions," *infra*, §245.)

3. Underwriters [§227]

The second group covered by the Act is "underwriters." Three classes of persons are considered "underwriters" within the meaning of the 1933 Act: (i) persons who purchase securities from the issuer with a view toward public distribution; (ii) persons who offer or sell securities for an issuer in connection with a distribution; and (iii) persons who "participate" in a distribution. [SA §2(a)(11)]

a. Purchasers who intend to distribute securities [§228]

One who purchases securities from an issuer with an eye toward *"distribution"* is an underwriter, provided a distribution in fact takes place. "Distribution" essentially means a *public offering*—i.e., an offering to a substantial number of unsophisticated investors. [SA §2(a)(11)]

b. Persons who offer or sell for an issuer [§229]

The definition of "underwriter" also encompasses persons who actually offer or sell securities *for an issuer* in connection with the issuer's public distribution.

Example: Members of a Chinese benevolent society in this country who gratuitously undertook to solicit offers for the purchase of Chinese government liberty bonds (without a contract or remuneration from the issuer) were held to be underwriters within the "selling for" definition. [**S.E.C. v. Chinese Consolidated Benevolent Association,** 120 F.2d 738 (2d Cir. 1941)]

---

c. Participants in a distribution [§230]

People who participate in a distribution are underwriters of the issuer's securities within the meaning of SA section 2(a)(11).

(1) Test of "participation" [§231]

The test of participation is simply whether the person in question took part in some *significant* fashion in the underwriting. It does not depend on whether the person receives any monetary compensation for the services.

(2) Presumptive underwriter doctrine [§232]

The S.E.C. has formulated an administrative rule of thumb—the *"presumptive underwriter doctrine"*—providing that any person who purchases a significant percentage of the securities offered in a registered public offering and then resells the securities without registering them is an "underwriter." However, the seller will not be charged with being an underwriter if the resales are in limited quantities—i.e., according to the limits set in rules 144 or 145 (*see infra*, §§659, 679). [*See* Nathan, "Presumptive Underwriters," 8 Review of Securities Regulation 881 (1975)]

(3) Exemptions [§233]

The 1933 Act exempts from underwriter status certain persons who participate in underwritings and would otherwise be deemed underwriters.

(a) Purchasers of unsold securities [§234]

Persons unaffiliated with the issuer or any principal underwriter who enter into an agreement with one of the principal *underwriters* (but *not* with the issuer), to purchase all or a portion of the securities unsold after a specified period of time, are excluded from underwriter status if their purchase of the securities is for *investment purposes*—*i.e.*, they intend to hold the securities for a significant period as an investment. [*See* SA Rule 142]

---

e.g. Example: An institutional investor, such as an insurance company, makes an advance commitment to the underwriter to purchase those securities not otherwise sold in the issuer's public distribution. This investor may purchase the securities at a discount from the public offering price without incurring liability as an underwriter.

(b) **Dealers selling for a normal commission [§235]**

Dealers who are part of the selling group in an underwriting would normally come within the participation test and hence be "underwriters." However, if such dealers merely receive from the underwriter or another dealer a commission which is "not in excess of the usual and customary distributors' or sellers' commission," they are *excluded* from the definition of "underwriters." [SA §2(a)(11); SA Rule 141]

1) **No payment from issuer [§236]**

To qualify for this exemption, the dealer must receive the commission from an *underwriter or other dealer*; the commission may *not* be received directly from the issuer. [SA §2(a)(11)]

2) **"Usual and customary commission" [§237]**

In addition, the commission must be for the "usual and customary" amount; *i.e.*, it may not exceed the amount typically allowed to other persons for comparable services in similar underwritings.

a) **"Spreads" [§238]**

Permissible commissions include remuneration commonly known as a "spread"—the difference between the purchase price and the sale price (*i.e.*, the amount received by a dealer who buys and sells as a principal)—as long as this is not more than customary or normal in the circumstances.

3) **Dealers performing additional functions [§239]**

Note that if a dealer's function is to *manage the distribution* of all, or a substantial part, of the particular issue of securities, or if it otherwise performs the normal functions of an underwriter or underwriting syndicate, it will be deemed an underwriter regardless of the amount of its commission. [*See* SA §2(a)(11)]

d. Underwriters for "control persons" [§240]

As defined above, an "underwriter" is a person who buys from, sells for, or participates in the issuer's public distribution of securities. Section 2(a)(11) of the 1933 Act provides that for the purpose of determining who is an underwriter, the term "issuer" includes "control persons." Thus, the term "underwriter" also includes a person who buys from, sells for, or participates in a distribution for a "control person" who makes a public distribution of her stock.

(1) "Control person" defined [§241]

A "control person" is someone having the power to direct the management and policies of the issuer. [SA Rule 405]

(a) Source of control [§242]

The control person's power may come through stock ownership, a position in management, influence with management, or a combination of these factors.

> **Example:** Anne owns 25% of the common stock in XYZ Corp. and is on the firm's board of directors. Anne would probably be a "control person" because she is in a position to influence the management and policies of XYZ.

(b) Control groups [§243]

Groups of persons who have the power to act in concert to influence the affairs of the issuer may be a "control group." Members of control groups are treated as control persons for the purposes of the 1933 Act.

(c) Control power need not be exercised [§244]

Power to control, not exercise of the power, is what makes someone a "control person." Thus, where the principal creditor of a corporation (who was also the principal source of its business) had options to acquire the interests of others in the company, and received 90% of the company's profits, the S.E.C. found that the creditor was a "control person" even though the creditor had not actively participated in the management of the company's business. [*In re* **Walston & Co.,** 7 S.E.C. 937 (1940)]

(2) Offerings by a control person [§245]

The public sale of securities owned by a control person or control group is called a "secondary distribution," because the stock was first issued by the issuer to the control person in the original distribution.

(3) Examples of underwriters

Key to understanding the 1933 Act is understanding that there are several ways to be an "underwriter," as defined by the Act, and that one can inadvertently (and unknowingly) achieve underwriter status. The following are examples of statutory underwriters.

Example: A owns 22% of XYZ Corp. common stock, has contributed another 67% of the stock to a trust whose trustees are his sons, controls another corporation that owns an additional 2% of the XYZ stock, and is the president of XYZ. A is a control person. Thus, an offering to the public of a substantial amount of A's stock over the New York Stock Exchange is a "secondary distribution" and must be registered. Furthermore, any broker-dealer who participates in the public distribution on behalf of A will be held to be an underwriter. [*In re* **Ira Haupt & Co.,** 23 S.E.C. 589 (1946)]

Example: XYZ sells 85,000 shares of common stock to S, the chairman of its board of directors. S already owns half of XYZ's common stock and a substantial percentage of the company's outstanding preferred stock convertible into common stock. S immediately converts the preferred stock into common stock and sells the converted stock and the newly acquired common stock to numerous persons without registration. S is a control person making an unlawful public distribution, and those selling for S in this distribution or buying from S and redistributing the stock to others are underwriters. [*In re* **Hazel Bishop, Inc.,** 40 S.E.C. 718 (1961)]

e. Pledgees of securities [§246]

The problem of defining who is an "underwriter" frequently arises when securities are pledged to a lender (such as a bank) as collateral for a loan. For example, suppose A, a control person owning stock in XYZ Corp., pledges his stock with a bank to secure a loan and then defaults on the loan. If the bank sells the shares publicly to repay the loan, is the bank an "underwriter" because it sold the securities to the public "for" a control person?

(1) Spurious pledge [§247]

If there is no bona fide pledge involved (*i.e.*, the "loan" is really a device to give the control person cash, and the pledgee bank intended from the beginning to sell the securities for reimbursement), the bank will be considered an underwriter. [**S.E.C. v. Guild Films Co.**, 279 F.2d 485 (2d Cir. 1960)]

(2) Weak loan [§248]

The result is the same where the bank has not reasonably investigated whether it is making a good loan—*i.e.*, where there is no reasonable basis for determining that the pledgor can repay the loan without a sale of the securities. [*See* **S.E.C. v. Guild Films Co.**, *supra*]

(3) Bona fide pledge and loan [§249]

The difficult cases occur where the loan is bona fide. No court has expressly held that a good faith loan and pledge requires registration of the control person's shares before the pledgee bank can publicly sell them. However, in dictum, the court in *Guild Films, supra,* indicated that *all* pledgees take with a view to distribution and must therefore register under the 1933 Act before making any public distribution of the securities. [*But see* **Fox v. Glickman Corp.**, Fed. Sec. L. Rep. (CCH) §91,682 (S.D.N.Y. 1966)—*contra*]

4. Dealers [§250]

The third group covered by the 1933 Act are "dealers." Thus, under section 4(1), dealers are also subject to the registration and prospectus requirements of the Act.

a. Those included as dealers [§251]

The definition of "dealer" given in section 2(a)(12) of the Act is based on a person's general activities rather than on conduct in a particular offering. A dealer is defined as any person who, either full or part-time, is *engaged in the business* of offering, buying, selling, or otherwise dealing or trading in securities issued by another person as *agent, broker,* or *principal.*

(1) Note

This definition of dealer expressly includes those performing the function of a broker.

b. Exemptions for dealers

(1) **"Dealer's exemption" from section 5 [§252]**

Under section 4(3) of the 1933 Act, dealers are exempt from section 5 as long as they comply with the prospectus delivery requirements of the Act. (*See supra*, §§212-220.)

(2) **Dealer's exemption from underwriter status [§253]**

Note that since dealers "participate" in the underwriting process, they would usually be defined as "underwriters," and hence would be subject to section 5 regardless of any exemption for "dealers." However, dealers are specifically *exempted* from underwriter status if they perform only normal dealer functions in return for a normal dealer's commission (*see supra*, §235).

c. **Exemption for brokers [§254]**

In addition to the limited exemption from registration provided for dealers, the Securities Act also provides an exemption for persons acting as brokers only. (*See infra*, §437.)

d. **Limitation on exemptions—underwriters [§255]**

If a dealer or broker is acting as an underwriter in a particular distribution (*i.e.,* going beyond the normal functions of a dealer or broker), the dealer or broker may *not* rely on the dealer or broker transaction exemption for transactions that are part of the distribution.

e. **Customers [§256]**

Even if the dealer or broker has an exemption, the selling customer must have his own exemption to avoid the prospectus delivery requirement. Usually the selling customer is not an "issuer, underwriter, or dealer," and so is exempt under section 4(1).

D. Property Interests Covered by the 1933 Act

1. **Act Applies Only to "Securities" [§257]**

To come within the registration requirement of section 5 of the 1933 Act, the property interest that is offered or sold must be a "security."

2. **Securities Subject to Registration [§258]**

Section 2(a)(1) of the 1933 Act defines three basic categories of "securities" subject to registration:

a. **Interests or instruments specifically mentioned in the Act [§259]**

The 1933 Act expressly classifies certain financial instruments or interests as "securities." However, the Act also provides that its definition of securities will not apply if "the context otherwise requires." Thus, even items expressly classified as securities in the 1933 Act may not be securities if the context dictates otherwise. The Supreme Court has provided some guidance for two such items: stock and notes.

(1) Stock [§260]

If so-called "stock" *possesses the characteristics normally associated with stock—i.e.,* it carries dividend and voting rights, it is negotiable, it can be pledged, and it can appreciate in value—then it is a security under the 1933 Act.

---

e.g. **Example:** A purchaser of 100% of the stock in a corporation can bring a claim under the 1933 and 1934 Acts, even though the transaction involved the purchase of an entire business, and even though the parties could have structured the transaction so as to avoid transferring stock (*e.g.,* by transferring the assets of the business). [**Landreth Timber Co. v. Landreth,** 471 U.S. 681 (1985)] *Note:* It may seem obvious that stock in a corporation is a security. However, before *Landreth, supra,* some courts had applied the "sale of business doctrine" to sales of 100% of the stock in closely held corporations. Under that doctrine, the federal securities laws did not apply.

---

cf. **Compare:** If so-called "stock" *lacks the normal indicia of stock*, then the courts may look to the economic realities of the situation to determine that no security is involved. Thus, the Supreme Court refused to hold that the sale of stock in a nonprofit housing cooperative involved a security. The stock lacked the usual indicia of stock: it was not transferable, there was no right to receive dividends, etc. The purchasers essentially bought living quarters for their personal use and were not investing in "stock." [**United Housing Foundation, Inc. v. Forman,** 421 U.S. 837 (1979)]

---

(2) Promissory notes [§261]

Like stock, promissory notes are specifically listed as "securities" in section 2(a)(1) of the 1933 Act. Notes, however, present a special problem, because many notes clearly are not securities (*e.g.,* mortgage notes, or the note signed by a consumer buying an automobile on credit).

(a) "Family resemblance" test [§262]

To determine whether a note is a security, courts apply the "family resemblance" test. The test includes a presumption and exceptions to the presumption.

1) Presumption that a note is a security [§263]

Because notes are specifically mentioned as securities in the 1933 Act, there is a presumption that every note is a security.

2) Exceptions [§264]

Recognizing, however, that not all notes are securities, the Supreme Court in **Reves v. Ernst & Young,** 494 U.S. 56 (1990), adopted a list of notes that are not covered by the presumption. These notes, and notes bearing a "family resemblance" to them, are deemed *not to be securities* under the 1933 Act. The list includes notes delivered in the following kinds of transactions:

a) *Consumer financing;*

b) *Home mortgages;*

c) *Short-term loans secured by assets of a small business;*

d) *"Character" loans* to bank customers;

e) *Short-term secured financing of accounts receivable;*

f) *Short-term, open-account debts incurred in the ordinary course of business* (especially when the debt is collateralized); and

g) *Commercial bank loans for current operations.*

3) Four factors for interpretation [§265]

In *Reves, supra,* the Supreme Court provided some guidance for deciding when a note bears a family resemblance to a note on the above list. Four factors should be examined:

a) *The motivations* of the seller and buyer of the note (*e.g.,* was the transaction one for investment, or instead to finance the purchase of a consumer item?);

b) *The plan of distribution* of the instrument, if any (*e.g.,* if the instrument is traded, the likelihood that it is a security increases);

c) *The reasonable expectations of the investing public* (*e.g.,* does the public reasonably expect to have the protections of the 1933 Act in this kind of transaction?);

1/ *Note:* In *Reves,* the Court stated that public expectations may result in defining a note as a security *even if an economic analysis of the transaction suggests that the note is not a security;* and

    d)   *Finally, the existence of a comparable scheme of regulation* diminishes the likelihood that a note is a security in a particular case. (*See* further discussion of the effect of comparable regulations, *infra*, §275.)

(3) Other interests or instruments specifically mentioned in the Act [§266]

The Act also expressly classifies the following additional items as "securities":

(a) *Preorganization subscriptions* for securities;

(b) *Fractional, undivided interests in oil, gas, or other mineral rights;*

(c) *Collateral trust certificates* (a type of bond secured by collateral, frequently other securities, deposited with a trustee);

(d) *Certain types of receipts for securities,* including American depositary receipts for foreign securities (*i.e.*, where a foreign company issues receipts in this country for shares deposited in banks in the foreign country) [*see* SA §2(a)(4)]; and

(e) *Equipment trust certificates* and certificates of interest in unincorporated investment trusts (*e.g.*, Massachusetts Trusts) [*see* SA §2(a)(4)].

b. Investment contracts [§267]

The broadest classification of securities in section 2(a)(1) is the catchall reference to "investment contracts." The S.E.C. and the courts have construed this phrase so as to apply the registration requirements of the 1933 Act to a wide variety of financial schemes.

(1) Traditional "*Howey* test" [§268]

The traditional test for whether a property interest constitutes an investment contract is the so-called *Howey* test, set forth by the Supreme Court in **S.E.C. v. W.J. Howey Co.,** 328 U.S. 293 (1946). This case holds that an "investment contract" is *any* contract or *profit-making scheme* whereby a person *invests his money* in a *common enterprise* and *expects to make a profit* solely from the *efforts of the promoter* or a third party who is responsible for management.

(2) Modern trend [§269]

For many years, court decisions tended to expand the scope of property interests regulated as securities under this provision of the 1933 Act. Thus, the cases occasionally went beyond the criteria of the *Howey* test to require registration in situations where the investors *participated* to some extent in management and where the benefits derived by them were something *other than cash profits.*

(a) Factors determining "investment" or "participation" [§270]

Under the modern test, the criteria for determining whether a particular property interest or participation in a profit-making venture is an "investment contract" are:

1) Does the investor have an *expectation of profit*?

2) Is there a *common enterprise*? This test suggests that there are a number of investors who stand in a similar relationship to a business in which they invest in common.

3) Does the success of the enterprise depend mainly on the efforts of persons *other than the investors*; or, even if the investors are active in management, does the scheme involve the raising of capital to finance the venture, which is then controlled by a third party (the "*risk capital*" test)?

4) Do the investors *need the protection* of the 1933 Act?

EXAM TIP   **gilbert**

If your exam includes a question in which you must determine whether something is a security under the 1933 Act (and most exams do include such a question), you should *state the traditional Howey test* (an investment contract is any profit-making scheme whereby a person invests his money in a common enterprise and expects to make a profit solely from the efforts of others, who are responsible for management). But you should *then note the modern test* discussed above.

(b) Requirement of a common enterprise [§271]

Under the so-called "horizontal" test for a common enterprise, there must be a sharing or pooling of funds or other assets by several investors and profits derived from these combined funds.

Example: There was *no* common enterprise where the plaintiff invested funds in a discretionary futures trading account with the defendant management firm (agreeing to share 25% of the trading profits with the defendant as compensation for its services) because there was no sharing or pooling of funds by more than one investor. [*See* **Hirk v. Agri-Research Council, Inc.**, 561 F.2d 96 (7th Cir. 1977)]

---

1) Horizontal test sometimes discounted [§272]

Note, however, that many courts seem to pay little attention to this horizontal (several investors) test. Instead, they rely on a "vertical" common enterprise test—a common enterprise will be found if the investor is relying on the efforts of the promoter to make a profit. Thus, "a common enterprise is one in which the fortunes of the investor are interwoven with and dependent upon the efforts and success of those seeking the investment." [**S.E.C. v. Glen W. Turner Enterprises, Inc.**, 474 F.2d 476 (9th Cir. 1973)]

a) Narrower test

A narrower vertical common enterprise test requires that the investment manager's fortunes rise and fall with those of the investor. For example, if a broker managing a discretionary commodities account is paid a fixed commission based on the dollar value of the trades he executes (and does not participate in the profits made in the account), some courts would hold that there is *no* vertical common enterprise but only a broker providing a service; thus, there is no security. [*See* **Schofield v. First Commodity Corp.**, 638 F. Supp. 4 (D. Mass. 1985), *aff'd*, 793 F.2d 28 (1st Cir. 1986)]

(c) Efforts of persons other than investors [§273]

In *Howey*, the Supreme Court noted that the test for an investment contract included a requirement that profits come "*solely*" from the efforts of others. It was perhaps inevitable that some would attempt to circumvent regulation by involving investors in the enterprise in one way or another, hoping thereby to avoid profits "solely" from the efforts of others. The courts have taken a dim view of these efforts, and the modern formulation of the *Howey* test requires only that the success of the enterprise depend *mainly* on the efforts of persons other than the investors. [*See* **S.E.C. v. Glen W. Turner Enterprises, Inc.**, *supra*; **S.E.C. v. Koscot Interplanetary, Inc.**, 497 F.2d 473 (5th Cir. 1974)]

1) Timing of third-party efforts [§274]

It might also make a difference when the efforts of the third party are made. For example, what if the third party expends effort seeking out the opportunities, and structures the acquisition of assets by the enterprise, but after the investment is made, the third party undertakes no significant additional tasks? In one such case, the court held that the enterprise does not involve "securities." [**S.E.C. v. Life Partners, Inc.**, 87 F.3d 536 (D.C. Cir. 1996)]

---

e.g. **Example:** LPI purchases life insurance policies from terminally ill persons, at a discount of 20-40% of the death benefit, depending on the insured's life expectancy. LPI obtains the money for these purchases by selling interests in the policies to third parties, who hope to make a profit when the insured dies and the insurance policy pays off. The S.E.C. sued LPI, claiming that the interests sold to third parties were securities and that LPI violated the securities laws by selling the interests in the policies without registration. The court held that the interests were not securities, because after the investment in the policy was made, there was nothing that LPI did or could do that would affect the profitability of the investment. Undeniably, LPI engaged in entrepreneurial effort in seeking out policies to purchase, and in making the actuarial calculations that were the basis for calculating the cost to LPI's investors of the policy. However, once the investment was made, it was the length of the insured's life that determined whether the investment was profitable, and nothing LPI could do had any effect on that. [**S.E.C. v. Life Partners, Inc.,** *supra; and see* **S.E.C. v. Tyler,** 77 S.E.C. Docket 60, 2002 WL 257645 (S.E.C.)—presence of secondary market-making justified departure from *Life Partners, supra*]

(3) The "comparable regulation" limitation [§275]

In 1975, the Supreme Court began to limit the scope of the federal securities laws to the regulation of the public trading markets and interstate investment promotions. [*See* **Blue Chip Stamps v. Manor Drug Stores,** 421 U.S. 723 (1975)] This trend has also narrowed somewhat the definition of a security. Thus, the Supreme Court has held that if a detailed scheme of federal regulation applies to a particular instrument or contract, the 1933 Act may not apply. [**Marine Bank v. Weaver,** 455 U.S. 551 (1982)]

Example: Plaintiffs purchased a six-year certificate of deposit from a bank. The bank then encouraged plaintiffs to pledge the certificate in a loan guarantee for one of the bank's customers. The bank never disbursed the loan but used it instead to pay off the customer's other loans and checking accounts that were in default. Four months later, the customer went bankrupt and the bank took the pledged certificate of deposit to pay off the remainder of the customer's loan. Plaintiffs sued the bank under rule 10b-5 of the 1934 Act, but the Supreme Court held that: (i) the certificate of deposit was not a security because banks were heavily regulated and the certificate was guaranteed by the Federal Deposit Insurance Corporation, and (ii) the agreement to guarantee a loan to one of the bank's customers was not a security because it was negotiated one on one, was private in nature, and was never intended to be publicly traded. [**Marine Bank v. Weaver,** *supra*]

> **Example:** Plaintiff was a participant in a noncontributory, compulsory union pension plan. Eligibility to receive benefits under the plan was determined by years of service. When plaintiff was found ineligible to receive benefits, he sued the union under rule 10b-5 of the 1934 Act and section 17 of the 1933 Act. The Supreme Court held that the enactment of ERISA (which requires pension plans to disclose specified information to employees and governs the substantive terms of pension plans) made application of the 1933 and 1934 Acts unnecessary. "Whatever benefits employees might derive from the effect of the securities acts are now provided in more definite form through ERISA." [**International Brotherhood of Teamsters v. Daniel,** 439 U.S. 551 (1979)—*see infra*, §296, for further discussion]

c. Any interest or instrument commonly known as a security [§276]

In addition to the items specifically listed in section 2(a)(1) and the ambiguous "investment contract," the 1933 Act also includes a catchall provision that sweeps into the definition of a security, "in general, any interest or instrument commonly known as a 'security.'"

3. Application of Definitions [§277]

The above definitions provide the courts with three tests for determining whether a property interest is a "security" within the 1933 Act: (i) is it *specifically mentioned* in the Act; (ii) is it an *investment contract*; or (iii) is it an *interest commonly classified as a security?*

a. Illustrations

The following are illustrations of property interests to which the above criteria have been applied.

(1) Interests in land [§278]

A "security" has been found where small tracts of land were sold to investors to be used for growing fruit. *Rationale:* The seller's company managed the land for the investors and was responsible for growing, harvesting, and selling the crops; the investors received a percentage of the net profits. [**S.E.C. v. W.J. Howey Co.,** *supra*, §268]

(a) And note

A security was found where leasehold rights on small plots of land were sold to investors in connection with the lessor's advertisement that he would drill a test well for the property. [**S.E.C. v. C.M. Joiner Leasing Corp.,** 320 U.S. 344 (1943)]

(2) Partnership and joint venture interests

(a) General partnerships [§279]

The sale of a general partnership interest normally does ***not*** constitute the sale of a security, because general partners ordinarily take an active part in the management of the business.

1) Exception—general partnership interests that are securities [§280]

General partnership interests may be securities if one or more of the following are true:

(i) An agreement among the parties leaves so *little power in the hands of the partner* that the arrangement in fact distributes power as would a limited partnership;

(ii) The *partner is so inexperienced and unknowledgeable in business affairs that he is incapable of intelligently exercising partnership powers*;

(iii) The *partner is so dependent on some unique entrepreneurial or managerial ability* of the promoter or manager that he cannot replace the manager of the enterprise or otherwise *exercise meaningful partnership power*.

[**Williamson v. Tucker**, 645 F.2d 404 (5th Cir. 1981)]

(b) Distinguish—limited partnership interests [§281]

Limited partnership interests are almost inevitably held to be securities, because limited partners obtain an interest in the partnership in return for a contribution of cash or other property, but have little or no role in managing the business.

1) Exception—limited partner retains significant control [§282]

Breaking with the tradition of holding that limited partnership interests are securities, a Third Circuit case held that a limited partner that, pursuant to the limited partnership agreement, retained significant control over the operation of the partnership was not a purchaser of a "security." [**Steinhardt Group Inc. v. Citicorp**, 126 F.3d 144 (3d Cir. 1997)]

a) Note—limited partnership agreement not typical [§283]

Steinhardt involved an unusual arrangement in which the limited partner-plaintiff, which owned 98.79% of the partnership, retained the right to (i) propose action outside the partnership's business plan (and if the proposal was not carried out by the general partner, to replace the general partner); and (ii) revise the partnership's business plan. The court characterized the arrangement as "far afield of the typical limited partnership agreement whereby a limited partner leaves control of the business to the general partners." [**Steinhardt Group, Inc. v. Citicorp,** *supra*]

(3) Limited liability companies [§284]

A limited liability company ("LLC") is a kind of hybrid of a corporation and a partnership. The owners (called "members") have limited personal liability for enterprise obligations (like shareholders in a corporation), but the enterprise may be managed and taxed like a partnership. The members of a limited liability company typically have the right to participate in management, raising the possibility that interests in such companies might not be securities. The S.E.C., however, has obtained preliminary injunctions against the sale of limited liability company memberships on the ground that the sales would violate SA section 5. [*See* **S.E.C. v. Parkersburg Wireless LLC,** 1995 WL 79775 (D.D.C. 1995); **Fransen v. Terps LLC,** 153 F.R.D. 655 (D. Colo. 1994)]

(a) "Sale of business" doctrine and LLCs [§285]

In **Landreth Timber Co. v. Landreth** (*supra*, §260), the Supreme Court held that when the sale of 100% of a business is structured as a sale of stock in a corporation, the transaction involves the sale of a security. So far, however, courts have not followed a similar rule in the case of LLCs. LLCs are not corporations, and the sale of an LLC, therefore, does not even technically involve the sale of stock. Instead, courts tend to analyze LLC interests to determine if they are investment contracts, and at least in cases in which the investors have substantial control, have declined to find sales of "securities" in these cases. [*See, e.g.,* **Great Lakes Chemical Corp. v. Monsanto Co.,** 96 F. Supp. 2d 376 (D. Del. 2000)]

Example: GLCC purchased 100% of a business from the business's founders, M Co. and STI. Later, GLCC came to believe that the business had been misrepresented to it by M Co. and STI. GLCC sued M Co. and STI on, among other things, federal securities law claims. The reasoning of *Landreth* applies to transactions in stock, and the question in *Landreth* was whether a sale of stock should ever be treated as something other than the sale of a security. Here, by contrast, the transaction involved no stock at all, and the question was whether it should be treated as though it did involve stock or an investment contract. The court declined to apply *Landreth*. The court also found that the LLC interests were not investment contracts, because the buyer exercised complete control over the enterprise after the sale was complete. [**Great Lakes Chemical Corp. v. Monsanto Co.,** *supra*]

(4) Franchises [§286]

The basic issue regarding franchises is the same as that for partnerships: Is the investor active in management of the franchise or merely a passive investor? If the franchisee is active, there is normally no security.

 Example: Franchisee paid $12,500 for a franchise to operate a tax center in a specified geographic area. The franchisor's participation was limited to providing initial training and assistance in establishing the center (in return for 10% of the gross sales). The court found that no security had been sold because Franchisee had to play a very active role in management. [**Wieboldt v. Metz,** 355 F. Supp. 255 (S.D.N.Y. 1973)]

(5) Pyramid sales plans [§287]

A "pyramid sales plan" exists when the promoter of a product creates a franchise system whereby she sells to franchisees both the right to distribute the product *and* the right to sell further distribution rights to others. The franchisees receive a flat fee for recruitment, or an override on sales by these "subdistributors." In essence, the scheme is one in which the participants (*i.e.,* each successive group of purchasers) try to sell distributorships and subdistributorships rather than the product itself.

(a) Investor's role [§288]

To avoid being classified as a "security" under the *Howey* test (*see supra*, §268), these plans initially required the purchasers to perform some minor management duties (*e.g.,* filing reports). However, the investors generally did not assume the major duties normally required of a person buying a business.

(b) Investor's benefit [§289]

The S.E.C. has also indicated that the benefit expected by the investor from such schemes need not necessarily be a share of cash profits in the enterprise. Any "economic benefit" may make the requisite property interest a "security." [SA Release No. 5211 (1971)]

Example: In one case, the court held that a pyramid scheme involved the sale of a security where:

(i) There was an initial *investment of money* to buy distributorships;

(ii) There was a *common enterprise* (the return to the investor-distributor depended in part on the efforts of the promoter to assist those who had already bought distributorships to sell others); and

(iii) The success of the scheme depended on the ***promoter's essential management efforts,*** even though the investor-distributors also contributed their own efforts.

[**S.E.C. v. Koscot Interplanetary, Inc.,** 497 F.2d 473 (5th Cir. 1974)]

---

(6) Condominiums [§290]

There are situations in which condominiums can be securities—generally when the purchaser, in addition to buying the condominium, receives some type of investment interest. For example, condominium units have been held to be securities where there is a rental arrangement whereby the condominium project manager rents the units to others when the owners are not using them and all units share expenses and revenues from rentals on a project basis. [SA Release No. 5347 (1973)]

(7) Club memberships [§291]

Memberships in social organizations or clubs (*e.g.*, memberships in country clubs) are normally ***not*** considered "securities"; however, memberships in clubs that have ***some business aspect*** are generally held to involve the sale of securities (*e.g.*, certificates issued to members for loans constitute "investment contracts" and hence are securities). [**United States v. Monjar,** 47 F. Supp. 421 (D. Del. 1942)]

(a) Construction of facilities [§292]

If memberships are sold to raise the *"risk capital"* to build a club, the promoters of the club operate it for their personal profit, and club members have an irrevocable right to use the club, a security is involved. [**Silver Hill Country Club v. Sobieski,** 55 Cal. 2d 811 (1961)]

1) Rationale

In *Sobieski, supra,* the California Supreme Court reiterated that profitmaking is not the only criterion of a security, but that the purpose of the securities laws was to protect against all schemes used to raise "risk capital."

2) Scope of *Sobieski*

Note that although *Sobieski* is a state securities law case, it has been frequently cited in *federal* decisions interpreting the 1933 Act.

(b) Distinguish—no "risk capital" [§293]

Whereas the court in *Sobieski* stressed the "risk capital" aspect of the venture, the court in *Wieboldt, supra,* §286, held that the "risk capital" test did *not* apply there because the franchisor had been in business for several years and was not using the money derived from franchisees to start the business.

(8) Employee pension and profit-sharing plans [§294]

Qualified employee pension and profit-sharing plans are tax-motivated arrangements. They allow employers to make a deductible contribution to a fund that defers any tax to the benefited employees, with respect to both the employer's contribution and the amounts of income generated by the plan, until the employee actually receives a deferred distribution (typically on retirement at age 65) from the plan. All such plans are conceivably investment contracts involving the pooling of individual investments in a medium through which profits are expected as a result of the efforts of another. The S.E.C.'s historical approach to such arrangements, however, has been dictated in large part by the extent to which it perceives the need to protect an investor interest.

(a) Voluntary contribution plans [§295]

If the offer or sale of an interest in these types of plans contemplates that the employee will make voluntary contributions to the plan, this has historically been held to be the offer and sale of a security. [*See* S.E.C. Release No. 33-6188 (1980)]

1) But note

If the contributions are used merely for the purchase of annuity or insurance contracts (themselves exempt under section 3(a)(8) of the 1933 Act), it may be that the plan does not involve the offer of a "security."

(b) No contributions or compulsory contribution [§296]

If the plan has no contributions by employees or if employee contribution is compulsory (*i.e.,* involuntary), historically the S.E.C. regarded such plans as involving no "sale" of a security and hence not covered by the 1933 Act. This position was affirmed in **International Brotherhood of Teamsters v. Daniel,** *supra,* §275. There, the court held:

1) *The plaintiff-employee's interest* in an involuntary and non-contributory union pension fund is *not* a "security."

2) The *plaintiff's interest is acquired "involuntarily"* (by becoming an employee), so there is no "sale" of the security to the plaintiff for value.

3) *The employee does not make an investment;* he does not give up specific consideration in return for a separable interest with

the characteristics of a security. He becomes an employee and as a result receives (commingled with many other rights) a compensation package. He is selling his labor to make a living—not primarily to make an investment. Also, the employer did not make a contribution specifically on behalf of the individual employees; the employer made contributions on the basis of actual weeks worked, and all qualifying employees (whether in service 20 or 40 years) got the same benefit.

4) *The return from the pension fund* comes to the employees mostly from employer contributions and only a minor amount from investment earnings on the contributed funds. Also, qualification to receive funds is not primarily a result of the management efforts of others, but rather of whether the individual can meet the requirements of the pension fund (such as length of service).

5) *The enactment of ERISA* in 1974 (which requires pension plans to disclose specified information to employees and governs the substantive terms of pension plans) severely undercuts all arguments for extending the federal securities acts to noncontributory, compulsory pension plans. The possible benefits employees might have derived from the securities acts are now provided in definite form by ERISA.

(9) Commodity silver purchases [§297]

The S.E.C. and the courts have begun to closely scrutinize commodity investment plans. Nevertheless, where the defendant firm offered and sold silver bars, touted silver as being a superior investment, and promised to buy the silver back at the spot price quoted in the *Wall Street Journal* on the date of sale, it was held that no security existed. [**Noa v. Key Futures, Inc.,** Fed. Sec. L. Rep. (CCH) ¶97,568 (9th Cir. 1980)] In reaching its decision, the court noted that any profits to be derived depended on the fluctuations of the silver market and not on the investment firm's management efforts. Also, the buy-back agreement saved the investor a brokerage fee but did not amount to an engagement in a common enterprise.

(10) Loan participations [§298]

When a commercial bank makes a loan, it often sells interests in the loan (known as "participations") to other banks. This practice is called "syndication," and the borrower may or may not be aware of it when it receives the proceeds of the loan. Thus, if a loan is syndicated, when the borrower makes a loan payment to its lender, the lender in turn will parcel out portions of the payment to the various syndicate member banks. The question then arises: Are such loan participations "securities"?

(a) Conditions under which loan participations are not securities [§299]
One court, applying *Reves* (*supra*, §§264-265), has concluded that loan participations are not securities, at least if certain conditions are met:

(i) Each participating financial institution agreed to **conduct its own credit analysis** of the borrower;

(ii) The overall **motivation of the parties was the promotion of commercial purposes**, rather than an investment in a business enterprise;

(iii) Loan participations were **marketed only to sophisticated financial or commercial institutions**, and resales of participations were restricted; and

(iv) Syndicate **members were on notice that they were participating in loans** and not investing in a business enterprise.

[Banco Espanol de Credito v. Security Pacific National Bank, 973 F.2d 51 (2d Cir. 1992)]

(b) "Participations" sold to the general public may be securities [§300]
A later case involved the sale to unsophisticated investors of participations in mortgages. Here, the court held that the participations were securities, distinguishing *Banco Espanol, supra*, because that case did not involve sales to the general investing public. [**Pollack v. Laidlaw Holdings, Inc.,** 27 F.3d 808 (2d Cir. 1994)]

E. The Registration Statement

1. In General [§301]
As previously indicated, prior to the original public issuance of securities, the issuer must file a registration statement with the S.E.C., the purpose of which is to disclose all of the material facts relating to the securities being offered. The prospectus, discussed above, constitutes Part I of the registration statement and contains the most important information in the registration statement. (Part II contains supplementary information.) Preparation of, and access to, the prospectus are principal aims of the 1933 Act.

2. Preparing the Registration Statement

a. **Investigation [§302]**

After the issuer decides to issue the securities, the issuer and its attorney normally conduct an investigation of the proposed underwriting firm. Similarly, the underwriting firm usually does a research study of the issuer before deciding whether to underwrite the securities issue (and, if so, at what price).

b. **Negotiation [§303]**

The managing underwriter (on behalf of all of the underwriters) and issuer generally do not sign a formal underwriting agreement until shortly before the registration statement is to be declared effective by the S.E.C. and the actual offering price of the security to be offered is determined. However, following their investigations, the issuer and managing underwriter do negotiate the terms of the underwriting—including the tentative offering price and the underwriter's commission—and they may sign a *letter of intent* (*i.e.*, an "agreement to agree"). At this point, the parties are ready to prepare the registration statement. Recall that such an agreement does not constitute an illegal offer because it takes place between the issuer and the underwriters.

c. **Drafting process [§304]**

Typically, the first step in drafting the underwriting agreement is to draw up a schedule of events assigning responsibility for each event to the various parties.

(1) **Legal responsibilities [§305]**

The legal duties in preparing the offering are generally split between counsel for the issuer and counsel for the underwriters, according to the background and experience of each. Normally, counsel for the underwriters prepares the underwriting agreement while counsel for the issuer drafts the registration statement.

(a) **Dual role of counsel for issuer [§306]**

The biggest concern during preparation of the registration statement is what the issuer must disclose in the statement. The law requires that all material facts be disclosed, but the issuer may balk at disclosing anything negative, wanting to make the statement as positive as possible for selling purposes. Counsel for the issuer may therefore find herself in a difficult position: She must represent the client's interests, but at the same time see that the client complies with the law.

(2) **Sources of guidance for drafter [§307]**

Drafting a registration statement is difficult, and much of the ability required to do an effective job can be acquired only by actual practice. However, the starting point for learning what is required is the statutory guidelines and the rules and forms prescribed by the S.E.C.

(a) Applicable sections and rules [§308]

The drafter of a registration statement should look first to sections 6 and 7 of the 1933 Act (governing the registration process) and regulation C (setting forth the rules that apply to the registration statement itself).

(b) Registration forms [§309]

In addition, the S.E.C. has prescribed a number of forms for use in complying with the registration requirements. These forms incorporate requirements stated in schedule A of the Act.

1) Basic registration forms [§310]

The S.E.C. has adopted a set of registration forms, including two basic forms:

a) Form S-3 [§311]

Form S-3 requires the least amount of disclosure and incorporates by reference 1934 Act reports filed by the issuer. To use form S-3 in a particular transaction, the *issuer* must meet the *registrant requirements* and the *transaction* must meet the *transaction requirements.*

1/ Registrant requirements [§312]

Form S-3 may be used by firms that (i) are required to file reports under the 1934 Act; (ii) have *timely* filed all reports under the 1934 Act for the preceding 12 months; and (iii) can meet certain standards of financial stability.

a/ Majority-owned subsidiaries [§313]

Majority-owned subsidiaries may register offerings on form S-3 if either: (i) the subsidiary itself meets the registrant requirements and the transaction requirements; (ii) the parent meets the registrant requirements and the offering is of investment-grade debt securities; or (iii) the parent meets the registrant requirements and the transaction requirements, and the parent unconditionally guarantees the subsidiary's payment obligations on the securities.

2/ Transaction requirements [§314]

Form S-3 is available for the following kinds of transactions:

a/ *Offerings of securities for cash,* if the issuer's "public float" (*i.e.,* the market value of common stock held by nonaffiliates of the issuer) is at least $75 million;

b/ *Offerings by the issuer of debt and nonconvertible preferred stock, for cash,* if the securities offered are rated "investment grade" by at least one nationally recognized rating agency;

c/ *Secondary offerings* (*i.e.,* offerings of the issuer's securities by persons other than the issuer), if securities of the same class are listed on a stock exchange or quoted in the NASDAQ system;

d/ *Rights offerings, dividend (or interest) reinvestment plans, and conversions or warrants*; and

e/ *Offerings of "asset-backed" securities* (*i.e.,* securities paid by flowing through the cash received on a pool of financial assets, such as accounts receivable), if the asset-backed securities are rated "investment grade" by at least one nationally recognized rating agency.

f/ *Automatic shelf registrations by WKSIs,* which are "pre-registrations" of securities with the S.E.C. They are effective immediately upon filing and usually omit details of the offering until the issuer is ready to actually sell securities. At that time, a prospectus supplement is prepared that outlines the particular offering. Shelf registration, including automatic shelf registration, is discussed in more detail, *infra*, §§411 *et seq.*

b) Form S-1 [§315]

Form S-1 is the general form used for the registration of the securities of most companies unless another form is prescribed or authorized. This form permits the least amount of incorporation by reference of 1934 Act filing information.

2) Other registration forms [§316]

Other, particularized forms also exist, such as form S-8 (for stock option plans) and forms SB-1 and SB-2 (generalized, simplified forms for use by qualified "small business issuers").

d. Contents of the registration statement [§317]

As noted above, the objective of the registration statement is disclosure of material information—*i.e.*, providing potential investors with *all* of the information that a reasonable investor would consider important in deciding whether to buy the securities registered.

(1) S.E.C. discretion [§318]

The S.E.C. exercises broad discretion in deciding what information is material and must therefore be included in the registration statement. For example, the registration statement must ordinarily contain the information specified in schedule A of the 1933 Act (*e.g.*, name of issuer, state of organization, location of principal office, etc.). [SA §7] Securities Act section 7, however, authorizes the S.E.C. to require more or less disclosure in a registration statement than is specified by schedule A. The primary way in which the S.E.C. exercises this discretion is in promulgating the various forms for registration statements. (*See, e.g.*, form S-3, discussed above, which abbreviates required disclosures for certain issuers on the theory that most such information has already been disclosed in reports the issuer filed under the 1934 Act.)

(a) Additional information [§319]

The form for a registration statement is only the starting point for disclosure. A registration statement must contain *all additional information needed to make the registration statement, as a whole, not misleading.* [SA Rule 408] For example, it would be misleading to include required information about a particular product manufactured by the issuer, but omit the fact that the issuer's management has plans to discontinue that product in the near future. Experienced practitioners include such information from the outset, without waiting for the S.E.C. to request it.

(b) Effect of disclosure [§320]

Although the S.E.C. does not approve or disapprove the investment merits of the securities being registered—*i.e.*, it does not protect the investor from risk, but merely sees that all material information is disclosed—the S.E.C.'s disclosure requirements may affect whether people ultimately buy the registered securities.

(2) Financial information [§321]

To make a wise investment decision, a potential investor will want to project the issuer's future sales and net earnings. Thus, financial data about the issuer are obviously an important part of the information that must be disclosed in the registration statement.

(a) Balance sheet [§322]

The issuer must release a balance sheet (*i.e.*, a statement showing its present or current financial condition) normally dated not more than *90 days* before filing; and if there is a delay in the effective date of the registration statement, the balance sheet must be updated. [SA Schedule A]

(b) Profit and loss statements [§323]

The S.E.C. also generally requires that the issuer include statements of its net income for at least the past three years (plus a statement for the year to date).

(c) S.E.C. accounting regulations [§324]

The S.E.C. has its own accounting regulations setting forth what it considers "generally accepted accounting principles." [*See* Regulation S-X] These regulations must be adhered to in preparing all financial information submitted to the S.E.C. in connection with the registration statement.

Example: S.E.C. accounting regulations require that balance sheets and profit and loss statements be prepared so as to permit meaningful financial analysis by investors. Thus, a profit and loss statement might have to be broken down so that investors can determine the source of the issuer's revenues by division, major product lines, etc.

(d) Certification by independent accountants [§325]

The accountants who certify that the issuer's financial statements comply with generally accepted accounting principles must be independent of the issuer, and must meet the requirements established by the Public Company Accounting Oversight Board. (*See infra*, §§1598-1604, 1607-1630.)

(3) Other material facts that require disclosure [§326]

Various Securities Act Releases and court cases, taken together, indicate that the following information is material and should be included in the registration statement:

(a) Facts affecting price or value of the securities [§327]

Facts affecting the price or value of the securities should be disclosed. These include:

1) *The difference between the book value* (*i.e.*, the excess of assets over all liabilities, or net assets) of the issuer's presently issued shares and the *offering price* of the new shares [*In re* **Universal Camera Corp.**, 19 S.E.C. 648 (1945)];

2) *Any substantial disparity* between the public offering price and the cost of shares owned by officers, directors, promoters, etc. [Regulation S-K, Item 506];

3) *The factors used to determine the offering price* of the securities, if the issuer is a new company [Regulation S-K, Item 505];

4) *The use to be made by the issuer of proceeds* from the offering [Regulation S-K, Item 504]; and

5) *Any restrictions on use* of the issuer's earned surplus (*e.g.*, because of loan agreements) which might limit the possibility of future dividends [SA Release No. 5278 (1972)].

(b) Facts that may make the securities a high risk [§328]

Facts that make the securities a high risk should be disclosed. These include:

(i) *Absence of any operating history* for the issuer;

(ii) *No earnings history,* or an erratic pattern of earnings;

(iii) *Competitive conditions in the industry;* and

(iv) *The issuer's reliance on only one product* or a limited product line.

[Regulation S-K, Item 503]

(c) Facts regarding status of issuer [§329]

Facts regarding the status of the issuer should be disclosed. These include:

1) *Government regulations* that could affect the business (*e.g.*, cost estimates of compliance with environmental laws) [Regulation S-K, Item 101(c)(xii); *see* SEA Release No. 34-16223 (1979)];

2) *Pending or threatened litigation* of a substantial nature against the issuer [Regulation S-K, Item 103]; and

3) *Proposals to (or the intention of) the issuer to enter new businesses* or lines of business [SA Release No. 5395 (1973); *see* Regulation S-K, Item 101(c)].

(d) Facts regarding conflicting interest transactions [§330]

Transactions (and proposed transactions) aggregating $60,000 or more must be disclosed if they are between the issuer (or any subsidiary) and any of the following:

(i)   Any *director or executive officer* of the issuer;

(ii)   Any *nominee for election* as a director;

(iii)   Any *security holder owning or voting more than 5%* of any class of voting securities of the issuer, *if* the issuer knows of this ownership or voting power; or

(iv)   Any member of the *immediate family of any of the above.*

[Regulation S-K, Item 404; *see* **In re Franchard Corp.**, 42 S.E.C. 163 (1964)]

(e) Facts regarding legal proceedings against directors and executives [§331]

Certain kinds of legal proceedings against directors, director-nominees, and executive officers of the issuer must be disclosed.

1) Disclosure required by Regulation S-K [§332]

The following proceedings must be disclosed if they took place with respect to a director, director-nominee, or executive officer *within five years before filing* the registration statement:

a)   Bankruptcy;

b)   Criminal convictions and pending criminal proceedings;

c)   Securities or commodities law violations; and

d)   Any injunction or order barring the executive from engaging in any type of business activity.

2) Other required disclosure [§333]

In addition, all other material facts of this nature, including facts regarding events that took place more than five years ago, and also *including material pending civil litigation*, must be disclosed. [*See* **Zell v. InterCapital Income Securities, Inc.**, 675 F.2d 1041 (9th Cir. 1982); **Bertoglio v. Texan International Co.**, 488 F. Supp. 630 (D. Del. 1980); SA Release No. 5758 (1976)]

a) Scope of "materiality" [§334]

Because these disclosure requirements are so broad, courts have sometimes limited the concept of what is considered material in order to render harmless the failure to disclose particular misconduct. Generally, claims that a director or officer received a personal benefit from a transaction are more likely to be deemed material than claims merely alleging illegality, without the element of personal profit to the individual director or officer. [*See, e.g.,* **Gaines v. Haughton,** 645 F.2d 761 (9th Cir. 1981)]

(f) Facts regarding environmental litigation [§335]

Environmental litigation to which the *government is a party* must be disclosed unless the issuer reasonably believes that any resulting sanction will not exceed $100,000. [Regulation S-K, Item 103, instr. 5]

(4) "Soft" information [§336]

One of the most important items of information to a prospective investor is whether the price of the security will go up or go down. This requires analysis of the issuer's likely future revenues, earnings, plans for expansion, and so on. Such information, which relies in part on subjective analysis and judgment, is often referred to as "soft" information, as distinguished from "hard" facts concerning past performance.

(a) The 1979 safe harbor provisions [§337]

The S.E.C. historically discouraged the use of soft information in a registration statement, because of its potentially misleading impact on investors. Over time, however, and in response to increasing criticism of its disclosure rules, the S.E.C. modified its stance and in 1979 adopted safe harbor rules for the disclosure of soft information. [SA Rule 175; SEA Rule 3b-6]

1) Safe harbor requirements [§338]

Under the S.E.C.'s 1979 safe harbor rules, a *forward-looking statement* should comply with the following requirements:

a) Good faith and reasonable basis [§339]

The projection must be made in "good faith" and with a "reasonable basis." Experience or past accuracy in making projections may indicate that projections were made in good faith and with a reasonable basis.

1/ Burden of proof [§340]

To prove a cause of action where actual results do not match earlier projections, a *plaintiff has the burden of proof* to establish the absence of a reasonable basis and good faith in making the projection. [**Wielgos v. Commonwealth Edison Co.,** 892 F.2d 509 (7th Cir. 1989)]

    2/   **Disclosure of assumptions [§341]**

Disclosure of assumptions behind projections is *not* mandatory, *but* in many cases may be necessary for the projections to meet the good faith and reasonable basis part of the test.

  b) **Duty to update [§342]**

Projections must be updated and assumptions must be restated when new information indicates that the earlier statements no longer have a reasonable basis.

  c) **Compliance with annual reporting requirements [§343]**

Companies that are required to file 10K (annual) reports with the S.E.C. under the 1934 Act must have filed their most recent report to qualify for the safe harbor protection.

2) Scope

  a) **Financial projections [§344]**

The safe harbor rule covers projections of revenues, earnings, and earnings per share and *other projections of financial items,* such as capital expenditures and financing, dividends, capital structure, statements of management plans and objectives for the future, etc.

  b) **Statements of outsiders [§345]**

Statements made by or on behalf of the issuer, or by *an outside* (expert) *reviewer* retained by the issuer, are also covered by the safe harbor rules.

  c) **Reporting companies and registered companies [§346]**

Companies that file reports under the 1934 Act *or* that are filing registration statements under the 1933 Act are covered. (Note that projections of these companies made prior or subsequent to these filings are also covered—not just their filings with the S.E.C.—if similar projections are also filed with the S.E.C., the companies are registered under the 1934 Act, or the projections are made in an annual report under the proxy rules of the 1934 Act.)

  d) **Investment companies [§347]**

The safe harbor rule does *not* apply to investment companies.

3) Role of risk factors and assumptions [§348]

The 1979 safe harbor was vague as to the manner in which

risk factors and assumptions underlying forward-looking statements should be disclosed, and as to whether disclosure of such underlying factors and assumptions could reduce an issuer's liability in the event that predictions did not come to pass. This gap in the safe harbor was filled, in part, by the judicially created "bespeaks caution" doctrine, *infra*.

(b) The "bespeaks caution" doctrine [§349]

The court-developed "bespeaks caution" doctrine in essence provides that optimistic (in hindsight, *overly* optimistic) statements about the future may be rendered harmless if they are surrounded by cautionary statements warning of the circumstances and events that might make the outlook less rosy. By the mid-1990s many circuit courts had endorsed the "bespeaks caution" doctrine. [*See, e.g.,* **Romani v. Shearson Lehman Hutton,** 929 F.2d 875 (1st Cir. 1991); **I. Meyer Pincus & Associates v. Oppenheimer & Co.,** 936 F.2d 759 (2d Cir. 1991); *In re* **Donald J. Trump Casino Securities Litigation,** 7 F.3d 357 (3d Cir. 1993), *cert. denied,* 510 U.S. 1178 (1994); **Rubinstein v. Collins,** 20 F.3d 160 (5th Cir. 1994); **Sinay v. Lamson & Sessions Co.,** 948 F.2d 1037 (6th Cir. 1991); **Mayer v. Mylod,** 988 F.2d 635 (6th Cir. 1993); **Polin v. Conductron Corp.,** 552 F.2d 797 (8th Cir. 1977)—"The terms thus employed bespeak caution in outlook and thus fall far short of the assurances required for a finding of falsity and fraud"; *In re* **Worlds of Wonder Securities Litigation,** 35 F.3d 1407 (9th Cir. 1994), *cert. denied,* 516 U.S. 909 (1995); **Saltzberg v. TM Sterling/Austin Associates, Ltd.,** 45 F.3d 399 (11th Cir. 1995)]

(c) The 1995 safe harbor for forward-looking statements [§350]

In 1995, as part of the 1995 Private Securities Litigation Reform Act (the "1995 Act"), Congress adopted an additional safe harbor for forward-looking statements. [SA §27A; SEA §21E] The 1995 safe harbor is based in large part on the bespeaks caution doctrine, *supra*.

1) Who may use the safe harbor [§351]

The safe harbor is available to:

(i) Issuers subject to the reporting requirements of the 1934 Act (*see infra,* §§875-877, 881);

(ii) Persons acting on behalf of such an issuer;

(iii) Outside reviewers retained by such an issuer; and

    (iv) The issuer's underwriters, with respect to information provided by the issuer or derived from information provided by the issuer.

[SA §27A(a); SEA §21E(a)]

2) Who is excluded [§352]
Certain issuers are excluded from using the safe harbor, even if they otherwise would qualify:

    (i)   Issuers of penny stock (*see infra*, §407); and

    (ii) Issuers that in the prior three years have been criminally convicted of securities fraud, or have been the subject of governmental decrees or orders relating to securities fraud.

[SA §27A(b); SEA §21E(b)]

3) Transactions excluded [§353]
Likewise, forward-looking statements made in connection with certain kinds of transactions are excluded from the 1995 Act's safe harbor, even if they would otherwise have been covered. Thus excluded are statements made in connection with:

    (i)   "Going private" transactions;

    (ii) Tender offers;

    (iii) Initial public offerings;

    (iv) Partnership "roll-up" transactions (*see infra*, §1334); and

    (v) Statements made in financial statements.

[SA §27A(b); SEA §21E(b)]

4) Two kinds of protection [§354]
The 1995 Act's safe harbor provides two alternative means of protection for forward-looking statements. Each is summarized below:

a) Plaintiff must prove actual knowledge [§355]
First, no plaintiff can recover against a covered person unless the plaintiff can prove that the forward-looking statement was made with *actual knowledge that it was false or materially incomplete.* Even if the plaintiff can

prove actual knowledge, however, the second means of protection (*see* below) may still apply to protect the statement.

b) Defendant may show adequate cautionary statements [§356]

The second variety of protection for forward-looking statements depends on whether the statement was written or oral.

1/ Written statements [§357]

A written forward-looking statement is protected if the statement is:

(i) *Identified* as a forward-looking statement; and

(ii) *Accompanied by meaningful cautionary statements* identifying important factors that could cause actual results to differ materially from those predicted in the forward-looking statement.

a/ "Meaningful" cautionary statements [§358]

"'Boilerplate' warnings will not suffice as meaningful cautionary statements identifying important factors . . . ." [H.R. Rep. No. 369, 104th Cong., 1st Sess. 43-44 (1995)] To qualify, a statement "must convey substantive information about factors that realistically could cause results to differ materially from those projected in the forward-looking statement . . . ." [*Id.*]

b/ Not all factors that could cause results to vary must be described [§359]

Congress does not expect issuers to show perfect foresight. Thus, not all factors that could cause the results to vary must be described, and indeed, *"failure to include the particular factor* that ultimately causes the forward-looking statement not to come true *will not mean the statement is not protected* by the safe harbor." [*Id.*]

2/ Oral statements [§360]

Oral statements can be protected on the same basis as written statements, above. In addition, however, an oral statement is protected if the oral statement *identifies a readily available written document* that contains the "meaningful cautionary statements" described in the safe harbor for written statements, *supra*. [SA §27A(c)(2); SEA §21E(c)(2)]

a/ Cross-reference to cautionary statements [§361]

The 1995 Act permits a cross-reference to cautionary statements *only* in the case of oral forward-looking statements. Written forward-looking statements must include written cautionary statements; the 1995 Act does not contemplate such cautions being incorporated by reference.

Example: Jan, the CEO of Jax Corp., makes a speech to a group of financial analysts. In the course of the speech, Jan makes several forward-looking statements. Jan can protect those statements by:

(i) *Identifying them* as forward-looking statements; and

(ii) *Referring (in the speech) to readily available written documents* that contain meaningful cautionary statements; *e.g.*, "I refer you to the Company's Annual Report on Form 10-K for a discussion of the various factors that might result in materially different results."

Note that the cautionary statements must be relevant to the forward-looking statements in Jan's speech.

---

b/ Note

"Boilerplate" cautionary statements *will not protect oral forward-looking statements*, just as they will not protect written forward-looking statements.

c) Illustration 1

Here is an example of the operation of the 1995 safe harbor.

1/ Facts

MFR, Inc., a manufacturing corporation, included in its prospectus the following statement:

> Management of the corporation expects to finish testing a new product by June next year and hopes to bring the product to market by the holiday selling season. Management expects that the new product will be highly profitable. This is a forward-looking statement, however, and there can be no assurance that the product will be brought to market on time, or, if it is brought to market on time, that it will be as profitable as management now expects. *See* "Risk Factors" for a discussion of important factors that could materially alter either the timetable, profitability, or both.

The "Risk Factors" section of the prospectus discloses, *inter alia*, that the availability of certain key raw materials is critical to the new product. It does not reveal, however, that management has been advised that at least one key material will probably not be available until January, well after the next holiday selling season. When MFR, one month after the offering is completed, announces by press release the unavailability of the material, MFR's stock price drops 15 points and a lawsuit is filed. The lawsuit alleges fraud in the prospectus because of the failure to reveal the likely inability to bring the product to market by the end of the year.

2/ Analysis

MFR's forward-looking statements in its prospectus are probably protected by the 1995 Act's safe harbor. The forward-looking statements were identified as such, and were accompanied by relevant "meaningful cautionary statements." The fact that management seemed to know that it was unlikely the predictions would come true does not make the safe harbor unavailable; management's state of mind is not relevant to the second avenue to protection under the safe harbor.

d) Illustration 2

Here is another example of the application of the 1995 safe harbor.

1/ Facts

Same as above, except that the prospectus does not reveal that management has been advised that a key employee, the marketing manager for the new product, has advised management that she is considering leaving MFR. One month after the offering is completed, MFR announces by press release the departure of the marketing manager, and MFR's stock price drops 15 points. Subsequently, a lawsuit is filed, alleging fraud in the prospectus because of the failure to reveal the possible departure of the marketing manager and the impact of that departure on MFR's predictions.

2/ Analysis

MFR's forward-looking statements in its prospectus are probably protected by the 1995 Act's safe harbor. The forward-looking statements were identified as such, and were apparently accompanied by relevant "meaningful cautionary statements" that identified "important" risk factors. The 1995 Act does not require that all risk factors be identified, and therefore the disclosure made by MFR would be adequate.

e) Illustration 3

Here is a final example of the operation of the 1995 safe harbor.

1/ Facts

Same as above, except that the prospectus does not reveal that the success of the new product is dependent on an increase in tourism in the geographic area of MFR's market. MFR's management simply assumed, without making any inquiry, that tourism would increase. Within several months, however, it becomes clear that tourism will not increase, but rather will decline. MFR issues a press release describing the decline in tourism and announcing that its profitability will suffer, notwithstanding the timely introduction of the new product. MFR's stock price drops 15 points. Subsequently, a lawsuit is filed, alleging fraud in the prospectus.

2/ Analysis

MFR's forward-looking statements in its prospectus are probably protected by the 1995 Act's safe harbor. Although the cautionary statements may have been insufficient to invoke the second avenue of protection under the safe harbor, the 1995 Act will still protect a forward-looking statement if the plaintiff cannot prove that the statement was made with "actual knowledge" of its falsity. While here it would seem that management was careless, and perhaps even reckless, there is no basis to conclude that management knew that tourism would not increase. Even though management had no reasonable basis for its assumptions about tourism, management's ignorance of the true state of affairs would seem to function as a shield against liability in this case.

3/ Discovery may be available

The safe harbor contemplates that, even though discovery is ordinarily stayed on the filing of a motion to dismiss, "discovery that is specifically directed to the applicability of the exemption provided for in this section [*i.e.,* the safe harbor section]" may be allowed. Therefore, on the facts set out in a), above, it is likely that a court would grant a plaintiff at least some discovery, in an attempt to show "actual knowledge" of falsity. [*See* SA §27A(c)(1)(B); SEA §21E(c)(1)(B)]

5) Areas for future clarification [§362]

While the 1995 Act's safe harbor for forward-looking statements is much clearer than the pre-1995 Act status quo, there are still a number of areas left for the courts to clarify. In particular, courts will probably have to decide:

a) What constitutes a forward-looking statement. One court has held that a mixed list of statements, some forward-looking and some not, taken as a whole qualified as a forward-looking statement. [**Harris v. Ivax Corp.,** 182 F.3d 799 (11th Cir. 1999)]

b) What is meant by a "meaningful" cautionary statement; and

c) How important the "important" risk factors need to be in order to protect the forward-looking statement. One

FINANCIAL INFORMATION	OTHER MATERIAL FACTS	"SOFT" INFORMATION (NOT REQUIRED)	MANAGEMENT'S DISCUSSION AND ANALYSIS
• Balance sheet, generally less than 90 days old • Profit and loss statements covering last three years	• Facts affecting price (*e.g.,* difference between book value and sale price) • Facts making security a high risk (*e.g.,* absence of operating history) • Facts regarding issuer's status (*e.g.,* threatened or pending litigation) • Facts regarding conflicts of interests (*e.g.,* transaction between the issuer and a director or officer of the issuer) • Facts regarding certain legal proceedings against directors and officers (*e.g.,* criminal convictions or proceedings, securities or commodities laws violations) • Facts regarding environmental litigation to which the government is a party unless issuer reasonably believes any resulting sanction will not exceed $100,000 • Other facts an investor would want to know	• Financial projections (*e.g.,* projections of future earnings and revenues)	• Short- and long-term analysis of the company's business, addressing key variables and other factors needed for an understanding and evaluation of the company

court has suggested that disclosure of important risks requires disclosing the principal risks as they were then understood, regardless of whether the risks disclosed were the risks that came to pass. [**Asher v. Baxter International, Inc.,** 377 F.3d 727 (7th Cir. 2004)]

6) Future expansion of the safe harbor [§363]

Finally, it should be noted that Congress considered the 1995 Act's safe harbor for forward-looking statements to be merely a beginning. "The Committee intends for its statutory safe harbor provisions to serve as a starting point and fully expects the S.E.C. to continue its rulemaking proceedings in this area. The S.E.C. should, as appropriate, promulgate rules or regulations to expand the statutory safe harbor by providing additional exemptions from liability or extending its coverage to additional types of information." [Joint Explanatory Statement of the Committee of Conference Accompanying H.R. 1058, 104 Cong., 1st Sess.]

(5) Management's Discussion and Analysis [§364]

Issuers must include a section entitled "Management's Discussion and Analysis" ("MD&A") in registration statements and in certain Securities Exchange Act filings. The MD&A affirmatively *requires* a certain amount of forward-looking disclosure.

(a) Purpose of MD&A [§365]

The MD&A section is intended to give the investor an opportunity to look at the company through the eyes of management by providing both a short- and long-term analysis of the business of the company. It requires management to address key variables and other factors peculiar to and necessary for an understanding and evaluation of the individual company. [SA Release No. 6835 (1989)]

(b) Compliance with MD&A requirements [§366]

Historically, few issuers have complied with the literal requirements of the MD&A. To encourage better compliance, the S.E.C. has made the MD&A an enforcement priority. [*See, e.g.,* **Matter of Sony Corp.,** SEA Release No. 34-40305 (1998); **Matter of Caterpillar, Inc.,** SEA Release No. 34-30532 (1992)]

3. Organization of Material in the Registration Statement [§367]

In addition to requiring that certain kinds of information be disclosed, the S.E.C. closely regulates the organization of the material, including the contents of the registration statement, the use of graphs, charts, etc., to ensure that the material included is communicated clearly.

a. **"Plain English" disclosure requirement [§368]**

In 1998, the S.E.C. began to require issuers to write certain sections of the prospectus and registration statement in "plain English," in order to improve the quality of disclosure by giving investors simpler, more readable documents. [*See* 1933 Act Release No. 7497 (1998); Regulation C Rules 421, 461, 481]

(1) **Prospectus cover page, summary, and risk factors [§369]**

The prospectus cover page, summary, and risk factors sections, probably the most widely read parts of the prospectus, are required to be written in plain English. [Regulation C Rule 421(d)]

(a) **Meaning of "plain English" [§370]**

To comply with the "plain English" requirements, the S.E.C. has instructed issuers to "comply substantially with six basic principles":

(i) *Short sentences;*

(ii) *Definite, concrete, everyday language;*

(iii) *Active voice;*

(iv) *Tabular presentation or bullet lists for complex material, whenever possible;*

(v) *No legal jargon or highly technical business terms;* and

(vi) *No multiple negatives.*

[1933 Act Release No. 7497, *supra*] It bears mention that the clarity and quality of most people's (including this author's!) writing would be improved by consistent adherence to these six principles.

(2) **Remainder of the prospectus [§371]**

Under rule 421(b), the entire prospectus is to be clear, concise, and understandable. Although the S.E.C. has not imposed a "plain English" requirement on sections of the prospectus other than those noted above, it has announced some guidelines to make the prospectus more readable. The guidelines include some "do's" and "don't's" for effective prospectus writing [*See* 1933 Act Release No. 7497, *supra*]:

(a) **Do**

1) Present information in *clear, concise sections, paragraphs, and sentences.* Whenever possible, use short explanatory sentences and bullet lists.

    2) *Use descriptive headings* and subheadings.

(b) Don't

    1) *Rely on glossaries* or defined terms as the primary means of explaining information in the prospectus. Define terms in a glossary or other section of the document only if the meaning is not clear from the context. Use a glossary only if it facilitates understanding of the disclosure.

    2) *Use legal or highly technical business terminology,* or legalistic or overly complex presentations that make the disclosure hard to understand.

    3) *Use vague boilerplate* explanations that are subject to differing interpretations.

    4) *Include complex information copied directly from legal documents* without any clear and concise explanation of the information.

    5) *Repeat disclosure* so as to increase the size of the document without enhancing the quality of the information.

4. Liability Based on Contents of Registration Statement [§372]
Section 11 of the 1933 Act imposes civil liability on those associated with preparation of a registration statement (including the prospectus) that contains material misstatements or omissions. (This topic is discussed in detail, along with other liability provisions, *infra*, §§774 *et seq.*)

5. Criticisms of S.E.C. Disclosure Policy [§373]
Several commentators have criticized the S.E.C.'s policies concerning disclosure, generally on the ground that they do not achieve their goal of ensuring that an investor will receive all material information concerning the offered securities. The following criticisms are among those heard most frequently.

a. Emphasis on negative information [§374]
There has been criticism of the fact that the S.E.C. requires the registration statement to focus on the negative aspects of the issuer (to avoid potential liability under the 1933 Act for misrepresentation), rather than allowing it to present a balanced picture of the company (relating the positive as well as the negative aspects of the company). The critics argue that because registration statements thus lack much information that is relevant to making an intelligent investment decision, and because all registration statements are uniformly negative, they may no longer be taken seriously by investors.

b. Presentation of complex information [§375]

Some also argue that the complex information the S.E.C. requires to be disclosed (*e.g.*, information on sophisticated products, financial information, accounting data, etc.) is impossible to present in a way that is understandable to the "average" investor. The S.E.C.'s response has been to adopt the "plain English" disclosure requirements, discussed *supra*. The solution offered by the commentators would be to draft the registration statement for the sophisticated or expert securities analyst, to whom the average investor looks for advice, and to dispense with the charade of trying to inform the investor himself.

c. Reliance on the "efficient capital market hypothesis" [§376]

The S.E.C. policies concerning disclosure are based to some extent on the idea that the market for securities is "efficient," that is, that prices of securities in the market are affected, if not dictated, by the information available with respect to those securities. Recently, these ideas have come under scrutiny, and the impact of other factors on securities prices (such as investor "sentiment," various trading strategies that are not based on information about issuers, etc.) has been examined. Ultimately, while no one theory adequately explains pricing in the securities market, it is probably safe to assume that information about the issuer and security will continue to be viewed as an important factor and that disseminating that information will continue to be a dominant goal of securities regulation.

6. Processing the Registration Statement

a. Effective date of statement [§377]

The registration statement becomes effective on the *20th* day after its filing with the S.E.C., unless it is the subject of a refusal or stop order issued by the S.E.C. (*see infra*, §§388 *et seq.*) or becomes effective sooner by an S.E.C. acceleration order (*see supra*, §§187-190).

(1) Amendments to the statement [§378]

Often, several amendments will be required by the S.E.C. before it declares the registration statement effective. An amendment starts the 20-day waiting period running anew. However, the S.E.C. normally accelerates the effective date as soon as all of the problems with the registration statement have been worked out, so that the delay affects the offering as little as possible (*see supra*, §§187-188).

b. Review of the registration statement [§379]

Once the registration statement is filed, the S.E.C. determines whether, and to what extent, it will review the statement to ensure that the issuer has complied with all disclosure requirements.

(1) S.E.C. authority [§380]

The S.E.C. cannot legally compel the issuer to amend a defective registration statement; but by commencing a formal examination or entering a "stop order" (*see* below), the S.E.C. can prevent the registration statement from becoming effective and thus effectively force the issuer to make the suggested amendments.

(2) S.E.C. review procedures [§381]

The S.E.C. employs different review procedures for examining registration statements. [SA Release No. 5231 (1972)]

(a) Deferred review [§382]

If an initial review of the registration statement indicates that it is poorly prepared or has other serious problems, the S.E.C. will simply notify the registrant of that fact (without specific comments) and allow the registrant to consider whether to go forward, withdraw, or amend the statement.

(b) Cursory review [§383]

If, after an initial review, the registration statement appears to be proper, the S.E.C. will indicate to the registrant that only a cursory review has been made and that the statement will be declared effective on the date and at the time requested in letters from the issuer and the managing underwriter. These acceleration requests are treated by the S.E.C. as a declaration that the various parties are aware of their statutory responsibilities under the Act.

1) Effect

This procedure saves the S.E.C. the administrative time normally consumed in a "full review" (below), but exposes the issuer to the risk of having mistakes in the documents which a more exhaustive review by the S.E.C. might have revealed.

(c) Summary review [§384]

This type of review means that the S.E.C. notifies the issuer that the statement will be declared effective on receipt of: (i) the same type of letters as required in a cursory review; *plus* (ii) adequate responses to limited comments made by the S.E.C. in its review.

(d) Full review [§385]

Here the S.E.C. gives a *complete* accounting, financial, and legal review—either on its own or when the issuer refuses to agree to the more limited cursory or summary review. The S.E.C. gives a full review to all first-time issuers.

TYPES OF S.E.C. REVIEW—A SUMMARY **gilbert**

THE FOLLOWING ARE THE MAIN TYPES OF REVIEW PROCEDURES USED BY THE S.E.C.

- *Cursory review:* S.E.C. notifies registrant that only a cursory review was performed and the registration will be declared effective on the date and time requested by the issuer and managing underwriter

- *Summary review:* S.E.C. notifies registrant that the registration will be declared effective on the date and time requested by the issuer and managing underwriter if the S.E.C. receives adequate responses to limited comments that it has made regarding the registration statement

- *Full review:* S.E.C. performs a complete accounting, financial, and legal review

c. **Formal proceedings by the S.E.C.**

(1) **Formal examination [§386]**

If either the S.E.C.'s initial review or the issuer's responses to that review indicate a serious problem, and the issuer appears uncooperative, the S.E.C. can institute a formal examination under SA section 8(e). The consequences of a formal examination are grave: The 1933 Act prohibits offers and sales of securities subject to such an examination if the examination began before the registration statement was declared effective. [*See* SA §5(c)] This essentially returns the offering to the pre-filing period, with all its restrictions, including the prohibitions on conditioning the market. (*See supra,* §§127 *et seq.*)

(a) **Duration of examination [§387]**

The 1933 Act does not impose any limit on how long a section 8(e) examination may take. Nevertheless, if the S.E.C. unreasonably delays completion of the exam, a court may compel it either to terminate the exam or to issue a stop order (discussed below). [*See* **Las Vegas Hawaiian Development Co. v. S.E.C.,** 466 F. Supp. 928 (D. Haw. 1979)]

(2) **Refusal and stop orders [§388]**

If, following an examination of the registration statement, the S.E.C. finds that the issuer has failed to comply with the Act's disclosure requirements, the S.E.C. may issue an order delaying or suspending the effectiveness of the registration statement.

(a) **Refusal order [§389]**

A "refusal order" may be issued within 10 days after the filing of a statement that is clearly inadequate on its face. Such an order *delays* the effective date in order to allow the S.E.C. to take appropriate action; therefore, it must always be issued *prior to* the effective date of the registration statement. [SA §8(b)] The impracticability of acting within 10 days after a registration statement is filed has made the refusal order rare, and the stop order (below) is the more common form of S.E.C. action.

(b) Stop order [§390]

A "stop order" either delays the effective date *or* stops the selling of securities (if it has begun), so as to permit an investigation of the issuer and the securities offered. The S.E.C. may issue a stop order at any time—whether before or after the effective date. [SA §8(d)]

(3) Effect of formal proceedings on underwriter [§391]

The institution of S.E.C. administrative proceedings against an underwriter can have a devastating effect on the underwriter's business. For example, in one case where the S.E.C. was investigating an underwriter's involvement in a regulation A offering, it sent letters to all issuers that were using the underwriter, indicating they would have to disclose in their registration statements that the S.E.C. was investigating the underwriter. [**Koss v. S.E.C.,** 364 F. Supp. 1321 (S.D.N.Y. 1973)]

(4) S.E.C.'s use of acceleration power [§392]

As a practical matter, the S.E.C. and issuers do not resort to formal grounds to delay the effective date. Issuers simply state on the registration statement that it will not be effective until S.E.C. approval. As a quid pro quo, the S.E.C. then accelerates effectiveness to the date requested by the issuer and the managing underwriter.

d. Withdrawal of registration statement [§393]

If, after filing, there are problems with the issuing company or its registration statement, the issuer may simply seek to withdraw the statement—in order to avoid adverse publicity and/or potential liability under the Act.

(1) S.E.C. approval required [§394]

The S.E.C. will grant the issuer's application for withdrawal only if withdrawal is consistent with the public interest and protection of investors. [SA Rule 477]

(2) Timing of request [§395]

The S.E.C. will generally honor a withdrawal request filed *before* the institution of stop order proceedings.

(a) But note

If a stop order has been instituted in the *post-effective* period, the S.E.C. obviously will *not* permit withdrawal—because the stock (or part of it) has already been sold.

e. Refusal of underwriter to proceed—material misstatements [§396]

The underwriter normally conducts an independent investigation of the issuer during the waiting period to determine whether all material facts have been disclosed in the registration statement. (This relates to the underwriter's defense of "due diligence" in case there are material misstatements or omissions in the registration statement; *see infra,* §793.) If there are material misstatements, the underwriter may *refuse* to proceed with the underwriting despite its contractual obligation to purchase and sell the issue (*see supra,* §99). *Rationale:* An underwriting contract that violates the 1933 Act because of material misstatements in the registration statement is void and therefore unenforceable. [**Kaiser-Frazer Corp. v. Otis & Co.,** 195 F.2d 838 (2d Cir. 1952)]

(1) Opinion from counsel for issuer [§397]

The underwriter also usually requires that the issuer's counsel (if the drafter of the registration statement) render the underwriter a legal opinion that he has no reason to believe that the registration statement contains any material omissions or misstatements.

f. Blue sky qualification [§398]

In some cases, the securities of a company going public must also be qualified under the "blue sky" or state securities laws of the states in which they are intended to be offered. Most companies going public do not need to qualify their securities under state law, however, because the securities fall within the definition of "covered securities" under the National Securities Markets Improvement Act of 1996. (State regulation of securities is discussed *infra,* §§2106 *et seq.*)

g. NASD clearance [§399]

The issuer must also receive clearance from the National Association of Securities Dealers that the underwriting commissions being paid are "fair" according to NASD rules.

7. Post-Effective Amendments and Updates to Registration Statement [§400]

There are two possible sources of error in the registration statement: (i) an intentional or unintentional material misstatement or omission may exist at the time the registration statement becomes effective; or (ii) everything may be correct at the time the registration statement becomes effective, but subsequent events may outdate the registration statement so that it contains material misstatements or omissions at the date of use. The Securities Act provides for a way to update the registration statement and the prospectus in each of these situations.

a. Errors existing at time of effectiveness [§401]

If the registration statement contains an error at the time it is declared effective, but the error is discovered only *after* the effective date, the appropriate way to update the prospectus is to file a "post-effective" amendment with the S.E.C.

b. Errors caused by subsequent developments [§402]

If developments *after* the effective date of the registration statement make the information in the registration statement or prospectus misleading or false (although it was accurate at the effective date), a correction may be made simply by placing a sticker on the cover of the prospectus and supplying the correct information in the body of the prospectus.

c. Updating requirement [§403]

Whether or not any errors are discovered, the 1933 Act requires that a prospectus still in use nine months after the effective date be updated to ensure that it contains information as of a date not more than 16 months prior to its use. The provision puts an outside limit on what can be considered "currently" accurate. [SA §10(a)(3)]

d. Special provisions for "blank check" offerings [§404]

During the 1980s, many promoters (*i.e.*, issuers, underwriters, and dealers) of "penny stock" (generally, low-priced stock that is not traded on a national exchange) were abusing the securities market with so-called "blank check" offerings. In a blank check offering, the promoter does not specify what the proceeds of the issuance will be used for. Such offerings usually involved start-up companies with no operating history or assets, and there were frequent allegations that the promoters diverted the offering proceeds into their own pockets. The Securities Enforcement Remedies and Penny Stock Act of 1990 was enacted to combat these abuses.

(1) Scope [§405]

The 1990 Act applies only to offerings by "blank check" companies. The Act defines a "blank check company" as a development stage company that is issuing penny stock, and that either has no business plan or purpose, or has indicated that its business plan is to merge with an unidentified company or companies. [SA §7(b); SA Rule 419]

(a) Distinguish—"blind pool" offerings [§406]

"Blind pool" offerings are not the same as "blank check" offerings. Blind pool offerings are less prone to abuse, and involve offerings by ventures that propose to invest in unspecified *businesses of a certain type*, for example, commercial real estate, or motels. They are not the subject of specific regulation, the way "blank check" offerings are.

(2) Definition of "penny stock" [§407]

Penny stock is defined in SEA rule 3a51-1, and includes any equity security *other than* a security:

(i) Registered on a national securities exchange (with an exception for certain "emerging companies");

(ii) Issued by a registered investment company;

(iii) That is a put (*i.e.*, option to sell) or call (*i.e.*, option to buy) issued by the Options Clearing Corporation (*see supra*, §39);

(iv) Authorized for quotation on NASDAQ;

(v) Whose issuer has at least: (i) $2 million in net tangible assets (if in operation at least three years), or (ii) $5 million in net tangible assets (if in operation less than three years), or (iii) average annual revenues of at least $6 million for the last three years.

[SEA §3(a)(51); SEA Rule 3a51-1]

(3) Additional investor protection [§408]

The "blank check" rules mandate certain forms of investor protection in addition to the usual disclosure obligations imposed by federal securities law. The regulations include the following:

(a) Escrow provisions [§409]

Securities sold in a "blank check" offering and the proceeds of the sale must be promptly deposited into an escrow account at a qualified institution until the disclosure and rescission requirements discussed below are met. [SA Rule 419] Trading in such securities is not permitted as long as they are in escrow. [SEA Rule 15g-8]

(b) Disclosure and rescission [§410]

When the issuer acquires assets for its business, it must describe the transaction in a post-effective amendment to the registration statement. A new prospectus describing the transaction must be distributed to the investors, who then have the right, if they wish, to rescind the transaction and to receive back their money. [SA Rule 419]

8. Shelf Registration [§411]

Many issuers are almost constantly involved in issuing new securities. It would be convenient for such issuers to simply prepare one registration statement, thereby registering all securities that they may offer at any time in the future (a so-called "shelf registration"). In addition to convenience, registration for the shelf offers some significant advantages to issuers. Among these are the ability to take advantage of favorable market conditions by selling preregistered securities immediately and reducing expenses by allowing issuers to register large quantities of securities in a single transaction.

a. General prohibition against shelf registration [§412]

As a general rule, the 1933 Act prohibits shelf registration. SA section 6(a) provides that a registration statement is deemed effective only as to the securities *specified* in the registration statement. *Rationale:* A single registration statement may not provide adequate disclosure to investors; *i.e.*, material events may occur subsequent to the filing of the registration statement that would make some of the information in the registration statement incorrect.

(1) And note

The S.E.C. has indicated that it may be materially misleading for an issuer to include in a registration statement more securities than are going to be offered *presently*; *i.e.*, it is misleading to include securities that are to be offered at some remote future date. [*In re* **Shawnee Chiles Syndicate,** 10 S.E.C. 109 (1941)]

b. Exceptions to prohibition [§413]

Despite SA section 6(a), there have always been situations in which "shelf registrations" were permitted; for example, where Company A is merged into Company B, and the controlling shareholders of Company A may wish to later offer their shares to the public, but cannot without registration. (*See* discussion of rule 145, *infra*, §634.) On the other hand, the S.E.C. has allowed more and more such exceptions, and today shelf registrations are available in a wide variety of offerings.

(1) Traditional shelf registration [§414]

SA rule 415 lists the traditional offerings for which the S.E.C. permits shelf registration. Rule 415 also provides that companies that are allowed to use registration form S-3 may shelf register their securities. S-3 companies are those that are widely followed in the marketplace and that file reports pursuant to the 1934 Act. (*See supra*, §§311-314.) These reports may be incorporated by reference, and the information in them need not be repeated again in the prospectus delivered to investors.

(2) "Automatic" shelf registration for WKSIs [§415]

In addition to the "traditional" shelf registration provided in SA rule 415, the 2005 SOR provided for "automatic" shelf registration for WKSIs. Recall that WKSIs are allowed to make written offers at any time, and in general are relieved of some of the more onerous requirements imposed on issuers during the pre-filing and waiting periods. In light of their relative freedom, it is understandable that WKSIs are also given broader freedom to register securities for the shelf.

(a) Immediate effectiveness [§416]

An automatic shelf registration statement is effective immediately when filed with the S.E.C. [SA Rule 462(e)]

(b) Unspecified quantities; pay-as-you-go [§417]

WKSIs do not need to specify the quantity of securities they are registering on an automatic shelf registration statement. Instead, they need specify only the name(s) and class(es) of the securities. [SA Rule 430B(a)] The fee for filing an automatic shelf registration statement is calculated based on the market value of the securities at the time they are actually offered (so-called "pay-as-you-go" registration). [SA Rule 456(b)]

    (c) Ability to add securities and classes of securities [§418]

Unlike most registration statements, which cover only the securities specifically registered at the time of effectiveness [SA Rule 413(a)], an automatic shelf registration statement can be amended to add additional securities (if a quantity was originally specified) and even to add additional classes of securities. [SA Rule 413(b)]

(3) Three-year limit and renewal provision [§419]

Shelf registration statements are effective for three years, but the issuer can file a new registration statement covering the same securities and continue offering them on a continuous basis. [SA Rule 415(a)(5)] Any unsold securities and filing fees paid in connection with unsold securities simply transfer over to the new registration statement. [SA Rule 415(a)(6)]

(4) Disclosure in shelf registration [§420]

When securities are registered for the shelf, not all the information about the offering(s) is known, because they are to be conducted in the future. An issuer in a shelf registration will typically file a "base prospectus" as part of the registration statement. This base prospectus describes what documents filed by the issuer under the 1934 Act will be incorporated by reference into the registration statement, but omits most specifics about the future offerings. [SA Rule 430B] Information about particular offerings following a shelf registration is disseminated by distribution or making available a prospectus supplement that contains the additional information, or by incorporating information from 1934 Act filings into the shelf registration statement by reference, or by a post-effective amendment to the shelf registration statement. [SA Rule 430B(d)]

F. Exemptions from Registration Requirements

1. In General [§421]

The cost and time required for a registered offering are high. Expenses include the S.E.C. registration fee, accounting and legal fees, printing costs (including stock certificates), state filing fees (in each state where the securities are sold), and insurance against Securities Act liabilities. The time required for a first-time issuer to complete the full registration and selling process is generally between 90 and 120 days. Therefore, if issuers can avoid having to go through the registration process, they will make every effort to do so. Thus, an issue frequently encountered under the 1933 Act is whether a particular distribution of securities qualifies under one or more of the *exemptions* from registration provided in the 1933 Act for certain types of *securities*, and certain types of securities *transactions*.

2. Exempted Securities [§422]

Certain types of securities are themselves exempt from registration under section 5 of the 1933 Act; *i.e.*, they may be sold and resold without ever being subject to registration. (*Note:* Such securities may be subject to the general antifraud and civil liability provisions of the Act; *see infra.*) Most of the exemptions for securities are covered in section 3 of the 1933 Act.

a. Bank and government securities [§423]

Section 3(a)(2) of the 1933 Act exempts from the registration requirements: (i) securities issued or guaranteed by the United States, its territories, or the states themselves; (ii) securities issued or guaranteed by banks; (iii) certain kinds of tax-free industrial revenue bonds; (iv) equity interests in certain trust funds maintained by banks in a fiduciary capacity; and (v) interests in insurance company "separate accounts" that fund pension or profit-sharing plans qualified under the Internal Revenue Code.

b. Short-term notes and other debt instruments [§424]

Notes or drafts arising out of current transactions are exempt if their maturity date does not exceed *nine months*. [SA §3(a)(3)]

c. Charitable organizations [§425]

Securities issued by religious, educational, or charitable organizations are also exempt from registration if the organization is organized and operated for charitable purposes only. [SA §3(a)(4)]

d. Savings and loan associations [§426]

Securities issued by savings and loan or related institutions are exempt if the issuer is supervised by state and/or federal authorities. [SA §3(a)(5)]

e. Railroad equipment trusts [§427]

Securities issued by common carriers to finance the acquisition of rolling stock are exempt. [SA §3(a)(6)]

f. Bankruptcy [§428]

Likewise, securities issued by a receiver or trustee in bankruptcy with the approval of the court are exempt. [SA §3(a)(7)]

g. Insurance policies [§429]

Finally, insurance, endowment, or annuity policies issued by companies supervised by state agencies are exempt. [SA §3(a)(8)]

EXAM TIP   **gilbert**

You are very likely to see an exam question involving exemptions from 1933 Act registration. Be familiar with the rather short list of *securities* that are *exempt from registration*: (i) bank and government securities, (ii) notes and drafts maturing in less than nine months, (iii) securities of charitable organizations, (iv) securities of savings and loans organizations regulated by state and/or federal authorities, (v) securities issued by common carriers to finance the purchase of rolling stock, (vi) securities issued by a receiver or trustee in bankruptcy with court approval, and (vii) insurance, endowment, and annuity policies issued by state-supervised agencies. Transactions in *all other securities must be registered* unless the *transaction* itself qualifies for an exemption (*see* below).

---

3. Exempted Transactions [§430]

It is important to distinguish exempted securities from exempted *transactions*. If the security *itself* is exempted, as above, it can be sold and resold without ever being subject to the registration requirements of section 5. On the other hand, if only the *transaction* is exempt, that transaction is not subject to section 5, but a later transaction in the same securities might be. For example, if XYZ Corp. issues stock to A under a transaction exemption, and A later transfers the stock to B, the transfer to B may not be exempt. However, if the *security* issued by XYZ to A is exempt, the transfer from A to B would be exempt. Exempted transactions are covered in section 4 of the 1933 Act and section 3(a)(9) - (12), 3(b), and 3(c).

a. Integration of offerings [§431]

Suppose an issuer sells $10,000 worth of securities to a single investor. The next day, the issuer sells $10,000 in securities to a different investor; the next day, to a third investor, and so on for a full year. Does this describe 365 separate transactions, or one transaction spread over a year? These facts raise the problem of *integration*: When an issuer has on separate occasions attempted several offerings under transaction exemptions, a question may arise as to whether the offerings were truly separate or only one offering disguised as multiple offerings to help the issuer evade registration. While the issuer might attempt to convey the appearance of having made two or more offerings, the S.E.C. might decide that the several offerings are *integrated* (*i.e.*, that all of the offerings are part of the same offering). The effect of having several offerings integrated into one can be disastrous for the issuer, because it is unlikely that the integrated offering will qualify for a transaction exemption. The issuer, relying on exempt status, has not registered the offering and, therefore, will violate the Securities Act. There are two basic approaches to integration under the Securities Act: the S.E.C.'s general five-factor test and safe-harbor tests particular to specific exemptions. The general five-factor test is discussed below. Each specific safe-harbor test will be discussed, *infra*, along with the particular exemption to which it applies.

(1) Five-factor test [§432]

In several releases pertaining to different exemptions, the S.E.C. has provided a list of five factors that it considers in determining whether offerings will be integrated:

(i) Whether the offerings are *part of a single plan of financing*;

(ii) Whether the offerings involve *issuance of the same class of security*;

(iii) Whether the offerings are *made at or about the same time*;

(iv) Whether the *same type of consideration* is to be received; and

(v) Whether the offerings are *made for the same general purpose*.

[*See, e.g.,* SA Release No. 4434 (1961)—§3(a)(11); SA Release No. 4552 (1962)—§4(2)]

(2) Note

It is important in considering the transaction exemptions, discussed below, to keep in mind the concept of integration and the possibility that a series of offerings might be integrated by the S.E.C.

b. Mortgage transactions [§433]

When certain mortgages are initiated by regulated financial institutions, and participating interests (*i.e.,* portions of the loan rights and duties) are sold to investors, the transactions may be exempt from registration. [SA §4(5)]

c. Transactions by particular persons

(1) Transactions by persons other than issuers, underwriters, or dealers [§434]

As noted *supra,* §225, the registration requirements of the 1933 Act apply only to issuers, underwriters, and dealers. Hence, transactions by other persons (*e.g.,* ordinary investors) are exempt from those requirements. [SA §4(1)]

EXAM TIP   **gilbert**

Remember that the registration requirements of the 1933 Act apply *only to issuers, underwriters, and dealers*. The majority of everyday securities transactions, therefore, are exempt from registration. However, it is possible for a person to become an "underwriter" for 1933 Act purposes without knowing it! Therefore, *before concluding that a transaction is exempt*, you should be sure that it does not involve an underwriter. The treatment of ordinary persons as "underwriters" is discussed *infra*, §§670 *et seq.*

---

(2) Dealer's transaction exemption [§435]

As previously discussed in connection with the post-effective period (*supra,* §§192 *et seq.*), dealers are subject to the prospectus delivery requirements of section 5 during the statutory distribution period. Dealer transactions after the distribution period are exempt from section 5. [SA §4(3); *see supra,* §§186-190]

(a) Exemption applies to illegal offerings [§436]

The exemption applies even when a registration statement should have been filed but was not. In such a case, if the unregistered securities are offered to the public, dealers are exempt from the prospectus delivery requirements after the distribution period ends. *Rationale:* Even though the offering was illegal, unsuspecting dealers trading in the securities should not be held to have violated the Act.

(3) Broker's transaction exemption [§437]

Brokers (*i.e.*, persons who sell a customer's securities for a commission) are exempt from the prospectus delivery requirement when they execute a customer's order to sell securities on any exchange or in the over-the-counter market. [SA §4(4)]

(a) Applies to specific transaction [§438]

The broker's exemption is only for a specific transaction—*i.e.*, the broker need only be acting as a broker (*e.g.*, on a commission basis) *in this transaction* to qualify.

1) Application to dealers [§439]

The Securities Act definition of "dealer" (*see supra*, §28) is broad enough to include persons performing the function of a broker. If a transaction by a dealer does not qualify for the dealer exemption, *supra* (because the time during which a prospectus must be delivered has not yet expired), the dealer can still rely on the broker's exemption for transactions in which the dealer is performing a broker's function.

(b) Not limited to "post-distribution" period [§440]

The 1933 Act contemplates that the ordinary investor should be able to sell her securities (purchased as part of a new offering) at any time—even when an S.E.C. stop order may have halted the original distribution process involving the issuer, the underwriters, and participating dealers. Hence, there is no "distribution" restriction on the broker's exemption, as there is in the case of the dealer's exemption.

1) Rationale—"open market" for investors [§441]

The broker's exemption allows brokers to execute *unsolicited* sell orders *at any time*, without complying with the prospectus delivery requirements. This ensures that there is always an open market in the securities, so that they may be traded at a price reflecting their current trading value.

> **e.g.** **Example:** XYZ Corp. issued 100,000 shares of its common stock to the public in a registered offering through Underwriter. Dealer had an allotment of 10,000 shares. A stop order would halt these parties from further distribution activity. But if Dealer had already sold 1,000 shares to Customer, then even during the period when the stop order was in effect, Customer could sell her 1,000 shares through Dealer (with Dealer using the broker's exemption) and receive whatever an unsolicited buyer was willing to pay.

(c) Does not apply to customer [§442]

The exemption applies only to the broker and does *not* extend to the selling customer. The customer must find her own exemption to sell the securities without violating the 1933 Act.

1) Note

The ordinary customer usually has no trouble in this regard, because she is usually not an "issuer, underwriter, or dealer" subject to the provisions of the 1933 Act (*see supra*, §434).

2) But note

Sales by a *control person* through a broker may result in liability for both the control person and the broker, because in such a case the broker will often be deemed to be an "underwriter" under section 2(a)(11) of the Securities Act (*see supra*, §§227-249; *and see* below). Similarly, sales by anyone of "restricted stock" may result in liability. [*See* SA Rule 144; *see supra*, §§227-249; *and see infra*, §§679 *et seq.*]

(d) "Usual brokerage function" [§443]

The broker exemption applies only if the broker is performing no more than the usual broker's function in this particular transaction.

1) More than usual commission [§444]

Receipt of more than the usual brokerage commission may take the transaction beyond the usual broker's function and eliminate the exemption.

2) Delegation of unusual authority [§445]

The transaction may also be deemed to be beyond the broker's function if the seller of the securities delegates unusual authority to the broker (*e.g.*, as to time and manner of executing the sell order).

e.g. **Example:** Authority to sell a "substantial block of securities" exceeds the usual brokerage function, because under such circumstances it is likely that the broker will *solicit* orders to buy so that he can dispose of the seller's block of securities (*see* below).

a) But note
The broker can always prove that the presumption of solicitation is wrong, thereby bringing itself within the exemption.

3) Broker's sales for control persons [§446]
The rules concerning a broker's sales for control persons are complex, mostly because for purposes of deciding who is an underwriter, control persons of issuers are deemed to *be* issuers. [SA §2(a)(11)] As a result, the following rules apply:

a) Where control person has exemption [§447]
If the control person has an exemption from the sale of unregistered securities (*e.g.*, under rule 144; *see infra*, §679), the broker that assists the control person in the sale may properly rely on the broker exemption in section 4(4).

b) Where control person has no exemption [§448]
However, if the control person has no exemption, and the broker knows or has reasonable grounds for believing this fact, the broker may be acting as an "underwriter" in selling the control person's stock (*see supra*, §240), in which case, he *cannot* rely on the broker's exemption. [*In re* Ira Haupt & Co., *supra*, §245]

c) Duty to investigate seller's status [§449]
Therefore, to claim the broker's exemption, the broker must make a reasonable investigation prior to any sale to determine whether the sale is for a control person and, if so, whether the control person has the requisite exemption. [SA Release No. 5168 (1971); SEA Release No. 9239 (1971)]

(e) No broker solicitation of buy orders [§450]
The broker's exemption is lost if the broker *solicits* orders to buy the seller's stock. *Rationale:* Soliciting buyers is the kind of activity normally associated with a distribution. When buyers are being solicited, they should receive all of the disclosure information required by the Act.

EXAM TIP   **gilbert**

If you see an exam question in which the broker's transaction exemption is in issue, remember the rationale for the rule—we want persons acting as brokers to be able to execute a customer's sell order without the trouble of delivering a prospectus so that *ordinary* sellers (*i.e.,* persons other than issuers, underwriters, dealers, and control persons) have an open market for their securities. The rationale may help you remember that the exemption does *not apply* if the broker is performing more than the *ordinary* broker function. Thus, if the broker receives *extraordinary* compensation, has *extraordinary* duties, or *solicits* buy orders, the exemption can be lost.

(f) Exemption does not apply to broker's transaction on behalf of underwriter [§451]

The Second Circuit has held that the exemption for broker's transactions does not apply when the broker's "customer" is in fact an underwriter of the securities. [**Byrnes v. Faulkner, Dawkins & Sullivan,** *supra,* §185]

DEALER'S TRANSACTION EXEMPTION VS. BROKER'S TRANSACTION EXEMPTION   gilbert

DEALERS	BROKERS
During the statutory distribution period (90, 40, 25 or 0 days, depending on circumstances; *see supra,* §§217-220) and until their allotment has been sold, dealers are required to deliver a prospectus to investors; *after the distribution period*, dealers are *exempt* from the prospectus delivery requirement.	Brokers are *generally exempt* from the prospectus delivery requirement when they execute a customer's order, *even during the statutory distribution period*, but note that the customer must have his own exemption (which is the usual case—unless the selling customer is an issuer, underwriter, dealer, or control person).

---

d. Private offering exemption [§452]

The registration requirements of section 5 apply only to an offering of securities that is made *to the public.* Therefore, transactions by an issuer that constitute a "private" (rather than public) offering of securities are exempt from registration. [SA §4(2)] Note, however, that securities offered privately are *not exempt from application of the anti-fraud provisions of the securities laws:* Exemption from registration does not mean exemption from the securities laws generally.

(1) Bases for exemption [§453]

The statutory basis for the private offering exemption is section 4(2) of the 1933 Act, which excludes from the registration requirements of SA section 5 "transactions by an issuer not involving any public offering." However, this statutory exemption is quite vague. In response to protests by issuers, underwriters, and their respective counsel, the S.E.C.

adopted a rule clarifying the circumstances under which the requirements of section 4(2) will be deemed to be met. (Such rules are often called "safe harbors," because compliance with the rule provides shelter from the stormy seas of statutory interpretation and litigation.) The modern section 4(2) safe harbor is SA rule 506, contained in regulation D. (*See infra*, §§477 *et seq.*, discussing regulation D in detail.) A complete understanding of the private offering exemption, therefore, requires knowledge of both the *statutory exemption* under section 4(2), and the *rule 506 safe harbor* under regulation D. This section discusses the statutory exemption; a discussion of the safe harbor follows in the discussion of regulation D.

(2) Section 4(2) exemption for private offerings [§454]

Whether an offering will be considered to be "private" under section 4(2), and hence exempt from registration, is a *question of fact* in each case. The party claiming the exemption has the burden of proof to show that the offering is private.

(a) Criteria for distinguishing private vs. public offerings [§455]

The following factors are considered by the courts in determining whether a given offering is public or private.

1) Need for protection of 1933 Act [§456]

In many courts, the primary question is whether, given the circumstances of the offering, potential purchasers need the protection of the registration provisions. [*See* **S.E.C. v. Ralston Purina Co.,** 346 U.S. 119 (1953)]

a) Sophistication of investors [§457]

The sophistication of the offerees is highly relevant to whether they need the protection of registration. Are they knowledgeable enough to ask the right questions, demand and get the information they need to make an intelligent investment decision, appreciate and bear the risk of securities investment, etc.? If so, this factor tends to support the conclusion that the offering is private.

2) Access to investment information [§458]

Investor sophistication by itself is not enough to establish applicability of the private offering exemption. The investor must *also* have access to all information material to the investment decision—*i.e.,* the same information as would be included in a registration statement. [SA Release No. 5487 (1974); *see* **S.E.C. v. Kenton Capital, Ltd.,** 69 F. Supp. 2d 1 (D.D.C. 1998)] Access to information can be shown in two ways:

a) Relationship with issuer [§459]

The first way to show access to information is to show that the offerees had a close relationship to the issuer and its management, because this provides the needed access to relevant information. [**Doran v. Petroleum Management Corp.**, 545 F.2d 893 (5th Cir. 1977); **S.E.C. v. Continental Tobacco Co.**, 463 F.2d 137 (5th Cir. 1972)]

b) Receipt of material information [§460]

The second way to demonstrate access to information is for the issuer to show that it *actually distributed* to its offerees the same type of material information as would be contained in a formal registration statement, and provided access to any additional information requested (no matter how sophisticated the offerees are). [**Doran v. Petroleum Management Corp.**, *supra*; **S.E.C. v. Continental Tobacco Co.**, *supra*]

3) Number of offerees [§461]

The concept of a "private offering" also seems to imply that the offerees will be *few* in number.

a) Application

The Supreme Court has stated that the number of offerees is not a major factor, but that the S.E.C. can adopt rules of thumb for purposes of administrative decisions. [**S.E.C. v. Ralston Purina Co.**, *supra*]

b) But note

Lower courts and the S.E.C. have emphasized the number of offerees in classifying the offer as public or private. Thus, when the number of offerees gets very large, the offering is likely to be deemed public and subject to registration—regardless of the other criteria discussed above (*i.e.*, no matter how sophisticated the investors might be, or how much information they are given). [**Hill York Corp. v. American International Franchises**, 448 F.2d 680 (5th Cir. 1971)]

c) Offerees, not purchasers

It is the number of *offerees—not* the number of actual *purchasers*—that is determinative.

4) Absence of resales [§462]

Resale of securities originally sold pursuant to the private placement exemption can destroy the exemption, because the reseller thereby may become an underwriter. Resales are discussed more fully *infra*, §§670 *et seq.*

5) Other relevant factors [§463]

It is clear from the case law that the fact that all offerees are sophisticated investors, or that they are given the same information they would get in a registration statement, may not be sufficient to bring the offering within the section 4(2) exemption. There are several additional factors that may also be relevant in determining whether an offering is public or private. *Rationale:* Actual registration with the S.E.C. gives the S.E.C. an element of control over the offering, allowing more protection for investors, and the S.E.C. believes that it should give up such control only in very limited circumstances. [**Woolf v. S.D. Cohn & Co.,** 515 F.2d 591 (5th Cir. 1975)]

a) Appearance of public offering [§464]

Most of the additional factors considered by courts stem from the notion that if an offering *looks* public (*i.e.*, is large and dispersed), it should be treated as such under section 4(2).

1/ Dollar value of offering [§465]

An offering of $4 million in securities looks more "public" than a $20,000 issue. [**Hill York Corp. v. American International Franchises,** *supra*]

2/ Marketability of the securities [§466]

Along the same lines, if the issuer has created a readily marketable security (*e.g.*, many units in small denominations such as $1 per share), there is more reason to find a distribution to the public. [**Hill York Corp. v. American International Franchises,** *supra*]

3/ "Diverse group" rule [§467]

Similarly, the more unrelated and diverse the offerees are, the more the offering appears to be public. [**S.E.C. v. Continental Tobacco Co.,** *supra*]

4/ Manner of offering securities [§468]

And the *manner* in which the offering is made may also be important—*e.g.*, an offering made through the use of *public advertising* is likely to be considered "public" for purposes of registration. [**Hill York Corp. v. American International Franchises,** *supra*]

b) Combination of all elements [§469]

Because various cases, S.E.C. releases, etc., tend to emphasize different important elements or tests, the careful securities lawyer tends to combine all of the tests into one comprehensive checklist of elements.

SECTION 4(2) PRIVATE OFFERING CONSIDERATIONS

IN DETERMINING WHETHER THE PRIVATE OFFERING EXEMPTION APPLIES, CONSIDER THE FOLLOWING:

☑ Need for protection of the 1933 Act (if the *offerees are sophisticated* in investing, the exemption is *more likely* to apply).

☑ Access to information (if the offerees had a *close relationship* with the issuer, or the issuer gave the offerees the *same type of information* that would be contained in a registration statement, the exemption is *more likely* to apply).

☑ Number of offerees (if there are *many offerees*, the offering will likely be deemed public and *not exempt* regardless of any other factor).

☑ Absence of resales (if the securities are *resold within a short time*, the exemption can be *destroyed*).

☑ Other factors that make the offering *look "public"* (e.g., if the offering involves millions of dollars, the securities are readily marketable, the offerees are a diverse group, or the offering is made through public advertising, the offering will likely be considered public and the exemption will *not apply*).

(b) Application of section 4(2) criteria [§470]

The following cases illustrate the application by the courts of section 4(2) criteria.

---

e.g. **Example—public offering:** An issuer offered stock to its employees at the rate of 400 employees per year. The employees represented all income levels, occupational levels, lengths of service, sophistication, etc. A public offering was found because the employees were deemed to need the protection of the Act. [**S.E.C. v. Ralston Purina Co.,** *supra*, §456]

---

e.g. **Example—public offering:** An issuer under an injunction for a previous violation of the private offering rules made an offering to an undetermined number of people of diverse and generally unsophisticated backgrounds. The court held this to be a public offering, notwithstanding the fact that the issuer had prepared an investment memo for the offerees and allowed them access to other relevant corporate information. [**S.E.C. v. Continental Tobacco Co.,** *supra*]

---

cf. **Compare—private offering:** On the other hand, an offering of the debt securities of a manufacturing firm to 80 institutional investors (banks, insurance companies, etc.) was held to be a private offering, as was an offering of an undivided interest in oil lease property to a single investor with experience in buying oil stocks. [**Garfield v. T.C. Strain,** 320 F.2d 116 (10th Cir. 1963)]

---

cf. **Compare—private offering:** And the exchange by five shareholders of their stock in a close corporation for stock of another company was held to be a private offering because they were in a position to obtain whatever information they wanted, and together had significant experience in running a manufacturing firm with nationwide sales distribution. [**Bowers v. Columbia General Corp.,** 336 F. Supp. 609 (D. Del. 1971)]

---

(3) Integration of private offerings into public offerings [§471]

If an issuer attempts to make two or more offerings under the private offering exemption, the S.E.C. may treat the several offerings as a single integrated offering. (*See supra*, §431.) It is difficult to be sure whether the several offerings will be deemed integrated under the S.E.C.'s general five-part test (*supra*, §432). Rule 506—the safe harbor provision for private offerings—contains its own, easier to predict integration provision, which, if followed, assures that the S.E.C. will not challenge separate offerings on the basis that they should be integrated. (*See infra*, §492.)

(a) Rule 152—private placement followed by public offering [§472]

SA rule 152 provides that the section 4(2) private placement exemption is not lost if the issuer later decides to make a public offering "and/or files a registration statement." This is potentially a very useful provision to issuers who might otherwise be deterred from conducting registered offerings because they had earlier done private placements and feared integration of the private and public offerings.

1) Rule 152 available for venture capital deals [§473]

The express terms of rule 152 are limited to situations where the issuer "decides" to do a public offering only after completing the private placement. The S.E.C. staff, however, has accorded no-action status to a number of issuers who first sought venture capital (by private placements), but even at the time of the private placement contemplated that a public offering would eventually take place.

(4) Integration of abandoned offerings—rule 155 [§474]

Suppose an issuer files a registration statement for its IPO, but then the market heads downward and the IPO is aborted. Can the issuer then successfully complete a private placement of its stock? Or, suppose an issuer approaches several institutions seeking private placement investors and discovers that there is so much interest, an IPO might be a better option? The problem in both of these scenarios is integration. Similar to SA rule 152, rule 155 provides a safe harbor from integration of abandoned public offerings into subsequent private offerings, and also protects abandoned private placements from being integrated into subsequent public offerings.

(a) Prior offering must be abandoned [§475]

Unlike rule 152, rule 155 requires that no securities be sold in the first offering and that the offering be abandoned.

(b) Meaning of "private offering" [§476]

In rule 155, the term "private offering" is strictly construed to include only offerings made under 1933 Act sections 4(2) or 4(6), or rule 506 under regulation D. [SA Rule 155(a)] Other exempt transactions are not considered "private," and, therefore, do not qualify for the integration safe harbor of rule 155.

(5) Exemption for offerings to "accredited investors" only [§477]

Section 4(6) provides an exemption from the Act's registration requirements for transactions involving offers and sales of securities by an issuer solely to one or more "*accredited investors*" if the aggregate offering price does not exceed the amount allowed under section 3(b) (currently $5 million, *see infra*, §484). No advertising or public solicitation is permitted in connection with such transactions. Although it has been largely superseded by Rule 506 under Regulation D, section 4(6) continues in existence.

(a) Exemption limited to "accredited investors" [§478]

Section 4(6) permits an offering only to "accredited investors." The term "accredited investors" is defined in SA section 2(a)(15) and SA rule 215 and is similar to the term "accredited investor" under regulation D (*see infra*, §489).

(b) No mandatory disclosure [§479]

Section 4(6) does not require the issuer to disclose information to accredited investors. However, the section does require any issuer relying on the exemption to file a notice of sale with the S.E.C.

(6) Incentive compensation plans in nonreporting companies—rule 701 [§480]

In the *Ralston* case, *supra*, an employer who offered company stock to its employees violated the act because the offering was unregistered. Reporting companies can easily overcome the *Ralston* problem by registering their incentive stock on Form S-8, which the S.E.C. has designed for just that purpose. It is more difficult for nonreporting companies, however, because they are not eligible to use Form S-8, and, therefore, such companies may take advantage of SA rule 701, which provides an exemption to nonreporting companies who issue stock as compensation to their employees.

(a) Not for raising capital [§481]

The exemption provided by rule 701 is not intended for raising capital, but only for compensating employees.

(b) Dollar limits [§482]

The dollar value of securities issued under rule 701 in any 12-month period may not exceed the greater of (i) $1 million, or (ii) 15% of the issuer's total assets at the end of its last fiscal year, or 15% of the outstanding securities of the same class (whichever is greater). Regardless which is the greater number, there is an aggregate cap of $5 million in any 12-month period.

(c) Integration [§483]

Rule 701 offerings are not subject to integration with other (presumably capital-raising) offerings. Aggregation of dollar amount is limited to rule 701 offerings in any 12-month period. [SA Rule 701(d)(3)(iv)]

e. Small issue exemptions [§484]

In addition to the other security and security transaction exemptions set forth in the Act, section 3(b) of the 1933 Act permits the S.E.C. to exempt security offerings from registration if the protection of the Act is not required and $5 million or less in securities is involved in the offering. Pursuant to this section, the S.E.C. has formulated several additional exemptions. Although the statutory basis for these exemptions is found in section 3 of the 1933 Act (which deals mostly with exempt securities), these small issue exemptions are really *transaction* exemptions.

(1) Regulation D

(a) Introduction [§485]

Regulation D contains some of the most-often-used exemptions from registration. It contains rules 501 through 508.

(i) *Rules 501 through 503* set forth definitions, terms, and conditions that apply generally throughout the regulation;

(ii) *Rules 504 and 505* provide small issue exemptions from registration under section 3(b) of the 1933 Act;

(iii) *Rule 506,* which as indicated above is based on the section 4(2) private offering exemption, rather than the section 3(b) small issue exemption, provides a private offering "safe harbor"—issuers complying with the provisions of rule 506 and regulation D will be deemed to have complied with all relevant provisions of section 4(2);

(iv) *Rule 507* bars issuers from using regulation D when the issuer (or any predecessor or affiliate) has been the subject of an injunction for failure to file required notices under regulation D; and

(v) *Rule 508* provides that an issuer that commits an *inadvertent and immaterial* violation of regulation D can, under some circumstances, still claim the regulation D exemption.

Regulation D *applies only to issuers*; control persons may not use regulation D.

1) **Purpose [§486]**

Regulation D is designed to:

a) *Simplify and clarify* existing exemptions;

b) *Expand the availability* of existing exemptions; and

c) *Achieve uniformity* between federal and state exemptions.

2) **Derivation causes differences [§487]**

As noted above, rule 506 is based on section 4(2) (the private offering exemption) of the 1933 Act, while rules 504 and 505 are based on section 3(b) (the small issue exemption). Perhaps the most immediate consequence of this difference is that offerings under rules 504 and 505 have specific dollar limitations (*see* below), but offerings under rule 506 have no dollar limitation; in a rule 506 offering the emphasis is on the nonpublic nature of the offering. Another difference is that under 1933 Act section 18, offerings exempt under rule 506 are not subject to state securities ("blue sky") regulation. [SA §18(a)(1), (b)(4)(D)] Blue sky regulation is discussed in more detail *infra,* §2106.

(b) **Definitions and terms used in regulation D [§488]**

Rule 501 sets forth definitions that apply to all of regulation D.

1) Accredited investor [§489]

One of the key concepts in regulation D is the "accredited investor," defined in rule 501 to include the following eight categories:

a) *Institutional investors* such as banks, insurance companies, pension plans, etc. [SA Rule 501(a)(1)];

b) *Private business development companies* [SA Rule 501(a)(2)];

c) *Corporations, partnerships, tax-exempt charities,* and the like, in each case (i) *not* formed for the specific purpose of acquiring the securities in question, and (ii) with total assets *exceeding $5 million* [SA Rule 501(a)(3)];

d) *Directors, executive officers, and general partners of the issuer* of the securities [SA Rule 501(a)(4)];

e) *Natural persons with $1 million in net worth* (individually, or jointly with spouse) [SA Rule 501(a)(5)];

f) *Natural persons with $200,000 in individual annual income* (or $300,000 joint income with spouse) [SA Rule 501(a)(6)];

g) *Trusts not formed for the specific purpose of acquiring the securities* in question, with total assets exceeding *$5 million,* if *directed by a "sophisticate"* (*see infra,* §515) [SA Rule 501(a)(7)]; and

h) Any *entity in which all the equity owners are accredited* investors [SA Rule 501(a)(8)].

2) Purchasers [§490]

As we will see, under rules 505 and 506 it is often important to determine how many "purchasers" there will be in a particular offering. Accredited investors are *not counted* in calculating the total number of purchasers in a regulation D offering. [SA Rule 501(e)(1)(iv)]

(c) General conditions to be met [§491]

There are several general conditions that apply to all offers and sales effected pursuant to rules 504 through 506 [*see* SA Rule 502]:

1) Integration [§492]

As noted earlier (*see supra,* §431), the concept of "integration" means that under certain circumstances, multiple offerings of securities may be deemed by the S.E.C. to be a single offering. This is often devastating for the issuer because it usually means that section 5 of the 1933 Act was violated. In this regard, regulation D provides some help to issuers, by providing a safe harbor for all offers and sales that take place at least six months before the start of, or six months after the termination of, the regulation D offering, as long as there are no offers and sales (excluding those to employee benefit plans) of securities of the same or similar class within either of these six-month periods. [*See* SA Rule 502(a)]

2) Information requirements [§493]

Regulation D specifies *when* disclosure is required in a regulation D offering, and *what kind* of disclosure is required. [SA Rule 502(b)]

a) When disclosure is required [§494]

Regulation D requires the delivery of a written disclosure document when securities are sold *under rules 505 or 506 to anyone that is not an accredited investor.* In such a case, delivery of the information specified in rule 502(b)(2) (*see* below) is required to be made to those persons that are not accredited investors.

1/ Note

When securities are sold under *rule 504, or only to accredited investors* under any provision of regulation D, there is *no mandatory disclosure.* However, in such a case, the issuer is still subject to the anti-fraud and civil liability provisions of the federal securities laws and *must comply with any applicable state disclosure requirements.*

b) What kind of disclosure is required [§495]

The nature of the required disclosure varies with the kind of issuer (*i.e.*, whether or not the issuer is a 1934 Act reporting company) and the dollar amount of the offering. [*See* SA Rule 502(b)]

1/ Issuers that are not 1934 Act reporting companies [§496]

Issuers that are not reporting companies under the 1934 Act must provide disclosure based on regulation A (*see infra*, §536) for offerings up to $2 million. If the offering is for more than $2 million, disclosure is based on the 1933 Act registration forms. At

$7.5 million, the requirements become somewhat more stringent, especially with respect to the financial statements that must be provided. [*See* SA Rule 502(b)(2)(i)]

2/ Issuers that are 1934 Act reporting companies [§497]

Reporting companies in essence can use the information they are already filing with the S.E.C.; *i.e.,* annual report, proxy statement, and the annual 10-K report. [*See* SA Rule 502(b)(2)(ii)]

3/ All issuers [§498]

In addition to the above, issuers in rule 505 or 506 offerings must give investors, prior to purchase, an opportunity to ask questions and to obtain additional information that the issuer can acquire without unreasonable effort or expense. [*See* SA Rule 502(b)(2)(v)] Issuers also must, prior to purchase, advise nonaccredited investors of the limitations on resale applicable to the securities (*see* below). [SA Rule 502(b)(2)(vii)]

3) Manner of the offering [§499]

Regulation D *prohibits the use of general solicitation or general advertising* in connection with rule 505 or 506 offerings. [*See* SA Rule 502(c)]

a) Rule 504 offerings in general [§500]

As a rule, regulation D also prohibits general solicitations in rule 504 transactions, but compliance with certain state-law registration procedures makes general solicitations permissible. General solicitations are permitted for offers and sales made:

(i) *Exclusively in one or more states that provide for the registration of the securities,* and require the public filing and delivery to investors of a substantive disclosure document before sale, and are made in accordance with those state provisions;

(ii) In one or more states that have no provision for the registration of the securities or the public filing or delivery of a disclosure document before sale, if the securities have been *registered in at least one state that provides for such registration, public filing, and delivery before sale;* offers and sales are made in that state in accordance with such provisions;

and the disclosure document is delivered before sale to all purchasers (including those in the states that have no such procedure); or

(iii) ***Exclusively according to state law exemptions from registration that permit general solicitation and general advertising*** so long as sales are made only to "accredited investors" as defined in Rule 501(a).

[SA Rule 504(b)(1)]

b) Rule 504 public offerings [§501]

Note that when general solicitations are permitted under rule 504 (*see* above), a rule 504 offering becomes a ***public offering, even though it is exempt from registration.*** This perhaps surprising result is justified because the manner of offering rules permit general solicitation only when the offering is subject to state regulation, and because rule 504 offerings are limited to $1 million during any 12-month period (*see infra,* §§509-510).

4) The meaning of "general solicitation" [§502]

Probably the single most important factor in avoiding a general solicitation under rule 502(c) is the presence of a preexisting relationship between the issuer and the offerees. Not just any relationship will do; the S.E.C. looks for a relationship that makes the ***issuer "aware of the financial circumstances or sophistication of the persons with whom the relationship exists."*** [Mineral Lands Research & Marketing Corp., S.E.C. No-Action Letter (Nov. 4, 1985); *see* E.F. Hutton & Co., S.E.C. No-Action Letter (Dec. 3, 1985)]

a) General solicitations and the Internet [§503]

After some initial reluctance, the S.E.C. has approved a procedure by which accredited investors who want to review private placement memoranda can do so on the Internet, without the issuer thereby violating rule 502(c)'s prohibition against general solicitation. An investor who is interested in reviewing such materials is required to complete a questionnaire, and the responses are assessed to determine whether the investor is "accredited" under rule 501. If so, the investor is provided a password that can be used to access private placement memoranda. [Lamp Technologies, Inc., S.E.C. No-Action Letter (May 29, 1997); IPONET, S.E.C. No-Action Letter (July 26, 1996)]

b) Solicitations by persons other than the issuer and its agents [§504]

Rule 502(c) prohibits only the issuer and persons acting in its behalf from engaging in general solicitations. The prohibition would not seem to reach third-party newsletters describing private placements, but in one case (in which the issuers had prepared the "news" items and paid for publication) the S.E.C. found that a general solicitation took place. [J.D. Manning, Inc., S.E.C. No-Action Letter (Jan. 29, 1986)] On the other hand, so-called "matching services," that match investment opportunities to investors, have not been found to be engaging in prohibited general solicitations, at least when they do not notify issuers of the identities of investors but rather notify the investors of offerings that might be of interest. [Texas Capital Network, Inc., S.E.C. No-Action Letter (Feb. 23, 1994)]

5) Limitations on resale [§505]

As will be discussed *infra* (§§670 *et seq.*), resales of securities issued under most transaction exemptions, including regulation D, are restricted.

a) Requirement of "reasonable care" [§506]

Issuers must exercise reasonable care to assure that the purchasers are not "underwriters" as defined in 1933 Act section 2(a)(11) (*see supra,* §227). Reasonable care may be demonstrated by:

(i) *Reasonable inquiry* to determine if the purchaser is acquiring the securities for himself or for other persons;

(ii) *Written disclosure* to each purchaser prior to sale that the securities are restricted and cannot be resold; and

(iii) *Placement of a legend* on the security certificates, stating that the securities have not been registered and noting the existence of restrictions on transferability and sale of the securities.

[*See* SA Rule 502(d)] Note that while these steps evidence reasonable care by the issuers, they are not the exclusive means to demonstrate such care.

b) Resale limitations and rule 504 transactions [§507]

Although as a general matter the resale restrictions and "reasonable care" requirements, *supra*, apply to rule 504 transactions, an issuer that complies with the procedures described above for avoiding the manner-of-offering limitations also thereby avoids the resale restrictions. [SA Rule 504(b)(1)]

(d) Filing of notices of sales [§508]

Within 15 days after the first sale of securities under regulation D, the seller must give the S.E.C. notice of the sale. There is a uniform notice of sales form for use in offerings under both regulation D and section 4(6) of the Act, called "form D." Issuers furnish information on form D mainly by checking appropriate boxes. [*See* SA Rule 503]

(e) Specific conditions of rules 504, 505, and 506

1) Rule 504 [§509]

Rule 504 provides an exemption for offers and sales not exceeding an aggregate offering price of *$1 million* during any 12-month period. This exemption is not available to investment companies, 1934 Act reporting companies, or blank check companies (*see supra*, §404). Commissions or similar remuneration *may* be paid to those selling the securities in a rule 504 offering.

a) Calculating $1 million limit [§510]

The aggregate offering price for an offering under rule 504 may not exceed $1 million, *less* the aggregate price for all securities sold (i) in the 12 months before the start of and during the rule 504 offering; (ii) in reliance on any exemption based on 1933 Act section 3(b); or (iii) in violation of 1933 Act section 5. [SA Rule 504(b)(2)]

2) Rule 505 [§511]

Rule 505 provides an exemption to any issuer that is not an investment company for offers and sales to an *unlimited number of accredited* investors, and to no more than 35 *nonaccredited* purchasers, where the aggregate offering price in any 12-month period does not exceed $5 million. [*See* SA Rule 505]

a) Calculating $5 million limit [§512]

The maximum dollar amount under rule 505 is calculated in the same way that the $1 million limit is calculated under rule 504. [*See* SA Rule 505(b)(2)(i)]

REGULATION D EXEMPTIONS—A SUMMARY   gilbert

	RULE 504	RULE 505	RULE 506
WHEN IS DISCLOSURE REQUIRED?	When required by state law	When sales are made to unaccredited investors	When sales are made to unaccredited investors
IS GENERAL SOLICITATION PERMITTED?	Yes, if state law is followed	No	No
ARE RESALES LIMITED?	No, if state law is followed	Yes	Yes
ARE THERE PRICE LIMITATIONS?	Yes, $1 million during any 12-month period	Yes, $5 million during any 12-month period	No
ARE THERE LIMITATIONS ON THE NUMBER OF BUYERS?	No	Yes, no more than 35 unaccredited buyers; any number of accredited buyers	Yes, no more than 35 unaccredited buyers, who must be sophisticated in financial matters; any number of accredited buyers

b) "Unworthy offering" disqualification [§513]

The rule 505 exemption is not available to issuers described in SA rule 262, the regulation A "unworthy offering" disqualification. (*See infra,* §524.)

3) Rule 506 [§514]

Like rule 505, rule 506—the private offering safe-harbor provision—provides an exemption for offers and sales to an *unlimited number of accredited investors* and to no more than *35 nonaccredited purchasers.* Unlike rule 505, there is *no dollar limitation* on rule 506 offerings (because of its origin under section 4(2) rather than section 3(b) and the corresponding emphasis on the nonpublic nature of the offering rather than its dollar amount; *see supra,* §487), and rule 506 has an additional requirement that the nonaccredited purchasers be *sophisticated* in financial and business matters or employ a representative who is sophisticated.

a) "Sophisticate" defined [§515]

To be a sophisticate, the purchaser or investment advisor must have "such knowledge and experience in financial and business matters that he is capable of evaluating the merits and risks of the prospective investment," or the issuer must reasonably believe that the purchaser meets that description. [SA Rule 506(b)(2)(ii)]

EXAM TIP   **gilbert**

The regulation D transaction exemptions are easy to test on, so watch for them on your exam. Be sure to remember the *general conditions* for the exemptions (*e.g.,* generally no public solicitation or advertising) and the *specific limits on the dollar amount* for the offering (*i.e.,* rule 504—$1 million; rule 505—$5 million; rule 506—unlimited) *and the number of purchasers* (rule 504—unlimited; rules 505 and 506—any number of accredited purchasers, but no more than 35 unaccredited purchasers).

---

(2) Regulation A exemption [§516]

Regulation A, which had largely fallen into disuse in the 1980s, was extensively revised in 1992 by the S.E.C. as part of its "Small Business Initiative." Nevertheless, regulation A has not become a very important exemption in the real world, perhaps in part because regulation D is often easier and just as useful. Many courses in securities regulation do not address regulation A, except for the "unworthy offering" rules (*see infra,* §§524-529), which also affect the availability of other, non-regulation A exemptions. (*See, e.g.,* rule 505, *supra,* §§511-513.) At a minimum, therefore, you should be familiar with the unworthy offering rules. If your class also covers other regulation A issues, you will find the rest of the exemption discussed below. If your class does not otherwise cover regulation A, you probably need only read the material on the unworthy offering rules.

(a) Shortened registration [§517]

Regulation A is *not a complete exemption* from registration. Instead, it provides a simplified form of registration which costs less to prepare and takes less time to complete than the standard registration (*see infra,* §§536-546). [SA Rules 251-263; Forms 1-A, 6-A]

(b) Issuers covered by regulation A [§518]

To use regulation A, an issuer must meet the following requirements:

1) Residence and principal place of business [§519]

The issuer must be a resident of, and have its principal place of business in, the United States or Canada. [SA Rule 251(a)(1)]

2) No 1934 Act reporting companies [§520]

The issuer must *not* be a 1934 Act reporting company immediately prior to the regulation A offering. [SA Rule 251(a)(2)]

3) No "blank check" companies [§521]

The issuer must *not* be a blank check company (*see supra,* §404, for a discussion of "blank check" companies). [SA Rule 251(a)(3)]

a) Note

The prohibition against blank check companies applies under regulation A whether or not the company proposes to issue penny stock (*see supra,* §407, for the definition of penny stock).

4) No investment companies [§522]

The issuer must not be an investment company subject to regulation under the 1940 Act. [SA Rule 251(a)(4)]

5) No oil or gas rights [§523]

The issuer must not be issuing fractional undivided interests in oil or gas rights. [SA Rule 251(a)(5)]

EXAM TIP   **gilbert**

Remember, regulation A technically is not a transaction exemption, but it gives issuers some relief from the burdens of the ordinary registration process by providing a *simplified form of registration*. It is available only for companies not required to register under the 1934 Act (*i.e.,* companies not registered on a national exchange, with fewer than 500 shareholders in any outstanding class, and with less than $10 million in assets), so it is an *option for small businesses* that wish to issue securities.

(c) Limitations on availability of regulation A

1) The "unworthy offering" rules [§524]

Regulation A may not be used when persons involved in the offering (*e.g.,* underwriters, officers, and directors of the issuer) have engaged in conduct indicating that potential investors may need the protection of a full registration under section 5. Such offerings are deemed unworthy of the regulation A exemption. [*See* SA Rules 251(a)(6), 262]

a) Previous conduct by issuer [§525]

If the issuer, its predecessors (*i.e.,* entities whose assets have been acquired by the issuer), or any affiliated issuer has engaged in prohibited conduct within the past five years (*e.g.,* has been convicted of a crime involving the sale of securities) or has been the subject within that time of certain S.E.C. orders (such as a stop order issued in connection with the filing of a registration statement), the regulation A exemption is not available. [SA Rule 262(a)]

b) Previous conduct by control persons and promoters [§526]

Similar disqualifications apply to control persons and promoters of the issuer. In addition, the regulation A exemption will *not* be available if any such person was *convicted of a securities-related offense within the previous 10 years.* [SA Rule 262(b)]

c) Previous conduct by underwriters [§527]

The disqualifications relating to underwriters are similar to those for control persons and promoters. In addition, if an underwriter was named as an underwriter in previous offerings that resulted in certain S.E.C. sanctions (*e.g.,* pending investigations, refusal orders, or stop orders under section 8), the regulation A exemption will not be available. [SA Rule 262(b), (c)]

d) Events occurring after filing [§528]

If any prohibited conduct, above, occurs after a regulation A offering statement is filed, the S.E.C. may issue a suspension order terminating the exemption. [SA Rule 258]

e) S.E.C. authorized exceptions [§529]

However, the S.E.C. has the power to make exceptions to these rules of conduct upon the issuer's showing of "good cause," so that persons otherwise disqualified may use regulation A. [SA Rule 262]

EXAM TIP   **gilbert**

Remember, an issuer will not be allowed to use regulation A if it appears that potential investors will need the protection of full registration. What makes an issuer unworthy of using regulation A is *bad conduct*. If an issuer has engaged in prohibited conduct within the past *five years* (*e.g.*, if it has been convicted of a crime involving the sale of securities within the past five years), it may not take advantage of regulation A. Similarly, use of regulation A is prohibited if a control person or promoter has been convicted of a securities-related offense within the past *10 years*.

---

2) Limitation on dollar amount of securities offered [§530]

The regulation A exemption is limited to the offering of a small amount of securities by the issuer (and related persons).

a) General rule [§531]

As a general rule, securities offered pursuant to regulation A by the issuer may not amount to more than $5 million worth of securities during any 12-month period. [SA Rule 251(b)]

1/ Limitations on sales by security holders [§532]

In addition, all security holders together may sell no more than $1.5 million worth of securities in any 12-month period. The securities sold by security holders are counted against the issuer's $5 million limit, but the issuer can control how much is sold by security holders under regulation A. All sales of securities issued under regulation A require the filing of a form 1-A with the S.E.C. (*see infra*, §536), which must be signed by the issuer. Thus, the issuer can prevent an investor from selling by refusing to sign the form. [SA Rule 251(b); *and see* SA Rule 251(d)(2)]

2/ Further limitations on affiliate sales [§533]

In addition to the above limitations on total sales and sales by security holders, sales by affiliates (control persons) are prohibited if the issuer has not had net income from continuing operations in at least one of its last two fiscal years. [SA Rule 251(b)]

EXAM TIP **gilbert**

Be sure to remember the dual *dollar limitations on securities offered under regulation A*. The offering generally cannot exceed $5 million in any 12-month period. In addition, the issuer's securities holders may not sell more than $1.5 million worth of the issuer's securities within any 12-month period. The issuer can control sales by its securities holders because no securities can be sold under regulation A unless the issuer signs a form 1-A and files it with the S.E.C.

b) Calculation of offering price [§534]

The $5 million/$1.5 million limitations apply to all securities offered under regulation A in the immediately preceding 12 months. The dollar amounts refer to the amount to be received by the issuer, including all non-cash consideration at its fair value. [SA Rule 251(b)]

c) Limitation due to integration of issues [§535]

Like regulation D (*see supra*, §§485-515), regulation A contains a safe harbor rule to protect issuers against the consequences of inadvertent integration of offerings. The integration safe harbor provides that sales made in reliance on regulation A will not be integrated with:

(i) *Prior offers or sales of securities* (although regulation A seems to provide that no prior offers or sales will be integrated, the release proposing the 1992 revisions stated that a regulation A offering will not be integrated with "any previously completed registered or exempt offering"; the implication is that the S.E.C. will integrate previous offers or sales made in violation of the SA section 5 [SA Release No. 6924 (1992)]); or

(ii) *Subsequent offers or sales* that are:

  i.   Registered under SA section 5;

  ii. Made in reliance on SA rule 701 (relating to employee benefit plans) or otherwise under employee benefit plans;

  iii. Made in reliance on regulation S (concerning unregistered offers and sales made outside the United States); or

  iv. Made more than six months after the completion of the regulation A offering.

[SA Rule 251(c)] Failure to meet the safe harbor provision requirements does not result in automatic integration; rather, the S.E.C. will apply its standard five-part test (set out in SA Release No. 4552; *see supra*, §432) to determine whether integration is appropriate.

(d) Regulation A procedures

1) Offering statement [§536]

The offering statement on form 1-A consists of three parts and is the basic form to be used by issuers for regulation A offerings:

a) Part I [§537]

Part I of the offering statement serves as a notification. It is filed with the S.E.C. and is publicly available, but it is not circulated by the issuer to investors.

b) Part II [§538]

Part II of the offering statement consists of the offering circular to be distributed to investors. A corporate issuer has a choice of three possible formats for the offering circular:

1/ Model A—50-question form U-7 [§539]

An issuer that is a corporation may use form U-7 (currently in widespread use for state "blue sky" disclosure). This form requires more extensive disclosure than the other two choices (below), but is a "fill in the blank," question and answer form that may be easier for inexperienced issuers to complete.

2/ Model B—previous regulation A format [§540]

Model B provides a "pool" of disclosure items, ranging from basic disclosure, such as a description of the business and management remuneration, to more specialized items, such as a description of the investment policies of a real estate investment trust. This format is available to corporate and noncorporate issuers.

3/ Form SB-2—new form for "small business issuers" [§541]

Finally, if the issuer qualifies as a "small business issuer" (*see infra*, §567), it may choose form SB-2 (*see infra*, §567) for the offering circular.

    c)   **Part III [§542]**

Part III of the offering statement specifies the exhibits that must be filed in a regulation A offering. They are filed with the S.E.C. and are publicly available, but are not circulated to investors.

2) S.E.C. processing procedures [§543]

A waiting period of at least 20 days must pass after filing of the offering statement before it is "qualified" by the S.E.C. and the selling of securities can begin. [SA Rule 252(g)(1)]

    a)   **Initial response after filing [§544]**

When the offering statement is filed by the issuer, the S.E.C. comments on any matters requiring an amendment of the offering statement.

    b)   **Acceleration [§545]**

As with a registered offering, the S.E.C. has a procedure whereby an issuer can obtain the S.E.C.'s reaction to a filing, make changes in response to S.E.C. comments, and obtain a green light from the S.E.C. when all comments have been addressed. Essentially, the procedure contemplates a kind of acceleration, similar to what usually takes place in a registered offering (*see supra*, §§187-188). [SA Rule 252(g)(2)]

    c)   **Continuing responsibility of issuer [§546]**

Whenever there has been a material change in the information presented in the offering circular, or subsequent developments have made the information misleading or incomplete, the issuer must update the offering circular and file the updated version with the S.E.C. [SA Rule 253(e)] In any event, the issuer remains responsible for any misstatements or omissions in the offering statement.

3) Reports of sales and use of proceeds [§547]

An issuer relying on the regulation A exemption is required to file a report of sales and use of proceeds of the offering every six months after the S.E.C. has qualified the offering statement, and within 30 days after the offering is completed. [SA Rule 257]

4) Substantial and good faith compliance [§548]

Failure to comply with all of the requirements of regulation A will not result in the loss of the exemption with respect to an offer or sale to a particular person or entity, *if* the issuer can prove that:

(i) The failure did not pertain to a term or condition directly *intended to protect* the offeree or buyer;

(ii) The failure to comply was *insignificant* with respect to the offering as a whole; and

(iii) *A good faith and reasonable attempt* was made to comply with all applicable requirements of regulation A.

[SA Rule 260]

(e) Offers and sales pursuant to regulation A

1) Solicitation of interest document [§549]

Regulation A permits an issuer to "test the waters" before committing to an offering. Under SA rule 254, "[a]n issuer may publish or deliver to prospective purchasers a written document or make scripted radio or television broadcasts to determine whether there is any interest in a contemplated securities offering." The issuer is not, however, permitted to solicit or accept any consideration or commitment, nor may any sales be made, until the offering statement is qualified (*see supra*, §543). [SA Rule 254(a)]

a) Copies to S.E.C. required [§550]

The issuer must submit a copy of the solicitation of interest document or script to the S.E.C. on or before the date of the document's first use. The document must contain or be accompanied by the name and telephone number of a person able to answer questions concerning the submission. [SA Rule 254(b)(1)]

b) Information required [§551]

Every solicitation of interest document or script must:

(i) State that *no money or other consideration is being solicited,* and if sent, will not be accepted.

(ii) State that *no sales will be made, nor commitments accepted,* until delivery of an offering circular that includes complete information about the issuer and the offering;

(iii) State that any indication of interest made by a prospective purchaser involves *no obligation or commitment* of any kind; and

(iv) Identify the *chief executive officer* of the issuer and describe briefly and generally the issuer's business and products.

[SA Rule 254(b)(2)]

c) Oral communications [§552]

After submitting copies of the solicitation of interest document to the S.E.C., the issuer is permitted to communicate orally with prospective investors. [SA Rule 254(a)]

2) Preliminary offering circular [§553]

Recall that in a registered offering, written offers may be made during the waiting period, provided they are in the form of a red herring prospectus (*see supra*, §§157 *et seq.*). Similar provisions apply to regulation A: After the offering statement is filed, but before it is qualified by the S.E.C. (*see supra*, §543), the offering circular may be used in the form in which it was filed, provided that it contains a legend specified by the S.E.C. alerting potential investors that the document has not yet been qualified under regulation A. [SA Rule 255(a)]

a) Oral offers permitted [§554]

After the offering statement is filed, oral offers are permitted. [SA Rule 251(d)(1)(i)]

b) No written offers except by preliminary offering circular [§555]

Once the offering statement is filed with the S.E.C., the solicitation of interest document may no longer be used. [SA Rule 254(b)(3)] The only permissible written offers after filing but before qualification are those made by the preliminary offering circular. [*See* SA Rule 255(a)]

c) Exception—"tombstone" advertisements [§556]

Regulation A contains a counterpart to the tombstone ad rule for registered offerings (*see supra*, §183). Once the offering statement is filed, advertisements are permitted if they state from whom an offering circular may be obtained and include no more than the following additional information:

(i) *Issuer's name;*

(ii) *Title of the security, amount* being offered, and per unit offering *price* to the public;

(iii) General type of the *issuer's business;* and

(iv) A brief statement as to the general *location and character of the issuer's property.*

[SA Rule 251(d)(1)(ii)(C)]

EXAM TIP   **gilbert**

On your exam, if regulation A comes into play, be sure to remember the parallels to the regular registration procedure under the 1933 Act: The issuer must *file an offering statement* (albeit a simplified one) with the S.E.C., and the offering statement is subject to a *20-day waiting period* before it can become effective (which begins anew after amendment, but which can be accelerated by the S.E.C.). There are also limitations on offers and sales under regulation A that are similar to those under the general registration requirements: The issuer may *not solicit sales of or accept consideration* for securities to be issued until the offering statement is qualified, but oral offers are permitted, a preliminary offering circular may be used, and "tombstone ads" may be placed. However, *unlike a traditional registered offering*, the issuer must file a report of sales and the use of proceeds of the offering every six months and within 30 days after the offering is completed.

---

3) Final offering circular required after qualification

a) As to offers [§557]

After the offering statement is qualified by the S.E.C., written offers may be made by means of the final offering circular. In addition, other written materials may be used, provided they are accompanied or preceded by a copy of the final offering circular. [SA Rule 251(d)(1)(iii)] This requirement is analogous to the "free writing" privilege accorded issuers in registered offerings. (*See supra,* §§193-194.)

1/ Tombstone ads permitted [§558]

Although generally, after qualification, written materials must be preceded or accompanied by a final copy of the offering circular, tombstone ads may be used after qualification without such delivery. [SA Rule 251(d)(1)(ii)(C)]

b) As to sales [§559]

No sale may be concluded unless an offering circular is furnished to the purchaser in accordance with the following rules:

1/ "Forty-eight hour" rule [§560]

As a general rule, a purchaser must be furnished a preliminary or final offering circular at least 48 hours before any mailing of confirmation of sale. [SA Rule 251(d)(2)(i)(B)]

2/ Delivery of final offering circular with confirmation [§561]

In addition, a copy of the final offering circular must be delivered to the purchaser at the time the confirmation of sale is delivered, unless it has been delivered earlier. [SA Rule 251(d)(2)(i)(C)]

3/ "Ninety-day" rule [§562]

The regulation A exemption recognizes that the offering may continue after all securities in the offering have been sold for the first time, until the issue really comes to rest in the hands of more or less permanent investors. Therefore, the S.E.C. rules arbitrarily designate the length of the secondary trading period as 90 days after qualification of the offering statement. [SA Rule 251(d)(2)(ii)]

a/ Effect of "ninety-day" rule [§563]

During this period, any dealer trading in the regulation A securities must furnish an offering circular to the purchaser no later than the time a confirmation of sale is delivered.

b/ To whom rule applies [§564]

These delivery requirements also apply to *underwriters* who have sold their allotments and are acting as dealers in the secondary trading markets. [SA Rule 251(d)(2)(ii)] However, if a dealer fails to comply with the 90-day rule, it does not destroy the regulation A exemption for *other persons* involved in the underwriting and distribution. [*See* SA Rule 260(a)(2)]

c) Period of circular's use [§565]

Unless used in connection with certain specific types of offerings (such as employee stock purchase plans), the original circular may be used only for a period of 12 months. After this time, a revised circular must be filed with the S.E.C. [SA Rule 253(e)(2)]

d) Post-effective amendments [§566]

The offering circular and sales material in a regulation A offering must continue to correctly represent all material facts throughout the period they are used. Hence, material changes in the issuer during the course of the offering may require suspension of the offering and an amendment to the circular. [SA Rule 253(e)]

(3) Registrations on form SB-2 [§567]

Form SB-2, which is available to "small business issuers," is designed to "facilitate capital raising by small businesses and reduce the costs of compliance with the federal securities laws." [SA Release No. 6949 (1992)]

(a) Definition of "small business issuer" [§568]

Essentially, a small business issuer is a United States or Canadian entity that is not an investment company (under the 1940 Act), has annual revenues of less than $25 million, and, if it is a majority-owned subsidiary, its parent corporation is also a small business issuer. [SA Rule 405]

1) Public float limitation [§569]

In addition to the above requirements, a small business issuer must have less than $25 million in public float; *i.e.*, the aggregate market value of securities of the issuer, held by nonaffiliates of the issuer, must be less than $25 million. [SA Rule 405]

f. Intrastate offering exemption [§570]

Securities offered and sold only to persons residing within a single state, by an issuer that is also a resident of and doing business in that state, are exempt from registration under section 5. [SA §3(a)(11)] *Rationale:* The intrastate offering exemption is designed to facilitate the raising of local capital for local businesses. The exemption is permitted on the grounds that local investors will be adequately protected both by their proximity to the issuer and by state regulations. [SA Release No. 5450 (1974)]

(1) Transaction exemption [§571]

Remember that the intrastate offering exemption is merely a transaction exemption, and securities sold under it may have to be registered when resold. [SA Release No. 5450 (1974)]

(2) Antifraud provisions apply [§572]

And even though an issuer qualifying for this exemption does not have to register its securities, the general antifraud provisions of the 1933 Act still apply to the offering (*see infra*, §§747 *et seq.*).

(3) Requirements for statutory intrastate offering exemption—section 3(a)(11)

(a) Entire issue must be intrastate [§573]

Under section 3(a)(11), the entire issue of securities must be offered and sold to residents of one state. Thus, a single offer to a nonresident will destroy the exemption. [SA Release No. 4434 (1961)]

EXAM TIP **gilbert**

This point is worth repeating. On an exam, be sure that the offering is *truly intrastate*. A single offer to a nonresident can destroy the section 3(a)(11) exemption regardless of how compelling the facts are.

---

1) Integration with other offerings [§574]

The issuer must be careful not to lose the exemption through integration of an attempted intrastate offering with other interstate offerings of securities. (*See supra*, §431.)

2) Limitation on resales—"coming to rest" test [§575]

Eventual resales to nonresidents are possible without destroying the intrastate offering exemption, but only after the original distribution to residents is complete—*i.e.*, only after the offering has "come to rest" in the hands of state residents.

a) Intent of purchaser determinative [§576]

Under section 3(a)(11), whether an issue of securities has "come to rest" depends on the intent of the original purchasers. If the securities were purchased with the intention of keeping them for investment, the issue is complete and resales to nonresidents may begin. But if the purchasers intend a further distribution or resale, the issue has not "come to rest" and any resale to nonresidents will destroy the exemption.

b) Objective test of intent [§577]

Whether the original purchasers intended to hold the securities for investment is a question of fact, to be determined by objective evidence. [SA Release No. 4434 (1961)]

Examples: A relatively long holding period of one year or more may be sufficient to prove the necessary investment intent. Conversely, a resident's resale within a short time to a nonresident supports an inference that the offering has not come to rest within the state, and may defeat the exemption. An even stronger inference is created when the original sale is to a broker-dealer, who resells within a short time to out-of-state residents. [SA Release No. 4434 (1961)]

(b) Issuer, offerees, and purchasers must reside within state [§578]

The intrastate exemption requires that the issuer, offerees, and purchasers *all* be residents of the same state.

1) Issuer [§579]

The issuer must meet two requirements to establish "residence" under section 3(a)(11):

a) Residence in state [§580]

First, the issuer must reside in the state where the offering is made. For a corporation, the state of residence is the state of incorporation.

b) Doing business in state [§581]

Second, because the purpose of the intrastate exemption is to finance local business, the issuer must also be "doing business" in the state. Under the statute, "doing business" is judged by: (i) whether the issuer is doing a majority of its business in the state; and (ii) whether the proceeds of the offering are used in the state.

---

e.g. **Example:** A Minnesota corporation with its only office in Minnesota sold unsecured installment notes to Minnesota residents. However, the intrastate offering exemption was not available because the proceeds of the offering were for loans to land developers outside the state. [**S.E.C. v. McDonald Investment Co.,** 343 F. Supp. 343 (D. Minn. 1972)]

---

2) Offerees and purchasers [§582]

With respect to offerees and purchasers, mere presence in the state is not sufficient to establish residence. Rather, the test is similar to that for "domicile." The purchaser must reside in the state *with an intent to remain.*

3) Underwriters, dealers, and control persons not included [§583]

Underwriters and dealers participating in the offering need *not* be from the same state as the issuer and offerees. And control persons may use the issuer's exemption, even though they are not residents of the state in which the offering is made.

(c) **No restrictions on use of facilities of interstate commerce [§584]**
The intrastate exemption is not lost merely because the mails or other instrumentalities of interstate commerce are used in the offering. Thus, the securities in question may be:

1) *Offered and sold through the mails* or other interstate facilities;

2) *Offered through general newspaper advertising*, as long as the advertisement indicates that offers are being made only to residents of the state; or

3) *Delivered through the facilities of interstate commerce* and transportation.

(4) **Rule 147 criteria for intrastate offering exemption [§585]**
Because intrastate offerings need not be reported to the S.E.C., the S.E.C. has little control over such offerings. This fact, plus uncertainty over the meaning of certain broad terms and conditions in the general section 3(a)(11) exemption (such as the definition of "doing business"), gave rise to numerous violations of the intrastate offering exemption. Consequently, the S.E.C. adopted rule 147, a safe harbor rule that provides specific criteria which, if followed, ensure that the issuer qualifies for the intrastate offering exemption. As with other safe harbors (for example, rule 506 under section 4(2)), if an issuance of securities does not qualify under rule 147, the issuer may still rely on the general terms of section 3(a)(11), as set out above.

(a) **Integration of offerings [§586]**
All securities transactions that are part of an integrated offering must meet the requirements of rule 147, or no part of the offering will qualify for an exemption under the rule.

1) **Integration safe harbor [§587]**
Rule 147 provides an integration safe harbor, so that transactions covered by other section 3 exemptions (*supra*, §§422 *et seq.*) or by the section 4(2) exemption (*supra*, §450), *and* which occur either six months or more before, or at least six months after the rule 147 transaction, will *not* be integrated with the intrastate offering, as long as there are no offers, offers to sell, or sales of securities of the same or similar class by or for the issuer during either of these six-month periods. [SA Rule 147(b)(2)]

a) **Note**
Where there have been offers or sales during one of the six-month periods, so that rule 147's integration safe harbor

is not available, reference must be made to the S.E.C.'s traditional five-factor test in determining whether issues will be integrated (*see supra*, §432.) [*See* also SA Release No. 5450 (1974)]

(b) Requirement of coming to rest [§588]

Rule 147 also provides an objective standard for the "coming to rest" test (*see supra*, §575). The rule 147 offering has come to rest within the state if no sales are made to persons residing outside the state of issue during the time the securities are being offered and sold by the issuer *and* for an additional period of *nine months* following the last sale by the issuer. [SA Rule 147(e)]

1) Precautions against interstate resale [§589]

To ensure that securities issued under the rule 147 exemption do not enter the interstate securities markets prior to the time stipulated under rule 147(e) (*i.e.,* nine months from last sale by issuer), the S.E.C. requires the issuer to take the following precautions [SA Rule 147(f)(1)]:

a) Restrictive legend [§590]

The issuer must place a legend on each securities certificate, stating that the securities have not been registered under the 1933 Act and setting forth the limitations on resale contained in rule 147's "coming to rest" provisions, above.

b) Stop transfer instructions [§591]

The issuer must also issue instructions to its transfer agent prohibiting transfer of the securities until the securities have "come to rest," as described above. (Such instructions are often referred to as "stop transfer instructions.") If the issuer does not use a transfer agent, it must make a notation in its own records that transfers require special action.

c) Written representation from each purchaser as to residence [§592]

The issuer must also obtain a written representation from each purchaser as to the purchaser's residence.

(c) Requirements of residence [§593]

To qualify for an intrastate offering exemption under rule 147, the issuer, offerees, and purchasers must all be residents of the same state.

1) Issuers [§594]

Rule 147 sets forth two requirements to establish an issuer's "residence":

a) Residence in a state [§595]

State residence is defined in rule 147 as follows:

(i) For a corporation, the *state of incorporation*;

(ii) For a partnership, the state where the partnership has its *principal place of business*; and

(iii) For an individual, the state in which the party has his *principal residence*.

[SA Rule 147(c)(1)]

b) "Doing business" requirement [§596]

Under rule 147, an issuer is deemed to be "doing business" in a state if it meets the "triple 80% plus principal office" test:

(i) At least 80% of its consolidated *gross revenues* are derived from the operation of a business or property located in the state, or from the rendering of services within the state; *and*

(ii) At least 80% of the issuer's consolidated *assets* are held in the state; *and*

(iii) At least 80% of the *proceeds* from the securities transaction in question are to be used, and in fact are used, in the issuer's operations within the state; *and*

(iv) The issuer's *principal office* is located within the state.

[SA Rule 147(c)(2)] Rule 147 also indicates how to calculate the time for determining whether these criteria have been met. Basically, the tests have to be met at the time that any offers or sales in the offering are being made. [*See* SA Rule 147(c), (c)(2)]

---

e.g. **Example:** XYZ Corp., whose business is selling products throughout the United States through mail order catalogues, is incorporated in State A and has its only warehouse and office there. All products are manufactured at XYZ's plant in A. Orders are accepted in A, and all products are shipped from XYZ's warehouse in A. Under these circumstances, XYZ is deriving at least 80%

of its gross revenues from a business located in A and meets all of the other tests for application of rule 147 as well. [SA Release No. 5450 (1974)]

---

2) Offerees and purchasers [§597]

For purposes of establishing offerees' and purchasers' residence under rule 147, corporations and business organizations are deemed to be residents of the state in which their *principal business office* is located. Individuals are considered residents of the state in which their *principal residence* is located. [SA Rule 147(d)(1), (2)]

a) Verification of residence [§598]

Recall that rule 147 requires the issuer to obtain a written representation from each purchaser regarding his place of residence (*see supra*, §592). The value of such a representation is questionable, however, in light of the fact that rule 147 requires compliance as to offerees as well as purchasers, and the rule does not require any representations from offerees.

b) Domicile vs. principal residence [§599]

The residence of an individual offeree or purchaser frequently is crucial in an intrastate transaction. Under the statutory exemption, individuals are deemed to reside in the state in which they are domiciled (*see supra*, §582). Under the safe harbor rule, however, an individual is to reside in the state where she has her principal residence. This is significant, because domicile is established by the *individual's intentions* and thus is determined subjectively, in contrast to the objective question of principal residence. For example, if securities offered in an intrastate offering decline in value, the individual purchasers may try to establish a violation of section 5, in order to rescind the transaction and get their money back. If the availability of the exemption depends on the plaintiff purchaser's domicile (and thus on the plaintiffs' intentions at the time of the purchase), the plaintiffs have an incentive to claim that they lacked the intention to be domiciliaries of the state, regardless of what their actual intentions were. Such testimony can be very difficult to rebut. Rule 147's test of principal residence of the purchaser avoids this problem by looking to residence, rather than domicile.

KEY POINTS OF RULE 147—A SUMMARY	gilbert
INTEGRATION SAFE HARBOR	Sales of other securities are ignored if they occur six months or more before or after the rule 147 offering.
COMING TO REST SAFE HARBOR	Securities will be deemed to have come to rest within a state if no sales are made to nonresidents during the time the securities are being issued or within nine months after the last sale by the issuer.
TRIPLE 80% PLUS PRINCIPAL OFFICE TEST	An issuer will be considered to be doing business in a state if its *principal office* is in the state and: ● At least 80% of its *gross revenues* are derived from business in the state; and ● At least 80% of its *assets* are held in the state; and ● At least 80% of the *proceeds* from issuance of the securities are used in the state.
RESIDENCE	Under rule 147, an individual's residence is determined objectively, by the location of the individual's primary residence, rather than by the individual's domicile, which is determined by subjective intent.

g. **"Intrastate small issues"—regulation CE [§600]**

One of the least-used exemptions, SA regulation CE, closely tracks a California state-law exemption. It provides that "offers and sales of securities that satisfy the conditions of paragraph (n) of Sec. 25102 of the California Corporations Code . . . shall be exempt from the provisions of section 5 . . . ."

(1) **State connections [§601]**

To qualify under California law, the issuer must attribute more than 50% of its assets, payroll, and sales to California, and have more than 50% of its voting securities held by California shareholders.

(2) **Qualified purchasers [§602]**

Only qualified purchasers may purchase securities in a regulation CE offering. Qualified purchasers are determined according to rules similar to those for determining "accredited investors" under SA regulation D. (*See supra,* §489.)

(3) **Door open for other states [§603]**

When it adopted regulation CE, the S.E.C. indicated that it would consider adopting a similar exemption for other state-law exemptions incorporating the same standards used by California. To date, however, the S.E.C. has adopted no further exemptions under regulation CE.

h. Exempt reorganizations and recapitalizations [§604]

If XYZ Corp. is incorporated in California and later forms a new corporation (ABC) in Delaware and transfers all of its assets and liabilities to ABC, there has been a *reorganization* of the enterprise. Or if XYZ exchanges a new issue of debt securities for its outstanding preferred stock, there has been a *recapitalization* (*i.e.,* a reordering of the capital structure of the corporation). This section explores the instances in which such reorganizations and recapitalizations are exempt from the section 5 registration requirements for new issues of securities.

(1) Registration not required where no "offer or sale for value" [§605]

Some reorganizations and recapitalizations are exempt because the registration requirements of section 5 apply only if a security is offered or sold. Thus, unless there is an "offer" (which includes "every attempt to dispose of a security for value") or a "sale" (including "every contract of sale or disposition of a security or interest in a security, for value"), the section 5 requirements do not apply to the transaction. [SA §2(a)(3)]

(a) "Rights" given to existing shareholders [§606]

If a corporation transfers "rights" to its shareholders to purchase additional stock (*e.g.,* a stock "warrant," such as a right to purchase one new share of common stock for each share already owned), these rights—even if issued without consideration—are still "securities." However, since there is *no sale for value*, registration of the rights is not required.

1) Distinguish—exercise of rights [§607]

But note that the underlying security, which is purchased upon exercise of the rights (*e.g.,* the common stock, above), *is* being offered for value, and if the right is immediately exercisable, then the underlying security must be immediately registered under the Act.

(b) Stock dividends and stock splits [§608]

If a corporation issues a stock dividend (*e.g.,* one new share of common stock for each 10 shares of common stock already outstanding) or has a stock split (*e.g.,* splits each $10 par value common share into 10 $1 par value shares), there is no transfer for value, and the shares given in the dividend or stock split need not be registered.

1) Option—stock or cash dividend [§609]

Even if the corporation gives the shareholder a choice between the stock dividend and its cash equivalent, there is no "sale for value" if the shareholder takes the stock.

2) Cash dividend [§610]

But if the corporation declares a cash dividend and the shareholder is permitted to waive receipt of the cash, taking stock instead, there is a "sale for value." It is as if the shareholder received cash and then purchased the securities. [SA Release No. 929 (1936)]

(c) "Free stock" [§611]

In the late 1990s, some Internet companies formulated programs in which users would be enticed to the companies' websites with so-called "free stock" programs, in which the user would register on the issuer's website and in exchange receive stock in the issuer. Increased registrations made the issuer appear to be a more substantial presence on the Internet, which in turn helped the issuer's prospects in any future IPO. The S.E.C. *rejected issuer attempts to obtain no-action treatment for these programs*, however, determining that issuing stock in exchange for user registration or website visits would be a "sale" within the meaning of the 1933 Act. [*See, e.g.,* Simplystocks.com, 1999 WL 51836—S.E.C. No-Action Letter] Merely requiring the user to mail the issuer a self-addressed envelope was enough "value" to make the resulting issuance of shares a "sale." [*See* Jones and Rutten, 1999 S.E.C. No-Act. LEXIS 555 (June 8, 1999)]

(d) Pledges of securities [§612]

A pledge of securities to secure a loan is a sale, as it represents the "disposition of an interest in a security for value." Although a pledge is not a complete disposition of all interest in the securities, it clearly is a disposition of some interest and is, therefore, a sale. [**Rubin v. United States**, 449 U.S. 424 (1981)]

(e) "Spin-off" transactions [§613]

Issuers sometimes use spin-off transactions in attempts to exploit the theory of "no sale for value" to achieve a public distribution without registration.

1) Conventional (legitimate) spin-offs [§614]

In a conventional spin-off transaction, a parent corporation distributes the stock of a subsidiary to the parent's shareholders. Typically, no consideration is sought or received by the parent for the distributed stock. The parent's motivations for such a transaction may include antitrust concerns, "downsizing" issues, and the like.

2) "Shell game" spin-offs [§615]

Because a spin-off does not usually involve a sale for value, enterprising promoters in the 1960s conceived a technique for using a spin-off transaction to take a company public surreptitiously. One common variation involved a privately held company issuing a sizable amount of its (unregistered) stock to a publicly held "shell" corporation (*i.e.*, a corporation without assets).

a) No registration

The public shell would then distribute the unregistered stock of the privately held company to the shareholders of the public corporation. Registration was avoided on the theory that the stock in the spun-off private company was not being sold "for value."

b) Effect

With the stock of the private company now in the hands of a large number of the public company's shareholders (thereby permitting public trading and a public market), the promoters would begin to promote an active trading market in the private company stock so that they could sell their own shares to the public at a sizeable profit.

3) S.E.C. reaction

a) Early position [§616]

Recognizing that the shell game transaction amounted to a public distribution of the private company's securities without registration, the S.E.C. first warned that the public company helping to effect such a distribution could be considered an "underwriter" under the 1933 Act [SA Release Nos. 4982, 8638 (1969)], and this theory was upheld by the courts [**S.E.C. v. Harwyn Industries Corp.**, 326 F. Supp. 943 (S.D.N.Y. 1971)—public company using such scheme several times held liable as an underwriter].

b) Limitations on trading [§617]

In 1971, the S.E.C. adopted a rule requiring that any broker-dealer quoting a security in a dealer stock quotation system (*e.g.*, NASDAQ; *see supra*, §19) have available certain comprehensive information about the issuer in order to trade in the issuer's securities. (A very few companies are exempted from this rule.) [SEA Rule 15c2-11]

1/ The rule works to thwart the active trading of securities normally associated with spin-off transactions, since it is difficult to create an active market in a stock that is not listed on a dealer quotation system where it can be traded by many securities firms.

4) Judicial reaction [§618]

The courts support the S.E.C. position by interpreting the statutory requirements of the 1933 Act in a way that prevents spin-off transactions (at least those that have no apparent business purpose other than to effect the distribution of securities of private companies to the public without registration).

---

e.g **Example:** D, a public company, bound itself contractually to a group of promoters to distribute the stock of several private companies to its shareholders as dividends. D retained a portion of the stock in each transaction for itself, making a profit when the stock subsequently went up as part of the promotional scheme. [**S.E.C. v. Datronics Engineers, Inc.,** 490 F.2d 250 (4th Cir. 1973), *cert. denied,* 416 U.S. 937 (1974)]

- The court held that there were several violations of the 1933 Act in that:

  — D could be considered to be the "issuer" of the securities. (The court distinguished the transaction here from that of an ordinary dividend, because D had a *contractual obligation* to make the dividend distribution.)

  — There was a "sale" of the private companies' securities "for value" because D kept part of the stock that was distributed to its shareholders and, when subsequent trading began, D profited.

  — And D could also be held liable as an underwriter because it took the stock of the private companies with the *intent* of distributing it to the public.

- The court was careful to distinguish transactions by companies having legitimate business purposes, even though the effect of such transactions could be substantially similar to the results in this case (*i.e.,* the distribution of the securities of a privately held company to the public without registration).

---

5) Present status of spin-offs [§619]

Reacting to the shell game problem, the S.E.C. has taken the position that a spin-off involves a "sale" unless it meets the following five criteria: (i) the spin-off securities are distributed pro rata to the parent's shareholders; (ii) no consideration is provided; (iii) the parent provides adequate information to the public about the spin-off; (iv) the parent has a valid business purpose; and (v) if the spin-off securities are "restricted," the parent has held them for at least two years. [S.E.C. Staff Legal Bulletin No. 4 (Sept. 16, 1997)]

(2) Exemption for exchanges between issuer and existing shareholders [§620]

Any security that the issuer exchanges voluntarily and exclusively for its outstanding securities—with no commission or other remuneration for soliciting the exchange—is exempt from registration under section 5. [SA §3(a)(9)]

Example: XYZ Corp. exchanges a new issue of debt securities with a longer maturity date, but a lower interest rate, for an outstanding issue of shorter duration with a higher interest rate. XYZ pays no commission or other fee for initiating the exchange of securities. This exchange may be exempt from registration under SA section 3(a)(9). (Note, however, that this transaction clearly is a "sale.")

(a) Exemption for initial transaction only [§621]

Note that this is a transaction exemption; hence, later resales of the securities offered pursuant to this section (*e.g.,* sales by control persons) must be registered or find their own exemption. [SA Release No. 646 (1936)]

(b) Limitations on the exemption

1) Must be in good faith [§622]

To qualify for this exemption, an exchange offer must be made in good faith. An offer that is merely an attempt to evade the registration requirements of the 1933 Act will not be exempt under section 3(a)(9), even if it literally appears to comply with the requirements of the section. [SA Release No. 646 (1936)]

a) Factors considered [§623]

In deciding whether an offer is merely an attempt to evade the registration requirements, the following factors are relevant: length of time the outstanding securities were outstanding; the number of holders of the outstanding securities;

and whether the exchange is dictated by financial considerations of the issuer, as opposed to merely enabling one or a few security holders to distribute their shares to the public. [SA Release No. 646 (1936)]

2) Must be offered only to issuer's security holders [§624]

The exchange may occur only between the issuer and its existing security holders. For example, the exemption would be destroyed if the issuer sold part of an issue to its security holders and the remainder to the public. [SA Release No. 2029 (1939)]

a) And note

The issuer must guard against integration (*supra*, §431), so that securities issued at different times are not integrated into one issue and the section 3(a)(9) "exchange" exemption lost in the process.

3) No commission allowed [§625]

As noted above, no commission or other remuneration may be paid by the issuer for soliciting the exchange of the issuer's securities with its shareholders.

4) "Clean exchange" required [§626]

As a rule, a transaction is exempt under section 3(a)(9) only if it involves a "clean exchange" of the issuer's old securities for its new securities, with no additional payments changing hands between the issuer and security holders.

a) Exception—certain payments from securities holders permitted [§627]

Payments from securities holders to the issuer necessary to ensure that all holders of a class of securities receive the same treatment in an exchange transaction will not destroy the exemption. [SA Rule 149]

Example: An issuer wishes to exchange an outstanding issue of debentures for new debentures. A dividend is payable on the old debentures to holders of record on June 30. As a condition of the offer, persons surrendering the old debentures are required to waive receipt of the dividend. A purchaser who purchases an old debenture after June 30, however, has no legal right to receive (or to waive) the dividend; moreover, the price this purchaser paid for the debenture will have been adjusted downward for the fact that it is "ex-dividend." Under these circumstances, it is fair to require the purchaser to pay the amount of the dividend to the issuer in order to participate in the exchange offer; otherwise, the purchaser gets to buy the debenture at a reduced price (ex-dividend) but gets the same consideration in the exchange as those who paid full price.

---

b) Exception—certain payments from issuer permitted [§628]

If the plan of exchange calls for cash payments to be made by the issuer to security holders (*e.g.*, because the securities surrendered are more valuable than the new securities distributed by the issuer), the exemption will still be available. [SA Rule 150]

(c) Rationale for limitations [§629]

The rationale for each of the restrictions above is that the exemption is designed to apply only if the issuer is simply exchanging securities *as part of a corporate recapitalization*, and not if it is raising new capital (which requires that purchasers be protected by a registration statement and prospectus).

(3) Exemption for approved reorganizations [§630]

The 1933 Act also exempts those business reorganizations in which a new security is issued in exchange for outstanding securities, claims, or property interests (or partly in exchange for cash) and the terms and conditions of the exchange are approved by a court or government agency. [SA §3(a)(10)]

(a) Authorized agencies [§631]

Agencies authorized to approve reorganizations (*i.e.*, after a hearing on the fairness of the transaction) include: (i) any court with jurisdiction over the parties and the transaction, (ii) any official or agency of the United States, and (iii) any state banking or insurance commission (or other state governmental authority) expressly authorized by state law to grant such approval. [SA §3(a)(10)]

Example: Huge Corp., incorporated under New York law, wishes to settle a class action suit based on allegedly defective products sold by Huge. Huge's settlement proposal involves the issue of its common stock to the class members in exchange for the release of their claims. This settlement may be approved by a court of general jurisdiction in New York State, and if the proper notice to class members was given, and an appropriate hearing on the fairness of the offer was held, the offering of securities will be exempt under section 3(a)(10).

(b) State transactions [§632]

For this exemption to apply to state-agency-authorized transactions, the governmental authority in question must be specifically authorized under state law to approve the transactions and the fairness of their terms. [*See* SA Release No. 312 (1935)]

Example: XYZ Insurance Co. wishes to form a financial services holding company. It organizes a new corporation (ABC) and, after a hearing conducted by the state insurance department on the terms and conditions of the proposed transaction, exchanges stock in the holding company for stock of the insurance company. As long as the state insurance department is specifically authorized by state law to approve such transactions, the transaction is exempted from registration by section 3(a)(10).

(c) Comparison with section 3(a)(9) "exchange" exemption [§633]

If Company A were to make an exchange offer for Company B stock, section 3(a)(9)—which applies only to exchanges by an issuer with its *own* security holders (*supra,* §620)—would not apply. However, the section 3(a)(10) government "approval" exemption would still be available.

1) Note

Similarly, the section 3(a)(9) exemption is generally lost if the issuer solicits cash from the security holders, but cash may be taken in a section 3(a)(10) transaction.

2) And note

While furnishing remuneration or commissions to brokers who participate in soliciting an exchange will destroy the exemption under section 3(a)(9), such payments may be made under the "approval" exemption of section 3(a)(10).

(4) Business combinations and rule 145 [§634]

Rule 145 provides not an exemption, but rather a clarification that certain corporate transactions (including mergers, consolidations, reclassifications, and asset acquisitions) involve "offers" and "sales" of securities, and, therefore, must be registered if no exemption is available.

(a) Development of rule 145 [§635]

Former S.E.C. rule 133, a precursor to rule 145, provided that a "sale" of securities had to involve a volitional act on the part of the seller and buyer before registration was required. Therefore, in certain types of corporate reorganizations where this required volition was lacking, no registration was required.

1) Sale of assets [§636]

For example, suppose that A Corp. offered its common stock to B Corp. to buy B's assets. Although the shareholders of B had to vote as a body (state law generally requiring a majority of the shareholders to approve a sale-of-assets transaction), and although there was a transfer for value (*i.e.,* shares of A for the assets of B), no registration was required under rule 133.

a) Rationale

Because no *single* shareholder could determine whether to make the investment in the offered securities, there was no "sale" involving a volitional act by the individual shareholder-purchaser.

2) Stock-for-stock tender offers [§637]

On the other hand, if A Corp. offered its common stock *directly* to the shareholders of B in exchange for their common stock (*i.e.,* a tender offer), each shareholder of B *would* have to make up his own mind whether to sell. Accordingly, a "sale" would be involved and a registration of A's securities required—unless some other exemption were available.

(b) Replacement of rule 133 by rule 145 [§638]

Rule 133 was excessively formalistic—it focused on the final step in a corporate transaction and ignored the fact that each shareholder, when faced with a proposal for a transaction (such as a sale of assets), had to make an individual (and "volitional") decision as to whether the transaction was in her best interests. For this reason, the S.E.C., in a 180 degree reversal, *repealed* rule 133 and replaced it with rule 145.

1) Provisions of rule 145 [§639]

Rule 145 provides that securities issued in certain corporate reorganizations, previously exempted from section 5 by rule 133, must be registered (or find an independent exemption), and that transfer limitations must be placed on the stock received by certain shareholders of the acquired company (*e.g.,* control persons). [*See* SA Release No. 5316 (1972); SEA Release No. 9804 (1972)]

(c) Transactions covered by rule 145

1) In general [§640]

Rule 145 makes clear that proposals for certain business reorganization transactions that *require the approval of shareholders* of the target company are "offers" under the 1933 Act, and that consummation of such transactions is a "sale" under that Act.

2) Specific transactions covered

a) Reclassifications [§641]

Any reclassification of securities that involves the substitution or exchange of one security for another (other than simple stock splits or changes in par value) is subject to rule 145. [SA Rule 145(a)(1)]

1/ Thus, if XYZ Corp. issues a new debt security for an outstanding debt issue, this exchange is covered by rule 145.

b) Mergers or consolidations [§642]

Rule 145 also applies to a statutory merger, consolidation, or similar acquisition of one corporation (A) by another (B), in which shares held by A's security holders will become (or be exchanged for) securities of B.

1/ The only exception to this aspect of the rule applies when the transaction is solely for the purpose of changing the issuer's domicile (*e.g.*, where A Corp. is incorporated in California and forms a new B Corp. in Delaware in order to merge into B and become a Delaware corporation). [SA Rule 145(a)(2)]

c) Transfers of assets [§643]

A transfer of assets by one person or corporation (A) to another (B) in exchange for securities issued by B is likewise subject to rule 145, *but only if:*

(i) The plan or agreement of transfer provides for dissolution of the corporation whose security holders are voting (*i.e.*, A's security holders); *or*

(ii) The plan or agreement of transfer provides for a pro rata distribution of the exchanged securities (of B) to the security holders that are voting (*i.e.*, A's shareholders); *or*

(iii) The board of directors of A adopts resolutions with respect to the provisions in paragraphs (i) or (ii) above within one year after consent to the transaction has been given; *or*

(iv) Notwithstanding paragraphs (i), (ii), or (iii), above, a subsequent dissolution or distribution is part of a preexisting plan for distribution of the securities of B.

Note: In each of the above four situations, registration under rule 145 is required because the securities of the purchasing entity (B) are being distributed from B to A and then to the public (*i.e.,* A's shareholders) within a short time after the purchase-of-assets transaction occurs. In effect, the transaction is a liquidating distribution to A's shareholders when A winds up its affairs and dissolves. [SA Release No. 5316 (1972)]

d) Distinguish—stock-for-stock tender offers [§644]

Rule 145 does not apply to stock-for-stock exchanges—*e.g.,* where X Co. seeks to acquire 80% of the outstanding common stock in Y Co. by offering its stock to Y shareholders in a stock-for-stock transaction. [SA Release No. 5463 (1974); SEA Release No. 10661 (1974)]

1/ Rationale

Recall that rule 145 mandates registration for transactions that previously (under former rule 133, discussed above) did not require registration. (*See supra,* §639.) Stock-for-stock tender offers, however, obviously involve a sale requiring registration, and they were treated as such even under rule 133. Rule 145, therefore, does not address such exchanges.

3) Note—relationship of rule 145 to exemptions [§645]

It is important to keep in mind that rule 145 is merely a provision clarifying that *certain transactions*, which were formerly exempted from SA section 5 by rule 133, *are no longer per se exempt.* If, however, such a transaction—*e.g.,* a merger—fits into the requirements of some *presently existing exemption*, then the transaction will be exempt. Nothing in rule 145 makes unavailable any current statutory or rule-based exemption. Thus, a merger of A into B might be covered by rule 145, but exempt from section 5 under section 3(a)(10) (*i.e.,* as approved by a government agency).

(d) Registration under rule 145 [§646]

The S.E.C. has provided a form for registration of securities issued in business combination transactions (including transactions covered by rule 145).

1) **Form of registration [§647]**

Form S-4 is the proper registration form to be used in rule 145 transactions. It requires detailed information about the proposed transaction. The form also requires information about the acquiring company and the acquired (or selling) company; the level of detail about the companies varies depending on whether each company would use form S-3 or S-1 to register its securities. (*See supra*, §§309-315, for a discussion of these forms.)

a) **Proxy information [§648]**

In addition, recognizing that many transactions registered on form S-4 are also subject to federal proxy regulation (because votes of shareholders are being solicited; *see infra*, §1284), form S-4 contemplates the inclusion of proxy disclosure, and when such information is included, it is deemed "filed" under the proxy rules. [SEA Rules 14a-6, 14c-5]

1/ **Note**

Because corporate acquisitions by companies whose securities are publicly traded generally require the filing of such proxy statements, those companies need not incur any additional work or expense because of rule 145. Generally, stockholders of the acquired corporation receive a combined proxy statement/ prospectus on Form S-4, saving the time and expense of preparing separate disclosure documents.

2) **Delivery of prospectus [§649]**

A prospectus must be given to all those who are security holders of record in the acquired (or selling) company in a rule 145 transaction and who are entitled to vote on the proposed transaction. Delivery of the prospectus must be made prior to the time a vote on the transaction is taken. [SA Rule 153A]

3) **Communications not subject to prospectus requirement [§650]**

Certain written communications made to shareholders of the selling company are *not* deemed to be a prospectus (under section 2(a)(10) of the 1933 Act) or an "offer to sell" (under section 5), so that they may be distributed to shareholders without causing a "gun-jumping" violation of SA section 5. Such communications need not include all of the information that must be included in the section 10(a) final, or section 10(b) preliminary prospectus.

a) **Rationale—preventing delay [§651]**

This position facilitates getting key information about the transaction into the hands of investors as quickly as possible, before a registration statement can be prepared and filed.

b) **Exempt communications connected with business combinations [§652]**

Acquiring companies are permitted to make an offer to sell their—or offer to buy the target's—securities, as long as any written offers comply with specific requirements. [SA Rules 145(b), 165] To be exempt, a written offer in connection with a business combination must:

(i) Comply with SA rule 135 (*see supra*, §§142-145) or

(ii) Both of the following:

　　i.　Contain a prominent legend that urges investors to read the relevant document filed, or to be filed, with the S.E.C. (and describe where these documents are available); and

　　ii.　In case of an exchange offer, the written offer must be made in accordance with the tender offer rules (*see infra*, §§1127 *et seq.*), and in case of a vote of security holders, the offer must comply with the proxy rules (*see infra*, §§1281 *et seq.*).

[SA Rules 145(b), 165]

c) **Communication before the first public announcement [§653]**

The section 5 problem is not limited just to communications made to the public. A communication made among the participants in the transaction could also technically violate section 5 if it furthers a public offering to be made in the future. SA rule 166 provides an exemption for all communications made before the first public announcement of the offering, as long as the participants act reasonably to prevent further distribution or publication of the communication until the offering is publicly announced or a registration statement is filed. [SA Rule 166]

(e) "Underwriters" in rule 145 transactions [§654]

Certain parties to the transactions covered by rule 145 are deemed to be "underwriters" and, as such, are restricted in subsequent transfers of the securities they receive in a rule 145 transaction. The idea is to prevent a control person (A) of a company (X), who could not otherwise distribute his X stock to the public without a registration, from merging X into Company Y under rule 145 in order to sell his newly acquired Y stock to the public without registration.

1) "Underwriters" defined [§655]

Any party (or affiliate of a party) to a rule 145 transaction, *except* the issuer, is considered to be an underwriter if he publicly sells or offers to sell the securities acquired in connection with the rule 145 transaction. [SA Rule 145(c)]

a) Definition of "party" [§656]

"Parties" include any corporations or persons (other than the issuer of the securities) whose assets or capital structure are affected by the transaction. "Affiliate of a party" means a person who controls, is controlled by, or is under common control with a party.

Example: If A Corp. sells its assets to B Corp. in return for common stock in B, A would be a party to the transaction, since its assets are affected.

---

2) Effect on control persons of acquired company [§657]

The effect of these "underwriter" provisions is to limit the subsequent transfer of securities received by control persons of acquired companies ("affiliates of a party") in rule 145 transactions.

3) Registration [§658]

Underwriters in rule 145 transactions may subsequently distribute their securities if the distribution is registered. The most convenient means of registering such a distribution is on the same form S-4 used to register the rule 145 transaction initially.

4) Special exemptions from underwriter status [§659]

To promote the free alienability of securities in circumstances that do not seem to require application of the 1933 Act, rule 145 provides that persons who might otherwise have been considered "underwriters" (*see* above) will not be so considered in the following three cases:

a) *The person sells the securities in compliance with Rule 144* paragraphs (c)—current public information about the issuer, (e)—limitation on amount sold, (f)—manner of sale, and (g)—broker's transaction. (Rule 144 is discussed *infra,* at §§679-703.)

b) *The person has held the securities* of the acquiring company *for at least one year* after the business combination transaction; and

   (i) *The person is not affiliated* (*i.e.,* a control person) *with the issuer* (*i.e.,* B) of the securities;

   (ii) *The issuer (B) is subject to the periodic reporting requirements* of sections 13 or 15(d) of the 1934 Act and has been so subject for at least 90 days; and

   (iii) *The issuer (B) has filed all of the reports required* under these sections during the past year (or such shorter period as the issuer was required to file the reports).

   [SA Rule 145(d)(2)]

c) Finally, a person who is *not an affiliate* of the issuer (and has not been an affiliate for at least three months) and who has held securities acquired in a transaction subject to rule 145 for at least *two years* is not deemed an underwriter with respect to the sale of the securities, even if the issuer does not meet the information requirements. [SA Rule 145(d)(3)]

5) Application of "underwriter" rules [§660]

Suppose X Co. wants to acquire substantially all of the assets of Y Co. in exchange for X stock. If A, a control person of Y, will be a control person of X after the transaction, A cannot use rule 145 to resell her stock publicly. As a control person of X, A is governed by the resale terms of rule 144 (*including* the one-year holding period). [*See* SEA Release No. 10661 (1974); *and see infra,* §682]

a) *Assume instead* that A is a control person of Y who will *not* be a control person of X after the transaction. Here, A *can* use rule 145 to resell her X stock publicly after the transaction—as long as she complies with the provisions of rule 145(d) (*supra,* §§658-659).

b) *Assume* that B, who is not a control person of Y, has received Y stock in a private offering. B will be allowed to resell publicly the X stock he receives after a rule 145 transaction. [SEA Release No. 10661 (1974)]

i. Bankruptcy exemptions [§661]

Transaction exemptions can arise during bankruptcy proceedings. The main provision of the federal bankruptcy law involving exemptions to the registration requirements is chapter 11, which provides for the reorganization of bankrupt companies.

(1) Appointment of examiners [§662]

The basis for an acceptable reorganization plan is left to be determined by the bankruptcy court on a case-by-case basis. However, if the debts exceed assets by $5 million or more, the court is required to appoint an examiner to investigate the debtor for fraud of insiders, etc. This provision is meant to protect public shareholders of large public companies. In addition, the S.E.C., or any other party having an interest in the outcome of the reorganization plan, may attend and be heard at all public hearings involving the plan.

(2) Disclosure requirements [§663]

Restructuring of the debtor's capital and debt structure usually involves an exchange of new debt and/or equity securities for the outstanding securities. The Bankruptcy Code provides for disclosure obligations in issuing these securities, which is done under the supervision of the bankruptcy court. Thus, when the Bankruptcy Code applies, the issuer is exempt from the other federal and state securities laws. [*See* Bankruptcy Code §§1125, 1145]

(a) Information required [§664]

The Bankruptcy Code provides that the issuer must provide information that is adequate in light of the nature and history of the debtor and the condition of its accounting records so that the typical holder of claims or interests of the relevant class can make an informed judgment about the proposed exchange.

(b) Timing [§665]

This information must be given to creditors at or prior to the solicitation of acceptance of the reorganization plan.

(c) S.E.C. or state disclosure requirements [§666]

The S.E.C. and/or state securities commissioners may appear and contest whether the disclosure statement proposed by the bankruptcy court is adequate.

(3) Debt securities [§667]

The Bankruptcy Code does not allow the sale by the debtor of equity securities to raise new capital (equity securities may be issued only in exchange for old debts or equity interests). It does, however, permit the trustee to issue debt securities, without 1933 Act registration, to raise additional funds to operate the business. [*See* Bankruptcy Code §364] This is a transaction exemption. In addition, section 3(a)(7) of the 1933 Act provides an exemption for debt securities issued with court approval in order to finance post-bankruptcy operations. Note the difference: Bankruptcy Code section 364 provides a *transaction* exemption; SA section 3(a)(7) provides a *security* exemption.

(4) Resales, sales by control persons, and other provisions [§668]

The Bankruptcy Code also sets forth standards under which a creditor or control person acquiring securities under the reorganization plan can resell the securities. [*See* Bankruptcy Code §1145(b)] A limited exemption for brokers selling such securities is also provided. [*See* Bankruptcy Code §1145(a)]

(5) Inapplicability of section 3(a)(9) and (10) to bankruptcy proceedings [§669]

The section 3(a)(9) (exchanges between the issuer and its existing shareholders) and 3(a)(10) (exemption for approved reorganizations) exemptions do not apply in corporate reorganizations undertaken under the Bankruptcy Code.

4. Resales and "Statutory Underwriters" [§670]

The issue of resales arises for two reasons, and there are two corresponding ways in which section 5 may be violated. The first reason is that most exempt *transactions* do not involve exempt *securities*, and nonexempt securities that were sold in an exempt transaction cannot be resold without another exemption. In this way, a resale of securities can violate section 5 even when the initial sale did not. The second reason has to do with the definition of "underwriter" in 1933 Act section 2(a)(11): For purposes of deciding who is an "underwriter," persons who sell for an affiliate (control person) of the issuer are deemed to sell for the issuer itself. This means that anyone who purchases from a control person and resells in a public manner (for example, through a broker) risks becoming an "underwriter," which is a problem when one considers that underwriters are not eligible for the transaction exemption in section 4(1) (transactions by persons other than issuers, underwriters and dealers). On the issue of underwriters for control persons, and for a definition of "control person," *see supra,* §§240 *et seq.* In both the case of resale of securities first sold in an exempt transaction, and securities sold by a control person, a party may become an underwriter without expressly taking on the "business role" of an underwriter. Such parties are called "statutory underwriters."

e.g. **Example:** George acquires 50,000 shares of ABC Corp. common stock in an unregistered private placement (this could be under either section 4(2) or rule 506). One month after acquiring the stock, George resells to 500 unsophisticated investors. This transaction violates section 5, because ABC stock is not an exempt security and George's sale transaction does not qualify, as far as we know, for any exemption from the registration requirements under the 1933 Act. George's role here is that of an underwriter: He sold for an issuer in connection with a distribution.

e.g. **Example:** George is the CEO (a "control person") of ABC Corp. He also owns 50,000 shares of ABC common stock that he purchased on the stock exchange, using his brokerage account. George sells all 50,000 shares from his brokerage account, to raise money for a new vacation home. This transaction violates section 5. Although George is not an underwriter in this example (he purchased the stock on the open market), his broker has become an underwriter (purchased from a control person of the issuer—which, for this purpose, is the same thing as buying directly from the issuer—and sold publicly). So section 5 is violated when George's broker sold to the public. However, George is also in trouble, because his transaction was not within section 4(1). It involved an underwriter, and transactions by underwriters are not exempt. [*See* **United States v. Wolfson**, 405 F.2d 779 (2d Cir. 1968), *cert. denied*, 394 U.S. 946 (1969)]

e.g. **Example:** George is the CEO of ABC Corp. Over the last several years, ABC has issued stock to George under Rule 506 every time George exercised one of his stock options. George currently owns 50,000 shares of ABC stock, all which was issued to George by ABC and which George now sells through his broker. This transaction violates section 5 for *both* of the reasons discussed above: First, the securities were issued to George in a transaction exemption (rule 506) and, therefore, George is an underwriter when he resells publicly. Second, George's broker is purchasing from a[n] [control person of] issuer, and is reselling publicly. That makes George's broker an underwriter, too.

a. **Importance to the investor [§671]**

Restriction of resales is an important issue because the ease or difficulty of resale is often crucial to an investor and will affect the price an investor is willing to pay. For example, if an investor perceives that he will be unable to sell when the price of the security is dropping or when he has an unforeseen need for cash, the investor will demand a substantial discount from the price of the security that he would otherwise pay.

b. **Buyer's intent important [§672]**

Underwriter status frequently depends on *intent*. If a buyer purchases from the issuer (or a control person) with a "view to distribution," and a distribution takes place, the buyer has become an underwriter. (Note that the 1933 Act does not literally state that a distribution must occur. Under the statute, it is possible that one could become an underwriter by purchasing "with a view to distribution" and not distributing—*e.g.,* merely holding—the securities. However, it is highly unlikely a court would find underwriter status in such a transaction.

(1) Traditional factors showing investment intent [§673]

Whether the original purchaser bought for investment or for distribution is a *question of fact; i.e.,* what was the purchaser's intent at the time of purchase? In determining intent, the following factors have traditionally been held relevant by the courts:

(a) Investment letters [§674]

It is a common practice to require that the original purchasers give the issuer a letter indicating that they are buying for investment purposes rather than for resale. However, the purchaser's own statements on the matter are not conclusive; in particular, an investment letter will be given no weight if in fact the purchaser turns around and sells the securities shortly after purchasing them.

(b) Length of holding period [§675]

The longer the securities are held by the original purchasers before resale, the more likely it is that the original purchase was for investment and that the private offering exemption still applies. (At one time, the S.E.C. gave opinion letters on the subject—*i.e.,* that a one-year holding period was sufficient to show investment intent—but it no longer does so.) [SA Release No. 3825 (1957)] Here again, however, the length of time is not conclusive evidence of investment intent; the other factors must also be considered.

Example: Investment intent has been found where stock was purchased from a control person and then resold publicly after a period of two years. [**United States v. Sherwood,** 175 F. Supp. 480 (S.D.N.Y. 1959)]

(c) Restrictive legends on stock certificates [§676]

To show that the issuer has made a reasonable investigation, and also to establish reasonable precautions by making unlawful secondary transfers more difficult, the issuer claiming a private offering exemption often places a legend on its stock certificates to the effect that the certificates cannot be transferred without the issuer's permission. Permission to transfer is then normally conditioned on the opinion of the issuer's counsel that a transfer will not violate the securities laws. [SEA Release No. 5121 (1970)]

(2) "Change in circumstances" doctrine [§677]

A change in circumstances was sometimes asserted by purchasers seeking to avoid underwriter status under the 1933 Act. They purchased with an intent to invest, the argument went, but a later change in circumstances necessitated sale of the securities. This argument was seldom successful.

e.g. **Example:** G purchased convertible debentures directly from the issuer in a private placement. Ten months later, G converted the debentures into stock and sold the stock on the stock exchange. The S.E.C. brought an enforcement proceeding, claiming a violation of SA section 5 because G was an underwriter who had publicly distributed stock in violation of SA section 5. G argued that the issuer was losing money, and that this constituted a changed circumstance justifying his sale. The court held that G failed to establish investment intent, and G therefore was an underwriter. [**Gilligan, Will & Co. v. S.E.C.**, 267 F.2d 461 (2d Cir. 1959)]

(3) Fungibility [§678]

Another issue complicating the analysis of resales involves the fungibility of securities. If an investor bought 100 shares of ABC common stock in a private placement, and subsequently bought 100 more shares on the stock exchange, can she sell any of the 200 shares? Before the S.E.C.'s adoption of rule 144 (*see infra*), it was unclear whether any of the shares could be sold.

(4) Proof of "investment intent"—rule 144 [§679]

Because of frequent confusion and ambiguity in determining whether an investor had "investment intent" (and, therefore, was not an underwriter), the S.E.C. adopted rule 144 specifying an objective set of criteria that will establish investment intent. If these criteria are satisfied, purchasers in a private offering of securities may *resell* the securities (referred to in rule 144 as "*restricted securities*") without violating the Act.

e.g. **Example:** A buys 100 shares from XYZ in a private offering by XYZ to sophisticated investors. After holding the shares for two years, A desires to sell but does not wish to violate any securities laws in doing so. If she complies with rule 144, A can rest assured that her sales are not unlawful (*i.e.*, she will not be deemed to be an underwriter, and her sales to the public will not turn the private offering into an unregistered public offering).

(a) Preference for rule 144 standard [§680]

While a seller of privately purchased securities can still rely on the traditional pre-rule 144 criteria (above) to establish investment intent, the S.E.C. takes a dim view of resales outside of rule 144. Lawyers should be very careful in advising clients that investment intent has been established where the requirements of rule 144 are not satisfied. [SA Release No. 5223 (1972)]

(b) Scope of rule 144

1) "Restricted securities" [§681]

Rule 144 applies to the sale of "restricted securities," defined in rule 144 to include the following types of securities:

a) *Privately offered securities* acquired directly or indirectly from the issuer or a control person (discussed *supra*, §§452 *et seq.*);

b) *Securities issued pursuant to rules 505 or 506* (discussed *supra*, §§485 *et seq.*), *or* pursuant to rule 701(c) (employee benefit plans);

c) *Securities sold under Rule 144A* (discussed *infra*, §§718 *et seq.*); and

d) *Other securities that have not been previously offered to the public*, including securities acquired from the issuer pursuant to regulation CE, equity securities of domestic issuers acquired subject to certain provisions of regulation S (*see infra*, §§734-746) and securities acquired pursuant to rules 801 or 802, when the acquiror held restricted securities.

2) Sales of securities by control persons [§682]

Rule 144 also applies to the sale of securities owned by control persons; *i.e.,* describes how a control person may sell securities without making those that subsequently resell the securities "underwriters" (*see supra*, §240).

a) Rule applicable to both restricted and nonrestricted securities [§683]

If the securities of control persons are involved, rule 144 applies to sales of *both* restricted securities (*i.e.,* those purchased by the control person in a private offering) and nonrestricted securities (*e.g.,* securities acquired by the control person in stock exchange transactions).

---

e.g. **Example:** When XYZ Corp. was formed, A received 25% of the stock (restricted stock), and now serves on the board of directors; hence, A is a control person of XYZ. Over the next several years, A acquired additional stock in stock exchange purchases (nonrestricted stock). A now wishes to sell. If she does *not* comply with rule 144, she runs the risk of violating SA section 5 by selling either the restricted or unrestricted stock. Conversely, if she complies with rule 144, she will not violate section 5.

(c) Requirements of rule 144 [§684]

Rule 144 imposes five principal restrictions on resale of restricted securities by anyone, and on the resale of any securities by control persons (affiliates) of the issuer. The restrictions require: (i) adequate public information about the issuer; (ii) a minimum holding period for restricted securities; (iii) sales to be within certain volume limits; (iv) securities to be sold through a broker or market-maker; and (v) filing of a notice of sale with the S.E.C.

1) Unlimited resale for nonaffiliates with two-year holding period [§685]

The limitations of rule 144 do not apply to sales by persons *who are not affiliates* of the issuer, who *have not been affiliates for the last three months*, and *who have held the securities for at least two years* before selling them. [*See* SA Rule 144(k)] The two-year holding period is calculated in the same way as the "normal" one-year period applicable to other sales under rule 144. (*See infra,* §689.) For all other sales of restricted securities, or sales by affiliates of the issuer, the following requirements must be met.

2) Adequate public information about the issuer [§686]

Adequate information about the issuer (*i.e.,* information analogous to that contained in a registration statement) must be available to the public at the time of sale. [SA Rule 144(c)]

a) 1934 Act reporting companies [§687]

The information requirement is satisfied by all companies that have been required to report for at least 90 days before the rule 144 sale, and have actually filed all required reports, under sections 13 or 15(d) of the 1934 Act. [SA Rule 144(c)(1)] (*See infra,* §882.)

b) Other companies [§688]

Issuers not required to report under the 1934 Act may choose to report voluntarily, in order to make rule 144 available to their security holders. Alternatively, they may make publicly available the information required under the 1934 Act to permit brokers to quote an over-the-counter security. [SA Rule 144(c)(2); *see* SEA Rule 15c2-11]

3) One-year holding period for restricted securities [§689]

Second, rule 144 provides that *restricted securities* cannot be resold until a period of one year has elapsed from the date of their acquisition from the issuer (or an affiliate of the issuer). The holding period is "tolled" (*i.e.*, it does not begin to run) until the initial buyer has fully paid for the securities. [SA Rule 144(d)(1)] (*Note:* The holding period/full payment rule *applies only to restricted securities;* thus, a control person (*i.e.*, an affiliate) selling nonrestricted securities need not comply with this provision.) *Rationale:* This requirement ensures that the investor purchased the securities as an investment, rather than for public distribution.

a) Determining full payment [§690]

The original purchaser has fully paid for the securities if one of the following applies:

1/ *The purchaser has paid for them in cash.*

2/ *When a promissory note or installment contract was used*, the note or contract must have been a "full-recourse obligation"—*i.e.,* if the loan goes bad, the issuer has recourse to *all* of the borrower's assets and not just to the stock that was purchased. Furthermore, the note or contract must be secured by collateral *other than* the securities themselves, having a fair market value at least equal to the amount of the note. The holding period is tolled for any period in which the market value of the collateral is inadequate. Finally, the promissory note must be paid in full before any securities can be sold, even if the holding period has run.

3/ *When the purchaser has borrowed* the money to pay for the securities from a third party (and the loan is not guaranteed by the issuer), the securities are deemed to be fully paid even if the purchaser only pledges the restricted stock as collateral for his full recourse loan from the third party.

4/ *When the securities issued are options*, they are not fully paid until the option is exercised and the option price is fully paid. Thus, if A had an option on 100 shares of XYZ common stock for one year, at the end of which time she exercised the option and paid the option price, the one-year option period would not satisfy the one-year holding period.

b) Calculating the one-year holding period [§691]

There are special rules for computing the one-year holding period in certain situations.

1/ Stock dividends or stock splits [§692]

The holding period for securities acquired through stock dividends or splits relates back to the acquisition date of the original securities. Thus, where A buys 100 shares of XYZ common stock in 2006, and XYZ pays a dividend of one share for each 10 shares owned in 2007, the holding period for the 10 dividend shares would relate back to the 2000 date of purchase on the original securities. [SA Rule 144(d)(3)(i)]

2/ Pledged securities [§693]

If securities are pledged (*i.e.,* put up as collateral), the pledgee can relate the start of its holding period back to the acquisition date of the pledgor *if* the pledge was made in connection with a full-recourse loan (*see supra*, §690).

a/ Non-full recourse loans [§694]

If the loan is not full recourse, the holding period begins to run on the date of the pledge. [SA Rule 144(d)(3)(iv)]

---

e.g. **Example:** A acquires stock in XYZ Corp. in 2005. In 2007, he pledges the stock to C under a full recourse loan agreement. If A then defaults and C takes the stock, C can use A's 2005 purchase date in calculating the one-year period for resale under rule 144.

3/ Gifts [§695]

A donee's acquisition date relates back to the acquisition date of his donor. [SA Rule 144(d)(3)(v)]

4/ Trusts [§696]

Similarly, the trustee or beneficiary of a trust may use the date on which the settlor of the trust acquired the securities in computing his holding period. [SA Rule 144(d)(3)(vi)]

5/ Estates [§697]

And an estate wishing to sell securities pursuant to

rule 144 may relate back its date of acquisition to the date the decedent acquired the securities. [SA Rule 144(d)(3)(vii)]

a/ Note

No holding period is required if either (i) the *estate is not an affiliate* (control person) of the issuer or (ii) the securities are *sold by a beneficiary of the estate that is not an affiliate* of the issuer. [SA Rule 144(d)(3)(vii)]

4) Limitation on amount of securities sold [§698]

The volume of securities that may be resold under rule 144 is limited, so that during any three-month period only the following quantities may be sold:

a) Sales by affiliates and sales of restricted securities [§699]

Sales by control persons and sales of restricted securities may not exceed the greater of:

(i) *One percent of the shares of the outstanding class of security;*

(ii) *If the security is traded on an exchange,* the average weekly reported volume of trading in such securities on all exchanges and/or reported through the automated quotations systems of a registered securities association for the four weeks prior to the filing of the notice of sale (*see infra,* §702); and

(iii) *The average weekly reported volume* of trading in such securities reported through the consolidated transaction reporting system that is contemplated by rule 11Aa3-1 of the 1934 Act during the four-week period preceding a filing of the notice of sale.

[SA Rule 144(e)]

b) Securities otherwise acquired [§700]

When restricted securities are pledged, given as a gift, placed in trust, or acquired in a decedent's estate, the respective sales by the pledgor, donor, settlor, or decedent (as the case may be) must be *combined* with the sales made by the pledgee, donee, trust, or estate within the relevant time period in calculating the total volume for the rule 144 limitation. Similar provisions apply in cases where convertible securities are sold together with securities of the class into which they are convertible, and where two or more persons act in concert in selling securities of the same issuer. [SA Rule 144(e)(3)]

5) Limitation on manner of sale [§701]

Rule 144 requires that sales (except sales by nonaffiliate estates and beneficiaries) thereunder be made in transactions directly with a "market maker" (as defined in section 3(a)(38) of the 1934 Act) or in "broker's transactions," within the meaning of section 4(4) of the 1933 Act (*see supra*, §§437 *et seq.*). [*See* SA Rule 144(f), (g)] Thus, the following limitations apply in a broker's transaction:

a) *The person selling the securities may not:*

1/ *Solicit orders* to buy the securities; or

2/ *Make any payment* in connection with the transaction to anyone other than the broker.

b) In addition, *the broker:*

1/ May not do more than *execute the order* to sell and cannot receive more than the customary commission;

2/ May not *solicit orders* to buy, although he may contact other brokers who have expressed an interest within the previous 60 days, or customers expressing an interest within the previous 10 business days;

3/ May *publish bid and ask quotations* in an interdealer stock quotation system, as long as the broker has been "making a market" (*i.e.*, trading regularly) in the security to be sold; and

4/ Must *make a reasonable inquiry* to ensure that the person claiming the right to sell without registration is entitled to do so.

6) Notice of proposed sale [§702]

The final requirement of rule 144 is that a seller who intends to sell more than 500 shares, or any number of shares for an amount greater than $10,000, must file with the S.E.C. a notice of intention to sell the securities. [SA Rule 144(h)] The person filing this notice must have a bona fide intention to sell the securities within a reasonable time. [SA Rule 144(i)]

7) Nonexclusive rule [§703]

Rule 144 is not exclusive. A nonaffiliate may effect sales of restricted stock, and an affiliate may effect sales of any stock, pursuant to a registration statement, another exemption, or a regulation A offering. [SA Rule 144(j)]

(5) Alternatives to rule 144 [§704]

While rule 144 made the criteria for legal resales of securities more definite, it also made them more stringent. Therefore, sellers may seek alternatives to rule 144, while still avoiding "underwriter" status.

(a) Registered transactions [§705]

One option that may be available to the would-be seller is to register the transaction. This is usually quite expensive, however, and requires extensive cooperation from the issuer. As a rule, this route is chosen only if the issuer was already planning a registered public offering, and the selling shareholders simply "piggyback" their offering on the issuer's offering.

(b) Regulation A exemption [§706]

In cases where a registered transaction is not readily available, sellers sometimes take advantage of regulation A, a shortened form of registration available to certain persons (*see supra*, §517).

(c) "Section 4(1½)"—private sales of restricted securities [§707]

The discussion of resales so far has focused on *public* resales. The problem with these, as we have seen, is that the seller (when restricted securities are sold) or the seller's broker (when the seller is a control person selling *any* securities, restricted or not) is likely to be swept into the definition of "underwriter" contained in SA section 2(a)(11). But what if the seller, rather than selling publicly, sells *privately?* This would avoid underwriter status, since an underwriter is one who is involved in a "distribution," *i.e.,* a sale to the public.

1) No express exemption [§708]

The first obstacle to such a sale is that SA section 4(2), the standard private offering exemption, is available only to an issuer. Even without an express exemption, however, a private sale is possible. The standards that the S.E.C. has required for such a transaction in order for the seller (and the seller's broker) to avoid underwriter status have come to be known as "section 4(1½)," because they resemble in some respects the requirements of SA section 4(2) (the issuer's private placement exemption) and result in the transaction's being exempt under SA section 4(1), the exemption for transactions not involving an issuer, underwriter, or dealer.

CHECKLIST OF RULE 144 REQUIREMENTS

UNDER RULE 144, PURCHASERS MAY RESELL THEIR SECURITIES WITHOUT VIOLATING THE 1933 ACT, IF THE FOLLOWING CRITERIA ARE SATISFIED:

☑ Is the sale by a person who has **not been a control person** for the last three months, and who has held the securities for at least two years? If so, the securities may be freely resold. If not, the remaining issues should be checked.

☑ Does the **public have adequate information** about the issuer, either through reports filed under the 1934 Act or from voluntary disclosure?

☑ If the **securities are restricted**, have they been held for **at least one year** since they were acquired from the issuer and fully paid for?

☑ Have sales subject to rule 144 by any one person exceeded the following **volume limitations** over any three-month period?

- 1% of the shares of the outstanding class of securities in question.

- The average weekly trading volume for the security, if traded on a national exchange or in NASDAQ, for the four weeks prior to filing a notice of sale.

- The average weekly trading volume for the security reported through the consolidated transaction reporting system contemplated by rule 11Aa3-1 of the 1934 Act.

☑ Is the **manner of the sale** (by broker or market maker) proper (the seller generally may not solicit orders or pay a commission to anyone other than the broker, or the broker may not do more than execute the sale for the customary commission or solicit orders to buy, and must make reasonable inquiry to ensure that the seller has the right to sell without registering)?

☑ If the seller intends to sell more than 500 shares or any number of shares for more than $10,000, has a **notice of intention to sell been filed** with the S.E.C.?

2) Sales of restricted securities by noncontrol persons [§709]

Suppose, for example, that A, a noncontrol person of XYZ Corp., has purchased some of XYZ's common stock in a private offering by XYZ under section 4(2) of the 1933 Act. A desires to resell some of these restricted securities. He cannot appeal to section 4(2), because this section applies only to "issuers," and A is not an issuer. If A is also not an "underwriter" or "dealer," then presumably he can resell under section 4(1).

a) Determining underwriter status [§710]

A is not an underwriter if he does not purchase from, or sell or otherwise participate in a "distribution" for, the issuer (XYZ). [*See* SA §2(a)(11); *and see supra,* §227] The S.E.C. and the courts have traditionally resorted to the concepts related to a "public offering" to determine the meaning of the word "distribution." What is necessary, then, is for A to avoid participating in a "public offering." This will be accomplished if A does not himself sell to the "public" *and* effectively prevents his purchasers from reselling to the public without an exemption (because if the purchasers resell to the public, the securities will have been "distributed," and A will thereby become an underwriter).

1/ Avoiding sales to the public [§711]

Generally, the seller can avoid selling to the public by offering and selling only to those who can meet the SA section 4(2) requirements for offerees in a private placement.

a/ Note

The S.E.C. staff has been less rigorous in enforcing some of the "private placement" requirements in the "section 4(1½)" context, compared to SA section 4(2). The staff has been unpredictable in this regard, however, and no-action treatment is usually sought for such a transaction.

2/ Restricting further resales [§712]

The usual techniques for restricting sales apply here (*see supra,* §§673-676). A could require his purchasers to agree to contractual provisions limiting resales, place legends on the security certificates noting that the securities cannot be resold without registration or an exemption, give stop transfer instructions to the issuer's transfer agent, and so on.

3) Sales by control persons [§713]

Control persons may also rely on section 4(1) to resell their securities, whether or not restricted.

a) Restricted securities [§714]

Control persons face no additional obstacles with respect to their sales of restricted securities than are faced by noncontrol persons. The key in either case is to *avoid becoming an underwriter by selling to the public,* and to *avoid selling to an underwriter* (by selling to someone who in turn sells to the public).

b) Nonrestricted securities [§715]

In sales by control persons of nonrestricted securities, the key is to *avoid selling to an underwriter.* The control person is not concerned with her personal underwriter status, because the securities were not acquired from the issuer or an affiliate (the securities are not restricted). However, if a purchaser from the control person sells to the public in a nonexempt transaction, the purchaser will be deemed to have acquired the securities from an affiliate of the issuer (*i.e.,* the control person) with a view to a distribution; *i.e.,* the purchaser will be deemed to be an underwriter.

1/ Avoiding sales to an underwriter [§716]

The most effective technique for avoiding sales to an underwriter is to extract from purchasers the same sorts of agreements limiting resales that are needed to exempt a sale of restricted securities (*see supra*). In addition, an investment letter should probably be obtained in which the purchaser states that she is purchasing for investment and not for resale.

(6) Restrictions on certain resales [§717]

As discussed above, sections 3(a)(9) (exempt exchange offers), 3(a)(10) (approved recapitalizations), and 3(a)(11) (intrastate offerings) are transaction exemptions. Thus, offerings pursuant to these sections, like those pursuant to section 4(2) (private offering), do not permit automatic resales of the securities without registration. Some exemption from the 1933 Act must be found for these subsequent transfers. The same is true for parties (and their affiliates) to rule 145 transactions. The "section 4(1½) exemption" can often be used for resales in these cases. The specific authorizations for resale given in connection with rule 147 offerings (*see supra,* §588) have already been discussed.

(7) Rule 144A—resales to "qualified institutional buyers" of privately placed securities [§718]

Rule 144A is designed to make restricted securities (*i.e.,* securities purchased in a nonpublic transaction) easier to resell in certain cases.

(a) Policy [§719]

The idea underlying rule 144A is that restrictions on resales are not needed as long as resales are made only to large and financially savvy institutions.

(b) Implementation [§720]

Like rule 144 (*see supra,* §§679-703), rule 144A provides that a person complying with its requirements will be deemed not to be engaged in a "distribution" and, therefore, will not be an "underwriter" under SA section 2(a)(11).

(c) Requirements [§721]

Rule 144A is available for resales if the following requirements are met:

1) Seller not an issuer [§722]

The rule is *not available to offers or sales by issuers.* [SA Rule 144A(b)] The rule is not intended to provide an exemption for primary distributions.

2) Offers and sales only to QIBs [§723]

Offers and sales are permitted under rule 144A only to *qualified institutional buyers ("QIBs")* or persons whom the seller reasonably believes to be QIBs.

a) Definition of "QIB" [§724]

QIBs include the entities typically regarded as "institutional investors" (*e.g.,* insurance companies, mutual funds, pension funds). A QIB must own and have investment discretion for at least *$100 million in securities* of unaffiliated issuers. [SA Rule 144A(a)(1)]

b) Establishing "reasonable belief" that buyer is a QIB [§725]

Rule 144A specifies several nonexclusive means by which a seller may establish a reasonable belief that the buyer is a QIB, including examination of the buyer's publicly available financial information and written certifications from executive officers of the buyer attesting that the buyer owns and invests a sufficient dollar amount in securities.

3) Notice to buyer [§726]

The seller must take reasonable steps to notify the buyer that the seller may be relying on the exemption provided by rule 144A. "Reasonable steps" are neither defined nor illustrated in the rule, but presumably written disclosure of this fact will suffice.

4) Securities sold are "non-fungible" [§727]

The securities sold under rule 144A must not be of the same class as securities listed on a United States stock exchange or quoted on NASDAQ. *Rationale:* Investors receive less disclosure—and potentially less protection—under Rule 144A than they would in a registered distribution. Therefore, securities sold under the rule should not be permitted to find their way into the hands of public investors without registration. Because rule 144A securities are of different classes than those traded publicly, the likelihood that rule 144A securities will find their way into the hands of the public is greatly diminished.

5) Disclosure [§728]

Rule 144A requires that some information about the issuer be made available to the buyer and seller.

a) Securities of 1934 Act reporting companies [§729]

If the issuer of the securities is a 1934 Act reporting company (*see supra*, §65) or one of a limited number of foreign issuers, no information need be provided. The information already publicly available under the 1934 Act is sufficient for the purposes of the rule.

b) Securities of nonreporting companies [§730]

If the issuer does not file reports under the 1934 Act, the issuer must provide certain basic information about itself. The information required includes a "very brief" statement of the nature of the issuer's business and the issuer's balance sheet, income statement, and retained earnings statement for the last three years (or shorter period that the issuer was in operation). The financial statements should be audited if that is reasonably possible.

EXAM TIP **gilbert**

If an exam fact pattern presents you with a securities holder who wants to resell restricted securities without being deemed an underwriter, be sure to consider the possibility of a sale under rule 144A. Rule 144A allows a *reseller* (not an issuer) to sell to *qualified institutional buyers* ("QIBs"), which are organizations with at least $100 million in investment discretion. The seller must take reasonable steps to notify the buyer that the seller is relying on the rule 144A exemption, and if the issuer does not file reports under the 1934 Act, the seller must get the issuer to provide some basic information, such as the nature of its business and a balance sheet, income statement, and statement of retained earnings for the past three years. Be sure to remember, however, that the securities to be sold may *not be of the same class as securities listed on a United States stock exchange* or quoted on NASDAQ.

(d) Resales do not destroy private placement exemptions [§731]

Rule 144A includes an express provision that the fact that purchasers of securities from the issuer may purchase with a view to reselling under rule 144A does not affect the availability to the issuer of the section 4(2) and regulation D exemptions under the 1933 Act. [SA Rule 144A, preliminary note 7]

1) Rationale

Recall that one of the concerns faced by an issuer in a private placement transaction is that resales by the original buyers may cause the exemption to be lost, because a buyer who buys from the issuer "with a view to distribution" may be deemed to be an underwriter. If this were applied to rule 144A transactions, the purpose of the rule—to facilitate resales of privately placed securities and thereby to attract investors to those securities—would be defeated.

(e) Securities sold under rule 144A are "restricted" [§732]

Finally, securities sold in accordance with rule 144A are not thereby transformed into unrestricted securities. Public distribution of such securities is conditioned on the availability of an exemption from registration.

(f) PORTAL—electronic market for rule 144A trading [§733]

To facilitate trading under rule 144A, the S.E.C. allowed the NASD to create an electronic market for rule 144A transactions. This market is (of course) open only to QIBs and trades only securities that qualify under rule 144A. PORTAL has been a success and has added considerable liquidity to the market for privately placed securities.

(8) Regulation S—unregistered offshore offers and sales [§734]

Regulation S clarifies that the registration requirements of the 1933 Act do not apply to offers and sales made outside the United States. The S.E.C.'s primary concern in drafting the complex provisions of regulation S is that securities distributed outside the United States might eventually end up in the hands of United States investors, and most of the regulation is designed to minimize the likelihood that an offering nominally conducted outside the United States is actually aimed at United States investors.

(a) Structure [§735]

Regulation S comprises rules 901 through 905 under the 1933 Act. *Rule 901* sets out the *general statement* of the regulation, namely that for the purposes of SA section 5, the terms "offer," "offer to sell," "sell," "sale," and "offer to buy" do not include offers and sales occurring outside the United States. *Rule 902* includes *definitions* applicable to the regulation. *Rule 903* sets forth a *safe harbor for issuers and distributors*; compliance with the regulation means the transaction will be deemed to occur outside the United States. *Rule 904* sets out a similar *safe harbor for resales* by persons other than issuers and distributors. Finally, rule 905 defines securities sold pursuant to Regulation S to be restricted.

1) Definition of "distributor" [§736]

"Distributor" is defined in regulation S as "any underwriter, dealer, or other person who participates, pursuant to a contractual arrangement, in the distribution of the securities" in question. [SA Rule 902(d)]

2) Definition of "substantial United States market interest" [§737]

The conditions that must be met for the issuer's safe harbor depend, in part, on whether there is a "substantial United States market interest" in the securities. This term is defined in rule 902(j). Under the rule, the existence of a substantial U.S. market interest depends on the relative size of the U.S. market compared to the world market for the securities.

(b) General conditions [§738]

To take advantage of the regulation S safe harbor, two conditions must be met:

1) Offshore transaction [§739]

The offer or sale must be made in an offshore transaction (defined in rule 902 essentially as a transaction in which the buyer is outside the United States at the time the buy order is placed, and the execution of the transaction and delivery of the securities takes place outside the United States).

2) No United States directed selling efforts [§740]

In addition, directed selling efforts in the United States are prohibited. United States directed selling efforts are activities that are intended to, or could reasonably be expected to, result in conditioning the market in the United States for the securities offered. (*See supra*, §132, for a discussion of conditioning the market.)

(c) Issuer's and distributor's safe harbor [§741]

The safe harbor for issuers and distributors is divided into three categories, depending on the nature of the securities offered, the issuer's status as a 1934 Act reporting company, and the degree of United States market interest in the securities offered. The category into which an offering falls determines which, if any, additional conditions must be met for the safe harbor to apply.

1) Category 1—foreign issuers, certain debt offerings by domestic issuers, certain employee benefit plans [§742]

Category 1 securities are subject to no requirements other than the general requirements set forth above. The following are the Category 1 securities:

a) Securities of foreign issuers as to which there is no "substantial United States market interest" (*see supra*, §737);

b) Securities of foreign issuers directed into a single country other than the United States;

c) Debt securities of United States issuers that are denominated in a foreign currency and the offering of which is directed into a single country other than the United States;

d) Securities backed by the full faith and credit of a foreign government; and

e) Securities offered and sold to employees pursuant to a foreign employee benefit plan.

2) Category 2—foreign issuers not eligible for category 1 [§743]

If there is a substantial United States market interest in the securities, issuers of equity securities that are 1934 Act reporting companies and issuers of debt securities must comply with a set of requirements under the regulation, including placing legends on the offering documents and adherence to a "distribution compliance period" of 40 days, during which no offers or sales to United States persons are permitted.

3) Category 3—all other offerings [§744]

The final category applies to all other offerings. The requirements in this category are the most onerous, including a distribution compliance period of 40 days for debt offerings and one year for equity offerings, stop-transfer procedures for equity offerings, and certifications from buyers that they are not buying for the account of a United States person.

(d) Resale safe harbor [§745]

The resale safe harbor is available to persons other than the issuer or a distributor of the securities. Affiliates and persons acting on behalf of the issuer or a distributor likewise cannot use the resale safe harbor, but affiliates who are such solely because they are officers or directors of the issuer may use the safe harbor as long as no compensation other than a normal broker's commission is paid in connection with the transaction. In most cases, only the two general regulation S requirements (*see* above) must be met in the case of resales.

(e) Exemption only from registration requirement [§746]

While regulation S exempts certain transactions from the registration requirements of SA section 5, the other provisions of the 1933 and 1934 Acts still apply. Thus, for example, while the amount of disclosure required under regulation S is small, the issuer remains potentially liable for violating the antifraud or other liability provisions of the Acts.

G. Liabilities Under the 1933 Act

1. Introduction [§747]

The liability provisions of the 1933 Act are organized around the two basic objectives of the Act: providing full disclosure of material information to potential investors in newly issued securities and generally preventing fraud and/or misrepresentation in the interstate sale of securities.

a. Conduct resulting in liability [§748]

Accordingly, the kinds of conduct that may result in liability under the 1933 Act may be sorted broadly into two categories:

(1) Liability for improper disclosure or violation of section 5 registration provisions [§749]

Section 11 of the 1933 Act provides for liability where the issuer misrepresents or fails to state a material fact in the registration statement. In addition, liability may arise under section 12(a)(1) of the Act as the result of an improper offer in the pre-filing period (*see supra*, §127);

failure to deliver the required prospectus in the post-effective period (*see supra*, §224); or other violations of section 5.

(2) Liability for fraud or misrepresentation in general [§750]

In addition to the above, the 1933 Act includes liability provisions covering fraud or misrepresentation in the interstate sale of securities in general (*i.e.*, whether or not registration with the S.E.C. is involved). [SA §§12(a)(2), 17; *and see* discussion *infra*, §§833, 857]

b. Remedies for 1933 Act violations [§751]

A wide range of remedies is available in actions under the 1933 Act, depending in the first instance on the nature of the plaintiff. That is, there are different remedies available to the S.E.C. than are available to a private plaintiff (*e.g.*, an aggrieved investor).

(1) Private lawsuits [§752]

When investors sue under the 1933 Act, they are typically looking to receive payment in compensation for what has turned out to be a bad investment. This may be accomplished in two ways:

(a) Damages [§753]

A plaintiff entitled to receive damages does not receive the full amount invested in the securities, but rather receives the amount lost (subject to certain limitations). Section 11 of the 1933 Act, discussed below, gives purchasers the right to receive damages.

(b) Rescission [§754]

A plaintiff receiving rescission gets back the full amount invested in the securities. In effect, the sale is reversed, the plaintiff returns the securities and gets back her cash. Section 12(a)(1) and (2) of the 1933 Act, discussed below, give purchasers the right to rescission.

(2) S.E.C. lawsuits [§755]

The S.E.C., as part of its enforcement responsibility, may sue persons alleged to have violated the 1933 Act. (Enforcement actions by the S.E.C. are discussed in more detail *infra*, §§1673 *et seq.*) In such an action, the S.E.C. has several kinds of remedies available:

(a) Cease-and-desist orders [§756]

Cease-and-desist orders resemble injunctions, in that each directs the respondent to stop violating the Act.

1) Distinguish—injunctions [§757]

There are some important differences between cease-and-desist orders and injunctions, including the following:

a) The cease-and-desist order is issued administratively, *i.e., by the S.E.C. itself,* while an injunction is issued by a federal district judge;

b) Violation of a cease-and-desist order may result in a *civil monetary penalty* under 1933 Act section 20(d), while violation of an injunction may lead to a contempt proceeding; and

c) The S.E.C. can obtain a cease-and-desist order *without the need to show that future violations of the securities laws are likely,* while an injunction requires such a showing.

2) Types of orders [§758]

There are two kinds of cease-and-desist orders: temporary and permanent.

a) Temporary orders [§759]

Temporary cease-and-desist orders may be issued against *broker-dealers, investment advisers, investment companies,* and certain other regulated entities. [SA §8A(c)(2)]

1/ Note

The temporary cease-and-desist order *may be issued ex parte—i.e.,* without notice to the respondent or a hearing—if the S.E.C. deems it appropriate.

b) Permanent order [§760]

Permanent cease-and-desist orders may be issued against anyone violating the 1933 Act. Notice must be given to the respondent, who is also entitled to a hearing before an administrative law judge. [SA §8A(a)]

3) Order for an accounting and disgorgement [§761]

In connection with a proceeding for a permanent cease-and-desist order, the S.E.C. may also order the respondent to furnish an accounting and to disgorge any monies received in violation of the 1933 Act, including reasonable interest. [SA §8A(e)]

(b) Injunctive relief [§762]

Section 20(a) of the 1933 Act authorizes the S.E.C. to conduct investigations into possible violations of the Act. Section 20(b) gives the S.E.C. the power to seek injunctive relief from the federal courts whenever it appears that the Act or the rules thereunder have been or are about to be violated.

1) Civil fines available in injunctive actions [§763]

In addition to obtaining an injunction against future violations of the securities laws, the S.E.C. has the authority, in connection with any injunctive action, to seek civil monetary penalties. [*See* SA §20(d), SEA §21(d)(3)]

a) Amount of penalty [§764]
The penalties that can be imposed are:

1/ Up to the greater of (i) $5,000 ($50,000 for corporations) for each violation, or (ii) the gross amount of pecuniary gain to the defendant;

2/ Up to the greater of (i) $50,000 per violation ($250,000 for corporations), or (ii) the gross amount of pecuniary gain to the defendant for fraud, deceit, manipulation, or deliberate or reckless disregard of a regulatory requirement; and

3/ Up to the greater of (i) $100,000 per violation ($500,000 for corporations), or (ii) the gross amount of pecuniary gain to the defendant if the violation meets the requirements of 2/, above, and in addition directly or indirectly caused substantial losses or created a significant risk of substantial losses to other persons.

(c) Criminal sanctions [§765]
Section 24 of the 1933 Act imposes criminal penalties upon conviction of a *willful violation of any of the provisions* of the 1933 Act, including violation of section 17(a), the general fraud provision of the 1933 Act. (*See infra,* §§854 *et seq.*) "Willful" violation of section 17(a) means that the defendant had the intent to defraud or that he made representations without knowing whether or not they were true. It need not be shown that the defendant knew that a "security" (as defined by the 1933 Act) was being sold or that defendant knew he was violating some specific provision of the securities laws. [**United States v. Brown,** 578 F.2d 1280 (9th Cir. 1978)]

EXAM TIP   **gilbert**

If an exam question involves a person criminally charged under section 24 of the 1933 Act, remember that it is *not a defense* that the person did not know that the thing fraudulently sold was a security or that the sale violated the 1933 Act. The defendant need *only have intentionally defrauded* a victim or made representations *without knowing whether they were truthful*. Remember also that a willful violation of section 5 (*e.g.,* failure to register offers of securities) can also be a criminal violation.

REMEDIES UNDER THE 1933 ACT—A SUMMARY	gilbert
PRIVATE REMEDIES	**S.E.C. REMEDIES**
Damages equal to the amount lost by plaintiff. *Rescission*.	*Cease-and-desist orders* (temporary or permanent) issued by the S.E.C. requiring the defendant to stop violating the 1933 Act and, if the order is permanent, to disgorge any monies received in violation of the Act. *Injunctions* issued by a federal court prohibiting future violations of the 1933 Act; the injunction may include award of a civil monetary penalty. *Criminal sanctions* issued by a federal court for willful violation of the 1933 Act.

c. Comparison of 1933 Act anti-fraud provisions with common law fraud remedies

(1) Elements of common law action [§766]

At common law, a defrauded purchaser of securities had to prove the same elements to recover as any other defrauded purchaser of goods:

(a) Material fact [§767]

The plaintiff had to show that the defendant seller of the securities misstated, or failed to state, a *material fact* that the seller was under a duty to disclose.

(b) Reliance [§768]

In addition, the plaintiff had to show that she relied on the misrepresentation.

(c) Privity [§769]

The plaintiff also had to show that there was privity of contract between her and the defendant (*i.e.*, that plaintiff had purchased the security from the specific seller being sued).

(d) Causation [§770]

Also, the plaintiff had to show that the defendant's misrepresentation was the actual and the proximate cause of the plaintiff's loss.

(e) Scienter [§771]

Finally, the defendant had to have had actual knowledge of the misrepresentation or omission; *i.e.*, the defendant's misrepresentation must have been intentional.

(2) Lesser burden under 1933 Act [§772]

In general, the liability provisions of the 1933 Act are less demanding on defrauded purchasers than was the common law. The 1933 Act makes recovery easier for purchasers of securities by lightening the burden of proof they must carry with respect to the above elements (*see infra*, §§783 *et seq.*).

2. Express Civil Liabilities

a. Introduction [§773]

The 1933 Act contains three express liability provisions. With the exception of section 11 (for material misstatements in an effective registration statement), none of these historically has been of major importance. The reason for this is that plaintiffs have preferred an action under rule 10b-5 of the 1934 Act (*see infra*, §§932 *et seq.*) or some other *implied* civil liability provision. Courts generally held that these implied civil liabilities were subject to fewer restrictions than the actions under one of the express liability sections. However, these express liability provisions have become more important recently because the Supreme Court increasingly has restricted the availability of causes of action under rule 10b-5 and has held that no implied civil liability will arise merely as the result of a violation of some section of the statutes or an S.E.C. rule. (*See infra*, §922.)

b. Section 11—liability for misstatements or omissions in registration statement or prospectus [§774]

Section 11 of the 1933 Act imposes liability on designated persons for materially false or misleading statements or omissions in an effective registration statement or prospectus. [*See* SA §11(a)]

(1) Free writing prospectus not part of registration statement [§775]

A free writing prospectus (*see supra*, §§161 *et seq.*) is not part of the registration statement for an offering. Consequently, SA section 11 does not apply to statements made in a free writing prospectus. [*See* SA Rule 433(d)(1)]

(2) Persons subject to liability [§776]

The following persons can be held liable under section 11 for material misstatements in the registration statement or prospectus:

(a) Every person who signs the registration statement [§777]

Every person who signs a registration statement can be held liable for material misstatements or omissions in the statement. The following persons *must* sign the registration statement:

(i) *The issuer;*

(ii) *The principal executive officers* of the issuer;

(iii) *The principal financial officer* of the issuer;

(iv) *The comptroller or principal accounting officer* of the issuer; and

(v) *A majority of the members of the board of directors* of the issuer.

[SA §6(a)]

(b) Every director of the issuer [§778]

Every person who was a director of the issuer at the time the registration statement became effective can also be held liable, even if the director did not sign the registration statement.

(c) Every person named as "about to become" a director [§779]

In addition, every person who is named in the registration statement (with his consent) as about to become a director of the issuer may be held liable.

(d) Every "expert" who certifies preparation of registration statement [§780]

All "experts" who consent to being named as having prepared or certified part of the registration statement may be held liable under section 11. For example, accountants are "experts" as to the certified financial statements included in the registration statement.

(e) Every underwriter involved in the distribution [§781]

Underwriters may also be held liable under section 11.

(f) Control persons [§782]

Finally, persons who "control" any person who is liable under section 11 may be held jointly and severally liable with the liable persons, unless the controlling person had no knowledge of nor reasonable grounds to believe in the existence of the facts on which the liability of the controlled person is alleged to rest. [*See* SA §15]

(3) Elements of plaintiff's cause of action

(a) Material misstatements or omissions [§783]

To recover damages under section 11, the plaintiff must prove that there has been a misstatement of, or a failure to state, a "material" fact. [*See* SA §11(a)]

1) Definition of "material" [§784]

Material facts here are those matters to which there is a substantial likelihood that a reasonable investor would attach importance in deciding whether to purchase the registered security.

[SA Rule 405] Other tests for "materiality" are discussed *in-fra*, §§973-975.

2) Judicial expansion of definition [§785]

The rule 405 definition has been elaborated on by the courts, which have held that a fact is material when it is ***more probable than not*** that a significant number of traders in the security would have wanted to know it before deciding to deal in the security. [**Feit v. Leasco Data Processing Equipment Corp.**, 332 F. Supp. 544 (E.D.N.Y. 1971)]

---

e.g. **Example—material facts:** A Corp. decided to acquire B Corp. through an exchange of A's securities made directly with B's shareholders. However, A failed to disclose that a major reason for acquiring the target company (B) was the amount of surplus cash that could be drained from B into A. A's failure to make this disclosure and to disclose the estimated amount of such cash (when estimates were known or could have been obtained from B's management) were held to be material omissions. [*See* **Feit v. Leasco Data Processing Equipment Corp.**, *supra*]

(b) Limited reliance requirement [§786]

In general, the plaintiff need ***not*** prove that she purchased in reliance on the misstatement to recover.

1) Exception—after-acquired securities [§787]

However, if the issuer sends out an earnings statement covering the period of one year after the effective date of the registration statement, a person thereafter acquiring some of the registered securities must prove reliance on the misrepresentation or omission to recover. [SA §11(a)]

a) But note

The plaintiff need not actually have read the registration statement to prove reliance. It is sufficient that she relied on secondary sources that repeated the misstatement.

b) And note

If any post-effective amendments are filed, the one-year period will run from ***their*** filing date rather than the filing date of the original registration statement.

(c) Secondary market purchasers [§788]

The language of 1933 Act section 11 provides a cause of action to "any person acquiring" the security that was the subject of the defective registration statement. Most courts interpret this to mean that even persons who purchased a security in the secondary market (as opposed to those who purchased the security in the issuer's public offering) can recover under section 11, as long as they can prove that the specific securities purchased were issued in the offering registered by the defective registration statement (a procedure called "tracing" the securities). [*See, e.g.,* **Hertzberg v. Dignity Partners, Inc.,** 191 F.3d 1076 (9th Cir. 1999)]

1) Privity of contract not required [§789]

Privity of contract with the defendant is not required under section 11; *i.e.,* a purchaser with standing may sue any person described by the statute as a potential defendant.

(d) Causation and damages [§790]

The plaintiff need *not* prove that her loss (*i.e.,* decline in value of the securities) was caused by the misrepresentation.

1) Reduction of damages [§791]

However, the *defendant* may be able to reduce the damages by proving that all or some portion of the damages resulted from some cause other than the misrepresentation or omission of material fact in the registration statement. [SA §11(e)]

Example: A court has taken into account a general decline in stock market prices after the date plaintiff purchased the issuer's stock, and allowed the defendant issuer a discount in damages equal to the percentage decline in the Standard and Poor's index of stock market prices. [**Feit v. Leasco Data Processing Equipment Corp.,** *supra,* §785]

Example: Another court sustained a loss causation defense when the defendant's misstatement was "barely material," and the price of the security actually increased somewhat upon public disclosure of the misstatement. [**Akerman v. Oryx Communications, Inc.,** 810 F.2d 336 (2d Cir. 1987)]

(4) Defenses

(a) General affirmative defenses [§792]

Any defendant (*including* the issuer) subject to liability under section 11 may claim the following defenses [SA §11(a)]:

1) *That the alleged false statements were actually true;*

2) *That the misstatements or omissions were not of material facts;*

3) *That the plaintiff-purchaser knew* of the misleading statements or omissions and invested in the securities anyway; and

4) *That the statute of limitations has run.* Under section 11, the period of limitations is one year after discovery of the false statement, with an overall limitation of three years after the security is first bona fide offered to the public. [*See* SA §13] This means that if a portion of the issue remains unsold after three years, for example in a continuous offering, purchasers after that time are not protected by section 11 of the Act.

(b) **Due diligence defense—experts and nonexperts [§793]**

In addition to the above defenses, all defendants (*except* issuers) have a "due diligence" defense under section 11. In applying this "due diligence" defense, section 11 makes a distinction between "experts," *i.e.,* those who certify part of the registration statement as being true (such as certified public accountants who certify that the financial statements were prepared according to generally accepted accounting principles), and "nonexperts," or all others who may be held liable pursuant to section 11. (*See supra,* §§776-782.) Section 11 also draws a distinction between the standard of care (*i.e.,* what constitutes due diligence) required of nonexperts who review material prepared by other nonexperts, and that required of nonexperts reviewing statements of experts. [*See* SA §11(a)]

1) **Statements made by experts [§794]**

To avoid liability under section 11, experts may demonstrate that they have met the following test of "due diligence" as to representations they made in the registration statement:

a) *That they actually believed that the statements they made were true;* and

b) *That their belief was reasonable.*

1/ *For their belief to be reasonable*, the experts must have made a *reasonable investigation* into the facts supporting the statements made. Normally, this means that they must at least have performed up to the standards of their profession (*e.g.,* accountants must make an investigation of the facts that would conform to the standards of their profession and must state the issuer's financial results according to the generally accepted accounting principles set forth by the S.E.C.). [*See* **Escott v. BarChris Construction Corp.,** 283 F. Supp. 643 (S.D.N.Y. 1968)]

2/ While compliance with professional standards (*e.g.,* by an accountant) establishes a reasonable investigation, it does not automatically shield the professional from liability. For example, an accountant who conducts an investigation in accordance with GAAP (generally accepted accounting principles) and GAAS (generally accepted auditing standards) would still be liable under section 11 if she consciously chose not to disclose a known material fact on a registration statement. [**Monroe v. Hughes**, 31 F.3d 772 (9th Cir. 1994)]

2) Statements made by nonexperts [§795]

"Nonexperts" who make statements that appear in the registration statement are held to the same standard of "due diligence" as experts. Thus, nonexperts must actually believe that the statements made were true and their belief must be reasonable—*i.e.,* based on a reasonable investigation of the facts.

a) Test for reasonable investigation by nonexperts [§796]

Under section 11, the test for defining the scope of a "reasonable investigation" is *what a prudent person would do* in the management of her own affairs. [*See* SA §11(c)]

1/ No single standard

As a practical matter, however, there is no single standard. The court looks at each individual defendant and, based on the person's position with the issuer, responsibilities relative to the issuer and the registration statement, and background, skills, training, and access to information, the court determines what the person should have done to fulfill the obligation of a "reasonable investigation." In other words, the test is really what kind of investigation a prudent person *in the defendant's position*, with the same responsibilities, skills, etc., would have made. [**Escott v. BarChris Construction Corp.,** *supra*]

b) Application—attorney drafting registration statement [§797]

An attorney who is also a member of the issuer's board of directors and who drafts the issuer's registration statement (and collects facts from the issuer to do so) does not "certify" his work and thus is a "nonexpert" as to the registration statement in general. [**Escott v. BarChris Construction Corp.**, *supra*]

1/ Reasonable investigation by attorney [§798]

In *BarChris*, the court indicated that the attorney-director did not have to conduct an independent audit of the issuer, but that a reasonable investigation would go beyond merely trusting the opinions and responses of the issuer's officers as to material facts. Therefore, a reasonable investigation by the attorney would include:

a/ Looking at original written records (*e.g.*, written contracts) to verify statements in the registration statement;

b/ An examination of the issuer's facilities, operations, material contracts, corporate minutes and other documents, and major items important to its financial condition;

c/ Use of a comprehensive questionnaire for directors and officers to elicit information required to be disclosed (such as whether they had any conflicting interests); and

d/ Having an accountant check any suspicious items disclosed by the lawyer's investigation.

2/ Distinguish—drafting attorney as corporate insider [§799]

Note that if the lawyer drafting the registration statement becomes so involved with the issuer and the registration that he is held to be a "corporate insider" (like the other management officers), he will then be held to the same high standard of diligence as other officers (*see infra*, §804). [**Feit v. Leasco Data Processing Equipment Corp.**, *supra*, §791]

3/ Other attorneys as experts [§800]

It is also conceivable that an attorney might be requested to certify (as an expert) some portion of the registration statement. In this case, the attorney would be held to the due diligence standard of an expert (*supra*, §794).

EXAM TIP	gilbert

Don't let professional pride sway you on your exam. Remember that an accountant is considered an "expert" under rule 11—and so is held to the expert's standard of due diligence. An attorney who drafts the registration statement is **not considered an expert**. The difference lies in their jobs: The accountant **certifies** that financial statements were prepared in a certain way, while the drafting attorney makes no such certification.

3) Nonexperts reviewing statements by other nonexperts [§801]

A nonexpert not involved in the actual drafting of the registration statement (such as a member of the issuer's board of directors) may also be potentially liable under the 1933 Act for statements made in the registration statement by other nonexperts. To avoid such liability, the nonexpert must show that she exercised due diligence appropriate to her position in reviewing the statements made by other nonexperts.

a) Standard of diligence required [§802]

The standard of diligence required for nonexpert reviewers is the same as for nonexperts concerning their own representations in the registration statement (*see supra*, §795).

b) Application

1/ Underwriters [§803]

Underwriters qualify as nonexperts and so must make a reasonable investigation of the *nonexpert* portions of the registration statement. They cannot simply rely on assurances of accuracy from the issuer's management, attorneys, etc. [*See* **Escott v. BarChris Construction Corp.**, *supra*, §797]

a/ Note that normally the "lead underwriter" (usually the underwriting firm that first established contact with the issuer, and which structures and manages the underwriting for all of the other underwriting firms) will conduct an investigation of the issuer for all members of the underwriting syndicate to satisfy the due diligence requirement. However, if the lead underwriter conducts a faulty investigation, this does *not* absolve the other underwriters.

b/ The S.E.C. has stated that a participating underwriter must be satisfied that the managing underwriter has made the kind of investigation

that the participant would have performed if it had been the manager. [*See* SA Release No. 33-5275 (1972)]

2/ Inside directors and executive officers [§804]

The standard of diligence imposed on directors who are also part of management (*i.e.*, officers of the issuer) and on the principal executive officers of the issuer is even higher than that imposed on underwriters.

a/ Not all of the inside directors and executive officers will be required to do the same things to show due diligence. What is required of each depends on the person's position, access to information about the offering, etc.

b/ However, it is clear that these persons are virtual *guarantors* of the accuracy of the registration statement, and it will be difficult for them to escape responsibility for material misstatements. [*See* **Feit v. Leasco Data Processing Equipment Corp.**, *supra*, §799] For example, if there are misstatements made relating to the issuer's financial condition, the issuer's chief financial officer will have a hard time sustaining his burden of showing that he really did not know of the misrepresentations. [*See* **Escott v. BarChris Construction Corp.**, *supra*]

3/ Outside directors [§805]

Outside directors (those who are not employed by the issuer as part of management) must also meet the due diligence test for nonexperts. However, their position differs from inside directors in that although they must discharge the duty of a director, they cannot realistically be expected to do a great deal to check on the accuracy of the registration statement. Thus, the issue is how extensive is the duty of an outside director?

a/ It appears from the cases that outside directors will probably be expected to attend directors' meetings during the time registration is underway and will also be held responsible for reading directors' meeting minutes, reading the drafts of the registration statement before filing and, in a general way, questioning company management, accountants, and legal counsel. [*See* **Weinberger v. Jackson**, 1990 WL 260676 (N.D. Cal. 1990)] But if this investigation turns up apparent misstatements, the directors must personally check into these matters and require company counsel to check into them. [**Escott v. BarChris Construction Corp.**, *supra*—holding liable two directors who failed to read the registration statement and one who gave it only a cursory review]

b/ Note again that what is actually expected of any specific director will depend in part on his background and familiarity with the registration process. For example, a lawyer-director might be expected to make a more extensive investigation than a doctor-director. [*See* **Escott v. BarChris Construction Corp.**, *supra*]

4) **Nonexperts reviewing statements made by experts [§806]**
Nonexperts (such as outside directors) are held to a lower standard of care when reviewing statements made by experts than when reviewing statements made by other nonexperts.

a) **Normally no investigation required [§807]**
Because nonexperts are entitled to rely on statements made by experts, in most cases *no investigation need be made by the nonexpert.* Rather, the reviewing nonexpert need only show that he did not believe the statements made by the expert to be false and that he had no reasonable ground to believe they were false.

b) **Burden generally met [§808]**
Nonexpert defendants usually will be able to meet this burden of proof. For example, in the *BarChris* case, most of the nonexperts were held not liable for misrepresentations made by the issuer's expert accountants.

c) **When investigation is required [§809]**
However, if facts suggest that the portions of the registration statement supplied by experts contain misstatements, the underwriters must make a reasonable investigation. [*In re* **Software Toolworks, Inc.**, 50 F.3d 615 (9th Cir. 1994)]

gilbert

PARTY	STANDARD	HOW MET
EXPERTS	Actual and reasonable belief that statement was true	Requires reasonable investigation into facts, generally performed up to the standards of the profession.
NONEXPERTS REVIEWING STATEMENTS OF OTHER NONEXPERTS	Actual and reasonable belief that statement was true	*General standard:* What a prudent person would do in the management of her own affairs.
• **UNDERWRITERS**		Lead underwriter must conduct a reasonable investigation; other underwriters must be satisfied that the lead underwriter made such an investigation.
• **INSIDE DIRECTORS/ MANAGERS**		Virtual guarantors of the accuracy of the registration statement; probably liable no matter how diligent.
• **OUTSIDE DIRECTORS**		Must attend directors' meetings during registration process; read minutes of meeting, registration drafts, etc.
NONEXPERTS REVIEWING STATEMENTS OF EXPERTS	No actual belief that statement was false and no reason to believe it was false	Generally, nonexperts are entitled to rely on statements of experts, so no investigation is required unless facts show a potential problem.

> **e.g. Example:** In *Software Toolworks, supra*, the underwriters discovered a memo raising doubt as to whether the issuer was properly recognizing revenue. The underwriters confronted the issuer's accountants, who had approved the revenue recognition, demanded from the accountants reconfirmation in writing that the revenue recognition was appropriate, and contacted other accounting firms to verify the revenue accounting used by the issuer. The court held that the underwriters' investigation was reasonable.

(5) Measure of damages [§810]

Where the plaintiff proves that there was a material misrepresentation or omission in the registration statement and that the securities purchased are traceable to the registered offering, the plaintiff can recover any damages suffered as a result of a decline in value of the securities. [*See* SA §11(e)]

(a) If the stock is sold prior to filing suit [§811]

If the stock is sold prior to the filing of a lawsuit, the plaintiff may recover the difference between the price she paid for the stock (but not exceeding the price at which the security was offered to the public) and the price at which it was sold prior to suit.

> **e.g. Example:** X bought stock in a registered offering for $10; she sold it for $6 prior to filing suit, and it was selling at $5 at the time of the suit. X can recover only $4 per share (the difference between the price paid and the price at which she sold).

(b) If the stock has not been sold prior to suit [§812]

If the stock has not been sold prior to the suit, the purchaser may recover either:

(i) *The difference* between the price she paid (not exceeding the offering price) and the value of the security *at the time the suit is filed;* or

(ii) *The price at which the stock was sold after the suit was filed but before judgment,* if such damages are less than those that result from using the value at the time the suit was filed.

[SA §11(e)]

(c) Determining value [§813]

If a court is required to determine the value of the issuer's securities at the time of the suit, it may consider various factors besides the actual market value. For example, it may adjust market value to account for "panic selling" then taking place, which may depreciate the securities beyond their normal investment value. [**Beecher v. Able,** 435 F. Supp. 397 (S.D.N.Y. 1975)]

(d) Plaintiff not required to mitigate damages [§814]

If the plaintiff buys securities that decline in value due to misrepresentations made in the registration statement and then files suit, she need not sell the securities to mitigate damages just because the market price begins to rise.

---

e.g. **Example:** A buys debentures at $100 each. They decline to $75 at the time of the suit, rise to $100 while the suit is going on, but decline again to $70 just before judgment (at which time the plaintiff sells). The plaintiff's damages are measured by the difference in the price she paid ($100) and the value at the time the suit was filed ($75). [**Beecher v. Able,** *supra; and see* SA §11(e)(3)]

(e) Limits on recovered amount

1) Offering price as ceiling [§815]

In no case can the amount recovered exceed the price at which the security was offered to the public. [SA §11(g)]

2) Liability of underwriter [§816]

Also, the total liability of an underwriter cannot exceed the offering price of the securities that the underwriter sold to the public. [SA §11(e)]

3) Loss causation defense [§817]

Finally, the defendant is not liable for damages that are proven to result from factors other than the misstatement in the registration statement. (*See supra,* §§790 *et seq.*)

(f) Joint and several liability—contribution [§818]

All persons (except outside directors) who are liable under section 11(a) are jointly and severally liable, and every person who becomes liable to make any payment under section 11 may recover contribution from any person who, if had they been sued would have been liable, unless the person who has become liable was guilty of fraudulent misrepresentation and the person who has not become liable was not. [*See* SA §11(f)]

1) Exception—outside directors [§819]

In actions brought under SA section 11, outside directors of the issuer are liable:

(i) *Jointly and severally for knowing violations* of section 11; and

(ii) *Proportionately to their respective degrees of fault for all other violations* of section 11.

[SA §11(f)(2); SEA §§21D(f)(5), (f)(10)(C)(ii)]

c. **Section 12(a)(1)—liability for offers or sales in violation of section 5 [§820]**

Section 12(a)(1) provides that any person who offers or sells a security in violation of any of the provisions of section 5 of the 1933 Act shall be liable to the purchaser for: (i) the *consideration paid* (with interest) less the amount of any income received on the securities (*i.e.*, a suit for rescission); or (ii) for *damages* if the purchaser no longer owns the security.

(1) Liability for any violation of section 5 [§821]

Liability under section 12(a)(1) is absolute for any violation of any provision of section 5. Such violations include a sale of unregistered securities, failure to deliver the required prospectus, making an illegal offer in the pre-filing period, etc. (*See supra,* §§118 *et seq.*)

(a) Control persons [§822]

Persons who "control" any person liable under section 12(a)(1) may be held jointly and severally liable with the controlled person, unless the controlling person had no knowledge of, or reasonable grounds to believe in, the existence of the facts on which the liability of the controlled person is alleged to rest. [SA §15]

(b) Participant liability [§823]

Section 12(a)(1) imposes liability on those who offer or sell a security in violation of section 5. But the 1933 Act nowhere says who may, for these purposes, be regarded as a statutory "seller" (or offeror). Clearly the person who passes title to the security is a seller, but may anyone else be regarded as a "seller" for purposes of section 12(a)(1)? Courts were in conflict over this question until 1988, when the Supreme Court decided **Pinter v. Dahl**, 486 U.S. 622 (1988).

1) Facts of *Pinter* [§824]

Pinter, an oil and gas operator and securities broker, sold unregistered oil and gas interests to Dahl in an attempted private placement. Later, Dahl solicited some of his friends to purchase additional interests, because Dahl believed the interests were good investments. Pinter sold the interests to Dahl's friends on the strength of Dahl's representations that the friends qualified as private placement investors. It turned out that the friends were not qualified private placement investors, and when the investment became worthless, Dahl and his friends sued under section 12(a)(1). Pinter counterclaimed, alleging, among other things, that Dahl was a "seller" under section 12(a)(1) and therefore that Dahl was required to contribute toward the amounts awarded the other plaintiffs.

2) Definition of "seller" [§825]
The Supreme Court held in *Pinter* that a "seller" for section 12(a)(1) purposes includes:

a) The *person who actually passes title* to the security; and

b) *Persons who solicit the purchase* from the purchaser.

3) Persons who are not sellers [§826]
Under *Pinter*, however, the term "seller" does not include persons whose sole motivation in acting is to benefit the buyer.

(2) Defenses to a section 12(a)(1) cause of action

(a) No sale of a "security" [§827]
One defense to a section 12(a)(1) cause of action is to prove that there was no offer or sale of a "security" as that term is defined in the 1933 Act. (*See* discussion *supra,* §§118 *et seq.*)

(b) No violation of section 5 [§828]
Another defense is that no violation of section 5 ever occurred (*i.e.,* the offering of securities was exempt from the registration provisions of section 5 of the 1933 Act).

(c) No privity [§829]
Unlike section 11, section 12(a)(1) imposes a condition of privity of contract between the plaintiff-purchaser and the seller-defendant. Therefore, a common defense to a section 12(a)(1) action is that no privity of contract existed.

Example: Issuer sold to A, who resold to B, who resold to C (a broker), who resold to the plaintiff. Because the plaintiff is in privity only with C, C is the only person against whom the plaintiff can bring a section 12(a)(1) action. Consequently, if C were found not to have violated section 5 (even though A and B had committed violations), plaintiff could not sustain a section 12(a)(1) action. [**Winter v. D.J. & M. Investment & Construction Corp.,** 185 F. Supp. 943 (S.D. Cal. 1960)]

---

1) Persons soliciting may be in privity [§830]

Remember, however, that persons who solicit the plaintiff's purchase, although they do not actually pass title to the security, are nevertheless held to be "sellers." (*See supra,* §825.)

(d) Statute of limitations [§831]

As under section 11, the period of limitations is one year after the violation, but in no event more than three years after the security was bona fide offered to the public. As above, if a portion of the issue is sold after three years from the first bona fide offer to the public, section 12(a)(1) is unavailable.

1) Note—laches may not be available [§832]

One court has held that laches (an equitable counterpart to the statute of limitations that evaluates staleness of a claim in terms of the prejudice caused by a knowing delay in bringing a suit, rather than by the mere passage of time) is *not* a defense in a section 12(a)(1) action where the period of limitations has not yet run. [**Straley v. Universal Uranium & Milling Corp.,** 289 F.2d 370 (9th Cir. 1961)]

d. Section 12(a)(2)—general civil liability under the Act [§833]

The 1933 Act generally prohibits fraud in the interstate offer or sale of securities. Section 12(a)(2) of the Act provides that any person:

(i) Who offers for sale a security (whether or not exempted from the registration requirements of section 5, except for certain government and bank securities) by the *use of any means of interstate commerce;*

(ii) By means of a prospectus or oral communication that contains an *untrue statement or omission of material fact* (the purchaser not knowing of such untruth or omission); and

(iii) Who *cannot sustain the burden of proof* that he did not know and in the exercise of reasonable care could not have known of the untruth

is liable to the purchaser of the security. [*See* SA §12(a)(2)]

(1) Scope of section 12(a)(2) actions [§834]

Except with respect to securities exempt under section 3(a)(2) (certain government and bank securities), section 12(a)(2) applies whether or not the securities were registered pursuant to section 5 of the Act, whether or not they were offered under an exemption from the Act, and whether the securities were offered in writing or orally.

> **e.g.** **Example:** If XYZ Corp. makes an offering of its securities, section 12(a)(2) applies to any misrepresentations made by XYZ, whether the offering is registered or unregistered (*i.e.,* even though XYZ uses an exemption from registration, such as the private offering exemption).

(2) Plaintiff's cause of action [§835]

A buyer bringing a section 12(a)(2) action may sue for *rescission* to recover the consideration paid for the securities, plus interest, and less any income received; or for *damages*, if the securities have already been sold. In either case, the plaintiff must show the following:

(a) Sale of a security [§836]

The plaintiff must prove that there has been an offer or sale of a "security" as that term is defined in the 1933 Act (*see supra,* §131).

(b) Use of jurisdictional means [§837]

The language of section 12(a)(2) limits liability to persons "who offer or sell securities by the use of any means or instruments of transportation or communication in interstate commerce or the mails."

1) Note

Most decisions have indicated that this requirement is satisfied if any part of the sale (including delivery after the sale) involves such means. [*See, e.g.,* **Wigand v. Flo-Tek, Inc.,** 609 F.2d 1028 (2d Cir. 1979)]

2) Application

Thus, as long as any means of doing interstate commerce is used (*e.g.,* use of a phone or mail service), this is sufficient (even though the transaction itself does not involve more than one state). [**United States v. Kunzman,** 54 F.3d 1522 (10th Cir. 1995)]

(c) Sale by means of a prospectus or oral communication [§838]

Section 12(a)(2) also requires that the offer or sale of securities occur by means of a "prospectus or oral communication" that includes the misrepresentation or fails to disclose the material fact. Because section 12(a)(2) does not have a reliance requirement, individual plaintiffs need not actually read the writing that contains the misrepresentation. [*See* **Alton Box Board Co. v. Goldman, Sachs & Co.,** 560 F.2d 916 (8th Cir. 1977)]

1) Section 12(a)(2) applicable only to primary offerings [§839]

The Supreme Court has held that section 12(a)(2) does not apply to a private, secondary sale of a security. [**Gustafson v. Alloyd Co., Inc.**, 513 U.S. 561 (1995)]

a) Facts of *Gustafson*

Gustafson involved a closely held corporation that was sold to a partnership pursuant to a contract of sale. The contract contained what turned out to be misstatements regarding the corporation's financial condition. Although the contract itself provided for adjustments in the purchase price if the company's condition was not as represented, the purchasers elected to rescind under section 12(a)(2) rather than demand a contractual rebate of part of the purchase price.

b) The Court's analysis

The Supreme Court characterized the issue as whether the contract for sale of the corporation was a "prospectus" within the meaning of section 12(a)(2). The Court reasoned that "prospectus" ought to mean in section 12(a)(2) the same thing it means in section 10. "Prospectus" in section 10, however, does not include contracts for sale of the type at issue. (Recall that section 10 is the basis for the disclosure requirements under the 1933 Act. Few, if any, documents drafted for a purpose other than 1933 Act registration will contain adequate disclosure under section 10. (*See supra,* §§118 *et seq.*)) Section 10 includes only statutory and preliminary prospectuses used in public offerings, and these, held the Court, are the only "prospectuses" that can give rise to liability under SA section 12(a)(2).

c) Significance of *Gustafson*

Gustafson has been widely criticized because it reads very narrowly the definition of "prospectus" in SA section 2(a)(10) (*see supra,* §153). However, it seems clear that for now section 12(a)(2) will not apply to private, secondary sales of securities. Moreover, the Court apparently considers section 12(a)(2) to apply only to primary public offerings by issuers or their shareholders, thus foreclosing application of section 12(a)(2) to public sales in the secondary market. This restrictive reading of the 1933 Act parallels some of the Court's later decisions under the 1934 Act [*e.g.,* **Central Bank v. First Interstate Bank**, *infra,* §1567] and may foreshadow additional decisions still to come.

(d) Untrue statement or omission of material fact [§840]

The plaintiff must also show that there was an untrue statement of, or an omission to state, a material fact.

> **Example:** D was an exclusive dealer in Penn Central notes and sold a large note to P shortly before Penn Central went bankrupt. D knew that P was required by law to purchase only the highest quality notes, that Penn Central had large losses, and that other banking firms were removing Penn Central notes from their approved buying lists. D's opinion as to the quality of the security was a material fact under section 12(a)(2). [*See* **Franklin Savings Bank of New York v. Levy,** 551 F.2d 521 (2d Cir. 1977)] *Note:* The court in *Franklin* indicated that D's knowledge that P was required to purchase only the highest quality notes constituted a representation that the note it sold to P was of the highest quality. Such a representation is a misrepresentation (if untrue) unless D makes a reasonable investigation of the financial facts and exercises reasonable care in arriving at a conclusion as to quality.

(e) Defendant's knowledge of the untrue statement [§841]

The plaintiff must *plead* that the defendant knew, or in the exercise of reasonable care should have known, of the untrue statement. However, the defendant then must bear the burden of proof on the issue (*i.e.,* that he did not know, and in the exercise of reasonable care could not have known, of the untrue statement).

(f) No reliance or causation required [§842]

Note that the plaintiff need *not* prove reliance on the misrepresentation (*see supra,* §838). Section 12(a)(2) requires, however, that the sale be accomplished *by means of* a prospectus (or oral communication) that contains a material misstatement or omission. One court has suggested that this language requires a showing of "some causal relationship between the misleading representation and the sale." [**Alton Box Board Co. v. Goldman, Sachs & Co.,** *supra*]

(3) Defenses [§843]

To avoid liability under section 12(a)(2), a defendant may raise the following defenses:

(a) Lack of knowledge [§844]

The defendant may show that he did not know, and in the exercise of reasonable care could not have known, of the untrue statement. This is basically a simple negligence standard.

1) Investigation requirement [§845]

Whether an investigation is required depends on all of the circumstances, but an underwriter probably has to make a reasonable investigation of an issuer. [**Sanders v. John Nuveen & Co.,** 619 F.2d 1222 (7th Cir. 1980), *cert. denied,* 450 U.S. 1005 (1981)] According to the *Sanders* court, there is no substantive difference between the investigation required to establish reasonable care under section 12(a)(2) and that required to prove due diligence for a nonexpert under section 11. [*See also* **Ambrosino v. Rodman & Renshaw, Inc.,** 972 F.2d 776 (7th Cir. 1992)]

2) Standards [§846]

And note that different standards have not been established with regard to statements made by experts and nonexperts (as they have under section 11; *see supra,* §§774 *et seq.*).

(b) Waiver and estoppel [§847]

The defendant may claim the defenses of waiver and estoppel if it can prove that the plaintiff has shown sufficient approval or acceptance of the defendant's misconduct.

(c) Plaintiff's knowledge [§848]

The defendant can also show that the plaintiff knew of the untrue statement.

(d) Privity [§849]

Under section 12(a)(2) (as in section 12(a)(1), above), there must be privity of contract between the plaintiff and the defendant.

(e) Participant liability [§850]

Like section 12(a)(1), section 12(a)(2) imposes liability on persons who "offer or sell" a security. *Pinter* (*supra,* §825) addressed the question of participant liability and who is deemed a "seller," but only with respect to section 12(a)(1). The Court expressly reserved any decision on the parallel requirement in section 12(a)(2). Lower courts addressing the issue since *Pinter,* however, have generally held that *Pinter* applies to section 12(a)(2), as well as to section 12(a)(1). [*See, e.g.,* **Royal American Managers, Inc. v. IRC Holding Corp.,** 885 F.2d 1011 (2d Cir. 1989)] Consequently, the same rules presently apply to participant liability under section 12(a)(1) and (2).

(f) Statute of limitations [§851]

The period of limitations for a section 12(a)(2) cause of action is one year after discovery of the false statement or material omission, or after such discovery should have been made in the exercise of reasonable diligence, but not more than three years after the sale.

1) Laches [§852]

It is uncertain whether laches applies to section 12(a)(2) actions.

(g) Loss causation in section 12(a)(2) cases—section 12(b) [§853]

In an action brought under section 12(a)(2), the defendant can escape liability to the extent that she can prove that all or any portion of the loss otherwise recoverable under section 12(a)(2) was *caused by something other than the defendant's alleged misstatement or omission.* [SA §12(b)] This defense is similar to the defense available under section 11, where a defendant is permitted to establish that some or all of the plaintiff's loss arises from factors other than the misrepresentation. (*See supra,* §791.)

1) Note

The difficulty with this defense lies in its requirement that the defendant "prove" that something in particular caused the loss. It is notoriously difficult to prove why the price of a security changed at any particular time, and under new SA section 12(b), the burden falls on the defendant to do so. The great majority of cases under section 12(a)(2) (in which such proof is *not* available) will be unaffected by this defense.

3. Section 17—S.E.C. Anti-Fraud Enforcement

a. Criminal liability and injunctions [§854]

As discussed above, sections 11, 12(a)(1), and 12(a)(2) of the 1933 Act provide plaintiffs with express causes of action based on specific types of misconduct in connection with the issuance of securities. These sections, however, are not available to the S.E.C., which is not a party to securities transactions. The Act therefore contains a provision—section 17—generally prohibiting fraud in connection with any offer or sale of securities. The S.E.C.'s 1933 Act anti-fraud enforcement is based on section 17, which makes it unlawful for any person in the *offer or sale* of securities by use of any means or instruments of transportation or communication in interstate commerce or by the use of the mails, directly or indirectly:

(i) *To employ any device, scheme, or artifice* to defraud [SA §17(a)(1)]; or

(ii) *To obtain money or property* by means of any *untrue statement of a material fact* or *any omission* to state a material fact [SA §17(a)(2)]; or

(iii) *To engage in any transaction, practice, or course of business* which operates or would operate as a fraud or deceit upon the *purchaser* [SA §17(a)(3)].

(1) Scope [§855]

Note that section 17(a) is not limited to sales; it applies to *offers* as well.

(2) Who is protected [§856]

The Supreme Court has held that section 17(a)(1) prohibits fraud against brokers as well as against purchaser-investors. [**United States v. Naftalin,** 441 U.S. 768 (1979)]

(a) Rationale

The Court held that although section 17(a)(3) specifically mentions "purchaser," this term should not be read into sections 17(a)(1) or (2), which are more general and cover fraud on brokers. The thrust of *Naftalin* is that sections 17(a)(1) and (2) apply to persons generally, in addition to purchasers of securities.

b. Implied civil liability [§857]

There is a long-standing split in the federal circuit courts over whether section 17(a) of the 1933 Act includes an "implied" civil cause of action permitting private persons to sue under the section and thereby, perhaps, avoiding some of the more onerous requirements of other sections of the 1933 and 1934 Acts (*e.g.,* 1933 Act section 12(a)(2), *see supra,* §§833 *et seq.*; 1934 Act section 10(b) and rule 10b-5, *see infra,* §§932 *et seq.*) that create fraud remedies for private plaintiffs. The *trend is clearly away from an implied remedy under section 17(a)*. This is the better view, because an implied remedy would conflict with the express remedies contained in each act. [*See* **Landry v. All American Assurance Co.,** 688 F.2d 381 (5th Cir. 1982)]

c. Culpable conduct [§858]

In civil *injunctive* actions brought by the S.E.C., a distinction must be made between the various subsections of section 17(a). Subsection 17(a)(1) requires a showing of scienter, while the two remaining subsections require only a showing of negligence. [**Aaron v. S.E.C.,** 446 U.S. 680 (1980)]

4. Liability Under the Securities Exchange Act of 1934 [§859]

A complete understanding of the liability provisions of the 1933 Act is impossible without also considering the provisions of the 1934 Act. The provisions of each statute overlap, and each has advantages and disadvantages in comparison with the others. (*See* discussion of 1934 Act provisions *infra,* §§932 *et seq.*)

5. Indemnification

a. Officers, directors, and control persons [§860]

Officers, directors, and control persons of an issuer may be exposed to substantial liability under the securities laws and substantial litigation expenses in defense of securities actions. The laws of the various states vary as to whether and to what extent these persons (acting as representatives for the corporation) may be indemnified against such liability by the issuer.

(1) No judicial decision [§861]

There is no direct judicial authority on the question whether indemnification of officers, directors, or control persons by the issuer against liabilities and expenses incurred in connection with the 1933 Act is unlawful. When such a decision comes, it will undoubtedly be based on the policy considerations underlying the 1933 Act.

(2) Policy of the S.E.C. [§862]

It is currently the policy of the S.E.C. that before it will accelerate the effectiveness of a registration statement, indemnification must either be *waived* by such persons *or* a statement must be made in the prospectus to the effect that the S.E.C. considers such indemnification against the policy of the 1933 Act (and therefore unenforceable) and that such persons promise to submit the question (if it arises) to a court of competent jurisdiction for a decision. [Regulation S-K Item 512(h)]

b. Underwriters [§863]

Note that indemnification by the issuer of the *underwriters* is common. The S.E.C. has done nothing to discourage this, even though some scholars believe that there is no reason to make a distinction between officers and directors on one hand, and underwriters, on the other.

(1) Actual knowledge of misstatement [§864]

One court, however, has held that at least where the underwriter has *actual knowledge* of materially misleading statements or omissions contained in the prospectus, the underwriter cannot rely on an indemnification agreement to escape liability. Rather, public policy requires that such underwriters be equally liable with the issuer to investors who have received the incorrect prospectus. [*See* **Globus, Inc. v. Law Research Service, Inc.**, 418 F.2d 1276 (2d Cir. 1969), *cert. denied*, 397 U.S. 913 (1970)]

(2) Negligence [§865]

It is still questionable what the result would be in a case where the underwriter was only *negligent* with respect to the inclusion of inaccurate information in the prospectus.

6. Contribution [§866]

A related question involves whether contribution is available in actions brought under sections of the 1933 Act that do not expressly provide for contribution (*i.e.*, sections other than section 11; *see supra*, §818). The courts have been friendlier to the idea of contribution in these actions than they have been to claims for indemnification.

a. Distinguish indemnification [§867]

While indemnification is the payment of all of a party's costs and expenses, contribution involves only the allocation of the damages among the defendants.

b. S.E.C. policy [§868]

So far, the S.E.C. has not attempted to discourage claims for contribution.

(1) Rationale

Contribution does not violate the policies underlying the 1933 Act; witness section 11(f), which expressly provides for contribution in a section 11 case. In fact, contribution furthers the policies of the Act, insofar as contribution tends to ensure that all defendants will bear some of the burden of the violation.

7. Liability Insurance [§869]

Another important issue in the area of liability is whether an issuer can purchase insurance to cover potential liabilities that could *not* be properly indemnified under state law.

a. Availability of insurance [§870]

State law varies, but many states do allow such insurance, and commercial policies are available. Insurance policies are not uniform with respect to what conduct they insure against; however, most do not insure against willful misconduct.

b. S.E.C. policy [§871]

Thus far, the S.E.C. has drawn a distinction between indemnification and insurance and has not discouraged insurance. [SA Rule 461(c)]

(1) Rationale

The reasons for this distinction are:

(a) If insurance were unavailable, the cost to the issuer's shareholders arising from liability could be high;

(b) Underwriters might refrain from marketing securities; and

(c) Directors and others might be unwilling to serve companies involved in the registration process.

8. Stipulations Contrary to Liability Provisions Void [§872]

Any condition, stipulation, or provision (as in a contract of sale) purporting to bind any person acquiring any security to waive compliance by the seller with any of the provisions of the 1933 Act or its rules and regulations is *void*. [SA §14]

Example: A sold B stock in an unregistered public offering. Later, A offered to return the money for the stock and gave B 10 days in which to respond to the rescission offer. B did not respond. Still later, B sued for rescission under what is now section 12(a)(1) of the 1933 Act. The court held that B had not waived his rights under the 1933 Act by failing to respond to A's offer of rescission. [**Meyers v. C & M Petroleum Producers, Inc.**, 476 F.2d 427 (5th Cir. 1973)]

Chapter Three: Regulation of Securities Trading—The Securities Exchange Act of 1934

CONTENTS

Key Exam Issues

The previous section of this Summary dealt with the Securities Act of 1933 and its regulation of the original distribution of securities. This section will cover the Securities Exchange Act of 1934 and its regulation of the trading of securities *subsequent* to their original distribution. For example, if XYZ Corp. issues 100,000 shares of its common stock to the public and registers this stock for trading on the New York Stock Exchange, the 1934 Act will regulate many aspects of the trading of XYZ's common stock.

This chapter covers a lot of important information. For exam purposes, the most important topics for you to study are:

1. **Rule 10b-5**

   Rule 10b-5 is one of the most important remedy provisions of the 1934 Act; therefore, it is almost inevitable that it will appear in a question on your exam. The key approach is to memorize the elements of the cause of action and then sift through the facts of your question to determine if each element is present. Remember to consider rule 10b-5 whenever you see trading by persons having important information that is not yet available to the public.

2. **Tender Offers and Repurchases of Stock**

   This is an important area of securities regulation law. Be sure you discuss the requirements for making a tender offer (*e.g.*, disclosure of information) and what a corporation might do in defense of tender offers by corporate raiders (*e.g.*, buy its own shares).

3. **Proxy Solicitation**

   Although this topic is often covered in a Corporations class, at least a brief review of the information on proxy contests and remedies for violation of the proxy rules would be worthwhile.

4. **Short-Swing Profits on Insider Transactions**

   This is sometimes the subject of an exam question. If your professor has stressed this area of law, the best approach is to study the rules carefully until you know them in detail, because section 16 is a highly technical area of securities law. Also consider rule 10b-5 if there has been any misrepresentation or nondisclosure of significant information.

5. **Participants and Advisors to Securities Transactions**

   Some professors skip this subject altogether; others emphasize this topic because it addresses ethics and professional values. Consider the coverage of the topic in your class, and adjust your studying accordingly.

A. Overview of the 1934 Act

1. Purpose of the Act [§873]

The purpose of the Securities Exchange Act of 1934 ("SEA") is to protect interstate commerce and the national credit, and to ensure a fair and honest market for the trading of securities. [SEA §2]

2. Registration and Reporting Requirements—Section 12 [§874]

Section 12 of the 1934 Act requires that certain securities be registered with the S.E.C. Once a company has registered its securities, it thereafter must file reports with the S.E.C. on a periodic basis. In addition, many of the company's other activities are subject to regulation under other provisions of the 1934 Act.

a. Companies required to register their securities [§875]

Companies whose securities must be registered with the S.E.C. may be divided into two categories: *listed companies* and *over-the-counter (or "OTC")* *companies*. (*See supra*, §§13 *et seq.*, for a discussion of stock exchanges and over-the-counter trading.) Companies of either kind that have triggered the 1934 Act registration requirements and begun to comply with the 1934 Act are typically referred to as "*registered*" or "*reporting*" companies.

(1) Listed companies [§876]

All companies whose securities are traded on a national stock exchange must register the securities so traded. [*See* SEA §12(a), (b)]

e.g. **Example:** If the common stock of XYZ Corp. is traded on a national securities exchange (such as the New York Stock Exchange), XYZ must register the stock with the S.E.C. under section 12 of the 1934 Act.

(2) Over-the-counter companies [§877]

In addition to listed companies, the 1934 Act requires registration of securities of *all companies that have reached a certain size,* even if their stock is not traded on a securities exchange. "Size" is measured by reference to the company's total assets and the number of shareholders it has: A company that has *more than $10 million in assets* must register *each class of equity security that is held by 500 or more shareholders.* [SEA §12(g); SEA Rule 12g-1]

e.g. **Example:** If no securities of XYZ are traded on a national exchange, but XYZ has in excess of $10 million in assets and at least 500 shareholders who own its common stock, XYZ must register the stock with the S.E.C. under section 12.

b. **Information required with registration [§878]**

Section 12 requires that the registering company supply the S.E.C. with information similar to that submitted with an S-1 registration statement under the 1933 Act—*i.e.*, information concerning its organization, financial structure, and the nature of its business; its securities outstanding; the names of directors, officers, underwriters, and principal shareholders, and their remuneration and material contracts with the issuer; bonus and profit-sharing arrangements; management and service contracts; options outstanding with respect to the issuer's securities; and all other material contracts and important financial statements (duly certified by public accountants). [SEA §12(b)(1); *see* SEA Form 10]

c. **Exemptions from registration requirements [§879]**

There are numerous exemptions from the registration requirements of the 1934 Act. The following securities are among those that need not be registered with the S.E.C.:

(i) *The securities of investment companies* (*i.e.*, "mutual funds") which are registered under the Investment Company Act of 1940;

(ii) *The securities of savings and loan companies,* where the companies are supervised by state or federal agencies; and

(iii) *The securities of organizations operated exclusively for religious, educational, or charitable purposes.*

[SEA §12]

d. **S.E.C. exemptive power [§880]**

In addition to the statutory exemptions, the S.E.C. has the power to exempt securities from registration if the exemption is in the public interest and does not endanger investors. [SEA §3(a)(12)(A)(vii)]

e. **Reporting requirements of registered companies [§881]**

All companies that have securities registered with the S.E.C. pursuant to SEA section 12 must make periodic (annual and quarterly) reports to the S.E.C. In addition, if a significant event takes place, the issuer is required to file a "current report." [SEA §13(a); Forms 10-K, 10-KSB, 10-Q, 10-QSB, 8-K] SEA section 13 contains the substantive reporting requirements. Form 10-K is the annual report of the issuer and requires virtually the same information that is required of an issuer registering an offering of securities on form S-1 under the 1933 Act (*see supra,* §315). Form 10-KSB is similar to form 10-K, but is slightly scaled-back and is designed for use by small business issuers.

f. Reports required of companies offering their securities to the public [§882]

Every issuer of a security registered under the 1933 Act must also file periodic reports with the S.E.C. Like the section 12 registration requirements, above, the periodic report provisions refer to SEA section 13 for the content and nature of the reports that must be filed with the S.E.C. Reporting may be discontinued when the issuer has fewer than (i) 300 holders of the class of security so registered *or* (ii) 500 holders of the class of security so registered and has had total assets under $10 million at the end of each of its three most recent fiscal years. [SEA §15(d); SEA Rule 12h-3]

g. Effect is registration of the issuer [§883]

Note that technically what is registered under section 12 of the 1934 Act is a class of securities, but the net effect, under the associated reporting requirements, is to register the issuer and subject the issuer to periodic reporting requirements of the 1934 Act.

(1) Reporting requirements are the same, whether triggered by size, listing, or 1933 Act registration [§884]

Notice that we have discussed several events that may trigger the reporting requirements of 1934 Act section 13. (*See supra,* §§881-882.) It is important to realize that, regardless of which event triggers the reporting requirements, the obligation to report is essentially the same. [*See* SEA §§13, 15(d); SEA Rules 13a-1, 13a-11, 13a-13, 15d-1, 15d-11, 15d-13]

h. Integration of the disclosure requirements [§885]

In 1980, the S.E.C. began a shift toward reliance on the 1934 Act and continuous reporting through that Act's monthly, quarterly, and annual reports to keep disclosure about issuers current. Since then, the requirements for disclosure under the 1933 and 1934 Acts have largely been integrated. [*See, e.g.,* SA Form S-3]

i. Integrity of accounting [§886]

The S.E.C. has broad authority to regulate the accounting of publicly held companies. Regulation S-X provides detailed requirements for the accounting disclosures that issuers and registrants must make under the 1933 and 1934 Acts. In addition, SEA section 13(b)(2), which was added by the Foreign Corrupt Practices Act and various sections of the Sarbanes-Oxley Act of 2002 ("SOXA"), also touch on public company accounting. Each of these is discussed below.

(1) Requirement to keep accurate books and records—SEA section 13(b)(2) [§887]

SEA section 13(b)(2) (added by the Foreign Corrupt Practices Act) requires 1934 Act reporting companies to keep accurate books and records and to maintain reasonable internal accounting controls. This provision "gives the S.E.C. authority over the entire financial management and reporting requirements of publicly held United States corporations." [**S.E.C. v. World-Wide Coin Investments, Ltd.,** 567 F. Supp. 724 (N.D. Ga. 1983)] In addition, *knowing* violations of section 13(b)(2) are criminal offenses. [SEA §13(b)(2)]

(2) Signatures and certifications

(a) Signatures [§888]

The principal executive officer, financial officer, and accounting officer, as well as a majority of the board of directors, must sign the annual report on form 10-K filed with the S.E.C. [SEA Form 10-K Gen. Instr. D(2)] This signature requirement may produce liability for any misstatements made in the report (*i.e.*, create a duty of "due diligence" similar to that under 1933 Act §11).

(b) Certifications [§889]

Both the chief executive officer and the chief financial officer of reporting companies must certify as accurate the financial statements contained in the company's filings under the 1934 Act. [SOXA §302] In addition, 1934 Act filings must contain officer certifications that the company has in place adequate disclosure controls and procedures, which are the processes the company uses to ensure that management knows of all information necessary for the company to meet its disclosure obligations. [SOXA §404] These certifications have been combined into one, standard certification, separate copies of which must be executed by the CEO and CFO. These certifications must be in exactly the language prescribed by the S.E.C. and must be included in every periodic report of the company under the 1934 Act that contains financial statements. [*See* Regulation S-K Item 601 Ex. 31] Finally, SOXA section 906 also requires the CEO and CFO to certify that each periodic report under the 1934 Act fully complies with the reporting requirements of the Exchange Act and "fairly presents, in all material respects, the financial condition and results of operations" of the company. A false certification under section 906 is a criminal violation. [SOXA §906; Regulation S-K Item 601 Ex. 32; SEA Rules 13a-14(b), 15d-14(b); 18 U.S.C. §1350]

3. Registration of Securities Professionals Under the 1934 Act [§890]

In addition to the registration requirements of section 12, other provisions of the

1934 Act require the registration of national securities exchanges, broker-dealers, information processors, and clearing agencies.

a. Registration of national securities exchanges [§891]

The 1934 Act defines an "exchange" [SEA §3(a)(1); *and see infra,* §§1817 *et seq.*], and requires such an exchange to register with the S.E.C. unless exempt [SEA §6].

(1) Effect of registration requirement [§892]

It is unlawful for any broker, dealer, or other securities exchange to employ any means of interstate commerce for the purpose of using the facilities of a national exchange unless the national exchange is registered (or exempt from registration) under the Act. [SEA §5]

(2) Agreement to comply [§893]

National exchanges must also agree to comply with the 1934 Act and to enact rules governing the conduct of exchange members. [SEA §6]

(3) Regulation of transactions [§894]

The 1934 Act also regulates various types of transactions entered into by stock exchange members. For example, the S.E.C. tries to prevent any conflicts of interest, particularly where a member of the exchange is acting as a broker (agent) *and* as a dealer (buying or selling from his own inventory) at the same time. [SEA §11; *and see infra,* §1870]

b. Registration of broker-dealers [§895]

The 1934 Act provides for the registration with the S.E.C. of all brokers and dealers who transact securities business in interstate commerce. [SEA §15(b); *and see infra,* §1903]

(1) Standards of conduct [§896]

The 1934 Act authorizes the S.E.C. to adopt and enforce rules for broker-dealers with respect to training, qualifications, and financial responsibility. [SEA §15(b)]

(2) Censure, suspension, revocation, or denial of registration [§897]

As a means of enforcing its standards of conduct, the S.E.C. is authorized under the 1934 Act (after a hearing) to censure a broker-dealer, or to deny, suspend, or revoke its registration for various types of prohibited conduct (*e.g.,* a willful violation of the securities laws). [SEA §15(b)(4)]

(3) Indirect regulation [§898]

Not only does the S.E.C. regulate the conduct of brokers and dealers directly, but it also oversees the regulation of their conduct by regulating the organizations of which they are members. Section 15A of the 1934

Act, for example, permits self-regulatory organizations of brokers and dealers to register with the S.E.C. (one organization, the National Association of Securities Dealers or "NASD," has done so). All brokers and dealers doing an interstate securities business must belong to the NASD, which regulates their conduct. [SEA §15(b)(8)] Also, broker-dealers that belong to the national securities exchanges are regulated directly by the exchanges, which in turn are regulated by the S.E.C.

c. Registration of information processors [§899]

"Securities information processors" (*i.e.*, persons who distribute information about securities, price quotations, or transactions) are required to register with the S.E.C. and make periodic reports. [SEA §11A(b)]

d. Registration of back-office agencies [§900]

Transfer agents, clearing houses, and others involved in the mechanical completion of securities trades are also required to register and make periodic reports. [SEA §17A]

(1) Transfer agents [§901]

Banks often have stock transfer departments, and public corporations usually appoint outside transfer agents, who are responsible for keeping track of all shareholders and stock certificates and seeing that all transfers are completed properly.

(2) Clearing houses [§902]

The exchanges normally have clearing houses, through which all certificates that are part of exchange transactions pass, so that proper deliveries will be made.

PROFESSIONALS REQUIRED TO REGISTER UNDER THE 1934 ACT   **gilbert**

THE FOLLOWING MUST REGISTER UNDER THE 1934 ACT:

☑ *National securities exchanges*

☑ *Brokers and dealers* who transact business in interstate commerce

☑ *Securities information processors* (*i.e.*, persons who distribute information regarding securities)

☑ *Transfer agents, clearing houses, and similar persons* involved in the completion of securities trades

---

4. Additional Reporting Requirements Under the 1934 Act [§903]

In addition to the reports required of registered companies and 1933 Act issuers under section 13 of the 1934 Act (*see supra*, §§881-882), other persons and entities are also required to file reports which the Commission uses to administer the provisions of the 1934 Act.

a. Reports by five percent owners of registered securities [§904]

The 1934 Act requires that the purchaser of more than 5% of a class of equity security registered under the Act must file certain information with the S.E.C., the issuer of the security, and the securities exchange (if the securities are traded on a national exchange). [SEA §13(d); *see* SEA Rule 13d-1]

(1) Information to be included [§905]

The report must contain information concerning the purchaser, the source of the funds used to purchase the securities, any plans the purchaser may have to acquire more of the same securities, and any plans it may have to attempt to change the issuer's business or corporate structure. [*See* SEA Schedule 13D]

(2) Purpose [§906]

This provision is aimed at regulating "tender offers," *i.e.*, transactions in which Company A makes an offer to buy the shares of Company B directly from Company B's shareholders. (For a discussion of tender offers, *see infra*, §§1127 *et seq.*)

b. Reports by officers, directors, and ten percent security holders [§907]

Officers and directors of the issuing corporation and owners of more than 10% of a class of security registered under section 12 must file a report with the S.E.C. listing their holdings, and must also file a monthly update of any changes therein. This report helps the S.E.C. enforce section 16(b) of the Act (which prevents insiders from making profits on short-term purchases and sales of registered securities). [SEA §16(a); *and see infra*, §§1433 *et seq.*]

c. Reports by national securities exchanges and associations [§908]

National securities exchanges and securities associations are required to file many reports concerning changes in their rules, discipline of their members, etc. [SEA §§6, 15]

d. Reports by institutional investors [§909]

Section 13(f) of the 1934 Act and rule 13f-1 require investment managers (*e.g.*, banks) who exercise investment discretion over accounts having $100 million or more in exchange-traded or over-the-counter-quoted equity securities to file form 13F annually with the S.E.C. The form reports the number of shares of each security held, the aggregate fair market value of the shares, and information about the nature of the manager's investment discretion and voting authority.

ADDITIONAL PERSONS WITH REPORTING REQUIREMENTS **gilbert**

THE FOLLOWING PERSONS ALSO HAVE REPORTING REQUIREMENTS UNDER THE 1934 ACT:

☑ *Persons who purchase more than 5%* of a registered class of equity security must report, among other things, the source of funds used for the purchase and any plans to purchase more of the same securities or to change the issuer's business or structure.

☑ *Officers, directors, and holders of more than 10%* of a registered class of security must file a report of their holdings and file monthly updates.

☑ *National securities exchanges* and associations must file reports concerning changes in their rules, discipline of their members, etc.

☑ *Institutional investment managers* with investment discretion over accounts having at least $100 million in equity securities must report the number of shares of each security held and their aggregate value and the manager's investment discretion and voting authority.

---

   e. Liability for filing false reports [§910]

      Filing materially false reports with the S.E.C. under the 1934 Act can result in civil and criminal liability. [*See* **S.E.C. v. Jos. Schlitz Brewing Co.,** 452 F. Supp. 824 (E.D. Wis. 1978); *and see, e.g., infra,* §920]

5. Regulation of Practices Relating to Stock Ownership [§911]

   The 1934 Act also regulates the following matters relating to stock ownership:

   a. Proxy solicitation [§912]

      The Act governs the manner in which voting proxies are solicited from the shareholders of companies whose securities are registered under section 12 of the Act. [SEA §14; *and see infra,* §§1281 *et seq.*]

   b. Tender offers [§913]

      Sections 13 and 14 of the Act govern the practices used in making a tender offer (*see infra,* §1127).

6. Regulation of Accounting Records and Internal Controls [§914]

   The 1934 Act also requires that reporting companies (i) make and keep books, records, and accounts which, in reasonable detail, accurately and fairly reflect the financial transactions of the issuer, and (ii) devise and maintain a system of internal accounting controls sufficient to provide reasonable assurances that proper recording of transactions and control of assets is achieved. [SEA §13(b)(2)]

7. A National Securities Market [§915]

   The 1934 Act also establishes the goal of a "national market system" and directs the creation of a National Market Advisory Board to move the securities markets in that direction. [SEA §11A]

8. **Role of the S.E.C. in Administering the 1934 Act [§916]**

As with the 1933 Act, the S.E.C. has broad power in administering the 1934 Act, including the powers to investigate, make and enforce rules, and impose penalties.

a. **Good faith reliance on S.E.C. rules [§917]**

The 1934 Act provides that good faith reliance on a rule adopted by the S.E.C. is a complete defense to liability under the Act. [SEA §23(a)(1)] Even though an S.E.C. rule is amended or rescinded, or declared by the courts to be invalid, one who has relied thereon in good faith will not be liable under the Act. However, once a rule has been judicially declared invalid, it may no longer be relied upon. [**B.T. Babbitt, Inc. v. Lachner**, 332 F.2d 255 (2d Cir. 1964)]

9. **Role of Other Regulatory Agencies [§918]**

The 1934 Act also grants power to the Board of Governors of the Federal Reserve System over "margin requirements"—*i.e.,* requirements applicable to customer loans from banks, broker-dealers, and other lending sources to purchase securities, and broker-dealer borrowings from regulated banks. In addition, the Federal Reserve System, the Comptroller of the Currency, and the Federal Deposit Insurance Corporation have power under the Act to regulate the issuance and exchange of bank securities. [SEA §12(i)]

10. **Sarbanes-Oxley Act [§919]**

The Sarbanes-Oxley Act of 2002 ("SOXA") introduced detailed regulation of reporting companies' auditors and accountants. It also regulates lawyers and securities analysts, and changed the nature and frequency of disclosures made under the 1934 Act, as well as enhances fines and penalties for financial crimes. Where SOXA has changed the 1934 Act, the changes are discussed *infra* in the discussion of those portions of the 1934 Act. Other SOXA provisions are discussed *infra*.

11. **Liability Provisions of the 1934 Act [§920]**

Several provisions of the Securities Exchange Act provide for a private cause of action for damages resulting from a violation of its provisions.

a. **Express provision for damages [§921]**

Some of these liability provisions *expressly* provide for private damage actions. For example, section 18 of the 1934 Act provides for the liability of anyone making false or misleading statements in any document filed pursuant to the SEA or any rule or regulation adopted thereunder (such as misstatements made in a filing pursuant to sections 12(b) or (g)). Recovery is allowed to any person who purchased or sold a security in reliance on a false statement at a price that was affected by the statement.

(1) **Note**

Additional provisions for express liability include section 16(b) of the Securities Exchange Act, regulating short-swing trading (*see infra*, §1433) and section 9 of the same Act, regulating market manipulation (*see infra,* §1921).

b. Implied provision for damages [§922]

Although other regulatory provisions do not expressly provide for private damage actions, in many instances a private right of action has been implied by the courts. [*See, e.g.,* SEA §10(b); SEA Rule 10b-5, *infra,* §948] The trend of decisions, however, is away from implying private causes of action. This trend is reflected in the Supreme Court's strict interpretation of statutory language, the intent of Congress to avoid overlap of the federal securities laws, and the concern that in the past it has been too easy to recover under the securities laws, resulting in the filing of unwarranted suits in order to recover their settlement value.

(1) Cort v. Ash test [§923]

In **Cort v. Ash,** 422 U.S. 66 (1975), the Supreme Court established a four-prong test to determine whether a private right of action would be implied from a federal statute:

(a) Is the plaintiff one of the *class for whose benefit the statute was enacted?*

(b) Is there any indication of *legislative intent,* explicit or implicit, *to create or deny such a remedy?*

(c) Is implication of a private cause of action *consistent with the underlying purposes* of the legislative scheme?

(d) Is the cause of action one *traditionally relegated to state law?*

(2) Legislative intent governs [§924]

In cases decided after *Cort,* the Supreme Court has emphasized the first three prongs of the test. Ultimately the issue is whether Congress intended to create a private right of action. [*See* **Transamerica Mortgage Advisors, Inc. v. Lewis,** 444 U.S. 11 (1979); **Touche Ross & Co. v. Redington,** 442 U.S. 560 (1979)]

(3) Express remedy [§925]

Where the securities laws provide an express remedy for a specific situation, it is unlikely that the courts will also imply an additional remedy under some other provision of the 1934 Act. [*See, e.g.,* **Cramer v. General Telephone & Electronics,** 443 F. Supp. 516, *aff'd,* 582 F.2d 259 (3d Cir. 1978)]

(a) Exception for actions under 1934 Act section 10(b) and rule 10b-5 [§926]

Implied actions under 1934 Act section 10(b) and rule 10b-5 (discussed *infra*) are so well-established at this point that the existence of an express remedy under a different provision of the securities laws will not destroy the availability of an implied remedy under section 10(b) or rule 10b-5. [*See, e.g.,* **Herman & MacLean v. Huddleston,** 459 U.S. 375 (1983); **Wachovia Bank & Trust Co. v. National Student Marketing Corp.,** 650 F.2d 342 (D.C. Cir. 1980); **Ross v. A.H. Robins Co.,** 607 F.2d 545 (2d Cir. 1979), *cert. denied,* 446 U.S. 946 (1980)]

c. Defenses [§927]

There are a number of possible defenses to causes of action brought under the various sections of the 1934 Act. These defenses are discussed *infra* in connection with the various liability provisions to which they relate.

12. Role of the Courts

a. Jurisdiction [§928]

The district courts of the United States have *exclusive* original jurisdiction over violations of the 1934 Act or its regulations and over actions brought to enforce liabilities or duties thereunder. Nationwide service of process is available. [SEA §27]

b. Court powers

(1) Powers of subpoena and contempt [§929]

The district courts have the power to issue orders to appear, to give testimony, and to produce evidence. In addition, a district court can cite persons in contempt for any violations of its orders. [SEA §21]

(2) Mandamus [§930]

Upon application by the S.E.C., the district courts may issue writs of mandamus to compel various corporate acts.

c. Judicial review [§931]

Another function of federal courts is to review decisions of the S.E.C. These appeals are heard in the District of Columbia Circuit, or in the circuit in which the appellant resides or has its principal place of business. [SEA §25] S.E.C. decisions must be based on a record, and the S.E.C.'s decision on factual issues is conclusive if based on "substantial evidence." Appeal from district court decisions is also to the circuit courts, then by certiorari to the United States Supreme Court.

B. Civil Liability Under Rule 10b-5 of the 1934 Act

1. Introduction [§932]

Rule 10b-5 is one of the most significant remedy provisions of the 1934 Act. It was adopted by the S.E.C. to strengthen the remedies provided in the 1933 Act against fraud in the purchase and sale of securities. (*See supra*, §833.) A discussion of rule 10b-5 follows and will give substantive meaning to the many references to the rule throughout the remaining sections of this Summary.

2. Statement of Rule 10b-5 [§933]

Rule 10b-5, which was enacted by the S.E.C. pursuant to section 10(b) of the 1934 Act, makes it unlawful, in connection with the *purchase or sale of any security,* for any person, directly or indirectly, by the use of *any means or instrumentality of interstate commerce*, or of the mails, or of any facility of any national securities exchange:

a. *To employ any device, scheme, or artifice to defraud;*

b. *To make any untrue statement of a material fact, or to omit to state a material fact* necessary in order to make the statements made, in light of the circumstances under which they were made, not misleading; or

c. *To engage in any act, practice, or course of business which operates or would operate as a fraud or deceit* upon any person.

3. Securities and Transactions Covered

a. Securities covered [§934]

Rule 10b-5 is very broad in its application to securities transactions; however, a "security" must be involved before the rule will apply. The term "security" is broadly defined (about the same as under the 1933 Act; *see supra*, §§257 *et seq.*; *and see* section 3(a)(10) and (11) of the 1934 Act). However, the trend in the Supreme Court is to limit the scope of the federal securities laws to the regulation of public trading markets and large, interstate investment promotions. One way to do this is to narrow the definition of "security." [*See, e.g.,* **Marine Bank v. Weaver,** *supra*, §275—a certificate of deposit is not a security]

b. Transactions covered [§935]

The courts have indicated that all purchases and sales of securities are covered under rule 10b-5, whether on exchanges, over-the-counter transactions, or private transactions. [**Fratt v. Robinson,** 203 F.2d 627 (9th Cir. 1953)]

(1) Compared to 1933 Act [§936]

The antifraud provisions of the 1933 Act apply only to fraud committed *by the seller* against purchasers (*see supra*, §§747 *et seq.*). Thus, prior to the adoption of rule 10b-5, there was no general prohibition against fraud committed by a purchaser in inducing a seller to sell.

(2) Compared to other sections of 1934 Act [§937]

Section 9 of the 1934 Act applies to both purchases and sales, but only in the context of securities listed on a national exchange (*see infra,* §1933); *section 15* also applies to both, but only in securities transactions in which broker-dealers are involved. *Rule 10b-5* applies to both purchases and sales in *all contexts*.

c. Interstate commerce requirement [§938]

Before rule 10b-5 will apply to a transaction, some means of interstate commerce, or the mails, or a national securities exchange must be used "in connection with" the purchase or sale of securities.

(1) Any part of transaction "in commerce" [§939]

The courts have held that the misrepresentation itself need not be transmitted by these jurisdictional means; it is sufficient if *any part* of the securities transaction occurs in interstate commerce (*e.g.,* delivery of the securities). [**Fratt v. Robinson,** *supra*]

(2) Use of interstate means can be intrastate [§940]

Any use of the interstate means is sufficient; the transaction itself need not involve more than one state. Thus, most courts have held that an intrastate telephone call is sufficient to establish jurisdiction, because the phone lines also carry interstate messages. [*See, e.g.,* **Dupuy v. Dupuy,** 511 F.2d 641 (5th Cir. 1975)]

4. Jurisdiction, Venue, and Service of Process [§941]

One of the reasons that rule 10b-5 has been used so frequently is its broad procedural provisions.

a. Jurisdiction [§942]

The federal courts have exclusive jurisdiction over all civil actions arising under rule 10b-5, regardless of the amount in controversy.

b. Venue [§943]

Suit may be brought in the district court of any district in which any act or transaction in violation of the rule occurred; or in any district where the defendant is found, resides, or transacts business.

c. Service of process [§944]

Process may be served anywhere in the world.

d. Supplemental jurisdiction [§945]

In addition, under supplemental jurisdiction (*see* Civil Procedure Summary), state actions for common law fraud can be joined in federal court with the rule 10b-5 action.

5. Elements of Cause of Action [§946]

The elements of a cause of action under rule 10b-5 depend on whether the government (*e.g.*, the S.E.C. or the Justice Department) or a private plaintiff is seeking to establish liability. Each of these elements is discussed in detail below, but it is best to start with an overview.

a. Actions by the government [§947]

In a government action under rule 10b-5, the government must prove the following elements:

(1) *Fraud or deception;*

(2) With respect to a *material fact;*

(3) *In connection with*

(4) *The purchase or sale of a security;* and

(5) *Scienter* (*i.e.*, fraudulent intent).

b. Actions by private plaintiffs [§948]

Private (*i.e*, nongovernment) plaintiffs seeking to recover under an implied private cause of action under rule 10b-5 must *prove all the elements of a government cause of action, plus the following additional elements*:

(1) *Standing*;

(2) *Reliance* (*i.e.*, transaction causation); and

(3) *Loss causation* (*i.e.*, deception was a substantial factor in causing the loss).

EXAM TIP   **gilbert**

Chances are great that rule 10b-5 will be tested on your exam. Be sure to remember the basic cause of action. The plaintiff must prove: (i) *fraud or deception*; (ii) with respect to a *material fact*; (iii) in connection with (iv) the *purchase or sale* of a security; and (v) *scienter* (an intent to defraud). If the plaintiff is not the government, the plaintiff must also prove: (vi) *standing*; (vii) *reliance*; and (viii) *loss causation*.

---

c. Fraud or deception [§949]

Rule 10b-5 requires that there be some misrepresentation, omission, deception, or other fraud. [**Santa Fe Industries, Inc. v. Green**, 430 U.S. 462 (1977)]

(1) Breach of fiduciary duty is not fraud [§950]

A breach of duty under state corporate law (*e.g., breach of the directors'* fiduciary duty or duty of care) is not a sufficient "fraud" for 10b-5 purposes. [**Santa Fe Industries, Inc. v. Green**, *supra*]

(a) Breach of fiduciary duty plus deception as to state remedy may suffice [§951]

Cases involving breach of fiduciary duty often also involve deception. After *Santa Fe*, plaintiffs bringing such cases began to plead deception in that the defendants did not disclose that their actions breached state-law fiduciary duties, and also did not disclose that the plaintiffs would have remedies under state law for such breaches. [*See* **Mayer v. Oil Field Systems Corp.**, 721 F.2d 59 (2d Cir. 1983); **Goldberg v. Meridor**, 567 F.2d 209 (2d Cir. 1977), *cert. denied*, 434 U.S. 1069 (1978)]

1) Likelihood of success [§952]

If a plaintiff can show deception because state-law breaches and remedies were not disclosed, must the plaintiff also show she would have won a state-law case but for the failure to disclose? Courts differ on this question. For a discussion, *see* **Alabama Farm Bureau Mutual Casualty Insurance Co. v. American Fidelity Life Insurance Co.**, 606 F.2d 602 (5th Cir. 1979), *cert denied*, 449 U.S. 820 (1980).

(2) Breach of contract as fraud [§953]

Ordinarily, a state-law breach of contract claim would not give rise to an action under rule 10b-5. However, if a person sells a security with a secret intention not to honor it, then an action for fraud may lie under rule 10b-5. [**Wharf (Holdings) Ltd. v. United International Holdings, Inc.**, 532 U.S. 588 (2001)]

---

e.g. Example: W Corp. entered into an oral contract with U Corp. that U would be permitted to purchase securities in a new corporation, priced according to a formula to which the parties agreed. When U Corp. attempted to exercise this option, W Corp. refused to honor it. In a lawsuit by U Corp. against W Corp., the Supreme Court held that the oral contract constituted the sale of a security—namely, an option to purchase stock—and that W Corp.'s intention not to honor the option was fraud in connection with that sale. [**Wharf (Holdings) Ltd. v. United International Holdings, Inc.**, *supra*]

---

(3) Issuer's duty to correct or update [§954]

Outside the mandatory disclosure requirements of the securities laws, for example in registration statements under the 1933 Act and 1934 Acts, and periodic disclosure under the 1934 Act, issuers generally are not under a duty to disclose information. However, if an issuer makes statements that later become false or misleading, a duty to correct or update those statements may arise. The failure to correct or update in this case might be fraudulent or deceptive and, therefore, violate rule 10b-5.

(a) Disclosure misleading when made [§955]

If a statement is misleading when it is made, and the speaker thereafter learns this, a duty to correct the earlier statement arises. [**Backman v. Polaroid Corp.,** 910 F.2d 10 (1st Cir. 1990)]

1) Misleading omissions [§956]

If an issuer makes a nonmandatory disclosure, the disclosure should be complete. For example, if a corporation is pursuing a specific business goal and announces the goal, as well as an intended approach for accomplishing it, the corporation may be required to disclose other approaches when they are under active and serious consideration. [*In re* **Time Warner Inc. Securities Litigation,** 9 F.3d 259 (2d Cir. 1993)]

(b) Disclosure is accurate when made [§957]

Courts are divided as to whether a duty to correct exists when the issuer makes a statement that is accurate and complete at the time it is made, but is rendered false or misleading by later events. Some courts have held that if the statement has a forward intent or connotation on which persons can be expected to rely, a duty to correct the earlier statement arises. [*See* **Weiner v. The Quaker Oats Co.,** 129 F.3d 310 (3d Cir. 1997); **Stransky v. Cummins Engine Co.,** 51 F.3d 1329 (7th Cir. 1995); **Backman v. Polaroid Corp.,** *supra*] Other courts have held that as long as the disclosure was accurate at the time it was made, no duty to update or correct it arises later. [*See* **Grassi v. Information Resources, Inc.,** 63 F.3d 596 (7th Cir. 1995); *compare* **In re Burlington Coat Factory Securities Litigation,** 114 F.3d 1410 (3d Cir. 1997)—"voluntary disclosure of an ordinary earnings forecast does not trigger any duty to update"]

(c) Statements by third parties [§958]

Issuers are not required to correct or respond to rumors or inaccurate statements about them made by third parties. However, if the issuer is the source of the inaccuracy, or is responsible for disseminating the statements of third parties, the issuer may be required to correct or update the statements. [**Elkind v. Liggett & Myers, Inc.,** 635 F.2d 156 (2d Cir. 1980)]

d. With respect to a material fact [§959]

Rule 10b-5 requires that the misrepresentation or omission be of a material fact.

(1) Fact vs. opinion [§960]

In many areas of the law, a distinction is made between "fact" and "opinion"; however, this distinction is not always clear-cut in securities cases.

(a) Prediction of earnings [§961]

In general, issuers are not required to predict future income. However, such predictions are important factors for investors to consider, and partly for that reason the 1933 and 1934 Acts were amended in 1995 to provide a new safe harbor for forward-looking statements. (*See supra*, §§350-361.) Issuers, their agents and underwriters, and certain others are fully protected from liability under rule 10b-5 if they comply with the provisions of the safe harbor.

(b) Balance sheet figures [§962]

A fact/opinion problem may also exist with respect to financial figures in the balance sheet of a company. For example, XYZ may have purchased real estate for $100,000 and carried this cost figure on its balance sheet. However, the *market value* of the property may now be $200,000. The problem with disclosing market value is that this value is often uncertain, and hence such information is in the nature of an "opinion."

Example—failure to disclose market value: Where the controlling shareholder of a company bought additional shares from other shareholders without disclosing that the market value of the company's tobacco inventory was substantially higher than the book value reflected in the company's financial statements, the court sustained a cause of action based on material nondisclosure. [**Speed v. Transamerica Corp.**, 235 F.2d 369 (3d Cir. 1956)] Note that in this case, market price was easily determined, and the information was in the possession of a corporate "insider" who was taking advantage of other shareholders.

Compare: Compare the result in *Speed* to a later case—*Gerstle*—involving an alleged violation of the proxy rules. There the court held that a company (A) had no obligation to disclose in its proxy statement, seeking approval of merger with another company (B), opinions about the market value of B's properties. However, the court did say that if A had any firm offers to buy the properties of B, it would have to disclose this "fact." [**Gerstle v. Gamble-Skogmo, Inc.**, 478 F.2d 1281 (2d Cir. 1973)]

(c) "Fair" price statements [§963]

When one company attempts to acquire another, some form of proposal is often made to the target company's shareholders. For example, in a tender offer, the proposal is made directly to the shareholders; in a classic merger, the target's shareholders vote to approve the proposal (*i.e.,* the merger agreement). When such a proposal is made, the target's board of directors is usually called upon to recommend voting for or against the proposal. In making this recommendation, the board must take into account the fairness of the price proposed to be paid, and the recommendation will include the board's opinion as to the price. If the board states that it believes the price is "high," and in hindsight the price proves to be low, is the board's statement actionable as a misrepresentation of fact?

1) **Truth of belief distinguished from truth of subject matter [§964]**
   Statements of belief are factual in two senses:

   a) **Truth of the belief [§965]**
      A statement that "the board believes that $42 per share is a fair price for your stock" is false if, in fact, the board does not believe that the price is fair. [*See* **Virginia Bankshares, Inc. v. Sandberg,** 501 U.S. 1083 (1991)]

   b) **Truth of the underlying subject matter [§966]**
      A statement that "the board believes that $42 per share is a fair price" is also an *endorsement* of the price, and may be taken to mean that there is sufficient extrinsic evidence to support a price of $42. Thus, the statement may be false if in fact $42 is *not* a fair price; *i.e.,* if there is no reasonable basis to conclude that $42 is a fair price. [**Virginia Bankshares, Inc. v. Sandberg,** *supra*]

2) **Lawsuit must be based on untruth of both belief and subject matter [§967]**
   In *Virginia Bankshares, supra,* the Supreme Court held that under SEA rule 14a-9 (a provision of the proxy rules analogous to rule 10b-5), it is not sufficient for the plaintiff merely to prove that the belief stated was not actually held; in addition, the plaintiff must show that the *statement was false as to its subject matter* (e.g., in the example above, that $42 was not a fair price).

   a) **Rationale**
      To find liability on mere disbelief, without any proof that the statement was false as to its subject matter, would rest "an otherwise nonexistent section 14(a) liability on psychological enquiry alone." [**Virginia Bankshares, Inc. v. Sandberg,** *supra*] This, in turn, could produce frivolous litigation instituted in the hope of achieving a quick settlement; the alternative for the board, in such a case, would

be to undergo lengthy discovery aimed at determining what each board member believed at the time of the statement.

3) Note

While the holding in *Virginia Bankshares* appears to immunize the board from liability for false statements about their own beliefs, the Court pointed out that it would be "rare to find a case with evidence solely of disbelief . . . without further proof that the statement was defective as to its subject matter."

EXAM TIP   **gilbert**

In determining whether a misrepresentation or omission involves a material fact, you may start with the position that only *"historical facts" are facts*. But remember, *some opinions might count as fact as well*. For example, the market value of a specific asset of a corporation is just an opinion, but if it is easy to determine the asset's value, it may be treated as a fact. Similarly, sincerity of belief in an opinion can be treated as a fact (*e.g.*, if a speaker says that she believes a price is fair but actually believes otherwise, or has no reasonable basis for the belief, and the price is unfair, the misrepresentation can be treated as one of fact).

---

(2) Omission of fact [§968]

In some cases, it may be clear that a material fact (*i.e.*, one that would be important to an investor's decision) is left out of the disclosure document. For example, in soliciting proxies for a vote on a merger, management does not disclose that it has received an additional offer to merge with a different company at a higher price. But the question of *how much* must be disclosed—in order to disclose all that is important—is always difficult to answer.

(a) Standards for disclosure [§969]

Numerous court decisions, as well as the S.E.C.'s own "plain English" rules (*see supra*, §368), make it clear that the "average investor" must be able to understand the disclosures made and the essential features of the transaction. The information must also be concise and relevant; *i.e.*, not everything that is arguably related need be disclosed. [**Feit v. Leasco Data Processing Equipment Corp.**, *supra*, §804; *and see infra*, §973—materiality]

(b) Failure to disclose importance of facts [§970]

There have been a few cases in which the courts have found liability for an omission of material fact where the party failed to state the importance of facts that were disclosed. [*See, e.g.*, **Robinson v. Penn Central Co.**, Fed. Sec. L. Rep. (CCH) ¶93,334 (E.D. Penn. 1971)]

(c) "Buried" facts [§971]

Defendants may be held liable for burying the facts by disclosing them in a manner that de-emphasizes them, *e,g.,* placing them far toward the back of a prospectus or disclosing them piecemeal on several different pages. [**Gould v. American Hawaiian Steamship Co.,** 535 F.2d 761 (3d Cir. 1976); **Kohn v. American Metal Climax, Inc.,** 458 F.2d 255 (3d Cir. 1972)]

(d) Duty to disclose [§972]

In connection with the above discussion of omissions of fact, it is important to realize that a party does not violate rule 10b-5 merely by failing to disclose (that is, omitting) a material fact. Omissions result in liability only when (i) there is a duty to disclose, and (ii) that duty is breached by the defendant. When material facts are omitted from disclosure documents required by the S.E.C., the duty to disclose is established because the S.E.C.'s rules require disclosure. However, omissions of fact can become more complex when one party to a transaction fails to make a disclosure to another, and the question later arises whether the party was in fact under some duty to make the disclosure. This issue often arises in the context of insider trading. (*See infra,* §§1037 *et seq.*)

(3) Materiality [§973]

The misrepresented or undisclosed fact must be "material" to the investor's decision. A number of tests of "materiality" have been applied by the courts.

(a) Substantial likelihood of significance [§974]

In the context of a proxy statement, the Supreme Court has held that the test for materiality is whether there is a *substantial likelihood* that a reasonable shareholder would consider the fact of significance in determining how to vote. The Court did not require proof of a substantial likelihood that disclosure would have caused the reasonable shareholder to change his vote, but only that the omitted fact would have assumed *actual significance.* [**TSC Industries, Inc. v. Northway, Inc.,** 426 U.S. 438 (1976)] This "substantial likelihood" standard has also been adopted for rule 10b-5 cases. [**Basic, Inc. v. Levinson,** 485 U.S. 224 (1988)]

EXAM TIP	gilbert

You should memorize the *TSC Industries* test for materiality for your exam: Information is material if there is a *substantial likelihood* that *a reasonable shareholder would consider the fact significant* in determining how to act.

(b) Probability vs. magnitude [§975]

When it is uncertain whether an event will or will not occur, the *TSC Industries* test for materiality—whether there is a substantial likelihood that a reasonable shareholder would consider the event significant—is difficult to answer. The Supreme Court has adopted a test for such circumstances that balances two issues: First, *how likely* is the occurrence of the event? Second, if the event occurs, *how significant* would it be to the issuer (and, thus, to the investor in the issuer's securities)? [**Basic, Inc. v. Levinson,** *supra*]

Example: The stock of Company B began to trade heavily, due to rumors that B was engaged in preliminary merger negotiations with C. Officers of B were asked on several occasions whether merger negotiations were underway; each time, they denied the rumors. Eventually C made a tender offer for B, and B revealed that negotiations had in fact been underway for some time. The Court held that the proper test for materiality would balance, at the time of each denial, the likelihood that the negotiations would bear fruit against the significance (to B) of the merger if it were to take place. Thus, a very low probability (approaching zero) of success in the merger discussions would justify nondisclosure. Because the merger unquestionably would be very significant to B, however, even a small increase in the likelihood of success would make the fact of the negotiations material. [**Basic, Inc. v. Levinson,** *supra*]

(c) Numerical standards of materiality [§976]

There is a great temptation to treat quantitative measurements as conclusive on the question of materiality, and securities lawyers do tend to make rough calculations to determine the likelihood that a misstatement or omission is material. It is easy to understand that an error of 50% in reported earnings, for example, is more likely to be material than an error of 0.5%. However, it would be a mistake to rely only upon such numbers as determinants of importance. An S.E.C. Staff Accounting Bulletin describes factors that "may well render material a quantitatively small misstatement of a financial statement item," including whether the misstatement:

(i) Arises from an item capable of precise measurement or whether it arises from an estimate and, if so, the degree of imprecision inherent in the estimate;

(ii) Masks a change in earnings or other trends;

(iii) Hides a failure to meet analysts' consensus expectations for the enterprise;

(iv) Changes a loss into income or vice versa;

(v) Concerns a segment or other portion of the registrant's business that has been identified as playing a significant role in the registrant's operations or profitability;

(vi) Affects the registrant's compliance with loan covenant or other contractual requirements;

(vii) Has the effect of increasing management's compensation—*e.g.*, by satisfying requirements for the award of bonuses or other forms of incentive compensation; or

(viii) Involves concealment of an unlawful transaction.

[SAB 99, 70 S.E.C. 785 (1999)] One must conclude that while quantitative estimates can be helpful in some situations, they are always a matter of judgment and must be weighed in light of all the circumstances. [*See* **Ganino v. Citizens Utility Co.**, 228 F.3d 154 (2d Cir. 2000)—1.7% of total revenue material under the circumstances]

(d) Materiality and the "bespeaks caution" doctrine [§977]

Finally, the materiality of a particular disclosure is affected by the other disclosures that are made; *i.e.*, statements must be evaluated in context. The materiality of a prediction that the issuer will be able to maintain liquidity is diminished by other disclosures that "bespeak caution" regarding liquidity. [*In re* **Worlds of Wonder Securities Litigation**, *supra*, §349] In 1995, the "bespeaks caution" doctrine was codified. (*See supra*, §349.)

(e) Other standards [§978]

The standards for materiality developed in other contexts, for example, under the proxy rules, are also relevant here and should be consulted. (*See infra*, §§1399-1405.)

e. "In connection with" requirement [§979]

Rule 10b-5 requires that the defendant's misrepresentation or deception be "in connection with" the purchase or sale of a security.

(1) Defendant need not be an actual purchaser or seller [§980]

As we will see (*see infra*, §§1005 *et seq.*), a private plaintiff in a rule 10b-5 action must be a purchaser or seller of securities. However, the *defendant need not have engaged in a purchase or sale*. Rather, the defendant's fraudulent activity need only be "in connection with" the purchase or sale of securities.

e.g. Example: A defendant corporation was held liable for a misleading press release on which reasonable investors might have relied in the purchase or sale of the company's securities. [**S.E.C. v. Texas Gulf Sulphur Co.,** 401 F.2d 833 (2d Cir. 1968)]

EXAM TIP   **gilbert**

On the exam, it is important to remember that while a private *plaintiff* generally must be a purchaser or seller of securities, there is *no* such requirement for the *defendant*.

---

(2) Relationship to other rule 10b-5 requirements [§981]

In private (*i.e.,* nongovernment) actions under rule 10b-5, the "in connection with" requirement is conceptually related to the other rule 10b-5 requirements of reliance and loss causation.

(a) The reliance requirement [§982]

One of the requirements for application of rule 10b-5 in private litigation is that the plaintiff must have relied on the defendant's material misrepresentation or omission. A showing of such reliance would probably establish the necessary connection or "nexus" between the defendant's misrepresentation and the purchase or sale by the plaintiff by proving "transaction causation"—*i.e.,* that the misrepresentation was the cause of the plaintiff entering the securities transaction. (*See* discussion of reliance, *infra,* §§1012 *et seq.*)

1) But note

Meeting the "in connection with" requirement does not necessarily satisfy the reliance requirement. Reliance is a state of mind. It is possible that the deception, while sufficiently close to the transaction to be "in connection with" the purchase or sale, was not relied upon by the plaintiff. In other words, the deception might have been connected to the transaction, but not be the cause of the plaintiff's entering into the transaction.

(b) The loss causation requirement [§983]

Another rule 10b-5 requirement in private litigation is that of loss causation—*i.e.,* that the plaintiff's economic loss was caused by the defendant's wrongful conduct. If the plaintiff is able to show that the defendant's wrongful conduct "caused" such a loss, this will tend to establish the "in connection with" requirement between the defendant's conduct and the plaintiff's purchase or sale of securities. (*See* discussion of loss causation *infra,* §§1026 *et seq.*) However, as with reliance, it is possible that the defendant's conduct could be "in connection with" the plaintiff's purchase or sale of securities, without actually causing the plaintiff's loss. [*See* **Semerenko v. Cendant Corp.,** 223 F.3d 165 (3d Cir. 2000), *cert. denied*, 531 U.S. 1149 (2001)]

(3) Problem of remoteness [§984]

The most common issue in this area is whether the fraud or deception is so remote from the plaintiff's purchase or sale transaction as to sever the requisite "connection."

(a) Fraud as part of the securities sales transaction [§985]

If the defendant's fraud occurs as part of the securities transaction itself, it is clear that a sufficient connection exists. For example, A sells securities to B, without disclosing material inside information: Assuming fraud, the necessary connection with B's purchase exists. [*See* **Semerenko v. Cendant Corp.,** *supra*]

(b) Fraud separate from the sales transaction [§986]

The more difficult cases are those in which the defendant's fraud is not directly related to, and does not involve the terms of, the securities transaction itself. It is not clear how close to the sale of securities the fraud must be in order to meet the "in connection with" requirement. We can say that if the purchase or sale is merely incidental to the fraud, then the fraud is not "in connection with" the securities transaction. On the other hand, it is clear that the defendant's fraud does not have to be about the value of securities. A few examples may help to shed some light on this complex area.

---

e.g. **Example:** The articles of ABC Corp. provide that only current employees can own stock in the corporation. Defendants, through a series of deceptive maneuvers, induced ABC's board to remove plaintiffs (who owned 45% of the corporation's stock) from their positions as officers and employees. The court held that the defendant's deceptive maneuvers were not "in connection with" the purchase or sale of a security. First, the real purpose of the maneuvers was to remove the plaintiffs from their positions, not to induce the sale of their stock; the issue was one of management control, not of stock ownership. [**Ketchum v. Green,** 557 F.2d 1022 (3d Cir.), *cert. denied*, 434 U.S. 940 (1977)]

---

e.g. **Example:** A stockbroker induced an elderly man to invest more than $400,000 in a discretionary brokerage account, over which the broker had investment control and a power of attorney. The broker engaged in a series of transactions that left the account empty. The transactions themselves were not fraudulent, in the sense that the prices of purchases and sales were the market prices. The account was emptied by the broker's diverting the proceeds of the transactions to his own accounts, by writing checks on the account that were paid by liquidating a sufficient quantity of securities to cover the checks. The Court held that this fraud was in connection with the purchase or sale of securities. While the transactions, in isolation, appear not to be fraudulent, they were conducted in furtherance of a scheme to defraud the investor. While it is not automatically a violation of rule 10b-5 to steal money from a brokerage account, in this case, the securities transactions were initiated and concluded in furtherance of a scheme to defraud. [**S.E.C. v. Zandford**, 535 U.S. 813 (2002)]

Example: W Corp. sold U Corp. an option to purchase stock in T Corp. W Corp. never intended to honor the option, if U should attempt to exercise it. The Court held that this was a fraud "in connection with" the purchase or sale of a security, and not merely a breach of contract (the option) to sell securities in the future. The option itself is a security, and the sale with the secret intent not to honor the option was fraudulent, "in connection with" the sale of the option. [**Wharf (Holdings) Ltd.**, *supra*, §953]

---

(4) Significance of the "in connection with" requirement [§987]

Because private plaintiffs must establish reliance and loss causation, and establishing those elements will almost inevitably meet the "in connection with" requirement [*see* **Semerenko v. Cendant Corp.**, *supra*], the significance of the "in connection with" requirement lies chiefly in the fact that in a rule 10b-5 action by the government, the government must establish that a fraudulent or deceptive act was connected to the purchase or sale of a security.

(5) Privity not required [§988]

The "in connection with" requirement *does not require privity*, and there is *no requirement* that the plaintiff and defendant be in privity with one another in an action under rule 10b-5. [**Superintendent of Insurance v. Bankers Life & Casualty Co.**, 404 U.S. 6 (1971)]

f. Purchase or sale requirement [§989]

Rule 10b-5 requires that the deceptive transactions occur in connection with the "purchase or sale" of a security.

(1) Definition of "purchase or sale" [§990]

"Purchase" and "sale" are defined to include "any contract to purchase or sell." [SEA §3(a)(13), (14)] Thus, something *beyond a mere offer* to purchase or an offer to sell must be involved. [**Blue Chip Stamps v. Manor**

Drug Stores, *supra,* §275] But at the same time, an actual completed purchase or sale need not be involved. So, for example, it has been held that a pledge of securities as collateral in a loan transaction constitutes a "sale" of the securities to the pledgee, so that the pledgor is a "seller" and the pledgee a "purchaser." [**Rubin v. United States,** 449 U.S. 424 (1981)]

(2) Oral contracts [§991]

Some doubt exists as to whether an oral contract makes the parties purchasers or sellers so as to give them standing under rule 10b-5. Some courts hold that an oral contract is sufficient. [*See, e.g.,* **Threadgill v. Black,** Fed. Sec. L. Rep. (CCH) (Transfer Binder) ¶91,402 (D.C. Cir. 1984)] Other courts hold that an oral contract is not enough, at least when it is not enforceable under the Statute of Frauds. [*See, e.g.,* **Kagan v. Edison Bros. Stores, Inc.,** 907 F.2d 690 (7th Cir. 1990); **Pelletier v. Stuart-James Co.,** 863 F.2d 1550 (11th Cir. 1989)]

(3) Merger [§992]

A merger transaction is an example of a purchase and sale transaction; *i.e.,* A, a shareholder in X Corp., exchanges his shares for shares in Y Corp. when X and Y are merged. [**S.E.C. v. National Securities,** 393 U.S. 453 (1969)]

g. Scienter [§993]

For liability to exist under rule 10b-5, it must be shown that the defendant had "*scienter,*" *i.e.,* intent to deceive, manipulate, or defraud. [**Ernst & Ernst v. Hochfelder,** 425 U.S. 185 (1976)]

(1) Facts of *Hochfelder* [§994]

In *Hochfelder,* the defendant (an accounting firm) audited the books of a small securities firm and prepared its financial statements filed with the S.E.C. and the Midwestern Stock Exchange. Plaintiffs were customers of the firm who had given the firm's president money to be invested in "escrow accounts." The president, however, embezzled the money, and, to prevent detection of his fraud, had a firm rule that no mail addressed to him could be opened by any other person. Plaintiffs claimed that if the defendant had not been negligent in its audit, it would have discovered the rule against opening the president's mail, would have investigated, and ultimately would have discovered the fraud. As it was, no reports of the escrow accounts ever showed up in the financial statements prepared by the defendant.

(2) Holding [§995]

The issue in *Hochfelder* was whether rule 10b-5 applies where the defendant has been **negligent** in performing its duties, thus aiding and abetting the perpetration of a fraud. The Supreme Court held that the defendant was *not* liable unless the plaintiff could prove that the defendant acted with scienter (which, said the Supreme Court, does not include merely negligent conduct).

(3) Reckless conduct [§996]

The Supreme Court in *Hochfelder* reserved the question whether a defendant who lacked actual knowledge of a fraud, but acted recklessly, might be liable under rule 10b-5. Circuit courts addressing the issue after *Hochfelder*, however, have uniformly held *that recklessness is enough* to establish liability under rule 10b-5.

(a) Definition [§997]

Reckless conduct has been defined as "highly unreasonable [conduct], involving not merely simple, or even inexcusable negligence, but an extreme departure from the standards of ordinary care, and which presents a danger of misleading buyers or sellers that is either known to the defendant or is so obvious that the actor must have been aware of it." [**Sundstrand Corp. v. Sun Chemical Corp.**, 553 F.2d 1033 (7th Cir.), *cert. denied*, 434 U.S. 875 (1977)]

EXAM TIP   **gilbert**

Remember on your exam that scienter can be established not only by *actual intent to deceive*, but also by *recklessness as to truth* (*i.e.*, conduct exhibiting an extreme departure from ordinary care that presents a danger of misleading buyers or sellers).

(b) Recklessness applies to historical facts [§998]

In 1995, Congress added a "safe harbor" to the 1934 Act (and to the 1933 Act) providing that a private plaintiff cannot recover for a fraudulent forward-looking statement unless it was made with *actual knowledge* of its falsity. [SEA §21E; SA §17A; *see supra*, §350] The effect of the safe harbor is that recklessness will constitute scienter only with respect to statements of historical fact.

1) Note

The safe harbor itself applies only to claims brought by private plaintiffs; the government (*i.e.*, the S.E.C.) can still bring an action based on reckless forward-looking statements.

(c) Defense of lack of "due diligence" [§999]

At common law, plaintiffs in fraud cases were sometimes stymied by the "lack of due diligence" defense, the essence of which was that the plaintiff's reliance on the defendant's omissions or misrepresentations was not justified, and would have been prevented had the plaintiff exercised "due diligence." However, in rule 10b-5 cases this defense is limited.

1) Negligence insufficient [§1000]

Mere negligence on the plaintiff's part is not enough to preclude a rule 10b-5 action. Before the contributory fault of the plaintiff will override the defendant's fraud, the plaintiff's action must reach the level of gross conduct, comparable to the action of the defendant. [*See, e.g.,* **Holdsworth v. Strong**, 545 F.2d 687 (10th Cir. 1976)—plaintiff was not denied a cause of action under rule 10b-5 for failing to ascertain the corporation's financial status, because plaintiff justifiably relied on defendant's representations; plaintiff's conduct may have been negligent, but was not reckless; *and see* **Teamsters Local 282 Pension Trust Fund v. Angelos**, 762 F.2d 522 (7th Cir. 1985)]

2) Defense applicable to face-to-face transactions only [§1001]

Note that to the extent the rule 10b-5 due diligence defense survives *Hochfelder*, it is properly applied only to face-to-face transactions. It would be manifestly unreasonable to require a purchaser on a securities exchange to investigate independently the condition of the company whose securities she is purchasing.

3) Plaintiff must read written disclosure [§1002]

What if the defendant makes oral misrepresentations, but at the same time delivers a written disclosure document clearly spelling out the risks of a transaction? The 10th Circuit has held that such a plaintiff cannot claim reliance on the oral misrepresentations. [**Zobrist v. Coal-X, Inc.**, 708 F.2d 1511 (10th Cir. 1983)]

4) Account statements [§1003]

Would-be plaintiffs are also well-advised to read their brokerage account statements. Should they fail to do so, they may find that transactions disclosed on the statements cannot later become the basis for a rule 10b-5 action. In a case in which a tax lawyer failed to follow up on allegedly unauthorized transactions in his account, and large losses were caused by additional unauthorized transactions a year later, the lawyer's 10b-5 claim was dismissed based on the plaintiff's failure to monitor his account after notice that there was unauthorized activity. [**Stephenson v. Paine Webber Jackson & Curtis, Inc.**, 839 F.2d 1095 (5th Cir.), *cert. denied*, 488 U.S. 926 (1988)]

(4) Standard of culpability for S.E.C. injunctions [§1004]

The standard of culpability that must be proved by the S.E.C. to obtain an injunction is the same as that applicable to private plaintiffs. Civil injunction actions brought under section 21(d) for violations of rule 10b-5 require a showing of scienter by the defendant. [**Aaron v. S.E.C.**, *supra*, §858]

h. Standing [§1005]

In a private action under rule 10b-5 the *plaintiff* must either be an actual "purchaser" or an actual "seller" of securities to have standing to maintain a 10b-5 cause of action. [**Blue Chip Stamps v. Manor Drug Stores**, *supra*]

---

e.g. **Example:** Plaintiff, a shareholder of Newport Steel Corp., brought a shareholder derivative suit alleging a rule 10b-5 violation against the president of Newport. The president had caused Newport to reject a merger proposal (which would have benefited all Newport shareholders), and then sold his own 40% controlling interest for double the market price to the same interested purchaser. The court held that the plaintiff had no standing to sue, because *neither* the corporation nor the plaintiff was a purchaser or seller as required by rule 10b-5. [*See* **Birnbaum v. Newport Steel Corp.**, 193 F.2d 461 (2d Cir.), *cert. denied*, 343 U.S. 956 (1952)]

---

(1) Purpose of requirement [§1006]

The purpose of the "purchase or sale" requirement is to prevent vexatious litigation, because plaintiffs might otherwise bring rule 10b-5 actions simply to extract a settlement from the defendant, by threatening to use the liberal federal discovery rules to disrupt the defendant's business. [**Blue Chip Stamps v. Manor Drug Stores**, *supra*]

(2) Contexts in which the issue arises

(a) Depreciation in value [§1007]

The "purchase or sale" issue may arise when the plaintiff has not actually sold his stock, but argues that the stock has depreciated in value due to the misrepresentations made by the defendant. [*See, e.g.,* **Greenstein v. Paul**, 400 F.2d 580 (2d Cir. 1968)—plaintiff had no standing because there was no purchase or sale]

(b) Transaction prevented [§1008]

The issue may also arise when the plaintiff claims he would have purchased stock but for the negative statements made by the defendant. [**Blue Chip Stamps v. Manor Drug Stores**, *supra*—no rule 10b-5 cause of action because no actual purchase or sale]

(3) Exceptions to requirement of purchase or sale by plaintiff

(a) Derivative suits [§1009]

Normally, a plaintiff who brings a rule 10b-5 action to enforce a fiduciary responsibility of corporate management will sue in a representative capacity on behalf of the corporation (*i.e.,* a shareholder derivative suit). In such a suit, the courts have held that the individual plaintiff shareholder need *not* be an actual purchaser or seller; it is sufficient if there is a purchase or sale *by the corporation.* [**Superintendent of Insurance v. Bankers Life & Casualty Co.,** *supra,* §988]

(b) Injunction plaintiffs [§1010]

Courts are divided as to whether plaintiffs who merely seek an injunction against continued violations of rule 10b-5 must be purchasers or sellers of securities. Some cases have held that standing exists as long as the plaintiff owns the securities that are the subject of the violation. [*See, e.g.,* **Mutual Shares Corp. v. Genesco, Inc.,** 384 F.2d 540 (2d Cir. 1967); **Kahan v. Rosenstiel,** 424 F.2d 161 (3d Cir.), *cert. denied,* 398 U.S. 950 (1970)] Other courts have held that injunction plaintiffs are not entitled to an exception to the *Blue Chip* rule. [*See, e.g.,* **Cowin v. Bresler,** 741 F.2d 410 (D.C. Cir. 1984)]

(c) Forced sale [§1011]

If the plaintiff in effect is forced to sell his stock, the purchase-sale requirement will be held to have been met. [**Alley v. Miramon,** 614 F.2d 1372 (5th Cir. 1980)]

---

e.g. **Example:** Through a series of deceptions, the defendant liquidated a corporation, and the plaintiff shareholder received none of the liquidation proceeds. The liquidation was held to be a "forced sale." Because it was an objectively verifiable event, the court found that there was no chance that the basic rationale of the *Blue Chip Stamps* case would be offended by this decision. [**Alley v. Miramon,** *supra*]

---

i. Reliance and transaction causation [§1012]

In private actions, in addition to the elements the government must prove, the plaintiff must show that he *actually relied* on the material fact that was misrepresented. There are essentially two elements of reliance that must be proved in a rule 10b-5 case: (i) the plaintiff must have actually *believed* the misrepresentations, and (ii) the belief must have been the *cause* of (*i.e.,* a "substantial factor" in) the plaintiff's entering the transaction ("transaction causation"). [**List v. Fashion Park, Inc.,** 340 F.2d 457 (2d Cir.), *cert. denied sub nom.* **List v. Lerner,** 382 U.S. 811 (1965)] In addition, reliance is treated differently in cases arising from face-to-face transactions than in those arising

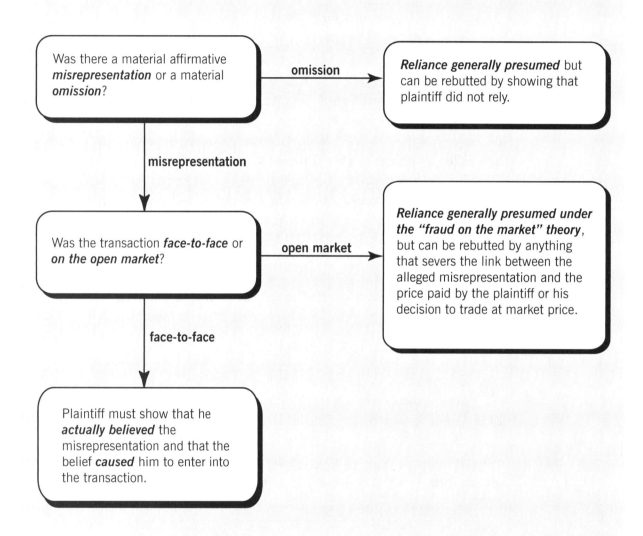

Was there a material affirmative *misrepresentation* or a material *omission*?

omission → *Reliance generally presumed* but can be rebutted by showing that plaintiff did not rely.

misrepresentation ↓

Was the transaction *face-to-face* or *on the open market*?

open market → *Reliance generally presumed under the "fraud on the market" theory*, but can be rebutted by anything that severs the link between the alleged misrepresentation and the price paid by the plaintiff or his decision to trade at market price.

face-to-face ↓

Plaintiff must show that he *actually believed* the misrepresentation and that the belief *caused* him to enter into the transaction.

from impersonal transactions on a securities exchange. Both kinds of cases are discussed below.

(1) Substantial factor test [§1013]

In showing transaction causation (*i.e.*, reliance), the plaintiff must be able to show that his belief in the misrepresentation was a "substantial factor" in his having entered the transaction. [**List v. Fashion Park, Inc.,** *supra*]

(a) Relationship to loss causation [§1014]

Reliance in the "substantial factor" sense is closely related to loss causation, because this kind of reliance requires the plaintiff to show that the misrepresentation or omission caused the plaintiff to enter into the transaction. (For a complete discussion of the loss causation requirement, *see infra*, §§1026-1034.)

(b) Relationship to materiality [§1015]

When a fact is shown to be material, this is a strong indication that it was a substantial factor in causing the plaintiff to enter the transaction. On this basis, reliance would seem to flow as a logical assumption from a showing of materiality; however, one does not necessarily follow the other. For example, the defendant might be able to prove that the plaintiff knew that a material fact was misrepresented, but entered the securities transaction anyway. [**List v. Fashion Park, Inc.,** *supra*]

(2) Face-to-face security transactions [§1016]

The role of reliance in face-to-face transactions differs according to whether the plaintiff claims that an *affirmative misrepresentation* was made by the defendant, or that the defendant *failed to disclose a material fact.*

(a) Affirmative misrepresentations [§1017]

Cases involving material misrepresentations (rather than omissions) and a personal, face-to-face relationship between plaintiff and defendant usually require the plaintiff to show that he *actually relied* on defendant's material misrepresentation. [*See, e.g.,* **Reeder v. Mastercraft Electronics Corp.,** 363 F. Supp. 574 (S.D.N.Y. 1973)]

(b) Nondisclosure cases [§1018]

If, on the other hand, the defendant failed to disclose a material fact, in a case involving a face-to-face relationship between the plaintiff and the defendant *reliance by the plaintiff is generally presumed.* This is so in part because of the difficulty of proving that the plaintiff "relied" on something that was not said. The presumption of reliance can be rebutted by showing that the plaintiff did *not* rely.

Note, however, that in many cases such a showing will amount to a demonstration that the particular undisclosed facts or circumstances were not "material" to this plaintiff. [*See, e.g.,* **Affiliated Ute Citizens v. United States,** 406 U.S. 128 (1972); **Barnes v. Resource Royalties, Inc.,** 795 F.2d 1359 (8th Cir. 1986); **Shores v. Sklar,** 610 F.2d 235 (5th Cir. 1980)]

(3) Open-market (impersonal) transactions [§1019]

Most securities transactions now occur over an exchange or in the over-the-counter market; the buyer and seller remain unaware of each other's identities, and the transactions, in that sense, are impersonal. These transactions pose their own set of problems regarding "reliance." First, in an impersonal market, "reliance" in the conventional sense seldom, if ever, exists—because the plaintiff does not know who the defendant is, she is also ignorant of the other's misrepresentations (and certainly of any omissions), at least until after the transaction is consummated. In addition, cases arising out of market transactions are usually brought by large classes of plaintiffs. To require proof of reliance, in the conventional sense, would make such class actions difficult or impossible to maintain: The individualized element of reliance would overwhelm the common elements of the case, and, therefore, no class could be certified. Such cases would have to be brought individually, and as a result, many smaller investors (who lack the resources to bring such a suit) would have no remedy at all. The "fraud on the market" doctrine is a judicial attempt to address these concerns.

(a) The "fraud on the market" doctrine [§1020]

"Fraud on the market" is premised on the idea that investors rely "generally on the supposition that the market price is validly set and that no unsuspected manipulation has artificially inflated the price, and thus [rely] indirectly on the truth of the representations underlying the . . . price." [**Blackie v. Barrack,** 524 F.2d 891 (9th Cir. 1975), *cert. denied,* 429 U.S. 816 (1976)]

1) Effect of the doctrine [§1021]

When the fraud on the market doctrine is applied, its effect is to raise a rebuttable presumption of reliance on any material misrepresentations or omissions. [**Basic, Inc. v. Levinson,** *supra,* §975] In effect, rather than having affirmatively to establish reliance, the plaintiff need only show the materiality of the misrepresentation or omission.

2) Efficient capital market hypothesis [§1022]

Underlying the fraud on the market doctrine is the efficient capital market hypothesis. (*See supra,* §376.) In an efficient capital market (*i.e.*, a market in which pricing reflects all publicly available information about a security), material misrepresentations or omissions cause a distortion in the price. *Basic* and *Blackie* accept the efficient capital market hypothesis and overcome the difficulty of proving individual reliance by establishing a presumption of reliance on the fairness of the price set by the efficient market.

a) When is the market efficient? [§1023]

Courts have identified five factors useful in determining whether the market for a security is efficient:

(i)   A large weekly trading volume;

(ii) The existence of a significant number of reports by security analysts;

(iii) The existence of market makers and arbitrageurs in the security;

(iv) The issuer's eligibility to file an S-3 registration statement under the 1933 Act (*see supra*, §§311 *et seq.*); and

(v)   A history of immediate movement in the price of the security in response to unexpected corporate events or financial developments.

[**Freeman v. Laventhol & Horwath**, 915 F.2d 193 (6th Cir. 1990); **Cammer v. Bloom**, 711 F. Supp. 1264 (D.N.J. 1989)]

b) Newly issued securities and fraud on the market [§1024]

Courts have struggled with application of the fraud on the market doctrine to newly issued securities. Because no established trading market for these securities exists, the market is not efficient and investors cannot be said to have relied on the integrity of the market price. Some courts would permit recovery if the newly issued securities are completely worthless, based on the notion that at a minimum the market "certifies" that securities offered for sale have at least *some* value. [*See, e.g.,* **Shores v. Sklar**, *supra*, §1018] Other courts decline to apply the doctrine in the absence of an efficient market. [*See, e.g.,* **Eckstein v. Balcor Film Investors**, 8 F.3d 1121 (7th Cir. 1993), *cert. denied*, 510 U.S. 1073 (1994)]

3) Rebutting the presumption of reliance [§1025]

In *Basic, supra*, the Court noted that the presumption of reliance can be rebutted by "[a]ny showing that severs the link between the alleged misrepresentation and either the price paid by the plaintiff or his decision to trade at a fair market price."

Example: If Company B publicly denies that it is negotiating its own buyout by Company A, but market makers in Company B stock in fact know that the negotiations are taking place, then the market price of Company B stock would not be affected by Company B's denial and the presumption would be rebutted. [**Basic, Inc. v. Levinson,** *supra*]

---

a) Note

As a practical matter, the presumption of reliance will be very difficult to rebut, because of the difficulty of establishing what various market participants knew.

j. Loss causation [§1026]

Courts have consistently stated that "causation" is a necessary element in a private action for damages under rule 10b-5. That is, the defendant's action must have "caused" the plaintiff's injury.

(1) Relationship to other elements of a rule 10b-5 cause of action [§1027]

The loss causation requirement is conceptually related to other elements of a rule 10b-5 cause of action—specifically, materiality (*supra*, §§973 *et seq.*), reliance (*supra*, §§1012 *et seq.*), and the "in connection with" requirement (*supra*, §§979 *et seq.*).

(a) The materiality requirement [§1028]

It seems almost inevitable that a court would find that loss causation has been shown once materiality has been proved (*i.e.*, that a reasonable investor would have considered the fact important in making a decision). In cases arising from nondisclosure in face-to-face transactions, the Supreme Court has held that loss causation (and reliance) may be presumed when material facts are withheld in violation of an obligation to disclose them. [*See* **Affiliated Ute Citizens v. United States,** *supra*, §1018]

1) Materiality without loss causation [§1029]

It is also conceivable, however, that a fact could be material but not the cause of loss. For example, it may be material to know that management engages in transactions in which their interest and the corporation's conflict, but this may not be the cause of the plaintiff's loss (*i.e.*, the price of the stock that the plaintiff bought might have gone down due to general market factors).

(b) The reliance requirement [§1030]

The plaintiff establishes reliance on a material fact—that is, transaction causation—by showing that the fact was (or, in nondisclosure cases, would have been) a substantial factor in causing him to *enter the transaction* in which he experienced a loss. (*See supra,* §§1012-1025.) Loss causation takes this one step further, requiring the plaintiff to show that the deception caused not only the transaction but the loss.

1) Transaction causation and loss causation [§1031]

Discussions of causation under rule 10b-5 can become confusing, because of the different kinds of causation that can exist. Essentially, a private rule 10b-5 plaintiff must show two kinds of causation: *transaction causation* and *loss causation*.

(c) The "in connection with" requirement [§1032]

In private securities litigation under rule 10b-5, a plaintiff who carries the burden of establishing loss causation will probably also satisfy the "in connection with" requirement. That is, if defendant's conduct actually caused the plaintiff's loss, then defendant's conduct was necessarily "in connection with" the purchase or sale of a security by the plaintiff.

(2) Loss causation amounts to proximate cause in misrepresentation cases [§1033]

To show loss causation in a misrepresentation case, the plaintiff must be able to show that the defendant's deception directly caused the loss and that the loss was a foreseeable outcome of the deception. In other words, loss causation is equivalent to proximate cause. [*See* **Suez Equity Investors, L.P. v. Toronto-Dominion Bank,** 250 F.3d 87 (2d Cir. 2001)]

---

e.g. **Example:** C Corp. made a tender offer for A Corp., which caused the price of A stock to rise. During the course of the tender offer, C discovered accounting irregularities that eventually caused C to restate its financial statements for several years and that turned ostensible profits into actual losses. Throughout the several months in which C investigated its accounting problems, C issued statements to the effect that it was financially healthy and that it remained committed to the merger. Eventually C abandoned the merger, and the price of A stock declined substantially. The court held that the element of loss causation was adequately pleaded on these facts. [**Semerenko v. Cendant Corp.,** *supra,* §987]

---

(3) Loss causation in nondisclosure situations [§1034]

The most difficult loss causation questions arise from an omission to disclose material facts. In these situations, the courts have at times proved willing to infer loss causation (and even reliance) upon a showing of materiality.

> **Example:** Bank officers who were "making a market" (*i.e.*, buying and selling as principals) in restricted securities of the Ute Tribal Development Corporation failed to disclose to sellers of the securities that the price defendants were paying was less than could be obtained in the trading market (which the defendants were helping to create). The Court held that both *reliance and loss causation* would be established if the facts withheld were found to be material. [**Affiliated Ute Citizens v. United States,** *supra*]

(a) Presumption not always available [§1035]

When it is feasible to prove actual loss causation, courts may not be willing to indulge a presumption that loss causation exists.

> **Example:** In a merger case, the bidder sued third parties that had found out about the proposed transaction and had purchased shares of the target, driving up the market price of target shares. The court held that the bidder had to show loss causation, meaning in this case that the plaintiff had to show that the target company board had been influenced by the market price of the company's shares in deciding whether or not to accept the bidder's offer. [**Litton Industries, Inc. v. Lehman Bros. Kuhn Loeb Inc.**, 967 F.2d 742 (2d Cir. 1992)]

k. Burden of proof [§1036]

In private civil causes of action for damages, the burden or proof is on the plaintiff to prove the rule 10b-5 cause of action by a *preponderance of the evidence.* [**Herman & MacLean v. Huddleston,** 459 U.S. 375 (1983)]

6. Insider Trading and the Duty to Disclose [§1037]

Trading on material, nonpublic information (so-called "insider trading") has been found by the courts to be a "fraud." Rule 10b-5 does *not* specifically require that a person having material information not publicly known disclose this information in a securities transaction. Nevertheless, the S.E.C. and the courts have applied rule 10b-5 to such transactions.

a. Elements of rule 10b-5 in insider trading cases [§1038]

The elements of a rule 10b-5 cause of action for insider trading are the same as those required for other actions based on rule 10b-5. (*See supra,* §§932 *et seq.*) The chief analytical difficulty presented by insider trading cases is whether the activity is fraudulent. In other words, given that the rule does not expressly prohibit trading on the basis of material, nonpublic information, when does such trading become fraudulent? The evolution of the insider trading prohibition under rule 10b-5 is to a great extent the story of the courts' and the S.E.C.'s struggle to answer this question. The earliest cases focused on the duty of the person with the information to disclose it to the person(s) with whom trading was carried on, and the courts described this duty as the duty to "*disclose or abstain* [from trading]." As the law has evolved, the understanding of the duty has become more refined, and today it is clear that "the purchase or sale of a security of any issuer, on the basis of material nonpublic information about that security or issuer, in breach of a duty of trust or confidence that is owed directly, indirectly, or derivatively to the issuer of that security or the shareholders of that issuer, or to any person who is the source of the material nonpublic information" violates rule 10b-5. [SEA Rule 10b5-1]

EXAM TIP   **gilbert**

Insider trading is a common exam issue. Remember, the cause of action for insider trading is the same as for any other rule 10b-5 case. However, the main focus usually is whether the defendant traded on the basis of **material, nonpublic information** about the security or its issuer **in breach of a duty of trust or confidence** owed to the issuer, its shareholders, or (in a case by the government) any person who is the source of the material, nonpublic information.

---

(1) Persons who may be liable for insider trading [§1039]

The persons who may be liable for insider trading under rule 10b-5 may be sorted into three categories: insiders, tippees, and misappropriators.

(a) Insiders [§1040]

An "insider" is an officer, director, controlling shareholder, or corporate employee of an issuer. There are two key elements of insider status:

1) *The person must have a relationship that gives access*—directly or indirectly—to information about the issuer's securities intended only for business purposes and not for personal benefit; and

2) *There must be an inherent unfairness* resulting from the insider taking advantage of the information, knowing that it is unavailable to those with whom the insider is dealing.

(b) "Constructive" insiders [§1041]

In addition to traditional insiders, courts treat persons such as accountants, lawyers, investment bankers, and others as "insiders" when they enter "into a special confidential relationship" with the issuer "and are given access to information solely for corporate purposes," with an expectation that the information will be kept confidential. [**Dirks v. S.E.C.,** 463 U.S. 646 (1983)]

---

e.g. **Example:** An investment banker, working on a proposed public offering for the issuer, received material nonpublic information about the issuer and traded on the basis of that information. The court held that the investment banker (and his employer) were liable as insiders. [**Shapiro v. Merrill Lynch, Pierce, Fenner & Smith, Inc.,** 495 F.2d 228 (2d Cir. 1974)]

(c) Tippees [§1042]

Tippees are persons who receive a tip from insiders and subsequently trade securities related to the tipped information. [*In re* **Investors Management Co.,** SEA Release No. 9267 (1971); *In re* **Cady, Roberts & Co.,** 40 S.E.C. 907 (1961); *and see* **Dirks v. S.E.C.,** *supra*]

(d) Misappropriators [§1043]

Finally, persons who misappropriate material nonpublic information for securities trading purposes, in breach of a duty to the source of the information, may be liable for insider trading. [**United States v. O'Hagan,** 521 U.S. 642 (1997)]

(2) Breach of duty [§1044]

The typical insider trading case consists of a purchase or sale by the defendant over an exchange without disclosing inside information. In such cases, the Supreme Court has held that *no violation of rule 10b-5 occurs unless the defendant breaches a duty* in so trading. [*See* **United States v. O'Hagan,** *supra*; **Chiarella v. United States,** 445 U.S. 222 (1980)] This duty may be a duty of trust and confidence owed by the insider (or constructive insider) to the issuer, to the issuer's shareholders, or, in the case of a misappropriator, to the source of the information. The key is that some *identifiable duty not to use the information for personal benefit* must be breached.

(3) "On the basis of" material nonpublic information [§1045]

Suppose a person is in possession of material nonpublic information with respect to a security, and then trades, but proves that the information did not cause the trade (*i.e.,* that the trade would have taken place even if the person had not learned the information)? In other words, does a person violate rule 10b-5 merely by trading while in possession of material nonpublic information, or must she actually use the information before a violation takes place?

Example: On September 14, D, a director of Computronix Corp., learned that a major customer of Computronix was going to either terminate or substantially curtail its orders. On September 19 through September 26, D sold 20,000 shares of Computronix stock. If D introduces credible evidence showing that the sales were part of a plan that had been in place before D learned of the reduced orders, has D violated the prohibition against insider trading? [*See* **S.E.C. v. Adler,** 137 F.3d 1325 (11th Cir. 1998)]

(a) Resolution—rule 10b5-1 [§1046]

Prior to 2000, there was some conflict in the cases on the "use vs. possession" question. In 2000, however, the S.E.C. adopted rule 10b5-1, under which a person will be deemed to have purchased or sold a security on the basis of material nonpublic information if the person was aware of the information when purchasing or selling.

1) "Awareness of" information [§1047]

Rule 10b5-1 does not indicate the circumstances under which a person is "aware of" material nonpublic information. Often it will be clear, for example when the C.E.O. of an issuer makes a business decision that will affect the company's stock price, and then buys or sells the company's stock. In other cases, however, there may be only indirect evidence of awareness, for example when the defendant's telephone records reveal calls to persons with inside information, but there is no direct proof that inside information was discussed.

2) Scienter and rule 10b5-1 [§1048]

Rule 10b5-1 does not modify the requirement that scienter be established before rule 10b-5 is violated. It merely defines trading "on the basis of" material nonpublic information to include all trading taking place while the defendant is aware of such information.

3) Affirmative defenses under rule 10b5-1 [§1049]

Rule 10b5-1 includes two affirmative defenses, either of which will shield the defendant from liability for trading "on the basis of" material nonpublic information. As with all affirmative defenses, the defendant must carry the burden of proof to establish the defense.

a) Prearranged trading [§1050]

The first affirmative defense requires proof that the challenged trading took place pursuant to a binding contract, trading instruction, or written *plan that existed before the defendant became aware of material nonpublic information.* [SEA Rule 10b5-1(c)(1)]

---

e.g. Example: On the facts of *Adler, supra,* D may be able to establish that the sale of shares was not made "on the basis of" material nonpublic information, because it took place pursuant to a plan that was established before D became aware of the reduced orders.

---

b) Institutional trading [§1051]

The second affirmative defense is available to anyone *other than a natural person.* For this defense, the defendant must prove that:

(i) The individual making the investment decision for the institution was *not aware of the material nonpublic information*; and

(ii) The institution had *reasonable policies* in place to ensure that the individuals making investment decisions would not violate the insider trading rules.

[SEA Rule 10b5-1(c)(2)]

(4) Application [§1052]

The principles above have been applied to various parties as follows:

(a) Trading insiders [§1053]

Insiders who trade on confidential, nonpublic information are liable under rule 10b-5 to the persons with whom they trade.

1) Controlling shareholders, directors, and officers [§1054]

Shareholders with a controlling interest, directors, and officers of a corporation are all insiders who can be held liable for trading on inside information with respect to the securities of their corporation. [**S.E.C. v. Texas Gulf Sulphur Co.,** 312 F. Supp. 77 (S.D.N.Y. 1970), *aff'd*, 446 F.2d 1301 (2d Cir. 1971)]

2) Corporate employees [§1055]

A group of corporate employees who accepted stock options knowing material facts about the company unknown to the company were held liable under rule 10b-5. [**S.E.C. v. Texas Gulf Sulphur Co.,** *supra*]

3) Tippees can sue insiders [§1056]

Note that tippees who are given supposedly inside information by corporate officer-insiders that turns out to be false and misleading can sue the insiders for recovery of their losses. [**Bateman Eichler, Hill Richards, Inc. v. Berner,** 472 U.S. 299 (1985)]

a) Note

The common law defense of in pari delicto (*i.e.*, equal fault) does not bar a private damages action under the federal securities laws against corporate insiders and broker-dealers who fraudulently induce investors to purchase securities by misrepresenting that they are conveying material, nonpublic information about the issuer. A private cause of action by such tippees will be barred only when the tippee's culpability for the violation is as great as that of the insiders against whom recovery is sought. [**Bateman Eichler, Hill Richards, Inc. v. Berner,** *supra*]

(b) Issuers [§1057]

An issuer may be held liable if material information is not properly disclosed to shareholders and the public before trading in the corporation's securities begins.

Example: In *Texas Gulf Sulphur, supra*, the S.E.C. sought an injunction against the corporation to prevent further violations of rule 10b-5. At issue was the corporation's failure to make complete and accurate disclosure in a news release with respect to its ore exploration activities. The court held that the news release misleadingly described certain material facts, and that *if the issuer does disclose material facts,* the disclosures must be timely and accurate. In addition, an issuer may be under a duty to update or correct earlier statements that have become misleading or untrue. (*See supra*, §§954-958.)

(c) Tippers [§1058]

"Tippers" (*i.e.,* insiders who, in breach of a duty, provide material nonpublic information to others, who then trade on that information) *are liable* under rule 10b-5, *even if they do not themselves trade on the information.*

Example: In *Texas Gulf Sulphur, supra*, one of the defendants tipped his friends, who traded on the information. The defendant was held liable for the profits made by his friends.

Example: A brokerage firm, participating as an underwriter in a public offering of securities, learned adverse information about the issuer. Before this information became public, the brokerage firm disclosed the adverse information to certain of its clients, who then sold securities of the issuer and thereby avoided substantial losses. The brokerage firm was held liable to contemporaneous buyers of the issuer's securities. [**Shapiro v. Merrill Lynch, Pierce, Fenner & Smith, Inc.,** *supra,* §1041]

(d) Tippees [§1059]

Those who receive inside information from tippers—"tippees"—and subsequently trade on it may be liable to the persons selling to, or buying from, the tippee.

1) *Dirks* and the derivative breach of duty [§1060]

Recall that liability under rule 10b-5 for insider trading is premised on the breach of a duty of trust and confidence owed to the issuer, its shareholders, or the source of the information. (*See supra,* §1044.) Clearly an insider breaches such a duty by trading with a shareholder of the issuer, but in most cases a ***tippee, as an unrelated party, is not bound by such duties.*** What, then, supports a tippee's liability for insider trading? In **Dirks v. S.E.C.,** *supra,* the Supreme Court held that tippee liability is premised on breach by the tipper of a duty; *i.e.,* the tippee derivatively breaches the tipper's duty.

a) Facts of *Dirks* [§1061]

Dirks, a stock analyst, was told by a corporate insider that the assets of the issuer were vastly overstated. The insider was not motivated by any personal gain but sought only to reveal the corporate fraud. Dirks gave this information to his clients, who then sold the issuer's stock to unknowing purchasers.

b) Result [§1062]

The Supreme Court held that neither the insider (the tipper) nor Dirks (the tippee) violated rule 10b-5. A tippee is liable for acting (either trading, or tipping others) on a tip only if, in giving the tip:

1/ The insider-tipper has ***breached duties owed to the issuer or its shareholders;***

2/ The insider-tipper has ***acted from a motive of "personal benefit";*** and

3/ The tippee knew, or should have known, that the information was provided by the tipper in breach of a duty.

c) The "personal benefit" requirement

1/ Gifts [§1063]

The requirement that the insider act to receive a "personal benefit" is satisfied if the insider receives a pecuniary gain or a reputational benefit that might translate into future earnings. The Supreme Court in *Dirks*, however, stated that this requirement is also met when an insider makes a *gift of confidential information to a trading relative or a friend.*

a/ Rationale

According to the Supreme Court, such a "tip and trade resemble trading by the insider himself followed by a gift of the profits to the recipient." Note that while the Court's statement is true, it is difficult in this situation to see the requisite "benefit" to the insider.

2/ Commissions [§1064]

In another case, a tippee who passed information to others but who bought no stock himself (but nevertheless benefited from the trading by receipt of broker's commissions) was held liable for insider trading. [**Shapiro v. Merrill Lynch, Pierce, Fenner & Smith, Inc.,** *supra*]

(e) Misappropriators and other corporate outsiders [§1065]

Corporate insiders (officers, directors, or employers) almost by definition possess a relationship to the issuer and its shareholders that makes them culpable if they trade on inside information. This concept has been extended to "constructive insiders" (*see supra*, §1041) and to tippees (who derivatively breach the insider's duty—*see supra*, §§1059-1064). Corporate "outsiders," however, may stand on a different footing since they acquire information in a variety of situations.

1) Rumors [§1066]

An outsider may hear rumors from several sources concerning a company, invest based on this information, and not be liable for abuse of inside information. [*See* **S.E.C. v. Monarch Fund,** Fed. Sec. L. Rep. (CCH) ¶97,148 (2d Cir. 1979)]

Example: In *Monarch Fund*, the defendant was an attorney responsible for advising two investment funds. He heard that a company in which the funds owned shares was receiving additional financing. He confirmed the rumors with a partner in the firm providing the financing. The court held this was not improper "inside" information because the information lacked "specificity" (defendant did not know the specific facts of what was going to happen); it was not clear that the information actually was confidential and nonpublic; and defendant's inquiries were reasonable under the circumstances.

2) "Outsider" has no fiduciary duty [§1067]

In **Chiarella v. United States,** *supra,* §1044, the Supreme Court significantly limited the concept of who is an "insider." *Chiarella* involved an employee of a financial printing firm who discovered information about pending tender offers from print orders from the bidders; he invested in the target companies based on this information. The Court held that no criminal action could be brought against the employee because he was not an "insider" of the target companies; *i.e.,* there was no relationship of trust and confidence between the defendant and the target companies or their shareholders, as there would be between management of a company and its shareholders. Furthermore, the defendant had not received the information directly from one of those insiders (*i.e.,* he was not a "tippee").

3) "Market information" and misappropriation [§1068]

At issue in *Chiarella, supra,* was information about the supply and demand for stock of the target companies, rather than "inside information" about the companies. This kind of information is called "market information," and it is often very valuable, particularly in the period immediately preceding a big change in demand, *e.g.,* just before a takeover is announced.

4) The misappropriation theory of liability [§1069]

In *Chiarella,* the government attempted to argue that the printer's employee misappropriated the employer's confidential information and that the employee was liable under rule 10b-5 by virtue of that breach of duty, notwithstanding that the employee breached no duty to the target or its shareholders. This "misappropriation theory" had not been argued at trial, however, and for that reason it was rejected by a majority of the Supreme Court. In 1997, however, the Supreme Court endorsed the misappropriation theory in a criminal case alleging violation of rule 10b-5. [**United States v. O'Hagan,** *supra,* §1043]

a) Facts of *O'Hagan* [§1070]

In *O'Hagan,* a law firm was retained in connection with a tender offer. O'Hagan, a lawyer with the firm, learned of the tender offer and purchased securities of the target, later selling them for a profit of more than $4.3 million. The Supreme Court, applying the misappropriation theory in a criminal case, held that O'Hagan violated rule 10b-5.

b) Basis of misappropriation liability [§1071]

A person violates rule 10b-5 when he misappropriates confidential information for securities trading purposes in breach of a duty to the source of the information. [**United States v. O'Hagan**, *supra*]

1/ Distinguish—traditional theory of liability [§1072]

The traditional theory of liability under rule 10b-5 is premised on the breach of a duty owed to the issuer or its shareholders; thus, the issuer as well as its insiders, constructive insiders, and (derivatively) the tippees of its insiders may all be liable. Under the misappropriation theory, however, the duty is not owed to the issuer or its shareholders, but rather it is owed to the source of the information.

2/ Misappropriation and the "in connection with" requirement [§1073]

The misappropriation theory bases rule 10b-5 liability on the taking of information "for securities trading purposes" and, in this way, meets the "in connection with" requirement of rule 10b-5. (*See supra*, §§979-988.) That is, the misappropriation becomes a rule 10b-5 violation because the information is taken in order to give the defendant an advantage in trading securities. If the defendant took the information but did not trade, there would be no rule 10b-5 case. The majority in *O'Hagan* distinguished the hypothetical case of a defendant who misappropriates money and uses it to trade in securities; money, said the majority, has a value independent of the subsequent trading and the fraud would not be "in connection with" the purchase or sale of a security.

EXAM TIP   **gilbert**

Remember that in a case **by the government,** a rule 10b-5 action can be based on the misappropriation of market information (*i.e.,* information relevant to the supply of or demand for a security) from **any source** if the misappropriation breaches a **duty owed to the source** and was for the purpose of trading in securities.

---

c) Misappropriation resulting from personal relationships [§1074]

Difficult questions sometimes arise when family members reveal material nonpublic information to one another. In such cases, the *Dirks* analysis often results in no liability, because the insider-tipper does not act from a motive of personal gain. Moreover, it is not always clear that a family member who trades on the information, or passes it on to someone who does, has "misappropriated" the information in breach of a duty to the source of the information.

Example: An insider tells his sister about a pending tender offer for the issuer, to help the sister tender her shares. The sister tells her daughter, who tells her husband, who tells his stockbroker. The stockbroker purchases the issuer's stock, believing (correctly, as it turns out) that the price of the issuer's shares will rise when the tender offer is announced publicly. Has the stockbroker violated rule 10b-5? Under *Dirks*, there is no violation. [**United States v. Chestman,** 947 F.2d 551 (2d Cir. 1991), *cert. denied*, 503 U.S. 1004 (1992)]

1/ Rule 10b5-2—"family" misappropriation [§1075]

In 2000, the S.E.C. adopted rule 10b5-2 to help clarify application of the misappropriation theory in family or personal relationships. Rule 10b5-2 sets out three nonexclusive circumstances in which a person has a duty of trust or confidence that will be breached if that person uses information for personal gain or reveals it to a third party. The breach of this duty, in turn, will support a cause of action under the misappropriation theory of insider trading. The circumstances in which such a duty exists include:

(i) When the recipient of the information *agrees to maintain the information in confidence*;

(ii) When the source of the information and the recipient have a *history, pattern, or practice of sharing confidences*, so that the recipient knows or should know that the source expects the information to remain in confidence; and

(iii) When the recipient of the information obtains the information from *her spouse, parent, child, or sibling,* unless the recipient can demonstrate that she did not know, nor reasonably should have known, that the information was expected to be kept confidential and that there was no actual agreement to keep it confidential.

[SEA Rule 10b5-2]

d) Misappropriation not available in private actions [§1076]

Although the Supreme Court has not addressed the question, circuit courts have held that private plaintiffs in insider trading cases cannot rely on the misappropriation theory—they must show breach of a duty owed to them. In other words, a private plaintiff must show that the defendant owed *her* a duty, and that the defendant breached that duty. [**Moss v. Morgan Stanley, Inc.,** 719 F.2d 5 (2d Cir. 1983)] The government, however, may assert the defendant's breach of duty to the source of the information in a case based on the misappropriation theory. [**United States v. O'Hagan,** *supra*]

b. "Selective disclosure" and regulation FD [§1077]

Dirks appeared to condone at least one kind of activity that the S.E.C. considers unlawful—the selective disclosure by insiders of material nonpublic information to securities analysts. Recall that under *Dirks,* disclosure by an insider gives rise to a cause of action under rule 10b-5 only if the insider acts from a motive of personal benefit (*see supra,* §§1062-1064). Thus, an insider can reveal material nonpublic information, as long as there is no quid pro quo. The S.E.C. has long been suspicious that in many cases where insiders selectively disclose material nonpublic information to securities analysts, there actually is a benefit back to the issuer, namely, favorable reports concerning the issuer by the analyst. There have been few cases brought claiming this as a violation of rule 10b-5, however, in part because it would be very difficult to prove the illicit benefit obtained by the issuer. To remedy the problem of selective disclosure, in 2000 the S.E.C. adopted regulation FD (for "Fair Disclosure"). Regulation FD is extremely complex, but some of its highlights are summarized below.

(1) Requirements—in general [§1078]

The essence of regulation FD is that if a disclosure of material nonpublic information is made by a regulated person and to a regulated person, the issuer must simultaneously (in the case of an intentional disclosure) or promptly (in the case of an inadvertent disclosure) make the information public.

(2) Applies to 1934 Act reporting companies [§1079]
Regulation FD is a reporting provision, rather than an antifraud provision. Thus, it applies to most companies that are required by either 1934 section 13(a) or section 15(d) to file reports with the S.E.C.

(3) Persons to whom disclosures are subject to regulation [§1080]
A disclosure of material nonpublic information is subject to regulation FD if it is made by the issuer or by a regulated person in its behalf (*see* below) to:

(a) A broker-dealer;

(b) An investment adviser:

(c) An investment company;

(d) Persons associated with any of the above; or

(e) Holders of the issuer's securities, if it is reasonably foreseeable that the holders will buy or sell securities on the basis of the disclosed information.

(4) Excluded persons [§1081]
Specifically excluded from the list of regulated disclosees are:

(a) Ratings agencies that publish their ratings, if disclosure is made solely for rating purposes;

(b) Persons subject to a duty of confidentiality; and

(c) Persons who agree to keep the information confidential.

(5) Persons by whom disclosures are subject to regulation [§1082]
Disclosures are regulated if made by senior officials of the issuer or by anyone else who regularly communicates with any of the persons to whom disclosures are regulated.

(6) Timing of public disclosure [§1083]
The key obligation under regulation FD is to make the information available to the public. How long the issuer has to accomplish this depends on whether the regulated disclosure was intentional or unintentional.

(a) Intentional disclosures—simultaneous public disclosure required [§1084]
A regulated disclosure is intentional if the regulated person making the disclosure knew, or was reckless in not knowing, that the information disclosed was material and nonpublic. The obligation in this

case is to make the information public simultaneously with the disclosure to the regulated disclosee.

(b) **Unintentional disclosures—prompt public disclosure required [§1085]**

A regulated disclosure is unintentional if the regulated person making the disclosure did not know, and was not reckless in not knowing, that the information disclosed was material and nonpublic. When an unintentional disclosure happens, the issuer must make the information public "as soon as reasonably practicable."

c. **Specific insider trading legislation [§1086]**

The securities markets of the 1980s were turbulent and produced two significant statutes dealing with insider trading: the Insider Trading Sanctions Act of 1984 and the Insider Trading and Securities Fraud Enforcement Act of 1988.

(1) **Insider Trading Sanctions Act [§1087]**

In 1984, Congress gave the S.E.C. additional enforcement powers against insider trading by enacting the Insider Trading Sanctions Act of 1984. Under this statute, the S.E.C. can seek a civil penalty of up to *three times* the amount of the insider's ill-gotten profits (or avoided losses). There are many unanswered questions under this Act, for example, would successive actions under the Act and for criminal violations violate the constitutional prohibition against double jeopardy? In view of the Act's provisions establishing the possibility of penalties at three times the insider's trading profits, would a nontrading tipper be covered by the Act? [*See* SEA §21A]

(2) **Insider Trading and Securities Fraud Enforcement Act of 1988 [§1088]**

In 1988, Congress adopted the Insider Trading and Securities Fraud Enforcement Act (the "1988 Act"). This statute, which added section 20A to the 1934 Act, provides a cause of action to persons who sold or purchased a security in the market at the time that the defendant purchased or sold a security of the same class, if the defendant's transaction violated "any provision of [the 1934 Act and the rules thereunder]."

(a) **Establishes cause of action [§1089]**

The 1988 Act does not prohibit any activity; instead, it relies on the existing provisions of the 1934 Act to establish a violation. Once a violation is established, however, the 1988 Act establishes a cause of action in favor of contemporaneous traders in the market.

(b) **Remedies under the 1988 Act [§1090]**

The 1988 Act limits the amount recoverable to the *defendant's profit gained or loss avoided*. This amount is then further reduced by the amount of any profits the defendant has already disgorged relating to the same securities transactions. [SEA §20A(b)(1), (2)]

7. Remedies

a. Rescission [§1091]

Rescission undoes the bargain between the parties; *i.e*, each party receives back what she gave in the transaction. Although most actions under rule 10b-5 seek damages, there is some authority permitting rescission—permitting the plaintiff to recover whatever (money or securities) she parted with. [*See, e.g.,* **Randall v. Loftsgaarden,** 478 U.S. 647 (1986)—rescission may be appropriate in an action under rule 10b-5] There are equitable limitations applicable to rescission, however, such as waiver, laches, estoppel, and impracticality (as in unwinding the merger of two publicly traded companies or if the defendant-purchaser has sold the securities purchased from the plaintiff).

b. Damages [§1092]

There are several basic formulas for awarding damages in private actions: (i) plaintiff may be awarded *restitution, i.e.,* the difference between the value of what she gave up and the value of what she received in the transaction (out-of-pocket losses); (ii) plaintiff may recover damages based on the *defendant's profits*; or (iii) plaintiff may recover the "benefit of her bargain." Regardless of the formula used, the damages recoverable by a private plaintiff were capped in 1995. (*See infra,* §1752.)

(1) Restitution [§1093]

Most courts grant the plaintiff damages based on restitution (what she has lost), but the restitution formula is applied differently by different courts.

(a) Value measured after "reasonable time" [§1094]

Some courts have placed a time limitation on measuring the plaintiff's damages. Thus, the plaintiff would recover the difference between the value of what she gave up—as of a reasonable period of time after the discovery of the fraud—and the value of what she received. [**Mitchell v. Texas Gulf Sulphur Co.,** 446 F.2d 90 (10th Cir. 1971)]

Example—plaintiff as seller: XYZ Corp. knows, but does not disclose, very favorable news about its ore exploration activity, which has resulted in the discovery of a rich vein of gold. During this time, A sells 100 shares of XYZ stock for $10 per share. Shortly thereafter, XYZ discloses the news and its stock quickly goes to $20 per share. A discovers the fraud soon after the news is disclosed. Her damages will be measured as of a reasonable time after the discovery of the fraud, when a reasonable person would have sought to mitigate damages by repurchasing the shares she had sold (*e.g.*, at the time the stock reached $20 per share). Her damages will thus be $1,000 ($20 minus $10 equals $10 per share × 100 shares). Even though the stock may continue to appreciate to $30, A cannot measure her damages at this amount.

> **Example—plaintiff as buyer:** XYZ Corp. knows, but does not disclose, highly unfavorable information about its ore exploration activity, which has been both expensive and utterly fruitless. During this time, A buys 100 shares of XYZ stock for $20 per share. Shortly thereafter, XYZ discloses the news and its stock quickly falls to $10 per share. A discovers the fraud soon after the news is disclosed. Her damages will be measured as of a reasonable time after the discovery of the fraud, when a reasonable person would have mitigated damages by selling the shares (*e.g.*, at $10 per share). Her damages will thus be $1,000, calculated exactly as in the preceding example. Even though the stock may continue to fall to $5, A cannot measure her damages at this amount.

(b) Value measured at time of trial [§1095]

Some courts are more lenient, giving the plaintiff damages based on the difference between the value of the securities at the time of the trial and the value of consideration paid by or to the plaintiff. [*See* **Myzel v. Fields,** 386 F.2d 718 (8th Cir. 1967), *cert. denied*, 390 U.S. 951 (1968)]

(2) Defendant's profits [§1096]

Some courts prefer a "disgorgement of profits" rule to mere restitution. In such a court, a defrauded seller would sue for the profit the buyer had made on the transaction. [*See* **Ohio Drill & Tool Co. v. Johnson,** 498 F.2d 186 (6th Cir. 1974)]

(3) Benefit of the bargain [§1097]

Alternatively, the plaintiff may request damages in the amount she expected to receive compared to what she actually received (*e.g.*, the acquiring company promised to pay shareholders of the acquired company $62.50 per share of common stock and only paid $59 per share). Plaintiff may bring an action to recover the difference of $3.50 per share. [**Osofsky v. Zipf,** 645 F.2d 107 (2d Cir. 1981)]

(4) Damages in insider trading cases [§1098]

Insider trading cases often present a difficult case for damages, especially when the securities are traded in an impersonal market. Suppose, for example, that D (defendant) is "tipped" to inside information, and as a result, sells 10 shares of IBM stock. By selling, D avoids a loss of $5 per share, or $50 in all. Now, suppose further that plaintiffs' attorneys get wind of this sale and bring a class action against D, on behalf of all those who purchased IBM stock on the day defendant sold. Plaintiffs seek to recover $5 per share for every share sold on that day, some 460 million shares in all. D's $50 avoided loss now exposes her to potentially huge damages. In this case, the word "draconian" seems too weak to describe D's liability. [*But see* **Shapiro v. Merrill Lynch, Pierce, Fenner & Smith, Inc.,** *supra,* §1058]

(a) Limiting insider trading liability [§1099]

To address the massive liability faced by insider trading defendants, which far exceeds the profits realized or loss avoided, courts tend to limit damages.

Example: A corporation disclosed material nonpublic information to a financial analyst in advance of general disclosure to the public, and the analyst used the information to trade in the company's shares (without, of course, disclosing the information). The court limited the recovery to the amount gained by the tippee as a result of selling at the earlier date (rather than delaying sale until after the disclosure). [*See* **Elkind v. Liggett & Myers, Inc.,** *supra,* §958] The evidence showed that the plaintiffs purchased and the defendant sold stock over the exchange when the information was undisclosed (at $55 per share); the disclosure was made and the stock dropped to $52, and a day later was at $46 per share. The defendant tippee's maximum liability is the price realized on sale ($55) minus the price of the stock within a reasonable time after disclosure (here $46 per share). If the total damages of plaintiffs exceed the total liability of the defendants, then the amount paid to each plaintiff is a pro rata share of the defendant's total liability amount. [*See also* **Fridrich v. Bradford**, 542 F.2d 307 (6th Cir. 1976), *cert. denied,* 429 U.S. 1053 (1977)]

---

c. Punitive damages [§1100]

Punitive damages are *not* available under rule 10b-5.

d. Liability of multiple defendants [§1101]

If there are multiple defendants in a rule 10b-5 action, two questions arise: First, what is the individual liability of each defendant? And second, can one defendant recover from another (that is, is there a right of contribution)?

(1) Liability of each defendant [§1102]

Until 1995, the liability of multiple defendants under rule 10b-5 was joint and several—*i.e.*, all defendants were individually liable for the total damages. In 1995, however, Congress added section 21D(f) to the 1934 Act, which provides that in *private actions* under the 1934 Act: (i) persons who knowingly commit securities fraud are jointly and severally liable; and (ii) all others are liable in proportion to their respective fault.

(2) Contribution [§1103]

In 1993, the Supreme Court confirmed the holdings of numerous lower courts that a defendant in a private action under rule 10b-5 has a right of contribution against other defendants found liable in the case. [**Musick, Peeler & Garrett v. Employers Insurance Co.**, 508 U.S. 286 (1993)]

e. S.E.C. actions [§1104]

When the S.E.C. brings an action under rule 10b-5, it may seek remedies different from those sought by private plaintiffs. The S.E.C. may recommend a criminal action to the Justice Department under rule 10b-5 or may itself sue for an injunction or to recover trading profits made by the defendants. [**S.E.C. v. Texas Gulf Sulphur Co.**, *supra*, §1058] Where the S.E.C. sues a defendant that purchased securities based on inside information, the proper measure of damages is the difference between the price paid (*e.g.*, $5/share) and the price at which the security traded within a short time after the material information was disclosed to the public (*e.g.*, $10/share). [*See* **S.E.C. v. MacDonald**, 699 F.2d 47 (1st Cir. 1983)]

8. Defenses [§1105]

The following defenses are available to a defendant in a rule 10b-5 action.

a. On the merits [§1106]

The defendant may be able to defend on the merits of the case, *e.g.*, that full disclosure of the facts was made, that the statements made were true, that the untruthful statements were not material or did not cause the plaintiff's loss, or that the defendant lacked scienter.

b. Other defenses [§1107]

Other, procedural defenses may also be available to the plaintiff.

(1) Failure to plead with particularity [§1108]

Under the Private Securities Litigation Reform Act of 1995 ("PSLRA") (*see infra*, §§1731 *et seq.*), actions based on fraud and filed under the 1934 Act by private parties must meet heightened standards of specificity at the complaint stage, before any discovery takes place. As a result, a common defense to an action under rule 10b-5 filed by a private party is a motion to dismiss for failure to plead fraud with sufficient particularity. To plead fraud successfully, a private plaintiff must:

(i) *Identify* each misleading statement;

(ii) *State the reason(s)* it is misleading;

(iii) With respect to allegations made on information and belief, *specify all facts on which that belief is formed*; and

(iv) *Specify facts* giving rise to a *strong inference that the defendant acted with the required state of mind*, *i.e.*, with scienter.

[SEA §21D(b)]

(a) Pleading scienter [§1109]

It can be very difficult for plaintiffs to plead scienter (*i.e.*, fraudulent or deceptive intent) with the necessary particularity. Before the PSLRA, the Second Circuit standard was prevalent and required the plaintiff to plead particular facts showing both motive and opportunity to commit fraud. After the PSLRA, not all courts are in agreement about what it takes to meet the standards, especially about what it takes to raise the strong inference of scienter that the PSLRA requires.

1) Second Circuit standard [§1110]

The Second Circuit has suggested that the required strong inference arises when a complaint sufficiently alleges that the defendants:

(i) *Benefited* in a concrete and personal way from the purported fraud;

(ii) *Engaged* in deliberately illegal behavior;

(iii) *Knew facts* or had access to information suggesting that their public statements were not accurate; or

(iv) *Failed to check* information that they had a duty to monitor.

[**Novak v. Kasaks**, 216 F.3d 300 (2d Cir. 2000)] The court further held that in pleading scienter, the plaintiff need not recite and specify every fact upon which the defendant's deceptiveness is based, but rather merely sufficient facts to support the belief that the defendants were being deceptive. [*Id.*]

---

e.g. **Example:** ATS Corp., which operated retail women's clothing stores, began to maintain a second category of inventory, which it called "Box and Hold." This inventory, most of which was very out of date, built up to nearly one-third of ATS's entire stock. Throughout this time, the corporation and the individual defendants (officers and directors of ATS) made misleading statements about ATS's inventory levels. Eventually the truth came out and the stock price declined substantially. The court held that "[w]hen managers deliberately make materially false statements concerning inventory with the intent to deceive the investment community, they have engaged in conduct actionable under the securities laws." The fact that the "Box and Hold" inventory was later liquidated at a substantial loss supported the allegations of the complaint, as did statements made by the individual defendants after the truth came to light. [*Id.*]

2) Ninth Circuit standard [§1111]

The Ninth Circuit has adopted a more demanding test, which requires the plaintiff to plead, in great detail, facts that constitute strong circumstantial evidence of (i) deliberately reckless, or (ii) conscious, misconduct. Mere recklessness is not enough in the Ninth Circuit; rather, something closer to intentional conduct must be shown. In addition, the Ninth Circuit is more demanding in requiring highly specific and detailed allegations of fact to support the inference of "deliberate recklessness" or intentional conduct.

e.g. Example: SGI Corp., a manufacturer of computer systems, announced a new product that required a so-called ASIC chip manufactured by T Corp. SGI projected continued rapid growth, based on projections of great demand for the new system and assumptions of continued supply of the ASIC chip from T. In fact, demand proved to be sluggish and T had trouble making the ASIC chip. The defendants, SGI and officers and directors of SGI, made optimistic statements, including "confirming" rapid growth projections and increasing demand for the new system, as well as assuring the market that supplies of the needed ASIC chip were plentiful. Eventually the truth came out and the price of SGI stock declined substantially. The court held that the complaint "lacks sufficient detail and foundation necessary to meet either the particularity or strong inference requirements of the PSLRA." The court noted that the complaint described internal reports detailing the company's problems, but did not detail the contents of the reports nor identify who prepared them, which officers reviewed them, and from whom the plaintiff received the information. [*In re* **Silicon Graphics Inc. Securities Litigation**, 183 F.3d 970 (9th Cir. 1999)]

(b) Scienter in insider trading cases [§1112]

Pleading scienter in insider trading cases is often easier than in other cases. It can still be difficult, however, if the plaintiff cannot prove that an insider had material nonpublic information, but instead relies on the timing of the insider's trades to raise the inference that the insider had such information. One court has concluded that "insider trading is suspicious only when it is dramatically out of line with prior trading practices at times calculated to maximize the personal benefit from undisclosed inside information." [**Ronconi v. Larkin**, 253 F.3d 423 (9th Cir. 2001)]

(c) Pleading requirements apply only to 1934 Act [§1113]

The enhanced pleading requirements of the PSLRA relate only to cases brought under the 1934 Act (*e.g.*, actions brought under rule 10b-5). The special pleading requirements do not apply to action brought under the 1933 Act (many of which do not require proof of fraud in any event).

(2) Statute of limitations [§1114]

The Sarbanes-Oxley Act of 2002 for the first time created an express statute of limitations that applies to private actions under rule 10b-5. Under SOXA section 804, a rule 10b-5 action must be brought within *two years after the discovery of the facts constituting the violation, and in no case later than five years after the violation occurred.* [SOXA §804; 28 U.S.C. §1658(b)] Before SOXA added this statute of limitations, the Supreme Court had held that the statute of limitations should be determined by reference to the express causes of action in the 1934 Act, and not by analogy to state statutes of limitation. [**Lampf, Pleva, Lipkind, Prupis & Petigrow v. Gilbertson,** 501 U.S. 350 (1991)] Although the specific holding of *Lampf* on the statute of limitations has been overturned by Congress in SOXA, the Supreme Court's reasoning that gaps in the statute ought to be filled by reference to federal legislation, rather than state law, remains relevant.

(a) Inquiry notice—what constitutes "discovery" [§1115]

Because plaintiffs must bring suit within one year of "discovery" of the facts constituting the violation, it is important to know when "discovery" of these facts has taken place. Although courts are not all in agreement, the trend is to begin the one-year period either when the plaintiff learned the facts or when, exercising reasonable diligence, the plaintiff should have learned them, whichever comes first. [*See, e.g.,* **Law v. Medco Research, Inc.,** 113 F.3d 781 (7th Cir. 1997); **Howard v. Haddad,** 962 F.2d 328 (4th Cir. 1992)]

(3) Other common law defenses [§1116]

Other common law defenses, such as in pari delicto (*i.e.*, equal fault), may be applicable to rule 10b-5 actions. However, courts are careful to subordinate such defenses to the primary objective of seeing that the purposes and policies of the securities acts are carried out. [*See* **Bateman Eichler, Hill Richards, Inc. v. Berner,** *supra,* §1056]

---

e.g. **Example:** In *Bateman*, the Court held that the defense of in pari delicto did **not** prevent a tippee (who had been given false information) from suing the corporate insiders who passed on the false information. The Court reasoned that barring such private actions would result in fraudulent schemes going undetected by the S.E.C., because there would be no incentive for plaintiff-tippees to bring such actions.

---

(4) Lack of plaintiff's "due diligence"
See discussion *supra*, §999.

9. Section 17(a) of the 1933 Act and Rule 10b-5 [§1117]

The language of section 17(a) of the 1933 Act (*see supra*, §854) and rule 10b-5 are almost identical; however, section 17(a)(3) applies only to fraud against purchasers, while sections 17(a)(1) and (2) are broader in scope. Also, section 17(a) contains the word "offer," so that it applies to fraud not only in connection with sales, but also with offers to sell (while rule 10b-5 requires an actual purchase or sale; *see supra*, §§989-992). Furthermore, the Supreme Court has held that in *injunction* actions pursuant to section 17(a)(2) and (3), the culpability standard is only negligence, while in rule 10b-5 actions, scienter must be shown. If the Supreme Court were to uphold private damage actions under section 17(a), then negligence may also be the applicable standard in these situations. [*See* **Aaron v. S.E.C.**, *supra*, §858]

a. Civil remedy under section 17(a) [§1118]

The question whether there is an implied civil remedy under section 17(a) is important because, if there is, it may afford a remedy in some situations not covered by rule 10b-5. At this point, however, the issue has not been decided by the Supreme Court, and the trend in the lower courts is away from an implied remedy under section 17(a). (*See supra*, §857.) The question will probably be ultimately decided by application of the standards of **Cort v. Ash**, *supra*, §923, and **Touche Ross & Co. v. Redington**, *supra*, §924.

10. Class Actions Under Rule 10b-5 [§1119]

Rule 10b-5 actions are frequently brought as class actions, because many shareholders may be similarly injured by the same rule 10b-5 violation.

a. "Class action" defined [§1120]

The class action is a suit in which a representative plaintiff presses her own claim and the claims of others similarly situated in a single action to establish the liability of the defendant and the gross amount of damages. It is in some respects an ideal method for enforcement of private rule 10b-5 rights, because it contributes to the efficient use of limited judicial resources, yet ensures that the interests of all plaintiffs (which may otherwise be too small to be asserted economically in individual actions) are given vindication in the courts, and thereby contributes to the effective enforcement of the federal securities laws.

b. Federal court jurisdiction [§1121]

The 1934 Act vests exclusive jurisdiction in the federal district courts over violation of its provisions and over all suits to enforce any liability or duty created by it or the rules and regulations thereunder. [SEA §27]

(1) Federal Rules of Civil Procedure applied [§1122]

The federal courts must apply the Federal Rules of Civil Procedure in all procedural matters; therefore, the Federal Rules apply to class actions brought under the federal securities laws.

c. Preconditions to the existence of a class [§1123]

Federal Rule 23(a) lists four mandatory preconditions to the existence of a class of plaintiffs:

(i) *The class must be so numerous* that joinder of all members is impracticable.

(ii) *There must be questions of law or fact common to the entire class* of plaintiffs.

(iii) *The claims or defenses of the representative parties must be typical* of the claims or defenses of the entire class.

(iv) *The representative parties must fairly and adequately protect* the interests of the entire class.

Even assuming that the above preconditions to the existence of a class are met, Federal Rule 23(b) imposes an *additional* requirement that the class representative (plaintiff) plead and show the existence of *one* of the following *special circumstances*:

(i) *That inconsistent, varying, or disadvantageous judgments are likely* if a class action is not permitted;

(ii) *That final injunctive or declaratory relief is appropriate; or*

(iii) That a *class action is superior to other available methods* for the fair and efficient adjudication of the controversy.

d. Exclusion from the class [§1124]

Under Federal Rule 23(c)(2), potential class members can avoid being bound by any judgment rendered in a class action by requesting exclusion from the class.

e. Application in rule 10b-5 case [§1125]

Cannon v. Texas Gulf Sulphur Co. provides a good example of application of the class action provisions to a rule 10b-5b situation. Over 364,000 shares had been sold during a five-day period following a misleading press release, and 26 actions involving 250 plaintiffs had already been filed. Although each plaintiff's reliance on the press release might have to be determined individually, the number of common questions predominated over those that had to be tried separately. The court concluded that a class action was appropriate on behalf of all shareholders who had sold their stock in the five-day period. [**Cannon v. Texas Gulf Sulphur Co.**, Fed. Sec. L. Rep. (CCH) ¶92,372 (1969)]

f. Private Securities Litigation Reform Act of 1995 [§1126]

The Private Securities Litigation Reform Act of 1995 (the "1995 Act") has made it considerably more difficult for private plaintiffs to bring securities fraud class actions. Most of the changes made by the 1995 Act are procedural and are summarized *infra*, §§1731 *et seq*.

C. Tender Offers and Repurchases of Stock

1. Introduction [§1127]

A "tender offer" is an offer by a person (the "bidder") to purchase the securities of a corporation (the "target"), made directly to the shareholders of the target. The purchase price may be paid *in cash*, *in securities*, or in a combination of both. The offer may be made with (a "friendly" offer) or without (a "hostile" offer) the cooperation of the target's management.

2. Inadequacies of Earlier Regulation [§1128]

Several provisions of the securities laws applied to tender offers prior to 1968, but there were gaps in the coverage of these provisions.

a. Securities Act of 1933 [§1129]

If the bidder made a cash offer to purchase, the 1933 Act would not be applicable (because it was an offer to purchase rather than an offer to sell securities) and there would be no affirmative disclosure requirement imposed on the bidder. Although 1933 Act section 5(c) does speak of "offers to buy," section 4(1) exempts most transactions, and the S.E.C. has never registered a cash tender offer under the Act. Also, the antifraud sections of the 1933 Act [SA §§11, 12, 17] are of limited use, because they apply only to defrauded *purchasers* of securities (*see supra*, §747).

b. Securities Exchange Act of 1934

(1) Rule 10b-5 [§1130]

The antifraud provisions of rule 10b-5 are available to plaintiff-sellers who sell their stock where there has been a material misrepresentation or omission by the bidder (*see supra*, §933). However, because rule 10b-5 requires the plaintiff to be an actual purchaser or seller of securities, it was questionable whether the target itself—or its shareholders who did not sell—could bring an action. Therefore, this rule did not adequately cover the tender offer area.

(2) Proxy rules [§1131]

The proxy rules under section 14 of the 1934 Act are of limited applicability, because tender offers usually do not require a shareholder vote, and therefore do not require any solicitation of proxies (*see infra*, §1281).

(3) Market manipulation [§1132]

If the bidder or the target engage in market manipulation (*see infra*, §1881), the other might have recourse to section 9 or rule 10b-5 of the 1934 Act. But the problems of proof and the limited coverage of section 9 (*see infra*, §1936) make this section inadequate for most of the problems that typically arise in tender offers.

3. Federal Regulation of Tender Offers [§1133]

Due to the limitations in the coverage of other provisions of the federal securities laws, in 1968 Congress passed the Williams Act (named after Senator Harrison Williams of New Jersey) specifically to regulate tender offers. The Williams Act added to the 1934 Act section 13(d) and (e), and section 14(d), (e), and (f).

a. Jurisdiction to regulate [§1134]

Jurisdiction of the federal government over tender offers is based on their effect on interstate commerce and on the use of the mails or other means of interstate commerce to effect the transaction.

b. Overview of SEA regulation of tender offers [§1135]

The following sections of the 1934 Act apply to tender offers:

(1) Reporting requirement [§1136]

Section 13(d) requires any party who acquires 5% or more of an equity security registered under section 12 of the 1934 Act (*see supra*, §§875-877) to report the acquisition and the party's intentions with respect to the issuer of the security. [*See also* Schedule 13D—sets forth the reporting requirements of section 13(d) in more detail]

(2) Disclosure requirements [§1137]

Section 14(d) is the basic section that regulates the making of tender offers. Under this section, the bidder must make an appropriate disclosure prior to commencing the tender offer. [*See also* Schedule TO] In addition, section 14(d)(4) requires disclosure by anyone making a "solicitation or recommendation to the holders of [the target's securities] to accept or reject a tender offer." [*See also* Schedule 14D-9] Rule 14e-2 requires the target's management to disclose its position on the tender offer; this disclosure triggers the target's obligation to file a Schedule 14D-9.

(3) Antifraud provision [§1138]

Section 14(e) is an antifraud provision that makes it unlawful for any party making a tender offer—or defending against one—to make untrue statements of material fact (or to omit to state material facts), or to engage in any fraudulent, deceptive, or manipulative act or practice in connection with any tender offer.

(a) Note

Although the language of section 14(e) is essentially the same as that of rule 10b-5, the two sections have been construed differently by the courts. [*See, e.g.,* **United States v. Chestman**, 947 F.2d 551 (1991), *cert. denied*, 503 U.S. 1004 (1992); *and see infra*, §§1205 *et seq.*]

(b) And note

While section 14(e) applies only in the context of tender offers, it is *not* limited to tender offers made for securities registered under the 1934 Act.

TENDER OFFER REPORTING—AN OVERVIEW

CHECKLIST OF REPORTING PROVISIONS:

☑ Anyone acquiring **5% *or more*** of an equity security registered under SEA section 12 **must report** the acquisition and his intentions.

☑ The bidder must file a **disclosure statement** (Schedule TO) prior to the tender offer.

☑ The target's management generally must **disclose its recommendation** with respect to the bid.

☑ It is unlawful for anyone to make **material untrue statements or omissions**, or otherwise commit fraud, with respect to a tender offer.

---

c. Remedies for violation of tender offer rules [§1139]

Although the 1934 Act says nothing about remedies for violation of the tender offer rules, the courts have filled in some of the gaps in the statutory provisions by *implying* remedies to enforce the provisions of the Act. However, since the mid-1970s the trend in the courts has been to limit implied private rights of action (*see* discussion *supra*, §922); thus the law with respect to each section of the Williams Act [SEA §§13(d), (e); 14(d), (e), (f)] must be checked carefully.

4. Preliminary Reporting Requirement—Section 13(d) [§1140]

The preliminary reporting requirements of section 13(d) are calibrated so that any-one making significant acquisitions of registered equity securities must disclose her plans with respect to the issuer of those securities at an early stage. Schedule 13D of the 1934 Act specifically requires disclosure of certain information. Note that some persons may use section 13(g) reporting, which requires less disclosure, when there is no intention to make any change in the control of the issuer. [*See* SEA Schedule 13G]

a. Ownership criteria [§1141]

Any person who acquires beneficial ownership in excess of 5% of a class of equity security registered under SEA section 12 must, within 10 days after the acquisition, file an information statement (usually Schedule 13D, sometimes Schedule 13G) with the S.E.C., sending copies to the issuer of the security and to any exchanges on which the security is traded. [SEA §13(d)(1), (6)(B)]

(1) Updating [§1142]

Section 13(d) requires the information to be updated if any material changes subsequently occur.

(2) Percentage requirement [§1143]

Section 13(d) applies to the acquisition of any class of registered equity security, and the 5% ownership requirement applies to *each class separately.*

---

e.g. **Example:** If A acquires 5% of the convertible debentures of XYZ Corp., the reporting requirements apply even though—if the debentures were converted into common stock—A would not own 5% of the underlying common stock. [**GAF Corp. v. Milstein,** 453 F.2d 709 (2d Cir. 1971)]

---

(3) Groups of persons [§1144]

Moreover, when two or more persons act as a partnership, limited partnership, syndicate, or other group for the purpose of acquiring, holding, voting, or disposing of the securities of an issuer, the group is deemed a "person" for purposes of section 13(d) (as well as for section 14(d)). [SEA §§13(d)(3), 14(d)(2); SEA Rule 13d-5]

(a) Formation of a group—five percent requirement [§1145]

A critical issue in group situations is the determination of when the group is "formed." The Second Circuit has held that the mere formation of a group of persons for the purpose of attempting to obtain control of an issuer triggers the section 13(d) filing requirement if the members of the group collectively own enough securities to trigger the filing requirement. There need be no additional stock purchases made by the group *as a group*. [**GAF Corp. v. Milstein,** *supra*]

---

e.g. **Example:** In *GAF Corp.*, the defendants were members of a family who each individually owned stock in GAF and collectively had the required percentage of shares prior to passage of section 13(d). After the Act was passed, and without purchasing additional stock, they formed a group with the intention to gain control of GAF and oust its management. Although section 13(d) requires a "person" to file only if acquiring more than 5% of a class of stock, the group was held to have "acquired" a beneficial interest in the prior, individual holdings of its members.

(b) Necessity of showing group "purpose" [§1146]

A group triggers the section 13(d) filing requirement only if it is formed for a purpose described in rule 13d-5 ("acquiring, holding, voting, or disposing of the securities of an issuer"). [*See* **Portsmouth Square, Inc. v. Shareholders Protective Committee,** 770 F.2d 866 (9th Cir. 1985)—committee of shareholders who solicited money from other shareholders to fund litigation against management not a "group" under §13(d)]

1) Purpose to dispose of securities [§1147]

One court found a "group" in five shareholders who had agreed that they would sell their stock if someone could be found to make a takeover proposal for the issuer. Although the five had not agreed on specific terms of sale, their collective willingness to sell was found to be sufficient purpose. [**Wellman v. Dickinson,** 682 F.2d 355 (2d Cir. 1982)]

2) Purpose to control must be more than mere desire [§1148]

In general, the purpose to control that triggers the filing requirement must be evidenced by some significant step to control the issuer, rather than merely a wish or desire to control. [**S.E.C. v. Amster & Co.,** 762 F. Supp. 604 (S.D.N.Y. 1991)]

(c) Stock "parking" [§1149]

Courts have sometimes held that defendants evaded the disclosure requirements of section 13(d) by arranging for others to purchase securities that, if purchased by the defendants, would have triggered the reporting requirements. This conduct has been penalized heavily, with both criminal sanctions [*see, e.g.,* **United States v. Bilzerian,** 926 F.2d 1285 (2d Cir.), *cert. denied,* 502 U.S. 813 (1991)] and disgorgement of profits realized on purchases made between the time the filing should have been made and the time it was actually made [*see, e.g.,* **S.E.C. v. First City Financial Corp., Ltd.,** 890 F.2d 1215 (D.C. Cir. 1989)].

b. **Information required [§1150]**

The following data must be disclosed in a section 13(d) information statement [*see* Schedule 13D]:

(1) **Information about the purchasers [§1151]**

The purchaser must disclose the background and identity of the persons involved in the purchase of securities.

(2) **Information about consideration [§1152]**

The sources and amounts of consideration used in the purchases must be disclosed.

(3) **Information about the purpose of the purchases [§1153]**

The purchaser must disclose whether or not the purpose of the purchases is to acquire control of the issuer and any plans or proposals that relate to (or would result in) liquidation of the issuer, sale of its assets, merger with any other entity, or any other major change in its business or corporate structure.

(4) **Information about ownership [§1154]**

The purchaser must disclose the number of shares she owns beneficially and the existence of any rights to purchase additional shares.

(5) **Information about contracts, etc. [§1155]**

The purchaser must disclose the existence of any contracts, arrangements, or other understandings relating to the issuer or its securities.

TENDER OFFERS AND SECTION 13(d) **gilbert**

PRELIMINARY REPORTING REQUIREMENTS

ANYONE WHO ACQUIRES OWNERSHIP OF MORE THAN 5% OF A CLASS OF EQUITY SECURITIES REGISTERED UNDER THE 1934 ACT MUST, WITHIN 10 DAYS AFTER THE ACQUISITION, FILE A STATEMENT WITH THE S.E.C. DISCLOSING:

☑ The *purchaser's background and identity*;

☑ The source and amount of *consideration* used in the purchase;

☑ The purchaser's *intent to acquire control of, liquidate, sell assets of, merge, or otherwise change* the corporate structure of the issuer;

☑ The *number of shares the purchaser owns* and any right to purchase additional shares; and

☑ *Any contracts or other understandings* the purchaser has relating to the issuer or its securities.

c. **Exemptions from section 13(d) [§1156]**
The following transactions are exempt from the reporting requirements of section 13(d).

(i) *Offers for and acquisitions of shares made by means of a 1933 Act registration statement*, because presumably the filing of the registration statement gives ample notice of the potential change in control. However, acquisitions made pursuant to any exemptions under the 1933 Act, or by means of a regulation A offering under the 1933 Act, are *not* exempt from section 13(d).

(ii) *Acquisitions made by the issuer of its own equity securities*—such acquisitions are governed by section 13(e), which includes similar, detailed disclosure requirements (*see infra*, §1240).

(iii) *Acquisitions made by the exercise of state-law preemptive subscription rights*, in an offering to all holders of the securities subject to the rights.

[SEA §13(d)(6); SEA Rule 13d-6]

d. **Relationship to section 16(a) of the 1934 Act [§1157]**
The provisions of sections 13(d) and 16(a) of the 1934 Act overlap somewhat. Section 13(d) requires that ownership of 5% or more of a registered equity security be reported, whereas section 16(a) requires the reporting of holdings by officers, directors, or persons owning 10%, including a purchase by a person who thereby becomes the owner of 10%. [*See* SEA §16(a); *and see infra*, §1439]

e. **Implied private rights of action**

(1) **By the target company [§1158]**
Courts generally agree that a target company has an implied private right of action against the bidder for a violation of section 13(d) (*e.g.*, for filing a false statement). [*See, e.g.*, **Gearhart Industries, Inc. v. Smith International, Inc.**, 741 F.2d 707 (5th Cir. 1984)]

(a) **Target's remedies under section 13(d) [§1159]**
Target companies suing under section 13(d) typically obtain a temporary injunction against the bidder, pending corrective disclosure. [*See, e.g.*, **Florida Commercial Banks v. Culverhouse**, 772 F.2d 1513 (11th Cir. 1985); **Gearhart Industries, Inc. v. Smith International, Inc.**, *supra*] Although the target usually would prefer an order directing the bidder's divestment of target stock, or "sterilization" of the bidder's target stock (*i.e.*, a prohibition on voting that stock), several courts have held that such remedies are *not* available. [**Liberty National Insurance Co. v. Charter Co.**, 734 F.2d 545 (11th Cir.

1984); **Dan River, Inc. v. Icahn,** 701 F.2d 278 (4th Cir. 1983); *and see* **Rondeau v. Mosinee Paper Corp.,** 422 U.S. 49 (1975)]

(2) By the shareholders of the target company [§1160]

Shareholders of the target company have standing pursuant to section 13(d), but damages are not available. [*See, e.g.,* **Kamerman v. Steinberg,** 891 F.2d 424 (2d Cir. 1989); **Sanders v. Thrall Car Manufacturing Co.,** 582 F. Supp. 945 (S.D.N.Y. 1983), *aff'd,* 730 F.2d 910 (2d Cir. 1984)]

5. Basic Tender Offer Rules—Section 14(d) [§1161]

Section 14(d) contains the basic regulatory provisions concerning the making of tender offers.

a. "Tender offer" within meaning of section 14(d) [§1162]

A "tender offer" is generally thought to be an offer to purchase that is made "publicly," to all or substantially all of the shareholders of a corporation. However, it is not defined in the 1934 Act.

(1) Broad interpretation by the courts [§1163]

The courts define the term "tender offer" on a case-by-case basis, and a broad definition will be used so as to effectuate the purposes of the 1934 Act and its tender offer provisions (*i.e.,* protection of the public and of investors). [**Hanson Trust PLC v. SCM Corp.,** 774 F.2d 47 (2d Cir. 1985)]

(2) Consideration of all relevant facts [§1164]

In short, all of the relevant facts must be considered in determining whether a tender offer exists.

(a) Eight-factor test [§1165]

Most courts refer to the eight-factor test given in **Wellman v. Dickinson,** 475 F. Supp. 783 (S.D.N.Y. 1979). Note that *not all eight factors need be present* for the court to find a tender offer.

1) Was there an *active and widespread solicitation of shares* by the offeror?

2) Was the solicitation *for a substantial percentage* of the outstanding stock?

3) Was a *premium price offered* over the market price before the offer?

4) Were the *terms of the offer firm and fixed*?

5) Was the offer *contingent* on the tender by shareholders of a fixed *minimum number of shares*?

6) Was the offer to shareholders *open for only a limited time*?

7) Was there *pressure put on the shareholders to sell*?

8) Were there *public announcements* accompanying the offer?

(b) *Hanson Trust* "totality of the circumstances" test [§1166]

In *Hanson Trust, supra*, the Second Circuit declined to elevate *Wellman* to a "litmus test," and stated that the question "whether a solicitation constitutes a 'tender offer' within the meaning of section 14(d) turns on whether, viewing the transaction in the light of the totality of the circumstances, there appears to be a likelihood that unless the pre-acquisition filing strictures [of section 14(d)] are followed, there will be a substantial risk that solicitees will lack information needed to make a carefully considered appraisal of the proposal put before them."

(3) Acquisitions over a stock exchange ("street sweeps") [§1167]

Normally, acquisitions made over a stock exchange in normal market transactions would not be a tender offer. However, under appropriate circumstances (*e.g.*, when enough of the *Wellman* factors are present, or when the "totality of the circumstances" so dictates), open-market purchases could amount to a tender offer. [*See, e.g.,* **Hanson Trust PLC v. SCM Corp.,** *supra*; **S.E.C. v. Carter Hawley Hale Stores, Inc.,** 760 F.2d 945 (9th Cir. 1985)]

(4) Negotiated purchases [§1168]

Similarly, although privately negotiated purchases ordinarily do not constitute tender offers, under appropriate circumstances (*e.g.*, when enough of the *Wellman* factors are present, or when the "totality of the circumstances" so dictates) negotiated purchases may amount to a tender offer. [*See, e.g.,* **Hanson Trust PLC v. SCM Corp.,** *supra*; **Hoover Co. v. Fuqua Industries, Inc.,** Fed. Sec. L. Rep. (CCH) ¶97,107 (N.D. Ohio 1979)]

(5) Alternative test for open-market and negotiated purchases—*S-G Securities* [§1169]

Still another test, broader than the eight-factor test of *Wellman, supra*, and designed to apply to open-market and negotiated purchases, was applied by the court in **S-G Securities, Inc. v. Fuqua Investment Co.,** 466 F. Supp. 1114 (D. Mass. 1978). Under the *S-G Securities* test, a tender offer is present if there is:

(a) *A publicly announced intention* by the bidder to acquire a block of the target's stock, for the purpose of acquiring control of the target; and

(b) *A subsequent rapid acquisition* by the bidder of large blocks of stock through open market and privately negotiated purchases.

b. Tender offers must satisfy conditions of section 14(d) [§1170]

It is unlawful for any person to make use of the means of interstate commerce to make a tender offer for any class of equity security registered under section 12 if, at the consummation of the tender offer, the bidder would be the beneficial owner of more than 5% of the class of securities tendered, *unless* the following conditions required by section 14(d) are met.

(1) Disclosure of information [§1171]

The bidder must make the following disclosures in connection with the tender offer:

(a) Schedule TO [§1172]

Pursuant to its authority under section 14(d), the S.E.C. has promulgated schedule TO (for "tender offer"), which a bidder must file with the S.E.C. (with copies to the target and all stock exchanges on which the target's stock is traded) *at or before the commencement of a tender offer.* The disclosures required by schedule TO resemble those required by schedule 13D (*see supra*, §§1150 *et seq.*), but schedule TO requires some additional disclosure as well. For example, schedule TO requires disclosure of:

1) Past contacts, transactions, or negotiations with the subject company (*i.e.*, the target);

2) Persons retained, employed, or to be compensated in connection with the offer;

3) If material to a decision by a potential tendering shareholder, financial statements of the bidder(s); and

4) If material to a decision by a potential tendering shareholder, certain additional information about: the relationships between the bidder, the target, and their respective officers and directors; regulatory and antitrust issues affecting the transaction; applicability of the margin regulations (governing the use of securities as collateral for loans); pending litigation affecting the offer; and other information material to the tendering shareholders.

TENDER OFFERS AND SECTION 14(d)   **gilbert**

DISCLOSURE REQUIREMENTS CHECKLIST

A bidder making a tender offer for any class of equity security registered under section 12 who, as a result, will own more than 5% of the class tendered, must disclose at or before commencement of the offer, among other things:

☑ Information similar to that required by schedule 13D;

☑ Past dealings with the target;

☑ Persons to be compensated in connection with the offer; and

☑ If material to a tendering shareholder:

- The bidder's financial statements;

- Information regarding relationships between the bidder, the target, and their officers and directors;

- Regulatory and antitrust issues affecting the offer; and

- Litigation affecting the offer.

(b) Identity of "bidder" and financial statement disclosure [§1173]

The requirement in schedule TO that the bidder(s) provide material financial disclosure was litigated in the late 1980s, in cases brought by targets seeking to enjoin the offer. Rule 14d-1(g)(2) defines a bidder as one who makes a tender offer, or on whose behalf a tender offer is made. Thus, the entity making the actual bid for the target's stock clearly is a bidder, but other participants might also be considered to be bidders.

1) Securities firms as bidders [§1174]

Investment banks are often heavily involved in tender offers, by providing financing for the offer (through, *e.g.*, the sale of "high-yield" (junk) bonds), and by providing financial and business advice in connection with the offer. In addition, it is common for an investment bank to own some of the equity in the company making the bid. If the investment bank is "central to the offer," and is "one of the principal planners and players," it may be deemed a "bidder" required to furnish financial statements. [**MAI Basic Four, Inc. v. Prime Computer, Inc.,** 871 F.2d 212 (1st Cir. 1989)—investment bank that played a central advisory and fundraising role, and that owned 14% of the bidder directly, plus additional indirect interests, deemed a "bidder"]

2) Minority interests in the bidder [§1175]

Courts are presently split as to whether an entity that owns only a minority position in the bidder may itself be deemed a "bidder" required to furnish financial statements. [*Compare* **MAI Basic Four, Inc. v. Prime Computer, Inc.,** *supra*—minority position not a bar to a finding that an entity is a bidder; **Koppers Co. v. American Express Co.,** 689 F. Supp. 1371 (W.D. Pa. 1988)—same, *with* **City Capital Associates, Ltd. v. Interco, Inc.,** 860 F.2d 60 (3d Cir. 1988)—"bidder" means the entity that will actually acquire the target's stock and those who control it]

(c) Disclosure and publication of tender offer documents [§1176]

In addition to filing the schedule TO, the bidder must (as both a practical and a legal matter) take steps to inform the public of the offer. [*See* SEA Rule 14d-6] This will happen in one of two ways: long-form publication or summary publication.

1) Long-form publication [§1177]

Long-form publication essentially requires the bidder to publish the offer (which must include or summarize the schedule TO) in a newspaper of general circulation. [SEA Rule 14d-6(a)(1)] Because this produces a rather lengthy (and expensive) advertisement, it is rarely used.

2) Summary publication [§1178]

Summary publication consists of a short advertisement, similar to a "tombstone" ad (discussed *supra*, §183) that gives the essential terms of the offer and states where copies of the complete offer materials may be obtained. [SEA Rule 14d-6(a)(2)]

(2) Substantive requirements [§1179]

In addition to requiring disclosure, section 14(d) imposes substantive requirements on tender offers, intended to ensure minimum standards of fairness and to curb abuses. Section 14(d) also gives the S.E.C. authority to modify its requirements through rules, and the S.E.C. has exercised this authority to protect offerees further.

(a) Withdrawal right [§1180]

The offeree may change her mind and withdraw the securities that she tendered and deposited with the offeror at any time while the offer remains open. [SEA §14(d)(5); SEA Rule 14d-7(a)(1)]

1) Exception—withdrawal rights not mandatory during the "subsequent offering period" [§1181]

The tender offer rules provide for a subsequent offering period, at the option of the bidder, for three to 20 business days, beginning after the expiration of the tender offer and meeting certain other conditions specified in rule 14d-11. During this period, the tender offer is essentially extended to those shareholders who did not tender in the original offer. The bidder must immediately accept and promptly pay for securities tendered in the subsequent offering period [SEA Rule 14d-11(d)] and, therefore, is not required to extend withdrawal rights to shareholders tendering in the subsequent offering period [SEA Rule 14d-7(a)(2)].

(b) Pro rata purchases [§1182]

If the bidder seeks to purchase less than all of the issuer's outstanding stock, and a greater number of shares are offered than the bidder intends to purchase, the bidder must purchase pro rata from each person who tenders shares. [SEA §14(d)(6); SEA Rule 14d-8]

(c) Equal treatment of security holders [§1183]

A tender offer must be open to all holders of the securities for which the offer is made, and the consideration paid to any security holder in the offer must be equal to the highest consideration paid to any other holder during the offer. [SEA §14(d)(7); SEA Rule 14d-10] Although the rule requiring equal treatment of security holders in tender offers is easy to state, in practice it can be difficult to apply.

1) Broad approach [§1184]

Some courts read the rule broadly, to include all contractual arrangements that depend on the success of the tender offer. Even transactions in shares taking place before or after the tender offer period may violate the "all holders" rules if the contractual obligations of the parties are conditioned in some way upon the success of the tender offer. [*See, e.g.,* **Epstein v. MCA, Inc.,** 50 F.3d 644 (9th Cir. 1995), *rev'd on other grounds,* 516 U.S. 367 (1996); **Field v. Trump,** 850 F.2d 938 (2d Cir. 1988)]

Example: M contemplated a tender offer for MI. W, the CEO and chairman of MI, negotiated an arrangement whereby his (rather substantial—about $350 million) holding of MI stock was placed in a corporation and was to pay him interest, before eventually being redeemed at the tender offer price. Apparently the goal of this arrangement was to make W's transaction tax-free. The obligations of both parties were conditioned on the success of the tender offer. The court pointed out that while W was not technically tendering his shares into the offer, had the offer failed, he would have remained the owner of his shares. Therefore, this arrangement violated the equal treatment rule, because W received consideration different from, and possibly more valuable than, the tendering shareholders. [**Epstein v. MCA, Inc.,** *supra*]

2) Narrow approach [§1185]

Some courts favor a considerably narrower approach to the equal treatment rule. Under the narrower approach, only persons selling shares during the period that the tender offer is open are subject to the equal treatment rule. [*See, e.g.,* **Lerro v. Quaker Oats Corp.,** 84 F.3d 239 (7th Cir. 1996)]

Example: Q contemplates a tender offer for S. L owns approximately 35% of the outstanding S shares. Q enters into a distributorship agreement with L, whereby L gets the exclusive right to distribute S products in some Midwestern states. After this agreement is negotiated, L tenders his shares. The court held that the distributorship agreement was signed before the tender offer commenced and, therefore, compensation paid under that agreement was outside the tender offer and not subject to the equal treatment rule. [**Lerro v. Quaker Oats Corp.,** *supra*]

3) Equal treatment and employment agreements [§1186]

One particularly difficult area involves the treatment of employment (and noncompete) agreements between the bidder and executives of the target. It is often in the bidder's interest to obtain such agreements, to protect its future competitive position by neutralizing competition from the target's former officers and by retaining their talent for itself. But when the officers also are paid for shares tendered, the question is raised whether they are receiving additional compensation in the tender offer, *e.g.,* by being "bribed" not to oppose the offer. Courts have gone both ways in such cases. [*Compare* **Gerber v. Computer Associates International, Inc.** 303 F.3d 126 (2d Cir. 2002), *with* **Harris v. Intel Corp.,** 2002 WL1758817 (N.D. Cal. 2002)]

(d) No purchases outside the offer [§1187]

The bidder is also prohibited from purchasing any securities of the class tendered outside the tender offer. The objective of this provision is to prevent the bidder from manipulating the market price during the offer or from giving a person selling outside the offer different terms than are given to one tendering shares under the offer. [SEA Rule 14e-5]

(e) Target company recommendations [§1188]

No later than 10 business days from the date a tender offer commences, the target company must disseminate to its shareholders a statement on schedule 14D-9 disclosing that it: (i) recommends acceptance or rejection of the bid; (ii) expresses no opinion and is remaining neutral; or (iii) is unable to take a position. The reasons for the position taken must also be stated. [SEA Rule 14e-2]

(f) Disclose or abstain from trading [§1189]

Any person who obtains information about a tender offer from either the bidder, the target, or officers, directors, or employees of either must disclose the information to the public *or* abstain from trading in the securities of the target. Bidders or those acting on their behalf are exempt. In addition, one may not "tip" such information to a tippee if it is "reasonably foreseeable" that the tippee will act in violation of this disclosure rule. [*See* SEA Rule 14e-3— passed by the S.E.C. in reaction to the Supreme Court's opinion in *Chiarella*; *and see supra*, §1044]

SECTION 14(d) SUBSTANTIVE REQUIREMENTS

TO ENSURE FAIRNESS IN TENDER OFFERS, S.E.C. RULES PROVIDE:

☑ A *right of withdrawal* during the time the offer is open for offerees who have tendered their securities.

☑ A requirement that *shares be purchased pro rata* from all offerees if more shares are tendered than the bidder intends to purchase.

☑ A requirement that all *security holders of the same class be treated equally* (e.g., all must receive the same compensation for each security).

☑ A *prohibition against purchasing securities of the class tendered outside the tender offer.*

☑ A requirement that the *target company recommend whether to accept or reject the tender offer* (or explain why it cannot make a recommendation).

☑ A requirement that persons obtaining tips about the tender offer from the bidder, the target, or their officers, directors, employees, etc., *refrain from trading or disclose the information*.

---

(3) Offers requiring registration under 1933 Act [§1190]

If a tender offer involves the public offer of the bidder's securities to the target's shareholders, the bidder must also register the securities in question under the 1933 Act (unless an exemption applies). In such a case, the bidder must file both schedule 14D-1 *and* the appropriate 1933 Act registration form with the S.E.C., and must distribute both the tender offer documents *and* the prospectus for the securities offered to the shareholders of the target.

(a) Note

All of the rules that apply to an announcement of an offer of securities (*e.g.,* rule 135) and to solicitations of interest prior to the effective date of the registration statement (*see supra,* §131) also apply in the tender offer situation.

(b) And note

What must be disclosed about the bidder in the registration statement under the 1933 Act goes far beyond the requirements of section 14(d). [*See, e.g.,* **Feit v. Leasco Data Processing Equipment Corp.,** *supra,* §785]

(4) When a tender offer begins [§1191]

A tender offer begins at 12:01 a.m. on the date that the bidder first provides the *means to tender* (*i.e.,* the instructions describing how to tender) to security holders. [SEA Rule 14d-2]

(a) Precommencement communications [§1192]

Recall that the bidder is required to file a schedule TO at or before the "commencement" of the offer. (*See supra,* §1172.) Because market conditions change quickly, however, a bidder may wish to announce the offer before the schedule TO has been completed and filed. In addition, if the market reacts poorly to the offer, the bidder may wish to withdraw it. The tender offer rules provide this flexibility to bidders by defining "commencement" as the date on which the *means to tender* are provided to security holders (*see supra*) and allowing for precommencement communications, which (as long as they do not include the means to tender) are deemed not to commence the offer. [SEA Rule 14d-2(b)]

1) Filing requirement [§1193]

Although precommencement communications do not officially commence the offer, they must be filed with the S.E.C., and copies must be delivered to the target and any other bidder for the same class of securities. [SEA Rule 14d-2(b)(2)]

c. Standards for complete disclosure [§1194]

Even if some disclosure has already been made, a court may require that the bidder provide *more complete disclosure.* For example, a court might require a person filing a section 13(d) or section 14(d) report to augment or more fully disclose his intention in the required report. But the issue of just how much of the bidder's plans must be disclosed is a difficult one.

(1) Excessive disclosure may incur liability [§1195]

The problem with disclosing "anything and everything" is that the offerees and public investors might unjustifiably rely on some statements, raising other liability problems (*e.g.*, for misrepresentation) if the plans of the offeror change.

(2) Disclosure of soft information [§1196]

One controversial area has to do with whether bidders must disclose "soft" information, like the value the bidder estimates for the target's assets, or the bidder's estimates of the future profitability of the target. Some courts have required at least some disclosure along these lines. [*See, e.g.*, **Radol v. Thomas**, 772 F.2d 244 (6th Cir. 1985); **Flynn v. Bass Bros. Enterprises, Inc.**, 744 F.2d 978 (3d Cir. 1984)]

(3) Disclosure of bidder's financing [§1197]

Another sometimes-litigated area concerns the requirement that the bidder disclose the source and amount of its financing for the tender offer. [*See* Schedule TO Item 7] The financing is not always in place when the offer commences, and it is a common practice for bidders to rely on letters from investment banks stating that the bankers are "highly confident" that the financing can be arranged in time for the offer to close. Although such letters are common, and offers have been allowed to proceed with disclosure of the letter and not much more [*see, e.g*, **Newmont Mining Corp. v. Pickens**, 831 F.2d 1448 (9th Cir. 1987)], there are still unanswered questions. For example, would the investment bank be liable if the financing were not obtained? Would the bidder be liable if the financing were obtained, but on more expensive terms than the bidder originally expected? There are presently no clear answers to these questions.

d. Exemptions [§1198]

The tender offer rules of section 14(d) do *not* apply to the following situations:

(1) Five percent limitation [§1199]

Section 14(d)(1) is *not* applicable by its own terms if, after consummation of the offer, the person making the offer is not the owner of at least 5% or more of the class of equity security tendered.

(a) Acquiring five percent [§1200]

Because a "person" for section 14(d) purposes includes a group of persons acting together (*see supra*, §1144), the 5% threshold can sometimes be exceeded in ways that are not obvious.

> **e.g. Example:** Three people, each of whom owns 2% of the equity in Target Corp., band together to make a tender offer for Target. A *schedule 13D report is due immediately*. The rationale for this result is that the group "acquired" 5% at the moment it was formed. The section 13(d) report, in turn, must disclose the group's intention to make a tender offer for Target. [**GAF Corp. v. Milstein,** *supra,* §1145]

(b) Beneficial ownership [§1201]

The 5% ownership test is determined by *beneficial ownership*, rather than by legal ownership. For tender offer purposes, a person beneficially owns a security if she has (or shares with another) either the *power to vote* the security or the *power to sell* (or otherwise dispose of) the security. It is common for persons to beneficially own securities to which they do not have legal title.

EXAM TIP   **gilbert**

On your exam, be sure to remember that while the tender offer rules apply only if the bidder will own at least 5% of the equity class tendered, the 5% threshold is based on *beneficial ownership* rather than legal ownership. Also, don't forget that if the bidder is a group of individuals, their shares will be combined and could trigger the section 13(d) reporting requirements as soon as the "group" is formed.

---

(2) Equity securities [§1202]

Only equity securities registered under section 12 are covered by section 14(d)(1)—*i.e.,* common or preferred stock as opposed to debt securities, such as bonds.

(3) Offers made by issuer for its own securities [§1203]

Offers made by the issuer for its *own* securities are not covered by section 14(d). These offers are governed by section 13(e), which includes similar, detailed disclosure requirements. (*See infra,* §1240.)

(4) Other exempted transactions [§1204]

The S.E.C. may exempt by rules or regulations other securities transactions that would normally be regulated by the tender offer rules.

6. Actions for Misstatements or Insufficient Disclosure—Section 14(e) [§1205]

Under section 14(e) it is unlawful for any person to make untrue statements or to omit to state material facts, *or* to engage in any scheme of deception or fraud in connection with any tender offer or in opposition thereto. (Note the similarity of language between section 14(e) and section 10(b) and rule 10b-5, discussed *supra,* §933.)

a. Private remedies for violation of section 14(e) [§1206]

Section 14(e) may be enforced by private persons (*e.g.,* shareholders of the target denied the opportunity to tender their stock by management's actions, or the bidder denied the opportunity to take over the target) or by the S.E.C. Private plaintiffs have three possible remedies: *damages, a temporary injunction* (usually to force corrective disclosure), *or a permanent injunction* (which may be sought by the target to prevent the bidder from going forward with the offer). Each remedy requires the plaintiff to prove different elements, and each is considered below.

b. Private action for damages [§1207]

A private plaintiff seeking damages for violation of section 14(e) must prove: standing to sue; misstatements, nondisclosure, or some other species of fraudulent act; materiality; (maybe) reliance (*i.e.,* transaction causation); (maybe) causation; and (maybe) scienter.

(1) Standing [§1208]

In **Piper v. Chris-Craft Industries, Inc.,** 430 U.S. 1 (1977), the Supreme Court held that a defeated bidder does not have an implied damages remedy under section 14(e).

(a) *Piper* [§1209]

In *Piper,* Chris-Craft had sought control of Piper Aircraft through several tender offers. It eventually gained 42% of Piper's stock, partly as the result of exchanging some of its shares for Piper shares in a tender offer. But a rival bidder, Bangor Punta, eventually gained control (slightly over 50%) of Piper. Chris-Craft alleged (and two lower courts agreed) that Piper, Bangor Punta, and Bangor Punta's underwriter had made material misstatements or omissions in connection with the tender offer. Nevertheless, the Court held that Chris-Craft had no cause of action for damages. The Court reasoned that Congress's intent in passing the Williams Act was *to protect shareholders of the target*, who prior to the Williams Act had been essentially at the mercy of "corporate raiders"; there was no evidence of intent to protect the defeated bidder. Furthermore, the Court held that application of the principles announced in **Cort v. Ash** (*see supra,* §§923 *et seq.*) suggested that a private damages remedy was inappropriate for a defeated bidder.

(b) Bidder *and* shareholder [§1210]

Many bidders are already shareholders of the target at the time they launch the tender offer. *Piper* left open the possibility that such a bidder would have standing, but one circuit court has held that a bidder that was also a shareholder would be considered merely a bidder for standing purposes, and hence would be barred from a damages action under *Piper.* [**Kalmanovitz v. G. Heileman Brewing Co.,** 769 F.2d 152 (3d Cir. 1985)]

(c) Rule 10b-5 as an alternative [§1211]

In the wake of *Piper*, one court has held that bidders do not have standing to sue for damages under section 9(e) or 10(b), or rule 10b-5 of the 1934 Act for injury allegedly incurred in a tender offer contest. [**Crane Co. v. American Standard, Inc.**, 603 F.2d 244 (2d Cir. 1979)]

(d) Comment

Piper is another case from the period in which the Supreme Court made it clear that the seemingly limitless expansion of antifraud securities law was at an end. Other cases establishing this point include *Blue Chip Stamps* (*supra*, §990) and *Hochfelder* (*supra*, §993).

EXAM TIP   **gilbert**

Be on the lookout for an exam fact pattern where the bidder is defeated in an attempted tender offer because the target has disseminated false information about the bidder or the offer. While the target's action may be unlawful—and the government may prosecute or sue the target for its wrongful conduct—the *bidder has no private cause of action for damages*, as unfair as this might seem. *Rationale:* In *Piper,* the Court held that Congress's intent in passing the Williams Act was to protect the *target's shareholders*; there is no evidence of any congressional intent to protect the bidder.

---

(2) Misstatements, nondisclosure, or fraudulent acts [§1212]

For a cause of action to exist under section 14(e), there must be a misstatement of a material fact, a failure to disclose a material fact, or some other scheme of fraud or deception. The Supreme Court has stated that the purpose of section 14(e) is to see that shareholders receive full disclosure, not to allow the courts to oversee the substantive fairness of tender offers. [**Schreiber v. Burlington Northern, Inc.**, 472 U.S. 1 (1985); *and see* the discussion of rule 10b-5, *supra*, §§949-951]

(3) Materiality [§1213]

The misrepresented or undisclosed fact must be material. The test for materiality is whether there is a *substantial likelihood that a reasonable shareholder would consider the information important* in deciding whether to accept the tender offer. [**Seaboard World Airlines, Inc. v. Tiger International, Inc.**, 600 F.2d 355 (2d Cir. 1979)] *See also* the definitions of materiality in rule 10b-5 cases, *supra*, §§973 *et seq.*, and in proxy cases, *infra*, §§1288 *et seq.* This is the same standard set for proxy cases in **TSC Industries, Inc. v. Northway, Inc.**, *supra*, §974.

(a) Application

In applying this standard, the courts have indicated that the marketplace conditions under which a tender offer takes place must be considered in testing materiality. The essential objective of the tender offer rules is to assure fair and honest dealing, not to impose an unrealistic requirement of "laboratory conditions." [**Electronic Specialty Co. v. International Controls Corp.,** 409 F.2d 937 (2d Cir. 1969)]

---

e.g. **Example:** Parties to a tender offer often act quickly, impulsively, and in angry response to the actions of the opposing party. They are not required to follow through on all statements of intent or preference (as long as the statements are truthful at the time given), neither are they required to correct erroneous reports in the news media. [**Electronic Specialty Co. v. International Controls Corp.,** *supra*]

---

(4) Reliance—transaction causation [§1214]

At present, courts are split as to whether the plaintiffs must show their individual reliance on a misrepresentation or omission. [*See, e.g.,* **Plaine v. McCabe,** 797 F.2d 713 (9th Cir. 1986)—reliance in a §14(e) case may be inferred from a showing that shareholders in general were misled into approving the transaction; **Lewis v. McGraw,** 619 F.2d 192 (2d Cir. 1980)—§14(e) cause of action fails absent a showing of individual reliance] In the future, it is likely that reliance will be handled in much the same way as it now is under rule 10b-5; *i.e.,* on a case-by-case basis, with certain presumptions that apply in cases where a reliance requirement seems incongruous (*e.g.,* in cases of fraudulent omission). (*See supra,* §§1012 *et seq.*)

(5) Loss causation [§1215]

As with reliance, the status of the law on loss causation in section 14(e) cases is uncertain.

(a) *Piper* [§1216]

Piper, supra, was decided by the majority on the issue of standing. Justice Blackmun, concurring, would have decided the case against the plaintiffs, because in his view they had not shown loss causation. A court might follow Justice Blackmun and hold that loss causation is a requirement in section 14(e) cases.

(b) Rule 10b-5 analogy [§1217]

On the other hand, it is possible that a court today will follow the cases under rule 10b-5 and hold that loss causation may, in an appropriate case, be presumed from a finding that a material fact was misrepresented or omitted. The best analogy is to a rule 10b-5 face-to-face transaction case, because in a tender offer situation, the bidder's and target's statements are made with the intention of encouraging or discouraging the tendering (or withholding) of the securities, much like similar statements made in a face-to-face securities purchase and sale transaction.

(6) Standard of culpability [§1218]

The Supreme Court has not addressed the question whether section 14(e) requires a showing of scienter. There are two analogous provisions that could influence a court deciding this question: section 17(a) of the 1933 Act and rule 10b-5 under the 1934 Act.

(a) Language in sections 17(a), 14(e) and rule 10b-5 [§1219]

The language used in section 17(a) of the 1933 Act is very similar to that used in 1934 Act section 14(e) and, for that matter, in rule 10b-5 under the 1934 Act. In other words, all three provisions are drafted in essentially the same way (although the paragraph structure varies among them).

(b) Significance [§1220]

The Supreme Court has held that 1933 Act section *17(a)(1) requires a showing of scienter,* while subsections *(a)(2) and (a)(3) do not.* [**Aaron v. S.E.C.**, *supra*, §858] On the other hand, the Court has held that *all three parts of rule 10b-5 require a showing of scienter.* [**Ernst & Ernst v. Hochfelder**, *supra*, §993] A court confronting the question whether section 14(e) requires a showing of scienter might follow *Aaron*, and hold that some parts of section 14(e) require scienter while others do not; or the court might follow *Hochfelder*, and hold that section 14(e) always requires scienter.

(c) Majority view [§1221]

Most courts adopt the analogy to rule 10b-5 and require a showing of scienter in all section 14(e) cases. [*See, e.g.,* **Connecticut National Bank v. Fluor Corp.**, 808 F.2d 957 (2d Cir. 1987)]

(7) Damages [§1222]

See the discussion of the measure of damages in connection with rule 10b-5 (*supra*, §1092).

7. Private Action for Injunction [§1223]

A plaintiff who is injured by a violation of the tender offer rules may, as an alternative to an action for damages, also sue for a temporary or permanent injunction.

a. Permanent injunctions [§1224]

Before a court will permanently enjoin the making or consummation of a tender offer, the plaintiff must show that it will suffer *irreparable injury* as a result of the defendant's violation of the tender offer rules. Permanent injunctions are exceedingly rare in tender offer cases.

> **e.g. Example:** An action was brought under section 13(d) for the defendant's failure to file the required report after acquiring 5% of the plaintiff's stock. Although the defendant had intended to make a tender offer, it had not actually done so at the time the plaintiff's action was brought. The Supreme Court found that the violation was not willful and that no irreparable injury resulted. [**Rondeau v. Mosinee Paper Corp.**, *supra*, §1159] Under these circumstances, the Court held that a permanent injunction would not issue against a mere *technical violation* of the tender offer rules. The Court stated that the plaintiff (the potential target company) would have to show that it would suffer an irreparable injury that could not be remedied at law, before an injunction would issue to bar the defendant from voting the shares it had acquired and from acquiring any more shares for a period of five years.

(1) Note

Rondeau probably sets the standard for permanent injunctions in section 14(d) and 14(e) cases as well.

b. Preliminary injunctions [§1225]

Unlike permanent injunctions, preliminary injunctions are fairly common in tender offer litigation and generally issue pending improved or corrective disclosure by the defendant. However, in some cases, the issuance of a preliminary injunction effectively is the end of the offer (*see infra*, §1235, discussing defensive tactics of target management). A plaintiff seeking a preliminary injunction must meet the burden of showing either (i) probable success if the case were to go to trial on the merits *and* the possibility of irreparable injury, *or* (ii) the existence of serious questions going to the merits *and* a balance of hardships in the plaintiff's favor. [**Stark v. New York Stock Exchange, Inc.**, 466 F.2d 743 (2d Cir. 1972)]

> **e.g. Example:** The plaintiff (the target company) was granted a preliminary injunction upon showing that the defendant had failed to disclose its intentions regarding the disposition of the plaintiff's assets if the tender offer were successful, and that the defendant had also failed to disclose that the English government had the statutory power to control the disposition of the plaintiff's assets. [**General Host Corp. v. Triumph American, Inc.**, 359 F. Supp. 749 (E.D. Wis. 1973)]

c. Bidder's standing to seek injunctions [§1226]

The question whether a bidder has standing to seek an injunction is unresolved at present.

(1) Recap—action for damages

Recall that the bidder has *no* standing under section 14(e) to bring a lawsuit for damages. [**Piper v. Chris-Craft Industries, Inc.**, *supra*, §1208]

(2) Injunctive relief

While *Piper* did not specifically address injunctions, the Court's opinion can be read to support the bidder's right to seek injunctive relief. A lower court has so held. [*See* **A & K Railroad Materials, Inc. v. Green Bay & Western Railroad,** 437 F. Supp. 636 (E.D. Wis. 1977)—bidder has standing to sue for an injunction, but mere negligence is insufficient to support the action; *and see* **Humana, Inc. v. American Medicorp, Inc.,** 445 F. Supp. 613 (S.D.N.Y. 1977)]

8. Enforcement by the S.E.C. [§1227]

The S.E.C. may use several means to enforce the tender offer rules:

(i) *Injunctions;*

(ii) *Criminal prosecutions;*

(iii) *Cease-and-desist proceedings;* or

(iv) *Orders for compliance* with section 13 or 14.

Each of these is explored in more detail in the materials on S.E.C. enforcement actions, *infra,* §§1674 *et seq.*

9. Tactics in Opposing a Tender Offer [§1228]

The target company's managers will usually attempt to fight (under threat of losing their jobs) the takeover attempt. While in many cases such a fight can be justified by sound business reasons, there is always some price at which fighting the tender offer can no longer be justified, because the shareholders' interests are best served by recommending acceptance of the tender. For managers to resist in these circumstances amounts to placing their self-interest (in their jobs) above the well-being of the shareholders, and may lead to liability under state law for breach of fiduciary duty. Generally, the question which defensive tactics are permissible is governed by the law of the state of the target's incorporation. (*See* Corporations Summary.) Some defensive techniques, however, raise federal securities law issues.

a. Staggered board of directors [§1229]

A common tactic to thwart potential takeovers is the use of a "classified," or "staggered," board of directors. A staggered board contains two or more classes of directors, with one class being elected at a time. In this way, the directors are elected over a period of years, making it more difficult for the bidder to gain control over the target's board. However, shareholders may not approve a staggered board of directors, because such a board reduces the power of the shareholders to vote in a new board, should they wish to do so.

b. Persuasion of the shareholders [§1230]

Management of the target may attempt to persuade the shareholders not to tender their shares to the bidder. However, any solicitation or recommendation to the target's shareholders must be made in accordance with the rules and regulations contained in section 14(d)(4) and rule 14d-9. Also, any recommendation that is made is subject to the antifraud provisions of section 14(e). (*See supra*, §1205.)

(1) Target's management must disclose its position [§1231]

In fact, quite apart from considerations of defense, the target's *management is required to make a statement to the target's shareholders* concerning management's position with respect to the offer. [SEA Rule 14e-2]

(2) Schedule 14D-9 [§1232]

Schedule 14D-9 sets forth the information that the target's management must send to the S.E.C. as soon as practicable on the date the information is first published, sent, or given to security holders.

(3) Stop-look-and-listen communications [§1233]

As soon as the offer is made, and while determining what it will recommend to shareholders, the target may transmit (without any filing with the S.E.C.) a communication to its shareholders stating that management is studying the proposal and will (before a specified date not later than 10 business days after commencement of the offer) give its recommendation. [SEA Rule 14d-9(f)]

c. Litigation [§1234]

Management may choose to bring an immediate action against the bidder, alleging that there have been misrepresentations or omissions of material facts in the tender offer.

(1) Suit for injunction [§1235]

If management is successful in obtaining a preliminary injunction, the tender offer may well be dropped; the bidder may be reluctant to spend large sums of money in litigation, with no assurance that conditions will be suitable for continuing the offer when the litigation is concluded. (*See supra*, §§1223 *et seq.*)

(2) Suit for rescission [§1236]

Rescission of a successful tender offer has never been granted and would be highly impractical. Many, if not most, of the former target shareholders (who may number in the thousands, or even tens of thousands) will have spent the money received in the offer by the time the suit is brought. Understandably, courts are extremely reluctant to attempt to "unwind" such transactions.

d. Merger with a "white knight" [§1237]

When a tender offer is attempted, the target often looks for another company with which to merge that will promise to employ the target's management.

[*See* **Paramount Communications, Inc. v. Time, Inc.,** 571 A.2d 1140 (Del. 1989)] Management's rationale for such a merger is typically that the merger is a "better deal" for shareholders than the tender offer.

e. Purchase of its own shares [§1238]

The target may attempt, directly or through its pension fund, to purchase enough of its own shares to cause the price to rise above the bidder's offer price or, in the case of a purchase by a pension fund, to prevent control from going to the bidder. Such a purchase could take place on the open market or in a self-tender by the target. If the result of such a stock purchase is to remove a company's stock from public ownership and trading, the transaction is known as "going private." Although issuer repurchases are not prohibited by the securities laws, they are extensively regulated.

(1) When a tender offer has been commenced [§1239]

If a bidder has already commenced a tender offer for the target, *the target must comply with 1934 Act rule 13e-1* before purchasing its own securities. Rule 13e-1 requires the target to file a statement with the S.E.C. disclosing certain information about the planned repurchase, including the securities to be repurchased, the markets in which the repurchase will take place, and the source of the funds to be used to make the repurchase.

(2) Self-tender offers [§1240]

If the issuer's purchase program amounts to a tender offer (*see supra*, §§1161 *et seq.*), the issuer must also comply with 1934 Act rule 13e-4. This rule requires the issuer to file a schedule TO with the S.E.C.; the disclosure required is substantially similar to that required of the bidder in a conventional tender offer (*see supra*, §§1172 *et seq.*).

(3) Pre-tender offer, open-market purchases [§1241]

Target companies purchasing their own shares during a third-party tender offer must comply with rule 13e-1, *supra*. But what if an issuer merely suspects that it may become a target in the future and decides to thwart a possible bid by purchasing its own shares in the open market, thereby causing the price of the shares to rise? The danger is that such purchases, designed to affect the price of the issuer's shares, will be deemed "manipulative" by the S.E.C., under 1934 Act section 9(a)(2). (*See infra*, §§1933 *et seq.*) The S.E.C. has promulgated a safe harbor rule, SEA rule 10b-18, which restricts the manner, time, price, and volume of issuer repurchases on the open market.

(a) Effect of noncompliance [§1242]

SEA rule 10b-18 is a safe harbor; compliance with the rule prevents the inference that the repurchases were manipulative under 1934 Act section 9(a)(2), but noncompliance does not raise any presumption that the repurchases *were* manipulative. [SEA Rule 10b-18(c)]

(b) Requirements of rule 10b-18 [§1243]

To take advantage of the rule 10b-18 safe harbor, an issuer (and its affiliated purchasers) must comply with the rule's purchasing conditions:

1) Single broker-dealer [§1244]

All rule 10b-18 purchases must be made from or through a single broker or dealer on any one trading day.

2) Time of purchases [§1245]

A rule 10b-18 purchase is not permitted to be (i) the opening purchase (*i.e.,* the first purchase) on any trading day or (ii) made within one-half hour of the end of trading on any day. An exception exists for NASDAQ-quoted securities, which may be the subject of a rule 10b-18 purchase at any time during which a current independent bid quotation is reported in NASDAQ.

3) Price of purchases [§1246]

Rule 10b-18 purchases must not be made at a price higher than the market price. (This is designed to limit the purchaser's ability to cause the market price to rise.)

4) Volume of purchases [§1247]

The daily volume of rule 10b-18 purchases may not exceed 25% of the average daily trading volume for the security over the preceding four weeks. For securities that are not publicly traded, rule 10b-18 provides that the volume over a six-day period may not exceed 1/20th of 1% of the outstanding shares (excluding shares held by affiliates) of the security.

(4) Regulation M and issuer repurchases [§1248]

Issuers repurchasing their own securities must also take note of regulation M rule 102, which prohibits an issuer from buying stock that is the subject of a distribution. This could cause problems, for example, when an issuer has outstanding both common stock and preferred stock convertible into common. In such cases, the issuer is deemed to be involved in an ongoing distribution of the common stock and must obtain a specific exemption from rule 102 by applying to the S.E.C.

f. "Poison pills" [§1249]

A "shareholder rights plan" (so called by its proponents; more commonly called a "poison pill") is a technique whereby the shareholders of a potential target are given the right either to purchase securities or to force a successful bidder to buy securities, in either case at a price highly favorable to the target's shareholders. As a rule, the price is so high that a takeover transaction is impossible for as long as the shareholders retain the rights. The target's board of directors, however, is given the power to redeem the rights; thus, poison pills are useful in forcing a bidder to negotiate with the target's board. Poison pills are typically structured in one of two ways:

(1) "Call plans" [§1250]

A call plan gives target shareholders the right to acquire additional securities of the target (or the survivor of a merger involving the target), at a greatly reduced price. The right is triggered by the happening of any one of several specified events, for example, the merger of the target and another company. The effect is to make a merger of the target prohibitively expensive for the bidder.

(a) Flip-over pills [§1251]

The pill discussed immediately above is an example of a "flip-over" pill, because the shareholders' rights "flip over" and become exercisable against the bidder in the event of a merger.

(b) Flip-in pills [§1252]

So-called flip-in pills are triggered by the bidder exceeding some specified limit, usually expressed in terms of percentage ownership of the target's stock. Thus, for example, a flip-in pill might be triggered when the bidder acquires more than 20% of the target's common stock, and the pill would then give the target's shareholders—other than the bidder—the right to acquire additional shares of the target at a greatly reduced price.

(2) "Put plans" [§1253]

A put plan gives the target shareholders the right to force the target (or the survivor of a merger involving the target) to buy stock of the target at a price specified by the plan. These are attractive mostly to smaller investors and to targets whose securities are held largely by smaller holders, because such shareholders may have difficulty raising enough money to buy significant quantities of securities in a call plan, even at discounted prices. Put plans, however, may constitute tender offers, because under such a plan shareholders sell their shares to a third party. As such, they may be subject to significant regulation that would not apply to a call plan.

(3) Proxy contests to counter poison pills [§1254]

Although poison pills can make a takeover prohibitively expensive and thus impossible, more commonly they have forced bidders to negotiate with target boards in order to get the board to redeem the pill. In some circumstances it might be a violation of the directors' fiduciary duty to the stockholders for the board to fail to redeem a pill, although the Delaware Supreme Court's decision in the *Time* case (*supra*, §1237) suggests that a board may justifiably "just say no" and refuse to negotiate with the bidder or redeem a pill. A bidder confronted by such a refusal might launch a proxy contest to unseat the directors and replace them with "friendly" directors who will redeem the pill. Targets have responded to this possibility in two ways.

(a) Proxy-triggered pills [§1255]

First, the board can attempt to institute a pill that is triggered by the solicitation of proxies or by someone forming a group with other shareholders to seek election to the board, without the approval of the incumbent directors. One way this can be implemented is by making the filing of a Schedule 13D the triggering event for the pill. Such triggers, however, raise significant fiduciary duty problems because they disenfranchise shareholders, at least to some extent, by limiting the director candidates for whom shareholders can vote.

(b) "Deadhand" pills [§1256]

Some poison pills include a provision that states that the pill can be redeemed only by directors in office prior to the start of a tender offer or proxy contest. This would make a proxy contest unavailing to defeat a pill, because only the ousted directors would be empowered to redeem the pill. These plans, too, raise serious questions about fiduciary duty.

g. "Greenmail" [§1257]

So-called "greenmail" is a payment from the target to the bidder in order to persuade the bidder to abandon its takeover plans. In the typical scenario, the target pays the bidder, in exchange for which the bidder executes a "standstill" agreement under which it agrees not to acquire additional shares in, or otherwise seek control of, the target for a specified period (often five or 10 years). The legal issues surrounding greenmail arise primarily under state law and involve conflicts of interest and the fiduciary duties of the target's management and board. Target shareholders are often understandably distressed by the thought of management using corporate assets to dissuade a bidder who, after all, might have offered the shareholders an attractive price for their stock.

(1) Tax consequences [§1258]

Under Internal Revenue Code section 5881, there is a 50%, nondeductible excise tax on profit received in a greenmail transaction. Section 5881 is relatively easy to avoid, however, because "greenmail" as defined under the statute includes only payments made to a person who has made or threatened to make a tender offer (and who meets certain additional criteria). Avoidance, then, is simply a matter of not explicitly threatening a tender offer, leaving the possibilities to the imagination of the target's management.

h. Employee stock ownership plans ("ESOPS") [§1259]

Originally intended as an employee benefit, ESOPS are sometimes used to thwart the takeover plans of a bidder. An ESOP can be structured so as to make it difficult or impossible for a bidder to gain control of the target's board of directors.

(1) Techniques for defensive use [§1260]

The following are examples of ESOP techniques that have been employed in efforts to defeat takeover attempts:

(a) Reset provisions [§1261]

Reset provisions provide target employees with economic incentives to vote against a takeover attempt. They permit the conversion price of target company preferred stock, issued to the ESOP, to be reset if the price of the target's common stock falls (*e.g.*, if a tender offer were to be withdrawn). Because employees are protected against this "downside risk," they have every reason to perpetuate the existing target management in office, especially since the ESOP would probably not survive if the bidder succeeds in obtaining control.

(b) Mirrored voting [§1262]

The trustees of an ESOP may be contractually required to vote unallocated shares held by the plan in the same proportion as shares allocated to (and therefore voted by) participants. Because the target's employees generally do not favor takeover attempts, this tactic usually produces a large, block vote against the bidder.

(c) "Heavy" voting [§1263]

An ESOP often holds senior securities (*e.g.*, preferred stock) that are convertible into common shares. When the senior securities are convertible into fewer shares of common stock than they carry votes, the voting power of the senior securities is said to be "heavy."

> **Example:** An ESOP holds preferred stock, each share of which is convertible into 8/10 of a share of common stock of the target. Each unconverted preferred share, however, carries one full vote, and as far as voting power is concerned, is the equivalent of a full common share. Voting is "heavy." [**NCR Corp. v. American Telephone & Telegraph Co.**, 761 F. Supp. 475 (S.D. Ohio 1991)]

(d) Leverage [§1264]

An ESOP is said to be "leveraged" when all shares allocated to the plan are issued at once, whether or not any participants have purchased or are likely to purchase them. An unleveraged ESOP, by contrast, receives shares incrementally, according to the plan's needs. Leveraged plans are more effective as takeover defenses, because they enable the target's management to reap the maximum benefit from mirrored and "heavy" voting.

(2) Enforceability of defensive ESOPS [§1265]

Although the techniques discussed above can be effective, ESOPS employing these techniques may be held to be unenforceable under state law or applicable stock exchange rules.

(a) Breach of fiduciary duty [§1266]

An ESOP must have a legitimate business purpose. In the absence of a legitimate purpose, an ESOP that consolidates control, or entrenches management, is a breach of fiduciary duty because it places the interests of management above those of the shareholders. [*See, e.g.,* **NCR Corp. v. American Telephone & Telegraph Co.,** *supra*]

(b) Stock exchange regulations [§1267]

The defensive issuance of shares to an ESOP may violate stock exchange rules prohibiting the issuance of large amounts of stock without shareholder approval. [*See* **Norlin Corp. v. Rooney, Pace, Inc.,** 744 F.2d 255 (2d Cir. 1984)]

i. Stock lockups [§1268]

Rather than issue shares to an ESOP, the target may issue shares to a "white knight"—*i.e.,* to a bidder whose offer the target views more favorably than the first bidder's. The ultimate goal of such a transaction might be to induce the white knight to make a tender offer at a price higher than the first bidder's. Alternatively, a stock lockup may be designed to force the first bidder to comply with state anti-takeover statutes (discussed *infra*), or to prevent the first bidder from obtaining enough shares to oust the incumbent board of directors.

j. "Crown jewel" lockups [§1269]

Takeover attempts are frequently launched in an effort to acquire control of the target's most desirable assets—its "crown jewels." Therefore, a target may grant an option on the crown jewels as a defense against the takeover attempt. These lockups typically are granted to white knights—*i.e.,* to potential bidders whose bids are viewed more favorably than those of the hostile bidder.

TACTIC	PROCEDURE	PITFALLS
ADOPT A STAGGERED BOARD OF DIRECTORS	Elect only part of the board each year	Generally allowed, but shareholders might not approve because it reduces their power to vote in a new board
PERSUADE SHARE-HOLDERS TO REJECT THE OFFER	Issue statements explaining why the offer should be rejected	The target's management must issue its recommendations anyway, but is prohibited from issuing false or misleading statements
SUE THE BIDDER	Bring a suit alleging misrepresentations or omissions	If proved, the target may obtain an injunction, but if the tender offer has been consummated, rescission generally cannot be granted due to the problems of unwinding the deal
MERGE WITH "WHITE KNIGHT"	Find another company with which to merge (that will promise to employ the target's management)	May breach management's state fiduciary duty if management is more concerned with its own welfare than that of the shareholders
PURCHASE OWN SHARES	Purchase corporation's own shares on the open market or in a self-tender	If the repurchase amounts to a tender offer, the issuer must file a schedule TO; if the repurchase is made on the open market, it could be deemed a scheme to manipulate price
ADOPT A SHAREHOLDER RIGHTS/POISON PILL PLAN	Adopt a "call plan" giving the target's shareholders the right to buy shares at a reduced price or a "put plan" requiring a successful bidder to buy shares at a price favorable to the shareholders	In a "call plan," shareholders might not have enough money to purchase the shares; a "put plan" could constitute a tender offer and be subject to significant regulation
GREENMAIL	Pay the bidder money not to go through with the tender offer	The plan may violate state fiduciary duties, and profits to the bidder may be subject to a 50% excise tax if the transaction is not structured properly
EMPLOY AN ESOP	Set up an employee stock ownership plan with provisions favorable to current management and employees	The plan may violate state fiduciary duties and stock exchange rules
LOCKUP STOCK	Issue shares to a "white knight"	May still result in a takeover, albeit by a third party more favorable to the target's management
LOCKUP "CROWN JEWELS"	Grant a third party an option to purchase the target's most desirable asset	May still result in a takeover, albeit by a third party more favorable to the target's management

10. State Anti-Takeover Legislation [§1270]

In **CTS Corp. v. Dynamics Corp.**, 481 U.S. 69 (1987), the Supreme Court upheld an Indiana statute imposing certain restrictions on bidders seeking to acquire Indiana targets. In the wake of *CTS*, many other states passed anti-takeover legislation. Although strictly speaking these statutes are not part of the field of securities regulation, belonging rather to the realm of state corporation law, they have a significant impact on the work of securities lawyers dealing with takeovers. For this reason, they are briefly discussed below.

a. Shareholder protection statutes [§1271]

The most common form of state anti-takeover legislation is the shareholder protection statute. Such statutes purport to protect the target's shareholders. Shareholder protection statutes may be grouped roughly into three groups, according to the approximate date of their passage and the manner in which the "protection" of the target's shareholders is implemented. [*See* **Amanda Acquisition Corp. v. Universal Foods Corp.**, 877 F.2d 496 (7th Cir. 1989)]

(1) First-generation statutes [§1272]

Before *CTS*, Illinois had attempted to limit takeovers of corporations with substantial assets in Illinois, by requiring approval of a public official before such an acquisition could be consummated. The Illinois statute was held unconstitutional under the Commerce Clause. [**Edgar v. MITE Corp.**, 457 U.S. 624 (1982)]

(2) Second-generation statutes [§1273]

Second-generation statutes do not impose any restrictions on the bidder's ability to buy the target's shares. Instead, they restrict the voting power of shares acquired by a hostile bidder. The voting power limitations can be eliminated by action of the target's management or by a vote of the target shareholders (excluding management and the hostile bidder). Second-generation statutes are fairly common today.

> **Example:** *CTS* involved a second-generation statute, which applied only to Indiana corporations and provided that, upon the acquisition of a threshold percentage of target shares, the acquired shares would lose their voting power unless the share acquisition was approved by either the target's board of directors or a majority of disinterested shareholders (*i.e.*, those not affiliated with the bidder or target management). The statute was held constitutional and not preempted by the Williams Act. [**CTS Corp. v. Dynamics Corp.**, *supra*]

(a) Comment

Whether second-generation statutes effectively restrict takeovers is debatable. Although few data are available, it would seem that if the number of shareholders wishing to tender is enough to give the hostile bidder control, those same shareholders would vote to restore the voting power of that bidder's shares. The chief restriction imposed by second-generation statutes is the delay resulting from the shareholder meeting necessary to conduct the required ballot, and equivalent delays are in any case achievable by means of a "poison pill" device.

(3) Third-generation statutes [§1274]

Most recently, state shareholder protection statutes have attempted to limit the ability of an "interested shareholder" (as defined by the statute) to effect a business combination with the target. Because most takeover attempts have as a goal a merger, liquidation or partial liquidation, or other similar transaction, all of which are usually included among the prohibited business combinations, such statutes have the effect of making hostile takeovers less common. These statutes have been held constitutional and not preempted. [*See, e.g.,* **Amanda Acquisition Corp. v. Universal Foods Corp.**, *supra*]

b. Challenges to state shareholder protection statutes [§1275]

Federal law challenges to state anti-takeover statutes have proceeded on two theories: that the state law is preempted by the Williams Act and that the state law is unconstitutional under the Commerce Clause.

(1) Williams Act challenges [§1276]

In general, the Williams Act will preempt a state law only if the law is in conflict with the Act. [*See* SEA §28(a); **CTS Corp. v. Dynamics Corp.**, *supra*] Precisely when a state anti-takeover law conflicts with the Williams Act remains unsettled. In *MITE, supra,* §1272, the Supreme Court decided—by a plurality—that the Illinois statute at issue was preempted because the statute favored management over the shareholders. Whether the Williams Act mandates state-law neutrality between these groups, however, remains questionable.

(2) Commerce Clause challenges [§1277]

Even if not preempted by the Williams Act, a state anti-takeover statute may be unconstitutional under the Commerce Clause. The circumstances under which a statute violates the Commerce Clause, however, are not entirely clear at this point. Certainly, a statute that overtly discriminates against bidders from other states would be unconstitutional. Also, states may not enact laws creating a significant risk that an activity will become subject to different, and inconsistent, regulation. Beyond this, however, it is difficult to predict in what direction the Supreme Court's Commerce Clause analysis will turn.

c. Other state anti-takeover statutes [§1278]

In addition to the shareholder protection statutes discussed above, many states have enacted other kinds of legislation designed to protect domestic corporations from takeover attempts. These may be loosely grouped into two categories: "constituency" statutes, and "disgorgement" statutes.

(1) Constituency statutes [§1279]

Constituency statutes permit a corporation's board of directors to consider the welfare of persons other than the shareholders. For the most part, however, the statutes are unclear as to whether such interests may be treated as superior to those of the shareholders, or whether they merely codify the common law rule that such interests may be considered when they are not in conflict with those of the shareholders.

(2) Disgorgement statutes [§1280]

Disgorgement statutes (to date, only Pennsylvania has adopted such a law) provide that investors must disgorge to the target profits received from shares acquired before the investors obtained control, if those shares are sold within some period of time after obtaining control. (Pennsylvania's law is similar in some respects to the "short-swing" disgorgement requirement by SEA section 16; *see infra,* §§1433 *et seq.*)

D. Regulation of Proxy Solicitations

1. "Proxy" Defined [§1281]

A proxy is a power of attorney to vote shares owned by someone else. At common law, proxies were illegal, but today they are permitted and regulated both by state statutes and by the Securities Exchange Act.

a. Power to revoke [§1282]

A proxy establishes an agency relationship that is revocable at any time, except under certain limited conditions.

(1) Irrevocable proxies [§1283]

Under state law, a proxy that is expressly made irrevocable *and* is "coupled with an interest" generally is irrevocable.

(a) Definition

"Coupled with an interest" means that some consideration was received by the shareholder for granting the proxy. For example, when a shareholder borrows money and pledges her stock as security, granting the lender an irrevocable proxy to vote the pledged shares, the proxy is coupled with an interest and is therefore irrevocable.

(b) But note

State statutes usually limit the duration for which even an irrevocable proxy coupled with an interest may be given (*e.g.,* to a period of five years).

b. What constitutes a proxy solicitation [§1284]

Under federal law, a "solicitation" is any communication to the shareholders reasonably calculated to result in the granting, withholding, or revocation of a proxy. [SEA Rule 14a-1]

(1) Note

The federal proxy rules may apply even though the party sending the communication is not soliciting a proxy for the purpose of voting.

---

e.g. **Example:** X may send a communication attempting to influence the shareholders of ABC Corp. not to give their proxies to management. The common stock of ABC Corp. is listed on the NYSE. This communication is covered by the federal proxy rules (although delivery of a proxy statement may not be required; *see infra,* §1313).

---

2. Regulation by the States [§1285]

Regulation of shareholder proxies is a central part of state corporate law. In addition to regulating the revocability of proxies, the states regulate many aspects of proxy solicitation, including the extent to which the expenses of a proxy contest can be paid by the corporation and how the shareholders' meeting is conducted (including permissible methods for counting the proxies, etc.).

a. State remedies [§1286]

State law remedies for fraud in the solicitation of proxies are usually available.

b. Federal jurisdiction over proxy rules exclusive [§1287]

However, the federal courts have exclusive jurisdiction over application of the federal proxy rules.

3. Federal Proxy Rules—An Introduction [§1288]

Because it favors the solicitation of proxies by corporate management, the proxy system is an effective tool for maintaining control over a large, public corporation. Due to the tremendous number of shares such a corporation will have outstanding, purchasing a majority of the outstanding voting stock—*e.g.,* in a tender offer—is often prohibitively expensive. Soliciting proxies from the many individual shareholders whose aggregate votes constitute the needed majority is not cheap, either—but it is far less expensive than purchasing a majority of the outstanding voting stock. Also, in most cases, state law permits management to use *corporate funds* to pay for the solicitation. To prevent abuses in the proxy solicitation process, authority to regulate proxies relating to securities registered under the 1934 Act has been given to the S.E.C. in section 14(a) of that 1934 Act.

a. Objectives of the S.E.C. rules [§1289]

Pursuant to its authority under section 14(a), the S.E.C. has adopted rules for the regulation of proxy solicitations. [*See* SEA Regulation 14A] These rules are designed to accomplish three objectives:

(1) To encourage full disclosure [§1290]

Those who solicit proxies (or attempt to dissuade shareholders from granting them) must fully disclose all material facts to the shareholders being solicited. [SEA Rules 14a-3 - 14a-6]

(2) To prevent fraud [§1291]

The federal rules specifically prohibit the use of fraud in the solicitation of proxies. [SEA Rule 14a-9]

(3) To provide for shareholder proposals [§1292]

Shareholders (other than management) may also solicit proxies from other shareholders, and the S.E.C. rules require management to include in its proxy statement proper proposals made by these shareholders. [SEA Rule 14a-8]

b. Scope of coverage of proxy rules

(1) Companies covered [§1293]

The federal proxy rules apply to all companies with securities registered under section 12 (*i.e.*, all "registered companies"). (*See supra*, §§875-877.)

(2) Securities covered [§1294]

Similarly, the proxy rules apply to all securities registered under section 12.

(a) Over-the-counter companies [§1295]

The proxy regulations apply only to the *registered equity securities* of the companies registered under section 12(g) (*i.e.*, "over-the-counter" companies). "Equity" securities are broadly defined under the Act and include, for example, convertible debentures.

(b) Listed companies [§1296]

Companies with securities listed for trading on a national securities exchange must register the securities with the S.E.C. under section 12(b). Therefore, the proxy rules apply to *any* such listed security, including listed *debt* securities.

1) Debt securities [§1297]

Although debt securities do not normally vote, any corporate action requiring the consent of debt security holders is subject to the proxy regulations.

Example: A solicitation of the vote of debenture holders, requesting them to waive a provision in the trust indenture covering the debentures, would require compliance with the proxy rules.

---

(3) Transactions and matters covered [§1298]

Whenever a registered company has a matter that calls for a shareholder vote, it is subject to the proxy rules. For example, the approval of a merger or the amendment of the articles of incorporation are subject to shareholder vote, and thus the proxy rules apply to these matters.

(4) Communications covered [§1299]

In the normal course of a corporation's affairs, management and others related to the corporation (*e.g.,* securities firms) may wish to distribute information to shareholders concerning the corporation. If such material is distributed immediately prior to or during a proxy solicitation, an issue may arise as to whether the material is distributed with the intent of influencing the proxy solicitation and, therefore, whether it is actually part of the proxy solicitation.

(a) Regular financial reports not a "solicitation" [§1300]

It is clear that the issuer may distribute its regular annual, semi-annual, or quarterly financial report and not have it deemed a "proxy solicitation." Indeed, the proxy rules *require* most issuers subject to the 1934 Act to send the annual report to their shareholders. [SEA Rule 14a-3]

(b) Statement of intended vote not a "solicitation" [§1301]

The proxy rules exclude from the definition of "solicitation" a communication by a security holder, who does not otherwise engage in a nonexempt solicitation, stating how the security holder intends to vote and the reasons therefor. [SEA Rule 14a-1(l)]

4. Proxy Disclosure Requirements [§1302]

There are two kinds of required disclosure under the proxy rules: the proxy statement and the annual report. Each is discussed below.

a. The proxy statement [§1303]

The proxy rules set forth what information must be disclosed in the proxy statement, essentially all material facts regarding matters to be voted on by the security holders and identification of the participants in the solicitation. [*See* SEA Schedule 14A; *see infra*, §1323]

(1) If proxies are not solicited—the information statement [§1304]

What if the issuer is not soliciting proxies? For example, there might be insiders of the issuer who control enough votes to constitute a quorum (and, perhaps, a majority of the votes present at any shareholder meeting). Can the issuer avoid the disclosure otherwise required under the proxy rules? The answer is no, because SEA section 14(c) requires the issuer to "file with the [SEC] and transmit to [the security holders] information substantially equivalent to the information which would be required to be transmitted if a solicitation were made . . . ." [*See* SEA Schedule 14C]

b. The annual report [§1305]

The second component of required proxy disclosure is the issuer's annual report. If directors are to be elected, before the meeting at which the election is to take place, the registrant must provide shareholders with an annual report. The contents of the annual report are specified in the proxy rules. [*See* SEA Rule 14a-3]

c. Antifraud provisions [§1306]

The proxy rules contain antifraud provisions in SEA rule 14a-9. These provisions apply to all proxy "solicitations" as defined in rule 14a-1, whether or not the particular solicitation is exempt from the delivery or filing requirements. If the activity in question is part of a solicitation, the antifraud rules apply to all materials used and statements made by the parties. [*See* SEA Rule 14a-9; *see infra*, §1396]

EXAM TIP | **gilbert**

Proxy issues come up from time to time in essay questions. Be sure to remember the basics. If a corporation calls for a shareholder vote on a matter, proxies will be solicited, and if the corporation's shares are registered under section 12, *all material facts concerning the matter must be disclosed*. The corporation's annual report must also be delivered to shareholders if directors are to be elected.

---

5. Proxy Statement Delivery Requirements [§1307]

In addition to specifying what information must be disclosed to shareholders when their proxies are solicited, the proxy rules specify the manner in which the information must be disclosed: by delivery of a preliminary or definitive proxy statement and, if directors are to be elected, an annual report.

a. Solicitation prohibited without delivery of proxy statement [§1308]

A solicitation subject to the proxy rules is not permitted to begin unless *each person solicited* has been furnished with a *written proxy statement containing the information required by schedule 14A.* [SEA Rule 14a-3]

(1) Proxy statement may be preliminary [§1309]

Note, however, that the written proxy statement required before a solicitation can begin *need not be in definitive form*—a preliminary proxy statement will meet the S.E.C.'s requirements, as long as it contains the information required by schedule 14A. [*See* SEA Rule 14a-3(a)]

(2) Proxy card prohibited until definitive proxy statement delivered [§1310]

Even though the proxy solicitation can begin before the definitive proxy statement is delivered, *the person soliciting* proxies may *not* deliver a proxy card (called the "form of proxy"—*i.e.*, the actual form on which the shareholders grant authority to vote their shares and specify how the shares are to be voted) *until a definitive proxy statement has been delivered* to the shareholders. [SEA Rule 14a-4(f)]

(3) Exceptions to delivery requirements [§1311]

The proxy statement delivery requirements do not apply to certain solicitations.

(a) Public solicitation [§1312]

Solicitations made by public broadcast, speech, advertisement, etc., need not be preceded or accompanied by delivery of a written proxy statement as long as:

(i) No form of proxy, consent, or authorization or means to execute such a document are provided in connection with the communication; and

(ii) At the time the communication is made, a definitive proxy statement is on file with the S.E.C.

[SEA Rule 14a-3(f)]

(b) Soliciting person not seeking proxy authority [§1313]

Similarly, if the person soliciting is not the issuer and is not actually seeking a proxy from the shareholders, no written proxy statement need be delivered. [SEA Rule 14a-2(b)]

(c) General exception and proxy contests [§1314]

Proxy contests (discussed *infra*, §1328) are high-stakes contests for corporate control. Because both sides in a proxy contest often need to act quickly, the proxy rules contain a general exception permitting solicitation before a proxy statement is filed. [SEA Rule 14a-12] Such solicitations are permitted if:

1) Each written communication to shareholders includes:

a) The identity of the participants in the solicitation and a description of their interest, or a prominent legend describing where such information is available; and

b) A prominent legend advising security holders to read the proxy statement when it becomes available.

2) A definitive proxy statement is provided to security holders at the same time, or before, the form of proxy is provided; and

3) All material used under this exception is filed with the S.E.C.

6. Proxy Statement Filing Requirements [§1315]

All written materials used in a solicitation must be filed with the S.E.C. [SEA Rule 14a-6] Some materials must be filed in preliminary, "draft" form before definitive copies are disseminated to the shareholders. Other materials need not be filed with the S.E.C. until final, definitive versions have been prepared and are actually disseminated.

a. Varieties of written proxy materials [§1316]

Written materials distributed to shareholders in connection with a proxy solicitation may be loosely grouped into three categories: the proxy statement, the form of proxy, and other soliciting materials.

b. Advance filing requirements [§1317]

The S.E.C. requires the following materials to be *filed in advance of their use*, to give the S.E.C. an opportunity to review and comment on them.

(1) Proxy statement and form of proxy [§1318]

Preliminary versions of both the proxy statement and the form of proxy must be filed with the S.E.C. *at least 10 days before the definitive versions are disseminated* to shareholders. [SEA Rule 14a-6(a)]

(a) Exception

The issuer need not file preliminary copies of the proxy statement or the form of proxy if the solicitation relates to any meeting of security holders at which the only matters to be acted upon are:

(i)   The *election of directors*;

(ii) Election, approval, or ratification of *accountants*;

(iii) A proposal by a security holder included pursuant to *SEA Rule 14a-8* (*see infra*, §1335);

(iv) The approval or ratification of a plan of *executive compensation*; or

(v)   *Certain matters affecting investment companies* registered under the Investment Company Act of 1940.

[SEA Rule 14a-6(a)]

(2) Other soliciting materials [§1319]

Materials other than the proxy statement and the form of proxy need not be filed in advance of their dissemination to shareholders.

c. Filing requirements for definitive versions [§1320]

All materials used in a solicitation must be filed (or mailed for filing) with the S.E.C. and with each national securities exchange on which securities of the registrant trade *no later than the day on which they are first used.* If the materials have been filed in preliminary form, the final versions are prepared with a view to the S.E.C.'s comments on the previously filed versions.

(1) Note

If preliminary versions of proxy materials have been disseminated, the above rule applies also to those; *i.e.,* copies must be filed with the S.E.C. no later than the day on which they are first used.

EXAM TIP — gilbert

On your exam, be sure to remember the **two filing requirement dates**: Generally, preliminary versions of the form of proxy and proxy statement must be filed with the S.E.C. at **least 10 days** before the final versions are disseminated, and all other soliciting materials must be filed **no later than the day on which they are first used**.

---

d. Antifraud provisions applicable [§1321]

Note that whether or not the S.E.C. requires advance filing of particular solicitation documents, the antifraud provisions of the 1934 Act apply to all materials used and statements made by the parties. [*See* SEA Rule 14a-9; *see infra*, §1395]

7. The Proxy Statement [§1322]

The following information must be included in the proxy statement (or the information statement, if proxies are not solicited):

a. Details about solicitation [§1323]

A statement identifying for whom the solicitation is being made, the means (mail, etc.) being used, who bears the cost, the amount already spent, and an estimate of the total amount to be spent in the proxy solicitation. [Schedule 14A]

b. Details about director election [§1324]

In addition, if directors are to be elected at the shareholders' meeting, the proxy statement must name and give detailed information about (i) the nominees of the person who is soliciting the proxy, (ii) other directors whose terms of office continue beyond the meeting, and (iii) the officers of the registrant. The statement must include information regarding transactions during the past year between the specified persons and the registrant. [Schedule 14A]

c. Details about specific matters [§1325]

Detailed information must be disclosed relating to the specific matters for which the proxy is being solicited. [Schedule 14A] Specific rules cover the information required in situations of merger, sale of corporate assets, liquidation or dissolution, or the purchase of another company.

(1) Reorganizations

With respect to mergers and other reorganization transactions, cross-reference the requirements of SA rule 145 (*supra*, §634). In rule 145 transactions, a registration statement on form S-4 is usually filed and serves as both the schedule 14A proxy statement and as a 1933 Act prospectus.

(2) Note

Financial statements must also be filed in connection with certain transactions, such as mergers and authorizations to issue new securities.

d. Details about executive compensation [§1326]

If the solicitation is made on behalf of the registrant, the proxy statement must also disclose details about the registrant's compensation of its executive officers. Information is required about the person serving as chief executive officer, the four most highly compensated officers other than the CEO, and up to two persons for whom disclosure would have been provided but for the fact that they were no longer serving as executive officers at the end of the most recent fiscal year. [Schedule 14A; Regulation S-K Item 402(a)(3)]

e. Details about general matters [§1327]

There are some general matters that must also be disclosed, including significant changes in control, the fact that securities owned by control persons have been pledged as collateral for loans, the vote required on each issue, the shares entitled to vote, and the record date for voting. [Schedule 14A]

8. Proxy Contests [§1328]

A proxy contest typically results from a fight between management and other shareholders for control of the company. Most often, the insurgent shareholders will have acquired a substantial position in the company and either (i) want to control the company through election of a majority of the directors or (ii) will have proposed a merger or made a tender offer for the shares of the company, and management seeks to avoid a loss of control by merging with another company. In the first situation, the insurgents will solicit shareholder proxies in order to elect their slate of directors; while in the second situation, a so-called "defensive merger," management will solicit proxies in support of the merger.

a. Exception to filing requirements [§1329]

Proxy contests frequently require quick action, and for this reason participants often rely on the general exception to the filing requirements to solicit proxies before actually filing a proxy statement. (*See supra*, §1314.) Before a form of proxy can be provided to security holders, however, the proxy statement and form of proxy must be filed with the S.E.C., and copies must be delivered to security holders.

b. Shareholder lists [§1330]

Normally, the question of a shareholder's access to the registrant's shareholder list is governed by state law. For 1934 Act reporting companies, however, the S.E.C.'s involvement in proxy regulation means that *federal law plays a part in the issue.*

(1) General rule [§1331]

If management is soliciting proxies and a shareholder wants to send proxy soliciting material (usually in opposition to management), either (i) the shareholder must be given *access to the registrant's shareholder list,* or (ii) the *registrant must mail the materials to its shareholders on behalf of the requesting shareholder.* The choice belongs to the *registrant,* which will most often choose to send the materials rather than give the shareholder access to the shareholder list. [SEA Rule 14a-7; *see infra*, §1371]

(2) Special rule for "going private" and "roll-up" transactions [§1332]

If management proposes a "going private" or "roll-up" transaction, the option of having the registrant send the materials or having access to the registrant's shareholder list *belongs to the requesting shareholder, not to the registrant.* [SEA Rule 14a-7(b)]

(a) "Going private" transaction defined [§1333]

Going private transactions are transactions in which a publicly held company becomes closely held, usually by means of a tender offer.

(b) "Roll-up" transaction defined [§1334]

A roll-up transaction is one in which limited partnerships are either combined or reorganized; usually, the interests of the limited partners are purchased by a successor entity, which then either sells securities or is itself acquired by the former general partner.

(c) Rationale

Going private and roll-up transactions involve the purchase of investors' interests, frequently by the managers of the enterprise. When the buyers are the managers, they have access to substantially more information about the business than do the investors. These transactions thus pose a greater risk of abuse than do run-of-the-mill transactions. The S.E.C., therefore, has given the choice to the requesting shareholders—they decide whether to demand a shareholder list, and to mail directly to shareholders, or alternatively to permit the registrant to do the mailing.

EXAM TIP   **gilbert**

Remember, generally if a shareholder wants to oppose the registrant's position in a proxy solicitation, the *registrant* has the choice of giving the shareholder access to the shareholder list or mailing the opposing shareholder's materials. However, if management is proposing "going private" (buying up shares to become a nonpublic company) or a "roll up" (combining or reorganizing limited partnerships), the *choice belongs to the shareholder*.

---

9. Shareholder Proposals [§1335]

As an alternative to an independent proxy solicitation, a shareholder may serve

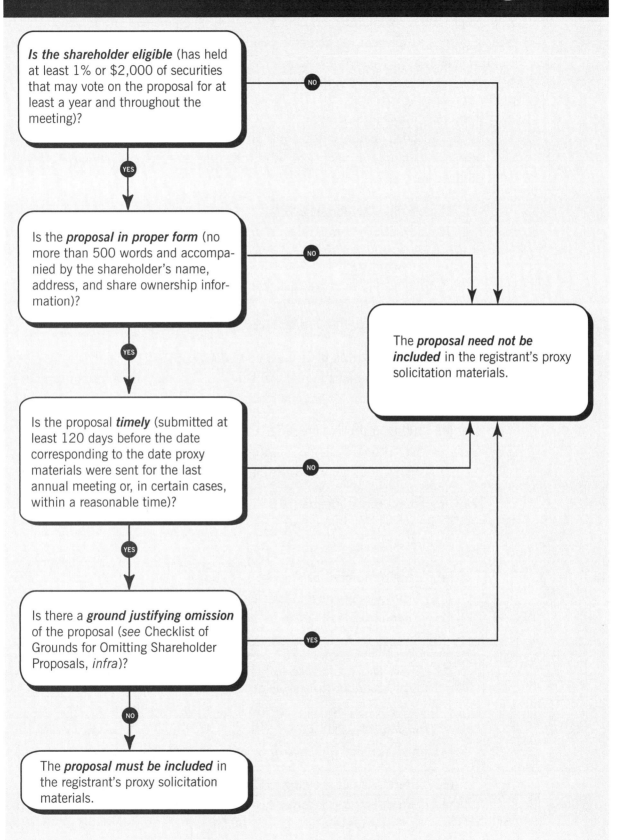

Is the shareholder eligible (has held at least 1% or $2,000 of securities that may vote on the proposal for at least a year and throughout the meeting)?

NO

YES

Is the **proposal in proper form** (no more than 500 words and accompanied by the shareholder's name, address, and share ownership information)?

NO

YES

Is the proposal **timely** (submitted at least 120 days before the date corresponding to the date proxy materials were sent for the last annual meeting or, in certain cases, within a reasonable time)?

NO

YES

Is there a **ground justifying omission** of the proposal (*see* Checklist of Grounds for Omitting Shareholder Proposals, *infra*)?

YES

NO

The **proposal need not be included** in the registrant's proxy solicitation materials.

The **proposal must be included** in the registrant's proxy solicitation materials.

notice on management of her intention to propose action at the shareholders' meeting. Then, in order to put the matter before the shareholders at the meeting, the shareholder may, under certain circumstances, compel management to include the proposal in the registrant's proxy statement. [SEA Rule 14a-8] Management, however, will in almost every case attempt to exclude the proposal from the proxy statement, relying on SEA rule 14a-8(c), which provides a list of permissible reasons for not including an otherwise proper shareholder proposal.

a. Requirements [§1336]

To be included in the registrant's proxy statement, a shareholder proposal must meet the requirements of SEA rule 14a-8(a) and (b), which are briefly outlined below.

(1) Eligible shareholders [§1337]

The proponent of the proposal must meet the following requirements:

(a) Holds at least one percent or $2,000 market value [§1338]

The proponent must be the record or beneficial owner of at least 1% or $2,000 in market value (whichever is less) of the registrant's securities entitled to be voted at the meeting.

(b) Holding period of at least one year [§1339]

The proponent must have held no less than the minimum quantity of securities for at least one year.

(c) Holds at time of meeting [§1340]

The proponent must continue to hold no less than the minimum quantity of securities through the time of the meeting.

(2) Procedural requirements [§1341]

Shareholder proposals must be submitted in accordance with the following procedures.

(a) Length; number of proposals [§1342]

A proponent may submit only one proposal, together with an accompanying statement in support. The proposal together with the supporting statement may not exceed 500 words.

(b) Shareholder information [§1343]

Together with the proposal, the proponent must provide her name and address, the number of voting securities she holds of record or beneficially, the dates on which she acquired the securities, and documentary evidence of beneficial ownership.

(c) Attendance at meeting [§1344]

Either the proponent or her representative (if allowed to present the proposal under state law) must attend the meeting and present the proposal.

1) **Failure to attend or to present proposal [§1345]**

If the proposal is not presented at the meeting and the failure is not excused by good cause, the registrant is not required to include in its proxy statement any proposals submitted by the shareholder for the next two years.

(d) **Timeliness [§1346]**

The proponent must submit the proposal far enough in advance to permit the registrant to consider it, and potentially to include it in the printed proxy statement sent to the shareholders.

1) **Annual meetings [§1347]**

Proposals that are to be presented at the registrant's annual meeting of shareholders must be received by the registrant 120 days before the date corresponding to the day and month on which the proxy statement was delivered to shareholders for the previous year's annual meeting.

a) **If there was no annual meeting in the previous year [§1348]**

If the registrant had no annual meeting in the previous year, or if the current year's meeting date was changed by more than 30 days from the previous year's, the proponent of the proposal must deliver the proposal to the registrant a reasonable time before the solicitation is made.

2) **Other meetings [§1349]**

Proposals to be presented to shareholders at meetings other than annual meetings must be delivered to the registrant a reasonable time before the solicitation is made.

b. **Management's omission of shareholder proposals [§1350]**

If management opposes the shareholder proposal, it must file the proposal and the reasons for opposing it with the S.E.C. [SEA Rule 14a-8(j)] The S.E.C. staff will review the proposal and give an indication of whether it agrees or disagrees with management (*i.e.,* whether it would recommend an enforcement action or, alternatively, "no action" if management omits the proposal from its proxy solicitation). Note, however, that a "no action" position expressed in the staff's letter is not binding on the proponent of the proposal, who remains free to litigate the propriety of excluding the proposal in federal court. Management may properly omit shareholder proposals in the following situations [SEA Rule 14a-8(i)]:

(1) **Proposal not a "proper subject" [§1351]**

If the shareholder's proposal is not a "proper subject" for action by the shareholders, it may be omitted from management's proxy solicitation.

The law of the state in which the issuer is incorporated applies to determine what is a "proper subject."

(2) Proposal illegal [§1352]

Management need not include a proposal that, if implemented, would require the registrant to violate any state or federal law or the law of any foreign jurisdiction to which the registrant is subject.

(a) Note

If compliance with a foreign law would cause the registrant to violate United States law, this basis for exclusion does not apply to a proposal that would cause violation of the foreign law.

(3) Proposal contrary to S.E.C. rules or regulations [§1353]

If the proposal or its supporting statement violates any of the proxy rules (including rule 14a-9, prohibiting false or misleading statements), it need not be included in the registrant's proxy statement.

(4) Proposal relates to redress of personal claim [§1354]

Management need not include proposals that are designed primarily to further some personal interest of the proponent not shared with other shareholders in general, *e.g.,* redressing a grievance against the registrant.

(5) Proposal relates to insignificant operations of the registrant [§1355]

Management need not include a proposal that relates to insignificant operations. To establish that the shareholder proposal relates to operations that are not significantly related to the registrant's business, two elements must be shown:

(a) No economic significance [§1356]

The operations in question must account for *less than 5%* of the registrant's *total assets* at the end of its most recent fiscal year, and less than 5% of its *net earnings* and *gross sales* for its most recent fiscal year; *and*

(b) No other significance [§1357]

The operations *must not be significant in some other way* to the registrant's business.

Example: Acme Corp. had revenues last year of $141 million and profits of $6 million. One Acme line of business is the importation and sale of paté de foie gras. Its paté sales last year grossed $79,000, with a net loss of $3,126. A shareholder sought to include in Acme's proxy statement a proposal that Acme form a committee to study the methods by which its French supplier produced paté and to determine whether the geese used in production were mistreated. Acme attempted to exclude the proposal on the ground that it was insignificant to its business. When the dispute arrived in court, the court held that Acme could not exclude the proposal; although the *economic* insignificance of the paté business to Acme was clear, the court ruled that the proposal might raise *policy questions* important enough to be considered "significantly related" to Acme's business. The court held that the rule is not limited to economic significance—the absence of policy significance must be shown before a proposal can be excluded. [**Lovenheim v. Iroquois Brands, Ltd.**, 618 F. Supp. 554 (D.D.C. 1985)]

(6) Proposal deals with matter beyond registrant's power [§1358]

Management need not include proposals relating to issues or situations over which the registrant has no control.

(7) Proposal deals with ordinary business operations of registrant [§1359]

Management may exclude proposals relating to the conduct of the ordinary business operations of the registrant. [SEA Rule 14a-8(i)(7)] *Rationale:* Matters related to the ordinary business operations of the registrant are the business of either the registrant's board of directors or its management; they are not matters over which shareholders have authority.

(a) Exception [§1360]

Even if a proposal arguably relates to the conduct of the registrant's ordinary business operations, it may not be excluded from the proxy statement if it also involves important political or social issues. Whether a particular proposal involves such issues can be difficult to determine, however, and the S.E.C. decides these questions on a case-by-case basis. [SEA Rel. No. 34-40018 (S.E.C. 1998)]

Example: In 1969, shareholders proposed to Dow Chemical Corporation that the board of directors should consider adopting a policy that the corporation would not manufacture napalm. Although this could be called an ordinary business decision involving the company's product line (and the S.E.C. staff issued a no-action letter permitting the proposal's exclusion on that basis), the shareholders brought an action in federal district court to force the company to include the proposal. The court ruled that the proposal must be included, because of its political and social significance. [**Medical Committee for Human Rights v. S.E.C.**, 432 F.2d 659 (D.C. Cir. 1970), *vacated as moot*, 404 U.S. 403 (1972)]

(8) Proposal relates to election to board [§1361]

Management may exclude proposals relating to an election to the registrant's board of directors; shareholders have a say in such matters simply by voting for or against the candidate.

MANAGEMENT MAY EXCLUDE A SHAREHOLDER'S PROXY SOLICITATION PROPOSAL IF THE PROPOSAL IS:

- ☑ *Not a proper subject* for shareholder action

- ☑ One that would require the registrant to *violate any law*

- ☑ *Contrary to S.E.C. rules or regulations*

- ☑ Related to *redress of a personal claim* not shared with other shareholders in general

- ☑ Related to *insignificant operations* of the registrant, both in economic terms (*i.e.,* involves less than 5% of assets, earnings, and sales) and in terms of policy

- ☑ Related to *issues over which the registrant has no control*

- ☑ Related to conduct of the registrant's *ordinary business operations* not involving important political or social issues

- ☑ Related to *election to the registrant's board*

- ☑ *Counter to a proposal to be submitted by the registrant*

- ☑ *Moot*

- ☑ *Substantially duplicative of an earlier proposal*

- ☑ *Substantially the same as a proposal previously rejected* by shareholders at a previous meeting (but the rules vary according to the vote received at those previous meetings)

- ☑ Related to the *amount of a dividend*

(9) Proposal counter to proposal to be submitted by registrant at the meeting [§1362]

Similarly, if the proposal runs counter to a proposal to be submitted by the registrant, the shareholders initially will have their say by voting for or against management's proposal. In such a case, it generally adds little to put a second proposal on the agenda, and management is permitted to exclude such proposals.

(10) Proposal moot [§1363]

Proposals that are moot (*e.g.*, because they have already been substantially implemented) need not be included in the proxy statement.

(11) Proposal duplicative [§1364]

If the proposal would substantially duplicate another proposal previously submitted by another proponent, and the earlier proposal will be included in the registrant's proxy materials, the later proposal need not be included.

(12) Proposal previously rejected [§1365]

If the proposal deals with substantially the same subject matter as a proposal submitted at any shareholder meeting (regular or special) in the preceding five years, it may be omitted from the proxy materials for any shareholder meeting held within three years after the latest such submission *if*:

(a) The proposal was submitted at only *one such prior meeting* and it received *less than 3%* of the vote;

(b) The proposal was submitted at *two such prior meetings*, and at the time of its second submission, it received *less than 6%* of the vote; *or*

(c) The proposal was submitted at *three or more* such prior meetings, and at the time of its latest submission, it received *less than 10%* of the vote.

(13) Proposal relates to specific amounts of cash or stock dividends [§1366]

State corporation law provides that dividends are within the board's discretion. Dividends are also of particular interest to shareholders. To avoid inundation by proposals to censure the board for slashing the dividend, or demanding that the board consider raising the dividend, such proposals may be excluded.

10. Participation of Broker-Dealers in Proxy Contests

a. Stock held in "street name" [§1367]

A substantial majority of corporate stock in the United States is held in "street name," *i.e.*, registered on the books of the corporation in the name of a bank or brokerage firm, rather than that of the beneficial owner. S.E.C. rules require that the corporation take certain steps to see that proxy solicitation material is forwarded by banks and brokers to these beneficial owners. [SEA Rule 14a-13]

(1) Broker-dealer rules [§1368]

The S.E.C. has also adopted rules requiring banks and broker-dealers holding securities in street name to forward promptly to the beneficial owner any proxy material received from the registrant. [SEA Rules 14b-1, 14b-2]

(2) Exchange rules [§1369]

The national exchanges (and the National Association of Securities Dealers ("NASD") with respect to its member firms that trade over-the-counter securities) have also adopted solicitation rules pertaining to securities held in street name.

(a) *If stock is held by the broker-dealer in a fiduciary capacity* (*e.g.*, as trustee), the broker-dealer can give the proxy without soliciting the consent of the beneficial owner.

(b) *However, if the stock is held in street name merely for safekeeping* on behalf of the beneficial owner, the broker-dealer must transmit all solicitation material to the beneficial owner and secure the beneficial owner's direction as to giving the proxy. For example, the rules of the New York Stock Exchange provide that if there is a proxy contest involving a security listed on the exchange, the broker-dealer must get appropriate instructions from the beneficial owner.

(3) Direct communication between registrant and beneficial owners [§1370]

Until 1986, direct communications between the registrant and the beneficial owners of its securities were not possible. There existed no mechanism by which the registrant could determine the identities of the beneficial owners. In 1986, however, the S.E.C. adopted rules that permit registrants to request and receive, from the record holders, lists of the names, addresses, and the number of shares beneficially owned of those beneficial owners who do not object to the disclosure of this information. [SEA Rules 14b-1(b)(3), 14b-2(b)(4)(ii), (iii)] (Such owners are usually referred to as "NOBOs," for "nonobjecting beneficial owners.") The availability of NOBO lists makes communications between the registrant and its shareholders much easier, and thereby eases the burden of proxy compliance, at least a little bit.

(a) **Insurgent shareholders need not be given access to NOBO lists [§1371]**

Federal law provides access to NOBO lists only to registrants. No other party has a federal right to obtain a NOBO list from the record holder of the securities. This gives management a sizable advantage in a proxy contest, because management has the ability to communicate directly with the NOBOs, while the insurgent group has only the right to request that management either provide a list of owners, or mail the insurgent group's materials on behalf of the insurgents. Management generally chooses to mail the insurgents' materials to avoid disclosing its NOBO information. [*See* SEA Rule 14a-7]

(4) State law [§1372]

If no federal laws apply, proxy solicitation of securities held in street name is governed by state law. The laws of most states provide that the beneficial owner may require the registered owner to give her a proxy to vote the shares.

b. Solicitations by broker-dealers [§1373]

A broker-dealer must be careful in communicating with shareholders during a proxy contest because the broker-dealer risks becoming involved as a "participant" in a solicitation. If the broker-dealer is a participant, the proxy statement used by the registrant will be defective, because it will not disclose the broker-dealer's status as a participant or the information required by SEA Schedule 14A about the broker-dealer.

(1) "Participant" in a solicitation [§1374]

The term "participant" is defined in Schedule 14A, item 4, instruction 3. The definition *includes the registrant and anyone who solicits proxies, or finances their solicitation,* but it *excludes persons who merely transmit soliciting materials.* Thus, it is especially risky for a broker-dealer to contribute anything to the text of materials that are sent, because to do so might make the "merely transmits" exclusion unavailable.

(2) Note

The broker-dealer does not violate this rule by asking instructions of the beneficial owner on how to give the proxy. [SEA Rule 14a-2(a)(1)(iii)] But if the broker-dealer were to give favorable treatment to one soliciting party (*e.g.,* by delaying sending the materials of another), there would be a violation of the proxy rules (and also of the national exchange and NASD rules).

(3) But note

The broker-dealer may advise its customers how to respond to a proxy solicitation if there has been an unsolicited request for such advice. [SEA

Release No. 7208 (1964)] And rule 14a-2(b)(3) exempts *financial advisers* who furnish unsolicited proxy voting advice from the informational and filing requirements of rules 14a-3 through 14a-6, 14a-8, and 14a-10 through 14a-14. However, advisers must disclose to the recipient of any advice: (i) any significant relationship with the registrant, an affiliate, or shareholder proponent; and (ii) any material interest of the adviser in the matter to which the advice relates. In addition, the adviser may not receive remuneration for providing the advice, except from the recipient. However, this exemption does not apply to advice furnished on behalf of anyone soliciting proxies or a candidate in an election contest for directors under rule 14a-11.

11. Exemptions from the Proxy Rules [§1375]

SEA Rule 14a-2 contains a number of exemptions from regulation under the proxy rules. The more commonly encountered exemptions include the following:

a. Solicitation of ten persons or fewer [§1376]

Anyone (other than management) may solicit proxies from 10 or fewer persons without having to comply with the proxy rules. [SEA Rule 14a-2(b)(2)] This provision may be helpful to an insurgent group that must, under state law, own or control by proxy a certain percentage ownership of stock to obtain a shareholder list.

b. Solicitation by beneficial owners [§1377]

The *beneficial* owner of securities may solicit a proxy from the *registered* owner without having to comply with the proxy rules. [SEA Rule 14a-2(a)(2)] This is important if an insurgent is purchasing shares to gain control of the registrant and needs to be able to vote the shares against management.

Example: A may purchase 100 shares of XYZ Corp. from B and become the beneficial owner thereof after the date set by XYZ for determination of stock ownership on its record books (the "record date"). Thus, B would appear on the corporate records as the registered owner as of the record date. Under rule 14a-2(a)(2), A may solicit a proxy from B without complying with the proxy rules.

c. "Tombstone ads" [§1378]

The proxy rules do *not* apply to a "tombstone" newspaper ad if the ad indicates only where copies of the proxy statement, form of proxy, and other soliciting materials may be obtained, the name of the registrant, the reason for the ad, and the proposals to be voted on by the shareholders. [SEA Rule 14a-2(a)(6); *see supra*, §183]

d. Broker-dealer exemptions [§1379]

"Impartial transmission" of solicitation materials by broker-dealers is also exempted from the proxy rules (*see supra*, §1374).

e. **Statement of intended vote not a "solicitation" [§1380]**

The definition of "solicitation" excludes certain communications by a security holder, who does not otherwise engage in a nonexempt solicitation, *stating how the security holder intends to vote and the reasons therefor.* [SEA Rule 14a-1(l)(2)]

(1) Requirements [§1381]

To be excluded from the definition of "solicitation," at least one of the following must be true of the statement of intended vote:

(a) Communication made in public medium [§1382]

The communication will be excluded if it is made in a public medium; *i.e.,* the communication is made by means of: speeches in a public forum; press releases; published or broadcast opinions; or statements or advertisements appearing in a broadcast medium, newspaper, magazine, or other bona fide publication disseminated on a regular basis.

(b) Communication made by a fiduciary to beneficiary [§1383]

A communication directed to persons to whom the security holder owes a fiduciary duty in connection with the voting of securities of the registrant held by the security holder is excluded.

(c) Communication made in response to unsolicited request [§1384]

A communication made in response to unsolicited requests for additional information with respect to a prior exempt communication made under (a) or (b), above, is exempt.

(2) Persons eligible [§1385]

The exclusion from the definition of "solicitation" is available to all shareholders, including officers and directors of the registrant, as long as they do not otherwise engage in a regulated solicitation.

(3) Antifraud provisions may not be applicable [§1386]

One interesting effect of excluding these communications from the definition of "solicitation" is that the antifraud provisions of the proxy rules [SEA Rule 14a-9; *see infra*, §§1395 *et seq.*] are apparently *not* applicable to such communications. Rule 14a-9, by its terms, applies only to "solicitations subject to this regulation" (*i.e.,* regulation 14A).

EXAM TIP **gilbert**

On your exam, be sure to remember that not every form of solicitation triggers the requirements of the proxy rules. Perhaps the most important exemptions to remember are the ones allowing for solicitation of *10 or fewer persons*, and the exemption for communications *by a security holder stating how the security holder intends to vote* when made in a public medium, by a fiduciary to the beneficiary, or in response to an unsolicited request. The latter exemption is actually excluded from the definition of "solicitation" altogether.

f.   Exempt solicitations [§1387]

The following activities are considered to be "solicitations" under the rules, but nevertheless are exempt from some or all of the provisions of the proxy rules:

(1)   Exemption from delivery and disclosure rules—soliciting person not seeking proxy authority [§1388]

Under SEA Rule 14a-2(b), a solicitation by a person who, during the solicitation period (i) *does not seek the power to act as a proxy* for a security holder and (ii) *does not furnish or request a form* of revocation, abstention, consent, or authorization is exempt from the proxy statement delivery and disclosure rules. [SEA Rule 14a-2(b)(1)]

(a)   Ineligible persons [§1389]

Certain persons are specifically excluded from eligibility for the rule 14a-2(b) exemption, including:

1)   *The registrant, or any affiliate or associate* (meaning generally a 10% or more shareholder, or a relative or affiliate of such a person);

2)   *An officer or director of the registrant engaging in a solicitation financed by the registrant;*

3)   *A nominee for whose election as director proxies are solicited;*

4)   *Anyone soliciting in opposition to certain transactions* (*e.g.,* a merger, recapitalization, reorganization) recommended or approved by the board of directors of the registrant, if the soliciting person is proposing an alternative transaction to which it or an affiliate is to be a party;

5)   *Anyone who is required to report beneficial ownership of the registrant's securities on schedule 13D* (*see supra,* §1141), unless that person has filed the schedule and neither disclosed an intent nor reserved the right to attempt to take over the registrant; and

6)   *Anyone who would receive a special benefit* from a successful solicitation, not shared by all shareholders pro rata.

(b)   Irrevocable election [§1390]

To remain eligible for this exemption, the person claiming the exemption must refrain from all nonexempt solicitation throughout the relevant solicitation period. Thus, once a person has availed herself of this exemption, she is *deemed to have made an irrevocable election* to maintain exempt status throughout the solicitation period.

[S.E.C. Release No. 34-31326 (1992)] In other words, such a person will be barred from conducting any nonexempt solicitations during that period.

(c) Required notice to S.E.C. for $5 million holders [§1391]

Any person who at the beginning of a solicitation owns beneficially securities of the solicited class with a market value of over $5 million, and who avails herself of this exemption, must file a notice with the S.E.C. *not later than three days* after the written solicitation is first given to any security holder. [SEA Rule 14a-6(g)]

(2) Exemption from delivery rules—solicitations by public broadcast speech, advertisement, etc. [§1392]

A solicitation that is made by public speech; press release; or published or broadcast opinion, statement or advertisement appearing in a broadcast medium, newspaper, magazine, or other bona fide publication disseminated on a regular basis *is exempt* from the proxy statement delivery rules. [SEA Rule 14a-3(f)] That is, such solicitations can be made regardless of whether the persons solicited have received a copy of the proxy statement *if:*

(a) *No form of proxy, consent, or authorization or means to execute such documents is provided* to a security holder in connection with the communication; *and*

(b) *A definitive proxy statement is on file with the S.E.C.*

12. Enforcement Provisions [§1393]

An action may be brought for any violation of the proxy rules, and the courts will fashion whatever relief is appropriate under the circumstances.

a. Implied private cause of action [§1394]

As with 1934 Act section 10(b) and rule 10b-5, *supra*, neither section 14(a) nor the proxy rules explicitly confer a private right of action for violation of the proxy rules. However, in 1964 the Supreme Court held that *there is a private right of action for violation of the proxy rules.* [**J.I. Case Co. v. Borak,** 377 U.S. 426 (1964)]

b. Antifraud provisions [§1395]

Most actions claiming violation of the proxy rules are brought under SEA rule 14a-9, the antifraud rule relating to the solicitation of proxies. The purpose of the antifraud provisions is to ensure complete disclosure to shareholders of all material facts necessary to support an intelligent decision on matters in which proxies are solicited, thus protecting the shareholders and the integrity of the shareholder voting process. The elements of a cause of action under rule 14a-9 are: (i) a misrepresentation or omission, (ii) of a material fact, (iii) made at least negligently, if not recklessly or intentionally. In addition, private plaintiffs must establish causation, which, as we will see, is—for purposes of the proxy rules—defined in terms of materiality. These elements are discussed in detail below.

(1) Misrepresentations or omissions of fact [§1396]

Solicitations that are made by any proxy statement, form of proxy, notice of meeting, or other communication, either written or oral, and that contain any affirmative misrepresentation or omission of a material fact, are prohibited. Compare the broader prohibition of rule 10b-5 (*supra*, §933) and section 14(e) (tender offers, discussed *supra*, §1205).

(a) Requirement of a "fact" [§1397]

As to what constitutes a "fact," *see* the discussion of rule 10b-5, *supra*, §960.

 Examples: Rule 14a-9 includes the following examples of potential material misrepresentations of fact:

(i)   Predictions of specific future market prices for the issuer's shares;

(ii) Statements that impugn character, integrity, or personal reputation or that make charges concerning illegal, immoral, or improper conduct, without factual foundation;

(iii) Proxy statements, forms of proxy, or other soliciting materials that fail to distinguish themselves clearly from the soliciting material of others soliciting for the same meeting or subject matter; and

(iv) Claims made prior to a shareholders' meeting concerning the results of the proxy solicitation.

[SEA Rule 14a-9]

(b) Proxy contests [§1398]

Many of the fraud cases involve a proxy contest, where two parties (management and insurgents) are fighting for control of the corporation. To some degree, the courts take this into account and do not require an exhaustive disclosure or even a perfectly balanced presentation of the facts by the soliciting parties. [**Abramson v. Nytronics, Inc.**, 312 F. Supp. 519 (S.D.N.Y. 1970)]

(2) Materiality [§1399]

The misrepresentation or omission must be of a *material* fact. The Supreme Court has stated that the test for materiality is whether there is a *substantial likelihood* that a reasonable shareholder would consider the fact of significance in determining how to vote. [**TSC Industries, Inc. v. Northway, Inc.**, *supra*, §974] The Court stated that this does *not* require proof of a substantial likelihood that disclosure would have caused the reasonable shareholder to change her vote, but only that the omitted fact would have had *actual significance* to the voter.

(a) The "total mix" of information [§1400]

In determining materiality, not only the information disclosed in the proxy statement is considered. Stockholders may be assumed to be aware of other information as well, and the "total mix" of information available to stockholders must be considered in deciding whether a statement or omission is misleading. This total mix includes "information already in the public domain and facts known or reasonably available to the shareholders." This information, however, does not necessarily include everything filed by a company under the 1934 Act: "Corporate documents that have not been distributed to the shareholders entitled to vote on the proposal should rarely be considered part of the total mix of information." [**United Paperworkers International Union v. International Paper Co.**, 985 F.2d 1190 (2d Cir. 1993)

(b) Information already in the other party's possession [§1401]

There is no requirement to disclose information to the other party that the other party already has, or that is already well-known in the securities market. [**Apple Computer Securities Litigation**, 886 F.2d 1109 (9th Cir. 1989), *cert. denied sub nom.*, **Schneider v. Apple Computer, Inc.**, 496 U.S. 943 (1990); **Seibert v. Sperry Rand Corp.**, 586 F.2d 949 (2d Cir. 1978)]

(c) Piecemeal disclosure and "buried facts" [§1402]

It is misleading to bury facts in voluminous disclosure, or to disclose facts piecemeal in such a way that a reasonable shareholder would not become aware of the significance of the facts. [**Werner v. Werner**, 267 F.3d 288 (3d Cir. 2001); **Kohn v. American Metal Climax, Inc.**, 322 F. Supp. 1331 (E.D. Pa. 1971)]

(d) Uncharged misconduct [§1403]

Misconduct that is not expressly required to be disclosed by an S.E.C. rule most often does not have to be disclosed. Thus, information that would support an inference of market manipulation does not have to be disclosed in the absence of a charge of market manipulation. [**TSC Industries, Inc., v. Northway, Inc.**, *supra*]

(e) Conflicts of interest [§1404]

The existence of an actual or potential conflict of interest is almost always material and must be disclosed. Thus, a parent company must disclose that it is considering spinning off an operating company subsidiary, reducing the likelihood that the parent would continue to support the operations of the subsidiary (even absent any legal obligation to do so). **[Kronfeld v. Trans World Airlines, Inc.,** 832 F.2d 726 (2d Cir. 1987), *cert. denied,* 485 U.S. 1007 (1988)]

(f) Other standards [§1405]

The standards of materiality developed in other contexts, for example rule 10b-5, are also highly relevant to proxy statements and should be consulted. (*See supra,* §§973-978.)

(3) Standard of culpability [§1406]

Section 14(a) of the 1934 Act offers no explicit standard of liability for proxy fraud. The courts that have considered the issue have come to different conclusions.

(a) Corporation—negligence suffices [§1407]

Courts have indicated that a corporation conducting a proxy solicitation can be held to have violated the proxy rules on a finding of negligence. **[Gerstle v. Gamble-Skogmo, Inc.,** *supra,* §962]

(b) Officers, directors, and employees—negligence may suffice [§1408]

Officers, directors, and employees may be liable for a proxy violation as principals or agents, as participants, or as aiders and abetters; and there are dicta that liability may be incurred upon a finding of negligence. [*See* **Gerstle v. Gamble-Skogmo, Inc.,** *supra*]

1) Distinguish—rule 10b-5 [§1409]

Although the language of rule 14a-9 is similar to that of rule 10b-5, it may be appropriate to require scienter in rule 10b-5 cases but not in rule 14a-9 cases. The S.E.C.'s authority under SEA section 10(b) is limited to regulating "manipulative or deceptive devices," which implies fraud. The S.E.C.'s authority under SEA section 14(a), by contrast, extends to all proxy regulation "necessary or appropriate in the public interest or for the protection of investors." This is substantially broader than the language of section 10(b) and can provide the basis for a broader reading of the regulations adopted pursuant to SEA section 14. **[Gerstle v. Gamble-Skogmo, Inc.,** *supra*]

(c) Outside accountants—scienter required [§1410]

A court has also held that in a private (*i.e.,* nongovernment) lawsuit brought against the outside accounting firm responsible for putting false financial statements in the proxy statement, liability could only be found if scienter was present. **[Adams v. Standard Knitting Mills,** Fed. Sec. L. Rep. (CCH) ¶97,382 (6th Cir. 1980)]

EXAM TIP	gilbert

On your exam, if you see an issue concerning a fraudulent statement or omission in a proxy statement, be sure to remember that the level of culpability to prove a violation of the proxy rules may vary depending on the *identity of the defendant*. Although this is not completely settled, most courts have indicated that a corporation and its officers, directors, and employees can be found liable if their conduct was *negligent*, but an outside accountant can be found liable (at least in a lawsuit brought by a nongovernmental plaintiff) only if the accountant acted *with scienter*.

(4) Loss causation [§1411]

To establish a cause of action under the antifraud provisions, the plaintiff must prove that the misrepresentation or omission of material fact was the cause of her loss.

(a) Question of fact [§1412]

The courts have held that the issue of causation is one of fact, to be determined at trial.

(b) Defined in terms of materiality [§1413]

Initially, plaintiffs were required to prove both reliance (*i.e.*, transaction causation) and loss causation (*i.e.*, that the misleading facts or omissions had actually caused their damages). These requirements, however, posed complex problems of proof for the plaintiffs (who typically sue in a class action). To require each member of the class to establish causation specific to that member is to make class certification impossible, because the individual question of causation will dominate the common questions. The problem is much the same as that raised by the requirement that the plaintiffs establish reliance and loss causation in an action under rule 10b-5 (as to which, *see supra*, §§1012 *et seq.*). In 1970, the Supreme Court held that the causation required in an action under rule 14a-9 is defined in terms of *materiality*. [**Mills v. Electric Auto-Lite Co.**, 396 U.S. 375 (1970)]

1) Solicitation an "essential link" [§1414]

Once materiality is shown, the plaintiff can prove causation simply by showing that the proxy solicitation itself was an essential link in effecting the transaction. In other words, the plaintiff need only show that the party soliciting the proxies needed the votes represented by the proxies to carry the proposition.

Example: In *Mills*, defendant, which owned 54% of the stock of A Corp., solicited proxies to get the two-thirds vote of the A shareholders required to effect a merger (*i.e.*, solicitation was necessary to accomplish the transaction). However, defendant failed to disclose to A's shareholders that it controlled 54% of A's stock. The Court held that causation was established by proof (i) of the materiality of the omission and (ii) that the solicitation was an essential link in the transaction.

---

2) Where solicitation not required for transaction [§1415]

Suppose that the party soliciting the proxies has enough votes by itself to approve the transaction, but nevertheless conducts a proxy solicitation, and there is a material misrepresentation or omission in the proxy statement. The Court took a relatively strict view of causation in such a case, holding that the causation required in a rule 14a-9 case *had not been established* when the plaintiffs' (minority shareholders') votes were not needed, under state law or corporate bylaw, to approve a merger, and the plaintiffs' vote did not foreclose any remedy that would otherwise have been available. [**Virginia Bankshares, Inc. v. Sandberg**, *supra,* §965]

a) Facts of *Virginia Bankshares* [§1416]

In *Virginia Bankshares,* proxies were solicited in connection with a proposed merger of First American Bank of Virginia ("the Bank") into Virginia Bankshares, Inc. ("VBI"). VBI owned about 85% of the voting stock of the Bank, making the merger a "freeze-out" merger in which the votes of the minority shareholders were not required by state law or by the corporate charter or bylaws. Nevertheless, the directors of the Bank solicited the proxies of the minority shareholders. The proxy solicitation materials contained the statement that "The Plan of Merger has been approved by the Board of Directors because it provides an opportunity for the Bank's public shareholders to achieve a high value for their shares." The materials also contained the statement that the merger plan was "fair" to the minority shareholders.

b) Plaintiff's claim [§1417]

Plaintiff claimed that the statements by the Bank's directors were false, because the directors believed neither that the $42 price was high nor that the merger terms were fair to the minority shareholders. To satisfy the "essential link" portion of the test set out in *Mills, supra,* the plaintiff made two arguments:

1/ Public relations

First, the plaintiff argued that although the votes of the minority shareholders were not legally required to effectuate the merger, the defendants would not be willing to proceed without them, because of the bad publicity and bad shareholder relations that would result.

2/ Deprivation of state remedy

Second, the plaintiff claimed that the transaction itself would have been potentially voidable because of a director's conflict of interest, and that to protect the transaction, the Bank's directors needed the affirmative vote of the "untainted" minority shareholders. By approving the merger based on the board's misleading statements, the plaintiff argued, the Bank's minority shareholders had been deprived of the state law remedy for the conflicting interest.

c) Supreme Court's holding [§1418]

The Supreme Court held that neither of the plaintiff's theories of causation satisfied the *Mills* "essential link" requirement.

1/ The "public relations" argument [§1419]

The Court rejected the public relations argument, reasoning that *such a claim could be made after almost any corporate action* and would be *difficult to disprove*, requiring a trial in virtually every case. "A subsequently dissatisfied minority shareholder would have virtual license to allege that managerial timidity would have doomed corporate action but for the ostensible approval induced by a misleading statement . . . . The issues would be hazy, their litigation protracted, and their resolution unreliable."

2/ The "deprivation of state remedy" argument [§1420]

The Court rejected the deprivation argument because under relevant state law, the allegedly defective disclosure resulted in defective approval by the minority shareholders. In other words, *no state remedy was lost*, because no minority approval valid under state law had been given.

d) Fraudulent statements of opinion [§1421]

Another issue raised by *Virginia Bankshares* was whether a statement of opinion—for instance, that $42 is a high value for the Bank's shares—is actionable under rule 14a-9.

1/ When actionable [§1422]

The Supreme Court held that a statement of opinion (or of reasons for a particular board action) can be actionable if:

a/ The board *did not in fact hold the opinion* stated; *and*

b/ The *fact underlying the opinion is also misrepresented*.

---

e.g. **Example:** The statement, "The Plan of Merger has been approved by the Board of Directors because it provides an opportunity for the Bank's public shareholders to achieve a high value for their shares," is actionable on a showing that:

- The board did not approve the plan because they believed it provided a high price to minority shareholders, but rather they approved the plan because they wanted to keep their jobs; and

- In fact, $42 is not a high price for the Bank's shares.

2/ Falsity of belief alone not enough [§1423]

The Court specifically held that it is not enough to prove that the board did not believe the statement in the soliciting materials. If the facts underlying the statement of opinion or belief are correctly stated, no cause of action will lie.

c. Remedies for violation of the proxy rules

(1) Actions by the S.E.C. [§1424]

The S.E.C. does *not* have the same administrative remedies available under the proxy rules as it does under the 1933 Act (*see supra*, §§747 *et seq.*). However, the S.E.C. may bring an action for an *injunction* to prevent the solicitation of proxies, to prevent the voting of proxies obtained through improper solicitation, to require resolicitation of proxies, etc.

(2) Implied private actions [§1425]

The courts will fashion whatever relief is appropriate to remedy the loss caused by the proxy violation, *e.g.*, damages, rescission of the transaction, etc. [**J.I. Case Co. v. Borak,** *supra*, §1394]

(a) Derivative and class actions [§1426]

A shareholder may bring a direct cause of action or join with others to bring a class action; or, alternatively, the shareholder may bring a derivative suit on behalf of the corporation. [**J.I. Case Co. v. Borak,** *supra*]

(b) Merger cases [§1427]

In *J.I. Case*, which involved a merger, the Court indicated that an appropriate remedy might be to *unwind* the merger. One factor to be considered in the decision whether to rescind a merger is the "fairness" of the terms of the transaction. However, practically speaking, rescission is seldom if ever feasible in merger cases.

1) For example, if the merger involved public companies, it would be difficult or impossible to trace back and return all of the shares traded at the time of the merger, since trading of the stock would inevitably have taken place since the time of the merger.

2) A case subsequent to *J.I. Case* indicated that, at least in that case, it was not feasible to unwind the merger. Hence, the plaintiffs were allowed to recover their share in the profits realized after their company was merged into the defendant and the assets of their company sold at a substantial profit. [**Gerstle v. Gamble-Skogmo, Inc.,** *supra*, §1409]

(c) Reimbursement of costs [§1428]

The successful plaintiff in an action alleging violation of section 14(a) is entitled to reimbursement of reasonable costs and attorneys' fees if the action is brought on behalf of a class of shareholders and benefits all members of the class. [**Mills v. Electric Auto-Lite Co.,** *supra*]

d. Reimbursement of proxy contest expenses [§1429]

The extent to which expenses incurred in the solicitation of proxies may be reimbursed by the corporation is primarily a matter of state law.

(1) Reimbursement of management [§1430]

If its expenses are "reasonable" in amount, management may be reimbursed for the solicitation of proxies whether it wins or loses. However, some courts limit reimbursement to situations where the proxy solicitation is concerned with a matter of "corporate policy," excluding expenses incurred in a personal contest for *control* of the corporation. [**Rosenfeld v. Fairchild Engine & Airplane Corp.,** 309 N.Y. 168 (1955)]

(a) Difficult to distinguish [§1431]

It is often difficult to distinguish what is a matter of corporate policy from what is merely a contest for control—because the contesting parties will always frame a contest for control in terms of a dispute over policy.

(2) Reimbursement of insurgents [§1432]

If the insurgents in a proxy contest are successful, they may be reimbursed for *reasonable* amounts expended in soliciting proxies. *Rosenfeld, supra*, held that for reimbursement to be proper it had to be *ratified by the shareholders* and that the contest had to be for the *benefit of the corporation*. Unsuccessful insurgents receive no reimbursement.

E. Insider Liability for Short-Swing Profits

1. Introduction [§1433]

Section 16 is designed to prevent corporate insiders from using inside information about their companies to make short-swing profits by buying and then selling, or selling and then buying, securities of their corporation within a six-month period. The provisions of SEA section 16 are so strict that avoiding them has provided employment to many a lawyer in private practice, and countering these avoidance strategies, in turn, has occupied many a government lawyer. The end product of this is a rather complex set of rules. This summary provides an overview of the rules, but it is not a complete guide. Nevertheless, the summary goes considerably deeper into section 16 than many courses in basic securities regulation. You should adjust your studies (and your readings in this book) to the degree of depth your professor has indicated will be appropriate for your course.

a. Basic rule—reporting and disgorgement [§1434]

SEA section 16 accomplishes its goal of deterring the use of inside information by requiring insiders to: (i) *file periodic reports* of their holdings of the issuer's securities [SEA §16(a)], and (ii) *disgorge any profits* resulting from any combination of sales and purchases taking place within six months of each other [SEA §16(b)].

b. Makes short sales by insiders unlawful [§1435]

In addition, section 16(c) makes it unlawful for insiders to engage in short sales of their company's equity securities.

(1) "Short sale" defined [§1436]

A "short sale" is a sale of securities that the seller does not yet own, but plans to purchase just in time to cover the obligations of the sale. This strategy can be thought of as a "bet against the company"—the short seller sells at today's price, hoping that later, when she has to cover the sale by delivering the securities, she will be able to purchase the securities more cheaply. (*See infra*, §1923.)

c. Distinguish—rule 10b-5 "insider trading" [§1437]

Although both rule 10b-5 and section 16 are sometimes said to prohibit "insider trading," the provisions operate entirely differently. A rule 10b-5 case is based on a fraudulent misrepresentation or failure to disclose (*see supra*, §§1037 *et seq.*). Section 16, on the other hand, is based on the amount of time elapsed between a purchase and sale (or a sale and purchase) of the issuer's securities by an insider. If the amount of time is too short, the insider must give up her "profits," regardless of whether information was misrepresented or withheld. The presence or absence of fraud is irrelevant to a section 16 case.

d. Limitations of section 16 [§1438]

Section 16 is not intended to be a comprehensive solution to the problem of insider trading. In fact, its narrow focus on short-swing trades makes it oblivious to even the most outrageous intentional frauds, as long as there are no purchases and sales within six months of one another.

Example: A, a director of X Corp., has owned 100 shares of X Corp. stock for three years. At a board meeting, A becomes aware that X Corp. is about to suffer a large loss of business. Before the news becomes public, A sells her X Corp. shares. A has not incurred any liability under section 16 (although she would be liable under rule 10b-5; *see supra*, §§1037 *et seq.*).

---

(1) Note

Rule 10b-5 and section 16(b) *can* apply to the same transaction. In the example above, had A owned the X Corp. stock for only three weeks, she could be liable to X Corp. under section 16(b) for her short-swing profits and concurrently liable under rule 10b-5 in an action by the S.E.C. or by contemporaneous purchasers of X Corp. shares.

2. Nature of a Section 16 Cause of Action [§1439]

Section 16(a) and (c) are enforceable by the S.E.C. and not by private plaintiffs. However, any shareholder of the issuer can bring a lawsuit under section 16(b) to recover for the issuer an insider's profit from short-swing trading. Section 16(b) provides that:

(i) Any officer, director, or owner of more than 10% of any class of an equity security registered under section 12;

(ii) Who realizes any profit;

(iii) From a purchase and sale, or sale and purchase, of;

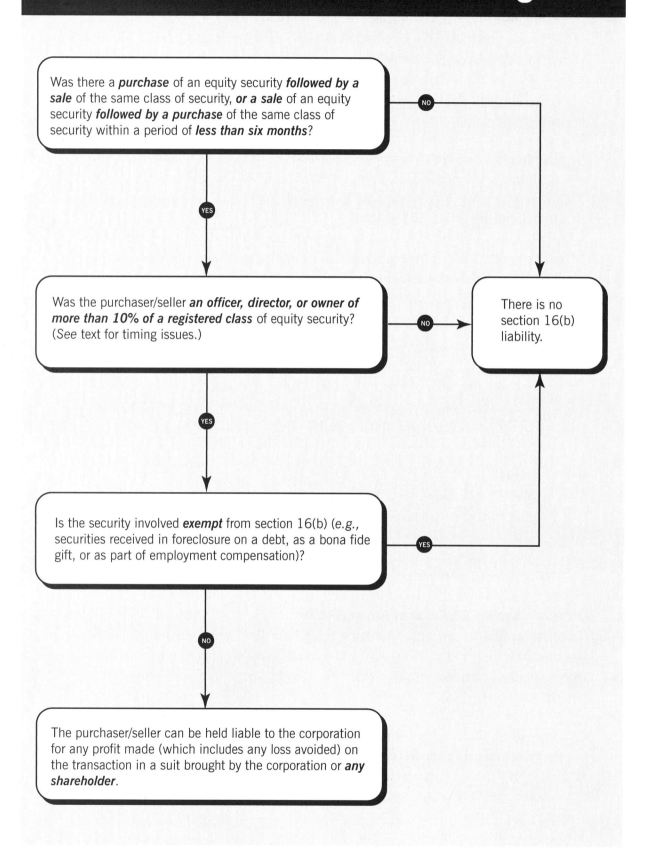

Was there a **purchase** of an equity security **followed by a sale** of the same class of security, **or a sale** of an equity security **followed by a purchase** of the same class of security within a period of **less than six months**?

NO

YES

Was the purchaser/seller **an officer, director, or owner of more than 10% of a registered class** of equity security? (See text for timing issues.)

NO

YES

There is no section 16(b) liability.

Is the security involved **exempt** from section 16(b) (*e.g.,* securities received in foreclosure on a debt, as a bona fide gift, or as part of employment compensation)?

YES

NO

The purchaser/seller can be held liable to the corporation for any profit made (which includes any loss avoided) on the transaction in a suit brought by the corporation or **any shareholder**.

(iv) Any nonexempt equity security of the issuer;

(v) Within any period of less than six months;

(vi) Shall be liable to the corporation for the profits made from the trading.

These elements are discussed in detail below.

3. All Equity Security Transactions Regulated [§1440]

To qualify as an "insider" by virtue of stock ownership, a person must beneficially own more than 10% of some class of *registered* equity security. But once qualified as an "insider" (either by owning more than 10% of a registered equity security, or by being an officer or director of a company with a class of registered equity security), purchases and sales of *any equity security of the issuer*—whether or not it is registered—may give rise to liability.

a. Note

This differs from other provisions of the 1934 Act (*e.g.*, the tender offer rule, *supra*, §1127), which apply only to transactions involving the *registered* equity securities themselves.

4. Beneficial Ownership [§1441]

The concept of "beneficial ownership" is critical in analyzing section 16 questions. A person may beneficially own securities to which she does not have record title; this is the usual case, for example, when a person purchases securities through a brokerage firm. Record title to the securities is held by the brokerage, while the buyer is the beneficial owner—meaning the benefits of ownership belong to the buyer, although the legal title is in the brokerage. For purposes of section 16, record title is not important: It is beneficial ownership that counts. Under section 16, there are two separate tests for determining beneficial ownership, depending on the purpose of the determination:

a. Beneficial ownership of more than ten percent of a class of registered equity security [§1442]

In deciding whether a person is the holder of more than 10% of a class of registered equity security, and is therefore an "insider" subject to section 16, all securities of that class beneficially owned by that person are counted. *For this purpose only,* beneficial ownership means having *voting power* with respect to those securities. In other words, all securities of that class which the person has the right to vote will be counted. [SEA Rule 16a-1(a)(1)]

b. All other section 16 purposes [§1443]

For all other section 16 purposes (*e.g.*, in reporting ownership of securities under section 16(a), or in calculating the profits from securities transactions under section 16(b)), beneficial ownership means having a direct or indirect *pecuniary interest in the shares.*

(1) Family ownership [§1444]

Officers and directors are presumed to have a pecuniary interest in, and therefore to be the beneficial owners of, *all securities held by virtually all relatives who share a household with the insider.* This includes in-laws and adopted relatives (all of whom are considered to be members of the insider's "immediate family"). [SEA Rules 16a-1(a)(2)(ii)(A), 16a-1(e)] However, the presumption may be rebutted by the insider.

c. Both methods may apply to one situation [§1445]

Suppose a person is the beneficial owner of more than 10% of a class of registered equity security based on voting power. The consequence of this is that she is required periodically to report ownership under section 16(a). However, the only securities reported under section 16(a) are the securities in which she had a direct or indirect pecuniary interest, which might be more (or less) than the securities over which she has voting power. [SEA Rule 16a-1(a), note]

EXAM TIP **gilbert**

On your exam, be sure to remember that there are two tests for beneficial ownership under section 16. The test concerning ownership of more than 10% focuses on *voting power*. The test for all other purposes focuses on *pecuniary interest* in the securities, and an officer or director will be assumed to have a pecuniary interest in securities of relatives who live with the officer or director unless the officer or director rebuts the presumption.

---

5. "Insiders" Defined [§1446]

"Insiders" covered under section 16 are officers and directors of a corporation with a class of equity securities registered under section 12 of the Act, *and* all persons who beneficially own more than 10% of any class of the corporation's equity securities registered under section 12. Courts have generally refused to expand the class of potential defendants beyond the persons described in section 16 (*e.g.,* to other persons who possess the same inside information as officers and directors).

a. Officers and directors [§1447]

Whether a potential defendant was an officer or director at a particular point in time is in most cases readily established through the corporate minute book.

(1) "Officer" defined [§1448]

An officer is defined as an issuer's president, principal financial officer, principal accounting officer (or, if there is no such accounting officer, the controller), any vice president of the issuer in charge of a principal business unit, division, or function (such as sales, administration, or finance), any other officer who performs a policy-making function, or "any other person who performs similar policy-making functions for the issuer." [SEA Rule 16a-1(f)]

(a) Officers of subsidiary and parent corporations [§1449]

Officers of subsidiary or parent corporations of the issuer may be deemed to be officers of the issuer, but only if they perform policy-making functions for the issuer.

(b) Honorary titles [§1450]

Merely holding an officer's title is not enough to cause section 16(b) liability to attach; the person in question must in fact perform the functions of an officer. It is the duties, rather than the title, that determine whether an employee is an officer under section 16(b). [**C.R.A. Realty Corp. v. Crotty,** 878 F.2d 562 (2d Cir. 1989); **Merrill Lynch, Pierce, Fenner & Smith, Inc. v. Livingston,** 566 F.2d 1119 (9th Cir. 1978)]

(2) Timing issues [§1451]

Section 16 raises three timing issues with respect to officers and directors: (i) What happens if a person was not an officer or director at the time of the first transaction (purchase or sale), but becomes one by the time of the second transaction (sale or purchase)? (ii) What is the result in the reverse situation; *i.e.*, the person was an officer or director at the time of the first transaction, but is no longer one at the time of the second? (iii) And finally, what happens if an officer or director of a company is not subject to section 16, because the company has no equity securities registered, and then the person becomes subject to section 16 when the company registers a class of equity securities?

(a) Transaction before person becomes an officer or director [§1452]

If a transaction takes place before the person becomes an officer or director, the policy underlying section 16 does not apply: *i.e.*, such a person generally has no access to inside information. The S.E.C. adopted this view in 1991, and dropped an earlier requirement that persons report all transactions taking place six months before becoming officers or directors.

(b) Transaction after person ceases being an officer or director [§1453]

A transaction that takes place after the person ceases to be an officer or director is subject to section 16 *only if it takes place within six months of a transaction that happened while the person was an officer or director.*

(c) Officer or director becomes subject to section 16 [§1454]

The last timing issue arises when an officer or director is not initially required to report a transaction, because the issuer has not registered a class of equity securities under the 1934 Act. If the issuer then registers a class of security, must the insider report the earlier transaction (and be liable for any profit when the transactions are matched)? The answer is yes, if: (i) the insider engaged in the second transaction after becoming subject to the reporting requirement (*i.e.*, after the issuer registered a class of equity securities), and (ii) the second transaction took place within six months of the first transaction. [SEA Rule 16a-2(a)]

1) Rationale

This rule is designed to trap transactions by insiders taking place shortly before the issuer goes public. The S.E.C. believes that in general, insiders of companies that are about to go public know about those plans far enough in advance to plan for section 16. In addition, the possibilities for abuse just before the company goes public are greater than they are later, when a market price has been established for the company's securities.

Example: Three weeks before XYZ Corp. goes public, XYZ's president, O, buys 1,000 shares of XYZ stock. At the time XYZ goes public, it must register its stock under 1934 Act section 12. Two weeks after the company goes public, O sells 1,000 shares of XYZ stock. O must report both the purchase and the sale, and will be liable for any profit on the transactions.

EXAM TIP	gilbert

On your exam, remember that transactions occurring *before* a person becomes an officer or director *are excluded* from section 16, but most other transactions by officers or directors *will trigger* section 16(a) reporting requirements and can trigger the section 16(b) disgorgement provision if the transaction can be matched with another transaction occurring within six months.

(3) Deputization [§1455]

Despite its general limitation to named insiders, section 16 may also apply to situations where an officer or director of one corporation has been appointed by that corporation to an inside position (such as director) in another corporation (*e.g.*, A Corp. appoints D to be a director of B Corp.). While the person might not engage in any prohibited purchases or sales in B stock for himself, the entity with which he is affiliated (A) might.

(a) Deputizing corporation may be liable [§1456]

Thus, A Corp. may be found to have "deputized" one of its own insiders to serve on the board or as an officer of B Corp.—and if A Corp. subsequently purchases and sells B Corp. stock, a section 16 plaintiff may seek to hold A Corp. itself liable as a director or officer of B Corp. (rather than the individual appointed by A Corp.).

(b) Rationale

The rationale behind deputization lies in agency law. An individual officer or director of A Corp. who is appointed to the board of another corporation, B Corp., with a view to representing A Corp.'s interests, is in a practical sense a surrogate for A Corp., and legally is A Corp.'s agent. It is not unreasonable, then, that A Corp. should be considered as though it itself were represented on the board of B Corp., as indeed, under agency law, it is.

(c) Question of fact

Whether a deputization has occurred is a question of fact.

---

e.g. **Example:** Martin-Marietta Corp. purchased a substantial number of shares of Sperry Rand. Rand then asked Bunker (president of Martin-Marietta) to join its board, which he did. While Bunker served on the board of Rand, Martin-Marietta continued to purchase additional shares of Rand stock; while this was going on, Bunker received reports on Rand's progress and discussed this information with other personnel at Martin-Marietta. After Bunker resigned from the board of Rand, Martin-Marietta sold all of its Rand stock at a profit. [**Feder v. Martin-Marietta Corp.,** 406 F.2d 260 (2d Cir. 1969)] Even though Rand had initiated Bunker's appointment to its board, the court found that he had been deputized by Martin-Marietta to represent its interests in Rand. Therefore, the profits made by Martin-Marietta on its purchases and sales of Rand stock were recoverable by Rand in a suit brought by a Rand shareholder under section 16(b).

---

cf. **Compare:** The Court has refused to find a deputization where A Corp.'s investment in and sale of B Corp.'s stock was made *independently* and *without the specific knowledge* of A's representative sitting on B's board of directors. [**Blau v. Lehman,** 368 U.S. 403 (1962)]

---

(4) Liability extends to all transactions in shares "beneficially owned" [§1457]

Keep in mind that officers and directors are required to report (and to disgorge profit from) all transactions in equity securities beneficially owned by them, and that for this purpose, "beneficial ownership" is defined as having or sharing any pecuniary interest in the securities. [*See* **Feder v. Frost,** 220 F.3d 29 (2d Cir. 2000); *and see supra,* §1443.)

b. More-than-ten-percent shareholder [§1458]

Every person who directly or indirectly is the "beneficial owner" of more than 10% of any class of registered equity security is subject to the provisions of section 16.

(1) Beneficial ownership [§1459]

It is important to remember that "beneficial ownership" is determined differently for purposes of calculating more-than-10% ownership than it is for other section 16 purposes. As discussed above (*supra*, §1442), in determining who holds more than 10%, "beneficial ownership" means having or sharing the power to vote the securities.

(2) Timing of ownership [§1460]

Although officers and directors need *not* occupy their positions at the time of both purchase and sale (*see supra*, §§1451-1454), the language of the statute indicates that 10% shareholders can be liable only if such ownership exists both at the time of purchase and at the time of sale.

> **Example:** A owns no stock in X Corporation. On March 3, A buys X Corporation common shares (which are registered under the 1934 Act) in an amount sufficient to make A an 11% shareholder. On May 1 (less than six months later), A sells all the X Corporation common shares. *Result:* Although A must report the May 1 sale under section 16(a), A is *not* liable to disgorge any profit under section 16(b). The purchase by which A became a more-than-10% shareholder is not counted for section 16(b) purposes, because at the time of that purchase, A was not a more-than-10% shareholder. [**Foremost-McKesson, Inc. v. Provident Securities Co.**, 423 U.S. 232 (1976)]

> **Example:** A owns 12% of a registered equity security, sells 3% on Monday, and sells the remaining 9% on Tuesday. A can be held liable for his profits from the sale of only the first 3%, because at this point he owned more than 10%; thereafter, at the time he sold the remaining 9%, he did not own more than 10%. [**Reliance Electric Co. v. Emerson Electric Co.**, 404 U.S. 418 (1972)]

(a) Limited applicability of section 16(b) [§1461]

If a 10% owner is careful, he may structure his purchases and sales so as to limit the applicability of section 16(b). For example, a person could buy over 10% in a series of separate purchases and only those acquired *after* he reached 10% could be matched with subsequent sales under section 16(b).

(3) Securities held in trust [§1462]

The existence of securities held in trust has the potential to complicate vastly the otherwise fairly routine application of section 16 to fact situations. Although the S.E.C.'s rules relating to section 16 treatment of securities held in trust were revised in 1991 and again in 1996, the revisions did not simplify matters much. They did, however, improve the consistency and fairness of the requirements applicable to trustees and beneficiaries. Below are some highlights of the rules relating to trusts.

(a) Trust as "beneficial owner"—section 16(a) reporting [§1463]

A trust is subject to section 16(a) reporting only if it is the *beneficial owner of more than 10% of a registered class of equity securities*. (This is because a trust cannot be an officer or director of the issuer.) Beneficial ownership of more than 10% is determined the same way for trusts as it is for natural persons; *i.e.*, the question is whether the trust has sole or shared voting power with respect to the securities.

1) Status of trustees and beneficiaries [§1464]

One of the issues that makes dealing with trusts complicated is that trustees and beneficiaries may personally be subject to section 16, quite apart from the trust. This is the case, for example, if the trustee (or beneficiary) is an officer or director of the issuer, or owns more than 10% based on voting power. When this happens, it is important to *separate the status of the trust from the individual status of the trustee or beneficiary*.

a) Trustee (personally) as beneficial owner [§1465]

Merely being a trustee of a trust does not make the trustee, personally, a beneficial owner of the securities in the trust. However, if the trustee or any member of her immediate family that shares the same household is a beneficiary of the trust, the trustee, personally, is a beneficial owner of the securities held in trust. [SEA Rule 16a-8(b)(2)] This becomes especially important when the trustee is personally subject to section 16, because trust transactions can then be matched with personal transactions to produce profit that must be disgorged under section 16(b).

b) Beneficiaries as beneficial owners [§1466]

Trust beneficiaries almost inevitably are beneficial owners of the securities held in trust, because they have the necessary pecuniary interest in the securities. [*See* SEA Rule 16a-1(a)(2)]

2) Trustee and beneficiary reporting requirements—investment control [§1467]

A trust that holds more than 10% must report transactions in the issuer's equity securities, and this is done by the trustee on behalf of the trust. However, there are also situations in which the trustee or beneficiaries, personally, must report such transactions.

a) Trustee reporting requirement [§1468]

A trustee must personally report trust transactions over which the trustee had investment control (which is by far the most common case), *if the trustee also was a beneficial owner of the securities.*

b) Beneficiary reporting requirement [§1469]

Beneficiaries must report trust transactions over which they had (or shared) investment control.

(b) Liability under section 16(b) [§1470]

The liability of a trust, trustee, or beneficiary to disgorge profit under section 16(b) follows reporting liability under section 16(a), as described above. [SEA Rule 16a-8(d)] Thus, if a trustee is required to report a transaction on behalf of the trust, the trust will be liable to disgorge any profit. Likewise, if the trustee was required personally to report the transaction (because the trustee was a beneficial owner of the securities held in trust), the trustee will be required personally to disgorge profit. Finally, if the beneficiary is required to report the transaction (because the beneficiary had or shared investment control over the transaction), the beneficiary will be liable to disgorge any profit from the transaction. [SEA Rule 16a-8(d)]

(c) Possible complications

1) Director is beneficiary [§1471]

Assume that D is a director of C Corporation. D is also the sole beneficiary of a trust that holds 5% of the outstanding common stock of C (which has been registered under the 1934 Act). D, however, has no investment control over any trust asset. If the trust buys C stock in January, and sells C stock in March, making a profit, must D report the January and March transactions under section 16(a)? Is D liable for that profit under section 16(b)?

a) Answer

No, to both questions. Under rule 16a-1, D is the beneficial owner of the C stock if she has the right to *vote* the stock. Normally, this would trigger D's reporting requirement, as a director who beneficially owns C stock. Likewise, as the sole beneficiary of the trust, D has the requisite pecuniary interest for section 16(b) liability to attach. However, because D lacks investment control (which is, in fact, the most common state of affairs for trust beneficiaries), rule 16a-8 *exempts D both from reporting and from disgorgement.* Finally, the fact that D is a director of C does not change this result: D owns no C stock directly, so any section 16 reporting or disgorgement liability arises only because of the trust's ownership, as to which the exemptions provided in rule 16a-8 are available. Moreover, in this case the trust itself has no section 16 reporting obligation or disgorgement liability, because it does not own more than 10% of C's stock.

2) Variation one—trustee is related to beneficiary [§1472]

Suppose the facts are the same as stated immediately above, *but* the trustee is the spouse of the director. Is D liable for the profit under section 16(b)?

a) Answer

Again, D has neither reporting nor disgorgement liability under section 16. If D has actually given her spouse inside information, and the spouse-trustee has traded on that information, then rule 10b-5 has been violated. (*See supra*, §§1037 *et seq.*)

3) Variation two—trust is eleven percent holder [§1473]

Suppose the same facts as in a), above, *except* that the trust holds 11% of the C common stock.

a) Answer

As before, D has neither reporting nor disgorgement liability under section 16. The *trust*, however, is liable, both to report the January and March transactions, and to disgorge the profit to C.

4) Variation three—director is trustee; family member is beneficiary [§1474]

Suppose, now, that D is the trustee of the trust, and that D's son, S, who shares a household with D, is the trust's beneficiary. Suppose also that D, personally, buys C stock in January, and that the trust sells C stock in March. Must D, personally, report the January and March transactions?

a) Answer

Yes, and D will be liable to disgorge any profit under section 16(b). D, as a director of C, must report the personal purchase of C stock. Moreover, because the beneficiary of the trust, S, is a family member sharing the same household, D is required personally to report the trust's sale in March. [SEA Rule 16a-8(b)(2)] If a profit is found by matching the transactions, D will be liable to disgorge it. Some cases, decided before the section 16 rules were amended, reached a different result. [*See, e.g.,* **CBI Industries, Inc. v. Horton**, 682 F.2d 643 (7th Cir. 1982)]

(4) Securities owned by corporation [§1475]

Another possibility complicating the question of beneficial ownership under section 16 involves corporate ownership of securities (rather than direct ownership, or ownership by a trust). Under SEA rule 16a-1(a)(2)(iii), a shareholder is generally not considered to be a beneficial owner of securities owned by the corporation.

(a) Exception—control plus investment power [§1476]

However, if a shareholder both controls the corporation and has investment power over the securities owned by the corporation, the shareholder is considered the beneficial owner of those securities. [SEA Rule 16a-1(a)(2)(iii)]

Example: F was CEO of I Corp. F also controlled a limited partnership, FP. Both F and FP together owned over 17% of N Corp. In addition, F and FP were parties to a shareholder agreement, which included over 50% of the voting shares of N. On several occasions, F and FP purchased I stock, while N sold I stock. The court reversed a grant of summary judgment for F, holding that there was at least an inference that F and FP were beneficial owners of the I stock owned by N Corp. [**Feder v. Frost**, *supra*, §1457]

---

6. "Equity Security" Defined [§1477]

Section 16 applies to transactions in equity securities. The 1934 Act defines "equity security" as "any stock or similar security; or any security convertible, with or without consideration, into such a security"; as well as certain "acquisition rights" to such securities; and "any other security which the Commission shall deem to be of a similar nature and consider necessary or appropriate . . . to treat as an equity security." [SEA §3(a)(11)]

a. Convertible securities [§1478]

A security convertible into an equity security (*e.g.*, a debenture convertible into common stock) is an equity security for the purposes of section 12. Thus, a holder of more than 10% of such a security is an "insider" and, therefore, is subject to the reporting requirements of section 16(a) and the disgorgement provisions of section 16(b).

(1) Calculating ten percent of convertible securities [§1479]

However, for purposes of determining whether the holder of convertible securities is a more-than-10% shareholder under section 16(b), the court will consider the relative amount of the *underlying security* (that is, of the security into which the convertible security can be converted) owned by the shareholder, *not* the relative amount of the convertible security itself. [SEA Rule 16a-4(a); *see* **Chemical Fund, Inc. v. Xerox Corp.**, 377 F.2d 107 (2d Cir. 1967)]

Example: In *Chemical Fund, supra*, an investment company held more than 10% of the corporation's convertible debentures. These debentures, however, if converted into common stock and added to the already outstanding common, would equal less than 3% of the corporation's common stock. The court held that the investment company was not a beneficial owner of more than 10% within the meaning of section 16.

(a) Rationale

Section 16 applies to more-than-10% holders because they have the opportunity to control (or at least to substantially influence) the corporation through voting. Thus, the court reasoned, it makes sense to consider the position of the shareholder after conversion and to disregard percentage ownership of unconverted, nonvoting securities. This reasoning has now been adopted by the S.E.C. [S.E.C. Release No. 34-28869, note 36 (1991)]

(b) Illustration

Corporation C has a registered class of common stock, and a registered class of preferred stock (which also has voting rights). A owns 12% of the C preferred stock, which is convertible into 4% of the C common stock. A buys and sells C common stock within a period of less than six months.

1) Result

A is a "10% holder" and is subject to section 16(a) reporting *and* to section 16(b) liability for her transactions in *any* equity security of C, including transactions in C common stock.

2) Rationale

The C preferred stock is an equity security in its own right, and it carries voting rights. Hence, ownership of more than 10% of this class of stock triggers the application of section 16. [S.E.C. Release No. 34-28869, note 36 (1991)]

3) Note

If the C preferred stock did *not* have voting rights, the result would be different—only securities that *have* voting rights are considered in deciding percentage ownership of a class of equity securities. The reasoning, per *Chemical Fund, supra,* is that the statute is aimed at abuses made possible by voting control, and this is manifestly not possible when the securities in question do not have voting rights. [*Id.*]

(2) Securities not immediately convertible [§1480]

In one case, the defendant owned convertible preferred stock that, if converted, would have made him the holder of more than 10% of the corporation's common stock. Nevertheless, the court held that the defendant was not a more-than-10% owner because the preferred stock was not immediately convertible. [**Levner v. Saud,** 61 F.3d 8 (2d Cir. 1995)]

7. Purchase and Sale Requirement [§1481]

To establish liability under section 16(b), there must be a matching purchase and sale, or sale and purchase. The general rule is that for purposes of section 16(b), a "purchase" occurs when the purchaser undertakes an irrevocable obligation to take and pay for the stock; and a "sale" occurs when the seller undertakes an irrevocable obligation to deliver and accept payment for the stock. Although these rules are easily stated, there are several types of stock transactions where it may not be clear if a "purchase" or "sale" has actually occurred. Many of these transactions involve the exchange of stock either for property or for other stock.

a. Security conversions [§1482]

There are various types of security conversions (*e.g.,* conversion of preferred stock or debentures into common stock), and the cases are split as to whether a "purchase" and/or a "sale" is involved in these transactions.

(1) Traditional approach [§1483]

Earlier judicial decisions seemed to take a simplistic approach to the question, defining all exchanges of stock as "purchases" or "sales."

---

e.g. **Example:** Where an issuer called for conversion of its preferred stock (*i.e.,* forced its preferred shareholders to convert their shares into common stock), the court held that the conversion was a "purchase" of the common stock. Similarly, the giving up of the convertible preferred stock would be a "sale." [**Park & Tilford, Inc. v. Schulte,** 160 F.2d 984 (2d Cir.), *cert. denied,* 332 U.S. 761 (1947)]

---

e.g. **Example:** Another court followed the *Park & Tilford* approach in a later case, holding that the conversion of convertible debentures into common stock involved a "sale" of the debentures and the "purchase" of the common. Here, the debentures had been purchased less than six months prior to the conversion, and some of the common stock was sold less than six months after the conversion. [**Heli-Coil Corp. v. Webster,** 352 F.2d 156 (3d Cir. 1965)]

SECURITIES CONVERSIONS	Split of authority: • **Traditionally** all conversions are deemed a purchase or sale • Some courts hold that the **involuntary conversion** of preferred stock is **not** a purchase or sale • Other courts look to the specific facts and hold that there is **no purchase or sale if** the transaction is not one that could support speculative, short-term profit-taking by insiders
STOCK OPTIONS	Acquisition of the option (rather than its exercise) generally is treated as the date of a **purchase or sale**
STOCK APPRECIATION RIGHTS	Stock appreciation rights (*e.g.,* cash bonuses given to officers equal to the increase in value of a specified number of the issuer's shares) generally are **exempt from section 16**
RECAPITALIZATIONS	Generally, the exchange of a new security for an already outstanding security is **not treated as a purchase or sale**
STOCK DIVIDENDS	Generally, stock dividends are held **not to constitute a purchase** by the recipient shareholder, but exercise of a warrant given as a dividend **is a purchase**
GIFTS	Receipt of a gift of stock is **not a purchase**
REORGANIZATIONS	Typical reorganizations (*e.g.,* merger of one company into another) are **treated as a sale** of the securities surrendered **and a purchase** of the securities received, although transactions pursuant to unsuccessful tender offers, other "unorthodox" transactions, and parent-subsidiary mergers may be exempt from section 16

(2) Involuntary conversions [§1484]

Some courts have held that a conversion of preferred into common is not a purchase of the common, at least if the conversion is "involuntary." If the holder is forced to convert or lose a large part of his investment, and has no control over the decision to call the convertible securities for redemption, such courts may find that the conversion does not constitute a purchase or sale. [**Petteys v. Butler,** 367 F.2d 528 (8th Cir. 1966), *cert. denied*, 385 U.S. 1006 (1967); **Ferraiolo v. Newman,** 259 F.2d 342 (6th Cir. 1958), *cert. denied*, 359 U.S. 927 (1959)]

(3) Policy approach [§1485]

Still other courts have looked at the rationale of section 16(b) in determining whether a conversion transaction involves a "purchase" or "sale." For example, the Second Circuit essentially overruled its earlier *Park & Tilford* case, *supra*, 19 years later, when it proposed a test for determining whether conversion transactions are within the scope of section 16(b): If the transaction is one that could support the speculative, short-term profit-taking by insiders that section 16(b) was designed to prevent, it will be deemed a "purchase" or "sale" within the meaning of the Act. [**Blau v. Lamb,** 363 F.2d 507 (2d Cir.), *cert. denied*, 385 U.S. 1002 (1967)]

EXAM TIP	gilbert

If a section 16 issue appears on your exam and the facts do **not present a danger of abuse of inside information**, be sure to mention this in your answer. Since the underlying policy of section 16 is to prevent such abuse, a court might exempt the transaction in question.

b. Stock options [§1486]

When determining whether there has been a purchase or sale of a security, the *acquisition* of a stock option (or other derivative security), rather than its exercise, is the significant event. *Exercise* of the option is viewed by the S.E.C. as merely a *change from indirect to direct beneficial ownership*, with no particular significance under section 16. [S.E.C. Release No. 34-23369 (1991)] *Rationale:* The S.E.C.'s position recognizes that derivative securities (for instance, stock options) are functionally equivalent to the underlying equity securities. Contrary to the general rule regarding "purchases" and "sales" (*see supra*, §1481), the S.E.C.'s position with respect to stock options is that the significant event is *not* a person's irrevocable obligation to take and pay, or deliver and accept payment. Rather, the critical event—the one providing the opportunity to profit from inside information—occurs when the person has the legal *right* to receive (or to deliver) the underlying equity security at a fixed price. This point is illustrated in the following examples. Notice how, in the last four examples, the right to receive or deliver a security is used to make a profit.

---

e.g. **Example—purchase stock/sell stock:** "If an insider of IBM purchased 1,000 shares of IBM common stock on February 23, 1990 ($102-5/8 per share NYSE), he would have paid $102,625. If the insider sold the 1,000 shares on April 16, 1990, for $110,750 ($110-3/4 per share NYSE), a profit of $8,125 would have been made." [S.E.C. Release No. 34-28869 (1991) (footnote omitted)]

---

e.g. **Example—purchase option/exercise option/sell stock:** "Similarly, the same insider could have bought 10 IBM call option contracts (covering 1,000 IBM common shares) on February 23, 1990, for $9,875 ($9-7/8 per share), exercisable on or before October 19, 1990, at $100 per share. If on April 16, 1990, the insider exercised the option and purchased the stock for $100,000 and sold the stock for $110,750 ($110-3/4 per share), the profit would be $875." [*Id.*]

---

e.g. **Example—purchase option/sell stock:** "If the insider purchased the same 10 IBM call option contracts (covering 1,000 IBM common shares) on February 23, 1990, for $9,875 ($9-7/8 per share), exercisable on or before October 19, 1990, but, instead of exercising the option and selling the underlying stock, he sold 1,000 shares of IBM common stock otherwise held on April 16, 1990, for $110,750 ($110-3/4 per share), the insider would lock in the ability to earn a profit of $875." [*Id.* (footnote omitted)]

---

e.g. **Example—purchase option/sell option:** "Suppose the same insider purchased 10 IBM call option contracts (covering 1,000 IBM shares) on February 23, 1990, for $9,875 ($9-7/8 per share), exercisable at $100 before October 19. On April 16, the insider sold the call options for $13,625 ($13-5/8 per share). The profit would have been $3,750." [*Id.*]

---

e.g. **Example—purchase stock/purchase put option:** "The same insider also could have bought 1,000 shares of IBM stock on February 23, 1990, for $102,625, and on April 16, 1990, bought 10 put option contracts (covering 1,000 IBM shares) expiring October 19 with an exercise price of $115, at a price of $7-1/2 per share, or $7,500. By purchasing the put options, the insider locked in the ability to earn a profit of $4,875, when the insider could receive $115,000 for the 1,000 shares under the put options." [*Id.*]

---

(1) Effect of rules [§1487]

The practical effect of the rules is that a purchase of an option is treated as the purchase (or sale, as appropriate) of the underlying security, and will be matched against any counterpart transaction—in the underlying security *or* in a derivative of the underlying security—to create a "profit" recoverable under section 16.

(a) Purchase of call option [§1488]

The purchase of a call option gives the option holder the right, for a fixed period of time, to buy the underlying security at a fixed price. This transaction is treated as a purchase of the underlying security, and can be matched against a sale of the underlying security, a sale of a call option, or a purchase of a put option.

(b) Purchase of put option [§1489]

A put option is essentially the reverse of a call option—it gives the option holder the right, for a fixed period of time, to *sell* the underlying security at a fixed price. This transaction is treated as a sale of the underlying security, and can be matched against a purchase of the underlying security, a purchase of a call option, or a sale of a put option.

(c) Exercise of an option [§1490]

The exercise of an option in most cases amounts to neither a purchase nor a sale under section 16. The opportunity for profit is created when the option is acquired, and its exercise, because it does not create a new opportunity for profit, is exempt.

1) Exception—exercise of "out-of-the-money" options [§1491]

There is an exception to the rule that the exercise of an option is exempt: Exercise by an insider of an out-of-the-money call option may constitute a purchase of the underlying security.

a) Definitions [§1492]

Understanding the scope of this exception requires us to understand three key terms relating to an option's exercise price.

1/ "In-the-money" [§1493]

An option is in the money if its exercise price represents a profit opportunity for the option holder. Thus, a call option is in the money if its exercise price is less than the current market price of the underlying security.

2/ "At-the-money" [§1494]

An option is at the money if its exercise price is the same as the current market price. (These are treated as in-the-money by the S.E.C.)

3/ "Out-of-the-money" [§1495]

An option is out of the money when its exercise would produce a loss to the option holder. (Options that are out-of-the money are also sometimes referred to as "under water.")

b) Rationale

The S.E.C.'s reluctance to treat the exercise of an out-of-the-money option as exempt from section 16 appears to be based on a general suspicion of such transactions, rather than on a specific perception of danger. In support of its decision, the S.E.C. noted merely that "there appears to be little economic justification for an insider to exercise an out-of-the-money option" and referred to unspecified "concerns as to the reasons that an insider would" do so. [S.E.C. Release No. 34-23369, *supra*]

(2) Stock appreciation rights [§1496]

Stock appreciation rights ("S.A.R.s") give officers a cash bonus equal to the increase in value of a specified number of the issuer's shares over the period of time between the grant of the S.A.R. and its exercise. In most cases, S.A.R.s are exempt from section 16, as are most awards pursuant to employee benefit plans and most employee compensation.

c. Recapitalizations [§1497]

Most recapitalizations (*i.e.,* transactions in which a corporation exchanges a new security for one of its already outstanding securities) do **not** involve a purchase or sale of the new stock. Insiders are generally unable to take advantage of inside information in recapitalizations because (i) all similarly situated shareholders are treated the same way, (ii) shareholder approval of the recapitalization is normally required, and (iii) each shareholder simply continues his investment in the corporation in a different form. [**Roberts v. Eaton**, 212 F.2d 82 (2d Cir.), *cert. denied*, 348 U.S. 827 (1954)]

(1) Leveraged recapitalizations [§1498]

Note, however, that *Roberts, supra,* did not deal with a "leveraged recapitalization." In such transactions, shares of the corporation's old stock are exchanged for a package typically including a share of new common stock, cash, and perhaps a debt security. The shareholder's incentive to participate is that the package offered by the corporation is worth considerably more than the market price of the old stock, just before the recap is announced. Such transactions pose obvious dangers of insider abuse, and a court confronting an insider who used her knowledge of a proposed leveraged recap to purchase and sell the company's stock at a profit might decline to follow *Roberts.*

d. Stock dividends and gifts [§1499]

A corporation may issue additional shares of common stock pro rata to its shareholders. Such a transaction may be effected by issuing "rights" to acquire additional shares, or warrants, or by simply issuing additional shares in the form of a stock dividend. These transactions have been held *not* to involve a "purchase" by the shareholder recipients. [**Shaw v. Dreyfus,** 172 F.2d 140 (2d Cir.), *cert. denied,* 337 U.S. 907 (1949); *see* SEA Rule 16a-9(b)]

(1) Exercise of rights is a purchase [§1500]

Note, however, that the *exercise* of such a right (or warrant) by a shareholder *is* a "purchase" of the securities received upon exercise. [**Shaw v. Dreyfus,** *supra; see* SEA Rule 16a-9, note] Although the exercise is reportable under section 16(a), it will be exempt from the "profit" calculation. [SEA Rule 16b-6(b)]

(2) Gifts [§1501]

A bona fide gift of stock is *not* a purchase by the donee under section 16. [**Shaw v. Dreyfus,** *supra;* **Truncale v. Blumberg,** 80 F. Supp. 387 (S.D.N.Y. 1948), 83 F. Supp. 628 (S.D.N.Y. 1949); *see* SEA Rule 16b-5] Note that this is consistent with the treatment of gifts under the 1933 Act.

e. Reorganizations [§1502]

Corporate reorganizations often fall within section 16(b). Generally, when a corporation is merged or sold in exchange for stock, a "sale" of the securities surrendered and a "purchase" of the securities received takes place. [*See* SEA Rule 16b-7—exempting certain mergers, and thus implying other mergers are covered by section 16]

(1) Opportunity for abuse [§1503]

The typical merger case presents opportunities for abuse, because those parties involved in the merger possess inside information that outsiders do not, and stock prices of target companies typically rise.

(2) Tender offers and defensive mergers [§1504]

A tender offer involves the direct purchase of the shares of the target company by the bidder.

(a) Typical situation [§1505]

The bidder (B) may begin by purchasing a minority interest in the target (A) and may then attempt to negotiate a merger of the two companies. Frequently, the target (A) will seek a defensive merger with a "white knight" (C). The bidder (B) may then find itself in a difficult situation with respect to section 16(b), as to its ownership of some of A's shares. This would be the case if B acquires 10% or more of a class of registered equity security, thus becoming an "insider" for section 16(b) purposes.

1) If B should fail in its tender offer and sell its A shares, B may be liable under section 16(b) if its purchase and sale of A's shares have occurred within less than six months.

2) Likewise, if C gains control and merges A into C, and B is then forced to exchange its A shares for C shares, B may be liable under section 16(b).

    a) However, it has been held that where B loses in its tender offer bid through a successful defensive merger of A into C, B's exchange of its A shares for C shares is *not* a "sale" within section 16(b). [**American Standard, Inc. v. Crane Co.,** 510 F.2d 1043 (2d Cir. 1974), *cert. denied*, 421 U.S. 1000 (1975)]

(b) "Unorthodox transactions" not within section 16 [§1506]

In 1973 the Supreme Court, departing from the normally strict interpretation of "purchase" and "sale" under section 16, held that certain merger transactions were "unorthodox" and, if such a transaction *did not present the dangers of abuse of inside information* that section 16 was designed to combat, the transaction would not be covered by section 16. [**Kern County Land Co. v. Occidental Petroleum Corp.,** 411 U.S. 582 (1973)]

1) Facts of *Kern County Land* [§1507]

Occidental Petroleum made a tender offer on May 8 for Kern County Land ("Kern") stock, acquiring by June 8 more than 10% of Kern common stock for $85 per share. Meanwhile, Kern successfully negotiated a defensive merger with Tenneco, pursuant to which Kern shareholders would receive one share of Tenneco preferred stock for each share of Kern stock they owned. Occidental (seeing that it was going to lose the battle) entered into an option agreement with Tenneco giving Tenneco the right to purchase all the Tenneco preferred stock that Occidental was to receive in the merger, for $105 per share. This option agreement was entered into within six months of the date Occidental had first acquired the 10% Kern interest. The option could not be exercised by Tenneco before December 9, 1967, a date six months and one day after the expiration of Occidental's tender offer. The option price paid by Tenneco to Occidental was $10 per share, to be part of the purchase price if Tenneco exercised the option. The Tenneco-Kern merger closed on August 30. On December 11, Tenneco exercised its option to buy Occidental's Tenneco preferred stock, which resulted in a profit to Occidental of more than $15 million. However, Tenneco then sued Occidental for this profit under section 16(b), alleging that both the execution of the option and the exchange of shares upon consummation of the merger were "sales" by Occidental, occurring within six months of its purchase of Kern shares.

a) The Court held that neither the execution of the option agreement nor the merger of Tenneco and Kern constituted a "sale" of the Kern stock by Occidental under section 16(b). The Court stated that the option price was not so large as to *compel* the exercise of the option by Tenneco. Furthermore, the merger-sale was involuntary as to Occidental (*i.e.*, once the merger was approved by Kern's shareholders, Occidental had no way to prevent its consummation), and was not motivated or caused by any abuse of inside information. In other words, the Court found no possibility of the kind of harm section 16(b) was intended to remedy.

b) To have held otherwise in this situation would have provided a powerful incentive for target companies to enter defensive mergers: If such mergers were concluded within six months of the time the unsuccessful bidder bought its shares, the successful bidder (after gaining control) would be able to collect damages against the unsuccessful bidder for a violation of section 16(b). [*See* **American Standard, Inc. v. Crane Co.**, *supra*, §1505]

(c) Case-by-case analysis [§1508]

Kern County Land opened a defense that previously appeared to be closed. At least in the context of "unorthodox" corporate combinations, the Supreme Court has approved a "subjective" approach—leading to a case-by-case determination of whether, in the factual context of the case, there has been a violation of the policy of section 16(b) against the speculative abuse of inside information.

(d) Parent-subsidiary combinations [§1509]

If Company A owns 85% or more of the equity securities of Subsidiary B (or 85% or more of the assets of B or a group of companies including B), and A is merged into B (or the group is consolidated into one company) and the shareholders of A receive a new security in exchange for their shares in A (*i.e.*, A is not the surviving company), the shareholders of A do *not* have a "purchase" or "sale" as part of the transaction. [SEA Rule 16b-7]

1) Rationale

This rule is designed to exempt shareholders of a controlling corporation which, for legal purposes, exchanges its shares for the shares of a controlled subsidiary.

2) But note

Not included within this exemption is an insider shareholder of A who purchases a security of one of the corporations involved in the merger and then sells the securities of another of these companies within a six-month period during which the merger occurs. However, the securities involved in the combination transaction itself do not count as a purchase or sale. [*Id.*]

8. "Within a Period of Less than Six Months" [§1510]

For section 16(b) to apply, the matching purchase and sale must occur within a period of *less than* six months.

EXAM TIP   **gilbert**

Remember, if the matched purchase and sale transactions occur exactly six months apart, or extend beyond six months, there is no liability, because the purchase and sale are not *within six months*.

---

a. Less than six months [§1511]

"The law does not take account of fractions of days." This maxim applies to section 16, as it does to most legal calculations of elapsed time. Application of this rule can, however, produce some confusion, especially if it is not clear whether to "not take account of fractions" means to disregard them altogether, or to count them as *full days* rather than as fractional days.

(1) Rule [§1512]

For section 16 purposes, *a fractional day counts as a full day*. Because a fractional day counts as a full day, the section 16 "period of less than six months" can be generically defined as a period that begins at any time on day 1 and *ends at midnight on the day that is two days before the corresponding date six months later*. [*See* **Morales v. Reading & Bates Offshore Drilling Co.**, 392 F. Supp. 41 (N.D. Okla. 1975)] This result follows because if the period were to extend to the following day, that *entire* day would be counted, and therefore the period would be *exactly* six months, rather than "less than six months" as the statute requires. In other words, because any fraction of a day counts as a full day, the statutory term "less than six months" amounts to "six months less at least one full day."

Example: D, a director of X Corporation, purchased 1,000 shares of X Corporation common stock (registered under section 12 of the 1934 Act) at 9:15 a.m. on January 20. At 3:15 p.m. on July 19, D sold all 1,000 shares. D's sale is *exactly six months* after her purchase, because January 20 is counted as a full day (the purchase at 9:15 a.m. is treated as though it took place immediately after midnight) and so is July 19 (the 3:15 p.m. sale is treated as though it took place precisely at the instant that the "six-month point" was reached).

---

b. **Special problems in determining time of transaction [§1513]**

Although the specific date on which a purchase or sale occurred is generally a matter of record, it may be difficult to determine the date of occurrence of some transactions.

(1) **Shares to be determined on contingent events [§1514]**

In some instances, shares are to be delivered as part of a purchase price based on future contingent events. For example, suppose Company A purchases Company B, and promises to pay additional shares of A stock to B shareholders in the event that the market price of A stock declines over a certain period of time. If the price of A stock does go down, A must pay more of its shares. When are these contingent shares of A "purchased" by B shareholders? Courts have split on this question.

(a) **Date of delivery [§1515]**

One possibility is that contingent shares are purchased on the date of their *delivery* (not the contract date, although the parties were committed as of this date). [**Booth v. Varian Associates**, 334 F.2d 1 (1st Cir. 1964), *cert. denied*, 379 U.S. 961 (1965)]

(b) **Date of commitment [§1516]**

Another possibility is that contingent shares are purchased on the date that the commitment to purchase (or sell, as the case may be) becomes complete. For example, in a case in which the purchase price of a closely held corporation was expressed in shares to be paid by the buyer over a number of years, the price of the additional shares was set at the outset but the *number* of additional shares to be delivered was contingent on future earnings. The court held that the purchase of the final installment of shares was made at the time the sale of the company closed, three years earlier. [**Prager v. Sylvestri**, 449 F. Supp. 425 (S.D.N.Y. 1978)]

(2) **Option agreements [§1517]**

Recall that an option to buy or sell stock is treated as a purchase or sale of the underlying stock, which can be matched against counterpart transactions either in options or in the underlying stock. (*See supra*, §1486.) The *time* at which a transaction takes place in a derivative security, such as a stock option, then, is the *time at which the option is acquired*. Neither the time the option becomes exercisable nor the time it is actually exercised has any significance for section 16 purposes, because the acquisition of the option is viewed as the purchase (or sale, as the case may be) of the underlying stock.

(a) **Effect [§1518]**

The effect of this rule is that a matching transaction must be found within a period of less than six months before or after the date of acquisition or no liability will result.

(b) Grant of employee stock option is usually exempt [§1519]

Options granted under an employee stock option plan are typically exempt from section 16, pursuant to rule 16b-3 (*see infra*, §1557). As a result, there normally is no section 16 liability resulting from the grant of an employee stock option.

9. "Profit" Under Section 16(b) [§1520]

The profit of the defendant under section 16(b) is calculated according to the statute and is unrelated to any real-world notion of buying low and selling high.

a. Any purchase or sale may be matched [§1521]

Section 16(b) may be applied to any matched "purchase" and "sale" (or "sale" and "purchase"), if the matched transactions occur within a period of *less than* six months.

Example: A, a director, buys 100 shares of XYZ stock on June 1 for $10 per share. On July 1, A sells the stock for $9 per share. On August 1, A buys 100 shares for $8 per share. Finally, on September 1, A sells the stock for $7 per share. In three months A has lost a total of $200, but is still liable under section 16(b), since the $9 sale can be matched with the $8 purchase (providing a $100 profit).

---

b. "Profit" from a sale followed by a purchase [§1522]

Section 16 profit can be earned not only from a purchase followed by a sale, but also from a sale followed by a purchase.

Example: B, a director of G Corp. (which has its common stock registered under section 12), sells 100 shares of G common stock on June 1, at $10 per share. Two months later, on August 1, B purchases 100 shares of G common stock at $5 per share. B is liable to G Corp. for her profit of $5 per share.

---

(1) Profit from loss avoidance [§1523]

Students are often puzzled that section 16(b) covers transactions like the one in the example above. The rationale for the $5 per share profit is that after making the August 1 purchase, B is in precisely the position she was in before the June 1 sale, except that she has $500 in cash that she did not have before. In other words, had she not engaged in the two stock transactions, she would have had 100 shares of G common stock on August 2. Having engaged in the transactions, she has 100 shares of

G common stock, *and* $500 in cash, which represents her profit on the transactions (and which is forfeitable to G Corp. under section 16(b)).

EXAM TIP   gilbert

On your exam, be sure to remember that the term "profit" under section 16(b) is broader than what is commonly thought of as profit. As explained above, it includes *avoided losses as well as traditional gains*.

---

c.   **Profit maximized [§1524]**

The matching of purchase and sale transactions that will produce the maximum profit is used, and there is no attempt made to trace particular securities bought and sold. For example, if 100 shares are purchased at $1 per share and 100 at $2 per share, and five months later 100 shares are sold at $10 per share, the recoverable profit is $9 per share.

(1)   **Loss transactions [§1525]**

Any transactions in the six-month period that produce losses are ignored.

EXAM TIP   gilbert

When determining profit in a section 16(b) fact pattern, it is very important to remember that transactions will be matched "coldheartedly" to produce the *maximum profit*. Do not be fooled by facts designed to convince you to discard this rule based on sympathy for the purchaser/seller. For example, suppose Doug is a director of Bigco and has owned 10,000 Bigco shares for many years. He decides to buy his dream home and sells 5,000 of his Bigco shares to his friend Pete President for the then current market value of $70 per share. Doug uses the $350,000 proceeds of the sale as a down payment on his new home. Five months later, Doug inherits $250,000. Although Bigco is as profitable as ever, because of a downturn in the economy, Bigco shares are now selling for $25 per share. Doug has faith in Bigco and believes that Bigco shares will return to a $70 per share market value within the next three years. Therefore, he uses his $250,000 inheritance to purchase 10,000 shares of Bigco stock on the open market. Is Doug liable under section 16(b)? You bet. The sale of 5,000 shares for $350,000 will be matched with 5,000 of the 10,000 shares Doug subsequently purchased for $25 each, leaving a profit of $225,000 ($350,000 - (5,000 × $25)). Doug's motivation for each transaction, the different number of shares involved in each, and the cause of the price differences *all are irrelevant*.

---

d.   **Matching transactions in derivative securities [§1526]**

Recall that the S.E.C. treats transactions in derivative securities (*e.g.*, stock options) as equivalent to transactions in the underlying security. (*See supra*, §1486.) For the purpose of calculating the "profit" on matching transactions in derivative securities, the S.E.C. has adopted special rules. [SEA Rule 16b-6(c)]

(1)   **Derivative securities with identical characteristics [§1527]**

"Profit" on the sale and purchase, or purchase and sale, of derivative securities with identical characteristics is calculated in the same way as it is for equivalent transactions in the underlying securities.

Example: D, a director of X Corporation, purchased and sold call options for X Corporation stock (which was registered under 1934 Act section 12). On February 1, D purchased 10 options for $10 each; on March 1, she sold 10 options for $9 each; on April 1, she purchased 10 options for $8 each; and on May 1, she sold 10 options for $7 each. D has made a "profit" of $10 under section 16, because the April 1 purchase (at $8) will be matched with the February 1 sale (at $9).

(2) Derivative securities with different characteristics, relating to the same underlying security [§1528]

Consistent with the idea that derivative securities are for most purposes equivalent to their underlying securities, the S.E.C. has limited the profits recoverable under section 16(b) in the case where the derivatives are based on the same security, but have different characteristics. In such a case, the maximum profit recoverable is the difference in price of the *underlying security* on the relevant dates.

Example: D, a director of X Corporation, on June 3 purchased 10 call options, each immediately exercisable for 100 shares of X Corporation common stock (which is registered under section 12 of the 1934 Act). On June 3, the price of X Corporation common stock is 46½. On July 1, D sold X Corporation convertible debentures, which in the aggregate could be immediately converted into 1,000 shares of X Corporation common stock at an effective conversion price of $25 per share. The market price of X Corporation common stock on July 1 was 51½. D's profit under section 16(b) is limited to the difference between the price of X common on the sale date, 51½, and the purchase date, 46½—that is, $5 per share—for a total of $5,000.

(3) Insiders who write options [§1529]

What happens when an insider does not purchase an option, but *writes* (*i.e.*, sells) an option? For example, an insider, D, might sell to someone the right to demand stock of an issuer *from D* at any time in the next three months. An insider who writes a call option is considered to have sold the stock on the date the option is written. Similarly, a put option written by an insider is treated as if the insider purchased the underlying stock on the date the option was written.

(a) Options expire without exercise [§1530]

But what happens if, as is often the case, an option written by an insider expires without being exercised? In such a case, the S.E.C. limits the section 16 profit recoverable to the amount of the fee, or premium, the insider received for writing the option. [SEA Rule 16b-6(d)]

e.g. **Example:** On January 1, D, a director of X Corporation, wrote a call option under which G could purchase from D 100 shares of X Corporation stock (which is registered under section 12 of the 1934 Act) at $100 per share. The option was exercisable on any date beginning January 1, 2007, through March 31, 2007. D received $10 from G for writing the option. The option expired without exercise. On April 10, D purchased 100 shares of X common stock for $80 per share.

1) Analysis

The writing of the call option is *treated as a sale of the underlying stock.* (*See supra,* §1529.) This transaction could then be matched with a purchase of the stock taking place within six months to produce liability, with a profit calculated by reference to the price of the stock on the relevant dates. In the example, this would produce a profit of $20 per share, or $2,000. However, because the option expired unexercised, the S.E.C. rule is that D is liable only for the option premium received—$10. [SEA Rule 16b-6(d)]

10. Other Elements of Damages Under Section 16(b) [§1531]

In addition to the defendant's profits, a section 16(b) plaintiff can also recover additional sums related to the case.

a. Interest [§1532]

Interest on the profit may be awarded in the discretion of the court, based on considerations of "fairness." [**Blau v. Lehman,** *supra,* §1456]

b. Dividends [§1533]

Dividends paid on securities that are held during the six-month period may be part of the "profit" realized, depending on the circumstances.

(1) Dividends not included [§1534]

Dividends are not included in the following situations [**Adler v. Klawans,** 267 F.2d 840 (2d Cir. 1959)]:

(a) Where they are declared *on stock prior to purchase by the insider;*

(b) Where they are declared *prior to the stockholder becoming an insider;* and

(c) Where they are declared *on specific certificates which were not sold at a profit.* However, there is authority to the contrary on this point. [**Western Auto Supply Co. v. Gamble-Skogmo, Inc.,** 348 F.2d 736 (8th Cir. 1965)—dividends paid on a number of shares equivalent to the number sold were held part of profit]

(2) Dividends included [§1535]

Dividends declared on the actual shares sold while the owner is an insider are held by all courts to be part of the "profit."

c. Attorneys' fees [§1536]

Attorneys' fees are recoverable in a section 16 action as part of the plaintiff's judgment.

(1) Practice note [§1537]

The provision for attorneys' fees often provides the main motivation for bringing a section 16(b) action. Lawyers may look for section 16 situations and then find a shareholder on whose behalf they can sue.

11. Strict Liability [§1538]

The general rule is that there are no defenses to a section 16(b) action if all elements of the cause of action are present (*i.e.*, an "insider," registered equity securities, and a matching purchase and sale within the required time period). Thus, it makes no difference that the insider cannot be shown to have had access to any inside information, or to have used any inside information in effectuating the matching purchase and sale. [**Smolowe v. Delendo Corp.**, 136 F.2d 231 (2d Cir. 1943)]

a. Exception—"unorthodox" transactions [§1539]

There is a narrow category of cases, involving what the Supreme Court has called "unorthodox" transactions, in which even though arguably a purchase and sale have taken place within six months, section 16(b) does not apply. These transactions typically involve mergers and acquisitions. (They are discussed in more detail *supra*, §§1506 *et seq.*)

12. Procedural Aspects of Actions Under Section 16

a. Jurisdiction [§1540]

Federal courts have exclusive jurisdiction over section 16 actions.

b. Service [§1541]

Nationwide service of process is available.

c. Venue [§1542]

The plaintiff may sue under section 16 in the district where any act or transaction constituting the violation occurred, or in the district where the defendant is found or transacts business, or if the transaction was consummated on a securities exchange, the action may be brought in the district in which the exchange is located.

d. Statute of limitations [§1543]

Section 16(b) provides for a statute of limitations of two years from the date when the profit is realized by the insider. The statute is tolled, however, if the insider has not filed the reports required by section 16(a), until such time as the profits are discovered or with reasonable diligence should have been discovered.

e. Jury trial [§1544]

The plaintiff may elect either a jury or a court trial.

f. Proper plaintiff [§1545]

The corporation may sue under section 16 for the profit made by its insider *or*, if the corporation declines to proceed, any security holder of the corporation may bring a *derivative action on behalf of the corporation*. Note that the S.E.C. has no authority to seek injunctive or other relief for the violation of section 16(b).

(1) No contemporaneous ownership requirement [§1546]

Section 16 lawsuits are easily brought because of the fact that *any* security holder is a proper plaintiff. The plaintiff need not be the owner of equity securities, nor must he have owned the securities at the time the wrong occurred. Thus, plaintiff can purchase securities subsequent to the date of the wrong and still bring an action. [**Blau v. Mission Corp.,** 212 F.2d 77 (2d Cir.), *cert. denied*, 347 U.S. 1016 (1954)]

(2) Sixty-day notice and demand [§1547]

A security holder may sue under section 16(b) only "if the issuer shall fail or refuse to bring such suit within 60 days after request or shall fail diligently to prosecute the same thereafter."

(3) Circumstances excusing sixty-day notice [§1548]

The 60-day notice period under section 16(b) has been excused in the following situations:

(a) Defendant dominates the corporation [§1549]

Notice is not required if the individual defendant dominates the corporation, so that a demand on the corporation to sue the individual would be futile. [**Weisman v. Spector,** 158 F. Supp. 789 (S.D.N.Y. 1958); **Netter v. Ashland Paper Mills, Inc.,** 19 F.R.D. 529 (S.D.N.Y. 1956)]

(b) Statute of limitations will run [§1550]

Likewise, the plaintiff-shareholder need not wait for 60 days to elapse after making demand on the corporation if the two-year statute of limitations applicable to actions under section 16(b) would run out during that time. [**Benisch v. Cameron,** 81 F. Supp. 882 (S.D.N.Y. 1948); **Grossman v. Young,** 72 F. Supp. 375 (S.D.N.Y. 1947)]

13. Exemptions [§1551]

The S.E.C. has provided a number of exemptions from section 16(b) liability.

a. Securities received in foreclosure on a debt [§1552]

Section 16(b) exempts a security acquired in good faith in connection with a debt previously contracted. Thus, the receipt of securities in connection with a foreclosure is not a "purchase" within the meaning of section 16(b).

b. Gifts and inheritance [§1553]

By rule, the S.E.C. has exempted bona fide gifts and transfers of securities by will or intestate descent. [SEA Rule 16b-5]

c. Exemption for dealers [§1554]

A problem might arise where a securities firm acts as a dealer in a registered equity security of a company and becomes an insider of that company (*e.g.,* by acquiring 10% of the security). In this event, the firm's trading activity in the company's securities could violate section 16(b).

(1) Exemption from section 16(b) [§1555]

The Act provides an exemption for dealers—with respect to securities *not* held in their investment accounts—to the extent that transactions are engaged in pursuant to maintaining an over-the-counter market in the security. [SEA §16(d)] Although such securities are *not* formally exempt from the reporting requirement of section 16(a), the S.E.C. has interpreted the 1934 Act not to require reporting. [S.E.C. Release No. 34-28869]

(a) "Securities in an investment account" [§1556]

Securities in an investment account are securities identified as such in the broker-dealer's records and for I.R.S. purposes. They are held for investment by the broker-dealer, rather than being purchased as part of market-making activity.

d. Employee benefit plans and compensation [§1557]

In general, transactions taking place between the issuer and its officers and directors are exempt from section 16(b) if they are either approved by the issuer's board of directors (or a committee containing at least two outside directors), or approved by the issuer's shareholders. [SEA Rule 16b-3(d), (e)] Transactions with an employee benefit plan are treated like transactions with the issuer. [SEA Rule 16b-3(a)]

F. Prohibition Against Insider Trades During Pension Fund Blackouts

1. The Rule [§1558]

"Pension fund blackouts" are periods of time during which pension fund participants may not engage in trades of the securities held in their accounts. In the *Enron* case (*infra* §1576), many employees were furious to learn that during a pension fund blackout—and while Enron's stock price was plummeting—senior executives were allegedly cutting their losses by selling large quantities of Enron stock. The employees were prohibited from selling during the blackout. SOXA responded to this by prohibiting the directors and executive officers of an issuer from selling the issuer's equity securities if a pension fund blackout is in effect. This prohibition applies to all equity securities acquired in connection with service or employment as a director or executive officer. Insider transactions are prohibited when a pension fund blackout (i) lasts for more than three business days, and (ii) suspends the ability of at least 50% of the plan participants to engage in plan transactions involving the issuer's equity securities. Issuers must notify plan participants, their directors and executive officers, and the S.E.C. of any blackout. [SOXA §306(a)(1); Regulation BTR]

G. Liability of Collateral Participants in Securities Transactions

1. Introduction [§1559]

This section of the Summary discusses the potential liability of persons who aid, abet, participate in, or render advice in connection with a transaction that violates the 1933 or 1934 Acts.

2. Liability of Collateral Participants [§1560]

"Collateral participants" are those who are involved in the securities transaction in some way, but are not directly responsible for the transaction.

a. Liability under 1933 Act

(1) Section 11 [§1561]

One court has held that a person may be liable as an aider or abettor under Securities Act section 11. [*In re* **Caesar's Palace Securities Litigation,** 360 F. Supp. 366 (S.D.N.Y. 1973)] This position appears to be unsound, however, because section 11 specifically lists the persons who may be liable under its provisions, and the list does not include aiders and abettors.

(2) Section 12(a)(1) [§1562]

Securities Act section 12(a)(1) provides a rescission remedy to purchasers of securities that were required to be registered under section 5, but were not registered. The action may be brought only against the "seller" of the securities. (*See supra*, §§820 *et seq.*) The question then becomes, who is a "seller" under the statute? For a time, the courts were split. The Supreme Court resolved the question to some extent in **Pinter v. Dahl,** *supra*, §§823 *et seq.*, by holding that under section 12(a)(1), a *"seller" includes persons who solicit the purchase.* "Sellers" do not include persons whose sole motivation in acting is to benefit the buyer. It remains to be seen how much "solicitation" of a purchaser is necessary to meet the standard of *Pinter.*

(a) Defenses [§1563]

Collateral participants in section 12(a)(1) cases have available essentially the same defenses that direct participants have: no sale of a "security," no violation of section 5, no privity, statute of limitations, and the jurisdictional defense (no activity in interstate commerce). (*See supra*, §§827 *et seq.*)

(3) Section 12(a)(2) [§1564]

Securities Act section 12(a)(2) provides a rescission remedy to purchasers of securities sold by means of a prospectus or oral communication that contained a materially misleading statement or omission. (*See supra*, §§833 *et seq.*) As with section 12(a)(1), the action may be brought only against the "seller" of the securities, and again the question arises as to who may be considered a "seller" within the statute. *Pinter, supra,* arose under section 12(a)(1), and the Supreme Court noted that it was not expressing any view about the scope of the term as used in section 12(a)(2). However, because the language is identical to that of section 12(a)(1)—in fact, most of it is literally *the same language*—one would expect the term "seller" to have the same meaning under each section. The circuit courts have so held. [*See, e.g.,* **Cyrak v. Lemon**, 919 F.2d 320 (5th Cir. 1990); **Royal American Managers, Inc. v. IRC Holding Corp.**, *supra,* §850]

(a) Defenses [§1565]

Again, collateral participants have available the same defenses as the direct participants: lack of knowledge of the misleading statement or omission (and the exercise of reasonable care would not have revealed the misleading statement or omission), plaintiff's knowledge of the true facts, lack of privity, the statute of limitations, lack of materiality, and the jurisdictional defense (no activity in interstate commerce). (*See supra*, §§843 *et seq.*)

(4) Section 17 [§1566]

It is highly unlikely that a private civil cause of action is available under Securities Act section 17. (*See supra*, §857.)

b. Liability under rule 10b-5 of the 1934 Act [§1567]

For many years, the courts and the S.E.C. upheld aider and abettor liability under rule 10b-5. In 1994, however, all this changed, when the Supreme Court decided **Central Bank v. First Interstate Bank,** 511 U.S. 164 (1994). *Central Bank* squarely held (albeit by a 5-4 vote) that *there is no implied private right of action against one who aids or abets a rule 10b-5 violation.*

(1) Facts of *Central Bank* [§1568]

Central Bank was the trustee on a bond issue. Before the bond issue closed, Central received information suggesting that the value of the land securing the bonds had declined significantly. Central's in-house appraiser recommended obtaining an independent appraisal of the land, but the bank failed to do so before the closing. Before the independent appraisal had been finished, the issuer defaulted on the bonds. Central Bank was sued as an aider and abettor of rule 10b-5 violations allegedly committed by the issuer and others.

(2) Supreme Court's analysis [§1569]

The Supreme Court began its analysis by observing that the text of the statute controlled its decision and that a private plaintiff may not bring suit under rule 10b-5 for conduct not prohibited by SEA section 10(b). Pointing out that Congress knew how to impose liability for aiding and abetting (*i.e.,* by using the words "aid and abet"), the Court held that because section 10(b) does not include such language, aiding and abetting liability does not exist under rule 10b-5.

(3) Significance of *Central Bank* [§1570]

Central Bank extended the restrictive interpretation of rule 10b-5 that began with **Blue Chip Stamps v. Manor Drug Stores** (*see supra,* §§990 *et seq.*) and continued with **Ernst & Ernst v. Hochfelder** (*see supra,* §§993 *et seq.*). It is clear that the Court intended to limit actions against lawyers, accountants, and other professionals. However, the case left some questions unanswered, and subsequent developments have raised the possibility that secondary liability for fraud might be reinstated.

(a) S.E.C. civil actions [§1571]

The broad language of *Central Bank* appeared to eliminate the power of the S.E.C. to bring civil actions against those who aided and abetted a violation of rule 10b-5. In 1995, however, Congress added section 20(e) to the 1934 Act, which made it clear that the S.E.C. has the power to bring civil actions against those who aid and abet any violation of the 1934 Act or the rules thereunder, including rule 10b-5. [*See* **S.E.C. v. Fehn,** 97 F.3d 1276 (9th Cir. 1996), *cert. denied,* 522 U.S. 813 (1997)]

(b) Effect on aiding and abetting actions under other provisions [§1572]

Central Bank left unclear the scope of private actions against aiders and abettors under other provisions of the securities laws, at least when the statute does not expressly provide for such an action. The Court's reasoning in *Central Bank* was extremely broad, and there is no apparent reason to confine it to SEA section 10(b) and rule 10b-5. Few cases on point have been decided since *Central Bank*, and the precise contours of aiding and abetting liability under the federal securities laws remain unclear.

(c) Sarbanes-Oxley and the scandals of 2001-2002 [§1573]

Less than a decade after *Central Bank*, the Enron, Worldcom, and Adelphia scandals, in which investors lost billions, presented a powerful argument for letting private investors sue secondary actors who facilitate the violations of those primarily liable. *Central Bank* may no longer be the insuperable obstacle to secondary liability that it was at first perceived to be. Both courts and Congress appear willing to consider the possibility that private remedies against aiders and abettors could be an important remedy in cases of fraud.

1) Secondary violator study [§1574]

Section 703 of SOXA directed the S.E.C. to study data from 1998 through 2001 to determine (among other things) how many accountants, accounting firms, investment bankers, investment advisers, brokers, dealers, lawyers, and other professionals practicing before the S.E.C. were found to have aided and abetted a violation of the securities laws but were not sanctioned as primary violators. In 2003, the Commission reported to Congress that approximately 1,600 individual violators were involved as aiders and abettors. To date, however, Congress has not taken legislative action to overrule *Central Bank*.

2) Primary liability for secondary actors [§1575]

Shortly after *Central Bank* was decided, courts began to explore the possibility that persons who previously would have been exposed to secondary liability might, notwithstanding *Central Bank*, be liable as primary violators. In fact, it appears that defendants who have themselves misrepresented or omitted a material fact may be liable as primary violators if the other requirements of the cause of action are met. In particular, accountants who sign a report expressing the opinion that financial statements present fairly the financial condition of a company may be liable if that is not in fact their opinion and if the financial statements do not fairly present the company's financial condition. [*See* **Wright v. Ernst & Young LLP**, 152 F.3d 169 (2d Cir. 1998); **Anixter v. Home-Stake Products Co.**, 77 F.3d 1215 (10th Cir. 1996)]

3) Secondary actors in the *Enron* litigation [§1576]

In the securities class action arising out of the Enron bankruptcy, the court has followed *Wright* and *Anixter, supra*, ruling that "secondary actors may be liable for primary violations" of SEA rule 10b-5, as long as the rule's requirements are met with respect to each secondary actor and the action is properly pleaded under the 1995 Act (*see supra*, §§1665 *et seq.*). [*In re* **Enron Corp. Securities Derivative & ERISA Litigation,** 235 F. Supp. 2d 549 (S.D. Texas 2002)] Although the court recognized that the 1995 Act was designed to cut back on securities litigation by private plaintiffs, the court noted that the 1995 Act "is a mechanism for winnowing out suits that lack [sufficient] specificity. It was not meant to let business and management run amuck to the detriment of shareholders." [*Id.—quoting* **Abrams v. Baker Hughes, Inc.,** 292 F.3d 424 (5th Cir. 2002)—Parker, C.J., concurring]

3. Liability of Controlling Persons [§1577]

Both the 1933 Act and the 1934 Act contain provisions making "controlling persons" liable for the securities law violations of persons they control. (*See supra*, §822.)

a. Liability under 1933 Act [§1578]

The 1933 Act provides that any person who controls another person found liable under sections 11 or 12 is jointly and severally liable along with the controlled party—*unless* the controlling person had no knowledge of, or reasonable grounds to believe in, the existence of the facts that form the basis of the controlled person's liability. [SA §15]

b. Liability under 1934 Act [§1579]

The 1934 Act provides that controlling persons are liable for the securities violations of persons they control, unless they acted in "good faith" and did not directly or indirectly induce the acts that are the basis of the controlled person's liability. [SEA §20(a)]

c. Who is a "controlling person" [§1580]

Whether a person is in a position of control with respect to another depends on the degree of power and influence the person has over the other. In general, persons have control over their *agents*, while they do not necessarily have control over *independent contractors*.

(1) Special rule for broker-dealers [§1581]

One court has held that *broker-dealers are always control persons* under SEA section 20(a) with respect to *their registered representatives*. [**Hollinger v. Titan Capital Corp.,** 914 F.2d 1564 (9th Cir. 1990) (*en banc*), *cert. denied*, 499 U.S. 976 (1991)]

(2) Directors [§1582]

Whether a director is a controlling person of the issuer depends on the nature of the director's involvement in the issuer's affairs. One court held that a director who was not involved in the issuer's day-to-day affairs, and did not participate in drafting the issuer's prospectus, was not a controlling person with respect to alleged securities fraud by the issuer. [**Burgess v. Premier Corp.**, 727 F.2d 826 (9th Cir. 1984)] Another court found that a director and sole shareholder, who claimed ignorance of the corporation's activities, was nevertheless a controlling person with respect to the issuer's sale of unregistered securities. [**San Francisco-Oklahoma Petroleum Exploration Co. v. Carstan Oil Co.**, 765 F.2d 962 (10th Cir. 1985)]

(3) "Culpable participation" not required [§1583]

A person can be liable as a controlling person without participating in the violation. [**Metge v. Baehler**, 762 F.2d 621 (8th Cir. 1985), *cert. denied sub nom.*, **Metge v. Bankers Trust Co.**, 474 U.S. 1057 (1986)]

d. Distinguish—"good faith" as a defense [§1584]

Ignorance (*i.e.*, no knowledge) is a clear defense to an action brought under section 15 of the 1933 Act, whereas section 20(a) of the 1934 Act requires the defendant to establish both that she did not induce the offense by the controlled party and that she acted in "good faith." Although the 1934 Act states these as independent requirements, it is questionable whether a party can act in good faith, but nevertheless induce violations by the controlled party. Arguably, good faith, at least, requires ignorance of the controlled party's actions. In that respect, it is parallel to the "ignorance" requirement of 1933 Act section 15. However, proving good faith might require more than merely proving ignorance of the controlled party's activities—but just how much more remains unclear.

(1) Affirmative action to prevent fraud [§1585]

To establish the "good faith" defense in a section 20(a) claim, the defendant generally must prove that it had some reasonable procedure for supervising the primary wrongdoer. In addition, other steps may be required, depending on the relationship between the controlling person and the primary wrongdoer, the nature of the business, and other circumstances. [*Compare* **S.E.C. v. First Securities Co.**, 507 F.2d 417 (7th Cir. 1974)—broker-dealer must take affirmative steps to prevent fraud, *with* **Zweig v. Hearst Corp.**, 521 F.2d 1129 (9th Cir.), *cert. denied*, 423 U.S. 1025 (1975)—newspaper not required to take affirmative steps to ensure fair and accurate reporting by financial columnist]

e. Application of agency principles [§1586]

On occasion, plaintiffs have asserted claims based on agency law against the employers of primary violators of the federal securities laws. For example, when an employee, acting within the scope of employment, violates rule 10b-5, it might be possible to sue the employer under the doctrine of respondeat superior. Earlier cases split on this question. However, the Supreme Court's decision in *Central Bank*, *supra*, makes it unlikely that a respondeat superior claim against an employer can be based on the federal securities laws. Such claims may be brought under state law (*i.e.*, where the employee has violated both rule 10b-5 and state law). [*See, e.g.*, **Bates v. Shearson Lehman Bros., Inc.**, 42 F.3d 79 (1st Cir. 1994)]

4. Liability of "Outside" Directors [§1587]

An "outside" director is a member of the board of directors who is not otherwise employed by the corporation. A frequent issue is to what extent outside directors may be held liable as collateral participants when the corporation participates in a transaction that violates the securities laws.

a. Liability under 1933 Act [§1588]

The subject of outside director liability under section 11 has been discussed *supra*, §805. In addition, a director might be held liable as a "controlling person" under section 15 on the theory that the director is responsible for management of the corporation. (*See supra*, §§1578, 1582.)

b. Liability under 1934 Act [§1589]

An outside director could be held liable under the 1934 Act in a number of different situations.

(1) Liability as an aider or abettor [§1590]

An outside director might be liable in an action by the S.E.C. if she knowingly aids or abets others in the corporation in committing a violation of the securities laws. [SEA §20(e)]

(2) Liability as a controlling person [§1591]

In addition, an outside director may be found liable as a "controlling person" under section 20(a). (*See supra*, §§1579, 1582.)

(3) Liability for negligence [§1592]

Even if an outside director has not aided or abetted a securities violation and is not liable as a controlling person, the question remains whether she can be held liable for negligently failing to discover a violation of the securities laws committed by others in the corporation.

(a) In rule 10b-5 cases [§1593]

In a case that specifically raised this question, a circuit court held that, absent actual knowledge of the misrepresentations or omissions made by company officers, rule 10b-5 imposed no duty on an outside director to investigate what information was communicated or omitted by company officers in the sale of the company's securities to another company. [**Lanza v. Drexel & Co.**, 479 F.2d 1277 (2d Cir. 1973)] This is consistent with the requirement of scienter under rule 10b-5.

> **e.g. Example:** In *Lanza*, officers of Company A had misrepresented A's financial condition to the owners of Company B, which was purchased for stock. An outside director of A knew of some material adverse information about the company, but did not know that A's officers had failed to disclose this information to B in the course of negotiations.

(b) In proxy cases [§1594]

Although negligence does not establish an outside director's liability under rule 10b-5, it may be sufficient in proxy cases. However, there is authority going both ways (*i.e.,* actual knowledge of the violation by an outside director must be shown vs. negligent failure to discover violation is sufficient). (*See supra*, §1408.)

5. Liability of Underwriters [§1595]

Underwriters generally act in the role of advisers and agents for the issuer in distributing the issuer's securities to the public and are a key link in the securities marketing chain.

a. Liability under 1933 Act [§1596]

Section 11 makes underwriters specifically liable for material misstatements or omissions in the registration statement. (*See supra*, §781.) However, liability is subject to the "due diligence" defense. (*See* defenses to section 11 liability *supra*, §§792 *et seq.*) The underwriter in a firm commitment underwriting might also be liable under section 12(a)(1) or (2) of the 1933 Act (*i.e.,* as the "seller").

b. Liability under 1934 Act [§1597]

The most commonly invoked liability provisions of the 1934 Act do not specifically mention underwriters as defendants, taking a broader approach instead. For instance, rule 10b-5 makes it unlawful for "any person" to do the prohibited acts. Because underwriters are "persons," they may be liable under the 1934 Act either as principals (underwriters, among other things, sell securities), as controlling persons, or, possibly, as aiders and abettors but (after *Central Bank, supra*) only in an action by the S.E.C. [*See* SEA §20(e)]

6. Liability of Accountants [§1598]

Accountants carry out two primary functions relating to disclosure under the securities laws: gathering information about the issuer (*the audit function*) and presenting that information in financial statements, which they certify and which become a part of the registration statement (*the accounting function*). In 2002, the Sarbanes-Oxley Act established the *Public Company Accounting Oversight Board* ("PCAOB") as a self-regulatory organization ("SRO"), similar in many respects to the other SROs (*see infra*, §§1717-1720, 1836-1841). [SOXA §101(a)] In addition, the Act prohibits certain relationships between auditors and their clients, discussed below, that might create a conflict of interest or provide a motive for the auditors to be less than exacting in their audit. In this section we will examine the nature of accountants' professional standards, including the relatively new standards promulgated under SOXA. We will conclude by looking at the traditional standards of liability for accountants in securities cases, which have not been changed under SOXA.

a. Public Company Accounting Oversight Board [§1599]

Formally, the PCAOB is *not* an agency of the United States government; it is a nonprofit corporation organized under the District of Columbia Nonprofit Corporation Act. [SOXA §101(b)]

(1) Composition [§1600]

The PCAOB is comprised of five members. Two (and only two) members must be certified public accountants. If the chair is a certified public accountant ("CPA"), he or she may not have been practicing as such for at least five years before being appointed to the PCAOB. PCAOB members serve five-year terms, one member's term expiring each year. No member may serve more than two terms on the PCAOB. [SOXA §101(e)]

(2) Duties [§1601]

The duties of the PCAOB include:

(i) *Registering public accounting firms* that prepare audit reports for issuers;

(ii) *Establishing standards* for audit reports, including standards for auditing, quality control, ethics, independence, and others as the PCAOB deems appropriate;

(iii) *Inspecting registered accounting firms;*

(iv) *Investigating and conducting disciplinary proceedings* regarding registered accounting firms;

(v) *Enforcing SOXA* with respect to registered accounting firms;

(vi) *Doing such other things that the PCAOB or the S.E.C. consider necessary or appropriate* to promote high professional standards among, and to improve the quality of audit services provided by, registered accounting firms.

[SOXA §101(c)]

(3) Obligation to register with the board [§1602]

Any public accounting firm that wants to prepare or issue an audit report for an issuer (or even "participate in the preparation or issuance of" such a report) *must register* with the PCAOB. [SOXA §102(a)]

(4) Consent to cooperate and testify [§1603]

An accounting firm's application for registration must contain the accounting firm's *consent to cooperate with the PCAOB and to produce documents and testimony to the board*, at the latter's request, or risk having its registration revoked. [SOXA §102(b)(3)] In effect, this means that *all issuers subject to the Act can be investigated by the PCAOB*, as documents produced by a registered accounting firm could (and probably would) relate to an audit report for an issuer.

b. PCAOB's standards and rules [§1604]

Accountants must carry out both the audit and accounting functions properly, in accordance with standards of good practice and the standards specifically adopted by the PCAOB.

(1) Manner of conducting an audit of the issuer [§1605]

Accountants gather information about the issuer, which is ultimately presented in the issuer's financial statements. The accounting profession has developed standards of good practice that apply to the process of gathering this information, called *"GAAS"* (for Generally Accepted Auditing Standards). GAAS standards are based on Statements of Auditing Standards ("SAS") promulgated by the American Institute of Certified Public Accountants. Although courts have resisted making GAAS a legal standard for liability under the securities laws, GAAS frequently is cited in support of the argument that accountants, on the facts, did all that could be expected of them. [*See, e.g.,* **S.E.C. v. Arthur Young & Co.,** 590 F.2d 785 (9th Cir. 1979)]

(2) Manner of presentation of the information [§1606]

Accountants have also developed practice standards governing the process by which the transactions and events of a business entity are measured, recorded, and classified. These standards are referred to as *"GAAP"* (for Generally Accepted Accounting Principles), which are based on Statements of Financial Accounting Standards ("SFAS") promulgated by the Financial Accounting Standards Board. As with GAAS, an accountant's compliance with GAAP will not immunize her from liability under the securities laws. [*See, e.g.,* **United States v. Simon,** 425 F.2d 796 (2d Cir. 1969), *cert. denied*, 397 U.S. 1006 (1970)] Just as with GAAS, however, in most cases compliance with the professional standard is significant in establishing a defense. [*See* **S.E.C. v. Arthur Young & Co.,** *supra*]

(3) PCAOB's standards [§1607]

In addition to the GAAS and GAAP standards with which accountants must comply, the PCAOB is empowered to establish standards for auditing, certifying and conducting quality control regarding audits, and ethics for public accounting firms. SOXA includes the following minimum standards which the PCAOB follows:

(a) Audit standards [§1608]

Each registered accounting firm must adhere to PCAOB standards providing, at a minimum, that:

(i) Audit work papers must be *kept for seven years*;

(ii) Each audit report issued by a registered accounting firm must be *approved by a second person* qualified under the PCAOB's rules (normally another person from the firm), in addition to the person in charge of the audit; and

(iii) Each audit report must include a report of the *testing of the issuer's internal control processes* and procedures.

[SOXA §103(a)(2)(A)]

(b) Quality control standards [§1609]

Each registered accounting firm must adhere to PCAOB standards addressing:

(i) Monitoring of *professional ethics* and independence from audit clients;

(ii) *Consultation within the firm on accounting and auditing questions*;

(iii) *Hiring, education, and promotion of personnel*;

(iv) *Agreeing to perform, and performing, accounting and auditing services*; and

(v) *Internal inspection and control.*

[SOXA §103(a)(2)(B)]

(c) Inspection requirements [§1610]

The PCAOB, in furtherance of its powers to regulate the accounting profession, must conduct a program of inspections to ensure the registered firms are in compliance with SOXA, the PCAOB's rules, the S.E.C.'s rules, and professional standards. [SOXA §104]

(4) Investigations and discipline [§1611]

The PCAOB has sweeping powers of investigation and discipline.

(a) Investigation [§1612]

In addition to its power to inspect (discussed above), the PCAOB has power to investigate registered firms suspected of violations of the securities laws, the S.E.C.'s rules, the PCAOB's rules, or professional accounting standards. The PCAOB may demand testimony and production of documents from the registered firm or its client(s), and can seek a subpoena from the S.E.C. compelling testimony or production of documents if necessary. The PCAOB may refer matters to the S.E.C., and, at the S.E.C.'s direction, to other authorities, including the Justice Department (for criminal violations).

(b) Discipline [§1613]

The PCAOB has the power to impose *discipline on registered accounting firms and associated persons* if it finds a violation of applicable law, rules, or standards. The nature of the discipline the PCAOB may impose depends on the nature of the violation; the most severe violations (those categorized as "intentional" or "knowing") can result in the accounting firm being permanently barred from auditing issuers, as well as substantial money penalties. Lesser violations may result in censure, mandatory training, lesser money penalties, and other sanctions to be determined by the PCAOB. [SOXA §105]

(5) Independence of auditors [§1614]

Congress was concerned that the financial scandals of 2001-2002 were caused partly because auditors had become too cozy with their clients. SOXA, therefore, contains provisions designed to ensure that *auditors remain independent*, so that audit reports represent an impartial conclusion regarding the accuracy of the clients' financial statements.

(a) Certain services prohibited [§1615]

Because of the possible conflicts of interest generated when auditors provide nonaudit services to issuers, auditors may not offer the following additional services *to their audit clients prohibited by the Act*:

(i) *Bookkeeping or other services related to the accounting records or financial statements* of the issuer;

(ii) *Financial information systems* design and implementation;

(iii) *Appraisal or valuation services*, fairness opinions, or contribution in kind reports;

(iv) *Actuarial services*;

(v) *Outsourcing internal audit services* for the issuer;

(vi) *Management or human resources services*;

(vii) *Broker, dealer, investment adviser, or investment banking services*;

(viii) *Legal services*, or other expert services, unrelated to the audit; and

(ix) *Other services prohibited* by the PCAOB in its regulations.

[SOXA §201(a); SEA §10A(g); SEA rule 10A-2; *see* Regulation S-X rule 2-01]

(b) Pre-approval of services [§1616]

Services not prohibited (*see* above) must be pre-approved *by the issuer's audit committee before they may be performed* by an issuer's outside auditor. The requirement of pre-approval applies to both audit and nonaudit services; "audit services" include comfort letters issued in connection with the issuer's offering securities. [SOXA §202; SEA §10A(i)(1)(A)]

1) De minimis exception [§1617]

De minimis nonaudit services do not require pre-approval if *each of the following conditions is met:*

(i) The services account for *less than 5% of the fees* paid to the auditor by the issuer in the year in which they were rendered;

(ii) The services were *not recognized as nonaudit services at the time* the outside auditors were engaged; and

(iii) The *services are promptly brought before the audit committee's attention and are approved before the completion of the audit.*

[SOXA §202; SEA §10A(i)(1)(B); Regulation S-X rule 2-01]

(c) Disclosure of nonaudit services [§1618]

Not only do all nonaudit services need to be approved (most of them in advance), but also their *approval must be disclosed in the issuer's periodic reports* filed under SEA section 13(a). [SOXA §202; SEA §10A(i)(2)]

(d) Delegation of power to approve [§1619]

The audit committee may delegate the power to pre-approve services to one or more members who are independent directors. However, if the delegated power is exercised, the delegated pre-approvals must be presented to the full audit committee at the next scheduled meeting. [SOXA §202; SEA §10A(i)(3)]

(e) Rotation of audit partners [§1620]

SOXA contemplates that a registered firm auditing an issuer will have one person responsible for supervising the audit and one person responsible for reviewing the supervisor's work. Neither of these persons may provide audit services to the issuer for more than five consecutive years. [SOXA §203; SEA §10A(j)]

1) Rotation of audit firms not required [§1621]

During the debate on the Act, a proposal was made to require rotation of auditing *firms*, rather than just *partners* within the same firm. This proposal was rejected after a SOXA-mandated study by the Government Accountability Office concluded that the expense of mandatory rotation outweighed its likely benefits. However, such a proposal could resurface in the future. [SOXA §207]

(f) Auditor reports to audit committee [§1622]

An issuer's outside auditor must timely report to the audit committee on certain matters. This has the effect of putting *all material communications between management of the issuer and the outside auditors before the audit committee*, which can thereby review the relationship between those two entities and ensure the independence of the auditors. The matters on which the auditors must report are:

(i) All *critical accounting policies and practices* to be used;

(ii) *Alternative treatments* of financial information (within GAAP) that have been discussed with management, the ramifications of such alternative treatments, and the auditor's preferred treatment; and

(iii) *All other material written communications* between management and the auditors.

[SOXA §204; SEA §10A(k); Regulation S-X rule 2-07]

(g) Issuer employment of auditor staff [§1623]

It is not uncommon for personnel from an issuer's accounting firm to take employment with the issuer; the outside accountants have in-depth knowledge of the issuer and the challenges it faces. However, to guard against conflicts of interest SOXA prohibits an accounting firm from auditing an issuer if the issuer's *CEO, CFO, controller, or chief accounting officer was employed by the accounting firm and participated in any capacity in the issuer's audit within the preceding 12 months*. [SOXA §206; SEA §10A(*l*)]

(6) Study of principles-based accounting [§1624]

Accounting in the United States is largely "rule-based," meaning it is governed by rules that define as precisely as possible the resolution of accounting issues. Unlike the United States, many countries have "principles-based" accounting, meaning that accounting is done under a set of principles that provide policy guidance for resolving individual issues. Each approach has its strengths and weaknesses. After the financial scandals of 2001-2002, however, some observers believed that the United States rule-based system encouraged issuers and accountants to stray too close to the edge, complying with the letter of the rule while avoiding its spirit. The rules might communicate precisely what not to do in order to avoid breaking the law, leaving it open for issuers and their auditors to accomplish the same result by other means. Section 108(d) of SOXA directed the S.E.C. to study the possibility of implementing a principles-based accounting system in the United States and to report to Congress on the results. In 2003, the S.E.C. reported to Congress that it was not recommending a wholesale change to principles-based accounting, but it was recommending that standards be set based on principles and that they be objective-oriented and avoid percentage or other bright-line tests that permit financial engineers to comply with the letter, while avoiding the spirit, of the accounting standards.

(7) Accountant discipline under S.E.C. rule 102(e) [§1625]

There are several bases upon which the S.E.C. may suspend or revoke the privilege of appearing or practicing before it. [S.E.C. Rule 102(e)]

(a) Qualifications [§1626]

The S.E.C. may bar an accountant because he lacks the requisite professional qualifications to represent others.

(b) Personal character [§1627]

An accountant who lacks character or integrity may be barred.

(c) Conduct [§1628]

An accountant who has engaged in unethical or improper professional conduct may be barred. Rule 102(e) defines improper professional conduct for accountants as any intentional or knowing conduct, including reckless conduct, that results in a violation of applicable professional standards. Negligent conduct may also be improper professional conduct, if it is either highly unreasonable or if it is repeated under circumstances that suggest incompetence. [S.E.C. Rule 102(e)(1)(iv)]

(d) Violation of securities laws [§1629]

An accountant may be barred if she has willfully violated, or willfully aided and abetted, the violation of any provision of the federal securities laws or the rules and regulations thereunder. The

S.E.C. has held that in this context "willful" means intentional (or at least reckless) conduct. [*In re* **Carter and Johnson,** 47 S.E.C. 471 (1981)]

(e) Collateral bar [§1630]

An accountant whose license to practice has been revoked or suspended in any state, or who has been convicted of a felony (or a misdemeanor involving moral turpitude) is automatically suspended from appearing or practicing before the S.E.C. [S.E.C. Rule 102(e)(2)]

c. Liability under 1933 Act [§1631]

A 1933 Act registration statement must contain certified financial statements. The accountants that certify the statements are subject to liability under section 11 as "experts." (*See supra,* §794.)

(1) Standard of negligence [§1632]

To avoid liability, accountants must have reasonable grounds to believe (after a reasonable investigation) and must actually believe (at the time the registration statement becomes effective) that the statements made by them are true and that there is no omission of a material fact. This holds the accountants to a standard of simple negligence ("reasonableness") with respect to both the audit function and the accounting function.

d. Liability under 1934 Act [§1633]

The cases that have been brought against accountants have primarily been rule 10b-5 cases.

(1) Standard of culpability [§1634]

It is important to remember that in an action under rule 10b-5, the plaintiff (or the government) must prove *scienter*, defined by the Supreme Court as an intention to commit fraud or deceit. [*See* **Ernst & Ernst v. Hochfelder,** *supra,* §993; **Aaron v. S.E.C.,** *supra,* §858]

(a) Recklessness [§1635]

Every circuit court to address the question whether recklessness can constitute scienter under rule 10b-5 has held that it can.

(2) Liability for material omissions [§1636]

A related question involves liability for omissions—that is, assuming that scienter can be established, must the plaintiff also prove a duty to speak (as is required, for example, in cases alleging insider trading violations of rule 10b-5)? (*See supra,* §§1044 *et seq.*) Courts typically hold that the plaintiff must establish such a duty, but differ as to whether the duty can arise simply from participation in a fraudulent scheme, or whether it must be established outside the securities laws. [*Compare* **Robin v. Arthur Young & Co.,** 915 F.2d 1120 (7th Cir. 1990), *with* **Roberts v. Peat, Marwick, Mitchell & Co.,** 857 F.2d 646 (9th Cir. 1988)]

(3) Scope of accountant's responsibility [§1637]

Financial statements prepared by accountants may be used to sell securities (*e.g.*, they may be used in a registration statement or in a document used in connection with a private offering) or may be filed with the S.E.C. pursuant to the filing requirements under the securities acts. In either case, a question arises as to the persons to whom the accountant may become liable if he breaches his duty of care.

(a) Duty to those who read financial statements [§1638]

If the accountant could reasonably expect that the financial statement would be used in making investment decisions, and persons actually did read the statement, there is actual reliance and the accountant will be held liable if he has acted culpably. [**Ernst & Ernst v. Hochfelder,** *supra*]

(b) Duty to those who have not read financial statements [§1639]

Some cases have gone even further, holding an accountant liable where he could *reasonably expect* that the financial statement would be used in making investment decisions, but where the persons dealing with the issuer did *not* actually read the financial statements (*i.e.*, there was no actual reliance). [*See, e.g.*, **Competitive Associates, Inc. v. Laventhol, Krekstein, Horwath & Horwath,** 516 F.2d 811 (2d Cir. 1975)]

Example: Where accountants intentionally falsified financial reports of an investment advisor, which were then filed with the S.E.C., customers of the investment advisor—who had not actually read the reports—were allowed to recover against the accountants.

(c) Duty owed where no expectation of reliance [§1640]

The courts have exculpated accountants in cases where they could have had no reasonable expectation that the financial statements would be relied on by anyone other than the members of the firm for which it was prepared. [**Landy v. Federal Deposit Insurance Corp.,** 486 F.2d 139 (3d Cir. 1973), *cert. denied*, 416 U.S. 960 (1974)]

e. Implied causes of action [§1641]

Of great importance to accountants and other professionals has been the recent trend of court opinions that have refused to imply private causes of action for violations of various sections of the securities acts that do not explicitly provide for causes of action. For example, section 17(a) of the 1934 Act requires broker-dealers to file certain financial reports with the S.E.C. and the national exchange. [*See* **Touche Ross & Co. v. Redington,** *supra,* §924—court refused to imply a private cause of action against defendant accounting firm for improper auditing procedures leading to filing of false financial statements on behalf of defendant's broker-dealer client]

f. Disclosure of accountant-client relationship [§1642]

The S.E.C. requires disclosure of the relationship between companies and their public accountants. [SA Release No. 5550; SEA Release No. 11147; Accounting Series Release No. 165 (1974)]

(1) *In monthly reports* required by the 1934 Act of registered companies, changes in a company's accounting firms (*e.g.,* resignation of a firm) and major disputes over accounting issues must all be disclosed.

(2) *In financial statements,* accountants must disclose any material disagreements with management, all events that gave rise to the disagreement, any matters accounted for differently than by a previous accounting firm's methods, how the result would come out under the previous accountants' methods, etc.

(3) *In proxy statements,* issuers must disclose the accounting firm to be used by the company, the name of any previous accountant, the existence and composition of any audit committee of the board of directors, etc.

(4) *In periodic reports,* the issuer must disclose any nonaudit services that it has approved to be performed by its accountants. (*See supra,* §1616.)

7. Liability of Lawyers [§1643]

In the traditional view of the lawyer's role, lawyers are responsible chiefly to their *clients*. In contrast, the S.E.C. occasionally suggests that securities lawyers ought to assume a "watchdog" function. Such a lawyer would normally resolve ambiguities (*e.g.,* whether a fact is "material") against her client, and would be expected to inform the government if the client declined to follow her advice. This view emphasizes the lawyer's responsibilities to the *public*. It is a response to the role that some lawyers have played in securities fraud—many complex fraudulent schemes would not have been possible without the diligent efforts of counsel. In particular, after the financial scandals of 2001 - 2002, SOXA extended regulation of securities lawyers beyond anything that had come before. In this section, we will look first at the liability of lawyers to clients and third parties, and then we will focus on the responsibilities of lawyers to the public as reflected in SOXA.

a. Liability to clients for malpractice [§1644]

Lawyers have always had the responsibility of performing competently for their clients; consequently, they may be liable to their clients for a knowing or negligent failure to do so. ***Third parties*** affected by the lawyer's malpractice may also have a cause of action against the lawyer.

b. Liability as principals [§1645]

A lawyer may also be liable for a violation of the securities laws as a principal in a business transaction. For example, a lawyer may own securities and make a material misrepresentation in connection with their sale, or purchase securities using material, nonpublic information.

c. Liability to those affected by securities transactions [§1646]

In addition, a lawyer may in some situations be liable to parties affected by a securities transaction. When such liability is alleged, it is important to determine whether it is claimed to result from the lawyer's involvement as a participant or as an aider and abettor.

(1) Liability as participant [§1647]

Often, lawyers participate in securities transactions in roles that go beyond simply counseling their client. In such cases, the additional roles played by such lawyers may become a source of liability under the securities laws.

(a) Liability as a director [§1648]

For instance, when the lawyer who drafted the issuer's registration statement is also a director of the issuer, the lawyer may be liable to purchasers of the issuer's securities under 1933 Act section 11. [*See* **Escott v. BarChris Construction Corp.**, *supra*, §797]

(b) Liability as an expert [§1649]

Similarly, lawyers participate in some transactions not as advisers to a party, but instead as experts with respect to a particular subject matter. For instance, a lawyer might render an opinion that title to real property has been passed to the issuer, and this opinion might be referred to in the registration statement. This can result in the lawyer's liability, not as a lawyer per se, but as an expert whose certification was material to the transaction. [SA §11; *see supra*, §794]

(c) Liability as a "seller" [§1650]

Occasionally, lawyers are alleged to be liable under 1933 Act section 12 as "sellers" of securities. To sustain such a claim, the lawyers would have to be heavily involved in the solicitation process. [*See* **Pinter v. Dahl**, *supra*, §1562] As a rule, such claims against lawyers fail. [*See, e.g.*, **Abell v. Potomac Insurance Co.**, 858 F.2d 1104 (5th Cir. 1988)—whatever the role of counsel, none of the investors can claim to have "bought bonds from" the law firm]

(2) Aiding and abetting liability [§1651]

Historically, aiding and abetting liability has been the most important source of lawyers' liability under the securities laws.

(a) Under the 1933 Act [§1652]

Most of the 1933 Act's remedial provisions specifically state who the proper defendants are; thus, they may not be useful for a person seeking to assert aiding and abetting liability. The government, however, may assert that a lawyer aided and abetted her client's violation of section 17(a) (the 1933 Act's general fraud provision).

1) Note

It remains unclear whether a private citizen can bring an action under section 17(a), but the better view is that she *cannot*. (*See supra*, §§857 *et seq.*)

(b) Under the 1934 Act [§1653]

For many years, probably the most common securities law claim made against lawyers was aiding and abetting the client's violation of 1934 Act rule 10b-5. [*See, e.g.,* **S.E.C. v. National Student Marketing Corp.,** 457 F. Supp. 682 (D.D.C. 1978)] In 1994, however, in *Central Bank, supra,* §1597, the Supreme Court held that *private* actions under rule 10b-5 could not be asserted against an aider and abettor. The S.E.C., however, can bring an action for aiding and abetting a rule 10b-5 violation. [SEA §20(e)]

EXAM TIP　　　　　　　　　　　　　　　**gilbert**

On your exam, be sure to remember that an attorney's liability for aiding and abetting a securities law violation is very narrow. A *private plaintiff* cannot bring an aiding and abetting claim against an attorney for violation of rule 10b-5 and probably cannot bring such a claim under section 17(a) of the 1933 Act, although the *government* can make such a claim under either provision.

---

(3) Legal opinion letters [§1654]

Regardless which Act is claimed to be violated, the most common factual basis for a lawyer's liability as an aider and abettor is the delivery of a legal opinion letter. Because the delivery of such letters is usually made a condition to closing a securities transaction, it is relatively easy to point to the delivery of the letter as a *sine qua non* of the transaction, and with hindsight, to find that the lawyer "must have" known her client's (fraudulent) intentions. [*See, e.g.,* **S.E.C. v. Spectrum Ltd.,** 489 F.2d 535 (2d Cir. 1973)—S.E.C. action for an injunction against lawyer who delivered opinion letter to the effect that a securities transaction did not require 1933 Act registration]

d. **S.E.C. injunctions against lawyers [§1655]**

The S.E.C. has traditionally used injunctions as a form of punishment (*i.e.,* public advertisement that a lawyer has engaged in wrongdoing), as well as a means of preventing future violations of the securities laws.

(1) **Basis for injunction [§1656]**

Although injunctions have traditionally issued on a showing of a negligent violation, after **Aaron v. S.E.C.** (*supra,* §1634), in rule 10b-5 actions the S.E.C. now has to show that the lawyer *knowingly* violated the securities laws. Possibly this might mean at the minimum reckless conduct. [*See* **McLean v. Alexander,** 599 F.2d 1190 (3d Cir. 1979)] On the other hand, negligence is a sufficient basis for an injunction in an S.E.C. action under section 17(a)(2) or (3) of the 1933 Act (although scienter must be shown under section 17(a)(1)). [**Aaron v. S.E.C.,** *supra; and see supra,* §858]

e. **Professional responsibility of lawyers under SOXA [§1657]**

SOXA addresses the professional responsibility of lawyers, although in a less comprehensive manner than it does for accountants. There is not, for example, a body similar to the PCAOB to register attorneys practicing before the S.E.C., nor are the duties applicable to attorneys spelled out in as much detail as they are for accountants. Nevertheless, as the following sections will reveal, the S.E.C.'s rules regarding attorneys are complex and require careful attention by practitioners. Under SOXA, the S.E.C. has adopted 17 C.F.R. part 205, Standards of Professional Conduct for Attorneys, which codifies and extends prior law. Part 205 is discussed below, together with other relevant provisions addressing the responsibilities of securities lawyers.

(1) **"Up-the-ladder" reporting [§1658]**

SOXA mandates "up-the-ladder" reporting of a material violation of securities law, breach of fiduciary duty, or similar violation by the issuer or any of its agents. Up-the-ladder reporting means that the lawyer who becomes aware of material evidence of such a violation must report it (i) first, to the chief legal officer of the issuer, and if that person does not appropriately respond; then (ii) further, to the audit committee or another board committee comprised of only independent directors. [SOXA §307]

(a) **Triggering up-the-ladder reporting [§1659]**

Up-the-ladder reporting is not triggered until the lawyer has "evidence of a material violation of securities law or breach of fiduciary duty or similar violation." [SOXA §307] This phrase is critical, as it triggers the requirement to report up the ladder.

1) **"Evidence of material violation" [§1660]**

The S.E.C. defines "evidence of a material violation" as "credible evidence, based upon which it would be unreasonable, under the circumstances, for a prudent and competent attorney not to conclude that it is reasonably likely that a material violation has occurred, is ongoing, or is about to occur." [17 C.F.R. §205.2(e)]

2) "Breach of fiduciary duty" [§1661]

Under the S.E.C.'s new rules, "breach of fiduciary duty refers to any breach of fiduciary or similar duty to the issuer recognized under an applicable federal or state statute or at common law, including but not limited to misfeasance, nonfeasance, abdication of duty, abuse of trust, and approval of unlawful transactions." [17 C.F.R. §205.2(d)]

3) "Appropriate response" [§1662]

The term "appropriate response" is important because if the reporting lawyer determines that the response she receives is not appropriate, she is required to go further up the ladder to the audit or other board committee. For purposes of the professional conduct rules, "appropriate response" means a response to an attorney regarding reported evidence of a material violation as a result of which the attorney reasonably believes:

(i) That *no material violation* (as defined above) has occurred, is ongoing, or is about to occur;

(ii) That the issuer *has taken appropriate measures* to remedy or prevent violations; or

(iii) That the issuer has *retained or directed an attorney to review* the reported evidence of a material violation and either:

    i   Has *substantially implemented any remedial recommendations* made by the attorney; or

    ii   The attorney *may assert a colorable defense* on behalf of the issuer or agent in any proceeding relating to the reported evidence of a material violation.

[17 C.F.R. §205.2(b)]

(b) Attorney-client privilege [§1663]

One of the more controversial aspects of the S.E.C.'s efforts to regulate lawyers has been its attempts to force lawyers to report wrongdoing by their clients to the government; this raises issues about attorney-client privilege when, for example, the attorney has learned of past wrongdoing in a privileged communication. The Act preserves attorney-client privilege because *up-the-ladder reporting remains within the corporate client* (*e.g.,* to chief legal officer, to audit committee, etc.) which has not thereby waived the privilege. If reporting to third parties were required, however, the privilege might well be waived and that could leave the lawyer open to professional discipline under state law.

(2) "Noisy withdrawal" [§1664]

What happens if lawyers report up the ladder to no avail? As originally proposed, the rules implementing SOXA section 307 required such lawyers to withdraw from representation of the client, notify the S.E.C. that they had done so for ethical reasons, and disaffirm any questionable S.E.C. filings made by the issuer. These rules were re-proposed after they drew a firestorm of criticism from the bar, together with a revised "noisy withdrawal" rule. Although the S.E.C. has not taken action on the new proposals yet, *securities lawyers eventually may become subject to a noisy withdrawal requirement in some form.* [*See* S.E.C. Rel. Nos. 33-8186, 34-47282; IC-25920 (Jan. 29, 2003)]

(3) Statutory basis for attorney discipline [§1665]

Rule 102(e) of the S.E.C.'s Rules of Practice gives the S.E.C. authority to discipline attorneys practicing before it. Prior to passage of SOXA, the S.E.C. did not have an express statutory basis for this rule, but rather relied on its general rulemaking powers and its inherent authority under the securities laws. Section 602 of SOXA provides an explicit statutory basis for the Commission's power to discipline attorneys. [SOXA §602; SEA §4C]

(4) Appearing and practicing before the S.E.C. [§1666]

The S.E.C. has disciplinary powers over lawyers "appearing and practicing before [it] in any way." [SOXA §602; SEA §4C(a)] The S.E.C.'s rules under Part 205 define "appearing and practicing" broadly, including any communications with the S.E.C., formal representation of a party in an S.E.C. proceeding, providing advice regarding United States securities law, advising on S.E.C. filings or whether a filing is necessary, and investigating matters reported "up-the-ladder" under SOXA. [17 C.F.R. §§205.2(a), 205.3(b)(5)] "Appearing and practicing" does *not* include a lawyer who:

(a) Conducts "appearing and practicing" activities, but is not providing legal services to an issuer with whom the attorney has an attorney-client relationship [17 C.F.R. §205.2(a)]; or

(b) Is a nonappearing foreign attorney (defined as a lawyer who is licensed outside the United States, who does not advise on United States securities laws except in conjunction with a United States attorney, and who only incidentally does things that would otherwise be "appearing and practicing" before the S.E.C. [17 C.F.R. §205.2(j)(2)].

f. Role of the "qualified legal compliance committee" ("QLCC") [§1667]

No discussion of the new rules governing securities lawyers would be complete without mention of the "qualified legal compliance committee" ("QLCC"). Issuers that form a QLCC may place much of the responsibility for legal compliance on the committee. The QLCC need not contain any lawyers, but perhaps that is not surprising because up-the-ladder reporting will in most cases terminate with the issuer's audit committee, which likewise need not contain any lawyers.

(1) Advantages of a QLCC [§1668]

Most issuers will probably establish a QLCC, because such a committee is more likely to prepare a coordinated response to evidence of securities law problems than the chief legal officer, who may not have procedures developed in advance to deal with such issues. In addition, a QLCC involves the issuer's board at an early stage of the response, perhaps making an adequate response more likely.

(2) Procedure for invoking the QLCC [§1669]

A QLCC comes into play in two situations: (i) when the reporting lawyer elects to report directly to the QLCC rather than to the chief legal officer; or (ii) the reporting lawyer reports the matter to the chief legal officer, who instead of taking action personally, refers the matter to the QLCC.

(3) Composition of the QLCC [§1670]

The QLCC must include at least one member of the issuer's audit committee and two or more members of the issuer's board of directors who are not employed, directly or indirectly, by the issuer. [17 C.F.R. §205.2(k)(1)]

(4) QLCC authority [§1671]

A QLCC must have *at least* the following authority [17 C.F.R. §205.2(k)(3)]:

(a) To *inform* the issuer's chief legal officer and chief executive officer of reports of evidence of a material violation;

(b) To *determine whether an investigation is necessary* regarding any report of evidence of a material violation and, if it determines an investigation is necessary or appropriate, to:

    1) Notify the audit committee or the full board of directors;

2) Initiate an investigation, which may be conducted either by the chief legal officer (or the equivalent thereof) or by outside attorneys;

3) Retain such additional expert personnel as the committee deems necessary; and

4) At the conclusion of any such investigation, to:

a/ Recommend, by majority vote, that the issuer implement an appropriate response to evidence of a material violation; and

b/ Inform the chief legal officer and the chief executive officer (or the equivalents thereof) and the board of directors of the results of any such investigation under this section and the appropriate remedial measures to be adopted; and

5) To take all other appropriate action, including notifying the Commission in the event that the issuer fails in any material respect to implement an appropriate response that the QLCC has recommended the issuer to take.

g. Sanctions for violation of the attorney conduct rules [§1672]

Under section 602 of SOXA, the S.E.C. may censure a violating lawyer, or deny the violator the privilege of appearing and practicing before it. The S.E.C.'s implementing rules echo this authority [17 C.F.R. §205.6(b)], and in addition, they expressly authorize the S.E.C. to "subject such attorney to the civil penalties and remedies for a violation of the federal securities laws available to the Commission in an action brought by the Commission thereunder." [17 C.F.R. §205.6(a)] This could potentially bring into play the full spectrum of remedies available to the S.E.C. in civil or administrative proceedings. (*See infra*, §§1673 *et seq.*)

H. S.E.C. Enforcement Actions

1. Introduction [§1673]

In this section we will consider the procedures involved in actions by the S.E.C. to enforce the federal securities laws, and the remedies available to the S.E.C. in such actions.

2. S.E.C. Investigations

gilbert

TYPICAL PROGRESS OF AN S.E.C. ENFORCEMENT ACTION

Information comes to the S.E.C. *indicating a possible securities law violation*, either through self-reporting or a complaint by an affected person.

↓

The S.E.C. staff conducts an *informal inquiry*, including interviews with willing witnesses. If the staff believes that there was a violation, it asks the Commission for a formal order to begin an investigation.

↓

The S.E.C. staff begins its *formal investigation*. It may subpoena witnesses but may not compel them to respond without a court order. If the staff believes there was a violation, it recommends that the Commission begin an enforcement action.

↓

The Commission *considers the staff's recommendation in a closed session* and has discretion to allow the target of the investigation to submit a written statement (a *Wells submission*). If the Commission believes that there was a violation, it can do *any or all* of the following:

↓

File an action in federal court seeking a temporary or permanent injunction, civil penalties, and/or to bar or suspend the target from serving as an officer or director of a 1934 Act reporting company.

Begin an administrative proceeding against the target seeking to: (i) impose a sanction for failure to make required filings, or (ii) issue a cease-and-desist order against the target.

Ask the Justice Department to bring a criminal action against the target under the 1933 or 1934 Act, the mail and wire fraud laws, or the RICO statute, among others.

a. Introduction [§1674]

Section 21(a) of the 1934 Act provides the S.E.C. with the power to conduct investigations regarding violations of the 1934 Act and the rules and regulations thereunder.

b. Stages of investigation [§1675]

Investigations typically go through two stages:

(1) Informal inquiry [§1676]

Initially, the S.E.C. begins an informal inquiry into a possible violation. Witnesses are interviewed but no one is required to talk with the S.E.C. if he does not wish to do so.

(2) Formal investigation [§1677]

The second stage is a formal investigation. The S.E.C. staff asks the Commission for an order based on a showing of the likelihood of a violation of the securities laws. A formal order then permits the staff to issue subpoenas and to examine witnesses under oath. At this stage, there is no punishment for failure to respond; the S.E.C.'s only recourse is to initiate a proceeding in court to enforce compliance.

(a) Right to counsel [§1678]

A person who is subpoenaed to testify in a formal investigation has the right to be represented by counsel during his own testimony. He has no right, however, to have counsel present during the taking of testimony from other witnesses. **[S.E.C. v. Meek,** Fed. Sec. L. Rep. (CCH) ¶97,323 (10th Cir. 1980)]

(b) Proper purpose [§1679]

The target of a formal S.E.C. investigation may believe that the Commission staff is acting with an improper motive (*e.g.,* that it was influenced by political pressure, or motivated by a personal conflict between the target's management and an S.E.C. Commissioner or staff member). In such a case, recourse is to the federal district court.

---

e.g. **Example:** W, the target of an S.E.C. investigation into proxy disclosure, believed that the investigation was the result of political pressure applied by a Senator, S, who was sympathetic to one of W's competitors. S had introduced legislation seeking to make ineligible for certain federal loans any person who was under S.E.C. investigation, and then contacted the S.E.C., urging an investigation of W. W brought an action in federal district court, seeking an order of protection against the S.E.C., which was refused. On appeal, the Court of Appeals ruled that while an informal investigation may be begun at any time, and for any reason, a formal investigation must be the result of the S.E.C.'s own, independent judgment, and may not be influenced by outside forces (such as the Senator). [**S.E.C. v. Wheeling-Pittsburgh Steel Corp.,** 648 F.2d 118 (3d Cir. 1981)]

(c) Confidentiality [§1680]

The S.E.C. takes the position that its investigations are secret, and witnesses are often warned that they may not disclose their testimony to anyone else. [*See* SA Rule 122]

(d) Wells submissions [§1681]

After the investigation is complete, the S.E.C. staff evaluates the information it has obtained and determines whether to seek the Commission's approval to commence an enforcement action. If the staff decides that enforcement is appropriate, the Commission considers the staff's recommendation in a closed session. Although the target of the investigation (and of any ensuing enforcement action) has no right to be heard at this stage, the S.E.C. has an informal practice of giving targets the opportunity to submit a written statement (a "Wells submission") to the Commission. But there is no legal right to make such a submission, and to do so can occasionally be perilous: Statements made in the Wells submission may later become evidence in court proceedings.

(e) Notice to target not required [§1682]

The target of an S.E.C. investigation has essentially no rights with respect to the investigation until administrative or court proceedings are begun. Thus, the target has no right to be advised of the identities of third parties from whom the S.E.C. is seeking to subpoena information, nor even a right to be informed that she is a target of the investigation at all. [**S.E.C. v. O'Brien,** 467 U.S. 735 (1984)]

EXAM TIP   **gilbert**

If an exam question involves an S.E.C. investigation, remember that the *target* of the investigation *basically has no right to be involved*. There is no right to know that the investigation is being done, no right to know who the S.E.C. is talking to, and no absolute right to make a statement concerning the investigation (although the S.E.C. generally does allow targets to make a written statement if the S.E.C. staff recommends an enforcement action).

---

c. Parallel proceedings [§1683]

S.E.C. investigations are potentially "parallel proceedings" from the time they are initiated because the end result of an investigation may be either a recommendation to file an injunctive action or a reference to the Justice Department with a recommendation that it initiate a criminal prosecution by bringing the matter before a federal grand jury. In other words, a prosecution could begin any time and run parallel with the civil action.

(1) Right to refuse to testify [§1684]

The witnesses in the investigation have the right to refuse to testify on the basis that their answers may tend to incriminate them. Exercise of this right, however, may come at a price, because in the civil proceeding, the factfinder (that is, the court or administrative law judge) is permitted to draw adverse inferences from the defendant's refusal to testify. The defendant, thus, has the choice to answer the questions, and risk the consequences in the criminal proceeding, or not to answer, and risk losing the civil case.

(2) Parallel investigations [§1685]

It may also happen that the S.E.C. is conducting an investigation at the same time that the Justice Department is conducting a grand jury investigation into the same matter, either as a result of referral by the S.E.C. or otherwise.

(a) I.R.S. proceedings [§1686]

In **United States v. LaSalle National Bank,** 437 U.S. 298 (1978), the Supreme Court held that a summons issued by the Internal Revenue Service after a recommendation for criminal prosecution had been made to the Department of Justice would not be enforced, because this might broaden the Justice Department's right of criminal litigation discovery or interfere with the role of the grand jury.

(b) S.E.C. proceedings [§1687]

On the other hand, the court in **S.E.C. v. Dresser Industries, Inc.,** 628 F.2d 1368 (D.C. Cir.), *cert. denied,* 449 U.S. 953 (1981), decided that the S.E.C.'s order for Dresser to comply with a subpoena of its corporate records in connection with an S.E.C. investigation into illegal payments to government officials should be enforced even though the Justice Department was pursuing the same matter before a federal grand jury. Perhaps *Dresser* is distinguishable from *LaSalle* in that in *Dresser* the court held that at least in the early stage of both proceedings, before any infringement of the defendant's rights in connection with the criminal proceeding, dual investigations should be permitted and cooperative sharing of discovered information is possible. When specific rights were threatened, the defendant could then seek relief from the courts.

d. Section 21(a) reports [§1688]

Section 21(a) of the 1934 Act allows the S.E.C., in its discretion, to publish information concerning violations of the securities laws. The S.E.C. has followed a policy of referring to this section as a basis for issuing reports documenting probable violations of the securities laws, without any formal administrative proceedings. The S.E.C. sometimes requires the target to confess wrongdoing and implement remedial action in exchange for the S.E.C.'s agreement not to institute a formal investigation or an injunctive action. [*See* SEA Release No. 15664 (1979)] Generally, the S.E.C. is unwilling to conclude an investigation with only a section 21(a) report unless the target's conduct is not clearly wrongful under established law. [*See, e.g., In re* **Carnation Co.,** SEA Release No. 22214 (1985)—disclosure of preliminary merger negotiations; *and see In re* **Spartek, Inc.,** SEA Release No. 15567 (1979)—statements of corporate officer to stock exchange official]

3. S.E.C. Administrative Proceedings

a. Overview [§1689]

An S.E.C. administrative proceeding is a quasi-judicial procedure that takes place before an administrative law judge, who is the S.E.C.'s employee. In these proceedings, the S.E.C. can impose a wide variety of sanctions, ranging from the relatively innocuous to the severe. (*See supra*, §§755-761.) In 1990, Congress added to the available administrative sanctions in the Securities Enforcement Remedies and Penny Stock Reform Act. This Act gave the S.E.C. a new cease-and-desist remedy, similar to an injunction, as well as civil fines and disgorgement, all available without the need to convince a federal district judge of the merits of the case (because these are administrative remedies). Because administrative proceedings involve the S.E.C. acting as legislature (pursuant to its rulemaking authority), prosecutor (because the Enforcement Division initiates the proceeding), and judge (its administrative law judge "tries" the case), concerns arise about fairness and due process protections for the target of the proceedings.

b. Notice and hearing [§1690]

In general, the S.E.C. may take action against a company or a person only after notice and an opportunity for a hearing. Furthermore, the proceedings must be conducted pursuant to the requirements of the Administrative Procedure Act (similar to a court trial, but with essentially no right of discovery for the "defendant" and greatly expanded admissibility of evidence).

c. Ex parte proceedings [§1691]

In addition, the S.E.C. may suspend trading in nonexempt securities, without any notice or hearing to the company involved, for a period of 10 days. [SEA §12(k)] Renewals of this period must be based on new circumstances arising after the original suspension notice. [**S.E.C. v. Sloan,** 436 U.S. 103 (1978)]

d. Burden of proof [§1692]

Most of the formal administrative proceedings conducted by the S.E.C. are disciplinary proceedings to punish alleged violations of the securities laws by persons required to be registered with the S.E.C. and expressly subjected by these laws to such administrative sanctions by the statutes (*e.g.*, registered broker-dealers, investment advisers, etc.).

(1) Hearings [§1693]

Hearings are conducted before an administrative law judge; the decision is then reviewed by the full S.E.C., and an appeal is available to the circuit courts.

(2) Preponderance of the evidence [§1694]

In a disciplinary proceeding before the S.E.C., the standard of proof to prove fraud is a *"preponderance of the evidence."* [**Steadman v. S.E.C.**, 450 U.S. 91 (1981)] The basis for this decision is the Court's interpretation of section 7(c) of the Administrative Procedure Act, which governs all agency hearings.

4. S.E.C. Injunctive Actions

a. Introduction [§1695]

When the S.E.C. files a lawsuit, it most often seeks an injunction in federal district court, enjoining those who have allegedly violated or are about to violate the securities laws. Injunctions may be either *temporary* or *permanent*. [*See* SEA §§21(d), 27—giving federal courts jurisdiction; *and see* SA §20(a)]

(1) Temporary injunction [§1696]

A temporary injunction is issued pending a final decision on the merits, usually because the defendant poses a danger to the public in the interim between the time the complaint is filed and the time final judgment is rendered. (*See infra*, §1704.)

(2) Permanent injunction [§1697]

A permanent injunction, on the other hand, is issued after the case has been determined on the merits. The focus, however, remains on the future. Thus, to obtain a permanent injunction the S.E.C. must show not only that the defendant has committed violations of the securities laws in the past, but also that she is likely to do so in the future. (*See infra,* §1705.)

b. Consents [§1698]

Frequently, defendants do not litigate; instead they agree to a "consent injunction," which is entered in court at the same time the complaint is filed.

c. Consequences [§1699]

An injunction can be a severe punishment. Many provisions of the securities laws disqualify a person from engaging in the securities business if the person has been enjoined in an S.E.C. action. Also, as a result of the injunction, private civil actions may be filed against the injunction defendant.

(1) Collateral estoppel [§1700]

If the S.E.C. injunction action is litigated, all of the factual issues that are litigated and decided by the court may not be litigated again in a separate action against the defendant. To avoid this possibility in subsequent civil actions by private plaintiffs based on the S.E.C.'s injunction action, defendants are highly motivated to settle actions with the S.E.C. without going to trial. Of course, in settlements, where defendants admit facts and these admissions become part of a consent injunction, the collateral estoppel effect is still present.

d. Culpability standard [§1701]

See the discussion of **Aaron v. S.E.C.**, *supra*, §1004.

e. Basis for injunction [§1702]

The purpose of an injunction, temporary or permanent, is to prevent future harm, and not to punish past misconduct. For many years, however, the S.E.C. was able to obtain injunctions with little evidence that future harm was likely to result. Courts did not consider an injunction to be a severe sanction, and so were not too concerned about its propriety in a particular case. Often the court would reason that an injunction, after all, was merely a command not to break the law again. Today, however, the severe consequences of an injunction to the defendant are more widely recognized, and the standards for imposing an injunction have become more important. [*See* **Aaron v. S.E.C.**, *supra*] Courts increasingly require the S.E.C. to produce substantial evidence of the likelihood that future violations will occur if an injunction is not issued.

(1) Distinguish private injunctions [§1703]

An action by the S.E.C. to obtain an injunction is different from an action by a private citizen to do so, because the S.E.C.'s action is statutory while the private citizen's is equitable. Thus, to obtain an injunction, the S.E.C. needs to show only what the statute requires, *i.e.*, that the defendant is presently committing a violation or is about to commit one, while a private citizen must show irreparable harm and the inadequacy of any remedy at law. [*See* **S.E.C. v. Caterinicchia**, 613 F.2d 102 (5th Cir. 1980)]

EXAM TIP   **gilbert**

If you have memorized the requirements for obtaining an injunction in your Remedies or Equity class, be sure to remember that the S.E.C. does *not* have to make the normal, equitable showings. The S.E.C. need only show that the defendant *has violated, or is about to violate, a securities law*. The S.E.C. need not show inadequacy of the legal remedy or irreparable harm.

---

(2) Standards for temporary injunction [§1704]

One court has held that the standard the S.E.C. must meet to obtain a temporary injunction *varies according to the conduct that the Commission seeks to enjoin*. A broad injunction against any future violations of the securities laws requires the S.E.C. to "make a substantial showing of likelihood of success as to both a current violation and the risk of repetition," but a lesser amount of evidence is needed to sustain a freeze order intended to preserve the defendants' funds to pay any judgment that might ultimately be rendered. [**S.E.C. v. Unifund SAL**, 910 F.2d 1028 (2d Cir. 1990)]

---

e.g. **Example:** In *Unifund SAL, supra,* there was evidence that the defendants had received information about a pending takeover. The court pointed out that while the evidence suggested that the defendants knew about the takeover discussions, the S.E.C. had not introduced any evidence establishing the *source* of the information. The identity of the source is crucial—an insider trading case rests on the breach of duty committed by the source, and the recipient's knowledge of that breach. (*See supra,* §§949 *et seq.*) Therefore, the court concluded that the S.E.C. had not provided enough evidence that a violation had actually been committed and refused to issue a broad injunction against future violations. However, the court continued, there was some basis to infer that insider trading had occurred, and therefore the S.E.C. was granted a freeze order for a limited period, requiring the defendant to maintain funds in its trading accounts adequate to cover a judgment in the event the S.E.C. prevailed.

---

(3) Permanent injunction [§1705]

When a permanent injunction is sought, the fact of past misconduct has already been adjudicated and the availability of the remedy turns on the likelihood that the defendant will violate the securities laws again. The S.E.C. must convince the court that the defendant's past conduct indicates *there is a reasonable likelihood of further violations* in the future. The decision whether to issue an injunction rests in the *sound discretion of the trial court.* [**S.E.C. v. First Jersey Securities, Inc.,** 101 F.3d 1450 (2d Cir. 1996)]

(4) Current trend of decisions [§1706]

Some courts, consistent with the view of injunctions as punishment for past wrongs, have found a "likelihood of future violations" (the basis for issuing an injunction) based on the defendant's one past violation. More recent decisions, however, indicate that courts now require the S.E.C. to demonstrate a realistic likelihood of recurrence of wrongdoing to get an injunction. [*See* **S.E.C. v. Commonwealth Chemical Securities, Inc.,** 574 F.2d 90 (2d Cir. 1978)]

(5) Factors considered in evaluating likelihood of future violations [§1707]

The following factors are looked at: the degree of scienter involved; the isolated or recurrent nature of the defendant's conduct; the sincerity of the defendant's assurances; and the defendant's recognition of wrongdoing. [**S.E.C. v. Universal Major Industries Corp.**, 546 F.2d 1044 (2d Cir. 1976), *cert. denied*, 434 U.S. 834 (1977)]

f. Ancillary relief [§1708]

The S.E.C., when it settles an investigative action with a defendant, often asks for and gets a variety of ancillary remedies designed to remedy both the consequences of past wrongs and to prevent future ones:

(1) Appoint receiver [§1709]

If the defendant is a corporation and its affairs are in bad condition, a receiver may be appointed to run the corporation.

(2) Disgorge profits [§1710]

The defendant may be required to disgorge profits made in connection with securities law violations (such as the use of inside information). [*See* **S.E.C. v. First Jersey Securities, Inc.**, *supra*—disgorgement of profit from fraud and excessive mark-ups]

(3) Appoint special counsel [§1711]

The defendant may be required to appoint "special counsel" to investigate and report on all past securities law violations.

(4) Require resignations [§1712]

Certain officers and directors may be required to resign.

(5) Appoint independent directors [§1713]

The defendant may be required to appoint independent persons, approved by the S.E.C., to the board of directors. [*See* **In re Occidental Petroleum Corp.**, SEA Release No. 16950 (1980)]

(6) Impose civil fines [§1714]

In the Securities Enforcement Remedies and Penny Stock Reform Act of 1990, the S.E.C. was given the ability to seek, in addition to disgorgement, a civil monetary penalty in specified amounts. (*See infra*, §§1721-1730, for further discussion of these provisions.)

(7) Bar officer or director from serving [§1715]

Another remedy introduced by the Securities Enforcement Remedies and Penny Stock Reform Act of 1990 is the power to ban or suspend a person from serving as officer or director of a 1934 Act reporting company. (*See infra*, §§1721-1730, for further discussion of these provisions.)

(8) Additional equitable relief for the benefit of investors [§1716]

Finally, SOXA authorized the S.E.C. to seek "any equitable relief that may be appropriate or necessary for the benefit of investors." [SOXA §305(a); SEA §21(d)(5)]

5. Self-Regulatory Enforcement [§1717]

Enforcement by the self-regulatory organizations ("SROs") has become increasingly important as the S.E.C.'s resources become more and more overcommitted. With much of the S.E.C.'s attention diverted to major investigations and enforcement proceedings, the SROs have become the parties primarily responsible for redressing more common, and more minor, infractions, such as account churning by brokers.

a. Scope [§1718]

The SROs enforce both the S.E.C.'s rules and regulations relating to the conduct of brokers, dealers, and other members, and their own rules and regulations, which in some cases are much more vague than the S.E.C.'s rules and correspondingly more flexible.

---

e.g. **Example:** Both the New York Stock Exchange and the National Association of Securities Dealers require their members to comply with "just and equitable principles of trade." Such a rule would be too vague to be enforceable by the S.E.C. [*See* **Colonial Realty Corp. v. Bache & Co.**, 358 F.2d 178 (2d Cir.), *cert. denied*, 385 U.S. 817 (1966)]

---

b. Appeal to the S.E.C. [§1719]

Rule 19d-1 under the 1934 Act provides that the S.E.C. must be notified whenever final disciplinary action has been taken by an SRO, and section 19(e) of the Act provides that final disciplinary action taken by an SRO can be appealed to the S.E.C.

c. Exclusivity [§1720]

Although the SROs can enforce the rules and regulations of the S.E.C., the S.E.C. has only a limited ability to enforce the rules of the SROs. Essentially, the S.E.C. must find that an SRO is "unwilling or unable" to act to remedy the situation, or that the S.E.C.'s intervention is otherwise required in the public interest.

6. Securities Enforcement Remedies and Penny Stock Reform Act of 1990 [§1721]

The Securities Enforcement Remedies and Penny Stock Reform Act of 1990 amended both the 1933 Act and the 1934 Act to enhance existing remedies and provide additional administrative remedies.

a. Enhancements [§1722]

The S.E.C. has typically sought disgorgement of profits as an ancillary remedy in cases in which it obtains an injunction against the defendant. (*See supra*, §1710.) Pursuant to the 1990 Act, the S.E.C. also may seek a civil monetary penalty and to bar an individual from serving as an officer or director of a 1934 Act reporting company.

(1) Civil monetary penalties [§1723]

Section 20 of the 1933 Act and section 21 of the 1934 Act, provide that the S.E.C. may seek civil monetary penalties in amounts:

(a) Up to $5,000 for a natural person, and $50,000 for a corporation, per violation; or

(b) If the violation involved fraud, deceit, manipulation, or deliberate or reckless disregard of a regulatory requirement, up to $50,000 for a natural person, and $250,000 for a corporation, per violation; or

(c) If the violation meets the requirements of (b), above (*i.e.,* it involved fraud, etc.), and in addition directly or indirectly resulted in either substantial losses or created the risk of substantial losses to other persons, or substantial monetary gain to the respondents, up to $100,000 for a natural person, and $500,000 for a corporation; and

(d) In any case above, if the gross amount of monetary gain accruing to the person as a result of the violation is greater than the amount of the penalty set forth, the penalty imposed can be up to the amount of the monetary gain.

(2) Officer and director bars [§1724]

In addition to imposing civil fines on the defendants, the S.E.C. can seek to bar or suspend a person from serving as an officer or director of a 1934 Act reporting company, either permanently or for a period of time. The Senate Report on the 1990 Act stated that these provisions were not intended to establish federal law qualifications for directors and officers (an area that has historically been reserved to the states), but noted that in some cases, the public interest requires that certain individuals be prevented from holding positions of trust with publicly held corporations.

(a) Permanent bar [§1725]

Before imposing a permanent bar, the court should consider whether a conditional bar (*e.g.,* one limited to a particular industry) or a bar limited in time might be sufficient. In addition, a court may consider any prior punishment that may have been imposed in a criminal proceeding. [**S.E.C. v. Patel,** 61 F.3d 137 (2d Cir. 1995)]

(b) Standards for bar [§1726]

Under SOXA, a bar may be imposed on any defendant who is unfit to serve. Prior to SOXA, the standard required a showing of "substantial" unfitness; SOXA elimination of the word "substantial" appears to indicate Congress's desire for a broader application of the bar.

b. Administrative cease-and-desist order [§1727]

S.E.C. cease-and-desist orders, authorized by section 8 of the 1933 Act and section 21C of the 1934 Act, resemble injunctions but are issued administratively. Because of their convenience for the S.E.C., they may be the most frequently used remedies under either Act. Like an injunction, the cease-and-desist order may be temporary or permanent. Unlike an injunction, the S.E.C. need not petition a court to obtain a cease-and-desist order; as an administrative remedy, it can be imposed by an administrative law judge, or in some cases by the S.E.C. itself, without a hearing and without notice to the respondent. (*See supra*, §§1695-1715.)

(1) Due process protections [§1728]

The defendant is entitled to a certain amount of due process in such a proceeding; just how much depends on the nature of the defendant and the nature of the order.

(a) Temporary cease-and-desist order [§1729]

Temporary cease-and-desist orders are available only against regulated entities, *e.g.,* broker-dealers and others over whom the S.E.C. and the SROs have oversight authority. A temporary cease-and-desist order can be issued ex parte, without a hearing and without notice to the defendant, if the Commission deems it in the public interest (or if notice and a hearing would be impracticable). The respondent can, however, appeal the order to the S.E.C., and from there to a federal district court.

(b) Permanent cease-and-desist order [§1730]

A permanent cease-and-desist order may be issued against anyone (not just persons regulated by the S.E.C.) violating the 1933 or 1934 Acts. The order directs the respondent to refrain from future violations and can also order disgorgement and take other steps to ensure compliance. Notice must be given to the respondent, who is entitled to a hearing before an administrative law judge. The judge's decision can be appealed to the S.E.C., and from there to a federal court of appeals.

I. The Private Securities Litigation Reform Act of 1995

1. **Introduction [§1731]**

    We have already discussed the Private Securities Litigation Reform Act of 1995 (the "1995 Act") and its safe harbor for forward-looking statements (*see supra*, §§350 *et seq.*). However, the 1995 Act made several other important changes to the securities laws, mainly dealing with the conduct of securities litigation by private parties. This section provides an overview of these changes. Impetus for the 1995 Act arose from the perception that fraud and abuse were widespread in securities litigation brought by private plaintiffs. As early as 1975, the Supreme Court noted that litigation under the federal securities laws "presents a danger of vexatiousness different in degree and in kind from that which accompanies litigation in general." [**Blue Chip Stamps v. Manor Drug Stores**, *supra*, §1570] The Act may be the most significant federal statute on the subject of securities litigation since the New Deal.

    a. **Comment**

        The Act received overwhelming congressional support (it was passed over a Presidential veto), which may mean that Congress intended the courts to interpret the new law to sharply limit questionable private securities litigation.

2. **Limitations of the 1995 Act [§1732]**

    The 1995 Act *does not apply* to:

    a. Actions brought by the federal government (including the S.E.C.) (*see supra*, §§755-765, 1674-1730);

    b. Actions brought by the securities self-regulatory organizations (*see supra*, §§1717-1720; *infra*, §§1836-1841);

    c. Actions brought by private plaintiffs under other federal laws (except that private civil RICO actions based on securities law violations are limited by the 1995 Act) (as to RICO, *see infra*, §§1794 *et seq.*);

    d. Actions brought by private plaintiffs under state securities laws (*see infra*, §§2106 *et seq.*);

    e. Actions brought by state securities regulators (*see infra*, §§2106 *et seq.*);

    f. Actions brought by private plaintiffs under common law fraud theories (*see supra*, §§766 *et seq.*).

3. **Major Provisions of the 1995 Act [§1733]**

    The 1995 Act made many changes relating to private securities litigation. The major provisions of the 1995 Act are summarized below:

    a. **Scope [§1734]**

        Keep in mind that the 1995 Act does not affect actions brought by the government, whether by the S.E.C. or by the Justice Department. The 1995 Act applies only to litigation filed by private plaintiffs.

b. 1934 Act fraud pleading requirements [§1735]

The provisions of the 1995 Act affecting pleadings have been discussed above. (*See supra,* §§1108 *et seq.*)

c. Special verdict [§1736]

At common law, proof of fraud had to include proof of the *defendant's intent* to defraud, called scienter. Scienter is also required in actions brought under SA section 17(a)(1) (*see supra,* §858) and in actions brought under rule 10b-5 (*see supra,* §993). To ensure that these requirements are met, the 1995 Act provides that a court hearing fraud claims by a private plaintiff must, on motion of the defendant, submit written questions to the jury regarding the defendant's state of mind. [SA §27(d); SEA §21D(d)]

d. Class action reform [§1737]

Class action lawsuits were among those perceived as most abusive under the former law; accordingly, the 1995 Act made some important changes in the way class action securities litigation is conducted. Under the 1995 Act:

(1) Notice to class members [§1738]

Within 20 days after a securities class action complaint is filed, the plaintiff must notify the members of the purported plaintiff class of the lawsuit. Up to 60 days after the filing, any member of the class can move the court to be named the lead plaintiff. [SA §27(a)(3)(A); SEA §21D(a)(3)(A)]

(2) Lead plaintiffs must meet certain criteria [§1739]

The motion filed by a would-be lead plaintiff must be decided by the court within 90 days after the filing of the complaint. The court must designate, as lead plaintiff for the class, the "most adequate plaintiff," *i.e.,* the class member or members "that the court determines to be the most capable of adequately representing the interests of all class members." [SA §27(a)(3)(B); SEA §21D(a)(3)(B)] The lead plaintiff "shall, subject to the approval of the court, select and retain counsel to represent the class." [*Id.*] *Rationale:* When a class of investors has been harmed by a securities law violation, it is often uneconomical for the holder of a small stake to sue, even when the defendant's liability is clear, because the cost of bringing such a case to judgment (or even to settlement) can easily exceed the value of the small investor's investment. Consequently, such cases are typically filed as class actions. (*See supra,* §§1119 *et seq.*) Moreover, class action litigation often results in awards of attorneys' fees to the plaintiffs' attorneys. Historically, this has led members of the plaintiffs' bar to race to the courthouse to file a class-action lawsuit, naming as the lead plaintiff a "professional plaintiff," who was often paid a "bounty" for his willingness to serve. Such plaintiffs are not good class representatives, because their entire interest in the litigation is limited to the bounty payment. (The real impetus for the lawsuit, of course, comes from the plaintiffs' lawyers, who decide to sue and who dominate the resulting proceedings in hopes of receiving a handsome fee award.) The 1995 Act, by requiring the appointment of the "most adequate plaintiff," sought to change the status quo by ensuring that the lead plaintiff will fairly represent the interests of the plaintiff class—rather than the interests of the plaintiffs' counsel.

(a) Presumption that large stake equals adequacy [§1740]

There is a rebuttable presumption that the plaintiff with "the largest financial interest in the relief sought by the class" is the most adequate plaintiff. [SA §27(a)(3)(B)(iii); SEA §21D(a)(3)(B)(iii)]

(b) Number [§1741]

More than one lead plaintiff can be appointed, especially when there is a logical group of plaintiffs to represent the plaintiff class, such as when two or more readily identifiable plaintiffs collectively have the largest financial interest in the relief sought. [*In re* **Cephalon Securities Litigation,** 1996 WL 515203 (E.D. Pa. 1996)]

(c) Grounds for challenging appointment [§1742]

While the defendant may challenge the appointment of a lead plaintiff on procedural grounds (for example, that the appointed lead plaintiff failed to file a certification with the complaint, or failed to serve notice to the class members), *the defendant lacks standing to challenge the appointment of a lead plaintiff* based on failure to meet the criteria set out by the 1995 Act. [**Greebel v. FTP Software, Inc.,** 939 F. Supp. 57 (D. Mass. 1996)]

EXAM TIP | **gilbert**

The 1995 Act class action reforms are important, and they could easily play a role in an exam question. Remember that to curtail lawsuits filed mainly to "make a buck" for the filing attorney, the Act requires the courts to assure that the lead plaintiff in a class action is the *most adequate plaintiff* (such as the person with the largest financial stake in the relief sought). On the other hand, you should also remember that a defendant has no standing to challenge the appointment of a lead plaintiff based on failure to meet the Act's criteria, so if the court fails in its duty, there is little a defendant can do about it.

---

(3) Certain payments are prohibited [§1743]

"Bounty" payments to the lead plaintiff, and similar arrangements, are not permitted. [SA §27(a)(4); SEA §21D(a)(4)]

(4) Restrictions on professional plaintiffs [§1744]

A person may serve as lead plaintiff in no more than five securities class actions brought in any three-year period, unless the court grants permission to serve in additional class actions. [SA §27(a)(3)(B)(vi); SEA §21D(a)(3)(B)(vi)]

e. The Securities Litigation Uniform Standards Act of 1998 [§1745]

One of the results of the class action reforms adopted in the 1995 Act was the migration of securities fraud class actions to the state courts, perhaps to avoid the new, more onerous requirements of the federal securities laws. In response, Congress passed the Securities Litigation Uniform Standards Act of 1998, which preempts class actions (and similar consolidated proceedings) based on state law if the action alleges misrepresentation or omission of a material fact, or the use of a manipulative or deceptive device or contrivance, in connection with the purchase or sale of a security. In effect, *state "blue sky" fraud litigation is preempted if* it is a class action or involves consolidated actions of more than 50 plaintiffs. (*See infra*, §§2108 *et seq.*)

f. Discovery

(1) Stay of discovery [§1746]

The 1995 Act provides for a *stay of discovery* upon the filing of a motion to dismiss by the defendant. [SA §27(b); SEA §21D(b)(3)] *Rationale:* Before the 1995 Act, critics of the status quo often asserted that the merits of a case had little relevance to the "settlement value" of the case. [*See, e.g.,* Janet C. Alexander, *Do the Merits Matter? A Study of Settlements in Securities Class Actions*, 43 Stan. L. Rev. 497, 511-13 (1991)] Plaintiffs in private securities litigation were typically allowed to conduct extensive discovery of an issuer's top management, even while a motion to dismiss the case was pending. Because such discovery consumes a lot of the managers' time, it can end up costing the issuer a great deal of money. Issuers confronting such scenarios often found it cheaper to settle the cases, even if they were frivolous. The 1995 Act stay of discovery provision seeks to end such abuse by the plaintiff, by staying discovery while the court considers the defendant's motion to dismiss.

(2) Exceptions [§1747]

Along with the stay of discovery, the 1995 Act provides for two important exceptions, when discovery will not be stayed. [SA §27(b); SEA §21D(b)(3)]

(a) The "undue prejudice" exception [§1748]

The exception to staying discovery for "undue prejudice" is available if the plaintiff would suffer *improper or unfair detriment even if less than* irreparable harm. [**Medical Imaging Centers v. Lichtenstein,** 1996 WL 156926 (S.D. Cal.), *aff'd*, 917 F. Supp. 717 (S.D. Cal. 1996)]

(b) The "loss of evidence" exception [§1749]

The 1995 Act also permits an exception to the stay of disclosure if the loss of evidence might result; however, the plaintiff must provide some proof. If the plaintiff merely makes speculative assertions regarding the loss of evidence, the stay of discovery will not be lifted. [**Novak v. Kasaks,** 1996 WL 467534 (S.D.N.Y. 1996)]

(3) Stay of discovery not the same as a stay of disclosure [§1750]

While the 1995 Act requires a stay of *discovery*, it does not require a stay of *disclosure* (*e.g.,* disclosure required under Federal Rule of Civil Procedure 26; *see* Civil Procedure Summary). [**Hockey v. Medhekar,** 932 F. Supp. 249 (N.D. Cal. 1996)]

(4) Discovery may be allowed to show "actual knowledge" [§1751]

Finally, while discovery is presumptively stayed upon the filing of a motion to dismiss, discovery may be permitted by the court if sought to show "actual knowledge" of falsity in a statement that the defendant claims is exempt under the 1995 Act's safe harbor for forward-looking statements. (*See supra,* §§350 *et seq.*)

g. Damages capped [§1752]

The 1995 Act caps damages in actions brought under the 1934 Act to the *difference between the price paid* by the plaintiff (or, in case of a sale by the plaintiff, the price received) *and the average trading price* of the security during the 90-day period beginning on the day corrective information (*i.e.,* the truth) is disseminated to the market. [SEA §21D(e)]

EXAM TIP | **gilbert**

Securities exam questions often involve rule 10b-5 violations. When answering such questions, be sure to keep in mind the damage cap imposed by 1934 Act section 21D(e): Damages are limited to the difference between the *price paid or received by the plaintiff* and the *average trading price* of the security during the 90 days after corrective information is disseminated.

---

h. Contribution and proportionate liability [§1753]

Before the 1995 Act, plaintiffs in securities cases often searched for the "deepest pocket"; *i.e.,* they would look for and sue the defendant able to pay the largest amount, even if that defendant's actions were merely collateral to the fraud. This strategy was encouraged by the rule of joint and several liability, which provides that any defendant can be required to pay the entire amount of a judgment. The 1995 Act sharply reduces the applicability of joint and several liability:

(i) In actions brought under the *1934 Act,* joint and several liability is limited to those who *"knowingly commit"* a violation of the securities laws.

(ii) In actions brought under *section 11* of the 1933 Act, joint and several liability of *outside directors* is limited to those who *"knowingly commit"* a violation of the securities laws.

(iii) In actions brought under either the *1933 or the 1934 Acts*, "knowingly commit" is defined as having *actual knowledge* of the falsity or fraud.

(iv) In actions brought under either the *1933 or the 1934 Acts, defendants are provided express rights of contribution.*

[SA §11(f)(2); SEA §21D(f)]

i. Loss causation [§1754]

In private actions under the 1934 Act, plaintiffs must prove that the defendant caused the loss. In private actions under section 12(a)(2) of the 1933 Act, the defendant may prove that all or part of the plaintiff's loss was caused by events or circumstances other than the defendant's alleged misstatement or omission. [SA §12(b); SEA §21D(b)(4)]

j. Settlement terms [§1755]

The 1995 Act requires that plaintiffs' counsel provide extensive disclosure of the terms of any settlement. In addition, counsel fees for plaintiffs' counsel are limited. [SA §27(a)(5) - (7); SEA §21D(a)(5) - (7)]

k. Mandatory sanctions [§1756]

In a case brought under the 1933 or the 1934 Acts, if the court finds that there was a violation of Federal Rule of Civil Procedure 11(b) as to the complaint, any responsive pleading, or any dispositive motion, the court *must* impose sanctions under Rule 11 against the party or attorney responsible. (Rule 11(b), among other things, prohibits presenting papers for an improper purpose and requires legal and factual contentions in papers to be supportable.) In addition, the court may require a bond against any sanctions to be imposed under Rule 11. [SA §27(c); SEA §21D(c)]

l. Mandatory reporting of fraud [§1757]

To enhance the ability of the government and the public to detect securities fraud, the 1995 Act requires:

(i) Audits of public corporations to include *procedures designed to detect illegal acts*;

(ii) Auditors to *inform management* and, if necessary, inform the board of directors of *illegal acts detected*; and

(iii) The issuer or the auditor to *inform the S.E.C. of illegal acts* detected, in certain cases.

[SEA §10A]

m. S.E.C. authority over aiding and abetting [§1758]

In **Central Bank v. First Interstate Bank**, *supra*, §1653, the Supreme Court held that there is *no implied right of action* against one who aids and abets a violation of SEA rule 10b-5. (*See supra,* §§1567 *et seq.*) Although *Central Bank* did not clearly hold that the S.E.C. (as opposed to a private plaintiff) lacked the power to sanction aiders and abettors, many commentators believed that the Court's reasoning would extend to actions brought by the S.E.C. In the 1995 Act, however, the S.E.C. was expressly given authority to seek both injunctions and money penalties against those who "knowingly provide substantial assistance" to others in violating the 1934 Act, "to the same extent as the person to whom such assistance is provided." This provision limits the effect of *Central Bank* to private litigants and makes it clear that the S.E.C. is not restricted by that case in its ability to pursue aiders and abettors. [SEA §20(f); **S.E.C. v. Fehn,** 97 F.3d 1276 (9th Cir. 1996), *cert. denied,* 522 U.S. 813 (1997)]

J. Criminal Enforcement and RICO

1. Overview [§1759]

When most people think of criminal conduct under the securities laws, they think of insider trading or complex stock frauds. In fact, the criminal provisions of the 1933 and 1934 Act cover much more than fraud and insider trading. *Willful violation of any provision* of either statute, or of any rule or regulation promulgated under either statute, is a *felony*. In addition, a "knowing and willful" false statement in a filing under the 1934 Act is a criminal offense. Each violation of the 1933 Act is potentially punishable by five years' imprisonment, and the penalty for violating the 1934 Act is even more severe: each infraction can result in up to 10 years in prison. [SA §24; SEA §32(a)]

a. Other statutes [§1760]

Charges arising from securities transactions are often brought under provisions other than the securities laws. Sometimes this is done to avoid difficult issues that have cropped up under the securities laws.

(1) Mail and wire fraud [§1761]

Thus, for example, in **Carpenter v. United States,** 484 U.S. 19 (1987), the prosecution charged violations of SEA section 10(b) and rule 10b-5, and also of the federal mail and wire fraud statutes. Ultimately, the securities law convictions were affirmed by an equally divided Court, but the mail and wire fraud convictions were affirmed unanimously.

(2) RICO [§1762]

The Racketeer-Influenced and Corrupt Organizations statute ("RICO") [18 U.S.C. §§1961-1968] is also frequently used in securities prosecutions. Its advantages include a pre-trial asset freeze, treble damages, and longer prison sentences.

b. Impact of Sarbanes-Oxley [§1763]

In 2002 SOXA created several new crimes and enhanced the penalties for others. These changes are discussed below. (*See infra*, §§1773-1781.)

2. Commencing a Criminal Action [§1764]

The S.E.C. does not have the authority to bring a criminal action, which can be done only by the United States Attorney's office in the relevant jurisdiction(s). Nevertheless, the S.E.C. is obviously heavily involved in, and very knowledgeable about, illegal securities activities, and securities prosecutions are usually the result of an informal referral from the S.E.C.'s Enforcement Division. A formal referral under 1934 Act section 21(d) is also possible, although such referrals (which require a vote of the Commission) are relatively rare.

a. Parallel proceedings [§1765]

There is a good deal of cooperation between the Justice Department and the S.E.C., and frequently both agencies pursue a defendant at the same time. Such parallel proceedings may raise troublesome procedural issues, as when the S.E.C. seeks discovery in its civil action and the defendant resists, claiming that the Justice Department (which will have access to everything the S.E.C. discovers) is improperly broadening the scope of its criminal discovery by "hiding behind" the S.E.C.'s civil discovery request. This argument, however, has not succeeded for defendants in securities cases. [*See, e.g.,* **S.E.C. v. Dresser Industries, Inc.**, *supra*, §1687]

b. Fifth Amendment [§1766]

Defendants in parallel proceedings may exercise their Fifth Amendment privilege and refuse to testify. In a civil proceeding, however, the factfinder is allowed to draw an adverse inference from the refusal to testify, and asserting this right might cost the defendant the case. On the other hand, if the defendant testifies, a transcript of the testimony will be made available to the Justice Department and can be used to impeach the defendant in later criminal proceedings.

3. Standard of Culpability [§1767]

Both the 1933 Act and the 1934 Act make it a criminal offense to "willfully" violate a provision of the statute, or of an S.E.C. rule or regulation thereunder. [SA §24; SEA §32(a)] The 1934 Act, however, goes on to provide that a false statement made in a 1934 Act filing is criminal if it is made "willfully and knowingly." Finally, the 1934 Act provides that if the defendant can prove lack of knowledge of the statute or rule allegedly violated, no prison term can be imposed. The crimes defined under SOXA have standards of culpability varying from "knowing" conduct, to "willful and knowing" conduct, to "corrupt" conduct.

a. Culpability under the 1933 Act [§1768]

The provisions of the 1933 Act relating to criminal intent are relatively straightforward: a "willful" violation is a crime. "Willful" under the Act means only the intent to do the act charged, together with knowledge that the act is wrongful. It does not mean that the defendant knew that the act violated any particular provision of a statute, or even that the act was unlawful. In a fraud case in which scienter is required, "willfulness" includes the intent to deceive, but not necessarily the intent to violate the securities laws.

Example: The defendant was charged with violating Securities Act section 17(a) by fraudulently selling securities. On appeal, he argued that the government had not met its burden of proving that he knew the items sold were "securities" under the Act. The court held that the government did not need to prove that the defendant knew the items were securities; it was enough to show that the items were in fact securities, and that the defendant intended to deceive the buyers in connection with the sales. [**United States v. Brown,** *supra,* §765]

---

b. Culpability under the 1934 Act [§1769]

The 1934 Act sets up two possible standards of culpability: "willfulness," relevant to any violation of the statute or rule; and "willful and knowing," relating to false statements made in filings under the statute or rules.

(1) "Willful" violation of the 1934 Act or rules [§1770]

"Willfulness" under the 1934 Act means much the same thing as it does under the 1933 Act; *i.e.,* intentional conduct and knowledge that the act is wrongful, but not necessarily that it is unlawful, nor that it violates any particular rule or regulation. [**United States v. Dixon,** 536 F.2d 1388 (2d Cir. 1976)]

(2) "Willful and knowing" false statements in filings under 1934 Act [§1771]

The courts have not reached a consensus on what the addition of the word "knowing" means in prosecutions for false filings under the 1934 Act. It might signify an intent to deceive, or perhaps specific knowledge of the provision of law that was violated. However, the former has rarely appeared in the cases, and courts have rejected the latter. [*See, e.g.,* **United States v. Dixon,** *supra*] Professors Loss and Seligman, eminent commentators, have concluded that the word "knowingly" in section 32(a) is redundant [10 Louis Loss & Joel Seligman, Securities Regulation 4692 (3d ed. 1993)]

(a) The 1934 Act "lack of knowledge" defense [§1772]

The 1934 Act also includes a provision that a defendant who proves that he did not know of the rule or regulation violated may not be sentenced to prison. The courts have construed this provision restrictively, holding that it is satisfied only if the defendant establishes that he had what amounts to a good faith belief that his conduct was lawful. The provision will not apply in a fraud case, in which proof of scienter forecloses the possibility of the innocence required for the "no knowledge" defense. [*See* **United States v. Lilley,** 291 F. Supp. 989 (S.D. Tex. 1968)]

c. **SOXA-defined crimes [§1773]**

Perhaps reflecting its hasty adoption in 2002, the crimes defined by SOXA have varying standards of culpability. One of the things that makes SOXA crimes potentially confusing is that it is not clear what the words "knowing" and "willful" mean under SOXA. It seems unlikely that they mean the same things they do in the 1933 and 1934 Acts, because the standard under those acts is "willful," and a somewhat higher standard (required for prison terms under the 1934 Act) is "willful and knowing." Under SOXA, by contrast, two crimes can be committed if the defendant acts "knowingly," without acting "willfully." (*See infra*, §§1774-1776.) A third crime requires both knowing and willful conduct (*see infra*, §§1777-1779), while a fourth is apparently complete if the conduct is "knowing"—but the penalty is doubled if the conduct is both "knowing" and "willful" (*see infra*, §1780). This is, in a sense, the reverse of the standard heretofore required by the 1934 Act, which enhances the penalty for "willful" acts if they are both "willful" and "knowing." Finally, a fifth crime requires neither "willful" nor "knowing" conduct: Its standard for culpability is whether the action is "corrupt." (*See infra*, §§1781.) It remains to be seen what courts make of the patchwork of standards that Congress adopted in SOXA. Each of these standards is discussed below in relation to the crimes to which it applies.

(1) **Crimes committed "knowingly" [§1774]**

The following offenses are committed when the actions taken are done "knowingly."

(a) **Tampering with or destruction of documents [§1775]**

SOXA created a new crime of knowingly tampering with, falsifying, or destroying any tangible object (or record or document) with the intention of impeding, obstructing, or influencing the investigation or proper administration of any matter within the jurisdiction of any agency or department of the United States, or any case under Title 11 (bankruptcy), or relating to or in contemplation of any such case or matter. The penalty for violation of this provision is a fine and up to 20 years in prison. [SOXA §802; 18 U.S.C. §1519]

(b) **Defrauding shareholders of public companies [§1776]**

Another crime created under SOXA is knowingly committing or attempting fraud in connection with a security of any issuer that has a class of securities registered under SEA section 12, or that reports under SEA section 15(d). The punishment is a fine and up to 25 years in prison. [SOXA §807; 18 U.S.C. §1348]

(2) Crimes committed "knowingly and willfully" [§1777]

The following crimes can be committed "knowingly and willfully." The first requires knowing and willful conduct; the second can be committed "knowingly" only, but the penalty is doubled if the defendant acted both knowingly and willfully.

(a) Failure to maintain audit records and workpapers [§1778]

Accountants are required to maintain all records related to an audit for five years after the audit. Knowing and willful failure to do so may result in a fine and imprisonment for up to 10 years. [SOXA §802; 18 U.S.C. §1520(a), (c)]

(b) Knowing false certification [§1779]

We have already encountered SOXA's requirement that the CEO and CFO of public companies certify the financial statements of their employers. (*See supra*, §§886-889.) In addition, a false certification, made knowingly, is a criminal offense with a penalty of a fine of up to $1 million and a prison term of up to 10 years. [SOXA §906(a); 18 U.S.C. §1350(c)(1)]

(c) Knowing and willful false certification [§1780]

If the certification referred to immediately above is knowingly and willfully false, the penalty is increased to a fine of up to $5 million and a prison term of up to 20 years. [SOXA §906(a); 18 U.S.C. §1350(c)(2)]

(3) Crimes committed "corruptly" [§1781]

Finally, SOXA amends the existing crime of "tampering with a record or otherwise impeding an official proceeding" by broadening it to include "corrupt" actual or attempted alteration, destruction, or concealment of a record or other object to impair its availability for use in an official proceeding, or other actual or attempted obstruction of or influence on an official proceeding. This crime is punishable by a fine and up to 20 years imprisonment. [SOXA §1102; 18 U.S.C. §1512(c)]

d. Statute of limitations [§1782]

The relevant statute of limitations for criminal prosecutions under the securities laws is five years; it is not contained in the securities statutes, but rather appears in the criminal code. [*See* 18 U.S.C. §3282]

4. Illegal Trading in Securities Under the 1934 Act [§1783]

In addition to fraud and the sale of unregistered, nonexempt securities, the securities laws are violated by selling or buying securities without complying with more technical, regulatory requirements of the 1934 Act. Because these violations are relatively easy to detect and prove, the government sometimes simply charges defendants with these offenses instead of more serious violations.

a. Stock parking [§1784]

Stock parking refers to an arrangement whereby one person holds title to securities on behalf of another person, who does not wish her ownership of the securities to be known. The arrangement can be implemented in numerous ways: for instance, the "true owner" may sell the securities to the counterparty, subject to a (usually secret) agreement to repurchase them at a fixed price. Or the counterparty may purchase the securities, subject to an agreement by the "true owner" to purchase them in turn at the counterparty's cost, plus commissions. Stock parking itself is not a crime, but the agreements that the various parties enter into to effectuate the scheme are seldom disclosed (secrecy being the whole point of "parking" the stock), and the securities business is so heavily regulated that the failure to disclose an arrangement of this sort inevitably causes a breach of a disclosure requirement at some point. [*See, e.g.,* **United States v. Bilzerian,** 926 F.2d 1285 (2d Cir. 1991)]

b. Price manipulation and rule 10b-5 [§1785]

"Manipulation" in the 1934 Act means "manipulation of the price of securities," and in section 9(e) the Act contains an explicit prohibition against doing so. (*See infra,* §1933.) The government has argued, however, that in addition to section 9(e), rule 10b-5 can be violated by price manipulation: specifically, when a person buys or sells a large block of securities with an intent to affect the price of that class of securities. The argument goes that the alleged manipulator should have disclosed her intention to affect the price, and by failing to do so, she violated rule 10b-5. While no court has expressly accepted this theory, the Second Circuit has held that to prove it, the government would have to prove that the defendant's sole intention was to affect the price of the class of security. A transaction effected with an investment intent is *not manipulative* under rule 10b-5, *even if the price is affected by the transaction.* [**United States v. Mulheren,** 938 F.2d 364 (2d Cir. 1991)]

5. Mail Fraud and Wire Fraud [§1786]

The mail fraud and wire fraud statutes [18 U.S.C. §§1341, 1343] are often used to prosecute persons for securities transactions, because they are relatively uncomplicated and the elements are conceptually simple (and often easy to prove).

a. Elements of mail or wire fraud [§1787]

To make out a case of mail fraud or wire fraud, the prosecution must prove:

(i) A *scheme to defraud;*

(ii) *Specific intent to defraud* (*i.e.,* scienter—but sometimes a reckless disregard for the truth will suffice); and

(iii) The *mailing of a letter, or sending a wire,* in furtherance of the scheme.

(1) Person mailing need not be defendant [§1788]

Note that while it is a requirement that a letter (or wire) be sent, *it is not required that the defendant be the one sending the letter.* A scheme in which the defendant, in face-to-face meetings, fraudulently convinces others to send him money through the mail is mail fraud, even though all the mailings were done innocently.

(2) Defendant need not have specific intent to use mail [§1789]
The government does not need to establish the defendant's specific intent to use the mail (or cause the mail to be used); it is enough if the *use of the mail was reasonably foreseeable.*

b. "Intangible business property" and the "intangible right of honest services" [§1790]
If a securities transaction is prosecuted as mail fraud, a problem may arise in identifying just what the victim was defrauded of. Insider trading cases, for instance, raise this issue. Prosecutors can make one of two arguments:

(1) Intangible business property [§1791]
This idea is closely linked to the "misappropriation" theory of insider trading (discussed *supra*, §§1069-1076). Essentially, the argument is that the tipper deprived the source of the exclusive use of the information. [*See* **Carpenter v. United States**, *supra*, §1761]

(2) Intangible right of honest services [§1792]
Alternatively, the prosecution can argue that the tipper (and the tippee) schemed to deprive the source of the information of her "intangible right of honest services." In 1988, Congress amended the criminal code specifically to add this possibility to the prosecutors' arsenal, by defining "scheme or artifice to defraud" to include "a scheme or artifice to deprive another of the intangible right of honest services." This appears to mean that a breach of fiduciary duty, if part of a fraudulent scheme, suffices as the basis for mail fraud. [*See* 18 U.S.C. §1346]

c. Enhanced penalties for mail and wire fraud [§1793]
SOXA increased the prison sentences for mail and wire fraud from five years to 20 years. [SOXA §903; 18 U.S.C. §§1341, 1343]

6. Racketeer-Influenced and Corrupt Organizations Act ("RICO") [§1794]
Finally, RICO has been important in both the criminal and civil enforcement of the securities laws. RICO was adopted in 1970 as a deterrent to the infiltration of legitimate business by organized crime. Beginning in 1980, however, prosecutors and private plaintiffs discovered its usefulness in many cases of simple fraud, unconnected to any organized crime activity. The result was a massive increase in the number of RICO claims.

a. RICO sanctions [§1795]
RICO's sudden increase in popularity may be accounted for in large part by

the severe sanctions it imposes on violators. Under RICO, both the criminal penalties and the civil damages remedy are unusually harsh.

(1) Criminal RICO [§1796]

The penalties for a RICO violation include 20-year prison terms, heavy fines, forfeiture (not only of the profits from the illicit activity, but also of the defendant's interest in the entire enterprise), and a pretrial freeze of the defendant's assets.

(a) Pretrial asset freeze [§1797]

RICO's pretrial asset freeze, in particular, has been sharply criticized. While its stated purpose is to ensure that the defendant does not conceal or liquidate his assets before the government can levy on them, it is often used by the prosecution to intimidate the defendant. A successful freeze essentially renders the defendant indigent pending the outcome of the trial. Consequently, the prospect of a pretrial freeze makes most defendants amenable to a negotiated plea.

(b) Constitutionality of the pretrial asset freeze [§1798]

The asset freeze has been challenged on the grounds that it renders the defendant unable to retain private counsel. But in **United States v. Monsanto,** 491 U.S. 600 (1989), the Supreme Court upheld the freeze, reasoning that the Constitution does not provide the right to counsel of the defendant's choice.

(2) Civil RICO [§1799]

Although RICO also includes a civil cause of action for anyone "injured in his business or property by reason of a [RICO violation]," civil RICO is *unavailable to private plaintiffs* suing "based on conduct that would have been actionable as fraud in the purchase or sale of securities," unless the defendant was criminally convicted* in connection with the fraud. [18 U.S.C. §1964(c)]

b. Establishing violation of RICO [§1800]

Establishing a RICO violation is a two-stage process:

(1) Pattern of racketeering activity [§1801]

The prosecution must prove that the defendant engaged in a "pattern of racketeering activity," defined to mean at least "two acts of racketeering activity, one of which occurred after October 15, 1970, and the last of which occurred within 10 years (excluding any period of imprisonment) after the commission of a prior act of racketeering activity." [18 U.S.C. §1961(5)]

(a) Acts of racketeering activity [§1802]

The acts of racketeering activity (sometimes referred to as the "predicate acts") are set forth in section 1961(1). They are all crimes under state or federal law, including the stereotypical "racketeering" acts or threats of murder, kidnapping, gambling, arson, robbery, bribery, extortion, and narcotics offenses, but also include fraud in the sale of securities, mail fraud, and wire fraud.

(b) Criminal conviction not required [§1803]

Note that while the acts of racketeering activity are all acts for which the defendant could be convicted, RICO does not require that the defendant actually be convicted of—or even charged with—any of them. [**Sedima, S.P.R.L. v. Imrex Co.**, 473 U.S. 479 (1985)]

(c) "Pattern" requires *relationship* plus *continuity* [§1804]

RICO requires *at least two predicate acts* to find a "pattern of racketeering activity." But merely proving two predicate acts will not suffice to establish a pattern. The prosecutor must in addition show that the *predicate acts* are *related to one another*, and that the predicate acts *amount to, or constitute a threat of, continuing racketeering activity*—i.e., continued commission of predicate acts. [**H.J. Inc. v. Northwestern Bell Telephone Co.**, 492 U.S. 229 (1989)]

---

e.g. Example: In *H.J. Inc.*, *supra*, the plaintiffs alleged that the defendants repeatedly bribed members of the Minnesota Public Utilities Commission with cash, promises of future employment, tickets to sporting events, and the like, to influence the commissioners to approve unfairly high rates for the telephone company. The Supreme Court held that the predicate acts (of bribery) were related to each other by their common purpose, and that the allegation that the acts occurred frequently over a six-year period could suffice to establish continuity. The Court stated further that continuity could also be established at trial by showing that the alleged bribes were a regular way of conducting Northwestern Bell's business, or a regular way of conducting the business of the RICO "enterprise."

---

1) Comment

The Supreme Court's formulation of the pattern requirement is vague and provides little guidance to lower courts or potential defendants. Justice Scalia, concurring in *H.J. Inc.*, *supra*, stated that the majority opinion is "about as helpful to the conduct of [the lower courts'] affairs as 'life is a fountain.'" Since *H.J. Inc.*, the lower courts have divided over what the proper test is for determining whether acts form a "pattern," and virtually every circuit has developed its own, distinctive approach to the problem.

(d) Single fraudulent scheme can violate RICO [§1805]

The "pattern" requirement of RICO requires multiple predicate acts, not multiple schemes that are furthered by the predicate acts. Thus, even a single fraudulent scheme, if it is supported by a pattern of racketeering activity, can be the basis for a RICO claim. [**H.J. Inc. v. Northwestern Bell Telephone Co.**, *supra*]

(2) Violative acts [§1806]

RICO is violated when the defendant engages in any of four expressly prohibited activities, each of which depends on the existence of a "pattern of racketeering activity." The RICO prohibitions are, in a sense, the "value added" (or perhaps "danger added") to a RICO offense. That is, the "pattern of racketeering activity" amounts simply to two felonies, and, standing alone, does not constitute a RICO offense. To prove a RICO offense, it must be proven that the defendant:

(i) *Invested income* from a pattern of racketeering activity in an "enterprise";

(ii) *Acquired or maintained an interest* in an "enterprise" through a pattern of racketeering activity;

(iii) *Conducted or participated in the affairs* of an "enterprise" through a pattern of racketeering activity; *or*

(iv) *Conspired to violate (i), (ii), or (iii), above.*

[18 U.S.C. §1962 (a) - (d)]

(3) The "enterprise" requirement [§1807]

RICO defines the term "enterprise" to include any "individual, partnership, corporation, association, or other legal entity, and any union or group of individuals associated in fact although not a legal entity." [18 U.S.C. §1961(4)]

(a) Defendant and enterprise cannot be the same person [§1808]

Most courts hold that the enterprise and the defendant must be different persons. [*See, e.g.*, **Bennett v. United States Trust Co.**, 770 F.2d 308 (2d Cir. 1985); **Haroco, Inc. v. American National Bank & Trust Co.**, 747 F.2d 384 (7th Cir. 1984); *but see* **United States v. Hartley**, 678 F.2d 961 (11th Cir. 1982)] *Rationale:* Section 1962(c) prohibits "conduct[ing] or participat[ing] in the conduct of [an] enterprise's affairs through a pattern of racketeering activity." If the defendant and the enterprise were the same person, section 1962(c) would make it illegal to conduct or participate in one's own affairs. Because this interpretation would be senseless, most courts have rejected it.

1) Group associated in fact [§1809]

The practical effect of the distinction between the defendant and the enterprise is that plaintiffs and prosecutors search for an "enterprise" separate from the deepest pocket defending the case. Here, the statute is accommodating. Usually the "enterprise" is identified as a "group of individuals associated in fact," which although at first appearing to exclude corporations (which are not usually considered to be individuals), has been held to be broad enough to include virtually any entity as a group member.

(b) "Pattern" and "enterprise" are not the same [§1810]

Another complexity arises from the Supreme Court's description of a RICO enterprise as "an entity separate and apart from the pattern of activity in which it engages." [**United States v. Turkette**, 452 U.S. 576 (1981)] Disagreement over the meaning of this statement and the nature and amount of proof required to establish such a separate enterprise continues.

(c) "Conduct" or "participate" [§1811]

In 1993, the Supreme Court held that to be liable under section 1962(c), the defendant must have participated in the operation or management of the enterprise. This does not imply upper management responsibilities; an ordinary day-to-day employee "participates in the operation" of the enterprise, in the Court's view. But it excludes liability for an accounting firm, whose involvement in the enterprise extended only to preparing financial statements based on the client's accounting system. [**Reves v. Ernst & Young**, 507 U.S. 170 (1993)]

(d) "Through a pattern" [§1812]

Similarly, section 1962(c) requires the plaintiff or prosecutor to prove that the defendant conduct or participate in the affairs of the enterprise "*through* a pattern of racketeering activity." Some courts have held that this requires that the affairs of the enterprise be furthered by or related to the predicate acts; others have held that it suffices if the defendant was enabled to commit the predicate acts by virtue of her position in the enterprise. [*Compare* **United States v. Kovic**, 684 F.2d 512 (7th Cir. 1982), *with* **United States v. Cauble**, 706 F.2d 1322 (5th Cir. 1983)] The D.C. Circuit has held that the defendant must exercise managerial control over the enterprise. [**Yellow Bus Lines, Inc. v. Drivers Local Union 639,** 913 F.2d 948 (D.C. Cir. 1990)]

c. **Respondeat superior [§1813]**

So far, courts have not been receptive to efforts to impose the RICO liability of an employee on the employer under an agency theory. Thus, in a case in which defrauded brokerage customers sought to recover against the broker's firm, the court held that the enterprise itself is not liable (and, in dictum, continued that this would be true even if the enterprise were "wholly illegitimate"). [**Schofield v. First Commodity Corp.,** 793 F.2d 28 (1st Cir. 1986)]

d. **Purchasers of securities [§1814]**

RICO includes as a predicate offense "fraud in the sale of securities." Does this language exclude fraud in the purchase of securities? Most courts have held that *fraudulent purchasers are liable under RICO.*

e. **Concurrent jurisdiction [§1815]**

The federal and state courts share jurisdiction over RICO cases. [**Tafflin v. Levitt,** 493 U.S. 455 (1990)]

Chapter Four: Regulation of the Securities Markets

CONTENTS

Key Exam Issues

The regulation of the national securities exchanges is very important to the well-being of the securities markets, but it is seldom tested on law school exams. However, you should learn the material in this chapter so that you have a basic understanding of how the securities markets work.

The topic most likely to appear on an exam concerns the regulation of trading activities of broker-dealers. In this area, you should watch for possible conflicts of interest between the brokers and their clients, and also be familiar with the rules that brokers must follow in working with clients.

A. Regulation of the National Securities Exchanges

1. Introduction [§1816]

As part of its purpose of regulating interstate trading of securities subsequent to their original distribution, the Securities Exchange Act of 1934 includes provisions regulating the "national securities exchanges" where many such securities are traded.

a. "Exchange" defined [§1817]

An "exchange" is any organization, association, or group of persons providing a marketplace or facilities for bringing together purchasers and sellers of securities. [SEA §3(a)(1)]

(1) Requirement of registration [§1818]

It is unlawful for a broker or dealer to use any means of interstate commerce for the purpose of trading or reporting the trade of a security on an exchange unless the exchange is registered with the S.E.C. as a "national securities exchange" or exempted from registration. However, the S.E.C. may exempt an exchange from registration if the volume of transactions on the exchange is so small that regulation is not necessary for the protection of the public interest or investors. [SEA §5]

(a) Section 6 [§1819]

The terms and conditions with which a national securities exchange must comply are set forth in section 6 of the 1934 Act (*e.g.*, the rules of the exchange must be designed to prevent fraudulent and manipulative practices).

b. Listing securities for trading [§1820]

To trade its securities on an exchange, an issuer must "list" the security with the exchange. The exchanges have rules under which an issuer can qualify its securities for trading (*e.g.*, requisite size of the firm in terms of sales and assets, net worth, etc.).

(1) Registration with the S.E.C. [§1821]

Once the issuer has listed a security with a national securities exchange, the security must then be registered with the S.E.C. under section 12 of the 1934 Act. (*See supra*, §876.)

c. Exchange membership [§1822]

Each national securities exchange sells memberships to securities firms or individuals in the securities business. Membership carries with it the privilege of executing transactions over the exchange.

d. Exchange disseminates price information [§1823]

Each exchange has developed an information system for disseminating information to market participants about the prices at which various securities have been bought and sold over the exchange. This information is sold and is becoming an important source of revenue for securities exchanges.

e. Exchange defines broker and dealer functions [§1824]

Also, to make the exchange work effectively, various broker and dealer functions have been developed for those members and their agents who participate in trading on the exchange. For example, the function of a "specialist" (*infra*, §1856) is to ensure a continuous market (*i.e.*, that a purchase or a sale in a listed security can always be made, at some price) in the securities for which the specialist is responsible.

2. Competition of Markets for Trading of Securities

a. Competing markets [§1825]

Many markets compete for the trading of securities.

(1) NYSE and regional exchanges [§1826]

For example, a security may be listed for trading on the New York Stock Exchange ("NYSE") and on one or more of the regional exchanges, such as the Pacific Coast Stock Exchange.

(2) Over-the-counter markets [§1827]

In addition, broker-dealers who are not members of an exchange may engage in buying and selling securities that are listed on an exchange in "over-the-counter" (*i.e.*, nonexchange) transactions.

(3) Institutional trading [§1828]

The institutions that own large amounts of securities may also engage in buying and selling securities directly with other such institutions.

(a) Alternative trading systems [§1829]

Institutional investors trade directly with one another on alternative trading systems, which are simply computerized facilities for bringing together buyers and sellers and disseminating information about price and availability. These trading systems increasingly compete with the more-established exchanges, and their growth has been fueled by rapid advances in, and deployment of, communications and information processing technology.

1) Regulation as broker-dealers [§1830]

Historically, the S.E.C. was willing to permit alternative trading systems to operate without registration as securities exchanges, as long as they registered as broker-dealers. [*See* S.E.C. Release No. 34-38672 (1997)] Although the more-established markets occasionally sued to overturn the S.E.C.'s decisions, those efforts were generally unsuccessful. [*See, e.g.*, **Board of Trade v. S.E.C.**, 923 F.2d 1270 (7th Cir. 1991)]

2) Rapid growth produced additional regulation [§1831]

In 1998, the S.E.C. estimated that almost 30% of the orders in over-the-counter stocks, and almost 5% of the orders in NYSE-listed securities, were handled by alternative trading systems. This heavy volume alerted the S.E.C. to the need to revisit its approach to alternative trading systems, and in 1998, the Commission promulgated regulation ATS, and revised certain rules under the 1934 Act to allow alternative trading systems to choose either registration as exchanges, or registration as broker-dealers and compliance with the new regulation ATS. [S.E.C. Release No. 34-40760 (1998)] This in turn has raised several issues, including whether alternative trading systems that register as exchanges can in fact carry out all of the functions of exchanges—for example, the self-regulatory function (discussed *infra*, §1837).

(4) Privatization of the established markets [§1832]

Responding to the competitive threat from alternative trading systems, both the NYSE and the NASD have become private, for-profit corporations. The change is intended to enable them to streamline decisionmaking and thereby compete more effectively. These developments raise some thorny problems, notably whether self-regulation (*see infra*, §1837) can be effectively carried out by an entity that is simultaneously seeking to maximize shareholder gain.

b. Development of national market system [§1833]

Congress has directed the S.E.C. to use its authority under the 1934 Act to facilitate the establishment of a "national market system" for securities. [SEA §11A]

(1) Projected elements of the national market system [§1834]
The following items have been suggested by Congress and the S.E.C. as important aspects of the national market system:

(a) *A nationwide system for disclosure* of market information so that price and volume information is available in all markets.

(b) *Elimination of artificial impediments to dealing* in the best available markets created by exchange rules or otherwise.

(c) *Establishment of terms and conditions* under which qualified broker-dealers could negotiate access to all exchanges.

(d) *An auction trading market* that would provide price and time priority protection for all public orders.

(e) *The type of securities to be included in the system* would be dependent on their characteristics (trading volume, etc.) and not on where they are traded (*i.e.*, which exchange, etc.). [*See* SEA Release No. 14416 (1978)]

(2) Progress toward the national market system [§1835]
Progress toward a national market system, in which there is intermarket competition, has been unsteady at best, due in large part to restrictions on the ability of exchange members to trade in listed securities off the exchange (*see infra*, §§1881 *et seq.*). However, overall there is far more price competition in the equity markets today than there was in 1975, when a national market system became a policy goal. This is primarily the result of technological and regulatory changes that facilitate the rapid dissemination of price information. Consequently, most investors today have access to timely and reliable information about securities prices, which tends to promote competition.

3. Self-Regulation of Exchanges vs. S.E.C. Supervision

a. Registration with the S.E.C. [§1836]
A broker-dealer is prohibited from effecting transactions on a securities exchange unless the exchange has registered with the S.E.C. pursuant to section 6 of the 1934 Act or is exempted from registration by other provisions of the Act. [SEA §5]

b. Self-regulation of exchanges [§1837]
Section 3(a)(26) of the 1934 Act provides that the national exchanges are

self-regulatory organizations ("SROs") that have the power to regulate their members' activities and business practices. [SEA §6]

(1) Rules, policies, and procedures [§1838]
The exchange may propose rules and adopt policies and procedures for implementing its rules.

(2) S.E.C. review [§1839]
Any proposed rule or change to an existing rule must be filed with the S.E.C., which then goes through an administrative notice and comment procedure, giving the public the right to comment on the proposal. [SEA §19(b)] In addition, the S.E.C. can, by its own rulemaking procedures, abrogate, add to, and delete rules from the rules of a self-regulatory organization. [SEA §19(c)]

(3) Disciplinary action [§1840]
If the exchange imposes any disciplinary sanction on an exchange member, or denies membership to a firm, the exchange must notify the S.E.C., which may then review (either on its own motion or on the motion of the aggrieved party) the actions taken by the exchange. [SEA §19(d)]

(4) S.E.C.'s power to sanction [§1841]
Finally, the 1934 Act empowers the S.E.C. to impose sanctions on the exchanges, exchange members, and persons associated with exchange members for violation of the federal securities laws. [SEA §19(h)]

EXAM TIP **gilbert**

Be sure to remember that while the securities exchanges are self-regulating, the S.E.C. may "ride shotgun" over the exchanges. It has the power to *add, modify, or abrogate rules* of self-regulatory organizations and *may punish* exchanges and exchange members for violating exchange rules as well as federal law.

---

4. Accommodation of Exchange Rules to the Antitrust Laws [§1842]
One of the principal "problem" areas concerning national exchanges concerns the application of the federal antitrust laws to exchange rules that restrain competition. Historically, exchanges have shown a tendency to protect the economic position of member firms from outside competition.

a. Rules in restraint of competition [§1843]
Historically, the anticompetitive impulses of exchanges have been expressed in three major ways:

(1) *Setting fixed commission rates* (*see infra,* §§1848 *et seq.*)*;*

(2) *Restricting membership on the exchange* and restricting the opportunity

to transact business on the exchange exclusively to members (*see infra*, §§1854-1855); and

(3) **Prohibiting exchange members from executing orders off the exchange** in securities that are listed on the exchange (*see infra*, §§1881 *et seq.*).

b. Securities laws do not preempt field [§1844]

The federal antitrust laws have been one of the tools used by those who wish to make the securities exchanges more competitive. The Supreme Court has indicated that the Securities Exchange Act does **not exclusively occupy the field** of securities regulation and that the 1934 Act must be reconciled or accommodated with the antitrust laws. However, with respect to particular conduct, if there is a "clear incompatibility" between the securities laws and the antitrust laws, the antitrust laws will not be enforced. [**Credit Suisse Securities (USA) LLC v. Billing**, 127 S. Ct. 2383 (2007)] *Rationale:* Antitrust regulation should not displace securities regulation.

(1) Guiding factors [§1845]

In *Billing*, the Court identified four factors that guide the determination whether a clear incompatibility exists:

(a) The challenged conduct is "*squarely within the heartland of securities regulations*";

(b) The S.E.C. has **clear and adequate authority to regulate** the conduct in question;

(c) The S.E.C. has conducted **active and ongoing regulation of such conduct**; and

(d) There is a **serious conflict between the antitrust and securities regimes**.

Example: Plaintiffs, purchasers in IPOs, brought an antitrust action against 10 major underwriting firms, claiming that the underwriters violated antitrust law by requiring IPO purchasers to (i) agree to purchase additional shares of the IPO security later at escalating prices ("laddering"); (ii) pay unusually high commissions to the underwriters on later purchases; and (iii) purchase from the underwriters other, less desirable, securities ("tying"). The Supreme Court held that application of the antitrust laws to the underwriters was precluded. The first factor is present because the challenged conduct—pricing and allocating IPO shares—is exactly the kind of activity that the S.E.C. regulates. The second factor is present because the law grants the S.E.C. authority to supervise all of the activities in question (as well as virtually every other activity in which underwriters engage). The S.E.C. has continuously exercised its legal authority to regulate underwriters, and thus the third factor is present. The fourth factor—conflict between the antitrust laws and the securities laws—is a bit more subtle, because both the securities laws and the antitrust laws appear to prohibit the alleged conduct. However, the Court found the securities and antitrust regulations to be in conflict. First, the complexity of the securities markets, and the difficulty of determining whether or not the securities laws allow conduct suggests strongly that one (and only one) authority should be in charge of regulation, and the authority best-equipped to regulate here is the S.E.C. In addition, application of the antitrust laws would result in different courts reaching different conclusions on the same activity, whereas the S.E.C. is presumably able to maintain consistency. (The Court did not address the very similar problem that can arise when different courts interpret the securities laws differently.) The need for antitrust enforcement in this case appeared small to the Court, because the plaintiffs would have a remedy under the securities laws. Finally, recent congressional attempts to make it more difficult for plaintiffs to bring securities lawsuits (*e.g.,* the PSLRA (*supra,* §1731) and the Securities Litigation Uniform Standards Act of 1998 (*supra,* §1745)) suggest that permitting antitrust lawsuits (which would circumvent these barriers) is not what Congress intended. [**Credit Suisse Securities (USA) LLC v. Billing,** *supra*]

---

(2) Antitrust laws inapplicable to rules fixing commissions [§1846]

Similarly, the Supreme Court has decided that the antitrust laws are *inapplicable* to exchange rules that fix commission rates to be charged by member firms. Because section 19(b) specifically gives the S.E.C. power to supervise exchanges in establishing commission rates, and the S.E.C. has a long history of actually exercising this power, the antitrust laws are preempted from limiting the exchange's self-regulatory power in this respect. [**Gordon v. New York Stock Exchange,** 422 U.S. 659 (1975)]

(3) Application to over-the-counter market [§1847]

Antitrust laws are applicable to the over-the-counter market (*see infra,* §§1896 *et seq.*) to the same extent as they are to the national securities exchanges.

c. Fixed commission rates as limiting competition [§1848]

As noted above, one of the classic anticompetitive strategies of the exchanges has been to fix the commission rates that its members must charge for transacting trades on the exchange.

(1) Minimum rates [§1849]

For a long time, the NYSE set *minimum* commission rates that its member firms could charge their customers. With pressure from the "third market" (*i.e.*, the trading of listed securities in the over-the-counter market), exchange members began to look for ways to avoid these minimum rates in order to offer their customers lower rates and thus preserve their business.

(2) "Give-up" of commission [§1850]

Under one method of avoiding the minimum rates, a customer would pay the exchange member the full commission on the trade, but would then direct the member firm to "give up" part of the commission to a specified third party (regardless of any involvement of this third party in the transaction). In either a direct or indirect way, the customer of the member firm would have an interest in the "give-up" (*i.e.*, the customer might have received other services from the party receiving the "give-up").

(3) Negotiated commissions [§1851]

Finally, the 1934 Act was amended to abolish fixed commission rates. It now provides that no national securities exchange may impose any schedule or otherwise fix the rates of commission charged by its members. [SEA §6(e)]

(a) Exceptions [§1852]

However, under SEA section 6(e) the S.E.C. may permit exceptions if it finds that:

1) *The fixed rates are reasonable* in relation to the costs of services; and

2) *The rates do not impose any unnecessary or inappropriate burden* on competition.

(b) "Soft dollars" [§1853]

Although the commission rates for trading of securities are now competitive, money managers worried that they would have to use the lowest-priced broker or risk liability for breach of fiduciary duty to their customers. Responding to this concern, Congress adopted SEA section 28(e), which permits money managers to pay higher commissions without incurring liability, if the commissions are *reasonable in relation to the "brokerage and research services"* provided by the recipient of the commission. Such extra payments are called "soft dollars" in the securities industry. Soft dollars must be expended for products or services that provide lawful and appropriate assistance to the money manager in the performance of investment decision-making, or the manager's fiduciary duty may be breached. [S.E.C. Release No. 34-23170 (1986)]

EXAM TIP   **gilbert**

Remember, a money manager's fiduciary duty does not require choosing "the cheapest broker in town"; the broker's commission need only be *reasonable in relation to the brokerage and research services* provided by the broker.

---

d. Exchange membership as limiting competition [§1854]

A second anti-competitive strategy of the exchanges has been to restrict membership on the exchange and to limit the opportunity to transact business on the exchange to its members.

(1) Institutional membership [§1855]

Financial institutions, which own most of the securities traded on national exchanges, for a long time desired to have membership on the NYSE either directly or to acquire as subsidiary corporations broker-dealers who had such membership. In this way, a financial institution that was constantly trading in securities listed on an exchange could save the commission expenses it would otherwise have to pay exchange members.

(a) But note

With the abolition of fixed minimum commission rates, however, the demand for institutional membership was almost completely extinguished. In addition, in 1975 Congress amended SEA section 11(a) to provide that a member of an exchange cannot effect a trade on the exchange for its own account or the account of an affiliate or person for whom the member exercises investment discretion (subject to limited exceptions, *e.g.,* where a member is acting as a specialist; *see* below). This abolishes the principal benefit sought by the financial institutions seeking memberships.

5. The Specialist System

a. "Specialist" defined [§1856]

A specialist is a member of a stock exchange who engages in the buying and selling of one or more specific securities listed on the exchange. He may act either as a broker (buying and selling for other brokers on the exchange) or as a dealer (buying or selling for his own account).

b. Function of the specialist [§1857]

The function of a specialist is to buy when stock is offered for sale but other bids for the purchase of the security are not available, and to sell when there are offers to buy but other offers to sell are not available. In other words, the specialist is supposed to see that there is a *continuous trading market* in the specific securities for which he is responsible, *i.e.,* to see that a security may *always* be bought or sold. In addition, as auctioneers, specialists set the opening price and establish the "bid" and "asked" spread within which others trade.

(1) Note
One specialist is responsible for each security listed on a national exchange.

(2) Effect of specialists
The specialists occupy a key position in the functioning of the stock exchanges; they purchase and sell a substantial portion of all the securities sold on the exchanges.

c. Types of orders executed [§1858]
Typically, the specialist executes the following types of orders:

(1) Limit orders [§1859]
A limit order is an order to buy or sell a stated amount of a security at a *specified price*, or at a better price if obtainable. For example, the specialist may receive an order to buy 100 shares of XYZ when the price drops to $10 per share or less.

(2) Stop-loss orders [§1860]
A stop-loss order is an order to buy or sell a stated amount of a security at the *market price*, if and when a transaction occurs at a designated price. For example, the specialist may receive an order to sell 100 shares of XYZ if the price ever drops below $10 per share (and the specialist may then sell at the market price).

(3) Market orders [§1861]
Specialists execute very few orders to buy or sell at the current market price (market orders), because these orders are normally executed between brokers at the "post" (the location on the exchange where the particular stock is traded). But where the order is at a price different from the current market price, the order is typically given to the specialist (who remains permanently at one post) to execute.

d. Recording of orders [§1862]
The specialist records each buy or sell order to be executed at a price above or below the current market price. As the market moves up or down, the specialist executes these orders.

e. Objections to the specialist system [§1863]
Most objections to the specialist system arise in connection with specialists trading for their own accounts (*i.e.,* acting as principals in stock transactions).

(1) Advantage of position as specialist [§1864]

The specialist has the advantage of special knowledge and superior bargaining power in buying and selling for her own account. For example, knowing that the limit orders to sell are above the market price may tell the specialist whether or not a stock can advance in price.

Example: If there are a lot of sell orders at $4.10 per share, just above the market price of $4 per share, the specialist would probably not buy for her own account. As soon as a price advance begins, it will run into all of the sell orders at $4.10 per share and the stock will probably retreat back to the $4 price.

---

(2) Potential for market manipulation [§1865]

By personal trading, the specialist is able to stimulate public interest and encourage market speculation. There is no question that specialists are in a position to manipulate the market.

(a) "Churning" to create commissions [§1866]

Specialists receive income from commissions on buying and selling; the more trading activity in a stock, therefore, the more money they make. Specialists may thus be motivated to create interest in a stock by stimulating the trading volume. Knowing when all of the buy orders are below the market price, the specialist might begin to "churn" (*i.e.*, buy and then immediately resell) the stock to create interest in a security.

(b) Specialist trading may accentuate price trend [§1867]

Rather than stabilizing the market, the specialist who trades excessively for her own account may actually accentuate an existing price trend.

f. Arguments supporting the specialist system [§1868]

There are also some strong arguments in favor of the specialist system:

(1) *Specialist trading contributes to price continuity and increases liquidity* of stock ownership; and

(2) *Acting as a dealer* (and profiting thereby) enables the specialist to assume substantial risks to *ensure an orderly market*.

g. Regulating the activities of specialists [§1869]

Because the position of specialist carries a significant potential for abuse, the 1934 Act regulates the trading activities of specialists. [SEA §11(a)]

(1) Trading limitations [§1870]

Specialists function both as brokers and as dealers. However, a specialist must restrict her activities as a dealer to those "reasonably necessary" to permit her to "maintain a fair and orderly market." [SEA Rule 11b-1]

EXAM TIP	gilbert

Specialists play an important role on the exchanges. They buy when there are offers to sell and no one else is willing to buy, and they sell when there are offers to buy and no one else is willing to sell. In other words, they are responsible for **maintaining a continuous market** for the securities on an exchange. But remember, because of their position, specialists can easily manipulate market prices. Therefore, their activity is closely regulated. A specialist must restrict her activities as a dealer in the stock in which she is a specialist to those **reasonably necessary to maintain a fair and orderly market**.

---

(2) NYSE rules governing specialists [§1871]

Numerous rules have been adopted by the NYSE to implement the basic objective to be achieved by specialists, *i.e.*, maintaining an orderly market.

(a) Registration [§1872]

Specialists are required by the NYSE to be registered with the exchange.

(b) Orderly market [§1873]

A specialist cannot exercise a trade in which she is personally interested unless the objective is to maintain an orderly market. Moreover, if a specialist is found to have engaged in "continued dealings" for her own account, and not for the objective of maintaining an orderly market, she can be suspended. [NYSE Rules 103, 104]

1) Specialists in market crashes [§1874]

Market crashes provide perhaps the ultimate test of the specialist system. Specialists who are solely or primarily self-interested would use their knowledge of the imbalance of buy and sell orders (in a crash, everyone wants to sell and no one is buying) to sell off their own securities. By and large, however, specialists performed well in the October 1987 market crash. That is, specialists purchased large quantities of securities on October 19, in a market that was heading down quickly. Then, on October 20, when the market rebounded upward, specialists sold large quantities of securities. These purchases and sales were clearly not done in the short-term financial interest of the specialists, but rather in discharge of their obligation to maintain a fair and orderly market.

(c) Capital requirements [§1875]

In addition, NYSE rules seek to establish fiscal responsibility of specialists by requiring that specialists be able to assume positions of a certain amount in each stock for which they are responsible, and that specialists have net liquid assets of a certain amount. These requirements are a necessity if specialists are to adequately perform their assigned functions.

1) Capital requirements after the 1987 crash [§1876]

Since the October 1987 market crash, the capital adequacy requirements have become stricter. In a significant stock market crash, specialists may be called on to buy huge quantities of securities, and the capital requirements at the time of the 1987 crash were not strict enough to ensure that all specialists were ready to meet those needs. As a result, several specialists were bankrupted by the 1987 crash, further contributing to the panic that accompanied the market crash.

(d) Dealer transactions on the exchange [§1877]

The 1934 Act prohibits any member of a national securities exchange (including a specialist) from effecting transactions on the exchange for its own account (*i.e.*, acting as a principal), the account of an associated person, or an account with respect to which it or an associated person has investment discretion (so-called "covered accounts"). [SEA §11(a)]

1) Dealer transactions exempted from prohibition [§1878]

The 1934 Act provides for specific exemptions from the prohibition against dealer transactions by members of the exchange. [SEA §11(a)]

a) Market-maker transactions [§1879]

A specific exemption is given in the Act for transactions by a dealer acting in the capacity of a "market-maker." [SEA §11(a)(1)(A)] A "market-maker" is a person who holds himself out as willing to buy and sell a particular security on a regular or continuous basis. [SEA §3(a)(38)] However, on the exchanges, only the specialists are permitted to make a market; thus, this exemption permits specialists to carry out their market-stabilization function but does not permit other dealers to compete with the specialists.

b) When outside orders are given priority [§1880]

The Act also provides that transactions may be effected for the account of exchange members, if: (i) the member is primarily engaged in the securities business and its principal income is derived from the securities business, and (ii) the transaction is effected in such a way as to yield "priority, parity, and precedence" to orders of persons who are neither members nor associated with members. [SEA §11(a)(1)(G)]

6. Regulation of Off-the-Exchange Transactions [§1881]

In addition to regulating trading on the national securities exchanges by exchange members, the S.E.C. and the national exchanges also regulate the trading in listed securities by exchange members *off the exchange.*

a. Background [§1882]

Historically, the stock exchanges sharply limited trading in listed securities elsewhere than on the exchange floor. The reason for this was simple: If a security was available only on the exchange floor, from an exchange member, a customer who wanted to buy or sell the security had no choice but to pay the usual commission on the transaction. In the 1970s, however, large customers (*e.g.,* financial institutions like banks, trusts, and insurance companies) began to apply pressure to exchange members to participate in off-exchange transactions.

(1) Birth of the "third market" [§1883]

As long as the exchanges were unwilling to permit member firms to participate in off-exchange transactions, financial institutions that wanted to avoid paying broker's commissions had to deal directly with one another and with nonmember firms. As the number of participants in this market grew, it became known as the "third market."

(2) Third market today [§1884]

The elimination of fixed minimum commissions (*see supra,* §1851) nearly eliminated the third market, which declined and, for a time, almost ceased to exist. In the late 1980s, however, the third market was reborn as trading volume increased dramatically.

b. Block transactions [§1885]

Many exchange member firms also found that they were unable to handle in normal exchange transactions the purchase or sale of the large blocks of securities being traded by financial institutions. These firms found that to facilitate such transactions for their customers, they often had to negotiate the transaction off the exchange—either by finding off-the-exchange brokers or dealers willing to participate, or by finding other institutions in the third market that wished to participate.

c. NYSE Rule 390 [§1886]

The New York Stock Exchange eventually responded to the pressure from members and their customers, and on the recommendation of the S.E.C., the Exchange amended its rule 390 to permit member firms, at least in theory, to engage in off-exchange transactions. Such transactions, however, were subject to strict requirements, discussed immediately below.

(1) Permission required [§1887]

Member firms were required by rule 390 to obtain permission from the Exchange before engaging in an off-the-exchange transaction involving a listed security.

(2) Solicitation of nonmember market-makers [§1888]

Once permission was granted, an exchange member firm could, under certain conditions, approach a nonexchange broker-dealer making a market in the listed security (provided the market-maker was a broker-dealer registered with the S.E.C.) to participate in an off-the-exchange transaction. However, efforts had to first be made to fill the order or make the sale over the exchange, and the relevant specialists also had to be given a chance to participate at the same price as those participating in the off-the-exchange transaction.

d. S.E.C. permission to trade off the exchange [§1889]

The S.E.C. viewed the amended rule 390 as merely an interim measure and, in the late 1970s, adopted rules 19c-1 and 19c-3. These rules preempted portions of rule 390 of the New York Stock Exchange as it then existed and eliminated some of the restrictions on off-exchange trading by member firms.

(1) Where member firm acts as broker [§1890]

When acting as a broker (*i.e.*, agent), a member firm may effect an off-exchange transaction in a listed security. [SEA Rule 19c-1]

(a) But note

The exchange rules may still require that members effecting such transactions first satisfy orders, at the same or better price, that are listed with the exchange specialist.

(b) And note

The exchanges may also still adopt rules that would prohibit member firms from effecting transactions "in house" (*i.e.*, acting as agent for both the buyer and the seller).

(2) Where member firm acts as principal [§1891]

Where, however, the member firm acts as a *principal* in the transaction (*e.g.*, by selling securities it owns in its investment account), the member firm must comply with exchange rules regulating off-the-exchange sales.

(3) Newly listed securities [§1892]

The S.E.C. has also adopted a rule removing off-exchange trading restrictions on securities first listed after April 26, 1979. [SEA Rule 19c-3] This allows exchange-member brokerage firms to compete directly with exchange specialists on transactions involving these stocks.

7. Civil Liability for Violations of Exchange or NASD Rules [§1893]

In a number of cases, a plaintiff has brought a *private action* against an exchange or a member firm, alleging an implied federal cause of action based on violation of a stock exchange or NASD rule.

a. Pre-*Blue Chip* view [§1894]

The older cases hold that under limited circumstances, such an action is possible. [*See, e.g.,* **Landy v. Federal Deposit Insurance Corp.**, *supra*, §1640; **Buttrey v. Merrill Lynch, Pierce, Fenner & Smith, Inc.**, 410 F.2d 135 (7th Cir.), *cert. denied*, 396 U.S. 838 (1969); **Colonial Realty Corp. v. Bache & Co.**, *supra*, §1718]

b. Modern view [§1895]

After the Supreme Court decided the *Blue Chip* case (cutting back implied liability under the securities laws; *see supra*, §990) the lower courts have refused to recognize implied actions based on violations of stock exchange or NASD rules. [*See, e.g.,* **Carrott v. Shearson Hayden Stone, Inc.**, 724 F.2d 821 (9th Cir. 1984); **Thompson v. Smith Barney, Harris Upham & Co.**, 709 F.2d 1413 (11th Cir. 1983); **Sacks v. Reynolds Securities Inc.**, 593 F.2d 1234 (D.C. Cir. 1978); **Heubach v. Friedman**, No. 95-3991-E (CGA) (S.D. Cal. May 1, 1997)]

B. Regulation of the Over-the-Counter Market

1. In General [§1896]

Securities that are traded outside the exchanges are said to be traded "over-the-counter." This trading, like that which occurs on the national securities exchanges, is also subject to regulation under the 1934 Act.

2. Role of Securities Firms [§1897]

Securities firms act as the agents (*i.e.*, as brokers) of the buyer and seller in over-the-counter securities transactions. And sometimes the securities firms may act as principals (*i.e.*, as dealers) as well, owning the security and acting as either buyer or seller in the transaction.

3. Transaction Information Systems [§1898]

There are several systems that disseminate information about the prices at which over-the-counter ("OTC") securities are bought and sold.

a. Local newspapers [§1899]

For example, local newspapers may collect information on local OTC stocks and publish this information daily.

b. NASDAQ system [§1900]

One of the most important information systems for the over-the-counter market is the NASDAQ system. This is a national, computer-based information network that lists OTC securities meeting NASD requirements and the firms that are making a market in these securities (*i.e.*, firms that have indicated a willingness to buy or sell the security at a quoted price). Securities that are quoted on NASDAQ are also referred to as National Market System ("NMS") securities. NASD members that quote prices on NASDAQ are required to execute trades at the quoted prices. In addition, NASD members must report transactions in NMS securities within 90 seconds of execution. This information has contributed to competition in the equity markets and has benefited consumers by enabling them to rely on price information.

c. "Pink sheets" [§1901]

Another important source of price information about OTC securities are the so-called "pink sheets," published by the National Daily Quotations Bureau. The pink sheets contain quotations for securities that are not carried in the NASDAQ system.

d. OTC Bulletin Board [§1902]

The OTC Bulletin Board is a computer bulletin board system ("BBS") operated by the NASD as an electronic interdealer quotation system. Securities not quoted in the NASDAQ system may be quoted on the OTC BBS, which makes price information more current and more accessible. Eventually the OTC BBS will replace the pink sheets altogether, although it has not yet done so.

4. Regulation of Broker-Dealers [§1903]

The 1934 Act provides for the registration with the S.E.C. of all broker-dealers transacting a securities business in interstate commerce. [SEA §15] This requirement applies to essentially all broker-dealers, including those in the OTC market, because it is difficult for a broker to avoid using instrumentalities of interstate commerce.

a. Self-regulation required [§1904]

In addition to registering with the S.E.C., broker-dealers must be members of a national securities association which is itself registered with the S.E.C. Only one such association exists today; that association is the National Association of Securities Dealers ("NASD").

b. Authority of the NASD [§1905]

The NASD is authorized by the Act to adopt and enforce rules for member broker-dealers addressing a wide variety of matters, including training, broker qualifications, and capital requirements. [SEA §15(b)] The S.E.C., however, continues to exercise authority over both the NASD itself and over NASD members. [SEA §15A]

(1) *The NASD's proposed rule additions, deletions, or changes must first be approved by the S.E.C.* [SEA §19(b)]

(2) *In addition, the S.E.C. may exercise its power to abrogate, add to, delete, or amend the rules* of the NASD when necessary to ensure its fair administration and to accomplish the purposes of the Act. [SEA §19(c)]

(3) *If the NASD imposes any disciplinary sanction on any member, or denies membership* to a broker-dealer, the NASD must inform the S.E.C. The S.E.C. may then review the actions taken by the NASD, either on its own motion or on the motion of an aggrieved party. [SEA §19(d)]

(4) *Finally, the S.E.C. has the power to sanction NASD members* and persons associated with members. [SEA §19(h)] The S.E.C. may exercise this authority even after an NASD member has been sanctioned by the NASD and may impose its own penalties for conduct that has already been the subject of NASD discipline. [**Jones v. S.E.C.**, 115 F.3d 1173 (4th Cir. 1997)]

c. Regulation of dealer markups [§1906]

One issue that frequently arises with respect to OTC securities not quoted on NASDAQ (*i.e.*, non-NMS securities) involves the amount of profit a dealer may make on a sale. The NASD's Rules of Fair Practice require dealers to "sell at a price which is fair, taking into consideration all relevant factors." Informally, the NASD has a guideline of 5% as a reasonable markup, but in some cases, a 5% markup may be unreasonable. For more detailed information regarding dealer markups, *see infra*, §§1996 *et seq.*

(1) NASD sanctions [§1907]

A dealer that marks up prices excessively is subject to NASD discipline. [*See, e.g.*, **Lehl v. S.E.C.**, 90 F.3d 1483 (10th Cir. 1996)]

(2) S.E.C. sanctions [§1908]

In addition, the S.E.C. has brought administrative actions under rule 10b-5 against dealers charging excessive markups, based on the failure to disclose the excessive markup to the customer. [*See, e.g.*, **Trost & Co.**, 12 S.E.C. 531 (1942)]

(3) Private actions [§1909]

Finally, the customer who has paid an excessive markup may succeed in a private action against the dealer, usually based on rule 10b-5. [*See, e.g.*, **Ettinger v. Merrill Lynch, Pierce, Fenner & Smith, Inc.**, 835 F.2d 1031 (3d Cir. 1987)] When the customer is an institution, however, such actions often fail. [*See, e.g.*, **Banca Cremi, S.A. v. Alex. Brown & Sons, Inc.**, 132 F.3d 1017 (4th Cir. 1997)]

5. Regulation of the "Penny Stock" Market [§1910]

A significant segment of the OTC market is composed of "penny stocks," low-priced (under $5 per share) stocks of small, new companies with little or no operating history. Congress reacted to widespread fraud and abuse in the penny stock market by passing the Securities Enforcement Remedies and Penny Stock Reform Act of 1990.

a. Administrative sanctions and registration provisions [§1911]

The 1990 Act provides for several administrative remedies (*see supra*, §§1673 *et seq.*) and stringent regulations governing the distribution of securities issued by "blank check" companies (*see supra*, §§404-410).

b. Broker-dealer regulation under the 1990 Act [§1912]

The 1990 Act also provides for extensive regulation of brokers and dealers who deal heavily in penny stocks, and authorizes the S.E.C. to make rules regulating participants in the penny stock market. [SEA §15(g)]

(1) Suspensions and bars [§1913]

Under the 1990 Act, the S.E.C. may suspend or bar persons from "being associated with any broker or dealer, or from participating in an offering of penny stock," if they have violated the 1933 or 1934 Acts in connection with a penny stock offering. [SEA §15(b)(6)(A)] It is illegal for such persons to work for a broker or dealer, or participate in a penny stock offering, in violation of the bar. [SEA §15(b)(6)(B)(i)] Likewise, it is illegal for a broker or dealer to hire such persons. [SEA §15(b)(6)(B)(ii)]

(2) Risk disclosure document [§1914]

A broker or dealer selling penny stock to a retail customer is required to deliver a document containing the information in schedule 15G, which sets out in detail many of the risks and dangers associated with an investment in penny stocks. Schedule 15G includes as an instruction the statement that "No material may be given to a customer that is intended in any way to detract from, rebut, or contradict the Schedule." [SEA Rule 15g-2]

(3) Written purchase agreement [§1915]

The dealer must obtain from the customer a written agreement to purchase the stock, setting forth the identity and quantity of the penny stock to be purchased. [SEA Rule 15g-9(a)(2)(ii)]

(4) Price information [§1916]

Penny stock dealers must also disclose to the customer available "inside" price information (the *wholesale* bid and asked prices) for the security sold. If the inside price is not available (*e.g.,* because the dealer has not consistently traded the security with other dealers), that fact and the reasons therefor must be disclosed. [SEA Rule 15g-3]

(5) Dealer compensation disclosure [§1917]

Penny stock dealers must disclose to the customer the aggregate amount of all compensation received in connection with the penny stock transaction. [SEA Rule 15g-4]

(6) Salesperson compensation disclosure [§1918]

In addition to disclosing the dealer's compensation, *supra*, the individual salesperson must disclose to the customer the total amount of compensation that she will receive from all sources (including the issuer or other promoters). [SEA Rule 15g-5]

(7) Account statements [§1919]

Penny stock dealers must provide their customers with a monthly account statement setting out price information for each penny stock owned by the customer. [SEA Rule 15g-6]

(8) Customer suitability [§1920]

Finally, before a broker-dealer is permitted to engage in any penny stock transaction with a customer, the *dealer must approve the customer's account.* This requires that the dealer obtain from the customer *information about the customer's financial situation, investment experience, and investment objectives.* Once that information is obtained, the dealer must determine, based on the information, that penny stock investments are suitable for the customer, and that the customer is capable of evaluating the risks of such an investment. Finally, the customer's financial information must be summarized in a written document and presented to the customer for signature, along with the statement that the broker-dealer is required by law to do so. [SEA Rule 15g-9]

CHECKLIST OF BROKER-DEALER REQUIREMENTS IN SALES OF PENNY STOCKS · gilbert

WHEN SELLING PENNY STOCKS TO RETAIL CUSTOMERS, A BROKER-DEALER MUST:

☑ *Deliver a document* to the customer including the information in schedule 15G (which sets out common risks of investing in penny stocks)

☑ *Obtain a written purchase agreement* from the customer identifying the stock and quantity to be purchased

☑ *Disclose "inside" pricing* (*i.e.,* wholesale bids) for the stock

☑ *Disclose the aggregate compensation the dealer* will receive

☑ *Disclose the compensation the salesperson* will receive

☑ *Provide purchasers with a monthly account statement*

☑ *Obtain information about the customer's financial situation*, investment experience, and investment objectives and determine that the customer is capable of evaluating the risks involved and that *penny stocks are suitable* for the customer

C. Regulation of Market Manipulation and Stabilization

1. Introduction [§1921]

The previous two sections of this Summary discussed the general regulations relating to the two principal markets for the trading of securities—the national stock exchanges and the OTC market. This section concerns the prohibitions in the 1934 Act against manipulation of the trading that occurs in these markets.

2. Regulation of Short Sales [§1922]

Short sales are one of the more controversial kinds of trading activities. Although an outright ban on short sales was considered in 1934, ultimately Congress decided to let the S.E.C. determine what kinds of short-selling practices to forbid.

a. Short sale defined [§1923]

A short sale is a sale of securities that the seller does not own, or any sale consummated by the delivery of a security borrowed by or for the seller. [SEA Rule 3b-3]

b. Why sell short [§1924]

Traders sell securities short because they believe that the price of the security will drop. Thus, a short sale is a "bet" that the market price of the securities will fall, and is sometimes cited as one way in which a sophisticated trader can make money even in a falling market.

---

e.g. Example: Cathy does not own any Acme Corp. stock, but she believes that Acme stock will fall in price. Her trading strategy, then, might be to sell short Acme stock. She will sell, say, 1,000 shares of Acme stock today. Under normal market practice, her sale will not "settle" (and Cathy will not have to deliver the Acme stock) until three business days after the contract date. If Cathy is correct, and the price of Acme stock falls, she can "cover" her sale of three days ago with cheaper stock purchased today.

---

(1) Note

An alert reader may wonder how Cathy in the example above can obtain Acme stock for delivery the same day in order to cover her earlier short sale. The answer lies in the ability of traders to borrow stock from one another: To implement her short-sale strategy, Cathy will borrow enough shares of Acme stock to cover the short sale. This borrowed stock is available to her when she needs it, at the then-current market price.

c. **Dangers of short sales [§1925]**

Short sales increase the volatility of market prices. That is, it is relatively easy and cheap to sell short a large quantity of an issuer's shares, and if the sales are accompanied by rumor-mongering, it is probable that other investors, hearing of the sales and the rumors, will choose to sell their shares. The effect of all this is to drive down the price, which of course fits the short-seller's strategy perfectly—the lower the price goes, the more easily and cheaply the short sales can be covered, and the greater the short-seller's profit.

(1) "Bear raids" [§1926]

A bear raid is a concerted effort to drive down the price of a security, using techniques similar to those described immediately above.

(2) Dangers to short sellers [§1927]

Selling short may be an appropriate strategy for a sophisticated investor, but it is seldom the best choice for others. The chief danger is that the short seller is exposed to liability that increases every time the price of the security goes up, until the sale is covered. Unlike an investor with a "long" position, whose risk is limited to the amount invested, the short seller's risk is hard to measure and is limited only by the potential increases in the price of the security.

d. **Regulation of short selling [§1928]**

To mitigate somewhat the potential dangers of unlimited short selling, the S.E.C. has promulgated several rules governing the practice.

(1) Short sales must be identified [§1929]

First, all sales of exchange-traded securities (whether or not taking place on the exchange) must be identified as "long" or "short." [SEA Rule 10a-1(c)]

(2) Short sales prohibited on downtick [§1930]

Next, short sales are not permitted to be made at a price lower than the last reported sale price. In addition, short sales are not permitted to be made at the last sale price, *unless* that price is higher than the immediately preceding reported sale price. [SEA Rule 10a-1(a)(1)]

---

e.g. Example: At 11:15 a.m., Acme stock sold for $35.75. At 11:20, Acme stock sold for $35.60. At this point, no short sales are permitted (unless they are made at a price higher than the current market price), because the last reported sale price ($35.60) is lower than the immediately preceding price ($35.75). (This is called a "*downtick*" or "*minus tick*.")

---

e.g. Example: Same facts as above, but at 11:25, Acme stock sold for $35.60 (again). At this point, short sales at the market price are still not permitted, because the last reported sale price ($35.60) was the same as the preceding price, and that price was lower than the next preceding price ($35.75). (This is called a *"zero-minus tick."*)

---

e.g. **Example:** Same facts as above, but at 11:30, Acme stock sold for $35.75. At this point, short sales at the market price are permitted, because the price for the sale ($35.75) is higher than the immediately preceding price ($35.60). (This is called an *"uptick"* or *"plus tick."*)

---

e.g. **Example:** Same facts as above, but at 11:35, Acme stock sold for $35.75 (again). At this point, short sales at the market price are permitted, because the price for the sale ($35.75) is the same as the immediately preceding price, and that price is higher than the next preceding price ($35.60). (This is called a *"zero-plus tick."*)

---

(3) Short sales prohibited during distributions [§1931]

During a distribution of securities (*see supra*, §§96 *et seq.*), the influx of new securities into the market tends to depress the price. Because the price is likely to decline at least a little, the short-seller's risk is reduced. Short sales were thus more likely to occur during a distribution. On the other hand, short sales during a distribution may make it impossible for the issuer to complete the distribution. In response to the NASD's request, the S.E.C. adopted rule 10b-21 (which now appears as regulation M, rule 105). The rule applies after the filing of a registration statement or notification under regulation A, relating to the class of securities sold short, and prohibits covering a short sale made in the five days before an offering is priced with securities purchased from an underwriter or broker participating in the offering.

e. Comment

The short sale regulations may discourage abuses, but they cannot prevent them. Virtually anything that can be accomplished by selling short can also be accomplished by using derivative securities, such as options, which do not carry similar restrictions. Nevertheless, the short sale regulations may be valuable if only because they tend to inhibit short sales by investors who lack the financial sophistication to understand and manage the risks that short sales entail.

EXAM TIP **gilbert**

If an exam question involves a short sale, there are a few rules you should know. First, the short sale *must be identified* as such. Second, short sales are *prohibited on a downtick and during a distribution*. Finally, the rules do not apply to derivative securities and so *may be easily circumvented* by a sophisticated investor.

---

3. Prohibition of Market Manipulation [§1932]

Market manipulation is an attempt to set stock prices—or other important criteria of stock market performance, such as the volume of shares traded—by entering into transactions for the specific purpose of such manipulation. There is a series of provisions in the 1934 Act aimed at prohibiting market manipulation.

a. Manipulation of listed securities prohibited—section 9 [§1933]

Section 9(a) of the 1934 Act prohibits "any person" from using the instrumentalities of interstate commerce or the facilities of "any national securities exchange" to engage in certain specified manipulative activities with respect to securities listed on a national securities exchange. Although SEA section 9 applies only to listed securities, its prohibitions are incorporated into sections 10(b) and 15(c), and thus the substance of the Act's anti-manipulation provisions applies to both listed and unlisted securities. [*See* **S.E.C. v. Resch-Cassin & Co.,** 362 F. Supp. 964 (S.D.N.Y. 1973)]

(1) Per se violations [§1934]

A series of "per se violations" are listed in section 9. These include activities such as attempting to create a misleading appearance of active trading; effecting a series of transactions on the exchange creating the appearance of active trading, to induce a purchase or sale of a security by others; or disseminating misleading information with respect to the listed security. [SEA §9(a)(1) - (5)]

(2) Violation of S.E.C. rules [§1935]

Other types of market transactions may also violate the 1934 Act if effected in contravention of rules adopted by the S.E.C. [SEA §9(a)(6), (b), (c)]

(a) Section 9(a)(6)

Section 9(a)(6) relates to "market stabilization," and makes it unlawful to engage in transactions in a listed stock for the purpose of "pegging, fixing, or stabilizing the price of such security" in contravention of such rules as may be adopted by the S.E.C.

(b) Note

Rather than adopt rules regulating stabilization pursuant to section 9, the S.E.C. regulates stabilization in regulation M. (*See infra,* §1957.)

(3) Limited use of section 9 [§1936]

Section 9 has received only limited use by the S.E.C., due to several factors.

(a) Applies only to listed securities [§1937]

One reason for its limited use is that section 9 applies only to securities listed on a national securities exchange. Other sections that are used because of their broader coverage are rule 10b-5, which applies to both listed and over-the-counter securities, and rule 15c1-2 (which is limited, however, to broker-dealer transactions).

(b) Must show "intent" or "willfulness" [§1938]

Under section 9, the S.E.C. must prove the defendant's "intent" or "purpose" to engage in an unlawful act before it can obtain injunctive relief. And a plaintiff in a private damage action must be able to show defendant's "willfulness." [SEA §9(e)]

b. General prohibition against market manipulation—rule 10b-5 [§1939]

As noted above, rule 10b-5—a general prohibition against fraud in the purchase and sale of securities—applies to both listed and over-the-counter securities. Because of this, and the burdensome requirement of proving intent or willfulness under section 9, rule 10b-5 has had broad application in market manipulation cases. Moreover, the specific prohibitions of section 9 with respect to listed securities have been held to be incorporated in rule 10b-5. [**S.E.C. v. Resch-Cassin & Co.**, *supra*]

c. Liability provisions applicable to broker-dealers—section 15(c) [§1940]

Section 15(c) is a general fraud provision worded similarly to section 9 and rule 10b-5, but specifically applicable to transactions involving broker-dealers in the over-the-counter market. (*See supra*, §1932.)

(1) S.E.C. rules [§1941]

Pursuant to section 15(c), the S.E.C. has adopted rules prohibiting certain manipulative and deceptive practices in securities trading. [SEA Rules 15c1-2 - 15c1-9]

(2) No "willfulness" element [§1942]

Note that the specific element of "willfulness" (required in a private damage action brought under section 9) is *not* present in a section 15(c) action. [*See* SEA §15(c); *infra*, §§1990 *et seq.*]

(3) S.E.C. enforcement powers [§1943]

In addition to private damages actions that may be brought under section 15(c), the S.E.C. has specific enforcement powers against broker-dealers for any violations of its rules adopted pursuant to section 15(c). In addition, it may review disciplinary proceedings brought by the NASD against any of its broker-dealer members. (*See supra*, §1840.)

d. Manipulation during a distribution—regulation M [§1944]

Before and during an offering of securities, the issuer, underwriters, and other participants in the offering may have an incentive to manipulate the price of the offered securities by making purchases. For example, an issuer that already has securities trading in the market would normally offer additional securities at the current market price of the securities already issued. That price could be raised, however, if the issuer or others connected with the offering were to purchase sizeable quantities of the securities just before commencing the new offering. Or, in the case of an initial public offering, the issuer or underwriters might wish to maintain the price of the securities at the offering price by making purchases even as the offering is underway. These practices have been heavily regulated by the S.E.C., first by rule 10b-6, and, beginning in 1997, by regulation M.

(1) What is regulated [§1945]

Persons subject to regulation M may not purchase or bid for securities that are being distributed until their participation in the distribution is over.

(2) Who is regulated [§1946]

Regulation M applies to issuers, underwriters, participating brokers and dealers, and affiliated purchasers (including persons acting in concert with any of the foregoing).

(3) When the prohibition begins [§1947]

The beginning "restricted period" during which persons may not purchase or bid depends on how heavily traded the security is.

(a) Heavily traded securities—one day [§1948]

If the security has an average daily trading volume ("ADTV") of at least $100,000 and a public float (*i.e.*, the aggregate market value of all outstanding securities) of at least $25 million, the restricted period begins one business day before the offering is priced (or, if later, the day on which the person becomes a participant in the offering).

(b) Other securities—five days [§1949]

If the security does not meet the above criteria, the restricted period begins five business days before the offering is priced (or, if later, the day on which the person becomes a participant).

(4) Exceptions [§1950]

There are a number of exceptions to regulation M, three of which are of primary interest here:

(a) Very heavily traded securities [§1951]

Securities with an ADTV of at least $1 million and a public float of $150 million are not subject to the trading restrictions of regulation M. The price of such securities is difficult, if not impossible, to manipulate by making purchases, so the prohibitions are not needed.

(b) Stabilization [§1952]

Stabilization of the price of securities during an offering is a common, if manipulative, practice. Stabilizing activities and their regulation are discussed *infra*, §§1957 *et seq.*

(c) **NASDAQ passive market-making [§1953]**

Underwriters and dealers are permitted to continue making a market in NASDAQ securities being distributed. However, bids or purchases by distribution participants must not exceed the highest independent bid or purchase price at any given time during the restricted period.

(5) Regulation M not a safe harbor [§1954]

Finally, note that regulation M is not a safe harbor. That is, if the S.E.C. can prove manipulative intent, even activity complying with regulation M would be a violation of rule 10b-5 or another, more specific, prohibition. This is the result of regulation M's structure, which broadly prohibits activities contravening its provisions, without insulating compliant activities from S.E.C. enforcement.

TRADING RESTRICTIONS UNDER REGULATION M **gilbert**

ISSUERS, UNDERWRITERS, PARTICIPATING BROKERS AND DEALERS, AND AFFILIATED PURCHASERS ARE PROHIBITED FROM PURCHASING OR BIDDING ON THE SECURITIES BEING DISTRIBUTED AS FOLLOWS:

TYPE OF SECURITY	TRADING LEVELS	RESTRICTED TRADING PERIOD
Very heavily traded securities	ADTV ≥ $1 million and public float ≥ $150 million	Excepted from regulation M
Heavily traded securities	ADTV ≥ $100,000 and public float ≥ $25 million	Beginning one business day before offering is priced until participation in distribution ends
Other securities	ADTV < $100,000 or public float < $25 million	Beginning five business days before offering is priced until participation in distribution ends

e. **Application of anti-manipulation provisions [§1955]**

Stock market manipulation usually involves persons who have ready access to the market mechanism (such as broker-dealers). Such persons are in a position to run the price of a security up (*e.g.*, by devices such as false market quotes) while at the same time refusing to accept sell orders from customers owning the security. The broker-dealers can then sell their own positions in the security at a very substantial profit, thereafter allowing the market for the security to collapse.

(1) Methods of attack [§1956]

In these situations, the S.E.C. might attempt to attack the manipulation scheme directly under one of the antifraud provisions discussed above. More often, an action will be brought for some technical violation of the securities acts (due to the less demanding requirements of proof), and the offending broker-dealer will be disciplined.

---

e.g. **Example—section 9:** Defendant, a brokerage firm, ran the price of a stock up by 75% in 20 days by putting successively higher bids in the quotation sheets, giving the public false indications of trading activity. After defendant sold its interest, the price of the stock collapsed. The court found defendant liable for a violation of section 9(a)(2). [**S.E.C. v. Resch-Cassin & Co.,** *supra*, §1933]

---

e.g. **Example—section 15:** Company X sold $300,000 of its common stock to the public in a regulation A offering. The underwriter of the securities issue was the defendant broker-dealer and its branch office manager (who was also on the board of directors of Company X). Personnel of the defendant purchased a significant number of X shares, gave out false information about the prospects of X to the defendant's customers, and arbitrarily raised the daily quotation price. Furthermore, no-sell orders were accepted from customers unless orders to buy an equal amount of shares were available at the time (thus permitting an artificial market price to exist). Finally, defendant's personnel sold all their own shares in preference to sell orders of other customers, and then allowed the market for X stock to collapse. [*In re* **Shearson, Hammill & Co.,** SEA Release No. 7743 (1964)] The S.E.C. found numerous violations of the securities acts, including section 5 of the 1933 Act and SEA Rule 15c1-2. The agency brought an action for suspension of the offending brokers associated with the defendant under sections 15(b), 15A, and 19(a)(3) of the 1934 Act. In addition, members of the defendant's executive committee were suspended for a substantial period of time. This sanction was imposed, rather than a general broker-dealer suspension or revocation, because the offending sales personnel had already been terminated by the firm, the firm was either involved in lawsuits or had settled the claims of customers who had been hurt, and the firm had instituted closer supervision practices. Nevertheless, the S.E.C. believed that the public interest still demanded the sanction imposed as a penalty for the lax supervision methods employed by the firm.

---

4. **Regulation of Market Stabilization [§1957]**

Market stabilization is a specific form of market manipulation and, as such, is regulated under the 1934 Act. [*See* SEA §9(a)(6); Regulation M, Rule 104]

a. **"Stabilization" defined [§1958]**

"Stabilization" is an attempt to maintain a fixed market price for a security by purchasing all of the shares that are offered at a price lower than the desired price.

(1) Occurs in original public distributions [§1959]

Market stabilization usually occurs in connection with an original public distribution of shares, where the underwriters stabilize the price until the entire issue is sold. It is critical to maintain the market for a new issue at the offering price until the entire issue is sold out, particularly in situations where securities of the same class are already outstanding.

(2) May determine success of public offering [§1960]

Stabilization can be extremely important to a successful public offering of securities, which ultimately depends on whether the underwriter is able to sell the securities to the public at the offering price.

(a) Note

Even when the underwriter is able to quickly sell the entire issue, there is *always* some immediate reselling by purchasers before the entire issue is sold out. The early purchasers may change their minds about owning the stock, or they may have bought purely for speculation, with the hope of selling immediately for a profit in the case of an early price rise.

(b) And note

If such reselling is not absorbed through public buying pressure, the market price of the remaining stock will drop below the initial offering price and the entire issue will not be sold at the price originally set. For this reason, the ability of the underwriters to purchase the resold shares as they come to the market, thereby stabilizing the market at the initial offering price, is of critical importance to a successful public offering.

b. Arguments against stabilization [§1961]

The argument against stabilization is that it is a form of manipulation, and when the manipulative activity ceases, the price returns to its natural level.

Example: The classic, nonstabilizing manipulation case involves a defendant who artificially raises the price of a security, gets people to purchase it at this price, and then withdraws from the market by selling her shares of the manipulated security. As soon as the defendant withdraws, the price goes down.

(1) Note

In the public distribution context, stabilizing can result in losses to purchasers, just as classic manipulation does. [*See* SEA Release No. 34-2446 (1940)]

c. Regulation of stabilization in public distributions [§1962]

The 1934 Act prohibits transactions for the purpose of pegging or stabilizing the price of a security *only* when such transactions are in violation of the rules and regulations adopted by the S.E.C. [SEA §9(a)(6)] The S.E.C. has adopted rule 104 of regulation M to regulate stabilization in distribution situations. Note that while regulation M generally does not operate as a safe harbor (*see supra*, §1954), in the case of stabilization, **rule 104 is a safe harbor**. Stabilization is inherently manipulative and if rule 104 did not insulate stabilization from liability, all stabilizing activities would violate rule 10b-5.

(1) Trading generally prohibited [§1963]

Regulation of stabilization begins with a fundamental rule: Any stabilization in contravention of regulation M, rule 104 is prohibited.

(2) Stabilization permitted to prevent price decline [§1964]

Stabilization in support of a public distribution is permitted "for the purpose of preventing or retarding a decline in the market price of a security." [Regulation M, Rule 104(b)]

(a) Stabilizing price level [§1965]

Stabilization may not be made at a price higher than the highest independent bid price for the security. In no event may stabilization be made at a price higher than the offering price. The stabilizing bid may follow the market up and down, provided it does not exceed the offering price or the highest independent bid price. Offerings made "at the market," *i.e.*, at other than a set price, may not be stabilized. [Regulation M, Rule 104]

(b) Disclosure of stabilizing [§1966]

The fact that the underwriters may be stabilizing the price of an issued security must be disclosed to a purchaser at or before the completion of the transaction. In addition, if stabilization is contemplated, a specific disclosure of that fact must be made in the prospectus. The stabilizer must also report all actual stabilizing transactions to the S.E.C. [Regulation M, Rule 104(h); Regulation S-K, Item 502]

(3) "Shelf registrations" [§1967]

Stabilization problems sometimes arise in "shelf registrations," where the securities to be sold are offered over a significant period of time.

e.g. **Example:** Certain shareholders of Company S stock registered a secondary offering of their stock, to be sold at *various times* (thus making the offering a "shelf registration") at the "market price" by a specific broker-dealer, Jaffee & Co. The broker began to sell the stock, and while the offering was in progress, Jaffee himself (as an individual) made purchases of the stock. Likewise, other shelf shareholders made market purchases at times when they personally were not selling, but when the shelf shareholders as a group were still engaged in distributing the stock. The court held that Jaffee's activities violated rule 10b-6 (now regulation M, rule 104), and noted that as long as the selling group was engaged in the distribution, the danger of manipulation existed. [**In re Jaffee,** 44 S.E.C. 285 (1970), *aff'd and vacated in part,* **Jaffee & Co. v. S.E.C.,** 446 F.2d 387 (2d Cir. 1971)] *Note:* Because the offering was at the market, no stabilizing was permissible. [Regulation M, Rule 104(e); *see supra,* §1965]

(a) Coordination among shelf shareholders [§1968]

Probably the biggest problem raised by *Jaffee* was the suggestion that to avoid the prohibition on purchases during a distribution, the activities of the shelf shareholders had to be highly coordinated. That is, as long as *any* shelf shareholder was selling, the distribution was not over and it was unlawful for any other shelf shareholder to purchase.

(b) Modern S.E.C. view [§1969]

In 1986 the S.E.C. revised its interpretation so that the restricted period applies only to the individual activities of that shareholder. The same is true for the time the distribution is considered to end— for each shareholder, it ends when she has distributed all *her* shares.

1) Exception for affiliated shareholders [§1970]

The revised interpretation, however, does not apply to shareholders who are "affiliated purchasers" with the issuer or with other shareholders. "Affiliated purchasers" are defined as purchasers who either are acting in concert with the specified party, or are in a normal affiliate relationship with the party.

5. The "Hot Issue" Problem

a. "Hot issue" defined [§1971]

A "hot issue" is a security offered through a public distribution for which there is tremendous demand. Thus, a "hot issue" will typically be over-subscribed; *i.e.,* there will be more initial offers to purchase than there are shares available.

b. "Hot issue" problems [§1972]

Normally, a "hot issue" rises immediately to a premium price over the initial offering price at which it comes to the market. Underwriters and dealers may attempt to profit from this situation, to the detriment of the public, by:

(1) *Holding back a portion of the initial issue* to be sold, so that it can be sold later at higher prices;

(2) *Allocating part of the issue to employees, relatives,* etc., for later sale;

(3) *Allocating part of the issue to other broker-dealers*—who will immediately put quotes in the quotation services raising the price of the issue—and then, as demand rises, all parties (*i.e.,* the underwriters and cooperating broker-dealers) will sell to the public at a substantial premium over the stated offering price;

(4) *"Laddering"*—allocating shares in a hot issue only to customers who agree to purchase shares in the secondary market after the initial offering. This gives the aftermarket price a boost as customers fulfill their promises in the days after an offering. Customers who agree to such aftermarket purchases are not harmed by this practice, but it may injure the public, which purchases at the market price, knowing nothing of these contractual arrangements to maintain that price; or

(5) *"Spinning"*—allocating shares in a hot issue to those whom the underwriter wishes to court, because they might bring underwriting business back to the underwriter. For example, an underwriter might want to allocate generous portions in hot issues to the CEO of a company that will conduct a significant offering later in the year, or to partners of venture capital firms that can steer IPO business to the underwriter.

c. Violation of the securities acts [§1973]

The S.E.C. and the NASD consider all of the above practices to be violations of the securities acts. [SEA Release No. 6097 (1959)]

(1) Note

Possible violations include violation of sections 11 and 12(a)(2) of the 1933 Act for misrepresenting that the offering will be made *to the public*, at the offering price, and for not identifying the trading firms as underwriters; and the antifraud provisions of the 1934 Act, including rules 10b-5 and 15c1-8, and regulation M.

(2) Distinguish

It is not a violation of the "hot issue" rules for the dealers to sell the issue to relatives and friends where the stock (which appreciated rapidly) was held for investment (at least six months) and maintained or increased in price even after the original purchasers sold (*i.e.,* no one was left "holding the bag"). [*See* **In re Institutional Securities of Colorado**, S.E.C. Admin. Proc. File No. 3-5104 (1978)]

d. "Free riding" prohibited [§1974]

"Free riders" are another of the problems associated with hot issues. Free riding broadly refers to several different types of broker-dealer misconduct, all of which involve "riding" the market upward as the price of a hot issue rises. The NASD has adopted rules prohibiting free riding. [*See* NASD Manual (CCH) ¶2151.06] The NASD rules describe free riding as, among other things, holding back part of the allotment of the securities, selling the securities (at the offering price) to a person affiliated with the broker-dealer, or selling to others upon whom the broker-dealer wishes to bestow a favor. [*Id.*]

D. Regulation of Securities Analysts

1. Introduction [§1975]

In addition to regulating accountants and lawyers, SOXA regulates securities analysts. The problems that arose during 2001-2002 regarding analysts were independent of the problems regarding financial reporting, but they came at about the same time.

a. The analysis and research scandal [§1976]

In spring 2001, New York state investigators announced an investigation of securities analysts at several major securities firms. The analysts were allegedly compensated in part by fees generated from investment banking deals with the issuers; the more successful an issuer was in the markets, the more investment banking business the issuer would bring to the securities firm. Analysts, thus, were caught in a conflict of interest—favorable recommendations of an issuer's securities would generate business for the analyst's employer, in turn generating substantial bonuses and salary increases for the analyst. In this way, analysts were transformed from impartial researchers of a company's prospects to promoters of the company's stock. After the market bubble burst in 2000, analysts continued to issue optimistic forecasts for securities whose prices were plunging, prompting an investigation by the Attorney General of New York that was ultimately joined by federal regulators. Among other things, the investigators made public certain emails among analysts and other brokerage employees in which the analysts spoke derisively of securities they were simultaneously recommending to public investors. The ensuing scandal severely eroded investor confidence in the markets, and ultimately led to a settlement between regulators and the securities firms totaling approximately $1 billion.

2. Analysts and Regulation AC [§1977]

Reacting to the analyst scandal, SOXA includes provisions addressing analyst conflicts of interest. Section 501 of SOXA requires either the S.E.C. or the SROs to adopt rules regulating securities analysts and research reports. In spring 2003, the S.E.C. adopted regulation AC ("Analyst Certification"), pursuant to SOXA and the antifraud provisions of the 1933 and 1934 Acts. [S.E.C. Rel. Nos. 33-8193, 34-47384 (April 14, 2003)] Among other things, regulation AC requires:

a. Certification in written statements [§1978]

Written research reports must include:

(i) A certification that all of the views expressed in the research report *accurately reflect the analyst's personal views* about any and all of the subject securities or issuers; and

(ii) A statement attesting that the *analyst's compensation is not related to the specific recommendations or views expressed* in the research report, or, if that is not the case, *accurate disclosure of the source, amount, and purpose of such compensation*, and that the compensation could influence the recommendations or views expressed in the research report.

[Regulation AC, rule 501]

b. Certification regarding public appearances [§1979]

In addition to providing written research, analysts also often appear publicly to speak about their views of particular securities and issuers. In some respects, public appearances are even more fraught with danger than written reports; it is possible that investors would respond even more rapidly to a public appearance, for example on television, than to a written report. Accordingly, regulation AC *prohibits outright any analyst compensation based on the views the analyst expresses in a public appearance*. Under regulation AC, analysts must certify once each calendar quarter that:

(i) The views expressed by the analyst in all public appearances during the quarter accurately reflected the analyst's personal views at that time about any and all of the subject securities or issuers; and

(ii) That no part of the research analyst's compensation was, is, or will be, directly or indirectly, related to the specific recommendations or views expressed by the research analyst in the public appearances.

[Regulation AC, rule 502]

3. Additional SOXA Requirements Concerning Analysts and Research [§1980]

Regulation AC does not completely discharge the burden of analyst regulation under SOXA, and so more rulemaking is likely, either from the S.E.C. or from the SROs. Specifically, SOXA section 501 requires the S.E.C. to promulgate rules:

(i) Restricting prepublication clearance or approval of research reports by investment bankers or others not directly responsible for investment research (other than legal or compliance staff);

(ii) Prohibiting supervision and evaluation of analysts by investment bankers;

(iii) Prohibiting retaliation against analysts for negative or unfavorable reports that may adversely affect the securities firms' investment banking relationships;

(iv) Defining periods of time during which securities firms involved in a public offering are prohibited from publishing research reports related to the offered securities;

(v) Requiring disclosure by analysts of any investments they have in the issuer that is the subject of their report;

(vi) Establishing institutional protections for analysts against pressure from investment bankers;

(vii) Requiring disclosure whether an issuer whose securities are recommended in a report is, or in the past year has been, a customer of the securities firm;

(viii) Addressing other issues that the S.E.C. or SRO deems appropriate.

[SOXA §501; SEA §15D]

E. Regulation of Broker-Dealer Trading Activities

1. Registration of Broker-Dealers with the S.E.C. [§1981]

The 1934 Act provides for registration with the S.E.C. of all broker-dealers who engage in securities transactions in interstate commerce (unless they deal exclusively in exempt securities).

a. Definition of broker and dealer [§1982]

Section 3 of the 1934 Act defines "broker" and "dealer."

(1) *A broker* is a person engaged "in the business of" effecting transactions in securities for the account of others. [SEA §3(a)(4)]

(2) *A dealer* is a person engaged "in the business of" buying and selling securities for his own account, but does not include such persons when they are not doing so as part of "a regular business." [SEA §3(a)(5)]

(3) *What is a "regular business"* is a fact question, but the buying and selling would have to be fairly regular to qualify. Thus, a single, isolated transaction does not qualify. [**De Bruin v. Andromeda Broadcasting Systems Inc.**, 465 F. Supp. 1276 (D. Nev. 1979)]

b. A "security" must be sold [§1983]

For the provisions of the 1934 Act relating to brokers and dealers to apply, a "security," as defined in the 1934 Act, must be involved. The definition in the 1934 Act is only slightly different from that of the 1933 Act. [*See* SEA §3(a)(10)]

c. Requirement of registration [§1984]

Section 15(a) of the 1934 Act forbids a broker or dealer who does any interstate business to use the mails or any means or instrumentality of interstate commerce to effect any transaction in, or to induce or attempt to induce the purchase or sale of, securities (other than securities exempted under the 1934 Act), unless the broker or dealer is registered with the S.E.C. under section 15(a) of the Act.

(1) Note

This section exempts broker-dealers *whose business is exclusively* intrastate. The interpretation of what is intrastate turns principally on the location of the broker-dealer's customers. [SEA §15(a)(1)]

d. Regulation by the S.E.C. [§1985]

Under section 15(b) of the 1934 Act, the S.E.C. has established qualification standards for registration of all brokers and dealers and any persons associated with them. Registration subjects the registrant to certain standards of operational capability, training, experience, and competence. It also subjects the broker-dealer to the requirement of passing certain examinations relating to the securities business and to maintaining certain financial stability standards. Registered broker-dealers must also file periodic reports with the S.E.C. Finally, the S.E.C. may, on notice and after a hearing, censure, suspend, or revoke the registration of any broker or dealer for statutory violations.

2. Sources of Authority to Regulate [§1986]

Besides direct regulation by the S.E.C., broker-dealers may also be subject to indirect regulation through the regulation of organizations of which the broker-dealers are members.

a. Self-regulation [§1987]

The 1934 Act provides for the self-regulation of registered broker-dealers through a registered national securities association, the National Association of Securities Dealers ("NASD"), subject to supervision and review by the S.E.C. [SEA §15(a); *and see supra*, §§1903 *et seq.*]

b. Regulation by national stock exchanges [§1988]

As noted above (*see supra*, §1837), the 1934 Act requires national securities exchanges to regulate their members, and the S.E.C. exercises supervisory power over such regulation.

c. Regulation of investment advisers [§1989]

An "investment adviser" is one who engages in the business of advising others whether to invest in, purchase, or sell securities. While investment advisers do not perform the same functions as broker-dealers, they do occupy an important position in the securities business where they are trusted by, and able to take advantage of, those purchasing and selling securities. For this reason, the S.E.C. regulates the activities of such advisers pursuant to the Investment Advisers Act of 1940.

3. Regulation Under General Antifraud Provisions [§1990]

The 1934 Act contains several general antifraud provisions (*e.g.*, rules 10b-5 and 15c1-2) that regulate the activities of broker-dealers. Section 17(a) of the 1933 Act (*see supra*, §854) is similar to these antifraud provisions; its language is essentially the same language used in rules 10b-5 and 15c1-2.

a. Comparison of antifraud provisions [§1991]

The differences between the three antifraud provisions are summarized in the chart below:

A COMPARISON OF ANTIFRAUD PROVISIONS **gilbert**				
PROVISION	APPLICABLE TO SALES OF SECURITIES?	APPLICABLE TO PURCHASES?	APPLICABLE TO BROKER-DEALERS?	APPLICABLE TO OTHER PERSONS?
SA §17(a)	Yes	No	Yes	Yes
SEA RULE 10b-5	Yes	Yes	Yes	Yes
SEA RULE 15c1-2	Yes	Yes	Yes	No (only to broker-dealers)

b. Requirement of intent [§1992]

The language of the above provisions seems to require that actions brought thereunder be based on a showing of actual fraud by the defendant (*i.e.*, intentional fraudulent conduct or misrepresentations) for plaintiff to recover. However, the Supreme Court has held that *in S.E.C. civil injunctive actions*, a cause of action may be proved only by showing scienter under section 17(a)(1), but that *negligence is sufficient under section 17(a)(2) and (3)*. (*See* the discussion *supra*, §858.) Also, there is considerable doubt as to whether a private cause of action will be implied pursuant to section 17(a) (*see supra*, §857).

(1) "Shingle theory" [§1993]

Also, the courts have held that when a broker-dealer goes into business (*i.e.*, "hangs out its shingle"), it impliedly represents that it will deal fairly and competently with its customers, and that there will be an adequate basis for any statement (*e.g.*, as to a security's value) or recommendations it makes to its customers. This "shingle theory" sometimes allows a court to find a cause of action against a broker-dealer under one of the three statutes mentioned above where an intentional misstatement or omission by the broker-dealer might not otherwise be proved. [**Charles Hughes & Co. v. S.E.C.,** 139 F.2d 434 (2d Cir. 1943)] In effect, the "intent" is proved by showing that defendant intentionally *did an act* that was unlawful, not that defendant intentionally committed fraud.

Example: Where a broker-dealer made optimistic statements to its customers about a security without having any actual basis for doing so, the broker-dealer was held liable. [*In re* **Alexander Reid & Co.,** SEA Release No. 6727 (1962)]

Example: Likewise where a broker-dealer sold securities to a customer at a price far in excess of their market value, without disclosing the actual market value, it was held liable. [**Charles Hughes & Co. v. S.E.C.,** *supra*]

Compare: A broker-dealer's implied representation about the value of a security probably does not amount to an absolute warranty, giving rise to liability if the security turns out to be worth less than the price the customer paid for it. Thus, the broker-dealer is probably not liable for unavoidable errors of fact. However, the broker-dealer must act "reasonably" and in "good faith"—*i.e.,* the broker-dealer must at least not be negligent in recommending the security to the client. [*See* **S.E.C. v. Capital Gains Research Bureau,** 375 U.S. 180 (1963)—action under the Investment Advisers Act of 1940; **Charles Hughes & Co. v. S.E.C.,** *supra*]

(2) Not as rigidly applied in private actions [§1994]

The "shingle theory" is probably not as rigidly applied in private actions against defendant broker-dealers; *i.e.,* in private actions, the plaintiff may have to prove actual fraudulent intent. However, in disciplinary actions brought by the S.E.C., the "shingle theory" is usually vigorously enforced. [**Hanly v. S.E.C.,** 415 F.2d 589 (2d Cir. 1969)]

EXAM TIP   **gilbert**

If an exam question raises the liability of a broker or dealer for false statements, don't forget to mention the "shingle theory" in your analysis. The "shingle theory" lowers the level of intent that must be proved *in an action by the government*: The government need only show that the defendant intentionally did an act that was unlawful; it need not show that the defendant intended fraud. The theory is based on an implied assumption that when a broker or dealer hangs out its shingle, it promises to *deal fairly and competently* with customers. *But note:* The theory probably is *not applicable in a private cause of action*.

4. Regulating Conflicts of Interest [§1995]

The S.E.C. has focused on several basic areas in its supervision of broker-dealers: situations where there is a conflict of interest between the broker-dealer and the client's financial interest; situations where the broker-dealer makes a recommendation to a client without adequate information; and situations where the broker-dealer has failed to adequately supervise the activities of those involved in his firm. This section discusses common conflict of interest problems.

a. Dealer markups [§1996]

When securities are listed on a national exchange, or traded in the NASDAQ system, customers have ready access to up-to-date price information. However, for OTC securities not traded in the NASDAQ system, customers may not have access to price information. This enables dealers to mark up excessively the prices of securities sold to the customer.

(1) NASD policy regarding markups [§1997]

The NASD has adopted a policy that its members may neither effect securities transactions at a price "not reasonably related to the current market price of the security" nor charge an unreasonable commission. [NASD Rules, art. III, §§1, 4]

(a) Five percent markup policy [§1998]

The NASD has indicated that a markup (*i.e.*, an increase over the market price to dealers or over the dealer's actual cost) of 5% (10% in the case of low-priced securities) would probably not violate sections 1 and 4 of the NASD rules. The following factors, however, are to be considered in determining whether a markup is "reasonable":

(i) *The type of* security involved;

(ii) *The availability* of the security in the market generally;

(iii) *The unit price* of the security;

(iv) *The total amount of dollars involved* in the transaction;

(v) *Whether disclosure of the markup is made* to the customer;

(vi) *The pattern of the broker-dealer's markups*; and

(vii) *The types of services and facilities* offered by the broker-dealer.

[*See generally* **Lehl v. S.E.C.**, *supra*, §1907; NASD Notice to Members 92-16 (1992); **Kevin B. Waide**, 51 S.E.C. 252 (1992); **LSCO Securities., Inc.**, SEA Release No. 34-28,994 (1991); **Alstead Dempsey & Co.**, 47 S.E.C. 1034 (1984)]

(b) Markup base [§1999]

The NASD rules indicate that the markup is to be based on the "market price" *or,* where evidence of market price is not available, on the broker-dealer's own contemporaneous cost.

Example: Appropriate markup bases include (i) the broker-dealer's cost for security purchases and sales occurring on the same day, and (ii) the "ask quotations" published in the quotation sheets of the National Daily Quotations Bureau, where the broker-dealer did not make any purchases and sales on the same day. One court stated that although the "ask quotations" are not firm offers to sell, they are prima facie evidence of market value. [**Merritt, Vickers, Inc. v. S.E.C.**, 353 F.2d 293 (2d Cir. 1965)]

---

1) Cost used as base [§2000]

If the base used for markups is the broker-dealer's cost, the markup rule might limit the broker's ability to earn profits on his dealer transactions. For this reason, the court in *Merritt, Vickers, Inc.* used cost as a basis only for a transaction where the broker-dealer bought the stock (*e.g.,* at $5 per share) and sold it on the same day (where a selling price of $5.25 would represent a 5% markup). In other transactions, the courts approved using quotes on market prices as a basis for markups.

Example: If a broker-dealer bought the stock of XYZ Corp. on January 1 at $5 per share, and held it until March 1 when its "market price" was quoted at $10 per share, it could base its selling price on a markup of 5%—*i.e.,* a sales price of $10.50 per share—without violating the rules.

---

2) Market price used as base [§2001]

For securities traded on the NASDAQ, determining the market price is simply a matter of surveying the NASDAQ-quoted prices, much as would be done for exchange-traded securities. But for securities traded neither on an exchange nor on the NASDAQ, it can be more difficult to determine what the market price is.

a) NASD requirements [§2002]

Since 1988, the NASD requires broker-dealers to mark customer order tickets for each transaction in a non-NASDAQ, non-exchange-traded security, to show the name of each dealer contacted and the price quotation received, in order to determine the prevailing market price. [NASD Notice to Members 88-33 (1988)]

b) Determining market price [§2003]

In a 1988 interpretation restating its "5% rule" (*see supra,* §1998), the NASD set out four factors for determining the market price for a security:

1/ Competitive market [§2004]

If the securities trade in a competitive market, the prices paid by other dealers to the market-maker whose markup is being reviewed should be the basis for the markup.

2/ Broker-dealers trading as principals with clients [§2005]

A market-maker dealing with a client as a principal is entitled only to the "inside spread"; *i.e.,* the best available price (to another dealer) is used to calculate the markup. If the dealer is not making a market in the security, its cost is used as the basis for the markup.

3/ No independent market for the security [§2006]

If the market-maker dominates the market, or there is otherwise no independent market for the security, the market-maker's contemporaneous cost should be used as the basis for calculating the markup.

4/ Price quotes [§2007]

A dominant market-maker should never use its own quoted price as the basis for a markup, but instead should use its actual contemporaneous cost.

3) Burden of proof [§2008]

The burden of proof is on the broker-dealer to show special circumstances justifying an "excessive" markup. [**Merritt, Vickers, Inc. v. S.E.C.,** *supra*]

(2) S.E.C. policy [§2009]

There are no specific S.E.C. rules against excessive markups, but the S.E.C. has regulated markups via the general antifraud provisions of the 1934 Act.

---

e.g. **Example:** A dealer who sold securities at a price substantially higher than the prevailing market price was held to violate rule 10b-5, because the dealer made a false "implied representation" that its price bore a reasonable relationship to the market price. [**Charles Hughes & Co. v. S.E.C.,** *supra,* §1993]

(a) **Fraud per se [§2010]**

The S.E.C. considers a markup of more than 10% of the prevailing market price to be fraud per se. [*See, e.g.,* **Alstead Dempsey & Co.,** SEA Release No. 34-20825 (1984)]

(b) **Offer quotations from other dealers [§2011]**

Although the NASD relies to some extent on price quotes from other dealers to establish the prevailing market price (*see supra*), the S.E.C. considers such quotations unreliable and whenever possible uses the dealer's contemporaneous cost. [**Lehl v. S.E.C.,** *supra,* §1998; **Alstead Dempsey & Co.,** *supra*]

(c) **Rule 10b-10 [§2012]**

Rule 10b-10 requires broker-dealers to disclose price-related information to the customer on the order ticket. In some cases, the markup must be disclosed; in other cases, the dealer must disclose whom it contacted and what prices were quoted in order to inform the customer about the basis for the asserted market price. [SEA Rule 10b-10; *and see infra,* §2020]

b. **Underwriter's compensation [§2013]**

Many states have securities laws limiting the amount and type of compensation that an underwriter may receive in an original distribution of securities. The NASD also has undertaken to regulate underwriter compensation and requires that such compensation be fair and consistent with just and equitable principles of trade. [NASD Rules, art. III, §1]

(1) **Standard [§2014]**

Compensation received by the underwriter must be "*fair and reasonable*" under all of the circumstances (taking into consideration the size of the offering, the type of security, the type of underwriting, etc.). [NASD underwriting guidelines, NASD Manual (CCH) ¶2151.02]

(2) **Advance review [§2015]**

Underwriting agreements for "unseasoned" companies (new companies or those without an established earnings record) must be reviewed by the NASD in advance of the underwriting.

(3) **Compensation factors and guidelines**

(a) **Excessive compensation [§2016]**

Compensation that exceeds 18 to 20% of the gross dollar amount received by the issuer in the offering will probably be held to be excessive.

(b) **What is included in "compensation" [§2017]**

All types of the issuer's securities received or purchased (prior to, at the time of, or subsequent to the underwriting) by the underwriter may be considered part of the underwriter's compensation. The rule of thumb is that securities amounting to no more than 10% of the total number of shares offered by the issuer may be received by the underwriter as compensation.

(c) Other factors [§2018]

Other factors involved in underwriter compensation are expenses payable by the issuer, cash commissions received, consulting and advisory fees, optiomns and warrants granted to the underwriter, etc.

EXAM TIP   **gilbert**

If an exam question raises underwriter compensation as an issue, remember that the basic standard is *"fair and reasonable"* compensation. Generally, compensation greater than 18-20% of the gross amount that the issuer will receive is excessive, and compensation generally should not include more than 10% of the securities being issued.

---

(4) Resale price maintenance [§2019]

The typical underwriting agreement requires all underwriters and members of the selling group to adhere to the public offering price as stated in the prospectus. Furthermore, the NASD has rules that prohibit various forms of price discounting in underwritings (such as by having a purchaser swap securities above their market value for securities being offered in the underwriting). [SEA Release No. 15807 (1979)] The S.E.C. has upheld the right of the NASD to enforce such administrative rules. [SEA Release No. 16956 (1980)]

c. Duty to disclose nature of relationship [§2020]

Broker-dealers may also be in a position of conflict with their customers' interests where they are representing their own or others' interests in the same transaction. Therefore, under SEA Rule 10b-10, broker-dealers are required to furnish their customers with written confirmation of securities transactions entered into on behalf of the customer, and these confirmations must disclose the nature of the broker-dealer's relationship to the customer—*i.e.,* whether it is acting as broker for the customer, as dealer for its own account, as broker for some other person, or as broker for both the customer and some other person. Where the broker-dealer is acting as an agent, it must also disclose the source and amount of any commission received. [SEA Rule 10b-10, *and see* NASD art. III, §12]

Example—acting in dual capacity: A broker-dealer who failed to disclose to customers that it was acting as agent for *both* the seller and the buyer of the same securities, and therefore was receiving a double commission, was held to have violated article III, section 12 of the NASD rules. [**Merritt, Vickers, Inc. v. S.E.C.**, *supra*, §1999]

---

d. Duty to disclose role as market-maker [§2021]

Failure by a broker-dealer to disclose the fact that it is making a market in stocks it has recommended to a customer may also be in violation of the 1934 Act.

(1) Function of a market-maker [§2022]

A "market-maker" is a broker-dealer who publishes (either in the NASDAQ or other quotation service) bona fide "two-way" quotations with respect to any other over-the-counter security. This means that the broker-dealer is quoting both a bid price (the price at which it will buy the security) and an ask price (the price at which it is willing to sell the security).

(a) Note

Functioning as a market-maker also implies that the broker-dealer stands ready to either buy or sell a given security in reasonable quantities. Usually the broker-dealer is carrying an inventory of the security for its own account as well.

(b) And note

The market-maker may also engage in simultaneous transactions, where it buys from one customer and sells to another. Such transactions are subject to the NASD "markup" policy discussed *supra*, §1997.

(2) Single market-makers [§2023]

Where a broker-dealer is the only firm making a market in a security (*i.e.*, the only firm regularly quoted as willing to buy and sell the security), there will be no market for the security other than that created by the broker-dealer. A single market-maker may not represent to its customers that transactions in the security are made at the market price. [SEA Rule 15c1-8]

(a) Close scrutiny [§2024]

This situation often occurs in the over-the-counter market, and any price representations made to customers will be closely scrutinized.

(b) Duty to disclose [§2025]

In addition, if there is only one market-maker in a particular security, the market-maker must disclose its role and the noncompetitive nature of the market to its customers. [**S.E.C. v. First Jersey Securities, Inc.**, 101 F.3d 1450 (2d Cir. 1996)]

(c) Shingle theory applies [§2026]

Under the general antifraud provisions, every sale by a broker-dealer carries with it the implied representation that the price is reasonably related to that prevailing in the open market. (*See supra*, §1993.)

(3) Multiple market-makers [§2027]

Even when there are several firms making a market, it is still necessary for a broker-dealer to disclose its position as a market-maker to its customers in order to avoid liability. Under rule 10b-5, for example, this is a *material fact* that must be disclosed. [**Chasins v. Smith, Barney & Co.,** 438 F.2d 1167 (2d Cir. 1971)]

(a) Note

In *Chasins,* the defendant broker-dealer *had* disclosed its role as principal in the transaction. Nevertheless, the court held that defendant's failure to disclose its position as a market-maker violated the securities laws.

(b) Comment

Chasins was controversial when it was decided. Since then, however, SEA rule 10b-10 mandates disclosure of the information required by *Chasins.*

e. Duty to fulfill expected role as agent [§2028]

Where a broker-dealer has implied in its dealings with customers that it is acting as an agent for them, it is a violation for the broker-dealer to trade with its customers as a principal, even if this fact is disclosed in the written confirmations. [*In re* **Norris & Hirshberg, Inc.,** 177 F.2d 228 (D.C. Cir. 1949)— broker-dealer traded as principal with its customers' discretionary accounts, without disclosing that it was acting as a dealer]

f. Duty of best execution [§2029]

Broker-dealers have a duty to "use reasonable diligence to ascertain the best interdealer market of the subject security and to buy or sell in such market so that the resultant price to the customer is as favorable as possible under the prevailing market conditions." [NASD Conduct Rule 2320] While this does not ordinarily present problems, there are occasions (*e.g.,* when a stock is not traded on the NASDAQ system) when the best market can be difficult to identify. Disputes over this rule most often arise between customers and broker-dealers and are resolved through arbitration (to which broker-dealers require their customers to agree, when the latter open their accounts).

g. Prohibition against causing sales [§2030]

It is also unlawful for a broker-dealer to cause, or attempt to cause, a customer to enter into a transaction not actually agreed upon, *e.g.,* by sending a written confirmation of a sale that the customer did not agree to. [NASD Manual (CCH) ¶2152]

(1) Regulatory provisions [§2031]

"False confirmations" are prohibited by article III, sections 1 and 18 of the NASD rules. Such conduct also violates the general antifraud sections of the 1934 Act.

Example: Approximately 5% of the confirmations sent by a broker-dealer were canceled. The sales had been solicited by telephone calls. The S.E.C. found these facts to constitute a violation. [*In re* **Palombi Securities Co.,** SEA Release No. 6961 (1962)]

h. Prohibition against "churning" [§2032]

The 1934 Act also prohibits "churning," *i.e.,* excessive trading by a broker-dealer in a customer's account, for the primary purpose of generating commission income. [SEA Rule 15c1-7] Churning is facilitated when the broker-dealer has discretionary accounts for which it may effect trades without prior approval of the customer.

(1) Question of fact [§2033]

Whether the broker-dealer is guilty of churning is a question of fact. The key issue is whether the trading has been so excessive as to indicate that the primary purpose of the trading was to generate commissions for the broker. [**Hecht v. Harris, Upham & Co.,** 430 F.2d 1202 (9th Cir. 1970)]

(a) Elements of churning [§2034]

The decision whether churning has occurred must be based on consideration of all the relevant facts; no set turnover rate, commission ratio, etc., constitutes churning as a matter of law. To establish a claim of churning, the customer must show that: (i) the trading in her account was excessive in light of her investment objectives; (ii) the broker exercised control over the trading in the account; and (iii) the broker acted with the intent to defraud or with willful and reckless disregard for the interests of the client. [**Nesbit v. McNeil,** 896 F.2d 380 (9th Cir. 1990)]

Example: Where the account in question represented less than one-tenth of 1% of the original dollar volume in the broker-dealer's office, but generated 5% of the total commissions, the court found the broker-dealer guilty of churning. [**Hecht v. Harris, Upham & Co.,** *supra*]

> **Example:** Churning was found when trades over an 11-year period increased the value of an account by almost $183,000, but commissions on the numerous transactions aggregated $250,000. [**Nesbit v. McNeil,** *supra*]

> **Compare:** Where the investor's purpose was "short-term" profits, and all investments were closely supervised, the court concluded that the broker-dealer could *not* be held liable for churning. [**Marshak v. Blyth, Eastman, Dillon & Co.,** 413 F. Supp. 377 (N.D. Okla. 1975)]

(2) Duty of the customer [§2035]

The plaintiff in a rule 10b-5 cause of action for churning will recover if churning occurred unless (considering all of the facts) the plaintiff was guilty of recklessness or worse in not discovering or terminating the broker's activity. [**Petrites v. J.C. Bradford & Co.,** 696 F.2d 1033 (5th Cir. 1981)]

(3) Scope of doctrine [§2036]

Churning is not limited merely to accounts over which the broker-dealer has been given discretionary authority. It may be found in any appropriate situation where a broker, by virtue of the trust and reliance placed in her by the customer, is able to determine the volume and frequency of sales. [*In re* **Norris & Hirshberg, Inc.,** *supra*, §2028]

(4) Liability of broker-dealer [§2037]

If a salesperson is guilty of churning, the broker-dealer may also be liable for failure to exercise adequate control (pursuant to SEA section 20). [*See* **Kravitz v. Pressman, Frohlich & Frost, Inc.,** 447 F. Supp. 203 (D. Mass. 1978)]

(5) Damages [§2038]

Normally, the plaintiff customer may recover the total amount of commission paid on the securities transactions in question. The older cases held that no damages could be recovered for losses in the market value of the securities purchased. [*See, e.g.,* **Hecht v. Harris, Upham & Co.,** *supra*] The better view (and the current trend) is that a customer who can demonstrate harm to the value of her portfolio can recover damages for that harm, as well as the excessive commissions paid to the broker. [**Nesbit v. McNeil,** *supra*]

(a) Punitive damages may be available [§2039]

In some cases, courts have awarded punitive damages for churning.

> **Example:** An account belonging to an 87-year-old widow was churned. The account increased in value by some $53,000,

but the court found that it would have increased an additional $56,000 had it not been churned. The plaintiff was awarded $44,000 in damages for the churning (representing excessive commissions generated by the churning), plus $56,000 for the reduced performance of the account, plus $2 million in punitive damages. [**Davis v. Merrill Lynch, Pierce, Fenner & Smith, Inc.,** 906 F.2d 1206 (8th Cir. 1990)]

5. Broker-Dealers' Duty to Disclose Adequate Information [§2040]

One of the major regulatory purposes of the federal securities laws is requiring full disclosure of relevant information to potential investors. The 1933 Act requires public issuers to make full disclosure to investors. The 1934 Act requires issuers, and others trading in securities registered under the Act, to provide full disclosure in certain situations; it also requires broker-dealers to ascertain and disclose relevant information in making recommendations to clients.

a. "Boiler room" operations [§2041]

A "boiler room" operation is a high-pressure securities sales operation (*e.g.,* by unsolicited telephone calls) in which the broker-dealer typically provides inadequate or false information to its salespeople concerning the security being sold. Normally the securities of only a single issuer are involved.

(1) Proceeding against broker-dealer [§2042]

The 1934 Act authorizes the S.E.C. to shut down a boiler room operation by revoking the broker-dealer's license. To be successful, the S.E.C. must be able to prove that the broker-dealer *willfully* violated the securities laws. [SEA §15(b)]

(2) Proceeding against individual salespeople [§2043]

Prior to 1964, statutory law provided that broker-dealers registered with the NASD could not hire (without prior approval of the S.E.C.) any sales representative who had been found to "cause" the revocation of a broker-dealer's registration. This was a form of "indirect control" of the individual salesperson responsible for violating the securities acts, because nothing in the law authorized the S.E.C. to proceed directly against him.

Example: Berko, a salesman, participated in a high pressure telephone campaign to sell 100,000 shares of a company's securities. A brochure sent out to potential customers contained substantial misrepresentations about the company's financial condition. The S.E.C. found that rules 10b-5 and 15c1-2, as well as section 17(a) of the 1933 Act, had been violated and revoked the registration of the broker-dealer that employed Berko. Besides using the misleading sales information provided by the broker-dealer, Berko made additional representations that the stock would double in price in a year, without having adequate information as to the financial condition of the company. The court approved the S.E.C.'s finding that Berko caused the revocation of the broker-dealer's registration, and, therefore, no other registered securities firm could hire Berko without the S.E.C.'s approval. [**Berko v. S.E.C.,** 316 F.2d 137 (2d Cir. 1963)]

(a) Salesperson must be cautious [§2044]

In selling securities of an unknown issuer, a salesperson cannot rely without independent verification on information given him by the broker-dealer (as he might do in a different type of sales operation dealing with an established company's securities).

(b) Profit not a defense [§2045]

It makes no difference in such a nondisclosure case that some of the salesperson's customers may have actually profited by his recommendations.

(c) Direct action against salesperson [§2046]

In 1964, the 1934 Act was amended to allow the S.E.C. to proceed directly against "any person" (including the broker-dealer's individual salesperson), and to censure or bar him from associating with *any* broker-dealer if he has willfully violated the securities acts. [SEA §15(b)(6)]

1) Note

The S.E.C. can also proceed for revocation against the employer broker-dealer in a boiler room operation under section 15(b)(4)(E), on a charge that the employer has "wilfully aided, abetted, counseled, commanded, induced or procured the violation" by the employee.

(d) Private cause of action [§2047]

Customers who were damaged by the purchase of misrepresented securities can bring a private suit for damages or rescission against the salesperson under rule 10b-5.

b. Suitability—the "know thy customer" rules [§2048]

Both the NASD and the New York Stock Exchange have adopted rules that prohibit a broker from recommending securities to a customer unless the broker has reasonable grounds to believe that the *securities are appropriate for the customer* in light of the customer's other securities holdings, her financial situation, and other relevant data. [Art. III, §2, NASD Manual (CCH) ¶2152; NYSE Rule 405, NYSE Manual (CCH) ¶2405] While "churning" claims focus on the quantity of trading, suitability claims focus on the quality of the securities purchased for the customer.

(1) Duty applies to salespeople [§2049]

The cases have made it clear that this rule applies independently to all individual salespeople employed by a broker-dealer, as well as the broker-dealer itself. [**Hanly v. S.E.C.**, *supra*, §1994; *and see supra*, §1993]

(2) Duty to investigate [§2050]

In light of the "know thy customer" rules, what investigation, if any, must a broker make in order to discover information about the customer?

(a) NASD rules do not require investigation [§2051]

The NASD "know thy customer" rule does not expressly require a broker to investigate the customer's financial situation. [*See* Art. III, §2, NASD Manual (CCH) ¶2152]

(b) NYSE rules require investigation [§2052]

The New York Stock Exchange rules, however, require the broker to investigate "the essential facts relative to every customer." The broker's recommendations to the customer must be reasonable in light of these "essential facts." [*See* NYSE Rule 405, NYSE Manual (CCH) ¶2405]

(3) Violations of the rules [§2053]

The following actions are typical violations of the NYSE or NASD rules:

(a) *Recommending a speculative security to someone seeking a "safe" investment.*

(b) *Inducing a customer to withdraw interest-bearing funds prior to the interest date* in order to buy a misrepresented and speculative security. [*In re* **Boren & Co.**, SEA Release No. 6367 (1960)]

(c) *Failing to instruct sales employees about the "suitability" requirement,* and failing to adequately supervise its application. [*In re* **Boren & Co.**, *supra*]

(d) *Making optimistic statements or absolute representations* about the prospects of a company, *without any adequate basis in fact,* to convince the customer that the security involved fits her needs. [**Kahn v. S.E.C.**, 297 F.2d 112 (2d Cir. 1961)]

(e) *Making recommendations reflecting an undue acceptance of management's statements and financial projections without investigation,* failing to investigate "red flags" and "warning signals," and failing to disclose known adverse information. [*See* **Merrill Lynch, Pierce, Fenner & Smith, Inc.**, SEA Release No. 14149 (1977)]

(4) Scope of duty [§2054]

Difficult questions may arise concerning the scope of the broker-dealer's duty to ascertain suitability, especially concerning speculative securities and in situations where there is little or no reliance on the broker-dealer's recommendations.

(a) Speculative securities [§2055]

Speculative securities involve a greater degree of risk; they are not suitable for all investors. And because the customer is more likely to lose money in speculative securities than in more conservative securities, speculative securities are more likely to generate litigation. Courts are thus often confronted with customers who invest in speculative securities, lose money, and then sue the broker, claiming that speculative securities were an inappropriate investment. Often, the broker's defense is that (i) the customer's instructions were to invest in the speculative securities, and (ii) the customer is seeking the best of both worlds—potentially large gains from speculation *and* recourse to the broker's pocket if the investment loses money.

(b) Lack of reliance [§2056]

Does the scope of the broker-dealer's duty to ascertain suitability change, depending on the type of relationship that exists between the broker and the customer? In other words, do factors such as the duration of the relationship, sophistication of the customer, etc.—which tend to indicate whether the customer relied on the broker's judgment—affect the scope of the broker's duty?

---

e.g. **Example:** In applying the "shingle theory" (*supra*, §1993) to a security salesperson, one court indicated that the fact that the investor was sophisticated or did not actually rely on the salesperson's statements was *irrelevant*.

(i) The court went on to hold that even in situations where the customer does not rely on the broker, a salesperson may not make statements without adequate information. Furthermore, the salesperson is required to disclose any lack of essential information and the risks that arise therefrom.

(ii) The salesperson is also required to undertake a reasonable investigation and reveal what information is reasonably ascertainable. A recommendation implies that a reasonable investigation has been made and that the recommendation is based on the results thereof.

[**Hanly v. S.E.C.**, *supra*, §1994]

---

(5) Duty where customer has investment adviser [§2057]

Brokers often execute trades suggested by investment advisers. The broker can still be liable in these situations for improper recommendations. [*See* **Rolf v. Blyth, Eastman, Dillon & Co.,** 570 F.2d 38 (2d Cir.), *cert. denied,* 439 U.S. 1039 (1978)—broker suggested adviser who made recommendations which were executed by the broker; portfolio dropped from $1.4 million to $225,000]

(a) But note

Rolf should not be seen as establishing a duty of the broker to inquire about suitability in all situations. In *Rolf*, the broker was charged by the customer with supervising the investment adviser (not merely executing orders); the broker was aware that the adviser was buying "junk"; and the broker advised the client that the adviser's suggestions were consistent with the client's investment goals (when they were not).

(6) Implied causes of action for violating the suitability rules [§2058]

Although some cases have permitted actions by private plaintiffs based on violation of SRO suitability rules [*see, e.g.,* **Buttrey v. Merrill Lynch, Pierce, Fenner & Smith, Inc.,** *supra,* §1894], most courts today do not permit such actions [*see, e.g.,* **Jablon v. Dean Witter & Co.,** 614 F.2d 677 (9th Cir. 1980)].

(a) Rule 10b-5 actions based on unsuitability [§2059]

A plaintiff may, however, base a rule 10b-5 action on the unsuitability of securities purchased for her account. This can be analyzed in at least two ways:

1) Traditional misrepresentation or omission [§2060]

Under one approach, the broker has simply omitted telling the customer that the securities recommended or purchased were unsuitable. This analysis proceeds in accordance with the traditional elements of a rule 10b-5 action (*see supra,* §§946 *et seq.*).

2) Fraud by conduct [§2061]

Another approach views the purchase of unsuitable securities as fraud by conduct. The following elements must be established by the plaintiff to prove fraud by conduct based on unsuitability:

(i) The *broker recommended or purchased securities that were unsuitable* in light of the customer's objectives;

(ii) The broker *acted with an intent to defraud* or with reckless disregard for the customer's interests (scienter); and

(iii) The *broker exercised control* over the customer's account.

[**O'Connor v. R.F. Lafferty & Co.,** 965 F.2d 893 (10th Cir. 1992)]

EXAM TIP   **gilbert**

The *"know thy customer" rule* may rear its head on your exam. The rule prohibits a broker from recommending securities to a customer unless the broker has *reasonable grounds to believe that the securities are appropriate for the customer*. Remember that the scope of the duties under the rule are unclear and not necessarily consistent from exchange to exchange (*e.g.,* the NYSE requires brokers to investigate their customers' needs; the NASD does not). In any case, the fact that the customer did not rely on the broker's statement or that the customer had an investment adviser other than the broker will not necessarily let the broker off the hook (*e.g.,* where the broker recommended the investment adviser). Remember also that violation of the rule generally is *not* actionable by a private plaintiff unless the broker's conduct also violates rule 10b-5.

---

c.   **Duty of broker-dealers in submitting quotations [§2062]**
The S.E.C. has imposed a duty of care on broker-dealers in the submission of quotations on over-the-counter securities to any interdealer quotation system or in any other publication of such quotations. [SEA Rule 15c2-11]

(1) Permissible quotes [§2063]
A broker-dealer may not give a quote on over-the-counter securities that are not quoted on the NASDAQ unless:

(a)   *The issuer has registered its securities* under the 1933 or 1934 Acts and is current in filing the required reports under the 1934 Act; *or*

(b)   *The broker-dealer has obtained, and makes available* to any person on request, *certain financial information* relating to the issuer.

   1)   When the broker-dealer is permitted to give a quote on this latter basis, it must have no reasonable basis for believing that the information is untrue or incorrect. In addition, the information must be obtained from sources that the broker-dealer has a reasonable basis for believing to be reliable.

   2)   This obligation does *not* impose a duty on the broker-dealer to investigate the accuracy of information (other than to believe in the reliability of the source), but the threat of liability tends to make broker-dealers more conservative as to the types of securities in which they deal.

6. Broker-Dealer's Duty to Supervise [§2064]

The 1934 Act provides for censure or, alternatively, denial, suspension, or revocation of a broker-dealer's registration, for failure to adequately supervise its associates (*i.e.,* salespeople and employees) if the result is a violation of the securities acts. [SEA §15(b)(4)(E)]

a. NASD rules [§2065]

The NASD rules also require the registered principal (*i.e.,* the person in charge of the broker-dealer organization) to supervise all transactions and correspondence of its employees. [NASD Rules, art. II, §27] The following have been found to be violations of the duty to supervise:

(i) Failure to properly instruct employees *about the difference between principal and agency transactions;*

(ii) Failure to instruct employees about the *"know thy customer" rule* (*i.e.,* that the security sold to a customer must be suitable to the customer's needs);

(iii) Failure to adequately *explain sales literature;* and

(iv) Failure of the principal to *approve correspondence* by employees.

[*In re* **Boren & Co.,** *supra*, §2053—the above were found to be violations of both NASD Supervision Rules and the 1934 Act as inconsistent with "just and equitable principles of trade"]

b. Stock exchange rules [§2066]

The national stock exchanges have similar rules, as required under section 6 of the 1934 Act. [*See In re* **Shearson, Hammill & Co.,** *supra*, §1956]

c. Liability of controlling persons [§2067]

In addition to actions brought for a broker-dealer's failure to adequately supervise, the broker-dealer may also be held liable as a "control person" for the securities law violations of persons they control. [SEA §20]

7. Margin Requirements [§2068]

To generate greater sales volume, broker-dealers often encourage their customers to buy securities on credit (*i.e.,* on "margin"). The regulations developed in this area under section 7 of the 1934 Act are the province of the Federal Reserve Board, but the S.E.C. brings enforcement actions for violations by broker-dealers.

a. Federal Reserve Board regulations [§2069]

Below are the margin regulations:

(i) *Regulation T* governs the extension of credit by market intermediaries (such as broker-dealers) in securities transactions.

(ii) *Regulation U* governs extension of credit by commercial banks for the purpose of buying securities.

(iii) *Regulation G* governs lending by persons other than broker-dealers and banks, where the credit extended is secured by the stock purchased.

(iv) *Regulation X* governs borrowing from domestic or foreign lenders.

b. Margin amount [§2070]

Under Federal Reserve Board Regulation T, a "margin amount" may be set. Thus, if the margin is 50%, a broker-dealer may not loan a customer more than 50% of the market value of the securities.

c. Implied action for margin rule violations [§2071]

Neither section 7 nor regulation T expressly provide for a private civil cause of action to enforce their provisions or to compensate for damages caused by a violation of the rules. Generally, most courts that have considered the issue in recent years have ruled that there is no implied private right of action under section 7. However, a few courts have recognized an implied civil action against broker-dealers for such violations.

8. Civil Liability for Violations of NASD, Stock Exchange, or S.E.C. Rules [§2072]

There have been a number of instances where a plaintiff has brought a cause of action against a defendant broker-dealer for the defendant's violation of an NASD, national stock exchange, or S.E.C. rule. The recent trend of court opinions, however, has been to limit sharply the implication of private remedies under various sections of the securities laws, as well as pursuant to NASD or stock exchange rules. (*See supra*, §1893.)

Chapter Five: Application of Federal Securities Laws to Multinational Transactions

CONTENTS

Key Exam Issues

The material covered in this chapter is included for the sake of completeness. Unless your professor has covered this material during your course, it is doubtful that an exam question will be taken from the information in this chapter. Many securities transactions involve investors and firms in foreign countries as well as in the United States. Questions may arise as to the applicability of the federal securities laws to these multinational transactions (subject matter jurisdiction) and as to the capability of the court to obtain personal jurisdiction over the parties involved in the transaction. The question of subject matter jurisdiction is discussed in this chapter. *See* the Conflict of Laws Summary for discussion of personal jurisdiction over foreign defendants.

A. Registration Under the 1933 Act

1. Introduction [§2073]

The 1933 Act confers jurisdiction over multinational transactions whenever United States facilities of interstate commerce are used to effect a securities transaction. The 1933 Act defines "interstate commerce" to include commerce between any foreign country and the United States. [SA §2(a)(7)]

2. Territoriality as Basis for Application of 1933 Act [§2074]

The registration requirements of the 1933 Act are limited by geography: Offerings taking place within the United States must comply with the 1933 Act, regardless of the nationality of the issuer. Offerings outside the United States need not be registered under the 1933 Act, again irrespective of the issuer's nationality.

a. Offshore offerings [§2075]

The above leaves open the question whether a particular offering in fact is outside the United States. It is easy to imagine an offering in which all the initial buyers are located overseas, but those buyers promptly resell to United States persons. To clarify some of the questions relating to offshore offerings, the S.E.C. adopted regulation S in 1990.

(1) Regulation S [§2076]

Regulation S, discussed *supra*, §§734 *et seq.*, was intended in part to clarify that the registration requirements of the 1933 Act do not apply to offers and sales made outside the United States.

(2) Rule 144A and resale of regulation S securities [§2077]

Simultaneously with the adoption of regulation S, the S.E.C. adopted rule 144A. In conjunction with regulation S, rule 144A makes it possible for a foreign issuer in two steps to effect a distribution to "qualified institutional buyers" (defined *supra,* §724) in the United States. In the first step, the foreign issuer sells its securities abroad. In the second step, the overseas buyers resell under rule 144A to "qualified institutional buyers" in the United States. For a discussion of both of these provisions, *see supra,* §§718 *et seq.*

b. United States offerings [§2078]

With what regulations must a foreign issuer comply to conduct a registered offering in the United States? At one time, the United States capital markets were seen as so desirable that the S.E.C. did not concern itself much with the convenience of foreign issuers. However, the increasingly competitive nature of the global economy makes it essential that the United States accommodate foreign capital to the extent that this is consistent with the protection of United States investors. This is gradually being accomplished by efforts to streamline and harmonize domestic regulation with regulation in other countries.

(1) Registration forms [§2079]

There are two principal kinds of foreign issuers: sovereign issuers (*i.e.,* foreign governments) and private issuers (foreign corporations and other business entities).

(a) Foreign sovereign issuers [§2080]

Schedule B to the 1933 Act specifies the information required to be included in a 1933 Act registration statement by a foreign sovereign. Note that the S.E.C. has never adopted a form for use by foreign sovereign issuers.

(b) Foreign private issuers [§2081]

The S.E.C. has adopted forms F-1, F-2, F-3, and F-4 for foreign private issuers. These forms are intended to parallel those used by American domestic issuers, and in most cases are comparable to forms S-1, S-2, S-3, and S-4 (*see supra,* §§310-315) used by domestic issuers.

(2) Financial disclosure by foreign issuers [§2082]

Probably the most difficult hurdle that a foreign issuer needs to clear before conducting an offering in the United States is the requirement that its financial statements be reconciled to United States generally accepted accounting practices ("GAAP") and the S.E.C.'s regulation S-X. Often, foreign accounting practices vary substantially from those prevalent in the United States, and reconciliation is a lengthy (and expensive) task. To mitigate the burden somewhat, the S.E.C. recognizes two methods of reconciliation:

(a) Full reconciliation [§2083]

Full reconciliation requires that essentially all data (including geographic and industry segment data) be reconciled to GAAP and regulation S-X. Although full reconciliation is not required for periodic reports under the 1934 Act, it is required for 1933 Act registration statements.

(b) Measurement item reconciliation [§2084]

In cases where full reconciliation is not required, the S.E.C. accepts reconciliation of measurement items only—*i.e.*, of income statement and balance sheet data. While this is considerably less burdensome than full reconciliation, it nevertheless entails significant expense and potential delay.

3. American Depositary Receipts ("ADRs") [§2085]

One technique has been used since the 1920s to attempt to avoid extensive regulation under the 1933 Act. Under this approach, an American bank purchases (in exempt secondary-market transactions) shares of foreign issuers. The shares are held in a trust or other custodial arrangement by the bank, which then issues receipts evidencing beneficial ownership of a stated number of shares. ADRs are popular with investors—in 1990 the dollar volume of ADRs traded, $125 billion, was almost 70 times what it had been only seven years earlier.

a. Regulation of ADRs [§2086]

ADRs are, technically, securities issued by the depositary bank. Consequently, the bank must register the securities under the 1933 Act. Compliance with the 1934 Act, however, is the responsibility of the foreign issuer. If the ADRs are neither listed on a stock exchange nor traded in NASDAQ, filing of 1934 Act reports may be excused under rule 12g3-2 (*see infra*, §2090). If the ADRs are listed on a stock exchange or traded in NASDAQ, the issuer must report under the 1934 Act (usually on form 20-F, *see infra*, §2092).

4. Multi-Jurisdictional Disclosure [§2087]

The S.E.C. has proposed a number of possibilities for multi-jurisdictional disclosure, *i.e.*, a system of registration and disclosure that would satisfy the regulatory requirements of two or more nations at the same time. To date, however, only Canada and the United States have agreed to a system of multi-jurisdictional disclosure. [*See* SA Release No. 33-6902 (1991)]

B. Application of the 1934 Act

1. Introduction [§2088]

Like the 1933 Act, the 1934 Act defines "interstate commerce" to include commerce between any foreign country and the United States. [*See* SEA §3(a)(17)]

2. Regulation Under the 1934 Act [§2089]

The registration requirements of the 1934 Act [SEA §12(b), (g)] do not distinguish between foreign and domestic registrants. On its face, therefore, the Act seems to require registration and periodic reporting if a foreign issuer has securities listed on a United States exchange [SEA §12(b)] or has at least 500 shareholders and more than $10 million in assets [SEA §12(g)].

a. Exemption [§2090]

Under rule 12g3-2(b), however, all such foreign issuers are exempt from registration *if* they file with the S.E.C. all information that they make public abroad (*e.g.,* stock exchange reports, filings required by the laws of their domicile, voluntary statements released to shareholders, etc.) and if their securities are neither listed on any United States exchange nor traded in NASDAQ. [SEA Rule 12g3-2(b)]

(1) "Grandfather" provision [§2091]

Until 1983, it was possible for a foreign issuer to have securities traded on NASDAQ and still be exempt from the 1934 Act's registration and reporting requirements under rule 12g3-2(b). When the S.E.C. modified the exemption to require NASDAQ-listed issuers to register and report, they "grandfathered" foreign issuers that were listed on NASDAQ at the time the rule changed. Consequently, there are still a number of foreign issuers listed on NASDAQ who have not registered under the 1934 Act and who do not report on United States forms.

(2) Reporting for nonexempt foreign issuers [§2092]

Issuers whose securities trade on an exchange or NASDAQ, and who are not grandfathered under rule 12g3-2(b), must file an annual form 20-F. The form is generally similar to a domestic form 10-K (*see supra,* §881), but requires substantially less disclosure of self-dealing transactions and of management compensation than its United States counterpart. Financial statements filed with form 20-F need not be reconciled to GAAP (*see supra,* §2082).

(a) But note

If the form 20-F will be incorporated by reference into a 1933 Act registration statement (*see supra,* §84), the financial statements must be reconciled to GAAP (*see supra,* §1606).

(b) Other reports [§2093]

Foreign registrants are not required to file quarterly reports, because these are not common outside the United States. When material information becomes public abroad, however, a foreign registrant must file a form 6-K disclosing that information.

b. Foreign Corrupt Practices Act [§2094]

Finally, if a foreign issuer registers a class of securities under the 1934 Act, the issuer becomes subject to the Foreign Corrupt Practices Act ("FCPA"). The

FCPA imposes criminal penalties for certain corrupt practices (bribery of government officials and the like) and also requires the issuer to keep accurate and fair books and records and to devise a system of internal accounting controls to ensure that such payments are not being concealed.

3. International Securities Fraud [§2095]

The preceding section focused on regulation of foreign entities and their securities transactions. Other international issues arising under the securities laws involve misconduct and the extent to which United States authorities can pursue (or prosecute) those responsible. Often the potential defendant first raises a defense based on jurisdiction, under SEA section 30(b).

a. Interpretation of section 30(b) of the 1934 Act [§2096]

Section 30(b) provides that neither the 1934 Act nor its rules apply to any person insofar as he transacts "a business in securities without the jurisdiction of the United States." This section has been referred to on several occasions when the courts have considered the extraterritorial application of the 1934 Act. At issue is the meaning of the phrases "transacts a business in securities," and "without the jurisdiction of the United States."

(1) General rule [§2097]

United States courts appear willing to apply the provisions of the 1934 Act to securities transactions involving foreign nationals and foreign transactions when there are (i) substantial United States contacts with the transaction, and (ii) substantial United States interests to be protected. [**Schoenbaum v. Firstbrook**, 405 F.2d 200 (2d Cir. 1968)]

Example: Acquitaine (a Canadian corporation) purchased additional shares of its subsidiary Banff Oil (also a Canadian corporation) at an unfair price, based on inside information about an oil discovery. An American shareholder of Banff sued Acquitaine under rule 10b-5. Although all of the events took place in Canada, the court found jurisdiction under the 1934 Act because Banff was listed and traded on the American Stock Exchange and application of United States law *was necessary to protect American investors*. [**Schoenbaum v. Firstbrook**, *supra*]

(a) Note

In *Schoenbaum*, section 30(b) was held to exempt *only* transactions by foreign securities professionals (*i.e.*, those in the securities business), and even then, only where the transactions were outside the jurisdiction of the United States under the above rationale.

Example: A United States corporation sued, under section 16(b), a foreign corporation that held 10% of its common stock where the foreign corporation purchased and sold the stock within a period of six months. The cause of action was *not* barred by section 30(b) because the foreign corporation was a mutual fund and not a broker-dealer (*i.e.,* not a "securities professional"). Also, the court found that because the transactions were executed on the NYSE, the business was not "without the jurisdiction" of the United States. [**Roth v. Fund of Funds, Ltd.,** 405 F.2d 421 (2d Cir. 1968), *cert. denied,* 394 U.S. 975 (1969)] *Note:* Section 16(b) of the 1934 Act might have been applied in this case even if the trading *had* occurred abroad, rather than on a United States exchange, because jurisdiction under section 16 depends on whether the issuer's securities are registered under section 12 and not on the use of facilities of interstate commerce.

---

e.g. **Example:** A French bidder planned a tender offer for R, an American corporation. After the bidder leaked information about the transaction, foreign investors purchased R shares and options to buy R shares. The orders to buy were placed in Europe and the Middle East, but ultimately were executed in the United States, over the NYSE and the Philadelphia Options Exchange. The Second Circuit Court of Appeals held that the S.E.C's action for an injunction could proceed, even though the misconduct took place outside the United States, because the *trading* took place inside the United States. "The [misconduct] created the near certainty that United States shareholders, who could reasonably be expected to hold [R] securities, would be adversely affected." [**S.E.C. v. Unifund SAL,** *supra,* §1704]

---

(2) Interpretation by the S.E.C. [§2098]

In the view of the S.E.C., the 1934 Act applies to extraterritorial transactions whenever its application is necessary for the protection of American investors and markets. But the S.E.C. recognizes that Congress also built into each provision of the 1934 Act certain jurisdictional requirements that may limit its application.

(a) Factors considered [§2099]

In determining whether a particular section of the 1934 Act applies to extraterritorial transactions, the S.E.C. considers all provisions of the section as to use of jurisdictional means, involvement of a registered security, and whether the provisions seem to apply only to persons in the securities business.

b. Application of SEA rule 10b-5 [§2100]

Most of the cases involving extraterritorial application of the provisions of the 1934 Act have concerned rule 10b-5. The rationale for applying rule 10b-5 to securities transactions involving foreign nationals and foreign transactions is that (i) substantial United States contacts exist with respect to the transaction, and (ii) substantial United States interests need to be protected. (*See supra*, §2097.)

(1) Test used [§2101]

The Second Circuit Court of Appeals (which has had the most extensive experience in questions of extraterritorial securities fraud) has applied two tests for resolving transnational jurisdictional questions [*see* **Itoba Ltd. v. Lep Group PLC**, 54 F.3d 118 (2d Cir. 1995)]:

(a) Substantial effects test [§2102]

Under the substantial effects test, jurisdiction is premised on foreseeable and substantial effects from the transnational transaction within the United States, regardless of where the activity in question occurred.

Example: Foreign investors received material nonpublic information about a foreign tender offer planned for an American corporation. The investors, acting abroad, placed buy orders for shares of an American corporation. The orders were ultimately executed on American stock and options exchanges. The Second Circuit Court of Appeals held that jurisdiction existed in the United States, because of the predictable effects the insider trading had on American investors whose shares were purchased. [**S.E.C. v. Unifund SAL**, *supra*, §2097]

(b) Conduct test [§2103]

Under the conduct test, jurisdiction is based on the fact that some significant activity occurred within American territorial limits. The difficult part is, of course, "describing, in sufficiently precise terms, the sort of conduct occurring in the United States that ought to be adequate to trigger American regulation of the transaction." [**Kauthar SDN BHD v. Sternberg**, 149 F.3d 659 (7th Cir. 1998), *cert. denied*, 525 U.S. 1114 (1999)] In *Kauthar*, documents containing fraudulent misstatements were prepared in the United States, the documents were mailed to the (foreign) plaintiff from the United States, phone calls to the plaintiff soliciting its purchase of securities were made from the United States, and the defendants were alleged to have held meetings in the United States to discuss how to obtain the plaintiff's investment. On these facts, the court held that there was sufficient conduct within the United States to confer jurisdiction on a federal court. Courts have jurisdiction "when the conduct occurring in the United States . . . forms a substantial part of the alleged fraud and is material to its success. This conduct must be more than merely preparatory in nature," but it need not by itself satisfy all the elements of a securities violation.

(2) Conduct, effects, or both? [§2104]

Rather than applying one test or the other, courts have looked at both tests and are willing to mix elements of each in deciding whether they ultimately have jurisdiction over the violation. [**Itoba Ltd. v. Lep Group PLC**, *supra*]

4. International Tender Offers [§2105]

Corporate takeovers sometimes raise difficult and sensitive issues concerning the extraterritorial reach of the United States securities laws. Often cases are brought in the United States federal courts, even though the bidder expressly excluded United States citizens from the tender offer (to avoid the application of United States securities law).

Example: GEC, a British corporation, made a tender offer for Plessey, another British corporation, to all Plessey shareholders except those residing in the United States. Plessey ADRs trade in the United States and are listed on the New York Stock Exchange. After the bid was announced, the price of Plessey ADRs on the NYSE rose dramatically. Plessey sued GEC in Delaware federal court, seeking an injunction compelling GEC to file tender offer documents under the Williams Act. The Delaware district court held that, *inter alia*, GEC did not use jurisdictional means to carry out a securities transaction in the United States, all of its actions were taken outside the United States, imposition of United States requirements was not necessary to protect United States interests in the bid, and interfering in a transaction of immense magnitude to British interests would violate international norms and could hinder comity. [**Plessey Co., PLC v. General Electric Co., PLC**, 628 F. Supp. 477 (D. Del. 1986)]

---

a. But note

Plessey did not involve any allegations of fraud. When fraud is alleged, the court may be more willing to assert jurisdiction, perhaps on the theory that a foreign government will be less protective of one of its citizens if that person has committed fraud. On the other hand, allegations of fraud are merely allegations, and in the typical tender offer contest, allegations of fraud are commonplace, although most are never proved.

Example: M, a Luxembourg corporation, made a tender offer for the stock of C, a British corporation. Only 2.5% of C's shares were held in the United States, but C owned half of N, a Delaware corporation that controlled the largest gold producer in the United States. Defending itself against M's takeover attempt, C sued M in federal court in New York. The Second Circuit Court of Appeals held that the United States courts had jurisdiction over the bid and remanded the case to the district court with a suggestion that if the plaintiff should prevail, an injunction might be an appropriate remedy. [**Consolidated Gold Fields PLC v. Minorco, S.A.**, 871 F.2d 252 (2d Cir. 1989)]

Chapter Six: Regulation of Securities Transactions by the States

---

CONTENTS

Key Exam Issues

This chapter summarizes the state laws regulating securities and explains how federal and state securities laws interface. For more than 60 years, the Securities Act and the Securities Exchange Act preserved the power to the states to regulate securities. Every state had adopted some form of securities regulation, requiring issuers and other parties to comply not only with federal law, but also with the laws of the various states that might have contact with the transaction. All this changed in 1996, with the adoption of the National Securities Markets Improvement Act of 1996 (the "1996 Act"). This chapter will give you a very brief overview of the Uniform Securities Act, which is the model for many states' securities laws, and then discuss how federal laws have severely restricted state regulation of securities.

A. Uniform Securities Act

1. Structure of Act [§2106]
The Commissioners on Uniform State Laws have adopted the Uniform Securities Act, divided into sections addressing (i) fraud in general, (ii) broker-dealer registration, (iii) registration of new securities offerings, and (iv) remedies. Of these, (ii) and (iii) have been largely preempted by the 1996 Act, and (i) has been partially preempted by the Securities Litigation Uniform Standards Act of 1998 (the "1998 Act"), discussed below.

2. Adoptions by the States [§2107]
In drafting their own securities laws, most of the states have adopted some part of the Uniform Securities Act, have used some of the concepts found in the federal acts, and have added some provisions of their own choosing. In cases not preempted by federal law, nearly all the states regulate both the original distribution of securities and their subsequent trading (including the registration of broker-dealers).

B. Preemption of State Securities Laws

1. Introduction [§2108]
Securities Act section 18 effectively preempts most state securities laws (so called blue sky laws), although the states had voluntarily ceded a good deal of power to the federal government before section 18 was enacted by adopting broad exemptions

from state regulation for many distributions. In addition, the 1998 Act preempts state-law securities fraud class actions. Both Acts are discussed below.

2. Structure [§2109]

Section 18 describes four broad classes of securities ("covered securities") and prohibits the states from requiring registration or qualification of any covered security. In addition, the states are prohibited from imposing any conditions on the use of offering documents prepared by the issuer, or on disclosure documents that must be filed with the S.E.C. relating to a covered security or to the issuer of a covered security. [SA §18]

3. Four Classes of Covered Securities [§2110]

Section 18 exempts from blue sky regulation four classes of security:

a. Securities of issuers registered under the Investment Company Act of 1940 [§2111]

Any investment company registered with the S.E.C. under the 1940 Act (*see supra*, §80) may issue securities free of blue sky regulation.

b. Listed securities [§2112]

Even before the 1996 Act, most states had already exempted from state registration securities listed or approved for listing on the NYSE and the AMEX, as well as those traded on the NASDAQ, under the so-called blue chip or marketplace exemptions. Section 18 makes this common state exemption a federal requirement.

c. Offers or sales to "qualified purchasers" [§2113]

This exemption remains to be fleshed out by the S.E.C. Note that offers and sales to sophisticated institutions, such as "qualified institutional buyers" ("QIBs") under rule 144A (*see supra*, §724) were already exempt under the laws of most states.

d. Certain offers and sales exempt under the 1933 Act [§2114]

Section 18 also preempts state regulation of:

(1) Transactions exempt under Securities Act section 4(1) (transactions by any person other than an issuer, underwriter, or dealer) in securities of an issuer that is a 1934 Act reporting company;

(2) Transactions exempt under Securities Act section 4(4) (brokers' transactions);

(3) Transactions in securities exempt under Securities Act section 3(a), *except*:

    (a)   Securities of religious or charitable organizations;

    (b)   Securities issued in intrastate offerings; and

    (c)   Municipal securities offered in the state of their issue; and

  (4)   Private placements made pursuant to rules adopted under Securities Act section 4(2) (currently only one such rule is in effect—rule 506 of regulation D (*see supra*, §§514-515)).

4.   Left to the States [§2115]

Clearly, SA section 18 removes a substantial amount of authority from state securities regulators. However, the states still have authority to:

a.   Regulate penny stocks (which are a significant source of securities fraud litigation);

b.   Regulate many small, intrastate, and other offerings exempt from federal regulation under the 1933 Act;

c.   Bring actions against brokers for fraud and other illegal conduct relating to securities and securities transactions; and

d.   Require notice filings (*i.e.*, notifications of the sale of securities within the state) and the payment of fees to the state for such notice filings.

5.   1998 Act Preempts State Law Class Actions [§2116]

An unintended result of the class action reforms adopted in the Private Securities Litigation Reform Act of 1995 (the "1995 Act") was the migration of securities fraud class actions to the state courts, perhaps to avoid the new, more onerous requirements of the federal securities laws. In response, Congress passed the 1998 Act, which preempts class actions (and similar consolidated proceedings) based on state law if the action alleges misrepresentation or omission of a material fact, or the use of a manipulative or deceptive device or contrivance, in connection with the purchase or sale of a security. In effect, state "blue sky" fraud litigation is preempted if it is a class action or involves *consolidated actions of more than 50 plaintiffs*. [*See* SA §16(b); SEA §28(f)]

a.   Individual lawsuits not preempted [§2117]

Individuals may still sue under state law for securities fraud, but if more than 50 persons sue and the actions are consolidated, the resulting litigation will be preempted.

b.   Derivative actions not preempted [§2118]

The 1998 Act does not preempt derivative actions brought by shareholders in the name of the corporation (*see* Corporations Summary), or certain other claims based on breach of fiduciary duty by a corporation's management.

c. 1998 Act applies only to "covered securities" [§2119]

The 1998 Act applies only to lawsuits alleging fraud with respect to a "covered security," as defined in Securities Act section 18(b). (*See supra*, §§2110 *et seq.*)

SUMMARY OF SECURITIES EXEMPT FROM STATE REGULATION   **gilbert**

COVERED	NOT COVERED
• Securities of issuers registered under the Investment Company Act	• Securities that constitute "penny stocks" (*e.g.*, securities selling for less than $5)
• Securities listed on the NYSE and AMEX or traded on the NASDAQ	• Securities sold in small or intrastate offerings
• Securities offered or sold to qualified purchasers, such as banks	
• Securities sold in transactions exempt under SA sections 4(1), 4(4), and most of 3(a), or rule 506	

C. Secondary Distribution of Securities

1. General Fraud Provisions [§2120]

Many states have statutory provisions that regulate the trading of securities subsequent to their original distribution, as does the Securities Exchange Act of 1934. Nearly every state has some general provision against fraud, and a few states have provisions similar to rule 10b-5 of the 1934 Act. However, class actions under such provisions were preempted by the 1998 Act.

2. Registration of Broker-Dealers [§2121]

Many states also have provisions requiring the qualification and registration of persons involved in the securities business as broker-dealers. [Uniform Securities Act §204] Such laws have for the most part been preempted by the 1996 Act.

3. Tender Offer Statutes [§2122]

In addition, many states have adopted special provisions governing the regulation of tender offers made for companies domiciled within the state's borders. Where the state statute conflicts with the purposes and manner of regulation of the federal laws, state law may be preempted by federal law. Alternatively, the state law may also be invalid on the ground that it imposes an undue burden on interstate commerce.

a. Undue burden on interstate commerce [§2123]

A state tender offer statute may be found to be invalid under the Commerce Clause of the Constitution where it imposes an undue burden on interstate commerce. [**Edgar v. MITE Corp.**, *supra*, §1272]

Example: In *Edgar*, Illinois state law provided that any tender offer for the shares of a target company must be registered with the Illinois Secretary of State. A "target company" was defined as a corporation that had shareholders located in Illinois owning 10% or more of the class of equity securities subject to the offer, *or* that met any two of the three following conditions:

(i)   The corporation had its *principal office* in Illinois;

(ii)   The corporation was *organized* under Illinois law; or

(iii)   At least 10% *of the corporation's stated capital and paid-in surplus* were represented within the state.

Offers filed with the secretary of state became registered 20 days after a registration statement was filed, unless the secretary called a hearing. During this time, either the secretary, or a majority of the target company's outside directors, or Illinois shareholders owning 10% or more of the class of securities subject to the offer could require a hearing. If the hearing was held, state law required the secretary to deny registration if a full disclosure of all relevant information on the offer had not been made, or if the "tender offer is inequitable." The Court found that allowing the Illinois Secretary of State to block a nationwide tender offer on this basis had a substantial effect on interstate commerce.

---

b. Preemption of state law [§2124]

In *Edgar*, the Supreme Court held that the Illinois takeover law was unconstitutional under the Commerce Clause of the Constitution. However, a majority of the Court could not agree that the Illinois law was also preempted by the Williams Act. Thus, *Edgar* left open the question of how far states could go in regulating takeovers. For a discussion of the post-*Edgar* trend, *see supra*, §§1270 *et seq.*

Review Questions and Answers

Review Questions

1. Megacorp has issued 100,000 shares of common stock. This stock is listed for trading on the New York Stock Exchange. Megacorp's articles of incorporation authorize 200,000 shares, and so Megacorp now wishes to issue an additional 50,000 shares in a public offering. Will the 50,000 new shares be offered in the primary market? _____

2. Abbey buys and sells securities for her customers on a commission basis. Would Abbey generally be designated as a "dealer" under the securities acts? _____

3. The two basic purposes of the Securities Act of 1933 are (i) to ensure disclosure of all material facts concerning issuers in new offerings and (ii) to prevent fraud in the interstate sale of securities. True or false? _____

4. Megacorp offers a $15 million issue of debt securities to the public. Does Megacorp have to comply with both the Securities Act of 1933 and the Trust Indenture Act of 1939? _____

5. Microcorp has $3 million in assets and 496 stockholders who own its common stock. Its stock is traded on the New York Stock Exchange. Must Microcorp register and report to the S.E.C. under the SEA of 1934? _____

6. Nucorp sells a new issue of its securities to the public without registration under the 1933 Act. Nucorp does not use the facilities of interstate commerce to make the offering. Does the 1933 Act nevertheless apply to this transaction? _____

7. In a "firm commitment" underwriting, does the issuer initially sell its own securities to the public? _____

8. Xavier owns 2,500 of the 100,000 shares of Megacorp. He is not an issuer, underwriter, or dealer, as those terms are defined in the 1933 Act, and he holds no position with Megacorp. Xavier purchased the shares over the New York Stock Exchange. When Xavier goes to sell these shares to the public, must Xavier register them under the 1933 Act? _____

9. Issuer Corp. has decided to conduct an initial public offering of its common stock. When the offering is complete, Issuer will have approximately 3,000 stockholders and assets worth $30 million. When issued, the common stock is expected to trade on the NASDAQ. The issue price will be in the neighborhood of $10 per share. Issuer has contacted Underwriter Bros., a securities underwriting firm, to underwrite

the offering on a "firm commitment" basis. Using the telephone, fax machines, and email, Issuer and Underwriter negotiate over the terms of a letter of intent describing the proposed transaction and the role that each of the parties will play. Has either Issuer or Underwriter violated section 5 of the 1933 Act? _____

10. Issuer and Underwriter in question 9, above, execute a letter of intent. Does the letter violate section 5 of the 1933 Act? _____

11. Issuer from question 9, above, publishes an ad in the local newspaper, stating that Issuer plans a public offering of one million shares at $10 per share and that Underwriter will serve as underwriter. Has Issuer violated section 5? _____

12. Underwriter calls several local securities firms on the telephone and invites them to participate as members of the retail selling group in the Issuer offering under the facts in question 11. Has Underwriter violated section 5? _____

13. Assume that Issuer from question 9, above, rather than planning its initial public offering ("IPO"), instead is planning another offering, to take place six months after its IPO. Issuer publishes an ad in the local newspaper, stating that Issuer plans a public offering of one million shares at $10 per share and that Underwriter will serve as underwriter. Has Issuer violated section 5? _____

14. Assume that the issuer from question 9 completed its IPO 16 months ago and is eligible to use form S-3 for the proposed offering. Issuer publishes an ad in the local newspaper, stating that Issuer plans a public offering of one million shares at $10 per share and that Underwriter will serve as underwriter. Has Issuer violated section 5? _____

15. Assume that Issuer from question 9 completed its IPO 20 years ago and, in the interim, has conducted numerous additional public offerings of its stock. Today, Issuer has outstanding over $1 billion in common stock, nearly all of it held by persons unaffiliated with Issuer, and meets all the requirements to use form S-3 for the proposed offering. Issuer publishes an ad in the local newspaper, stating that Issuer plans a public offering of one million shares at $10 per share and that Underwriter will serve as underwriter. Has Issuer violated section 5? _____

16. Under section 5 of the 1933 Act, may actual sales be made during the waiting period (after filing but before the registration statement has become effective)? _____

17. Assume that Issuer (in questions 9 - 15, above) has filed the registration statement for its IPO, but the registration statement has not yet been declared effective by the S.E.C. Dealer Corp., a securities dealer, intends to accept an invitation from Underwriter to participate as a retail dealer in the Issuer IPO. Dealer lists Issuer's industry in its monthly report on "growth industries investors should watch." Has Dealer violated section 5? _____

18. Underwriter (from the facts above) emails copies of a preliminary prospectus for Issuer's IPO to dealers throughout the United States. In some cases, the emails have

attachments that contain the prospectus; in others, the emails contain a link to a page on Underwriter's website where the Issuer prospectus can be viewed. In many cases the emails include an invitation to the recipient to reply with an indication of whether the dealer might be interested in participating in Issuer's IPO after the registration statement is declared effective. Do the emails violate section 5?   _____

19. Dealer (from the facts above), having indicated it will participate in the Issuer IPO and that it will purchase 10,000 shares of Issuer stock, telephones Customer and offers to sell 1,000 shares of Issuer's stock at the public offering price. Customer accepts. Does this violate section 5?   _____

20. Assume (under the facts above) that Issuer, instead of filing the registration statement for its IPO, has filed the registration statement for another offering to take place six months after its IPO. Dealer Corp., a securities dealer, intends to accept an invitation from Underwriter to participate as a retail dealer in the Issuer offering. Dealer lists Issuer's industry in its monthly report on "growth industries investors should watch." Has Dealer violated section 5?   _____

21. Assume (under the facts above) that the registration statement for Issuer's IPO has been declared effective. Dealer calls another of its customers and offers the customer 1,000 shares of Issuer stock, and the customer accepts. Does this violate section 5?   _____

22. After the events described in question 21, above, Dealer emails a confirmation of sale to the customer. Nothing else is mentioned in the email. Does this violate section 5?   _____

23. One week after mailing the confirmation of sale in question 22, above, Dealer delivers to the customer the stock certificates for the Issuer stock. Nothing else is included in the envelope. Does this violate section 5?   _____

24. Under the facts in the questions above, Dealer mails a prospectus to a potential customer, including with it a separate written report compiled by Dealer's research department, which gives Issuer a highly enthusiastic recommendation. This material is never filed with the S.E.C. Is this a violation of section 5?   _____

25. Generally speaking, after the expiration of 40 days from the date on which securities are first offered to the public, dealers are exempt from the prospectus delivery requirements of the 1933 Act even if the public offering involved was illegal because the securities were not registered. True or false?   _____

26. Under the 1933 Act, may dealers who are still selling the securities originally allotted to them as part of the distribution dispense with the prospectus delivery requirements after 40 days from the date the securities are first offered to the public?   _____

27. Muriel purchases 100,000 shares of Siebco's common stock from Siebco, with the intent of reselling these shares immediately to the public. Is Muriel an underwriter?   _____

28. Suppose that Dirk hears that Selco is selling 100,000 shares of its common stock in a public offering. The offering, although made to the public, is not registered with the S.E.C. Dirk buys 10,000 shares. At a dinner party, Dirk is talking with Cheryl about his investments and describes his investment in Selco. The next day Cheryl buys 100 shares from Selco. Is Dirk an underwriter? _____

29. Alfred has a position on the board of directors of Batcorp and owns 25% of its outstanding common stock. Alfred originally formed the corporation, although he no longer is an officer or active in its day-to-day management. Alfred proposes to sell his 25% interest to the public through a brokerage firm. The stock is traded over the New York Stock Exchange. Must Alfred register his stock under the 1933 Act? _____

30. Would a subdivision of lots, where most purchasers are buying the lots for speculation, later to resell them for a profit, be an offering of a "security" under the 1933 Act? _____

31. Astrid purchased a large section of land, then subdivided it into very small parcels and leased it to many investors. The leases included an obligation by Astrid to drill test wells for oil. Is it likely that a court would find that Astrid had marketed a "security" to the lessees? _____

32. Are general partnership interests usually securities under the 1933 Act? _____

33. What is the general registration form to be used by commercial and industrial companies in registration under the 1933 Act where another form does not specifically apply? _____

34. Must the following facts about Regco be disclosed in its registration statements under the 1933 Act?

    a.   The recent earnings history of the company (its net profits). _____

    b.   A five-year projection of its net earnings made by the company's vice president of finance. _____

    c.   All significant personal financial dealings of each member of Regco's key management with Regco. _____

    d.   The fact that the president of Regco is seeing a psychiatrist. _____

35. Registration with the S.E.C. of a new issue under the Securities Act of 1933 guarantees the accuracy of the facts represented in the registration statement or the prospectus. True or false? _____

36. A stop order proceeding is not available under the 1933 Act once the registration statement has been declared effective. True or false? _____

37. Does an amendment filed by the issuer to a registration statement under the 1933 Act normally start the 20-day waiting period for effectiveness running again? _____

38. If the S.E.C. has already instituted stop order proceedings under the 1933 Act in a preeffective registration statement matter, may the issuer still withdraw the registration statement without the approval of the S.E.C.? _____

39. Shelfco wishes to register all of the securities it will issue in the future at one time, in order to avoid the expense of drafting and filing multiple registration statements under the 1933 Act. Is it true that such a registration procedure will probably not be permitted by the S.E.C.? _____

40. Technically speaking, the S.E.C. does not require the registration statement to be amended to account for changes that occur after its effective date, at least if a period of less than nine months has transpired. True or false? _____

41. Ishco issues its stock to the public through a registration statement and prospectus under the 1933 Act. At the time the registration statement is declared effective by the S.E.C., there are no material misstatements or omissions therein. But subsequent events, which occur while the offering is still going on, make some of the material statements in the prospectus misleading. May Alex, an investor in the Ishco securities, bring an action under section 11 for these misstatements? _____

42. If a security is exempted from registration under the 1933 Act, it may be sold and resold and never have to be registered, even if resold by a control person. True or false? _____

43. May a broker-dealer rely on either the dealer exemption (section 4(3)) or the broker exemption (section 4(4)) of the 1933 Act? _____

44. The broker's exemption covers not only the broker but also the selling customer. True or false? _____

45. Suppose that Lynch, a broker-dealer, has purchased some of Bigco's securities for its own account and has been trading these securities during the 40-day period after the new offering of Bigco's securities was declared effective. During this period, the S.E.C. enters a stop order suspending the distribution of the offering. Buffet, a customer, approaches Lynch and asks to buy some of the Bigco securities that Lynch has in inventory. May Lynch use the broker exemption to sell to Buffet without violating section 5 of the Act? _____

46. There are no hard and fast rules for determining whether an issuance of securities is a private offering. True or false? _____

47. One of the tests the S.E.C. uses for determining whether a security is being offered to the "public" is whether the purchasers thereof need the protection of the 1933 Act. True or false? _____

48. Privco contemplates a private offering of its securities under section 4(2). It offers and ultimately sells its securities to 11 people. Is the offering certain to be a private offering? _____

49. Privco makes a private offering of its common stock on January 1 and additional offerings on March 1, August 1, and November 1. Are these offerings in danger of losing their nonpublic offering exemption? _____

50. Regulation A is not a total exemption from registration under the 1933 Act; rather, it provides the opportunity for a shortened form of registration for offerings under a certain amount. True or false? _____

51. Blue Corp. issues 100,000 shares of its common stock pursuant to rule 147. Warren buys 50,000 of these and holds them for two years. He then wishes to resell his shares in a public distribution. Because he has met his investment intent pursuant to the rule, although he is a control person, may he sell without registration under the Act? _____

52. Sameco makes an intrastate offering pursuant to rule 147. All purchasers are residents of the same state as Sameco, but one of the offerees is not. Is the exemption therefore lost? _____

53. Bigco has 100,000 common stockholders. It issues "rights" to these stockholders to buy additional shares of common stock (ownership of 10 shares allows the stockholder to buy one additional share at a 5% discount from the then prevailing market price). No consideration is paid for the rights, which are good for six months. Must Bigco register the rights with the S.E.C.? _____

54. Emendco amends its corporate charter to provide that dividends that are in arrears on its cumulative preferred stock will be canceled and that dividends will no longer be cumulative. A majority of the preferred stockholders vote to approve this change. Emendco does not issue new stock certificates to the preferred stockholders. Is this a "sale" for "value" of new securities that, absent an exemption, must be registered under the 1933 Act? _____

55. Bondco has outstanding class A bonds. It proposes to issue new class B bonds in exchange for the A bonds, exchanging the bonds at equal face value. The B bonds have different maturity dates, interest rates, default provisions, etc. Bondco will pay the A bondholders a cash amount to account for the interest differential in the two bonds. May Bondco rely on the section 3(a)(9) exemption in making the exchange? _____

56. Tine, Inc. proposes to issue common stock in exchange for the assets of Warmer Co. Warmer Co. will first obtain the approval of its shareholders, as required by state law, to an agreement setting forth the terms and conditions of the exchange and providing for a distribution of the Tine, Inc. common stock to the Warmer Co. shareholders. May Tine, Inc. use rule 145 and the S-4 registration procedure? _____

57. XYZ Corp. sells to A, B, and C in a private offering. A and B (although representing that they are taking for investment) violate their representations and A sells to D through G, and B sells to H through L. Are A and B underwriters under the 1933 Act if the total offering amounts to a public offering? _____

58. Stern issues stock to Abbey in a private offering. Abbey is a control person who establishes her investment intent with respect to the offering. Abbey then sells all of her control stock through a broker over the stock exchange, without registration, to many purchasers. Has Abbey violated the 1933 Act by making a public distribution without registration? _____

59. Smith is the owner of 25% of the common stock of Oldboy Co. In addition, Smith sits on the board of directors of Barney Co. and is a good friend of the president. None of the stock that Smith owns is restricted stock. Smith has held the stock for six months and now desires to sell it. May Smith use rule 144? _____

60. Smallco is not subject to the reporting requirements of sections 13 or 15(d) of the SEA of 1934. Yanni owns restricted securities of Smallco and wants to sell them. He has held them for two years, and Smallco has furnished the information called for under rule 15c2-11 of the 1934 Act to the broker for Yanni. Can Yanni use rule 144 to sell the stock? _____

61. Barbie got her stock as a gift from her father. Her father got the stock in a private placement from Nattel Corp. and held it for six months. Barbie has now held it for eight months. She is not a control person. Barbie meets all of the other requirements of rule 144. May she sell under the rule? _____

62. Ronen Corp. has registered a public offering of its stock. Alex buys some stock and resells to Becky within a two-month period of the offering. There are material misrepresentations in the registration statement. Becky does not read the registration statement and knows nothing of the misrepresentations. However, when the misrepresentations are made public, Ronen stock goes down. Becky discovers the fraud and sues Ronen. Can Becky recover under section 11 of the 1933 Act? _____

63. Sellco sells stock to the public pursuant to a registration statement; the offering price is $10 per share. An hour after the offering begins, all of the stock has been sold for the first time, and the stock is trading at $15 per share. Matsuo buys 100 shares at $15. There is a material misstatement in the prospectus. A month later, when the stock has fallen to $10 per share, Matsuo sells. Thereafter, Matsuo discovers the misrepresentation and sues Sellco. Under SA section 11, what amount per share can Matsuo recover? _____

64. Ginsu Corp. sells stock directly to the public in a public distribution without registration. Penelope is one of the purchasers. Ginsu has never heard of section 5 of the 1933 Act; neither has Penelope. Penelope becomes disenchanted with the stock and sues under section 12(a)(1) of the Act to rescind the transaction. Will Penelope win? _____

65. Goldenco recruits an advisory board of influential business and civic leaders to advise the company about new marketing plans and ideas. Goldenco raises money through an intended private offering, which turns out to be a public offering. In the offering memorandum, the name, background, and experience of each member of the advisory board appear, and the memorandum states that offerees may call these people for recommendations about the company. Several offerees do so and receive assurances that the company is sound, as well as invitations to purchase Goldenco securities. The memorandum contains several material misstatements in its financial statements, and, in fact, the company is broke. May the purchasers sue the members of the advisory board under SA section 12(a)(2)? _____

66. Fraudco has no securities registered under section 12 of the 1934 Act and is not subject to 1934 Act periodic reporting. Fraudco engages in a fraudulent securities transaction. May it be sued under rule 10b-5 of the 1934 Act? _____

67. For rule 10b-5 to apply, there must be a sufficient connection between the activity complained of (*i.e.,* a misrepresentation, etc.) and the purchase or sale of securities. True or false? _____

68. Loadedcorp declares a cash dividend on its common stock but does not disclose this to the public. Hence, trading in Loadedcorp's stock is continued without awareness on the part of buyers and sellers that a dividend has been declared. Is this an omission of a material fact by the corporation? _____

69. Rule 10b-5 requires strict privity between plaintiff and defendant. True or false? _____

70. Delco, which has securities traded on the NYSE and is issuing additional securities, chooses to predict its future earnings for the coming year. The prediction is inaccurate and carelessly made. Is Delco subject to a rule 10b-5 suit on the basis of having misrepresented a material fact? _____

71. Cleopatra is a shareholder of Nile.com. She claims that her stock has depreciated in value in the market due to a series of misrepresentations made by the management of Nile.com to the public. Cleopatra has not actually bought or sold any Nile.com stock during the period of these misrepresentations. Cleopatra sues Nile.com under rule 10b-5. Does Cleopatra have standing to bring the suit? _____

72. In the audit of Ronen Corp., the auditing firm (Artie Anson & Co.) fails to accurately account for the corporation's liabilities from outstanding warranties given on Ronen Corp. products. As a result, Ronen Corp.'s published financial statements are substantially inaccurate. A shareholder who bought Ronen Corp. stock in the market at $100 per share sues when the stock drops to $50 per share after the true facts are published. One of the named defendants in the rule 10b-5 suit is Artie Anson & Co. At trial it is shown that Artie Anson & Co.'s omission of the material fact was the result of negligence. May the shareholder recover under rule 10b-5 against Artie Anson & Co.? _____

73. Ronen Corp. issues a materially false press release concerning its financial condition. Peter buys Ronen Corp. stock over the stock exchange at $10 per share. Later, when Ronen Corp. corrects the press release and discloses its true financial condition, the stock drops to $7 per share. Shortly thereafter, Ronen Corp. announces that merger discussions it has been carrying on with another corporation have terminated, at least for the present time. Peter then sues Ronen Corp. under rule 10b-5 on the basis of the false press release. At trial, Peter does not prove reliance on the false press release, but simply proves that Ronen Corp.'s financial condition was a material fact. Ronen Corp. proves that, in fact, Peter did not rely on the financial condition of the corporation, but would have bought the stock anyway (because Peter had inside information about the merger discussions, in which a bidder was considering the purchase of Ronen Corp. stock for $25 per share). Is this a valid defense to Peter's lawsuit? _____

74. Indicate whether the following persons are "insiders" of Bigco, as the term has been defined by the courts:

    a. Controlling shareholder of Bigco who is briefed by the corporation on all major developments. _____

    b. Directors of Bigco. _____

    c. Officers of Bigco. _____

75. May a corporation itself be held liable for damages under rule 10b-5 for failure to disclose a material fact to the investing public? _____

76. If a defendant violates rule 10b-5 by trading on inside information over an exchange, it is clear that the courts will allow unlimited recovery by all injured plaintiffs no matter what their total damages, even when the defendant's total profits are substantially less than the plaintiff's damages. True or false? _____

77. The statute of limitations for rule 10b-5 actions is three years from the date the misrepresentation or omission is discovered. True or false? _____

78. Acquireco offers cash to the shareholders of Target Corp. for their common stock in Target Corp. If the common stock of Target Corp. is registered under section 12 of the 1934 Act, would this be a tender offer for the purposes of section 14(d) of the 1934 Act? _____

79. Between February and April of this year, Acquireco acquires more than 5% of the 1934 Act registered common stock of Target Corp. It is Acquireco's intention to attempt to gain control of Target Corp. through a tender offer. Must Acquireco disclose this information to the management of Target Corp.? _____

80. Acquireco makes a tender offer for the common stock of Target Corp. Target Corp. sends out a letter to its shareholders which misrepresents the financial condition and the experience of Acquireco's management. Does Acquireco have standing in federal

court to bring an action for damages against Target Corp. under section 14(e) of the SEA?

81. In the above question, could Acquireco get an injunction against the mailing of such a letter?

82. For the federal proxy rules to apply, must a company have a class of its equity securities registered under section 12 of the 1934 Act?

83. Mergeco has a class of its equity securities registered under section 12 of the SEA of 1934. It schedules its annual meeting of shareholders, where one issue to be voted on is the merger of Mergeco into Consolid Corp. No proxies are solicited. Under the federal proxy rules, must Mergeco file with the S.E.C. and distribute to its shareholders prior to the shareholders' meeting the same information that would have been included in a proxy statement had proxies been solicited?

84. The antifraud provisions of the federal proxy rules do not apply to oral representations made in the course of a proxy solicitation. True or false?

85. Under the antifraud provisions of the federal proxy rules, in cases where proxies are needed to secure affirmative action on a matter proposed to the shareholders, the plaintiff in a private damage action need only show that a misstatement or omission was "material" in order to substantially meet the requirement that the proxy materials be shown to have caused the damage for which the complaint seeks relief. True or false?

86. Tish owns 15% of the common stock of Bankco. The common stock is registered under section 12 of the 1934 Act. Tish also owns 15% of the convertible preferred stock of Bankco, which is not registered under section 12. Tish buys and then sells shares of the convertible preferred stock within six months at a profit. May a shareholder of Bankco sue Tish in a derivative action for the profit under section 16(b)?

87. Martha owns 8% of the registered common stock of L-Mart Corp. She buys an additional 4% at $10 per share on March 1. On April 1, she sells 4% at $20 per share. Is Martha liable as an "insider" under section 16(b) of the 1934 Act for her profit in the sale on April 1?

88. Directors and officers may be held liable under section 16(b) as "insiders," even though they were not insiders both at the beginning and at the end of the matched purchase and sale (or sale and purchase), as long as they held office at either the time of the purchase or at the time of the sale. True or false?

89. Generally, when a corporation is merged or sold in exchange for stock, there is a "sale" of the securities surrendered by the selling company's shareholders and a "purchase" of the securities received from the buying company. Thus, section 16(b) would apply to such transactions. True or false?

90. As a general rule, for an insider to be liable under section 16(b) of the 1934 Act, she must be shown to have actually received and unfairly used "inside" information. True or false? _____

91. Abbey is a lawyer. She does not represent Macrosoft Corp., but she is a good friend of Macrosoft Corp.'s president, Bill. Macrosoft Corp. is having trouble selling a private offering of its securities. Bill asks if Abbey will help him market the issue, and Abbey agrees. Abbey takes no compensation for her services. Abbey calls several of her clients and suggests that they buy Macrosoft Corp. stock. They do so. In fact, the Macrosoft Corp. investment memorandum contained material misrepresentations concerning Macrosoft Corp.'s financial position. May the clients of Abbey successfully sue Abbey as an aider and abettor under rule 10b-5? _____

92. It has been clearly established by the courts that any employer can be held liable on the basis of traditional agency principles for the acts of employees that constitute a violation of either the 1933 or 1934 Acts. True or false? _____

93. The financial statements of an issuer used in a registration statement under the 1933 Act must be certified by an independent accountant. Arthur is an accountant. Is Arthur "independent" under the 1933 Act in the following circumstances?

    a. Arthur provides bookkeeping services for the issuer. _____

    b. Arthur provides human resources services for the issuer. _____

    c. Arthur designed the information system of the issuer. _____

94. Duncan, an accountant, assists Ronen Corp., Duncan's largest client, in the publication of materially false financial statements. (Duncan, knowing that Ronen Corp. has not stated its income according to generally accepted accounting principles, nevertheless certifies the financial statements as having been prepared correctly.) The financial statements are then used as part of an offering memorandum in a private placement of securities. Yoshi buys some of the stock after reading the financial statements. When the fraud is disclosed, may Yoshi bring suit for his losses against Duncan under rule 10b-5? _____

95. McCall is a lawyer representing Nationsco in a registration under the 1933 Act. In conferences with the president of the corporation, it is disclosed to McCall that the backlog of orders which Nationsco has stated that it has is really not as large as indicated. McCall considers this a material misstatement of fact in the draft of the registration statement. He asks the president to correct it, and the president declines, feeling that the sale of the stock issue depends on showing favorable prospects for the future. McCall must report the matter to Nationsco's chief legal officer. True or false? _____

96. Bigco has its common stock listed for trading on the New York Stock Exchange. May Bigco's stock be traded at the same time on other regional exchanges, over-the-counter, and directly between financial institutions? _____

97. The basic function of a "specialist" on the floor of a national securities exchange is to see that a continuous trading market exists for buying and selling specific securities listed on the exchange. True or false? _____

98. Under specific and limited circumstances, the courts will imply a private remedy for damages for violation of one of the rules of a national securities exchange (such as by a broker-dealer member). True or false? _____

99. Abbey is a broker-dealer doing a securities business in interstate commerce. She is not a member of any national securities exchange.

    a.   Must Abbey register with the S.E.C.? _____

    b.   Must Abbey belong to and be regulated by the National Association of Securities Dealers ("NASD")? _____

100. Stock market manipulation is any attempt to set prices or other criteria of stock market performance through transactions entered into with that specific purpose. True or false? _____

101. Market stabilization is one form of market manipulation that is specifically prohibited by the 1934 Act. True or false? _____

102. Smith Blarney is an underwriting firm selling a new issue of Sellco to the public in a registered offering. It plans to hold back 50,000 of the 500,000 shares being offered in the hopes that demand will lift the stock almost immediately above its $25 per share offering price. Once the price rises above $25, Smith Blarney will begin selling the 50,000 shares for its own account. Are such sales by Smith Blarney unlawful? _____

103. The "shingle theory" holds that a broker-dealer subject to one of several antifraud provisions of the securities acts may be held liable under one of these sections even though the broker-dealer's conduct does not amount to the statutorily required intentional wrongdoing. True or false? _____

104. Sheerson, a broker-dealer, buys 100 shares of Sellco on March 1 for $5 per share and sells the shares to its retail customers the same day for $10 per share. Could this be a violation of NASD and S.E.C. rules? _____

105. NASD and S.E.C. rules require that registered broker-dealers disclose their relationship with their customers where the broker-dealer is making a market in a security which the broker-dealer buys or sells to the customer. True or false? _____

106. In a "boiler room" operation, the crux of the 1934 Act violation is that the broker-dealer and its salespeople normally fail to comply with NASD and S.E.C. rules requiring that broker-dealers know the facts concerning any recommended security and give full disclosure of such facts to the customer. True or false? _____

107. May Charles Squabb, a broker-dealer, be held liable under the NASD or S.E.C. rules where it fails to exercise reasonable supervision over its sales personnel in the recommendations that such personnel give their customers? _____

108. The Federal Reserve Board, and not the S.E.C., is responsible for developing the margin rules pursuant to section 7 of the SEA of 1934. True or false? _____

109. Rule 10b-5 of the 1934 Act will be applied to foreign nationals and foreign securities transactions as long as there is some substantial U.S. contact and a substantial U.S. interest to be protected. True or false? _____

110. Regionalco wishes to sell a public offering of its stock to residents of seven states. If Regionalco registers its stock under the 1933 Act, will it be required to register in any of the seven states? _____

Answers to Review Questions

1. **YES** — The primary markets are the facilities for the first issuance of securities to the public. [§12]

2. **NO** — The securities acts define the terms "broker" and "dealer" in specific contexts. But, in general (in functional terms), a **broker** is one who buys or sells securities as an agent, for a commission. [§§27-28]

3. **TRUE** — Material disclosures are to be given in the registration statement and prospectus (liability provisions of sections 11 and 12(a)(1) relate thereto), and section 12(a)(2) of the SA is a general liability provision relating to fraud in the interstate sale of securities. [§§62-63, 108-112] Similarly, SA section 17 is a general antifraud provision that can be enforced by the government, although probably not by private plaintiffs. [§§854-857]

4. **YES** — The 1933 Act applies to public offerings of securities, and the Trust Indenture Act applies to specified large issues of debt securities. [§§62, 78]

5. **YES** — The registration provisions of the 1934 Act apply to (i) securities listed on a national securities exchange, and (ii) equity securities that are held by 500 or more shareholders, if the issuer has over $10 million in assets. Issuers with a class of securities registered under the 1934 Act must make periodic reports under that Act. [§§64, 874-882] Here, Microcorp has stock traded on the NYSE, so it is subject to 1934 Act registration and reporting.

6. **NO** — Interstate commerce must be involved. However, it is extremely unlikely that a public offering could be made without using some means of interstate commerce. [§§85, 90]

7. **NO** — A firm commitment underwriting is one where the underwriter buys the issuer's securities, marks them up, and sells them to the public. [§105]

8. **NO** — Section 4(1) of the Act indicates that registration applies only to issuers, underwriters, or dealers. Xavier is none of these. And he is not a control person, which would make him an issuer by the terms of the 1933 Act. [§§113, 241]

9. **NO** — The 1933 Act allows the issuer and the underwriters to conduct negotiations during the pre-filing period; such negotiations are expressly excluded from the definitions of "offer" and "sale." This is true for all categories of issuers, even nonreporting issuers (which is what Issuer currently is). It also applies to underwriters acting among themselves. [§§129-130]

10. **NO** — Although the letter may constitute a contract (it is hard to know for sure without carefully analyzing its specific terms), even contracts between issuers and underwriters (or among underwriters) are allowed during the pre-filing period. [§129]

11. **YES**   Issuer is a nonreporting company, which has the most severe limitations on what it is allowed to do during the pre-filing period. In this case, Issuer is allowed to make certain statements not referring to the proposed offering (*e.g.*, statements made more than 30 days before filing, under rule 163A, and statements of regularly communicated factual business information, under rule 169). Here, however, Issuer mentioned the offering. Consequently, the statement must be within rule 135 or it is a violation. Rule 135 does not allow Issuer to name the underwriters; hence the ad violates section 5. [§§121, 133, 142]

12. **YES**   The calls are unlawful offers during the pre-filing period. Although negotiations and agreements between the issuer and the underwriters (and among underwriters) are permitted, retail sellers are not included. [§§127, 129]

13. **YES**   In this case, Issuer is an unseasoned issuer, rather than a nonreporting issuer. [§122] Such issuers are permitted to communicate factual business information, plus forward-looking information, during the pre-filing period. [§§137-139] However, the offering must not be mentioned, or section 5 is violated. Rule 135 still applies, as it did to a nonreporting issuer, but it does not permit naming the underwriter. [§142]

14. **YES**   In this case, Issuer is a seasoned issuer [§123], but the limitations on its activities during the pre-filing period are the same as those that apply to an unseasoned issuer. The ad violates section 5. [§§137-139]

15. **PERHAPS NOT**   In this case, Issuer is a WKSI (well-known seasoned issuer) [§124], and as such Issuer has nearly—but not quite—unrestricted ability to make oral and written offers, even during the pre-filing period. Here, the conditions that the ad would have to meet are: (i) it must be filed with the S.E.C. if and when a registration statement ultimately is filed; and (ii) it must contain the warning legend specified by rule 163(b)(1). Even if these conditions are not met, however, the offer may not be considered illegal if Issuer can show that it made a good faith and reasonable effort to comply with the conditions. [§135]

16. **NO**   However, certain *offers* are permissible in this period. [§§151, 154-157]

17. **YES**   Although dealers participating in an offering are sometimes allowed to include information about issuers and their industries in research reports, this rule does not apply to issuers conducting IPOs. [§149] This kind of publicity during the waiting period would be viewed by the S.E.C. as an illegal offer.

18. **NO**   Emails, websites, and the like are all within the definition of "graphic communications" and are regulated the same as other written materials. Widespread distribution of the preliminary prospectus is not only allowed, it is required in order to obtain acceleration of the effective date of a registration statement. [§186] That leaves the other statements in the emails. These, too, are treated as

writings. In this case, such writings would qualify as free writing prospectuses, and as long as they contain the appropriate statements and copies are filed with the S.E.C., free writing prospectuses are legal. The same analysis would apply if the preliminary prospectuses were mailed, with cover letters, to the dealers. In that case, the cover letters would be free writing prospectuses. [§§161-167]

19. **YES** The problem here is that sales are not allowed until the registration statement is effective. Although no sale has been consummated here, on the facts the parties have formed an executory contract of sale, and under the 1933 Act that is defined as a sale. [§§131, 154]

20. **NO** In general, participating dealers may publish reports on the industries of issuers that are 1934 Act reporting companies, provided the issuers are current in their reporting obligations. [§149]

21. **NO** The executory contract of sale created between Dealer and the customer amounts to a sale under the 1933 Act, but offers and sales are permitted in the post-effective period. [§192] There are no written offers involved and no securities or confirmation are being delivered, so the prospectus delivery rules are not implicated. [§194] Within two days after the sale, however, Dealer will have to send the customer a notice "to the effect that the sale was made pursuant to a registration statement or in a transaction in which a final prospectus would have been required" but for rule 172. [§§201-208]

22. **NO** A confirmation of sale may be sent to the customer as long as the requirements of rule 172 are met, which means essentially that a registration statement has been declared effective, a final prospectus has been filed with the S.E.C., and no S.E.C. stop orders or examinations are pending regarding the offering or the participants in the offering. [§§203-206]

23. **NO** As with confirmations, Dealer does not need to deliver a prospectus as long as the requirements of rule 172 are met. [§§203-206]

24. **NO** Dealer's research report qualifies as post-effective free writing, because it was accompanied by the final prospectus. As such it does not need to contain a legend or be filed with the S.E.C. [§194]

25. **TRUE** The Act gives dealers a limited prospectus delivery exemption, which begins after the end of the statutorily defined "distribution" period. [§§212, 218]

26. **NO** The delivery requirement continues as long as the dealer is selling part of its original allotment. [§216]

27. **YES** Muriel meets the definition of "underwriter" in section 2(a)(11) of the 1933 Act. [§227]

28. **NO**   The theory for finding Dirk an underwriter would be that he "participated" in the public offering. However, it is doubtful that there is sufficient participation here to warrant such a finding. [§§230-231]

29. **YES**   Alfred is a "control person," and therefore the brokerage firm with which he deals will be deemed an "underwriter" under the 1933 Act. Consequently, the exemption provided in SA section 4(1) will not be available to Alfred, because his transaction will involve an underwriter. [§§240-245] Alfred's alternative to registration is to sell under the provisions of SA rule 144. [§§679 *et seq.*]

30. **DEPENDS**   Such a plan, although dealing with a commodity (real estate) that is not normally thought of as a security, has the elements associated with a security—profit-making and services by central management (subdivision). However, if resales are totally the responsibility of the buyers, then perhaps there is no security because there is substantial involvement in management by the investors. [§§268-275]

31. **YES**   Under the *Howey* test, it appears to be an investment contract, with management provided by Astrid. [§278]

32. **NO**   General partnership interests are not usually securities under the 1933 Act. However, if the holder of the interest has no real partnership power or is expected to delegate most power, a general partnership interest may be treated as a security. [§279]

33. **FORM S-1**   The 1933 Act provides a number of forms for use by particular types of companies or for special types of securities offerings. S-1 is the general form. [§§310-315]

34.a. **YES**   As part of the financial statements. [§323]

   b. **NO**   However, the S.E.C. encourages disclosure of earnings projections, with appropriate cautionary statements. [§§336 *et seq.*]

   c. **YES**   This is material because it may disclose a conflict of interest between the key management and the issuer, which is relevant information to an investor. [*See* Regulation S-K item 404] [§330]

   d. **NO**   Not expressly required by any directive related to the 1933 Act, and yet it is potentially very important to investors because the performance of the company may be dependent on the emotional stability of the president and other key officers. However, if the omission of this fact would make the registration statement, as a whole, misleading, the psychiatric care must be disclosed. [*See* SA Rule 408] [§330]

35. **FALSE**   The S.E.C. does not make such a guarantee. The issuer and specified persons involved with the offering must take responsibility for any material inaccuracies. [§372]

36.	**FALSE**	A stop order proceeding is available at any time. [§390] There are limitations, however, on the issuance of a refusal order. [§389]
37.	**YES**	But the S.E.C. may, on request, shorten this period and declare the statement effective. [§378]
38.	**NO**	Withdrawal at this stage is at the discretion of the S.E.C. staff. [§394]
39.	**DEPENDS**	This is a "shelf registration," which is available to many issuers under certain circumstances and is automatically available to WKSIs. [§§411-415]
40.	**TRUE**	However, because section 12(a)(2) of the 1933 Act covers any misrepresentation in the sale of securities, an issuer would probably want to update the registration statement and prospectus if subsequent events made anything stated therein at the time of use a material misrepresentation. [§§402, 750]
41.	**NO**	Section 11 applies only to errors in the registration statement at the time it is declared effective. [§§401-402]
42.	**TRUE**	However, most exemptions under the 1933 Act are transaction exemptions; with a transaction exemption only the specific transaction is exempt. Later resales (as by a control person) may have to be registered. [§§422, 430]
43.	**YES**	Of course, where the dealer exemption applies, the dealer will have no need for the broker exemption. [§439]
44.	**FALSE**	The selling customer must find its own exemption. [§442]
45.	**NO**	The transaction does not come under the broker's exemption because it is a dealer sale (out of inventory). [§443]
46.	**IN GENERAL, TRUE**	Under section 4(2) of the Act, the S.E.C. and the courts look at a number of variables in making the private offering determination. [§§455-469] There are, however, specific "safe harbor" rules with objective criteria for determining whether an offering is a private one. [*See, e.g.,* rule 506] [§514]
47.	**TRUE**	This is a basic consideration underlying the S.E.C.'s application of the section 4(2) exemption for offerings not made to the public. [§456]
48.	**NO**	The S.E.C. and the courts consider several variables in deciding whether an offering is private and, therefore, exempt under SA section 4(2). While the number of offerees and the number of purchasers are both relevant, neither figure is determinative. An offering could be public, notwithstanding that it was made only to 11 offerees and purchasers. [§§452-469]
49.	**YES**	Where possible, the S.E.C. will argue that apparently separate private offerings should be integrated into one public offering, in order to prevent issuers from avoiding the registration provisions of the 1933 Act. [§§431-432, 471]

50. **TRUE**   Section 3(b) of the Act permits the S.E.C. to provide for exemptions in certain small offerings. The S.E.C. has allowed for a shortened registration procedure in the case of regulation A offerings. [§§516-517]

51. **NO**   A control person must always find an exemption for his sales. Rule 147 is a transaction exemption and does not cover secondary sales by control persons. [§§571, 585-599]

52. **YES**   All offerees and purchasers must be residents of the same state. [§593]

53. **NO**   There is no sale for "value." [§606] However, the additional stock that will be issued must be registered, unless the transaction independently qualifies for an exemption.

54. **YES**   Here there has been a change in the rights of the security holders. It is not a mere exchange of paper with no increase or lessening of the substantive rights of the preferred stockholders. [§§620, 626]

55. **YES**   But if Bondco required the class A bondholders to pay money to it on the exchange, the exemption might not apply. [§§626-627]

56. **YES**   The transaction is the type covered by rule 145—sale of all or substantially all assets. [§§643, 647]

57. **YES**   The distribution continues until it comes to rest in the hands of those taking for investment. A and B have participated in a public distribution. [§§670-671]

58. **YES**   It makes no difference that Abbey established investment intent. When a control person (an "affiliate of the issuer") sells through a broker, the broker becomes an underwriter and the 1933 Act section 4(1) exemption for transactions not involving an underwriter is not available. [§670]

59. **YES**   The one-year holding period of rule 144 applies only to sales of restricted stock. [§689]

60. **NO**   This is not sufficient disclosure of information concerning Smallco to apply rule 144. The S.E.C. requires that the rule 15c2-11 information about the issuer be "publicly available," *i.e.*, supplied to the issuer's shareholders, brokers, marketmakers, and any other interested persons. In addition, financial information about the issuer must be published in a recognized financial reporting service. [§§687-688; *and see* §617]

61. **YES**   Rule 144 provides that restricted securities cannot be resold until at least one year has passed since the date the securities were acquired from the issuer. In this case, 14 months have passed, and so rule 144 will apply to Barbie's sale. [§§689, 695]

62. **YES**   Most courts hold that persons who purchase a security in the secondary market can recover under section 11, as long as they can prove that the specific securities purchased were issued in the offering registered by the defective registration statement. [§788]

63. **$0**   Under SA section 11, when securities are sold before suit, the measure of damages is the price paid for the security (but not more than the offering price), less the price at which the security was sold. [§811] Applying this measure, Matsuo cannot recover damages under section 11, because the price at which Matsuo sold was the same as the offering price: $10 per share.

64. **YES**   It is a violation of section 5 to make a public offering without registration absent an exemption. Section 12(a)(1) relates to any violation of section 5. It makes no difference that Ginsu Corp. did not intentionally violate the Act. [§§820-826]

65. **YES**   Section 12(a)(2) is a general fraud provision for purchasers. Here, the issue is whether the advisory board members are "sellers" under section 12(a)(2). Because the advisory board members solicited the purchasers, the board members here become sellers. [§§825, 850]

66. **YES**   Rule 10b-5 applies to all types of securities and securities transactions, not just those securities registered under the 1934 Act. There is, however, an interstate commerce requirement; *i.e.*, in order for the rule to apply, some means of interstate commerce must be used in connection with the purchase or sale of securities. [§§935-940]

67. **TRUE**   Otherwise, nearly any fraud could somehow be connected with a purchase or sale of securities, and there would be no limitation on rule 10b-5 causes of action. [§979]

68. **YES**   Clearly, a reasonable investor would want to know that the company had declared a dividend. Hence, the fact of a dividend is a *material* fact, and it must be announced by the corporation to avoid liability under rule 10b-5. [§974]

69. **FALSE**   There is no privity requirement under rule 10b-5. [§988]

70. **PROBABLY NOT**   The facts state that the prediction was made "carelessly." This implies negligence. Negligence does not amount to scienter, which is required in an action under rule 10b-5. [§§993-995] This applies to actions brought by the government and by private plaintiffs. Moreover, the prediction may qualify as a forward-looking statement for purposes of the safe harbor in the 1995 Act. Under the safe harbor provision, no private plaintiff can bring a lawsuit under rule 10b-5 unless she can show actual knowledge that the statement was materially false or incomplete. [§998]

71. **NO**   For a plaintiff to bring a 10b-5 cause of action, she must be an actual purchaser or seller of securities. [§1005]

72.	**NO**	The shareholder must prove actual intentional wrongdoing by Artie Anson & Co. (or possibly recklessness). Negligence is not sufficient. [§§993-996]
73.	**YES**	Applying the "fraud on the market" doctrine raises a rebuttable presumption of reliance on any material misrepresentations or omissions. Here, Peter established that Ronen Corp.'s financial condition was material, and that it was misrepresented. However, the presumption is rebuttable by "[a]ny showing that severs the link between the alleged misrepresentation and either the price paid by the plaintiff, or his decision to trade at a fair market price." Here, Ronen Corp. has severed the link, by showing that Peter was not relying on the integrity of the market price, but rather was speculating about the success of the merger talks. [§§1020-1021, 1025]
74.	**YES as to all**	These persons are all insiders. [§1040]
75.	**MAYBE**	In certain circumstances; *see* discussion of the *Texas Gulf Sulphur* case. [§1057]
76.	**FALSE**	The trend is to limit damages to the plaintiff's gain (or avoided loss). [§§1098-1099]
77.	**FALSE**	The statute of limitations for rule 10b-5 actions provides that actions must be brought within one year after discovery of the facts constituting the rule 10b-5 violation, and in no event more than three years after the violation took place. [§1114]
78.	**YES**	A tender offer is an offer directly to a company's shareholders for their stock. Section 14(d) is the basic section that regulates the making of tender offers. [§§1127, 1137]
79.	**YES**	When a person acquires more than 5% of the registered equity securities of a company, that person must disclose her intentions with regard to the company to the management of that company. *See* discussion of section 13(d) of the 1934 Act. [§§1141-1143]
80.	**NO**	A bidder has no standing to bring a damages action in this circumstance. [§1208] However, if Acquireco is a shareholder of Target Corp., it may have standing as a shareholder to bring a damages action. [§1210]
81.	**YES**	Lower federal court opinions indicate that Acquireco would have standing here. [§1226]
82.	**YES**	The proxy rules apply only to companies reporting under the 1934 Act. [§1293]
83.	**YES**	If a matter requires a shareholder vote, an information statement must be filed and distributed, even if proxies are not solicited. [§1304]

84.	**FALSE**	Oral misrepresentations made by one soliciting proxies in the course of such solicitation are covered by rule 14a-9 of the proxy rules. [§1396]
85.	**TRUE**	The Supreme Court has indicated in the *Mills* case that causation is proved by showing materiality in a case where the proxy solicitation was an essential link in the accomplishment of the transaction. [§§1413-1414]
86.	**YES**	Tish qualifies as an "insider" under section 16 by virtue of her 15% ownership of a registered class of equity securities. Thereafter, purchases and sales of any equity security (*i.e.*, the convertible preferred stock), even if not registered, are covered by section 16. [§1440]
87.	**NO**	Section 16(b) requires that an insider for stock ownership must be a 10% owner at the time of a "purchase" *and* at the time of a "sale," if the purchase and sale are to be matched for section 16(b) purposes. Here, the purchase on March 1 does not qualify because Martha did not own 10% on that date. [§1460]
88.	**FALSE**	Transactions taking place *before a person becomes an officer* or director are not reportable and *will not be matched* with transactions taking place after the person takes office. However, transactions taking place *after the person leaves office will be matched* with transactions taking place less than six months previously, while the person was in office. [§§1451-1453]
89.	**TRUE**	But an exception has been made for certain defensive merger situations where the 10% owners must make such an exchange involuntarily. [§§1502-1507]
90.	**FALSE**	Section 16(b) applies if its specific requirements are met, whether or not inside information was actually used in the trading of securities by an insider. [§1538]
91.	**NO**	There is no implied private right of action against one who aids or abets a violation of rule 10b-5. [§1567] However, if Abbey meets the *Hochfelder* requirement of scienter, Abbey might be liable as a primary violator. Aiding and abetting, and other secondary liability theories, might be unnecessary.
92.	**FALSE**	The Supreme Court's decision in *Central Bank* makes it unlikely that a respondeat superior claim against an employer can be based on the federal securities laws. Such claims may be brought under state law (*i.e.*, where the primary violation is of state law). [§1586]
93.	**NO as to all**	SOXA prohibits an auditor from also performing the listed services. [§1614]
94.	**YES**	Duncan has intentionally participated in a violation of rule 10b-5. [§1634]
95.	**TRUE**	SOXA mandates up-the-ladder reporting of material violations of the securities law. [§1658]

96.	**YES**	A company's securities may be traded in many markets simultaneously. [§§1825-1831]
97.	**TRUE**	The specialist is in charge of specific securities and has the responsibility of seeing that those securities can always be bought or sold. [§1857]
98.	**FALSE**	Although the older cases implied such private damage actions, since the 1980s the trend is against the implication of such private remedies. [§§1893-1895]
99.	**YES to both**	Broker-dealers transacting an interstate business must be registered with the S.E.C. and must be members of the NASD (or, in theory, any other comparable body itself registered with the S.E.C.). As a practical matter, NASD membership is required because there are no other organizations comparable to the NASD that are registered with the S.E.C. [§§1903-1904]
100.	**TRUE**	Such manipulation is regulated by specific provisions of the 1934 Act and by the general liability provisions of the Act (*see* rule 10b-5). [§§1932-1938]
101.	**TRUE**	Currently, the S.E.C. has prohibited all stabilization not complying with regulation M, rule 104. However, if compliant stabilization transactions were to appear manipulative to the S.E.C., it would undoubtedly use the general liability provisions of the Act (rule 10b-5) to attack the transactions. [§1962]
102.	**YES**	The S.E.C. regulates such "hot issues" and prohibits Smith Blarney's conduct and similar conduct which gives the appearance that a stock is being offered at a specific price when in fact part of the offering is not really being sold to the public at the offering price at all. [§§1971-1973]
103.	**TRUE**	The courts have indicated that such broker-dealers make certain implied representations simply by entering the securities business (hanging out a shingle); these representations act as implied warranties, so that violation may be found under one of the antifraud provisions without proving actual intentional fraud. [§1993]
104.	**YES**	In a general policy statement, the NASD has indicated that its broker-dealers may not charge unreasonable commissions or markups. A markup limit of 5% has been set for same-day transactions. However, Sheerson could try to prove that 100% was not unreasonable if the actual market for the stock had moved up that much from the time it purchased the stock. [§1998]
105.	**TRUE**	To avoid conflicts of interest with customers, the rules require such disclosures to those with whom the broker-dealer is doing business. [§2021]
106.	**TRUE**	In a boiler room operation, a single security is promoted by high-pressure tactics. There is little or no concern for the rules requiring the broker-dealer to know the security and the customer and to make appropriate recommendations. [§§2041, 2046]

107. **YES**   The registered broker-dealer is held responsible for all of the transactions entered into by personnel registered under the broker-dealer. [§§2064-2067]

108. **TRUE**   But the S.E.C. has the responsibility of enforcement. [§2068]

109. **TRUE**   The position of the courts on this issue is about the same as it is with respect to application of any other United States law to foreign transactions. [§2100]

110. **DEPENDS**   Although most state "blue sky" laws were preempted in 1996, some offerings are still state-regulated. Regionalco will have to ensure that its securities are exempt from state regulation under 1933 Act section 18. [§2108]

Exam Questions and Answers

QUESTION I

A, who owns 25% of the stock of XYZ Corp., is a director and an officer of XYZ and is active in daily management. She pledges her stock in XYZ to a bank as collateral for a loan to buy some real estate. The stock of XYZ is publicly traded. Immediately after receiving the loan proceeds, A resigns as an officer of XYZ, knowing that the company is entering a period of financial difficulty. A enters the real estate business. As soon as the 90-day period of the loan is up, the bank calls the loan, and A refuses to pay. The bank resorts to the security (the XYZ stock), which it sells to pay off A's loan. Shortly thereafter, the news breaks that XYZ is in financial trouble, and the stock drops substantially in price. Applying only the Securities Act of 1933, is the bank an underwriter unlawfully engaged in a public distribution without registration?

QUESTION II

Without complying with the registration requirements of the Securities Act of 1933, XYZ Co. advertises in newspapers and over radio and television to find distributors for its product, a line of cosmetics. The distributors come from all walks of life, having had a great variety of former jobs, income levels, and educational backgrounds. Each distributor pays a fee of $5,000 for his "franchise," for which he receives an inventory of products which may be resold at a suggested retail price of $7,500. Also, the distributors receive the right to find other distributors, for which a finder's fee of $1,000 will be paid. Each distributor signs a contract with XYZ, which provides that the distributor is an "independent contractor." The company agrees to provide each new distributor with a one-week training course on how to recruit other distributors and for a fee will provide brochures, inspirational tape recordings, etc., which can be used in the recruiting meetings. But XYZ holds no meetings to assist its franchisees to recruit new distributors. All of XYZ's written materials and advertising allude to the tremendous profits that can be made under its program. But orally, before having the distributor sign a contract, the company warns potential distributors that selling the product and recruiting distributors is very hard work. The company acknowledges that the product line is really nothing special, and that the real money is to be made in recruiting other distributors. Actual results by distributors to date indicate that most have not earned their investment back; but a few have made substantial profits, mostly by selling other distributorships. One of the disgruntled distributors seeks advice as to whether he can get his $5,000 investment back if he returns the inventory unused. Consider only whether a "security" is involved under the 1933 Act.

QUESTION III

QRS Corp. registers an offering of its stock for public distribution through an underwriter. In the prospectus it indicates that its earnings for the coming year will be "nominal."

The stock is sold at $20 per share, which is the market price at the time of the offering. At the end of the year, the company announces that it has a loss of $25 million, or about one-third of its net worth. Immediately, the stock's price drops to $5 per share and remains there. Those who purchased QRS stock in the public offering bring a lawsuit to recover for material misstatements in the prospectus. At trial it is shown that the projection of earnings was done by the company's vice president of finance and accounting and that it was based on an "optimistic" outlook for the company's performance on existing government contracts which were behind schedule and experiencing cost overruns at the time the projection was made. Considering only section 11 of the 1933 Act, can the purchasers recover from QRS? (Do not consider the amount of damages.)

QUESTION IV

A is a successful promoter. She has a number of very wealthy friends who invest in the deals she puts together. She gets ideas, finds management, raises the money, puts the corporation together, and then, after several years of operation, merges the companies into larger companies.

A has a new idea for the manufacture of rotating widgets. She finds B (president), C (vice president of finance), D (vice president of marketing), E (vice president of manufacturing), and hires F as her attorney. F incorporates X Co., and for 10 cents per share, F issues common stock as follows:

A	=	50% or 50,000 shares
B	=	20% or 20,000 shares
C	=	9% or 9,000 shares
D	=	9% or 9,000 shares
E	=	9% or 9,000 shares
F	=	3% or 3,000 shares

Prior to the issuance of the stock, A explains to B, C, D, E, and F the basic idea, showing some feasibility studies concerning the development of the product, hands out some articles on the industrial applications involved, and talks about the plan for issuing stock and financing the company. B, C, D, and E are all experienced executives who have participated in forming companies before; they ask no more questions, simply trusting in A's track record. A has hired F because F's fees are low; this is F's first incorporation, and being impressed with the 3,000 shares offered, F asks no more questions. Also, A gives the impression that she does not want to hear any questions—the investors can simply take the deal or leave it. The group discusses the financing plans; all agree that this should be covered in the business plan which is to be written. All persons taking the common stock sign investment letters; F sees that a restrictive legend is placed on the shares and issues instructions to the transfer agent that no shares are to be transferred without an opinion from F. All shareholders become members of the board of directors.

State and resolve all issues raised by the above facts under section 4(2) of the Securities Act of 1933.

QUESTION V

X purchases 100,000 shares of privately offered (*i.e.*, restricted) securities from Y Co., a 1934 Act reporting company, giving Y a promissory note for the purchase price. The note is secured by collateral in the form of the restricted securities of Y that X purchased, the securities having a fair market value at least equal to the purchase price. The note is a nonrecourse note, meaning that in the event of default, the seller (Y) can look only to the collateral for payment; Y does not have recourse to X's other assets. One year later X, who is not a control person of Y, wants to sell these restricted securities over an exchange. The note has not been paid.

1.   Is rule 144 available to X for sale of his restricted securities?

2.   Assume that the facts are the same except that X gives Y securities other than the Y stock as collateral. A month after the purchase of the Y stock, the value of the collateral decreases to $50,000 less than the outstanding obligation on the note. X does not put up additional collateral. This condition continues for a period of six months, after which the market price of the collateral rises to a point above the amount owing on the note. Also, this time the note is a full-recourse note, and it is paid off prior to X wanting to sell the securities. One year after the purchase date, X wants to use rule 144 for sale of the restricted securities. Is it available?

3.   Assume that X buys the shares and pays Y cash, getting the money from a bank loan, for which he pledges the restricted securities. The securities drop in value below the amount of the bank note, and after one year they are still below the amount owed on the note. Finally, the bank's examiners require that the bank collect the under-secured loan, and so they ask X to sell the stock and pay off the loan. Can X use rule 144 to sell the restricted securities?

QUESTION VI

XYZ is a drug manufacturer. It is a public company, traded on the New York Stock Exchange. A, the head of research, has been working on a cure for cancer for 15 years. The company has spent $5 million on this research. The only other person in the company who knows about all of the ramifications of the project is B, the company president. On January 1, A mentions to B, while they are having lunch together, that he has made an interesting but puzzling breakthrough. Using an extract from cancerous cells of cattle, he had injected various cancerous animals and found that in some cases he has cured them. B becomes very excited. The stock of the company has been doing very poorly in the market, and B is under pressure from some shareholders and the board of directors to improve performance. A, however, has been down many blind alleys before, and he succeeds in calming B down, indicating that there are so many variables involved that it may be as long as five years before he knows whether they have really discovered anything. B goes away depressed, but he continues to think about the matter. Recalling vaguely the *Texas Gulf Sulphur* case, and thinking that his own situation might be helped if he disclosed the company's current progress, B calls C, an outside lawyer for XYZ. B calls a conference at which A, B, and C discuss the matter of company disclosure. They decide that it would be helpful to have the opinion of an outside consultant concerning progress of the project. They bring in D, a world-renowned researcher in cancer. He confirms A's estimate of the complexity of the remaining research and that it could take at least five years to know if something substantial would come from the project. When asked her opinion, C indicates that she thinks disclosure is not required and might even be misleading. Based on her opinion, all concur in the decision to delay an announcement.

S is a shareholder. On February 1, five days after the last meeting between A, B, and C, S sells 1,000 shares of XYZ at $5 per share. This is a transaction over the New York Stock Exchange.

In the meantime, B feels "in his bones" that A is on the verge of a dramatic breakthrough in cancer therapy. On February 10, he buys 1,000 shares on the exchange at $5 per share.

On the morning of March 1, A bursts into B's office with news that, working nonstop, he has miraculously succeeded in separating an element from the cancerous cells that, when injected into dogs with eye cancer, seems immediately to go to work curing the diseased cells. Word has already leaked out to the research staff; by midafternoon, the XYZ stock is trading at $10 per share. C is called in and issues a careful news release indicating that, as of March 1, the company has made progress in separating an element from cancerous cells of cattle that seems to have an effect in curing eye cancer in animals, but that nothing is known in the way of definitive research or what the possible effect may be on human beings.

The news release is sent to all shareholders and given to the major news services. By March 15, the stock has gone to $20 per share. By March 30, it is $25 per share. S checked with her broker on March 1 about her holdings and was told that XYZ stock had taken off, based on some cancer research breakthrough.

After checking into the facts, S hires you as an attorney and asks you to sue B, C, and XYZ under rule 10b-5. By the time the suit is brought, the stock of XYZ is selling at $30 per share.

While you are waiting to come to trial (18 months after the filing of the complaint), XYZ announces that further research indicates that there are harmful side effects from the extract and that all further research based on the extract has been discontinued. Within 24 hours, the stock of XYZ is trading at $3 per share.

C and her law firm have been counsel to XYZ for 10 years. C's name has appeared in XYZ's annual reports, registration statements, etc. Three months before she was asked for her opinion about whether to disclose the initial research findings, C resigned as a member of XYZ's board of directors.

Discuss the merits of S's lawsuit against B, C, and XYZ under rule 10b-5. Do not consider the measure of damages or contribution among parties, if you find one or more persons liable.

QUESTION VII

On December 15, the federal government issued new regulations, making the curing of tobacco more expensive.

On January 1 of the next year, X Corp., a conglomerate that had been very active in buying other companies, was approached by D, a shareholder in Y Corp., about buying D's 10% interest in Y Corp.'s common stock. Y Corp. is a small tobacco company. C, Y Corp.'s president, is 68 years old. He is also chairman of the board of directors. He owns 250 shares of Y Corp.'s 1,574,354 outstanding shares and has had an option to purchase 50,000 additional shares for many years. (The market price of the company's stock has never risen substantially above the option exercise price, which is $14 per share. The market price of the company's stock is now at $8 per share.) The rest of the board is comprised of C's cronies, who have been on the board for an average of 10 years; their average age is 66. The rest of the management (*i.e.*, the key officers) are all around age 60. D is the largest shareholder of Y Corp. and has been trying to get C to either get new management or sell the company. The earnings per share of the company have been dropping for the last five years and are now at 80 cents per share. The multiple of 10 times earnings for the stock price is just a little below the industry average.

D, finally tiring of feuding with C about the future of the company, has sought out X Corp. and offered the stock for sale. D tells the management of X Corp. that the new government regulations may have raised the value of Y Corp.'s inventory. He therefore offers his stock for $12 per share. The book value of the stock is $8 per share. X Corp. already owns a cigarette manufacturer (of the Superman brand), and, aware of the recent government regulation, its management has been looking for a tobacco company to buy.

After an investigation of Y Corp. (which involves no contact with its management), X Corp. buys D's stock for $12 per share. At the closing of the sale, on January 15, D has a conversation with the vice president of acquisitions for X Corp., suggesting that it would make a lot of sense for X Corp. to buy Y Corp. for a premium over the market price of the Y stock and then to liquidate Y Corp. The vice president of X Corp. makes no response.

The minutes of a directors' meeting of X Corp., held on January 30, indicate that the directors (including the vice president of acquisitions) authorized a tender offer for Y Corp.'s shares at $10 per share. The reason for the acquisition is stated to be that X Corp., concerned about the possible increased tobacco costs to its cigarette manufacturer, is seeking a stable source of tobacco.

The vice president of acquisitions of X Corp. then approaches C and indicates that X Corp. intends to bid for the shares of Y. During a lengthy discussion, the vice president makes it known that if C is willing to cancel his 50,000 stock options, once the acquisition is complete, X Corp. will see to it that C is given a five-year management contract at a substantial increase in salary. C gives his tentative agreement to this plan.

On February 15, X Corp. makes a cash tender offer for all of the Y stock at $10 per share (the market price being $8 per share). The offer states that it is contingent on the tender of at least 67% of the stock. In fact, 68% of the stock is offered, which X Corp. accepts. The tender offer discloses to Y shareholders all relevant financial information about X Corp., its management, the fact that an X Corp. subsidiary is in the cigarette manufacturing business, that over the past five years it had sought to expand sales and earnings by buying other companies in related businesses, that it has offered a five-year management contract to C, and that it is offering a price in excess of recent market values of Y's stock.

On February 28, a board meeting of Y Corp. is held. All directors except C resign. New directors are elected by X Corp. C gives up his stock options and is given a five-year management contract at a substantial increase over his present salary. A discussion is then held concerning the future of Y Corp. and ways to improve the running of the business are discussed in detail.

A month later, there is another board meeting of Y Corp., at which X Corp. has its nominees pass a resolution to liquidate Y Corp. State law requires a two-thirds vote of the shareholders, which X Corp. gets by voting its own shares. Y Corp. is liquidated within 30 days. It turns out that the value of its tobacco inventory is worth 100% more than its stated book value, which brings the asset value of each Y share to $16 per share.

The shareholders that sold to X Corp. in its tender offer bring a class action against X Corp. under rule 10b-5 of the 1934 Act. After discovery, plaintiffs stipulate that X Corp. did not receive any inside information from Y Corp. (or key persons associated with Y) in making its tender offer.

In discussing the issues in the above fact situation, consider only rule 10b-5 as applicable to the case. (If you find a cause of action, do not discuss the measure of damages.)

QUESTION VIII

A, who has a net worth of $150 million, buys on the stock exchange 5.1% of XYZ Corp. common stock. A has a history of taking companies over through tender offers. As soon as he completes the purchase, he files a section 13(d) information report with the S.E.C., as required under the 1934 Act, completing responses to all of the questions asked. In the report, A says he has no present intention to take over XYZ. But speculators, suspecting that A will make a move to take over XYZ, begin buying the XYZ stock in the market. The stock moves very rapidly from $5 per share to $10 per share. In the meantime, A goes back to running his other enterprises. A year goes by, and the stock of XYZ falls back to $5 per share. A now makes a tender offer for 51% of the XYZ stock at a price of $7.50 per share. In the section 14(d) information report required under the 1934 Act, A indicates that it is his present intention to gain control and remove the management of XYZ. B, a former shareholder of XYZ who sold out at $5 per share shortly before A's tender offer, now sues A for damages for a misleading section 13(d) report. Who wins?

ANSWER TO QUESTION I

The bank appears to be an underwriter who sold securities unlawfully without registration. A initially appears to be a "control person" because she is in a position to influence the direction of XYZ. Thus, the bank is potentially an underwriter of A's securities because it may be held to have "purchased" the securities from an issuer with a view toward distribution to the public. (Under section 2(a)(11) of the 1933 Act, control persons, like A, are "issuers" for purposes of determining those who are underwriters.) The 1933 Act requires underwriters to comply with the registration provisions of the Act unless they can distribute the securities in the offering under some exemption.

Before the bank can be found to be an underwriter, it must first be determined whether A's having left XYZ changes her status as a control person, so that the bank can claim that it is no longer selling for an issuer. The answer is *probably not*. A still owns 25% of the company's stock (even though it is pledged), which is probably enough to be influential in the direction of the company.

The next issue concerns the status of the loan. If it is spurious (*i.e.*, a device merely to give A cash for her securities), then it is clear under *Guild Films* that the bank is an underwriter. Here, the loan probably was not spurious. A's motivation was to get rid of her stock because she knew the company was in financial trouble, and she probably did not have time to register the stock (or to sell it under rule 144) before it fell in price. The bank would never have gone along with a pledge with this knowledge. Additionally, the loan was probably not a weak loan: The stock was pledged and A had the real estate she bought with the loan (and probably other property as well), so the bank had adequate security for the loan. But even if the loan was bona fide, that does not clear the bank. Although no court has expressly held that a good faith loan and pledge requires registration before a public resale by the pledgee, the S.E.C.'s position would probably be that the stock should have been registered before being sold. Here, the results of the sale would seem to support the S.E.C.'s position. Shortly after the sale, XYZ's difficulties were revealed and the stock dropped in price. Had the bank registered the securities, an investigation of XYZ would have revealed its problems, and the public would not have purchased overpriced securities. Hence, the bank should have gone after A for other security or to force her to register the stock before the sale, sold the securities in accordance with SA rule 144, or taken a loss on the loan.

ANSWER TO QUESTION II

The issue is whether a security is involved. There are several tests for a security, each one of which must be considered:

	Test	Answer	Analysis
a.	Is it listed as a security in section 2(a)(1) of the Act?	No	

b. Is it an investment contract? **Probably**

1) Is it an investment with the expectation of profit? **Yes**

2) Are the essential management functions performed by the promoter with the investor passive? **Yes**

3) Is there a "common enterprise"? **Yes**

The critical issue here concerns the degree of participation and effort by the company. *S.E.C. v. Koscot* held that the program for solicitation of distributors was an investment contract and could be separated from the sale of the product involved. A similar situation is present here. There is an investment of money, a return depends primarily on recruiting other distributors, the efforts of the company are an important part of this recruiting process, and finally, the success of the scheme as a whole is dependent on the essential managerial efforts of the company. Also, there is a "common enterprise" in that the efforts of management *and* the investor are necessary to the success of the scheme.

Counterarguments would be that the investors have to work very hard to make a profit and, therefore, the analogy should be to the purchase of a franchise. Investors are even called "independent contractors" and warned of the difficult work involved. They are given recruiting materials but are not assisted in the actual recruiting. Also, the conservative definition of a "common enterprise" is an investment by a group of investors whose pool of capital is necessary to fund the development of the scheme.

Nevertheless, the tendency is to find a security in this type of case, if the company is involved in performing at least some of the management functions critical to the success of the scheme. Thus, given the company's advertising program, the one-week training course, the fact that its product is "nothing special," and the above trend, it appears that the weight of the arguments is in favor of finding a security.

| c. | Do the investors need the protection of the Act? | Yes | The persons enlisted here appear to be relatively unsophisticated and the program involves a large number of people. |

ANSWER TO QUESTION III

The issues here concern what must be included in the registration statement, what (under section 11) is a "fact" and a "material" fact, and the application of the safe harbor for forward-looking statements.

The registration statement must include all of those facts that a reasonable investor would consider material in making an investment decision whether to buy the company's securities being offered. Traditionally, the S.E.C. indicated that only historical "hard" facts should be included, and (although relevant to investors) opinions on matters such as projected earnings should not be included. Hence, QRS would argue that all investors should take with a grain of salt the projected earnings in the registration statement (because it was only an opinion and not to be relied on), and there should be no recovery. However, including a projection in the registration statement, and an optimistic one at that, is almost certain to have an effect on the sale of the securities. The S.E.C. has encouraged issuers to include forward-looking statements, by providing a safe harbor for such statements.

QRS stock appears to be publicly traded because there was a market price at the time of the transaction in question ($20 per share). QRS is, therefore, a 1934 Act reporting company and is eligible for the safe harbor, in the absence of any information indicating that it is excluded. The transaction does not appear to be excluded from the safe harbor; therefore, it will apply. Under the safe harbor, private plaintiffs must prove that the defendant had actual knowledge that the forward-looking statement was false or materially incomplete. Whether the "optimistic" outlook here meets this test is unknown, but it will be difficult for the plaintiffs to make this showing. Even if they do so, if QRS can show that the statement was identified as a forward-looking statement, and was accompanied by meaningful cautionary statements, the plaintiffs will not recover. Here, it will be helpful to QRS if it fully disclosed: (i) that its government contracts were behind schedule and experiencing cost overruns; and (ii) the possible impact of continued schedule difficulties and overruns. Boilerplate warnings will not suffice for QRS.

All in all, it seems unlikely that the plaintiffs will win unless they can make the difficult "actual knowledge" showing.

ANSWER TO QUESTION IV

The issue here is whether this is a private offering of securities pursuant to section 4(2) and thereby exempt from registration under section 5 of the 1933 Act. The availability of the section 4(2) exemption turns on whether, considering all the circumstances of the offering, the potential purchasers need the protection of the 1933 Act. That question, in turn, depends on a number of factors:

1) *Manner of offering and number of offerees:* First, was the offering conducted in a "public" manner, reaching a large number of offerees (which would make it likely that at least some of the offerees need 1933 Act protection)? Here, it seems that the offering was not conducted in a public manner: No advertising was used, and there was no general solicitation. Likewise, the number of offerees was relatively small.

2) *Sophistication of the offerees:* Also relevant to the need for 1933 Act protection is the relative sophistication of the offerees, *i.e.*, their knowledge, experience, ability to bear the risk of the investment, and their ability to properly evaluate the merits of the securities offered. Here, there seem to be some questions that might be raised, especially with respect to F: B, C, D, and E have all participated in similar transactions before, and are "experienced executives" who presumably know a great deal about the risks of transactions like this one. F, however, has never incorporated a business, and evidently is far less experienced than the others. On the other hand, F is investing only $300 (3,000 × 10 cents), and therefore very likely can easily bear the risk of the investment. Moreover, F is a lawyer, and perhaps even a relatively unsophisticated lawyer is more savvy in business matters than a layperson.

   From a policy perspective, this is a "seed capital" sort of transaction, with a small group of people putting up the initial cash to get a business started. If the S.E.C. were to require all such transactions to be registered, economic growth would suffer tremendously.

   On balance, then, while F does not seem to meet precisely the criteria for a private placement investor, F is also not clearly unsuitable. This factor alone should not make the exemption unavailable.

3) *Type of information provided:* Another important factor examined in section 4(2) cases is the nature and amount of information provided. If the information is both qualitatively and quantitatively equivalent to the information that would be contained in a 1933 Act registration statement, or if the offerees at least had access to such information on request, the offering will be more likely to qualify under section 4(2). Here, however, that does not seem to be the case. Certainly F does not have access to this kind or amount of information, and it is at least questionable whether B, C, D, and E had such access. On balance, the information requirement has not been met in this case.

4) *Resale restrictions:* The facts indicate that a restrictive legend was placed on all share certificates and that the transfer agent was instructed not to transfer shares without F's approval. Therefore, appropriate restrictions on resale have been imposed on the securities to prevent their secondary distribution to the public by the initial participants.

5) *Other factors:* The remaining factors favor the exemption's availability in this case. The total dollar value of the offering is relatively small ($10,000); the securities were offered only to a reasonably homogenous group; and the securities, while marketable in theory, because they are relatively cheap, have been restricted and therefore are essentially unmarketable without the called-for legal opinion.

In conclusion, while not all the requirements of section 4(2) were met here, many businesses are formed this way. Given the small dollar amount involved and the nature of the participants, all of whom have some professional tie to the issuer, it is likely that a court would apply 1933 Act section 4(2) and find the transaction exempt from registration.

ANSWER TO QUESTION V

1. No. Rule 144, which sets forth objective criteria for those wishing to prove investment intent after purchasing and holding privately offered securities, is not available to X. One technique by which rule 144 achieves its goal of assuring the necessary investment intent is by requiring a purchaser to bear the full economic risk of the investment for one year before reselling. This one-year holding period is tolled until the purchaser has paid for the securities in full (because until the securities have been paid for, the risk of ownership is not really on the buyer). Although X acquired the securities one year ago, X has not yet paid the note delivered in exchange for the securities, and therefore the holding period requirement has not been satisfied.

    Rule 144(d)(2) provides that the holding period will commence if the securities are paid with a promissory note that (i) provides for full recourse against the purchaser of the securities, and (ii) is secured by collateral other than the securities purchased, having a fair market value at least equal to the purchase price. Neither of these requirements is met here, however. Finally, even if both requirements were met, rule 144(d)(2)(iii) requires that any note given in payment be paid in full before the securities are sold. Therefore, even if X had paid with a note otherwise meeting the requirements of rule 144, X would not be permitted to sell under the rule until the note is paid.

2. No. Rule 144 requires that collateral be equal in value to the outstanding amount of the loan *at all times* during the holding period. The holding period of rule 144 is tolled any time the value of the collateral drops below the amount of the debt—which it did here for a period of six months. Only in this way is X, the purchaser, subject to the full risk of having *purchased* the securities, rather than leaving that risk with the issuer.

3. Yes. Here, X (the purchaser) and the bank, but not the issuer (Y), bear the risk of the purchase of the securities; Y already has received the purchase price. Therefore, after one year X may use rule 144 to sell the securities.

ANSWER TO QUESTION VI

The first issue is whether any of the defendants is an "insider." The corporation (XYZ) is. So is B, the president. But is C such an insider? She has resigned from the board and represents the corporation only as its outside attorney. Still, as such, she was given access to the company's inside information and was bound by a fiduciary duty to the company; therefore, she is an insider.

Moving on, then, the next question is whether XYZ and C, neither of whom traded in securities, can be liable in this case. Certainly the issuer, XYZ, can be liable, as was the issuer in the *Texas Gulf Sulphur* case. But can C be liable? Although at one time an aiding and abetting theory might have resulted in C's liability, aiding and abetting is no longer available to private plaintiffs in rule 10b-5 cases (after the *Central Bank* decision). The facts do not support an inference of fraudulent intent on C's part. In the absence of any trading by C, then, it is unlikely that C can be liable under rule 10b-5.

B, on the other hand, traded in XYZ stock, albeit before the most promising information about the cancer therapy was known to anyone. The next issue, then, is whether B was under a duty to disclose the information in his possession on February 10 about A's research into cancer treatments. Was that information a "material fact"? *Texas Gulf Sulphur* might seem to indicate that the answer is "No."

Facts are material when a reasonable investor would want to know the information and would give it significance in making an investment decision. *Texas Gulf Sulphur* and *Basic* indicated that in making this determination, the probability of the fact actually coming to fruition should be considered along with the magnitude of the impact of such a fact on the market for the company's securities. Here, the impact of a cancer cure would be phenomenal, much like the discovery of ore in the *Texas Gulf Sulphur* case, or the takeover in *Basic*, or perhaps greater than both. But the probability of the cure becoming a reality is very small indeed. So it is a close question whether the company should have been required to issue a very cautionary press release, or whether, having checked out the probabilities, the chances for a cure were too remote to require disclosure. Certainly the chances of the cancer cure becoming reality were much smaller than the ore discovery becoming reality in *Texas Gulf Sulphur*.

Assuming that a press release should have been issued, there is still the issue of whether S can prove the necessary scienter to recover from B or XYZ. *Hochfelder* would seem to require that B have acted with the intent to defraud (with the possibility that reckless conduct would qualify).

Assuming that the required state of mind can be proved, the plaintiff will have no difficulty establishing that the nondisclosure was "in connection with" a sale of securities. Reliance and loss causation are the remaining elements. The fraud on the market doctrine can provide a presumption of reliance with respect to this transaction, but only if the plaintiff can establish materiality—which is in doubt. Loss causation will also be difficult for the plaintiff to show, because there is no evidence that S would have sold during the brief period in which XYZ stock was trading above $5 per share.

In conclusion, the case against C will fail. The case against B and XYZ is extremely weak, both because the materiality of the undisclosed facts is doubtful and because loss causation will be very difficult to establish.

ANSWER TO QUESTION VII

The overall rationale of rule 10b-5 is to protect the public interest in the integrity and fairness of the securities markets and securities transactions by ensuring that interstate purchase and sale transactions involving securities are free from fraud.

There are several elements that a private plaintiff must prove to sustain a rule 10b-5 cause of action: a security; a purchase or sale; fraud in connection with the purchase or sale; a material fact, if the fraud is misrepresentation or omission of a fact; reliance; scienter; and loss causation.

The main issues here concern whether there is an omission of a material fact and, if so, whether there was the required scienter.

a. *Material Fact?*

1) Was it an omission of a material fact to fail to disclose that a new government regulation made the curing of tobacco more expensive and that, therefore, Y Corp.'s inventory of tobacco had a market value much higher than its book value?

a) *Arguments that it is not a material fact:* The information is public knowledge (D, a Y Corp. shareholder knew about it; why should X Corp. have to specifically inform other Y Corp. shareholders about it?). X Corp. should not have to disclose information about another company to that company's shareholders (it should only have to disclose information about its own company). X Corp. is not an insider here, so it has no fiduciary duty to disclose information about Y Corp. to Y shareholders.

b) *Arguments that it is a material fact:* X Corp. owned 10% of the Y stock at the time of the offer and had had meetings with Y Corp. management, so it is an insider and as such has a special duty to Y shareholders to disclose what it knows that affects their interests. The *Leasco* case might be authority that X Corp. must disclose information that it knows about the company to be acquired, although that was a 1933 Act (section 11) case, not a rule 10b-5 case. Inventory of tobacco has an easily ascertainable value in the market; therefore, its value is a fact and must be disclosed.

2) Even assuming there was no omission of a material fact in failing to disclose the inventory value, was it an omission of a material fact to fail to disclose the intent to liquidate Y Corp.?

a) *Arguments that it was a material fact:* The intent to liquidate would have warned Y shareholders that there was greater value in Y Corp.'s assets than appeared on the books. There was clear intent to liquidate, as shown by X Corp.'s purchase of 68% of the stock and the fact that Y Corp. was liquidated shortly after its acquisition.

b) *Arguments that it was not a material fact:* There was no intent to liquidate at the time of the tender offer, as shown by the board minutes of X Corp., the giving of a five-year management contract to C, and the meeting on ways to make Y Corp. run effectively. Even if there was intent, it was not material because many companies buy other companies and liquidate them afterward—disclosure of such an intent would have told the Y shareholders nothing about a higher intrinsic value than was shown on the books.

b. *Scienter?* Was there intentional conduct (or possibly reckless conduct)? Certainly X Corp. and its key executive knew about the higher inventory value, and if it is shown that they had the intent to liquidate Y Corp., it could reasonably be inferred that they purposefully failed to disclose this information to Y shareholders.

c. *Purchase or Sale of a Security?* Yes. Y shareholders sold to X Corp., and the alleged fraud was directly connected with the sale.

d. *Reliance?* Would the Y shareholders have relied on the material undisclosed information had it been disclosed? Probably yes.

e. *Loss Causation?* Did the failure to disclose cause the loss to Y shareholders? In cases of deceptive omission, showing materiality generally suffices to establish loss causation unless X Corp. can show that some other cause was responsible for the loss.

ANSWER TO QUESTION VIII

The problem here is that A's real intentions at the time he completed the purchase of 5.1% of XYZ's common stock are unknown. Section 13(d) of the 1934 Act requires that the party acquiring equity securities of the issuer disclose his *present* intent with respect to the company ("present intent" includes changes to be made in management, whether a tender offer for control is contemplated, etc.). There are several possible explanations for A's conduct, some of which lead to liability, and some of which do not.

For example, A may have assumed that speculators would begin bidding up the price of XYZ's shares as soon as they discovered that A had taken a position in XYZ. This would increase the cost of a tender offer for XYZ, so A may have intended to wait until the price dropped back down before commencing his tender offer. But what if this was his intention? It is not clear when the tender offer would commence, or even if it ever would (the stock price might not decline). Moreover, if that was A's intention, disclosing it would make it less likely ever to be realized, because the speculators might just hang on, waiting for A's tender offer.

On the other hand, perhaps A had no present intention to make a tender offer at the time the section 13(d) report was filed. Maybe he bought the 5.1% purely as an investment. The intention to take control may not have arisen until after, perhaps long after, the report was filed.

Ultimately, a court may have to make a factual determination about A's intention and whether A misrepresented it. This can be very difficult, especially in the context of a tender offer, where business conditions can change a person's mind overnight. It is especially difficult in this case, which raises the question whether a person's intent to do something only after the passage of a significant period of time and the occurrence of events that might never happen, is a "present" intention.

Tables of Citations

CITATIONS TO SECURITIES ACT OF 1933

Section	Text Reference	Section	Text Reference	Section	Text Reference
2(a)(1)	§§258, 261, 267, 276		464, 470, 472, 476,	8A(c)(2)	§759
2(a)(3)	§§129, 130, 131,		485, 487, 514, 585,	8A(e)	§761
	192, 605		587, 708, 709, 711,	10	§§152, 154, 156, 191,
2(a)(4)	§§226, 266		717, 731, 2114		193, 198, 220, 839
2(a)(7)	§§86, 2073	4(3)	§§208, 212, 217,	10(a)	§§156, 157, 163, 182,
2(a)(9)	§164		252, 435		194, 198, 199, 200,
2(a)(10)	§§153, 158, 163, 182,	4(3)(B)	§218		206, 207, 220, 650
	201, 650, 839	4(3)(C)	§216	10(a)(3)	§§223, 403
2(a)(10)(a)	§§182, 194, 196,	4(4)	§§437, 447, 2114, 2119	10(b)	§§156, 157, 160, 191,
	207	4(5)	§433		199, 220, 650, 857
2(a)(10)(b)	§§182, 183	4(6)	§§476, 477, 478,	11	§§63, 95, 193, 224, 372,
2(a)(11)	§§227, 228, 230, 235,		479, 508		753, 773, 774, 775, 776,
	236, 239, 240, 442,	5	§§63, 110, 118, 120, 124,		780, 781, 782, 783, 788,
	446, 506, 670, 710,		169, 177, 209, 210, 216,		789, 792, 793, 794, 818,
	720		219, 226, 253, 257, 430,		819, 829, 831, 845, 846,
2(a)(12)	§§213, 251		452, 535, 599, 600, 604,		853, 854, 866, 888, 1129,
2(a)(15)	§478		605, 620, 645, 650, 653,		1561, 1588, 1596, 1631,
3	§§484, 587		670, 677, 746, 749, 820,		1648, 1649, 1753, 1973
3(a)	§§2114, 2119		821, 823, 828, 829, 833,	11(a)	§§774, 783, 787,
3(a)(2)	§§423, 834		834, 1563, 1956		792, 793, 818
3(a)(3)	§424	5(a)	§§127, 131, 151,	11(c)	§796
3(a)(4)	§425		152, 154	11(e)	§§791, 810, 812, 816
3(a)(5)	§426	5(a)(1)	§192	11(e)(3)	§814
3(a)(6)	§427	5(a)(2)	§§192, 202	11(f)	§§818, 868
3(a)(7)	§§428, 667	5(b)	§§152, 155	11(f)(2)	§§819, 1753
3(a)(8)	§§295, 429	5(b)(1)	§§152, 154, 192, 194,	11(g)	§815
3(a)(9)	§§430, 620, 622, 624,		198	12	§§224, 1129, 1650
	626, 633, 669, 717	5(b)(2)	§§111, 127, 152, 158,	12(a)(1)	§§749, 754, 820, 821,
3(a)(10)	§§430, 630, 631, 632,		159, 192, 202		822, 823, 825, 827,
	633, 645, 669, 717	5(c)	§§127, 131, 132, 152,		829, 831, 832, 849,
3(a)(11)	§§430, 570, 573, 576,		155, 386, 1129		850, 854, 872, 1562,
	579, 585, 717	6	§308		1563, 1564, 1596
3(a)(12)	§430	6(a)	§§412, 777	12(a)(2)	§§63, 95, 750, 754,
3(b)	§§430, 477, 484, 485,	7	§§308, 318		833, 834, 835, 837,
	487, 510, 514	7(b)	§405		838, 839, 840, 842,
3(c)	§430	8	§§188, 527, 1727		843, 845, 849, 850,
4(1)	§§209, 256, 434, 670,	8(b)	§389		851, 852, 853, 854,
	708, 709, 713, 1129,	8(d)	§390		857, 1564, 1596,
	2114, 2119	8(e)	§§386, 387		1754, 1973
4(2)	§§452, 453, 454, 463,	8A(a)	§760	12(b)	§§853, 1754

Section	Text Reference
13	§792
14	§872
15	§§782, 822, 1578, 1584, 1588
16(b)	§2116
17	§§63, 275, 750, 854, 1129, 1566
17(a)	§§224, 765, 855, 857, 858, 1117, 1118, 1652, 1653, 1768, 1991
17(a)(1)	§§854, 856, 858, 1117, 1220, 1656, 1736
17(a)(2)	§§854, 856, 1117, 1220, 1656
17(a)(3)	§§854, 856, 1117, 1220, 1656
17A	§998
18	§§2108, 2109, 2112, 2114, 2115
18(a)(1)	§487
18(b)	§2119
18(b)(4)(D)	§487
20	§1723
20(a)	§§762, 1695
20(b)	§762
20(d)	§§757, 763
24	§§765, 1759, 1767
27(a)(3)(A)	§1738
27(a)(3)(B)	§1739
27(a)(3)(B)(iii)	§1740
27(a)(3)(B)(vi)	§1744
27(a)(4)	§1743
27(a)(5)	§1755
27(a)(6)	§1755
27(a)(7)	§1755
27(b)	§§1746, 1747
27(c)	§1756
27(d)	§1736
27A	§350
27A(a)	§351
27A(b)	§§352, 353
27A(c)(2)	§360
27A(c)(1)(B)	§361

CITATIONS TO SECURITIES ACT RULES

Section	Text Reference
122	§1680
133	§§636, 638, 639, 644, 645
134	§§176, 182, 183, 184, 191, 220
134(d)	§184
135	§§142, 143, 145, 150, 181, 652, 1190
137	§§146, 147
137(b)	§148
138	§§146, 149
139	§146
139(a)(2)	§149
141	§§130, 235
142	§234
144	§§95, 232, 442, 447, 659, 660, 678, 679, 680, 681, 682, 683, 684, 685, 687, 688, 689, 694, 697, 700, 704, 708, 720
144(c)	§686
144(c)(1)	§687
144(c)(2)	§688
144(d)(1)	§689
144(d)(3)(i)	§692
144(d)(3)(iv)	§694
144(d)(3)(v)	§695
144(d)(3)(vi)	§696
144(d)(3)(vii)	§697
144(e)	§699
144(e)(3)	§700
144(f)	§701
144(g)	§701
144(h)	§702
144(i)	§702
144(j)	§703
144(k)	§685
144A	§§681, 718, 719, 720, 721, 723, 725, 726, 727, 728, 730, 731, 732, 733
144A(a)(1)	§724
144A(b)	§722
145	§§95, 125, 232, 413, 634, 635, 638, 639, 640, 641, 642, 643, 644, 645, 646, 647, 648, 649, 654, 655, 657, 658, 659, 660, 717, 1325
145(a)(1)	§641
145(a)(2)	§642
145(b)	§652
145(c)	§655
145(d)	§660
145(d)(2)	§659
145(d)(3)	§659
147	§§585, 586, 587, 588, 589, 590, 593, 594, 595, 596, 597, 598, 599, 717
147(b)(2)	§587
147(c)	§596
147(c)(1)	§595
147(c)(2)	§596
147(d)(1)	§597
147(d)(2)	§597
147(e)	§§588, 589
147(f)(1)	§589
149	§627
150	§628
152	§§472, 473, 474, 475
153A	§649
155	§§474, 475, 476
155(a)	§476
163	§§135, 141, 167, 169, 174
163(b)(1)	§§135, 174
163(b)(1)(iii)	§135
163(b)(2)(iii)	§135
163(A)	§§133, 167
164	§§167, 169, 174, 191, 196, 199, 200, 207
164(e)(2)	§176
165	§652
166	§653
168	§§137, 140, 141, 167
168(b)(1)	§138
168(b)(2)	§139
168(c)	§137
169	§§141, 167
169(b)	§141

Section	Text Reference	Section	Text Reference	Section	Text Reference
172	§§201, 202, 203, 204, 206, 207, 208	262	§§513, 517, 524, 529	501(e)(1)(iv)	§490
		262(a)	§525	502	§§485, 491
172(a)	§204	262(b)	§§526, 527	502(a)	§492
172(b)	§205	262(c)	§527	502(b)	§§493, 495
172(c)	§206	263	§517	502(b)(2)	§494
173	§§208, 212, 220	405	§§124, 163, 164, 165, 166, 241, 568, 569, 784, 785	502(b)(2)(i)	§496
174	§§208, 220			502(b)(2)(ii)	§497
174(d)	§219			502(b)(2)(v)	§498
175	§337			502(b)(2)(vii)	§498
215	§478	408	§319	502(c)	§§499, 502, 503, 504
251	§517	413(a)	§418	502(d)	§506
251(a)(1)	§519	413(b)	§418	503	§§485, 508
251(a)(2)	§520	415	§§414, 415	504	§§485, 487, 491, 494, 500, 501, 507, 508, 509, 510, 515, 516
251(a)(3)	§521	415(a)(5)	§419		
251(a)(4)	§522	415(a)(6)	§419		
251(a)(5)	§523	419	§§405, 409, 410	504(b)(1)	§§500, 507
251(a)(6)	§524	430(a)	§§158, 192	504(b)(2)	§510
251(b)	§§531, 532, 533, 534	430A(c)	§159	505	§§485, 487, 490, 491, 494, 498, 499, 508, 511, 512, 513, 514, 515, 516, 585, 670, 681
251(c)	§535	430B	§420		
251(d)(1)(i)	§554	430B(a)	§417		
251(d)(1)(ii)(C)	§§556, 558	430B(d)	§420		
251(d)(1)(iii)	§557	431	§160		
251(d)(2)	§532	433	§§167, 169, 179, 191, 196, 199, 200, 201	505(b)(2)(i)	§512
251(d)(2)(i)(B)	§560			506	§§453, 471, 476, 477, 485, 487, 490, 491, 494, 498, 499, 508, 514, 515, 516, 681
251(d)(2)(i)(C)	§561	433(c)	§175		
251(d)(2)(ii)	§§562, 564	433(c)(2)	§174		
252	§517	433(d)	§§177, 179		
252(g)(1)	§543	433(d)(1)	§775		
252(g)(2)	§545	433(e)(1)	§177	506(b)(2)(ii)	§515
253	§517	433(e)(2)	§178	507	§485
253(e)	§§546, 566	433(g)	§180	508	§485
253(e)(2)	§565	456(b)	§417	701	§§480, 481, 482, 483, 535
254	§§517, 549	460	§189		
254(a)	§§549, 552	461(c)	§871	701(c)	§681
254(b)(1)	§550	462(e)	§416	701(d)(3)(iv)	§483
254(b)(2)	§551	477	§394	801	§681
254(b)(3)	§555	501	§§485, 488, 489, 503	802	§681
255	§517	501(a)	§500	901	§735
255(a)	§§553, 555	501(a)(1)	§489	902	§§735, 739
256	§517	501(a)(2)	§489	902(d)	§736
257	§§517, 547	501(a)(3)	§489	902(j)	§737
258	§§517, 528	501(a)(4)	§489	903	§735
259	§517	501(a)(5)	§489	904	§735
260	§§517, 548	501(a)(6)	§489	905	§735
260(a)(2)	§564	501(a)(7)	§489		
261	§517	501(a)(8)	§489		

CITATIONS TO SECURITIES EXCHANGE ACT OF 1934

Section	Text Reference	Section	Text Reference	Section	Text Reference
2	§873	11A	§§915, 1834		1218, 1219, 1220, 1221,
3(a)(1)	§§891, 1817	11A(b)	§899		1224, 1226, 1230, 1396
3(a)(4)	§1982	12	§§65, 874, 876, 877,	14(f)	§§1133, 1139
3(a)(5)	§1982		878, 879, 882, 883,	15	§§71, 72, 73, 908, 1903
3(a)(10)	§§934, 1983		907, 912, 1136, 1138,	15(a)	§§1984, 1987
3(a)(11)	§934, 1477		1141, 1170, 1172, 1202,	15(a)(1)	§1984
3(a)(12)(A)(vii)	§880		1293, 1294, 1306, 1439,	15(b)	§§895, 896, 937, 1905,
3(a)(13)	§990		1446, 1478, 1512, 1578,		1956, 1985, 2042
3(a)(14)	§990		1776, 1821, 2097	15(b)(4)	§897
3(a)(17)	§§89, 2088	12(a)	§876	15(b)(4)(E)	§§2046, 2064
3(a)(26)	§1837	12(b)	§§876, 921, 1296, 2088	15(b)(6)	§2046
3(a)(38)	§§701, 1879	12(b)(1)	§878	15(b)(6)(A)	§1913
3(a)(51)	§407	12(g)	§§877, 921, 1295, 2088	15(b)(6)(B)(i)	§1913
4C	§1665	12(i)	§918	15(b)(6)(B)(ii)	§1913
4C(a)	§1666	12(k)	§1691	15(b)(8)	§§94, 898
5	§§892, 1818, 1836	13	§§65, 67, 659, 687,	15(c)	§§1933, 1940, 1941,
6	§§71, 891, 893,		881, 882, 884, 903,		1942, 1943
	908, 1819, 1837		913, 1227	15(d)	§§659, 687, 882, 884,
6(b)(5)	§92	13(a)	§§1079, 1618		1079, 1776
6(e)	§§1851, 1852	13(b)(2)	§§881, 886, 887, 914	15(g)	§1912
7	§§69, 2068, 2070, 2071	13(d)	§§904, 1133, 1136,	15A	§§73, 1905, 1956
8	§69		1139, 1140, 1142, 1143,	15A(b)(6)	§93
9	§§70, 921, 937, 1132,		1144, 1145, 1146, 1149,	16	§§68, 1280, 1433, 1437,
	1933, 1934, 1935,		1150, 1155, 1156, 1157,		1438, 1441, 1442, 1443,
	1936, 1937, 1938,		1158, 1159, 1160, 1194,		1445, 1446, 1451, 1452,
	1939, 1940, 1942		1201, 1224		1453, 1454, 1455, 1456,
9(a)	§1933	13(d)(1)	§1141		1458, 1459, 1462, 1464,
9(a)(1)	§1934	13(d)(3)	§1144		1474, 1475, 1479, 1483,
9(a)(2)	§§1241, 1242, 1934,	13(d)(6)	§1156		1485, 1486, 1487, 1490,
	1956	13(d)(6)(B)	§1141		1495, 1502, 1506, 1512,
9(a)(3)	§1934	13(e)	§§1133, 1139, 1156,		1519, 1522, 1537, 1539,
9(a)(4)	§1934		1203		1540, 1542, 1545, 1546
9(a)(5)	§1934	13(f)	§909	16(a)	§§907, 1157, 1434,
9(a)(6)	§§1935, 1957, 1962	13(g)	§1140		1439, 1443, 1445, 1454,
9(b)	§1935	14	§§66, 67, 912, 913,		1460, 1463, 1470, 1471,
9(c)	§1935		1131, 1227, 1409		1478, 1479, 1500, 1501,
9(e)	§§1211, 1785, 1938	14(a)	§§967, 1288, 1394,		1505, 1543, 1555
10(b)	§§74, 922, 926, 933,		1406, 1409, 1428	16(b)	§§907, 921, 1434, 1438,
	1205, 1211, 1394, 1409,	14(c)	§1304		1439, 1443, 1450, 1454,
	1569, 1572, 1761, 1933	14(d)	§§1133, 1137, 1139,		1456, 1460, 1461, 1465,
10A(g)	§1615		1144, 1161, 1162,		1470, 1471, 1472, 1474,
10A(i)(1)(A)	§1616		1166, 1170, 1172, 1179,		1478, 1479, 1481, 1485,
10A(i)(1)(B)	§1617		1190, 1194, 1198, 1200,		1502, 1507, 1508, 1510,
10A(i)(2)	§1618		1203, 1224		1520, 1521, 1523, 1525,
10A(i)(3)	§1619	14(d)(1)	§§1199, 1202		1528, 1531, 1537, 1538,
10A(j)	§1620	14(d)(2)	§1144		1539, 1543
10A(k)	§1622	14(d)(4)	§§1137, 1230	16(c)	§§1435, 1439, 1545,
10A(l)	§1623	14(d)(5)	§1180		1547, 1548, 1550, 1551,
11	§§894, 1578	14(d)(6)	§1182		1552, 1554, 1557, 2097
11(a)	§§1855, 1869, 1877,	14(d)(7)	§1183	16(d)	§1555
	1878	14(e)	§§1133, 1138, 1139,	17(a)	§§1641, 1991, 2043
11(a)(1)(A)	§1879		1205, 1206, 1207, 1208,	17(a)(1)	§1992
11(a)(1)(G)	§1880		1212, 1214, 1215, 1216,	17(a)(2)	§1992

Section	Text Reference	Section	Text Reference	Section	Text Reference
17(a)(3)	§1992	21	§§929, 1723	21D(e)	§1752
17A	§900	21(a)	§§1674, 1688	21D(f)	§§1102, 1753
18	§921	21(d)	§§1004, 1695, 1764	21(D)(f)(5)	§819
19	§73	21(d)(3)	§763	21D(f)(10)(c)(ii)	§819
19(a)(3)	§1956	21(d)(5)	§1716	21E	§§350, 998
19(b)	§§72, 1839, 1846, 1905	21A	§1087	21E(a)	§351
19(c)	§§72, 91, 1839, 1905	21C	§1727	21E(b)	§§352, 353
19(d)	§§1840, 1905	21D(a)(3)(A)	§1738	21E(c)(1)(B)	§361
19(e)	§1719	21D(a)(3)(B)	§1739	21E(c)(2)	§360
19(h)	§§1841, 1905	21D(a)(3)(B)(iii)	§1740	23(a)(1)	§917
20	§§2037, 2067	21D(a)(3)(B)(vi)	§1744	25	§931
20(a)	§§1579, 1581, 1584, 1585, 1591	21D(a)(4)	§1743	27	§§928, 1121, 1695
20(e)	§§1571, 1590, 1597, 1653	21D(a)(5)	§1755	28(a)	§1276
		21D(a)(6)	§1755	28(e)	§1853
20(f)	§1758	21D(a)(7)	§1755	28(f)	§2116
20A	§1088	21D(b)	§1108	30(b)	§§2095, 2096, 2097
20A(b)(1)	§1090	21D(b)(3)	§§1746, 1747	32(a)	§§1759, 1767, 1771
20A(b)(2)	§1090	21D(b)(4)	§1754		
		21D(d)	§1736		

CITATIONS TO SECURITIES EXCHANGE ACT RULES

Section	Text Reference	Section	Text Reference	Section	Text Reference
3a51-1	§407		1120, 1125, 1130, 1132,	11b-1	§1870
3b-3	§1923		1138, 1205, 1211, 1212,	11Aa3-1	§§699, 708
3b-6	§337		1213, 1214, 1217, 1218,	12g-1	§§65, 877
10a-1(a)(1)	§1930		1219, 1221, 1222, 1394,	12g3-2(b)	§§2090, 2091, 2092
10a-1(c)	§1929		1396, 1397, 1409, 1413,	12h-3	§882
10b-5	§§74, 95, 275, 773,		1437, 1438, 1472, 1567,	13a-1	§884
	857, 872, 922, 926,		1568, 1569, 1570, 1571,	13a-11	§884
	932, 933, 934, 935,		1576, 1586, 1593, 1594,	13a-13	§884
	936, 937, 938, 941,		1633, 1634, 1635, 1636,	13d-1	§904
	942, 945, 946, 947,		1653, 1656, 1736, 1752,	13d-5	§§1144, 1146
	948, 949, 950, 953,		1761, 1785, 1909, 1937,	13d-6	§1156
	954, 959, 961, 967,		1939, 1940, 1954, 1962,	13e-1	§§1239, 1241
	972, 974, 979, 980,		1973, 1990, 1991, 2009,	13e-4	§1240
	981, 982, 983, 987,		2027, 2043, 2047, 2060,	13f-1	§909
	988, 993, 995, 996,		2061, 2097, 2100, 2120	14a-1	§§1284, 1306
	999, 1000, 1001, 1003,	10b5-1	§§1038, 1046, 1047,	14a-1(l)	§1301
	1004, 1005, 1006, 1008,		1048, 1049	14a-1(l)(2)	§1380
	1009, 1010, 1012, 1026,	10b5-1(c)(1)	§1050	14a-2	§1375
	1027, 1031, 1032, 1037,	10b5-1(c)(2)	§1051	14a-2(a)(1)(iii)	§1374
	1038, 1039, 1044, 1045,	10b5-2	§1075	14a-2(a)(2)	§1377
	1048, 1053, 1055, 1057,	10b-6	§1944	14a-2(a)(6)	§1378
	1058, 1060, 1062, 1069,	10b-10	§§201, 2012, 2020,	14a-2(b)	§§1313, 1388, 1389
	1070, 1071, 1072, 1073,		2027	14a-2(b)(1)	§1388
	1074, 1077, 1091, 1100,	10b-18	§§1241, 1242, 1243,	14a-2(b)(2)	§1376
	1101, 1102, 1103, 1104,		1244, 1245, 1246, 1247	14a-2(b)(3)	§1374
	1105, 1108, 1113, 1114,	10b-18(c)	§1242	14a-3	§§1290, 1300, 1305,
	1116, 1117, 1118, 1119,	10A-2	§1615		1308, 1374

Section	Text Reference	Section	Text Reference	Section	Text Reference
14a-3(a)	§1309	14d-1(g)(2)	§1173	15g-8	§409
14a-3(f)	§§1312, 1392	14d-2(b)	§1192	15g-9	§1920
14a-4(f)	§1310	14d-2(b)(2)	§1193	15g-9(a)(2)(ii)	§1915
14a-6	§§648, 1290, 1315, 1374	14d-6	§1176	16a-1(a)	§1445
		14d-6(a)(1)	§1177	16a-1(a)(1)	§1442
14a-6(a)	§1318	14d-6(a)(2)	§1178	16a-1(a)(2)	§1466
14a-6(g)	§1391	14d-7(a)(1)	§1180	16a-1(a)(2)(ii)(A)	§1444
14a-7	§§1331, 1371	14d-7(a)(2)	§1181	16a-1(a)(2)(iii)	§1476
14a-7(b)	§1332	14d-8	§1182	16a-1(e)	§1444
14a-8	§§1292, 1318, 1335, 1374	14d-9	§1230	16a-1(f)	§1448
		14d-9(f)	§1233	16a-2(a)	§1454
14a-8(a)	§1336	14d-10	§1183	16a-4(a)	§1479
14a-8(b)	§1336	14d-11	§1181	16a-8	§1471
14a-8(c)	§1335	14d-11(d)	§1181	16a-8(b)(2)	§§1465, 1474
14a-8(i)	§1350	14e-2	§§1137, 1188, 1231	16a-8(d)	§1470
14a-8(i)(7)	§1359	14e-3	§1189	16a-9	§1500
14a-8(j)	§1350	14e-5	§1187	16a-9(b)	§1499
14a-9	§§967, 1291, 1306, 1321, 1353, 1386, 1395, 1397, 1409, 1413, 1415	15c1-2	§§1937, 1941, 1956, 1990, 1991, 2043	16b-3	§1519
				16b-3(a)	§1557
		15c1-7	§§1941, 2032	16b-3(d)	§1557
14a-10	§1374	15c1-8	§§1941, 1973, 2023	16b-3(e)	§1557
14a-11	§1374	15c1-9	§1941	16b-5	§1501, 1553
14a-12	§§1314, 1374	15c2-8	§189	16b-6(b)	§1500
14a-13	§1367, 1374	15c2-11	§§617, 688, 2062	16b-6(c)	§1526
14a-14	§1374	15d-1	§884	16b-6(d)	§1530
14b-1	§1368	15d-11	§884	16b-7	§§1502, 1509
14b-1(b)(3)	§1370	15d-13	§884	19c-1	§§1889, 1890
14b-2	§1368	15g-2	§1914	19c-3	§1889, 1892
14b-2(b)(4)(ii)	§1370	15g-3	§1916	19d-1	§1719
14b-2(b)(4)(iii)	§1370	15g-4	§1917	21D(c)	§1756
14c-5	§648	15g-5	§1918		
14d-2	§1191	15g-6	§1919		

Table of Cases

McDonald Investement Co., S.E.C. v. - **§581**

McLean v. Alexander - **§1656**

MAI Basic Four, Inc. v. Prime Computer, Inc. - **§§1174, 1175**

Manor Nursing Centers, Inc., S.E.C. v. - **§224**

Marine Bank v. Weaver - **§§275, 934**

Marshak v. Blyth, Eastman, Dillon & Co. - **§2034**

Matter of - *see* name of party

Mayer v. Mylod - **§349**

Mayer v. Oil Field Systems Corp. - **§951**

Medical Committee for Human Rights v. S.E.C. - **§1360**

Medical Imaging Centers v. Lichtenstein - **§1748**

Meek, S.E.C. v. - **§1678**

Merrill Lynch, Pierce, Fenner & Smith, Inc. v. Livingston - **§1450**

Merritt, Vickers, Inc. v. S.E.C. - **§§1999, 2000, 2008, 2020**

Metge v. Baehler - **§1583**

Metge v. Bankers Trust Co. - **§1583**

Meyers v. C & M Petroleum Producers, Inc. - **§872**

Mills v. Electric Auto-Lite Co. - **§§1413, 1414, 1417, 1418, 1428**

Mitchell v. Texas Gulf Sulphur Co. - **§1094**

Monarch Fund, S.E.C. v. - **§1066**

Monjar, United States v. - **§291**

Monroe v. Hughes - **§794**

Monsanto, United States v. - **§1798**

Morales v. Reading & Bates Offshore Drilling Co. - **§1512**

Moss v. Morgan Stanley, Inc. - **§1076**

Mulheren, United States v. - **§1785**

Musick, Peeler & Garrett v. Employers Insurance Co. - **§1103**

Mutual Shares Corp. v. Genesco, Inc. - **§1010**

Myzel v. Fields - **§1095**

N

NCR Corp. v. American Telephone & Telegraph Co. - **§§1263, 1266**

Naftalin, United States v. - **§856**

National Securities, S.E.C. v. - **§992**

National Student Marketing Corp., S.E.C. v. - **§1653**

Nesbit v. McNeil - **§§2034, 2038**

Netter v. Ashland Paper Mills, Inc. - **§1549**

New York City Employees' Retirement System v. S.E.C. (1995) - **§55**

Newmont Mining Corp. v. Pickens - **§1197**

Noa v. Key Futures, Inc. - **§297**

Norlin Corp. v. Rooney, Pace, Inc. - **§1267**

Norris & Hirshberg, Inc., *In re* - **§§2028, 2036**

Novak v. Kasaks - **§§1110, 1749**

O

O'Brien, S.E.C. v. - **§1682**

O'Connor v. R.F. Lafferty & Co. - **§2061**

O'Hagan, United States v. - **§§1043, 1044, 1069, 1070, 1071, 1073, 1076**

Occidental Petroleum Corp., *In re* - **§1713**

Ohio Drill & Tool Co. v. Johnson - **§1096**

Osofsky v. Zipf - **§1097**

PQ

Palombi Securities Co., *In re* - **§2031**

Paramount Communications, Inc. v. Time, Inc. - **§1237, 1254**

Park & Tilford, Inc. v. Schulte - **§1483, 1485**

Parkersburg Wireless LLC, S.E.C. v. - **§284**

Patel, S.E.C. v. - **§1725**

Pelletier v. Stuart-James Co. - **§991**

People v. - *see* name of party

Petrites v. J.C. Bradford & Co. - **§2035**

Petteys v. Butler - **§1484**

Pinter v. Dahl - **§§823, 824, 825, 826, 850, 1562, 1564, 1650**

Piper v. Chris-Craft Industries, Inc. - **§§1208, 1209, 1210, 1211, 1216, 1226**

Plaine v. McCabe - **§1214**

Plesse Co., PLC v. General Electric Co., PLC - **§2105**

Polin v. Conductron Corp. - **§349**

Pollack v. Laidlaw Holdings, Inc. - **§300**

Portsmouth Square, Inc. v. Shareholders Protective Committee - **§1146**

Prager v. Sylvestri - **§1516**

R

Radol v. Thomas - **§1196**

Ralston Purina Co., S.E.C. v. - **§§456, 470, 480**

Randall v. Loftsgaarden - **§1091**

Reeder v. Mastercraft Electronics Corp. - **§1017**

Reliance Electric Co. v. Emerson Electric Co. - **§1460**

Resch-Cassin & Co., S.E.C. v. - **§§1933, 1939, 1956**

Reves v. Ernst & Young (1990) - **§§95, 264, 265, 299**

Reves v. Ernst & Young (1993) - **§1811**

Roberts v. Eaton - **§§1497, 1498**

Roberts v. Peat, Marwick, Mitchell & Co. - **§1636**

Robin v. Arthur Young & Co. - **§1636**

Robinson v. Penn Central Co. - **§970**

Rolf v. Blyth, Eastman, Dillon & Co. - **§2057**

Romani v. Shearson Lehman Hutton - **§349**

Ronconi v. Larkin - **§1112**

Rondeau v. Mosinee Paper Corp. - **§§1159, 1224**

Roosevelt v. E.I. DuPont de Nemours & Co. - **§55**

Rosenfeld v. Fairchild Engine & Airplane Corp. - **§§1430, 1432**

Ross v. A.H. Robins Co. - **§926**

Roth v. Fund of Funds, Ltd. - **§2097**

Index

commission rates, §§1849-1884

definition, §25

development, §§1883-1884

TOMBSTONE ADS

after qualification of offering statement, §558

and regulation A, §§556, 558

during waiting period, §§183-184

proxy exemptions, §1378

TOTALITY OF THE CIRCUMSTANCES TEST, §1166

See also Tender offers

TRANSACTION INFORMATION SYSTEMS, §§1898-1902

See also Over-the-counter market

TRANSFER AGENTS, §901

TRANSFER OF ASSETS, §643

TRUST INDENTURE ACT OF 1939, §78

U

UNDERWRITERS

agreement with dealers, §100

agreement with issuer, §99

commissions, clearance by NASD, §399

compensation, §§2013-2019

    excessive, §2016

    fair and reasonable, §2019

    resale price maintenance agreements, §2019

    "usual and customary," §§237-238

definition of under SA, §§227-249

disclosure required by SA, §114

dissemination of information in pre-filing period, §§146-150

distribution of securities, §§94-107, 230-231

effect of S.E.C. formal proceedings on, §391

for control persons, §245

indemnification, §§863-865

liability

    in general, §§1595-1597

    registration statement or prospectus, §§781, 816

negligence concerning prospectus, §865

nonexperts and SA section 11 liability, §803

participants in distribution, §§94-107, 230-231

    test, §231

pledges of securities, §§246-249

preliminary negotiations and agreements with issuer or other underwriters, §129

presumptive underwriter doctrine, §232

previous conduct by and regulation A, §527

private sale of restricted securities, §§707-716. *See also* Registration, transaction exemptions

refusal to proceed and material misstatements, §§396-397

rule 145 transactions, §§654-660

SA exemptions, §§233-239, 253-256

SA registration requirement, §§227-249

statutory underwriters and resales, §§670-683. *See also* Registration, transaction exemptions

types of agreements between issuers and underwriters, §§103-107. *See also* Distribution of Securities

UNIFORM SECURITIES ACT, §§2106-2107

UNORTHODOX TRANSACTIONS, §§1506-1508

"UNWORTHY OFFERING" DISQUALIFICATION, §§513, 524-529

UPTICK, §1930

See also Market manipulation and stabilization

USUAL AND CUSTOMARY COMMISSION, §§237-238

USUAL BROKERAGE FUNCTION, §§443-449

V

VENUE

action for insider's short-swing profits, §1542

rule 10b-5, §943

VERTICAL COMMON ENTERPRISE, §272

WXY

WAITING PERIOD

See also Securities Act of 1933

registration statement, §§126, 377-378

regulation during, §§151-191

WAIVER

as defense to SA section 12(a)(2) action, §847

of compliance by seller with SA, §872

WELLS SUBMISSION, §1681

See also Enforcement actions

WHITE KNIGHT MERGER, §1237

WILLIAMS ACT

See Tender offers

WIRE FRAUD, §§1786-1793

Z

ZERO-MINUS TICK, §1930

ZERO-PLUS TICK, §1930